THE
INFORMED
ARGUMENT

A MULTIDISCIPLINARY READER AND GUIDE • second edition

THE INFORMED ARGUMENT

A MULTIDISCIPLINARY READER AND GUIDE • second edition

ROBERT K. MILLER
University of Wisconsin, Stevens Point

HARCOURT BRACE JOVANOVICH, PUBLISHERS

San Diego   New York   Chicago   Austin   Washington, D.C.
London   Sydney   Tokyo   Toronto

Preface for Students

This book has been designed to help you argue on behalf of your beliefs so that other people will take them seriously. Part 1 will introduce you to the basic principles of argumentation that you need to evaluate the arguments you read and to compose written arguments of your own. It will also introduce you to the conventions that writers must follow when they support their arguments with information they have acquired through reading.

The material assembled for you in Part 2 should give you adequate information to write on a variety of subjects. Some of these subjects may appeal to you more than others. I hope you will enjoy many of the essays you read, even if they concern subjects that were not previously of interest to you. I hope also that your reading will leave you better informed about the different subjects that are discussed in Part 2. But whatever you learn about these subjects is a bonus. The purpose of *The Informed Argument* is not to turn you into an expert on gun control, capital punishment, or animal experimentation; it is to help you master skills that you can subsequently apply to subjects of your own choice. Reading the essays in Part 2 and writing essays that draw upon your reading will help you to acquire skills that will remain useful to you long after you have completed this course.

In choosing the various essays that have been included in the book, I was guided by two basic principles. I have tried to give equal consideration to opposing viewpoints so that you can better understand different sides of the issues in question. I have also given you facts as well as opinions. To fulfill these goals, I have included a mixture of old and new essays. You will find that the date of original publication is printed in boldface within the introductory note that comes immediately before every selection in Part 2. An essay can embody a strong argument or interesting point of view many years after it was written. On the other hand, an old essay can also include outdated information, so you should consider the age of each source when deciding on the extent to which you can rely upon it.

If you read carefully, you will find that almost every written argument includes at least one weak point. This is because it is almost impossible to achieve perfection in writing—especially when logic is involved. One of the reasons people have been drawn to study philosophy is that some of the great minds of world civilization have occasionally composed arguments that are so brilliant they seem perfect. Most writers, however, usually have to settle for less than perfection, especially when time or space is limited. Experienced writers spend as much time revising their work as they possibly can, but they also know that they cannot expect to have the last word. In any written argument there is almost always going to be a point that has been overlooked or something that could have been better put. Therefore, don't feel that an argument automatically loses all credibility because you have discovered a flaw in it. Although you should be alert for flaws, especially in reasoning, you should consider the significance of the flaw in proportion to the argument as a whole. Some writers undermine their entire argument by contradicting themselves or making wild charges; others are able to make a strong argument despite one or two weak points.

I wrote this book because I saw that students often needed additional information before they could write well-supported arguments but did not always have time to do research. Some writers, however, enjoy doing their own research, and you may want to supplement your reading in this book with material that you have discovered on your own. Part 3, "A Guide to Research," discusses how to find sources in a library. Searching for your own sources will enable you to include recently published material within your arguments. If you discover unusual or surprising information, library research may also help make your arguments more interesting to readers who are already familiar with the material in *The Informed Argument.* The extent to which you decide to go outside the book, if at all, is something to be decided in consultation with your instructor. The book itself has been designed to make research an option rather than a necessity.

All three parts of the book contain essays written by students. These have been included so that you can see how other students have satisfied assignments similar to those you may be asked to undertake. These essays are intended to help you rather than impress you. As is the case with the reprinted essays by professional writers, some of the student essays are stronger than others. You should try to learn what you can from them, but you should not feel that they represent some sort of perfection that is beyond your grasp. All of the students in question are serious enough about writing that they will probably see things they'd like to change as soon as they see their essays in print, for revision is a never-ending task essential to good writing. I want to thank these students for giving me permission to publish their work and remind them that I hope they keep on writing. I also want to thank the many students who studied the first edition of this book and helped me to see how it could be improved.

Preface for Instructors

The second edition of *The Informed Argument* continues to reflect my belief that students resent being asked to write on topics that seem trivial or contrived. The readings in this book are assembled into the equivalent of eight separate casebooks, seven of which focus on important issues of the sort students often want to write about. Instructors are free to treat each section either as a self-contained unit or as a springboard to further reading. To facilitate class discussion, every essay has its own editorial apparatus and every section ends with a list of suggestions for writing. Some of these suggestions direct students exclusively to material within the book, while others ask them to incorporate their own experience or research. This allows instructors much flexibility. Readings can be assigned in whatever sequence is deemed appropriate. And there is plenty of material, so the readings chosen for assignments can vary from class to class.

The 82 selections, 42 of which are new to the second edition, are drawn from a variety of disciplines to help students master different types of writing and reading. Among the fields represented are biology, business, history, journalism, medicine, law, literature, philosophy, political science, psychology, and sociology. In selecting these readings, I have been guided by two primary concerns: to include different points of view within each section and to provide students with both model arguments and adequate data for composing essays of their own. Recognizing that students can tire of long reading assignments, I have included within the second edition a greater number of short selections than were in the first. But each section in Part 2 continues to include at least one long selection suitable for teaching paraphrase and summary.

Although I believe in the importance of writing across the curriculum, I also believe that literature should be part of the curriculum being written across. Consequently, the book still includes some poetry and a section on literary criticism as a type of argumentation. The thematically organized sections are followed by "Some Classic Arguments," a ninth section that does not focus on a particular issue. This section increases the variety of readings made available to students through inclusion of such well-known essays as "A Modest Proposal," "Politics and the English Language," and "Letter from Birmingham Jail," as well as excerpts from several important works in the history of ideas.

The readings are the heart of this book. But *The Informed Argument* is more than an anthology. Because books have become so expensive, I have designed a text that satisfies all the needs of students in a semester-long course and will be useful to them long afterward. Part 1 introduces students to the rhetorical principles they need to write argumentative essays of their own and profit from the readings in Part 2. I have tried to keep the explanations as simple as possible. Examples are provided for each of the concepts discussed, and student essays illustrate both inductive and deductive reasoning as well as the model for reasoning devised by Stephen Toulmin. In addition, two versions of the same student essay now illustrate the importance of rewriting.

Part 1 also explains the nature and importance of summary, paraphrase, and the responsible use of sources. To emphasize that the use of sources is not limited to only research papers, documentation is now discussed in Part 1—facilitating correct documentation of any essay that is supported by material from Part 2. All of the major documentation styles in use across the curriculum are discussed—not only those of the Modern Language Association (MLA) and the American Psychological Association (APA), which are discussed in detail, but also the use of documentary footnotes and of a numbered system favored in much scientific writing. MLA style is illustrated by several student essays in Part 2 and by the model research paper in Part 3. Other systems, including one recommended by *The Chicago Manual of Style,* are all illustrated by one or more of the essays in Part 2.

The pages on which documentation is discussed are identified by gray borders in this edition so that students can page back to the model entries and find them more easily. Another helpful change in the second edition is that the headnotes introducing the selections in Part 2 now include the date of original publication in boldface; this should help students who use APA style documentation.

One other change in the second edition calls for a brief explanation. Each section in Part 2 now concludes with a student essay. The first of these essays provides an example of summary, and it appears immediately after the selection it summarizes. The second of these essays illustrates synthesis by drawing upon many of the selections in the section it concludes. The other student essays provide additional examples of argument and documentation. I have included these essays because students often profit from studying the work of other students. Given the difficulty of arguing effectively and using sources responsibly, students using the second edition may welcome the chance to see how other students coped with assignments similar to their own.

Several of the suggestions for writing in Part 2 encourage students to do library research. How to do so is discussed in Part 3, "A Guide to Research." In keeping with the book's multidisciplinary character, I emphasize a search strategy that can be used to locate material in many different courses. Although this information appears at the end of the book, it can be taught at any time.

In completing this book, I have contracted many debts. I would like to thank my colleagues in the English Department at the University of Wisconsin at Stevens Point, especially Ruth Dorgan, Jean Rumsey, Mary Shumway, and Al Young. I would also like to thank the staff of the Albertson Learning

Resource Center, especially Donna Carpenter, Kathleen Halsey, and Margaret Whalen. For deeply appreciated assistance during the final stages of my work, I want to thank Gary, Linda, Phyllis, and Robert Stanley Miller. For encouragement and support without fail, I want to thank Warren Garitano. At Harcourt Brace Jovanovich, Marcus Boggs, Catherine Fauver, Eleanor Garner, Amy Krammes, Stuart Miller, Sandra Steiner, Kim Turner, Linda Wild, and Ellen Wynn deserve many thanks for their expert help. Kathy Walker, my manuscript editor, was untiring in both her attention to detail and her commitment to maintaining the production schedule. Finally, I want to thank Tom Broadbent, the editor whose help was essential in completing the first edition of this book and vital to planning the second.

Contents

Section 9 Some Classic Arguments   452

PART 3
A GUIDE TO RESEARCH 575

PART 1

An Introduction to Argument

Argument is a means of fulfilling desire. That desire may be for something as abstract as truth or as concrete as a raise in salary. When you ask for an extension on a paper, apply for a job, propose a marriage, or recommend any change that involves someone besides yourself, you are putting yourself in a position that requires effective argumentation. In the years ahead, you may also have occasion to argue seriously about political and ethical concerns. Someone you love may be considering an abortion, a large corporation may try to bury its chemical waste on property that adjoins your own, or you may be suddenly deprived of a benefit to which you feel entitled. By learning how to organize your beliefs and support them with information that will make other people take them seriously, you will be mastering one of the most important skills you are likely to learn in college.

Working your arguments out on paper gives you the luxury of being able to make changes as often as you want until you are satisfied that your words do what you want them to do. This is an important benefit because constructing effective arguments requires that you think clearly without letting your feelings dominate what you say, and this can be difficult at times. But it can also be tremendously satisfying when you succeed in making other people understand what you mean. You may not always succeed in converting others to your point of view, but you can win their respect. This, in a way, is what argument is all about. When you argue for what you believe, you are asking others to believe in you. This means that you must prove to your audience that you are worth listening to. If you succeed this far, you may have won the argument even if you lose the vote on the particular issue at hand. Argumentation is intellectual self-assertion designed to secure the consideration and respect of one's peers, and it should not be confused with quarreling.

Bearing this in mind, you should always be careful to treat both your audience and your opponents with respect. Few people are likely to be converted to your view if you treat them as if they are fools and dismiss their

1

beliefs with contempt. Reason is the essence of effective argumentation, and an important part of being reasonable is demonstrating that you have given consideration to beliefs that are different from your own and have recognized what makes them appealing. Since nobody likes a know-it-all, you should always try not to be narrow minded or overly opinionated.

Similarly, you should avoid the temptation of arguing all things at all times. Most points can indeed be argued, but just because something can be argued does not necessarily mean that it *should* be argued. You won't be taken seriously if you seem to argue automatically and routinely. Argument should be the result of reflection rather than reflex, and argumentation is a skill that should be practiced selectively.

CHOOSING A TOPIC

The first step in written argumentation, as in all forms of writing, is choosing a topic. In doing so, you should be careful to avoid subjects that could be easily settled by referring to an authority, such as a dictionary or an encyclopedia. There is no point in arguing about how to spell "separate" or about what is the capital of Bolivia, because questions of this sort can be settled quickly and absolutely, having only one correct answer. Argument assumes the possibility of more than one position on the issue being considered. When you disagree with someone about anything that could be settled by simply checking the facts, you would be wasting your time to argue, even if you are sure you are right.

Almost all intelligent arguments are about *opinions*. But not all opinions lead to good written arguments. There is no reason to argue an opinion with which almost no one would disagree. An essay designed to "prove" that puppies are cute or that vacations can be fun is unlikely to generate much excitement. Don't belabor the obvious. Nearly everyone welcomes the arrival of spring, and you will be preaching to the converted if you set out to argue that spring is a nice time of year. If you've been reading T. S. Eliot, however, and want to argue that April is the cruelest month (and that you have serious reservations about May and June as well) then you may be on to something. You should not feel that you suddenly need to acquire strange and eccentric opinions. But you should choose a topic that is likely to inspire at least some controversy.

In doing so, be careful to distinguish between opinions that are a matter of taste and those that are a question of judgment. Some people like broccoli, and some people don't. You may be the world's foremost broccoli lover, dreaming every night of broccoli crops to come, but no matter how hard you try, you will not convince someone who hates green vegetables to head quickly to the produce department of the nearest supermarket. A gifted stylist could probably write an amusing essay on broccoli, in the manner of Charles Lamb or E. B. White, that would be a delight to read. But it is one thing to describe our tastes and quite another to insist that others share them. We all have likes and dislikes that are so firmly entrenched that persuasion in matters of taste is usually beyond the reach of what can be accomplished through the written word—unless you happen to command the resources of a major advertising agency.

Taste is a matter of personal preference. Whether we prefer green to blue or daffodils to tulips is unlikely to affect anyone but ourselves. Questions of judgment are more substantial than matters of taste because judgment cannot be divorced from logic. Our judgments are determined by our beliefs, behind which are basic principles to which we try to remain consistent. These principles ultimately lead us to decide that some judgments are correct and others are not, so judgment has greater implications than taste. Should a university require freshmen to live in dormitories? Should men and women live together before getting married? Should parents spank their children? All these are questions of judgment.

In written argumentation, questions of judgment provide the best subjects. They can be argued because they are complex, giving you more angles to pursue. This does not mean that you must cover every aspect of a question in a single essay. Because good subjects have so many possibilities, the essays that are written on them will take many different directions. Good writers sound like individuals, not committees or machines, and it is easier to sound like an individual when you address a subject about which many different things can be said. Moreover, in making an argument the writer always hopes to surprise his audience with information—or an ingenious interpretation of information—that is not usually considered. If your audience consists of people who know almost nothing about your subject, then you may be able to build a convincing case by simply outlining a few basic points. But an educated audience will be converted to your view only if you move beyond the obvious and reveal points that are often overlooked. This is most likely to happen when the subject itself is complex.

It is important, therefore, to choose subjects that you are well-informed about or willing to research. This may sound like obvious advice, and yet it is possible to have an opinion with nothing behind it but a few generalizations that are impossible to support once you begin to write. You may have absorbed the opinions of others without thinking about them or may have prejudged a particular subject without knowing much about it. Nobody is going to take your views seriously if you cannot support them.

The readings that form the core of this book were chosen to make you better informed on some of the important questions of our time. After you have read six or seven essays on the same subject, you should be able to compose an argument of your own that will consider the various views you have encountered. But remember that being "better informed" does not always mean being "well informed." Well-educated men and women recognize how little they know in proportion to how much there is to be known. Don't suppose that you've become an expert on capital punishment simply because you have spent a week or two reading about it. What you read should influence what you think, but as you read more, realize that controversial subjects are controversial because there is so much that could be said about them—much more than you may have realized at first.

DEFINING YOUR AUDIENCE

Argumentation demands a clear sense of audience. Good writers remember whom they are writing for, and their audience helps shape their style. It would be a mistake, for example, to use complicated technical language when writing for a general audience. But it would be just as foolish to address an audience of experts as if they knew nothing about the subject. As the writer you should always be careful not to confuse people. On the other hand, you must also be careful not to insult the readers' intelligence. Although awareness of audience is important in all types of writing, it is especially true in written arguments. A clear sense of audience allows you to choose the points you want to emphasize in order to be persuasive. Just as importantly, it enables you to anticipate the objections your readers or listeners are most likely to raise if they disagree with you.

In written argumentation, it is usually best to envision an audience that is skeptical. Unless you are the keynote speaker at a political convention, rallying the members of your party by telling them exactly what they want to hear, there is no reason to expect people to agree with you. If your audience already agrees with you, what's the point of your argument? Whom are you trying to convince? Remember that the immediate purpose of an argument is almost always to convert people to your point of view. Of course, an audience may be entirely neutral, having no opinion at all on the subject that concerns you. But by imagining a skeptical audience, you will be able to anticipate the opposition and offer counterarguments of your own, thus building a stronger case.

Before you begin to write, you should list for yourself the reasons why you believe as you do. Realize that you may not have the space, in a short essay, to discuss all of the points you have listed. You should therefore rank them in order of their importance, considering, in particular, the degree to which they would probably impress the audience for whom you are writing. Once you have done this, compose another list—a list of reasons why people might disagree with you. Having considered the opposition's point of view, now ask yourself why it is that you have not been persuaded to abandon your own beliefs. You must see a flaw of some sort in the reasoning of your opponents. Add to your second list a short rebuttal of each of your opponent's arguments.

You are likely to discover that the opposition has at least one good argument, an argument which you cannot answer. There should be nothing surprising about this. We may like to flatter ourselves by believing that Truth is on our side. In our weaker moments, we may like to pretend that anyone who disagrees with us is either ignorant or corrupt. But serious and prolonged controversies almost always mean that the opposition has at least one valid concern. Be prepared to concede a point to your opponents when it seems appropriate to do so. You must consider and respond to their views, but your responses do not always have to take the form of rebuttals. When you have no rebuttal and recognize that your opponent's case has some merit, be honest and generous enough to say so.

By making concessions to your opposition, you demonstrate to your audience that you are trying to be fair minded. Far from weakening your own case, an occasional concession can help bridge the gulf between you and your opponents, making it easier for you to reach a more substantial agreement. It's hard to convince someone that your views deserve to be taken seriously when you have belligerently insisted that he or she is completely wrong and you are completely right. Life is seldom so simple. Human nature being what it is, most people will listen more readily to an argument that offers some recognition of their views.

You must be careful, of course, not to concede too much. If you find yourself utterly without counterarguments and ready to concede a half dozen points, you had better reconsider the subject you have chosen. In a short essay, you can usually afford to make only one or two concessions. Too many concessions are likely to confuse readers who are uncertain about what they think. Why should they be persuaded by you when you seem half persuaded by your opponents?

Having a good sense of audience also means illustrating your case with concrete examples your audience can readily understand. It's hard to make people care about abstractions; good writers try to make the abstract concrete. Remember that it is often easy to lose the attention of your audience, so try to address its most probable concerns.

There is, however, a great difference between responding to the interests of your audience by discussing what it wants to know and twisting what you say to please an audience with exactly what it wants to hear. You should remember that the foremost responsibility of any writer is to tell the truth as he or she sees it. What we mean by "truth" often has many dimensions, and when limited space forces us to be selective, it is only common sense to focus on those facets of our subject that will be the most effective with the audience we are attempting to sway. But it is one thing to edit and quite another to mislead. Never write anything for one audience that you would be compelled to deny before another. Hypocrites are seldom persuasive, and no amount of verbal agility can compensate for a public loss of confidence in a writer's character.

To better understand the importance of audience in argumentation, let us consider an example. The following essay was recently published as an editorial in the student newspaper at the university where I work.

TO SKIP OR NOT TO SKIP: A STUDENT DILEMMA

This is college right? The four-year deal offering growth, maturity, experience, and knowledge? A place to be truly independent? 1

Because sometimes I can't tell. Sometimes this place downright reeks of paternal instincts. Just ask the freshmen and sophomores, who are by class rank alone guaranteed two full 2 years of twenty-four hour supervision, orchestrated activities, and group showers.

But the forced dorm migration of underclassmen has been bitched about before, to no avail. University policy is, it seems, set in stone. It ranks right up there with in-grown toe nails for sheer evasion and longevity. 3

But there's another university pol- 4
icy that has no merit as a policy and
no place in a university. Mandatory
Attendance Policy: wherein faculty
members attempt the high school hall
monitor–combination–college instructor maneuver. It's a difficult trick to
justify as professors place the attendance percentage of their choice above
a student's proven abilities on graded
material.

Profs rationalize out a lot of argu- 5
ments to support the policy. Participation is a popular one. I had a professor
whose methods for lowering grades so
irritated me I used to skip on purpose.
He said, "Classroom participation is
a very important part of this introductory course. Obviously, if you
are not present, you cannot be participating."

Equally obvious, though not stated 6
by the prof, is the fact that one can be
perpetually present but participate as
little as one who is absent. So who's
the better student—the one who makes
a meaningless appearance, or the one
who is busy with something else? And
who gets the points docked?

The rest of his policy was charac- 7
teristically vague, mentioning that absences "could" result in a lower grade.
Constant ambiguity is the second big
problem with formal policies. It's tough
for teachers to figure out just how
much to let attendance affect grade
point. So they doubletalk.

According to the UWSP catalog, 8
faculty are to provide "clear explanation" of attendance policy. Right. Based
on the language actually used, ninety-
five percent of UWSP faculty are functionally incapable of uttering a single
binding statement. In an effort to offend no one while retaining all power
of action, profs write things like (these
are actual policies): "I trust students
to make their own judgments and
choices about coming, or not coming
to class." But then continues: "Habitual
and excessive absence is grounds for

failure." What happened to trust? What
good are the choices?

Or this "More than three absences 9
may negatively affect your grade." Then
again, they may not. Who knows? And
this one: "I consider every one of you
in here to be mature adults. However,
I reserve the right to alter grades based
on attendance."

You reserve the right? How? By vir- 10
tue of your saying so? Is that like calling the front seat?

Another argument that profs cling 11
to goes something like, "Future employers, by God, aren't going to put up
with absenteeism." Well, let's take a
reality pill. I think most students can
grasp the difference between cutting
an occasional class, which they paid
for, and cutting at work, when they're
the ones on salary. See, college students are capable of bi-level thought
control, nowadays. (It's all those
computers.)

In summary, mandatory attendance 12
should be abolished because:

1. It is irrelevant. Roughly the same 13
number of students will either skip or
attend, regardless of what a piece
of paper says. If the course is worth
anything.

2. It is ineffective. It automatically 14
measures neither participation, ability,
or gained knowledge. That's what tests
are for. Grades are what you end up
knowing, not how many times you sat
there to figure it out.

3. It is insulting. A college student 15
is capable of determining a personal
schedule, one that may or may not
always meet with faculty wishes. An
institution committed to the fostering
of personal growth cannot operate
under rules that patronize or minimize the role an adult should claim
for himself.

4. It is arbitrary. A prof has no right 16
and no ability to factor in an unrealistic
measure of performance. A student
should be penalized no more than what
the natural consequence of an absence

is—the missing of one day's direct delivery of material.

5. It abolishes free choice. By the   17
addition of a factor that cannot be
fought. We are not at a university to
learn conformity. As adults, we reserve
the right to choose as we see fit, even
if we choose badly.

Finally, I would ask faculty to con-   18
sider this: We have for some time upheld in this nation the sacred principle
of separation of church and state; i.e.,
You are not God.

Karen Rivedal
Editor

Karen chose a topic that would certainly interest many college students,
the audience for whom she saw herself writing. Her thesis is clear: mandatory
class attendance should not be required of college students. And her writing
is lively enough to hold the attention of many readers. All this is good.

Unfortunately, Karen's argument also has a number of flaws. In paragraph
6 she offers what logicians call "a false dilemma." By asking, "So who's the
better student—the one who makes a meaningless appearance, or the one
who is busy doing something else?" she has ignored at least two other possibilities. Appearance in class is likely to be meaningful to at least some students, and cutting class may be meaningless if the "something else" occupying
a student's attention is a waste of time. The comparison in paragraph 10
between reserving the right to lower grades because of poor attendance and
"calling the front seat" is confusing. (In conversation after the initial publication of this essay, Karen explained to me that she was making a comparison between professors who "reserve the right to alter grades" and children
who call "I got the front seat" when going out in the family car. I then pointed
out that this analogy could easily be used against her. The driver *must* sit in
the front seat, and surely whoever is teaching a class is analogous to the
driver of a car rather than one of its passengers). In paragraph 13 Karen
claims, "Roughly the same number of students will either skip or attend,
regardless of what a piece of paper says," but she offers no evidence to support this claim, which is really no more than guesswork. And since Karen
herself admits that many students skip class despite mandatory attendance
policies, her claim in paragraph 17 that required attendance "abolishes free
choice" does not hold up.

But these lapses in logic aside, the major problem with this argument is
that Karen misjudged her audience. She forgot that professors, as well as
students, read the school newspaper. Since students cannot change the policies of their professors, but professors themselves can usually do so, she has
overlooked the very audience that she most needs to reach. Moreover, not
only has she failed to include professors within her audience, but she has
actually gone so far as to insult them. Someone who is told that he or she is
"functionally incapable of uttering a single binding statement" is unlikely to
feel motivated to change. It's only in the very last paragraph of this essay
that Karen specifically addresses the faculty, and this proves to be simply
the occasion for a final insult. Although there may be professors who take
themselves too seriously, are there really that many who believe that
they are divine?

It's a shame that it's so easy to poke holes in this argument, because Karen deserves credit for boldly calling attention to policies that may indeed be wrong. Recognizing that her original argument was flawed, but still believing strongly that mandatory class attendance is inappropriate for college students, Karen decided to rewrite her essay. Here is her revision.

Absent at What Price?
Karen Rivedal

This is college, right? A place to break old ties, solve problems, and make decisions? Higher education is, I thought, the pursuit of knowledge in a way that's a step beyond the paternal hand-holding of high school. It's the act of learning performed in a more dynamic atmosphere, rich with individual freedom, discourse, and debate.   1

Because sometimes I can't tell. Some university traditions cloud the full intent of higher education. Take mandatory attendance policies: wherein faculty members attempt the high school hall monitor—college instructor maneuver. It's a difficult trick to justify as professors place the attendance percentage of their choice above a student's proven abilities on graded material.   2

This isn't to say that the idea of attendance itself is unsound. Clearly, personal interaction between teacher and students is preferable to textbook teaching alone. It's the mandatory attendance policy, within an academic community committed to the higher education of adults, that worries me.   3

Professors, however, offer several arguments to support the practice. Participation is a popular one. I had a professor whose methods for lowering grades so irritated me that I used to skip out of spite. He said, "Classroom participation is a very important part of this introductory course. Obviously, if you are not present, you cannot be participating."   4

Equally obvious, though, is the fact that one can be perpetually present, but participate as little as one who is absent. Participation lacks an adequate definition. There's no way of knowing, on the face of it, if a silent student is necessarily a learning student. Similarly, an instructor has no way of knowing for what purpose or advantage a student may miss a class, and therefore no ability to determine its relative validity.   5

As a learning indicator, then, mandatory attendance pol-   6
icy is flawed. It automatically measures neither participation, ability, or gained knowledge. That's what tests are
for. A final grade should reflect what a student ends up
knowing, rather than the artificial consequences of demerit
points.

Some faculty recognize the shortcomings of a no—excep-   7
tions mandatory attendance policy and respond with partial
policies. Constant ambiguity is characteristic of this approach and troublesome for the student who wants to know just
where he or she stands. It's tough for teachers to figure out
just how much to let attendance affect grade point. So they
doubletalk.

This, for example, is taken from an actual policy: "I trust   8
students to make their own judgments and choices about coming, or not coming, to class." It then continues: "Habitual
and excessive absence is grounds for failure." What happened
to trust? What good are the choices?

Or this: "More than three absences may negatively affect   9
your grade." Then again, they may not. Who knows? And this
one: "I consider every one of you in here to be mature adults.
However, I reserve the right to alter grades based on attendance."

This seems to say, what you can prove you have learned from   10
this class takes a back seat to how much I think you should
know based on your attendance. What the teacher says goes—
just like in high school.

Professors who set up attendance policies like these be-   11
lieve, with good reason, that they are helping students to
learn by ensuring their attendance. But the securing of this
end by requirement eliminates an important element of learning. Removing the freedom to make the decision is removing
the need to think. An institution committed to the fostering
of personal growth cannot operate under rules that patronize
or minimize the role an adult should claim for himself.

A grading policy that relies on the student's proven abil-   12
ities certainly takes the guesswork out of grade assigning
for teachers. This take—no—prisoners method, however, also
demands a high, some say unfairly high, level of personal
student maturity. Younger students especially may need,
they say, the extra structuring that a policy provides.

But forfeiting an attendance policy doesn't mean that a   13
teacher has to resign his humanity, too. Teachers who care to

can still take five minutes to warn an often absent student
about the possible consequences, or let the first test score
tell the story. As much as dedicated teachers want students
to learn, the activity is still a personal one. Students must
want to.

A "real-world" argument that professors often use goes   14
something like, "Future employers aren't going to put up
with absenteeism, so get used to it now." Well, let's take a
reality pill. I think most students can differentiate between cutting an occasional class, which they paid for, and
missing at work, when they're the ones on salary.

Students who intelligently protest an institution's poli-   15
cies, such as mandatory attendance requirements, are proof-
in-action that college is working. These students are thinking, and learning to think and question is the underlying
goal of all education. College is more than its rules, more
than memorized facts. Rightly, college is knowledge, the
testing of limits. To be valid, learning must include choice
and the freedom to make mistakes. To rely on mandatory attendance for learning is to subvert the fullest aims of that
education.

In revising her essay, Karen has retained both her thesis and her own
distinctive voice. Such phrases as "the high school hall monitor–college instructor maneuver," the "take-no-prisoners method," and "let's take a reality
pill" are still recognizably her own. But her argument is now more compelling. In addition to eliminating the fallacies that marred her original version,
Karen included new material that strengthens her case. Paragraph 3 offers a
much needed clarification, reassuring readers that an argument against a
mandatory attendance policy is not the same as an argument against attending class. Paragraph 7 begins with a fairly sympathetic reference to professors, and paragraph 11 opens with a clear attempt to anticipate opposition.
Paragraph 12 includes another attempt to anticipate opposition, and paragraph 13, with its reference to "dedicated teachers," is much more likely to
appeal to the professors in Karen's audience than anything in the original
version did. Finally, the conclusion of this essay is now much improved, and
it successfully links the question of mandatory attendance policies with the
purpose of higher education as defined in the opening paragraph.

DEFINING YOUR TERMS

If you want your arguments to be convincing, they must be understood by
your audience. To make sure that your ideas are understandable, you must
be careful to use words clearly. It is especially important to make sure that

any terms essential to your argument are clear. Unfortunately, many writers of argument fail to define the words they use. It is not unusual, for example, to find a writer advocating gun control without defining exactly what he or she means by "gun control." Many arguments use words such as "censorship," "society," "legitimate," and "moral" so loosely that it is impossible to decide exactly what the writer means. When this happens, the entire argument can break down.

You should not feel that you need to define every word you use, but you certainly should define any important word your audience might misunderstand. When doing so, always try to avoid defining the word by using another term that is equally complex. For example, if you are opposed to the sale of pornography, you should be prepared to define what you mean by "pornography." It would not be especially helpful to tell your audience that pornography is "printed or visual material that is obscene" since this only raises the question: What is "obscene"? In an important ruling, the Supreme Court defined "obscene" as material that "the average person, applying community standards, would find . . . as a whole, appeals to the prurient interest," but even if you happened to have this definition at hand, you should ask yourself if "the average person" understands what "prurient" means—not to mention what the Court may have meant by "community standards." Unless you define your terms carefully, avoiding unnecessarily abstract language, you can end up writing an endless chain of definitions that require further explanation.

The easiest way to define a term is to consult a dictionary. However, some dictionaries are much better than others. For daily use, most writers usually refer to a good desk dictionary such as *The American Heritage Dictionary, The Random House Dictionary,* or *Webster's New Collegiate Dictionary.* A good general dictionary of this sort may provide you with an adequate working definition. But you may also want to consider consulting the multivolume *Oxford English Dictionary,* which is available in most college libraries and is especially useful in showing how the usage of a word has changed over the years. Your audience might also appreciate the detailed information that specialized dictionaries in various subject areas can provide. Many such dictionaries are likely to be available in your college library. For example, if you are working on a paper in English literature, you might consult *A Concise Dictionary of Literary Terms* or *The Princeton Handbook of Poetic Terms.* For a paper in psychology you might turn to *The Encyclopedic Dictionary of Psychology,* or for a paper on a musical topic, *The New Grove's Dictionary of Music and Musicians.* There are also dictionaries for medical, legal, philosophical, and theological terms as well as for each of the natural sciences. When using specialized dictionaries, you will often find valuable information, but remember that the definition which appears in your paper should not be more difficult than the word or phrase you originally set out to define.

Instead of relying exclusively upon dictionaries, it is often best to define a term or phrase in words of your own. In doing so, you can choose among several strategies:

- You can give synonyms.
- You can compare the term with other words with which it is likely to be confused and show how your term differs.
- You can define a word by clarifying what it is *not.*
- You can provide examples.

Writers frequently use several of these strategies to create a single definition, and an entire essay could be devoted to such a definition. In argument, however, you will usually need to define your terms within a paragraph or two. When doing so, remember your various options and decide which will be the most effective for your purpose. (For an example of an essay in which definition is used as a prelude to argument, see "Separating Myth From Reality" by Ivan B. Gluckman, pp. 198–203.)

In addition to achieving clarity, definition helps to control an argument by eliminating misunderstandings that can cause an audience to be inappropriately hostile or to jump to a conclusion that is different from your own. By carefully defining your terms, you limit a discussion to what you want to discuss. This increases the likelihood of your gaining a fair hearing for your views.

ORGANIZING YOUR ARGUMENT

If you have chosen your subject carefully and given sufficient thought to your audience and its concerns (paying particular attention to any objections that could be raised against whatever you wish to advocate), then it should not be difficult to organize an argumentative essay. Considering the various concerns discussed in the previous sections will provide you with what amounts to a rough outline, but you must now consider two additional questions: "Where and how should I begin my argument?" and "How can I most efficiently include in my argument the various counterarguments that I have anticipated and responded to?" The answers to these questions will vary from one essay to another. But while arguments can take many forms, formal arguments usually employ logic, of which there are two widely accepted types: inductive and deductive reasoning.

Reasoning Inductively

When we use *induction,* we are drawing a conclusion based upon specific evidence. Our argument rests upon a foundation of details that we have accumulated for its support. This is the type of reasoning that we use most frequently in daily life. We look at the sky outside our window, check the thermometer, and may even listen to a weather forecast before dressing to face the day. If the sun is shining, the temperature high, and the forecast favorable, we would be making a reasonable conclusion if we decided to dress lightly and leave our umbrellas at home. We haven't *proved* that the day will be warm and pleasant, we have only *concluded* that it will be. This is all we can usually do in an inductive argument: arrive at a conclusion that seems likely to be true. Ultimate and positive proof is usually beyond the writer's reach, and the writer who recognizes this and proceeds accordingly will usually arrive at conclusions that are both moderate and thoughtful. He or she recognizes the possibility of an unanticipated factor undermining even the best of arguments. A lovely morning can yield to a miserable afternoon, and we may be drenched in a downpour as we hurry home on the day that began so pleasantly.

Inductive reasoning is especially important in scientific experimentation. A research scientist may have a theory which he or she hopes to prove. But to work toward proving this theory, hundreds, thousands, and even tens of thousands of experiments may have to be conducted to eliminate variables and gather enough data to justify a generally applicable conclusion. Well-researched scientific conclusions sometimes reach a point where they seem uncontestable. It's been many years since Congress required the manufacturers of cigarettes to put a warning on every package stating that smoking can be harmful to your health. Since then, additional research has supported the conclusion that smoking can indeed be dangerous, especially to the lungs and the heart. That "smoking can be harmful to your health" now seems to have entered the realm of established fact. But biologists, chemists, physicists, and physicians are usually aware that the history of science, and the history of medicine in particular, is an argumentative history full of debate. Methods and beliefs established over many generations can be overthrown by a new discovery. Within a few years, that "new discovery" can also come under challenge. So the serious researcher goes back to the lab and keeps on working—ever mindful that truth is hard to find.

Induction is also essential in law enforcement. The police are supposed to have evidence against someone before making an arrest. Consider, for example, the way a detective works. A good detective does not arrive at the scene of a crime with his or her mind already made up about what happened. If the crime seems to be part of a pattern, the detective may already have a suspicion about who is responsible. But a good investigator will want to make a careful study of every piece of evidence that can be gathered. A room may be dusted for fingerprints, a murder victim photographed as found, and if the body is lying on the floor, a chalk outline may be drawn around it for future study. Every item within the room will be catalogued. Neighbors, relatives, employers, or employees will be questioned. The best detective is usually the detective with the best eye for detail, and the greatest determination to keep searching for the details that will be strong enough to bring a case to court. Similarly, a first-rate detective will also be honest enough never to overlook a fact that does not fit in with the rest of the evidence. The significance of every loose end must be examined to avoid the possibility of an unfair arrest and prosecution.

In making an inductive argument, you will reach a point at which you decide that you have offered enough evidence to support the thesis of your essay. When you are writing a college paper, you will probably decide that you have reached this point sooner than a scientist or a detective might. But whether you are writing a short essay or conducting an investigation, the process is essentially the same. When you stop citing evidence and move on to your conclusion, you have made what is known as an *inductive leap*. In an inductive essay, you must always offer interpretation or analysis of the evidence you have introduced; there will always be at least a slight gap between your evidence and your conclusion. It is over this gap that the writer must leap; the trick is to do it agilely. Good writers know that their evidence must be in proportion to their conclusion: The bolder your conclusion, the more evidence you will need to back it up. Remember the old adage about "jumping to conclusions," and realize that you'll need the momentum of a running start to make more than a moderate leap at any one time.

If you listen closely to the conversation of the people around you, the chances are good that you'll hear examples of faulty inductive reasoning. When someone says, "I don't like Chinese food," and reveals, under questioning, that his only experience with Chinese food was something called "hamburger chow mein" in a high school cafeteria, we cannot take the opinion seriously. A sweeping conclusion has been drawn from flimsy evidence. People who claim to know "all about" complex subjects often reveal that they actually know very little. Only a sexist claims to know all about men and women, and only a racist is foolish enough to generalize about the various racial groups that make up our society. Good writers are careful not to overgeneralize.

When you begin an inductive essay, you might cite a particular observation that strikes you as especially important. You might even begin with a short anecdote. A well-structured inductive essay would then gradually expand as the evidence accumulates, so that the conclusion is supported by numerous details. Here is an example of an inductive essay written by a student.

In Defense of Hunting
David Wagner

I killed my first buck when I was fourteen. I'd gone deer   1
hunting with my father and two of my uncles. I was cold and
wet and anxious to get home, but I knew what I had to do when I
sighted the eight—point buck. Taking careful aim, I fired at
his chest, killing him quickly with a single shot.

I don't want to romanticize this experience, turning it   2
into a noble rite of passage. I did feel that I had proved my—
self somehow. It was important for me to win my father's respect, and I welcomed the admiration I saw in his eyes. But
I've been hunting regularly for many years now, and earning

the approval of others no longer seems very important to
me. I'd prefer to emphasize the facts about hunting, facts
that must be acknowledged even by people who are opposed
to hunting.

It is a fact that hunters help to keep the deer population   3
in balance with the environment. Since so many of their natural predators have almost died out in this state, the deer
population could quickly grow much larger than the land can
support. Without hunting, thousands of deer would die slowly
of starvation in the leafless winter woods. This may sound
like a self-serving argument (like the words of a parent who
beats a child and insists, "This hurts me more than it does
you; I'm only doing it for your own good"). But it is a fact
that cannot be denied.

It is also a fact that hunters provide a valuable source of   4
revenue for the state. The registration and licensing fees
we pay are used by the Department of Natural Resources to re-
forest barren land, preserve wetlands, and protect endangered species. Also there are many counties in this state
that depend upon the money that hunters spend on food, gas,
and lodging. "Tourism" is our third largest industry, and
all of this money isn't being spent at luxurious lakeside re-
sorts. Opponents of hunting should realize that hunting is
the most active in some of our poorest, rural counties—and
realize what hunting means to the people who live in these
areas.

It is also a fact that there are hundreds of men and women   5
for whom hunting is an economic necessity and not a sport.
Properly preserved, the meat that comes from a deer can help
a family survive a long winter. There probably are hunters
who think of hunting as a recreation. But all the hunters I
know—and I know at least twenty—dress their own deer and
use every pound of the venison they salt, smoke, or freeze.
There may be a lot of people who don't have to worry about
spending $3.00 a pound for steak, but I'm not one of them. My
family needs the meat we earn by hunting.

I have to admit that there are hunters who act irresponsi-   6
bly by trespassing where they are not wanted and, much worse,
by abandoning animals that they have wounded. But there are
many different kinds of irresponsibility. Look around and
you will see many irresponsible drivers, but we don't respond to them by banning driving altogether. An irresponsible minority is no reason to attack a responsible majority.

I've listened to many arguments against hunting, and it   7
seems to me that what really bothers most of the people who
are opposed to hunting is the idea that hunters <u>enjoy</u> killing. I can't speak for all hunters, but I can speak for myself
and the many hunters I personally know. I myself have never
found pleasure in killing a deer. I think that deer are beautiful and incredibly graceful, especially when in movement.
I don't "enjoy" putting an end to a beautiful animal's life.
If I find any pleasure in the act of hunting, it comes from
the knowledge that I am trying to be at least partially self-
sufficient. I don't expect other people to do all my dirty
work for me, and give me my meat neatly butchered and conveniently wrapped in plastic. I take responsibility for what I
eat.

So the next time that you hear someone complaining about   8
hunters, try to be fair-minded before going along with the
usual stereotypes. The men and women who hunt are no worse
than anyone else. Lumping us all together as insensitive
beer-drinking thugs is an example of the mindless stereotyping that logic should teach us to avoid.

David has drawn upon his own experience to make an articulate defense of hunting. He begins with an anecdote that helps to establish that he knows something about the subject he has chosen to write about. The first sentence in the second paragraph helps to deflect any skepticism his audience may feel at this early stage in his argument, and the last sentence in this paragraph serves as a transition into the facts that will be emphasized in the next three paragraphs. In the third paragraph, David introduces the evidence that should most impress his audience, if we assume that his audience is unhappy about the idea of killing animals. In paragraphs 4 and 5, he defends hunting on economic grounds. He offers a concession in paragraph 5 ("There probably are hunters who think of hunting as a recreation") and another concession in paragraph 6 ("I have to admit that there are hunters who act irresponsibly"). But after each of these concessions he manages to return smoothly to his own thesis. In paragraph 7 he anticipates an argument frequently made by people who oppose hunting and offers a counterargument that puts his opponents on the defensive. The concluding paragraph is a little anticlimatic, but within the limitations of a short essay, David has made a fairly strong argument.

Reasoning Deductively

Sometimes it is best to rest an argument on a fundamental truth, value, or right rather than on specific pieces of evidence. You should try to be specific within the course of such an essay, giving examples to support your case.

But in deductive reasoning, evidence is of secondary importance. Your first concern is to define a commonly accepted value or belief that will prepare the way for the argument you want to make.

The Declaration of Independence, written by Thomas Jefferson (pp. 473–76), is a classic example of deductive reasoning. Although Jefferson cited numerous grievances, he rested his argument on the belief that "all men are created equal" and that they have "certain unalienable Rights" which King George III had violated. This was a revolutionary idea in the eighteenth century, and even today there are many people who question it. But if we accept the idea that "all men are created equal" and have an inherent right to "Life, Liberty, and the pursuit of Happiness," then certain conclusions follow.

The right, value, or belief from which we wish to deduce our argument is called our *premise.* Perhaps you have already had the experience, in the middle of an argument, of someone saying to you, "What's your premise?" If you are inexperienced in argumentation, a question of this sort may embarrass you and cause your argument to break down—which is probably what your opponent had hoped. But whether we recognize it or not, we almost always have a premise lurking somewhere in the back of our minds. Deductive argument requires that we think about values we have automatically assumed and get them up front as a crucial part of our case.

A good premise satisfies two requirements. In the first place, it is general enough that your audience is likely to accept it, thus establishing a common ground between you and the audience you hope to persuade. On the other hand, the premise must still be specific enough so that it prepares the way for the argument that will follow. It usually takes much careful thought to frame a good premise. Relatively few people have their values always at their fingertips. We usually know what we want or what our conclusion is going to be—but it takes time to realize the fundamental beliefs that we have automatically assumed. For this is really what a premise amounts to: the underlying assumption that must be agreed upon before the argument can begin to move along.

Because it is difficult to formulate an effective premise, it is often useful to work backwards when you are outlining a deductive argument. You should know what conclusion you expect to reach. Write it down, and assign to it number 3. Now ask yourself why you believe statement 3. This should prompt a number of reasons which you can group together as statement number 2. And now that you can look both at your conclusion and at the immediate reasons that seem to justify it, ask yourself if there's anything you've left out—something basic that you skipped over, assuming that everyone would agree with that already. When you can think back successfully to what this assumption is, knowing that it will vary from argument to argument, you have your premise, at least in rough draft form.

This may be difficult to grasp in the abstract, so let us consider an outline for a sample argument. Suppose that the forests in your state are slowly dying because of the pollution known as acid rain—one of the effects of burning fossil fuel, especially coal. Coal is being burned by numerous industries not only in your own state, but in neighboring states as well. You hadn't even realized that there was a problem with acid rain until last summer when fishing was prohibited in your favorite lake. You are very upset about this and declare, "Something ought to be done!" But as you begin to think about the problem, you recognize that you'll have to overcome at least two obstacles in deciding what that something should be. Only two years ago, you participated in a demonstration against nuclear power, and you'd also hate to see the United States become more dependent upon foreign oil. So if you attack the process of burning coal for energy, you'll have to be prepared to recommend an acceptable alternative. The other question you must answer is "Who's responsible for a problem that seems to be springing from many places in many states?" Moreover, if you do decide to argue for a radical reduction in coal consumption, you'll have to be prepared to anticipate the opposition: "What's this going to do to the coal miners?" someone might well ask. "Will you destroy the livelihood of some of the hardest working men and women in America?"

You realize that you have still another problem. Your assignment is for a 750-word deductive argument, and it's due the day after tomorrow. You feel strongly about the problem of acid rain, but you don't think that you should have to become an energy expert to pass freshman English. Your primary concern is with the effects of acid rain, which you've witnessed with your own eyes. And while you don't know much about industrial chemistry, you do know that acid rain is caused principally by public utilities burning coal that has a high percentage of sulfur in it. Recognizing that you lack the expertise to make a full scale attack upon coal consumption, you decide that you can at least go so far as to argue on behalf using low sulfur coal. In doing so, you will be able to reassure your audience that you want to keep coal miners at work, recognize the needs of industry, and do not expect the entire country to go solar by the end of the semester.

Taking out a sheet of paper, you begin to write down your outline in reverse:

3. Public utilities should not burn coal that is high in sulfur content.
2. Burning high sulfur coal causes acid rain, and acid rain is killing American forests, endangering wildlife, and spoiling local fishing.

Before going any farther, you realize that all of your reasons for opposing acid rain cannot be taken with equal degrees of seriousness. As much as you like to fish, recreation does not seem to be in the same league with your more general concern for forests and wildlife. You know that you want to describe the condition of your favorite lake at some point in your essay, because it gave you some firsthand experience with the problem and some vivid descriptive details. But you decide that you'd better not make too much of fishing in order to avoid the risk of sounding as if you care only about your own pleasure.

You now ask yourself what lies behind the "should" in your conclusion. How strong is it? Did you say "should" when you meant "must"? Thinking it over, you realize that you did mean "must," but now you must decide who or what is going to make that "must" happen. You decide that you can't trust industry to make this change on its own because you're asking businessmen to spend more money than they have to. You know that as an individual you don't have the power to bring about the change you believe is necessary, but you also know that individuals become powerful when they band together. Individuals band together in various ways, but the most important—in terms of power—is probably the governments we elect to represent us. You should be careful with a term like "government" and avoid such statements as "The government ought to do something about this." Not only is the "something" hopelessly vague, but we don't know what kind of government is in question. Most of us are subject to government on at least three levels: municipal, state, and federal. Coming back to your topic, you decide to argue for *federal* legislation, since acid rain is being generated in several different states—and then carried by air to still others.

You should now be ready to formulate your premise. Since your conclusion is going to demand federal regulation, you need, at the very beginning of your argument, to establish the principle that supports this conclusion. You realize that the federal government cannot solve all problems; you therefore need to define the nature of the government's responsibility so that it will be clear that you are appealing legitimately to the right authority. Legally, the federal government has broad powers to regulate interstate commerce, and this may be useful to you since most of the industries burning coal ship or receive goods across state lines. More specifically, ever since the creation of Yellowstone National Park in 1872, the U.S. government has undertaken a growing responsibility for protecting the environment. Acid rain is clearly an environmental issue, so you would not be demanding anything new, in terms of governmental responsibilities, if you appealed to the type of thinking that led to the creation of a national park system in 1916 and of the Environmental Protection Agency in 1970.

You know, however, that there are many people who distrust the growth of big government, and you do not want to alienate anyone by appealing to Washington too early in the essay. A premise can be a single sentence, a full paragraph, or more—depending on the length and complexity of the argument. Since its function is to establish a widely accepted value which even your opponents should be able to share, it would probably be wise to open this particular argument with a fairly general statement. Something like: "We all have a joint responsibility to protect the environment in which we live and preserve the balance of nature upon which our lives ultimately depend." As a thesis statement, this obviously needs to be developed in the paragraph that follows. In the second paragraph you might cite some popular examples of joint action to preserve the environment, pointing out, for example, that most people are relieved to see a forest fire brought under control or an oil slick cleaned up before it engulfs half the Pacific coastline. Once you have cited examples of this sort, you could then remind your audience of the role of state and federal government in coping with such emergencies, and emphasize that many problems are too large for states to handle. By this stage in your essay, you should be able to narrow your focus to acid rain, secure in the knowledge that you have laid the foundation for a logical argument. *If* the U.S. government has a responsibility to help protect the environment, and *if* acid rain is a serious threat to the environment of several states, then it follows logically that the federal government should act to bring this problem under control. A brief outline of your argument would look something like this:

1. The federal government has the responsibility to protect the quality of American air, water, soil, and so on—what is commonly called "the environment."
2. Acid rain, which is caused principally by burning high sulfur coal, is slowly killing American forests, endangering wildlife, and polluting lakes, rivers, and streams.
3. Therefore, the federal government should restrict the use of high sulfur coal.

Once again, this is only an *outline.* An essay that made this argument, explaining the problem in detail, anticipating the opposition, and providing meaningful concessions before reaching a clear and firm conclusion, would amount to at least several pages.

By outlining your argument in this way, you have followed the pattern of what is called a *syllogism,* a three-part argument in which the conclusion rests upon two premises, the first of which is called "the major premise" because it is the point from which we begin to work to a specific conclusion. Here, for example, is a simple example of a syllogism:

MAJOR PREMISE:	All people have hearts.
MINOR PREMISE:	John is a person.
CONCLUSION:	Therefore, John has a heart.

If the major and minor premises are both true, then the conclusion we have reached should be true. Note that the minor premise and the major premise share a term in common. In an argumentative essay, the "minor premise" would usually involve concrete evidence that helps support the more general statement with which the essay began.

A syllogism such as the one just cited may seem very simple. And it can be simple—if you're thinking clearly. On the other hand, it's even easier to write a syllogism (or an essay) that breaks down because of faulty reasoning. Consider the following example:

MAJOR PREMISE:	All women like to cook.
MINOR PREMISE:	Elizabeth is a woman.
CONCLUSION:	Therefore, Elizabeth likes to cook.

Technically, the form here is *valid.* The two premises have a term in common, and if we accept both the major and minor premises, then we will have to accept the conclusion. But someone who thinks along these lines may be in for a surprise, especially if he has married Elizabeth confidently expecting her to cook his favorite dishes every night just as his mother used to do. Elizabeth may *hate* to cook, preferring to go out bowling at night or read the latest issue of the *Journal of Organic Chemistry.* You should realize, then, that while a syllogism may be valid in terms of its organization, it can also be *untrue,* because it rests upon a premise that can be easily disputed. Always remember that your major premise should inspire widespread agreement. Someone who launches an argument with the generalization that "all women like to cook," is likely to find he's lost at least half of his audience before he even makes it to his second sentence. Some generalizations make sense and some do not. Don't make the mistake of confusing generally accepted truths with privately held opinions. You may argue effectively on behalf of your opinions, but you cannot expect your audience to accept an easily debatable opinion as the foundation for an argument on behalf of yet another opinion. You may have many important things to say, but nobody is going to read them if alienated by your major premise.

You should also realize that there are many arguments in which a premise may be implied but not stated. You might have a conversation like this:

> "I hear you and Elizabeth are getting married."
> "Yes, that's true."
> "Well now that you've got a woman to cook for you, maybe you could invite me over for dinner sometime."
> "Why do you think that Elizabeth will be doing the cooking?"
> "Because she is a woman."

The first speaker has made a number of possible assumptions. He may believe that all women like to cook, or perhaps he believes that all women are required to cook whether they like it or not. If the second speaker had the patience to continue this conversation, he would probably be able to discover the first speaker's premise. A syllogism that consists of only two parts is called an *enthymeme.* The part of the syllogism that has been omitted is usually the major premise, although it is occasionally the conclusion. Enthymemes usually result when a speaker or writer decides that it is unnecessary to state a point because it is obvious. Of course, what is obvious to someone trying to convince us with an enthymeme is not necessarily obvious to those of us who are trying to understand it. Although an enthymeme might reflect sound reasoning, the unstated part of the syllogism may reveal a flaw in the argument. When you encounter an enthymeme in your reading, you will often benefit from trying to reconstruct it as a full syllogism. Ask yourself what the writer has assumed, and then ask yourself if you agree with that assumption.

One sign of a faulty deductive argument is that a questionable point has been assumed to be universally true, and we may need to discover this point before we can decide that the argument is either invalid or untrue.

Deductive reasoning, which begins with a generalization and works to a conclusion that follows from this generalization, can be thought of as the opposite of *inductive reasoning*, which begins with specific observations and ends with a conclusion that goes beyond any of the observations that led up to it. So that you can see what a deductive essay might look like, here is a short essay written by a student:

The Weaker Sex

Wendy Mekler

National responsibilities should be equally shared by all   1
citizens, especially during a world crisis, when unity plays
a vital role. And there is no reason why these duties should
not be shared by everyone.

Women make up a large percentage of the United States popu-   2
lation. They are becoming more and more a major influence in
the social, economic, and political aspects of our country.
And yet, in certain areas, they are still dealt with as
frail, over-emotional, and super-sensitive creatures.
This is most obvious in the recent debate on reinstating
the draft, or more importantly, in the question of drafting women.

It has been argued that drafting women would be immoral,   3
illogical, and even unconstitutional. (Females just aren't
tough enough to handle the rigors of military life.) It appears to make little difference to legislators and the public that women have survived experiences equal to if not more
strenuous than any wartime conditions. There have been female explorers, dictators, and warriors. In Israel women
play a major role and take an active part in warfare.

Granted, not all women have the physical strength of most   4
men. And not all women have the mental capacity to deal capably with the atrocities of battle. However, not all men can
cope with these pressures either. For example, consider the
debilitating effect the Viet Nam War had on many of its veterans.

I am not trying to present participation in a war as a glo-   5
rious objective that should be sought after. On the contrary, war is a horrifying experience, especially in the

nuclear age. What I am attempting to point out is that Ameri—
can women have a responsibility to do their share—typing
reports and rolling bandages is not enough.

If a person has to risk his life on the battlefield because   6
he is a man, there is no reason why a woman should be exempt
from the same risk because she is a woman. I feel that if the
draft is reinstated, females should not only be inducted but
should be involved in active, front—line duty. How can women
expect equality if they are not willing to give up their spe—
cial privileges and accept their responsibilities?

This is not a perfect essay. In her opening paragraph, for example, Wendy
should have been more cautious in writing of "all citizens." One might ask if
she intended to imply that the physically and mentally handicapped should
also be drafted in the event of a national emergency. Nonetheless, the argument is clearly deductive. The premise with which it opens ("National responsibilities should be shared equally by all citizens . . .") is broader than
the minor premise ("Women make up a large percentage of the United States
population") and both are considerably broader than the conclusion they join
to support: "I feel that if the draft is reinstated, females should not only be
inducted but should be involved in active, front-line duty."

The strength of this argument lies in its careful organization. I have read
the essay to several classes, and students almost always agree with the opening paragraph, finding it a reasonable generalization. Many of these students
are subsequently disturbed to see where the logic of this argument eventually takes them. But the conclusion is implied by the premise. Anyone who
agrees with the first paragraph has been led halfway down the road toward
agreeing with the last.

As you can see from this example, deduction allows a writer the chance
to prepare the way for a controversial argument by strategically opening with
a key point that draws an audience closer, without immediately revealing
what exactly is afoot. With a genuinely controversial opinion, one must always face the risk of being shouted down—especially with a potentially hostile audience. Deductive reasoning increases our chance of gaining a fair
hearing. Logic may be difficult, but it is essential to effective argumentation.

Before turning away from "The Weaker Sex," you should note that Wendy
demonstrates good audience awareness. She anticipates opposition at the
beginning of the third paragraph ("It has been argued that drafting women
would be immoral . . .") and in the next two paragraphs concedes that "not
all women have the physical strength of most men," and that some women
lack "the mental capacity to deal capably with the atrocities of battle." These
are concessions that deserve to be taken seriously; they are especially likely
to appeal to the men and women who would be most opposed to drafting
young women. But the author was too sophisticated to let these concessions

simply sit on the page and possibly fester. She immediately returns to her thesis by claiming that many men also lack the physical strength and mental stamina that war demands. Having made this generalization, she then backs it up: "For example, consider the debilitating effect the Viet Nam War had on many of its veterans." This is a strong comeback, and should show you that concessions need not weaken an argument. On the contrary, they can strengthen an argument by making it more subtle and complex.

Since this essay was originally written for an audience of college freshmen, Wendy was also wise to emphasize that "war is a horrifying experience, especially in the nuclear age." College students frequently criticize the military and oppose whatever legislation seems likely to add to its already formidable power. A student audience might easily dismiss an argument on behalf of drafting women if the writer herself seemed especially eager to get her hands on a submachine gun and march off to Central America. But after reassuring us about the importance of avoiding war whenever possible, the author once again ends her paragraph by reaffirming her thesis that women need to do more than "typing reports and rolling bandages."

The moment at which writers choose to anticipate the opposition will usually vary; it depends upon the topic, how much the author knows about it, and how easily he or she can deal with the principal counterarguments that others might raise. But whether one is writing an inductive or a deductive argument, it is usually advisable to recognize and respond to the opposition fairly early in the essay. You will need at least one or two paragraphs to launch your own thesis, but by the time you are about one-third of the way into your essay, you may find it useful to defuse the opposition before it grows any stronger. If you wait until the very end of your essay to acknowledge that there are points of view different from your own, your audience may have already put your essay aside, dismissing it as "one-sided" or "narrow-minded." Also, it is usually a good idea to put the opposition's point of view at the beginning of a paragraph. By doing so, you can devote the rest of that paragraph to your response. It's not enough to recognize the opposition and include some of its arguments in your essay. You are a writer, not a referee, and you must always try to show your audience why it should not be persuaded by the counterarguments you have acknowledged. If you study the organization of "The Weaker Sex," you will see that the author begins her third, fourth, and fifth paragraphs with sentences that acknowledge other sides to the question of drafting women. But in each case, she was able to end these paragraphs with her own argument still marching clearly forward.

Reasoning with the Toulmin Model

Although both inductive and deductive reasoning suggest useful strategies for writers of argument, they also have their limitations. Many writers prefer not to be bound by a prefabricated method of organization and regard the syllogism, in particular, as unnecessarily rigid. To make their case, some writers choose to combine inductive and deductive reasoning within a single essay—and other writers can make convincing arguments without the formal use of either induction or deduction.

In an important book first published in 1958, a British philosopher named Stephen Toulmin demonstrated that the standard forms of logic needed to be reconsidered because they did not adequately explain all logical arguments. Emphasizing that logic is concerned with probability more often than certainty, he provided a new vocabulary for the analysis of argument. In Toulmin's model, every argument consists of three elements:

> *claim:* the equivalent of the conclusion or whatever it is a writer or speaker wants to try to prove;
>
> *data:* the information or evidence a writer or speaker offers in support of the claim; and
>
> *warrant:* a general statement that establishes a trustworthy relationship between the data and the claim.

Within any argument, the claim and the data will be explicit. The warrant may also be explicit, but it is often merely implied—especially when the arguer believes that the audience will readily agree to it.

To better understand these terms, let us consider an example adapted from one of Toulmin's:

CLAIM:	Raymond is an American citizen.
DATA:	Raymond was born in Puerto Rico.
WARRANT:	Anyone born in Puerto Rico is an American citizen.

These three statements may remind you of the three elements in a deductive argument. If arranged as a syllogism, they might look like this:

MAJOR PREMISE:	Anyone born in Puerto Rico is an American citizen.
MINOR PREMISE:	Raymond was born in Puerto Rico.
CONCLUSION:	Raymond is an American citizen.

The advantage of Toulmin's model becomes apparent when we realize that there is a possibility that Raymond was prematurely born to French parents who were only vacationing in Puerto Rico, and he is now serving in the French army. Or perhaps he was an American citizen but became a naturalized citizen of the Soviet Union after defecting with important U.S. Navy documents. Because the formal logic of a syllogism is designed to lead to a conclusion that is *necessarily* true, Toulmin argued that it is ill-suited for working to a conclusion that is *probably* true. Believing that the importance of the syllogism was overemphasized in the study of logic, Toulmin argued that there was a need for a "working logic" which would be easier to apply in the rhetorical situations in which arguers most often find themselves. He designed his own model so that it can easily incorporate *qualifiers* such as "probably," "presumably," and "generally." Here is a revision of the first example:

CLAIM: Raymond is probably an American citizen.
DATA: Raymond was born in Puerto Rico.
WARRANT: Anyone born in Puerto Rico is entitled to American citizenship.

You should note that both the claim and the warrant have now been modified. You should also note that Toulmin's model does not dictate any specific pattern in which these three elements must be arranged, and this is a great advantage for writers. The claim may come at the beginning of an essay, or it could just as easily come after a discussion of both the data and the warrant. Similarly, the warrant may precede the data or it may follow it—or, as already noted, the warrant may be implied rather than explicitly stated at any point in the essay.

If you write essays of your own using the Toulmin model, you may find yourself making different types of claims. In one essay you might make a claim that can be supported entirely by facts. For example, if you wanted to argue that the stock market should be subject to greater regulation, you could define the extent of current regulation, report statistics from the stock market crash of 1987, and cite specific abuses such as scandals involving insider trading. In another essay, however, you might make a claim that is easier to support with a mixture of facts, expert opinion, and appeals to the values of your audience. If, for example, you wanted to argue against abortion, your data might consist of facts (such as the number of abortions performed within a particular clinic in 1988), testimony on which it is possible to have a difference of opinion (such as the point at which human life begins), and an appeal to moral values that you believe your audience should share with you. In short, you will cite different types of data depending on the nature of the claim you want to argue.

The nature of the warrant will also differ from one argument to another. In may be a matter of law (such as the Jones Act of 1917 which guarantees U.S. citizenship to the citizens of Puerto Rico), an assumption that one's data have come from a reliable source (such as documents published by the Securities and Exchange Commission), or a generally accepted value (such as the sanctity of human life). But whatever your warrant, you should be prepared to back it up if called upon to do so. No matter how strongly you may believe in your claim, or how compelling your data may be, your argument will not be convincing if your warrant cannot be substantiated.

It is important to realize that the Toulmin model for argumentation does not require that you abandon everything you've learned about inductive and deductive reasoning. These different systems of logic complement one another and combine to form a varied menu from which you can choose whatever seems best for a particular occasion. Unless your instructor specifies that an assignment incorporate a particular type of reasoning, you will often be able to choose the type of logic you wish to employ just as you might make any number of other writing decisions. And having choices is ultimately a luxury, not a burden.

For an example of a student essay that reflects the Toulmin model for reasoning, consider the following argument on the importance of studying history.

History Is for People Who Think
Ron Tackett

Can a person consider himself a thinking, creative, responsible citizen and not care about history? Can an institution that proposes to foster such attributes do so without including history in its curriculum? Many college students would answer such a question with an immediate, "Yes!" But those who are quick so answer do so without reflecting on what history truly is and how and why it is important.

History is boring, complain many students. Unfortunately, a lot of people pick up a bad taste of history from the primary and secondary schools. Too many lower level history courses (and college level, too) are just glorified Trivial Pursuit; rife with rote memorization of dates and events deemed important by the teacher and textbooks, coupled with monotone lectures that could induce comas in hyperactive children. Instead of simply making students memorize when Pearl Harbor was attacked by the Japanese, teachers should concentrate on instilling an understanding of why the Japanese felt they had no alternative but to attack the United States. History is a discipline of understanding, not memorization.

Another common complaint is that history is unimportant. But even the most fanatic antihistory students, if they were honest, would have to admit that history is important at least within the narrow confines of their own disciplines of study. Why be an artist if you are merely going to repeat the past (and probably not as expertly, since you would have to spend your time formulating theories and rules already known and recorded in Art's history)? Why write <u>The Great Gatsby</u> or compose <u>Revolution</u> again? How could anyone hope to be a mathematician, or a scientist, without knowing the field's history? Even a genius needs a base from which to build. History helps provide that base.

History is also important in being a politically aware citizen. Knowing that we entered World War I on the side of

1

2

3

4

the Allies in part because Woodrow Wilson was a great Anglo-
phile, as some historians charge, is not vital to day-to-day
life. But it is important to know that the economic repara-
tions imposed on Germany after the war set the stage for the
rise of Hitler and World War II and that that war ended with a
Russian domination of Eastern Europe that led to the Cold
War, during which political philosophies were formulated
that still affect American foreign and domestic policies.
This type of history enables citizens to form an intelligent
world view and possibly help our nation avoid past mistakes.
Of course, this illustration is simplified, but the point is
as valid as when Santayana said that without history, we are
"condemned to repeat it." This does not mean that history
will repeat itself exactly, but that certain patterns recur
in history, and if we understand the patterns of what has
gone before, perhaps we can avoid making the mistakes our
ancestors made.

A person can live a long life, get a job, and raise a family   5
without having any historical knowledge. But citizens who
possess a strong knowledge of history are better prepared to
contribute intelligently to their jobs and their society.
Thus, knowing which Third World nations have a history of de-
faulting on loans can help a bank executive save his or her
institution and its customers a great deal of grief by avoiding, or seeking exceptional safeguards on, such loans. And
knowing the history of U.S. involvement in Central and South
America, from naval incidents with Chile in the 1890s to
trying to overthrow the Sandanistas in Nicaragua in the
1980s, can help Americans understand why many people and nations are concerned about U.S. policies in the region. More
importantly, Americans cannot intelligently determine what
those policies should be without a knowledge of history.

Now, if history is important enough to be required in col-   6
lege, how many credits are enough and what sort of history
should be taught? American, European, Eastern, Latin American, or yet another? First, a course in American history must
be required. Students can little appreciate the history of
others, without first knowing their own. Secondly, since we
more and more realize that we are members of a "global community," at least one world history course should be mandated.
Though there is no magic number of credits that will ensure
the student becoming a thinking, creative member of society,
history can help fulfill the collegiate purpose of fashion-

ing men and women with the potential for wisdom and the ability to critically appraise political, economic, and moral
issues. Thus, history should be a required part of the college curriculum.

In arguing on behalf of history, Ron shows that he is well aware that many students would like to avoid history courses. Paragraphs 2 and 3 are devoted to anticipating and responding to opposition. Although Ron concedes that history can be boring if it is badly taught, and makes an additional concession at the beginning of paragraph 5, he still insists that all college students should be required to take at least two history courses. The *claim* of this essay is "history should be a required part of the college curriculum." The *warrant* behind this claim is a value that is likely to be widely accepted: a college education should help people to think critically and become responsible members of society. This warrant underlies the entire argument, but it can be found specifically in the last paragraph where Ron refers to "the collegiate purpose of fashioning men and women with the potential for wisdom and the ability to critically appraise political, economic, and moral issues" immediately before making his claim.

Providing *data* to support this claim presented the writer with a challenge, since it would be difficult to provide statistics or other factual evidence to prove that the claim fulfills the warrant. A reader might agree with the warrant and still doubt if requiring college students to study history would give them the ability to think critically about political and moral issues. Ron chose to support his claim by defining history as "a discipline of understanding, not memorization" and providing several examples of historical events that are worth understanding: the Japanese attack on Pearl Harbor, the consequences of World War I, and the nature of U.S. involvement in Central and South America. Additional support for the claim is provided by appeals to other values which Ron has assumed his audience to possess. Paragraph 3 includes an appeal to self-interest: knowing the history of your own field can save you from wasting time. This same strategy is employed in paragraph 5 where Ron suggests that the knowledge of history can lead to better job performance. All of the examples found within the essay are clearly related to the values that the argument has invoked, and within the limitations of a short essay Ron has done a good job of supporting his claim.

AVOIDING LOGICAL FALLACIES

An apparently logical argument may reveal serious flaws if we take the trouble to examine it closely. Mistakes in reasoning are called logical *fallacies*. This term comes from the Latin word for deceit, and there is some form of deception behind most of these lapses in logic. It is easy to deceive ourselves into believing that we are making a strong argument when we have actually lost our way somehow, and many fallacies are unintentional. But others are used deliberately by writers or speakers for whom "winning" an argument is more important than looking for truth. Here is a list of common fallacies that you should be careful to avoid in your own arguments and that you should be alert to in the arguments of others.

Ad Hominem Argument   An ad hominem argument is an argument that attacks the personal character or reputation of one's opponents while ignoring what he or she has to say. *Ad hominem* is Latin for "to the man." Although an audience may often consider the character of a writer or speaker in deciding whether it can trust what he or she has to say, most of us realize that good people can make bad arguments, and even a crook can sometimes tell the truth. It is almost always better to give a logical response to an opponent's arguments than to ignore those arguments and indulge in personal attacks.

Ad Misericordiam Argument   An ad misericordiam argument is an appeal to pity. Writers are often justified in appealing to the pity of their readers when the need to inspire this emotion is closely related to whatever they are arguing for and when the entire argument does not rest upon this appeal alone. For example, someone who is attempting to convince you to donate one of your kidneys for a medical transplant would probably assure you that you could live with only one kidney and that there is a serious need for the kidney you are being asked to donate. But in addition to making these crucial points, the arguer might also move you to pity by describing what will happen to the person who has been denied a needed transplant.

When the appeal to pity stands alone, even in charitable appeals where its use is fundamental, the result is often questionable. On my way to work this semester, I have been driving past a large billboard advertising for the American Red Cross. It features a closeup photograph of a distraught (but nevertheless good-looking) man, beneath which in large letters runs this caption: PLEASE, MY LITTLE GIRL NEEDS BLOOD. Although I already believe in the importance of donating blood, and I also believe it is important for the Red Cross to encourage people to donate it, I find myself questioning the implications of this ad. Can we donate blood and ask that it be reserved for the exclusive use of little girls? Is the life of a little girl more valuable than the life of a little boy? Are the lives of children more valuable than the lives of adults? Of course, few people would donate blood unless they sympathized with those who need transfusions, and it may be unrealistic to expect logic in advertising. But consider how weak an argument becomes when the appeal to pity has little to do with the issue in question. Someone who has seldom attended class and failed all his examinations but then tries to argue, "I deserve to pass this course because I've had a lot of problems at home," is making a fallacious appeal to pity because the "argument" asks his instructor to overlook relevant evidence and make a decision favorable to the arguer because the instructor has been moved to feel sorry for him. You should be skeptical of any appeal to pity that is irrelevant to the conclusion or that seems designed to distract attention from other factors which you should be considering.

Ad Populum Argument   An ad populum argument, which means "argument to the crowd," plays upon the general values of an audience often to the point where reasonable discussion of a specific issue is no longer possible. A newspaper that creates a patriotic frenzy through exaggerated reports of enemy "atrocities" is relying on an ad populum argument. But the ad populum argument can also take more subtle forms. A politician may remind you that he was born and raised in "this great state," that he loves his children, and admires his wife—all of which are factors believed to appeal to the average man and woman but which nevertheless are unlikely to affect his performance in office. When a candidate lingers on what a wonderful family man he is, it may be time to ask a question about the economy.

Argument by Analogy   An analogy is a comparison that works on more than one level, and it is possible to use analogy effectively when reasoning inductively. To do this, you must be sure that the things you are comparing have several characteristics in common and that these similarities are relevant to the conclusion that you intend to draw. If you observe that isolation produces depression in chimpanzees, you could argue that isolation can cause a similar problem for human beings. The strength of this argument would depend upon the degree to which chimps are analogous to humans, so you would need to proceed with care and demonstrate that there are important similarities between the two species. When arguing from analogy, it is important to remember that you are speculating. As is the case with any type of inductive reasoning, you can reach a conclusion that is likely to be true but not guaranteed to be true. It is always possible that you have overlooked a significant factor that will cause the analogy to break down.

Unfortunately, analogies are often misused. An argument from analogy that reaches a firm conclusion is likely to be fallacious, and it is certain to be fallacious if the analogy itself is inappropriate. If a congressional candidate asks us to vote for him because of his outstanding record as a football player, he might be able to claim that politics, like football, involves teamwork. But because a successful politician needs many skills and will probably never need to run across a field or knock someone down, it would be foolish to vote on the basis of this questionable analogy. The differences between football and politics outweigh the similarities, and it would be fallacious to pretend otherwise.

Begging the Question   In the fallacy of "begging the question," a writer begins with a premise that is acceptable to anyone who will agree with the conclusion that is subsequently reached—a conclusion often very similar to the premise itself. Thus, the argument goes around in a circle. For instance, someone might begin an essay by claiming, "Required courses like freshman English are a waste of time," and end with the conclusion that "Freshman English should not be a required course." It might indeed be arguable that freshman English should not be required, but the author who begins with the premise that freshman English is a waste of time has assumed what the argument should be devoted to proving. Because it is much easier to claim that something is true than to prove it is true, you may be tempted to beg the question you set out to answer. This is a temptation that should always be avoided.

Equivocation   Someone who equivocates uses vague or ambiguous language to mislead an audience. In argumentation, equivocation often takes the form of using one word in several different senses, without acknowledging that this has been done. It is especially easy to equivocate if you are addicted to abstract language. Watch out in particular for the abuse of such terms as "right," "natural," "liberal," "revolutionary," "freedom," "law," "justice," and "real." When you use words like these, make sure you make your meaning clear. And make double sure your meaning doesn't shift when you use the term again.

False Dilemma   A false dilemma is a fallacy in which a speaker or writer poses a choice between two alternatives while overlooking other possibilities and implying that other possibilities do not exist. If a freshman receives low grades at the end of his first semester in college and then claims, "What's wrong with low grades? Is cheating any better?" he is pretending that there is no other possibility—for example, that of earning higher grades by studying harder, a possibility that is recognized by most students and teachers.

Guilt by Association   This is a fallacy that is frequently made in politics, especially toward the end of a close campaign. A candidate who happens to be religious, for example, may be maneuvered by opponents into the false position of being held accountable for the actions of all the men and women who hold to that particular faith. Nothing specific has been *argued*, but a negative association has been either created or played upon through hints and innuendos. Guilt by association may take the form of an ad hominem argument, or it may be more subtle. A careless writer may simply stumble into using a stereotype to avoid the trouble of coming up with a concrete example. But whatever its form, guilt by association is a fallacy in which prejudice takes the place of thought.

Ignoring the Question   When someone says, "I'm glad you asked that question!" and then promptly begins to talk about something else, he or she is guilty of ignoring the question. Politicians are famous for exploiting this technique when they don't want to be pinned down on a subject. But students (and teachers) sometimes use it too when asked a question that they want to avoid. Ignoring the question is also likely to occur when friends or lovers have a fight. In the midst of an emotional quarrel, criticism is likely to evoke remarks like, "What about you!" or "Never mind the budget! I'm sick of worrying about money! We need to talk about what's happening to our relationship!"

Jumping to Conclusions   This fallacy is so common that it has become a cliché. It means that the conclusion in question has not been supported by an adequate amount of evidence. Because one green apple is sour, it does not follow that all green apples are sour. Failing one test does not mean that you will necessarily fail the next. An instructor who seems disorganized the first day of class may eventually prove to be the best teacher you ever had. You should always try to have more than one example to support an argument. Be skeptical of arguments that seem heavy on opinion but weak on evidence.

Non Sequitur   This term is Latin for "it does not follow." Although this can be said of almost any faulty argument, the term "non sequitur" is usually applied more precisely. The most common type of non sequitur is a complex sentence in which the subordinate clause does not clearly relate to the main clause, especially where causation is involved. An example of this type of non sequitur would be "Because the wind was blowing so fiercely, I passed the quiz in calculus." This is a non sequitur because passing calculus should not be dependent on the weather. A cause-and-effect relationship has been claimed but not explained. It may be that the wind forced you to stay indoors, which led you to spend more time studying than you usually do, and this in turn led you to pass your quiz. But someone reading the sentence as written could not be expected to know this. A non sequitur may also take the form of a compound sentence: "Mr. Blandshaw is young, and so he should be a good teacher." Mr. Blandshaw may indeed be a good teacher, but not just because he is young. On the contrary, young Mr. Blandshaw may be inexperienced, anxious, and humorless. He may also give you unrealistically large assignments because he lacks a clear sense of how much work most students can handle. So watch out for non sequiturs the next time you register for classes.

Non sequiturs sometimes form the basis for an entire argument: "William Henderson will make a good governor because he is a friend of the workingman. He is a friend of the workingman because he was a plumber before he became a millionaire through his contracting business." Before allowing this argument to go any further, you should realize that you've been already asked to swallow two non sequiturs. Being a good governor involves more than being "a friend of the workingman." And there is no reason to assume that Henderson is "a friend of the workingman" just because he used to be a plumber. It may be over thirty years since he last saw the inside of a union hall, and he may have acquired his wealth by taking advantage of the men and women who work for him.

Post Hoc, Ergo Propter Hoc   If you assume that an event is the result of something that merely occurred before it, you have committed the fallacy of post hoc, ergo propter hoc. This is a Latin phrase which means "after this, therefore because of this." Superstitious people offer many examples of this type of fallacious thinking. They might tell you, "Everything was doing fine until the lunar eclipse last month; *that's* why the economy is in trouble." Or personal misfortune may be traced back to spilling salt, stepping on a crack, or walking under a ladder.

This fallacy is often found in the arguments of writers who are determined to prove the existence of various conspiracies. They often seem to amass an impressive amount of evidence—but the "evidence" is frequently questionable. Or, to take a comparatively simple example, someone might be suspected of murder simply because of being seen near the victim's house a day or two before the crime occurred. This suspicion may lead to the discovery of evidence, but it could just as easily lead to the false arrest of the meter reader from the electric company. Being observed near the scene of a crime proves nothing by itself. A prosecuting attorney who would be foolish enough to base a case on such a flimsy piece of evidence would be guilty of post hoc, ergo propter hoc reasoning. Logic should always recognize the distinction between *causes* and what may simply be *coincidences.* Sequence is not a cause because every event is preceded by an infinite number of other events, all of which cannot be held responsible for whatever happens today.

This fallacy can be found in more subtle forms in essays on abstract social problems. Writers who blame contemporary problems on such instant explanations as "the rise of television" or "the popularity of computers" are no more convincing than the parent who argues that all the difficulties of family life can be traced to the rise of rock and roll. It is impossible to understand the present without understanding the past. But don't isolate at random any one event in the past, and then try to argue that it explains everything.

A final caution: be careful not to accidentally imply a cause-and-effect relationship where you did not intend to do so. Trying to be concise, you might find yourself writing something like "Castro took over Cuba in 1959, and Hemingway killed himself only two years later." If you really believe that Hemingway killed himself *because* of the Cuban revolution, then you'll need to work hard to prove it. To simply link these two events together in one sentence is to fall into the fallacy of post hoc, ergo propter hoc.

Slippery Slope   According to this fallacy, one step will inevitably lead to an undesirable second step. An example would be claiming that legalized abortion will lead to euthanasia or that censoring pornography will lead to the end of freedom for the press. Although it is important to consider the probable effects of any step that is being debated, it is fallacious to claim that men and women will necessarily tumble downhill as the result of any one step. There is always the possibility that we'll be able to keep our feet firmly on the ground even though we've moved them from where they used to be.

Straw Man   Because it is easier to demolish a man of straw than to beat a live opponent fairly, arguers are sometimes tempted to pretend that they are responding to the views of their opponents when they are only setting up a type of artificial opposition which they can easily refute. The most common form of this fallacy is to exaggerate the views of others or to attribute to them views that they do not actually hold. This fallacy almost always avoids the real issue. An example would be arguing against defense spending by claiming that peace is more desirable than war. Since almost everyone believes that war is undesirable, this argument avoids the more difficult question of how peace is best secured.

UNDERSTANDING OTHER FORMS OF PERSUASION

Of the various forms of persuasive writing, logical argument is the most honorable. Its object is truth, not manipulation—although logic, like any other tool, can be abused. It appeals to the mind and works only to the extent that it moves ahead with mathematical clarity and precision. This is why logic is difficult: whether we are writing a logical argument or simply trying to understand one, we have to be actively involved with ideas. To put it simply, we have to *think*. And behind any logical argument is the assumption that reasonable men and women should agree with its outcome—not so much because it is gracefully written (although it may be that), but because it is *true*.

There are other types of writing that rely upon an indirect appeal to the mind, exploiting what is known about the psychological makeup of an audience or its most probable fears and desires. Successful advertising is *persuasive* in that it encourages us to buy one product or another, but there is nothing logical about it. Few people have the money, time, or inclination to sample every product available for consumption. When we buy a particular mouthwash, toothpaste, soap, or soft drink—and even when we make purchases as large as a car—we may simply choose the cheapest product available. But bargain hunting aside, we are frequently led to purchase brands that advertising has taught us to associate with health, wealth, and happiness. A prominent greeting card company insists that we send their cards if we really and truly care about someone. Love has also been used as the justification for piling up extravagantly high phone bills. (After all, who wants to worry about money when doing something as noble as "reaching out to touch someone"?) One popular cigarette is associated with the masculinity of mounted cowboys, and another implies a dubious link with the women's movement. Even in an age that pretends to have outgrown sexual stereotyping, Detroit continues to suggest that beautiful women can be acquired through the purchase of a beautiful car. Almost no one really believes this sort of thing when forced to stop and think about it. But we often act without thinking, and this is one of the reasons why advertising has been able to grow into a billion dollar industry. Through the clever use of language and visual images, advertisers can lead people into a variety of illogical and possibly ruinous acts.

This, then, is the principal distinction between argument and persuasion: argument seeks to clarify thought, while persuasion often seeks to obscure it. Argument is dependent on facts and does not necessarily dictate any one particular course of action. Persuasion, on the other hand, can work altogether independent of the facts as we know them (such as how much money we can afford to spend before the end of the month), and it is almost always designed to inspire action—whether it is buying a new kind of deodorant or voting for the candidate with the nicest teeth. Persuasion is thus a form of domination. Its object is to make people agree with the will of the persuader, regardless of whether the persuader is "right" or simply selling his or her services by the hour.

In addition to utilizing psychology, persuasion often works by appealing to our emotions. A persuasive writer or speaker knows how to evoke feelings ranging from love, loyalty, and patriotism to anger, envy, and xenophobia. An audience may be deeply moved even when nothing substantial has been said. With a quickened pulse or tearful eyes, we may find ourselves convinced that we've read or heard something wonderfully profound. But a few days later, we may realize that we've been inhaling the intoxicating fumes of a heavily scented gasbag, rather than digesting genuine "food for thought."

Although you may often find it useful to appeal to the heart as well as to the head, you should try to avoid appealing to the heart alone. People can be fickle, and the audience you move on Friday may have forgotten your name by Monday. An argument or speech that works primarily by inspiring an emotional response can succeed only when an audience can be called upon for immediate action. If a senator can inspire his colleagues moments before a critically important vote, or an evangelist move a congregation to generosity just as the collection plate is about to be passed, then the results of such persuasion may be significant. But opportunities of this sort are rare for most writers. Almost everything we write can be put aside and reconsidered at another time. Irrespective of the ethical importance of arguing what is true and not just what is convenient, there is also a very practical reason for trying to argue logically: the arguments that carry the greatest weight are usually the arguments that are capable of holding up under analysis. They make more sense as we think about them, not less. Whereas persuasion relies upon impulse, argument depends upon conviction. Our impulses may determine what we do this afternoon, but our convictions shape the rest of our lives.

In addition to the various types of fallacious reasoning that we have already discussed, persuasive writing sometimes becomes dishonest—which is worse than being illogical. When analyzing persuasion, you should be especially on guard against the following three tricks.

Bogus Claims   A claim can be considered "bogus," or false, whenever a persuader promises more than he or she can prove beyond dispute. If a Chicago restaurant offers "fresh country peas" in the middle of January, you might want to ask where these peas were freshly picked. And if a large commercial bakery advertises "homemade pies," try asking whose home they were made in. You'll probably get some strange looks, because many people don't really expect words to mean what they say. But good writers become good writers in part because they have eyes and ears—eyes that see and ears that hear.

If a toothpaste promises to give your mouth "sex appeal," you'd still better be careful about whom you try to kiss. A claim of this sort is fairly crude, and therefore easily recognizable. But bogus claims can take many forms, some more subtle than others. A television advertisement for a new improved designer laxative may star an unnamed man in a white coat, with a stethoscope around his neck. The advertisement implies—without necessarily saying so—that the product in question is endorsed by physicians. Ads of this sort are also likely to speak vaguely of "recent studies," or better yet, "recent *clinical* studies," which are declared to prove a product's value. The product may indeed have value; on the other hand, it may be indistinguishable from its competition except in price and packaging. You might like it when you try it. But well-educated men and women should always be a little skeptical about promises from strangers.

When writing an essay, it is easy to fall into the habit of making bogus claims when reaching for generalizations to support your point of view. Imitating the style of the advertisements with which they grew up, careless writers like to refer to those ever popular "recent studies" which conveniently seem to support whatever is being argued. Such phrases as "recent studies have shown" enable writers to avoid identifying who did the research. A recent study may provide the evidence to prove a point, but a good writer should be prepared to cite it, especially when the claim is surprising. It is one thing to write "Recent studies have shown that nutrition plays an important role in maintaining good health," for the generalization in this case enjoys wide acceptance. It would be something else altogether to toss off a claim like, "Recent studies have shown that apricot pits can cure cancer." This example is only a slight exaggeration of the type of unsupported claims that can be made by sloppy writers who are desperate to complete an assignment.

Writers who like to refer to "recent studies" are also fond of alluding to unspecified statistics, as in "Statistics have shown," or "according to statistics." If you look hard enough, you can find statistics to prove almost anything, so don't make the mistake of assuming the word itself is filled with such dazzling appeal that further documentation is unnecessary. Similarly, you should turn a critical eye on claims like "It is a well-known fact that . . ." or "Everybody knows that . . . ." If the fact *is* well known, why is the writer boring us with what we already know? And if the fact is *not* well known, as is usually the case when lines of this sort are thrown about, then the writer had better explain how he or she knows it.

In short, if you want to avoid bogus claims, never claim anything that would leave you speechless if you were called upon to explain or defend what you have written.

Loaded Terms   Good writers have good diction; they know a lot of words, and just as important, they know how to use them accurately. They know that most words have positive or negative *connotations*—associations with the word that go beyond its standard definition or *denotation.* "Placid," "tranquil," or "serene" might all be used to describe someone who is "calm," but each word creates a slightly different impression. An experienced writer is likely to pause before choosing the adjective that best suits his or her subject.

A term becomes *loaded* when it is asked to carry more emotional weight than its context can legitimately support. A loaded term is a word or phrase that goes beyond connotation into the unconvincing world of the heavy handed and narrow minded. To put it simply, it is *slanted* or *biased.*

Loaded terms may appeal to the zealous, but they mislead the unwary reader and offend the critically minded. For example, when an aspiring journalist denounces the Reagan "regime" in the school newspaper, he is taking what many men and women would consider a cheap shot—regardless of their own politics. "Regime" is a loaded term because it is most frequently used to describe military dictatorships. Even someone who opposed everything Reagan stood for should still be clearheaded enough to speak of the Reagan "Administration," which is the term best suited for a political discussion of the U.S. Presidency.

Like "regime," many words have such strong connotations that they can become loaded terms very easily. In the United States, for example, "Marxist" is almost always used as a type of rebuke. (And in communist countries, "capitalist" is used in a similar way.) When most Americans hear that an idea is "Marxist," they become immediately hostile toward it. Nevertheless, when Salvador Allende became the democratically elected president of Chile in 1970, American newspapers seemed unable to report news from Chile without repeated references to "Marxist President Salvador Allende," as if "Marxist" was part of his job title. Even now, so many years after his assassination, "Marxist President Salvador Allende" can still be found making occasional appearances in the American press.

Within a particular context, a seemingly inoffensive word may become a loaded term. In order to manipulate reader response, a writer may sneak unnecessary adjectives into his or her work. A political correspondent may write, "Mr. D'Arcy, the wealthy candidate from Park Ridge, spoke today at Meryton High School." The candidate's income has nothing to do with the news event being reported, so "wealthy" is a loaded term. It's an extra word that serves only one function: to divide the candidate from the newspaper's audience, very few of whom are "wealthy." It would not be surprising if some readers began to turn against this candidate, regardless of his platform, simply because they had been led to associate him with a background that is alien to their own.

Do not make the mistake of assuming that loaded terms occur only in political discourse. They can be found almost anywhere, if you take the trouble to read critically and intelligently. You may even find some in your textbooks.

Misrepresentation   Misrepresentation can take many forms. Someone may come right out and lie to you, telling you something you know—or subsequently discover—to be untrue. In the course of writing a paper, someone may invent statistics or alter research data that point to an unwelcome conclusion. And then, of course, there is *plagiarism*—which means taking someone else's words or ideas without acknowledgment and passing them off as your own.

There are always going to be people who are tempted to lie, and there isn't much we can do about this except to keep our eyes open, read well, and choose our friends with care. As for how to do research, we will discuss this subject separately in Part 3 of this book. Another type of misrepresentation exists that must be understood as part of our introduction to the principles of argument and persuasion: dishonest writers will often misrepresent their opponents by twisting what others have said.

The most common way in which writers misrepresent opposing arguments is to oversimplify them. The ability to summarize what others have said or written is a skill that cannot be taken for granted, and we will turn to it shortly. There is always the possibility that someone may misrepresent an opponent accidentally—having failed to understand what has been said or having confused it in reporting it. But it is also possible to misreport others *deliberately*. A complex argument can be reduced to ridicule in a slogan, or an important element of such an argument could be entirely overlooked, creating a false impression.

Political campaigns are especially likely to inspire deliberate misrepresentation. Republicans are said to favor the rich, and Democrats are blamed for big government. Biologists are accused of tampering with life, and physicists with trying to destroy it. Feminists have been said to favor single-sex toilets, and homosexuals accused of corrupting children. And so forth. A list of misrepresented realities would be very long indeed. *Don't add to it.* What's more, have the courage to ask for evidence whenever someone seems drifting off into an ideological fantasy.

Also, if you ever find it necessary to quote someone, make sure you do so not only correctly but also *fairly*. The concept of "quoting out of context" is so familiar that the phrase has become a cliché. But clichés sometimes embody fundamental truths, and here is one of them: quotations should be more than accurate; they should also reflect the overall nature of the quoted source. When you select a passage that truly represents the thesis of another's work, you can use it in good conscience—as long as you remember to put it in quotation marks and reveal to your readers where you got it. But if you fasten onto a minor detail and quote a line that could be misunderstood if lifted away from the sentences that originally surrounded it, then you are guilty of a type of misrepresentation as dishonest as oversimplification.

Whether you are writing persuasion, or simply trying to defend yourself against it, it is important to be aware of the ways in which the techniques of persuasive writing can be abused. And they are abused—frequently. As a result, many people automatically distrust anyone who seems unusually persuasive, convinced that smooth talkers will always prove to be con men of one sort or another. In *Gulliver's Travels*, Jonathan Swift defined lawyers as "a society of men among us, bred up from their youth in the art of proving by words multiplied for the purpose, that white is black, and black is white, according as they are paid." Lawyers are still regarded skeptically by many people, even if they have never read Swift. Advertisers, actors, and public relations experts also have reputations that often suffer because people question the integrity of anyone who uses language too glibly.

There is nothing new about this. Over two thousand years ago, there was a group of philosophy teachers in ancient Greece known as the Sophists. They were smart, and they were articulate. But according to Plato, they were a little too slick. The Sophists could argue anything—and do so eloquently. They were famous for ingenuity rather than wisdom or honesty. Their name lives on in the word *sophistry,* which means "a clever and tricky argument that makes sense only superficially." If you make a genuinely logical argument, you may make some people angry with you, but you will not be accused of dishonesty. When you abandon logic for the techniques of persuasion, make sure that this is simply a change in writing strategy. Never write anything that you don't believe. This does not mean that there's anything wrong with writing fiction or satire. But it does mean that good writers shouldn't tell lies.

Working with Sources

SUMMARIZING

On many occasions you will be required to summarize what others have said or written—or even what you yourself have written. This skill is especially important in argumentation. You will have to be able to summarize the main arguments of your opponents if you want to write a convincing argumentative essay. And research papers will become ridiculously long, obscure, and unwieldy if you lack the ability to summarize your reading.

Equipped with a yellow felt pen, some students make the mistake of "highlighting" nearly everything that they read. Unable to distinguish the main points from the supporting details, such students end up with yellow-coated pages that offer little help when the time comes to review. When you are reading material for a college class, and especially when you think you may need to summarize this material, you should read it at least twice. Instead of marking in ink, you might find it useful to make a small check (√) in the margin whenever a line seems important the first time you are reading something (assuming, of course, that the book is your own). Use a pencil so that you can erase these marks later if you wish to. It's hard to erase ink and almost impossible to erase highlighting, and you don't want to be distracted by permanent marks that you later decide you don't need.

There is no clear rule to determine what passages are more significant than others. Every piece of writing must be judged on its own merits, and this means that you must consider every paragraph individually. The first sentence of a paragraph may be important if it introduces a new idea. Unfortunately for writers of summary (but fortunately for readers, who would be easily bored if every paragraph followed the same mechanical pattern) the first sentence may simply be a transitional sentence, linking the paragraph with whatever has preceded it. The *topic sentence* (also called the *thesis sentence*) is the single most important sentence in most paragraphs—the exception being the very short paragraphs that serve only as transitions. (Transitional paragraphs do not advance a new idea, but simply link together longer paragraphs devoted to ideas that are related, but not closely enough so that the paragraphs can flow smoothly together). It is also important to realize that the *topic sentence can occur anywhere in the paragraph.*

41

As you read the material you want to summarize, limit yourself to marking no more than one or two sentences per paragraph. You should identify the topic sentence, and you may want to mark a line that contains an important supporting detail. At this point, you may choose to copy all the material you have noted onto a separate sheet of paper. But do not think that this means you have completed a summary. What you have are the notes for a summary: a collection of short quotations that are unlikely to flow smoothly together. A good summary should always be easy to read. So you must now take your notes and go to work shaping them into a clear, concise piece of writing.

Writers of summary must be prepared to *paraphrase,* which means to restate something you've read or heard into your own words. There are many different reasons for paraphrasing, and you've probably been practicing this skill since you were a child. We frequently paraphrase the words of others to soften unpleasant truths. Sometimes we may even be tempted to restate a relatively mild statement more harshly to make trouble for someone we don't like. But in writing summary, we should paraphrase only to make complex ideas more easily understandable. A paraphrase can be as long as the original material; under some circumstances, it may even be longer. So don't confuse paraphrase with summary. Paraphrasing is simply one of the skills that we call upon to write a coherent summary.

Reading over the quotations you have compiled, look for lines that seem longer than they have to be and ideas that seem unnecessarily complicated. Lines of this sort are likely subjects for paraphrase. As you restate these ideas more simply, you may also be able to include details that appeared elsewhere in the paragraph and seem too important to leave out. You should not have to restate everything that someone else has written, although there's nothing necessarily wrong in doing so. A summary can include direct quotation, so long as the quotations are relatively short and have a clarity that you yourself cannot surpass.

You should now reread your paraphrasing and any quotations that you have included. Look for gaps between sentences, where the writing seems awkward or choppy. Rearrange any sentences that would flow more smoothly once you have done so. Eliminate any repetition and add transitional phrases wherever they can help smooth the way from one idea to the next. After you have made certain that your sentences follow in a clear and easily readable sequence and have corrected any errors in grammar, spelling, or syntax, you should have an adequate summary of the material you set out to cover. But you would be wise to read over what you have written at least one more time, making sure that the content accurately reflects the nature of whatever is being summarized. And be absolutely sure that any direct quotations are recognizable as such by being placed within quotation marks.

Writing summary requires good judgment. A writer has to be able to distinguish what is essential from what is not, and the judgment that summary demands should be editorial only. If the material being summarized has a particular bias, then a good summary should indicate that that bias is part of the work in question. But *writers should not interject their own opinions into a summary of someone else's work.* The tone of summary should be neutral. You may choose to summarize someone's work so that you can criticize it later, but do not confuse summary with criticism. When summarizing, you are taking the role of helping another writer speak for him- or herself. Don't let your own ideas get in the way.

Good summaries vary in length, depending on the length and complexity of the original material and on how much time or space is available for summarizing it. It's unusual, however, to need more than 500 words to summarize most material, and you may be required to summarize an entire book in less than half that. When summary is being used as a preliminary to some other type of work—such as argument or analysis—it is especially important to be concise. For example, if you are summarizing an argument before offering a counterargument of your own, you may be limited to a single paragraph. The general rule to follow is to try to do justice to whatever you are summarizing in as few words as possible and to make sure that you have a legitimate reason for writing any summary that goes on for more than a page or two.

Experienced writers know that summary is a skill worth practicing. If you find summary difficult, remind yourself that it combines two skills of fundamental and inescapable importance: reading and writing. Well-educated men and women must be proficient in both. Summarizing tests not only your ability to write simply and clearly, but also your ability to comprehend what you read. The selections in Part 2 of this book will provide you with many opportunities for summarizing. You will also find an example of summary in the student essay by James McClain at the end of the section on mandatory drug testing (pp. 99–101).

SYNTHESIZING

Synthesis is closely related to summary, and it demands many of the same skills. The principal difference is that while summary involves identifying the major points of a single work or passage, synthesis requires identifying related material in two or more works and tying them smoothly together according to your purpose. Synthesis is often an extension of summary since writers may need to summarize various sources before they can relate these sources to one another, but synthesis does not necessarily require that a writer cover *all* the major points of the individual sources. You may go through an entire article or book and identify only one point that relates to another work you have read. And the relationships involved in your synthesis may be of various kinds. For example, two different authors may have made the same claim, or one might provide specific information that supports a generalization made by the other. On the other hand, one author might provide information that makes another author's generalization seem inadequate or even wrong.

When reading material that you may need to synthesize, always try to ask yourself: "How does this material relate to whatever else I have already read on this topic?" If you are unable to answer this question, consider a few more specific questions: Does the second of two works offer support for the first or does it reflect an entirely different thesis? If the two sources share a similar position, do they arrive at a similar conclusion by entirely different means or do they overlap at any points? Would it be easier to compare the two works or to contrast them? This process of identifying similarities and differences is essentially what synthesis is all about.

When you have determined the points that link your various sources to one another, you are ready to write a synthesis. To see how a synthesis can be organized, let us consider an example. Suppose you have read several articles on the subject of AIDS. The first article was by a scientist, the second by a clergyman, the third by a gay activist, and the fourth by a government official. You were struck by how differently these four writers responded to this epidemic. Although they all agreed that AIDS is a serious problem, each writer advanced a different proposal for fighting this disease. To write a synthesis, you would probably begin with an introductory paragraph that includes a clear thesis statement. In this case, it might be: "Although there is widespread agreement that AIDS is a serious problem, there is no consensus about how this problem can be solved." Each of the following four paragraphs could then be devoted to a brief summary of a different point of view. A final paragraph might emphasize the relationship of the several sources either by reviewing the major points of disagreement among them or by emphasizing one or two points about which everyone agreed. An outline for this type of synthesis would be something like this:

Paragraph one: Introduction
Paragraph two: Summary of first writer
Paragraph three: Summary of second writer
Paragraph four: Summary of third writer
Paragraph five: Summary of fourth writer
Paragraph six: Conclusion

Of course, any good outline should allow for some flexibility. Depending upon the material and what you want to say, your synthesis might involve fewer than six paragraphs or it might involve more. For example, if two of your sources were especially long and complex, there is no reason why you couldn't devote two paragraphs to each of these sources even though you were able to summarize your other two sources within single paragraphs.

An alternative method for organizing a synthesis involves linking two or more writers within paragraphs that focus on specific issues or points. This type of organization is especially useful when you have detected a number of similarities that you want to emphasize. Suppose that you have read six essays on the topic of abortion. Three writers favored legalized abortion for much the same reasons; three writers opposing abortion also used similar arguments. Your assignment is to identify the most common arguments made by people who favor legalized abortion and those made by people who oppose it. In this case, your synthesis might be organized like this:

Paragraph one: Introduction
Paragraph two: One argument in favor of abortion that was made by different writers
Paragraph three: A second argument in favor of abortion that was made by different writers.
Paragraph four: One argument against abortion that was made by different writers.
Paragraph five: A second argument against abortion that was made by different writers.
Paragraph six: Conclusion

During the course of your reading, you identified several other arguments both for and against legalized abortion, but you have decided not to include them within your synthesis since each of these points came up only within a single work and your assignment was to identify the most commonly made arguments on this subject. If you feel uneasy about ignoring these additional points, you can easily remind your audience in either your introduction or your conclusion that other arguments exist and you are focusing only on those most commonly put forward.

For an example of a synthesis written by a student, see the essay by Pamela Schmidt at the end of the section on gun control (pp. 139–41).

AVOIDING PLAGIARISM

You are guilty of plagiarism if you take someone else's words or ideas without giving adequate acknowledgment. Plagiarism is one of the worst forms of dishonest writing, and you may be severely penalized for it even if you did not intend to do it.

The most obvious form of plagiarism is to submit someone else's paper as your own. No one does this accidentally. Another form of plagiarism is to copy long passages from a book or article and pretend that the words are your own. Once again, anyone doing this is almost certain to know that he or she is cheating.

But students sometimes plagiarize without intending to do so. The most common form of plagiarism is an inadequate paraphrase. Some students will read a passage in a book, change the wording, and then convince themselves that they have transformed the material into their own work. You must always remember that it is important to give credit to the *ideas* of others, as well as their words. If you take most of the information another writer has provided and repeat it in essentially the same pattern, you are only a half-step away from copying the material word for word. Here is an example:

Original source:

Hawthorne's political ordeal, the death of his mother—and whatever guilt he may have harbored on either score—afforded him an understanding of the secret psychological springs of guilt. *The Scarlet Letter* is the book of a changed man. Its deeper insights have nothing to do with orthodox morality or religion—or the universal or allegorical applications of a moral. The greatness of the book is related to its sometimes fitful characterizations of human nature and the author's almost uncanny intuitions: his realization of the bond between psychological malaise and physical illness, the nearly perfect, if sinister, outlining of the psychological techniques Chillingsworth deployed against his victim.

Plagiarism:

Nathaniel Hawthorne understood the psychological sources of guilt. His experience in politics and the death of his mother brought him deep insights that don't have anything to do with formal religion or morality. The greatness of *The Scarlet Letter* comes from its characters and the author's brilliant intuitions: his perception of the link between psychological and physical illness and his almost perfect description of the way Roger Chillingsworth persecuted his victim.

This student has simplified the original material, changing some of its wording. But he is clearly guilty of plagiarism. Pretending to offer his own analysis of *The Scarlet Letter,* he owes all of his ideas to another writer who is unacknowledged. Even the organization of the passage has been followed. This "paraphrase" would still be considered a plagiarism even if it ended with a reference to the original source (p. 307 of *Nathaniel Hawthorne in His Times,* by James R. Mellow). A reference or footnote would not reveal the full extent to which this student is indebted to his source. Here is an acceptable version:

Paraphrase:

As James R. Mellow has argued in *Nathaniel Hawthorne In His Times, The Scarlet Letter* reveals a profound understanding of guilt. It is a great novel because of its insight into human nature—not because of some moral about adultery. The most interesting character is probably Roger Chillingsworth because of the way he was able to make Rev. Dimmesdale suffer (307).

This student has not only made a greater effort to paraphrase the original material, but he has also introduced it with a reference to the writer who inspired it. The introductory reference to Mellow, coupled with the subsequent page reference, "brackets" the passage—showing us that Mellow deserves the credit for the ideas in between the two references. And additional bibliographical information about this source is provided by the list of works cited which is included at the end of the paper. Turning to the bibliography we find:

Mellow, James. *Nathaniel Hawthorne in His Times.* Boston: Houghton, 1980.

One final caution: it is possible to subconsciously remember a piece of someone else's phrasing and inadvertently repeat it. You would be guilty of plagiarism if the words in question embody a critically important idea or reflect a distinctive style or turn of phrase. When you revise your rough draft, look for such unintended quotations; if you use them, show who deserves the credit for them, and *remember to put quoted material within quotation marks.*

DOCUMENTING YOUR SOURCES

"Documenting your sources" means revealing the source of the information you report. You must provide documentation for:

- any direct quotation,
- any idea that has come from someone else's work, and
- any fact or statistic that is not widely known.

The traditional way to document a source is to footnote it. Strictly speaking, a "footnote" appears at the foot of the page, and an "endnote" appears at the end of the paper. But "footnote" has become a generic term covering both forms. Most writers prefer to keep their notes on a separate page since doing so is easier than remembering to save adequate space for notes on the bottom of each page. The precise form of such notes varies, depending upon the style manual being followed. Here is how a documentary footnote would look in the style recommended by the Modern Language Association:

A. Bibliographic Form

Manchester, William. <u>American Caesar: Douglas MacArthur 1880–1964</u>. Boston: Little, 1978.

B. Note Form

[1]William Manchester, <u>American Caesar: Douglas MacArthur 1880–1964</u> (Boston: Little, 1978) 65.

The indentation is reversed, the author's name is not inverted, and the publishing data are included within parentheses. Also, the author is separated from the title by a comma rather than a period. A subsequent reference to the same work would follow a shortened form:

[5]Manchester 182.

If more than one work by this same author is cited, then a shortened form of the title would also be included:

[7]Manchester, <u>Caesar</u> 228.

Documentary footnotes require what many authorities now regard as unnecessary repetition, since the author's full name and the publishing data are already included in the bibliography. And many readers object to being obliged to turn frequently to another page if they want to check the notes. Some writers still use notes for documentation purposes. (You can find examples of such notes in the essays by Shurr and Singer in Part 2.) But most important style guides now urge writers to provide their documentation parenthetically within the work itself, reserving numbered notes for additional explanation or discussion that is important but cannot be included within the actual text without a loss of focus. Notes used for providing additional information are called *content* notes. (The essays by Shurr and Singer also include content notes, as do the essays by Gluckman, Orwell, and Ring which are found elsewhere in Part 2).

The form of your documentation will vary, depending upon the subject of your paper and the requirements of your instructor. Students in the humanities are usually asked to follow the form of the Modern Language Association (MLA) or that recommended by *The Chicago Manual of Style*. Students in the social sciences are often expected to follow the format of the American Psychological Association (APA). And students in the natural sciences are usually required to use either a parenthetical system resembling that of the APA or else a system that involves numbering their sources. Make sure that you understand the requirements of your instructor, and remember that you can consult a specific manual in your field if you run into problems. Here is a list of manuals that can be found in many college libraries:

American Institute of Physics. Publication Board. *Style Manual for Guidance in the Preparation of Papers*. 3rd ed. New York: American Inst. of Physics, 1978.

American Chemical Society. *American Chemical Society Style Guide and Handbook*. Washington: American Chemical Soc., 1985.

American Mathematical Society. *A Manual for Authors of Mathematical Papers*. 7th ed. Providence: American Mathematical Soc., 1980.

American Psychological Association. *Publication Manual of the American Psychological Association*. 3rd ed. Washington: American Psychological Assn., 1983.

The Chicago Manual of Style. 13th ed. Chicago: University of Chicago Press, 1982.

Council of Biology Editors. Style Manual Committee. *CBE Style Manual: A Guide for Authors, Editors, and Publishers in the Biological Sciences*. 5th ed. Bethesda: Council of Biology Editors, 1983.

Gibaldi, Joseph, and Walter S. Achtert. *MLA Handbook for Writers of Research Papers*. 3rd ed. New York: Modern Language Assn., 1988.

Harvard Law Review. *A Uniform System of Citation*. 13th ed. Cambridge: Harvard Law Review Assn., 1981.

A detailed discussion of all of these styles is beyond the range of this chapter. But the following pages provide model entries for the most frequently used styles.

Parenthetical Documentation:
The MLA Author/Work Style

In 1984 the Modern Language Association adopted parenthetical documentation to take the place of endnote or footnote citations. In MLA form, the author's name is followed by a page reference. It is not necessary to repeat within the parentheses information that is already provided within the text. If you are used to using footnotes for documentation, this format may seem a little strange at first, but it has the great merit of being easy to use and easy to understand. (Remember that additional information on these sources will be provided in a separate bibliography.)

A. *A Work by a Single Author*

Henry James often identified wickedness with sexual duplicity (Kazin 227).

or

Alfred Kazin has argued that Henry James identified wickedness with sexual duplicity (227).

There is no punctuation between the author's name and the page reference when both are cited parenthetically. Note also that the abbreviation "p." or "pp." is not used before the page reference.

B. *A Work with More Than One Author*

According to Cleanth Brooks and Robert Penn Warren, "indirection is an essential part of the method of poetry" (573).

or

Although this sonnet may seem obscure, its meaning becomes clearer when we realize "indirection is an essential part of the method of poetry" (Brooks and Warren 573).

Note that when a sentence ends with a quotation, the parenthetical reference comes before the final punctuation mark. Note also that the ampersand (&) is not used in MLA style. When referring to a work by more than three authors, you should follow the guidelines for bibliographic entries and list only the first author's name followed by "et al." (Latin for *et alii,* "and others").

Comley et al. have produced a fine anthology.

C. A Work with a Corporate Author

When a corporate author has a long name, you should include it within the text rather than within parentheses. For example:

In 1980 the Council on Environmental Quality reported that there is growing evidence of ground water contamination throughout the United States
(81).

rather than

There is growing evidence of ground water contamination throughout the
United States (Council on Environmental Quality 81).

Although both of these forms are technically correct, the first is preferred because it is easier to read. Long parenthetical references are unnecessarily intrusive, interrupting the flow of ideas.

D. A Work with More Than One Volume

When you wish to cite a specific part of a multivolume work, include the volume number between the author and the page reference:

As Jacques Barzun has argued, "the only hope of true culture is to make
classifications broad and criticism particular" (2: 340).

Note that the volume number is given in an arabic numeral, and a space separates the colon and the page reference. The abbreviation "vol." is not used unless you wish to cite the entire volume: (Barzun, vol. 2).

E. More Than One Work by the Same Author

If you cite more than one work by the same author, you need to make your references distinct. You can do so by putting a comma after the author's name and then adding a shortened form of the title: (Hardy, *Mayor* 179). But your paper will be easier to read if you include either the author or the title directly in the text:

Twain's late work reflects a low opinion of human nature. But when Satan
complains that all men are cowards (<u>Stranger</u> 184), he is only echoing Col.
Sherburn's speech in <u>Huckleberry Finn</u> (123–24).

F. A Quotation Within a Cited Work

If you want to use a quotation that you have discovered in another
book, your reference must show that you acquired this material sec-
ondhand and that you have not consulted the original source. Use
the abbreviation "qtd. in" (for "quoted in") to make the distinction
between the author of the passage being quoted and the author of
the work in which you found this passage:

In 1835 Thomas Macaulay declared the British to be "the acknowledged
leaders of the human race" (qtd. in Davis 231).

G. A Quotation of Poetry

Identify line numbers when you quote poetry, but do not use the
abbreviations "l." or "ll." These abbreviations can easily be confused
with numbers. Write "line" or "lines" in your first citation of poetry;
subsequent citations should include only the line numbers. Quotations of three lines or less should be included directly into the text
of your paper. Separate the lines with a slash (/), leaving an extra
space both before and after the slash:

Yeats returned to this theme in "The Second Coming": "The best lack all
conviction, while the worst / Are full of passionate intensity" (7–8).

Each line of longer quotations should begin on a new line, indented
ten spaces from the margin.

Parenthetical Documentation: The APA
Author/Year Style

The American Psychological Association requires that in-text documentation
identifies the author of the work being referred to and the year in which this
work was published. This information should be provided parenthetically, although it is not necessary to repeat any information that has already been
provided directly in the sentence.

A. One Work by a Single Author

It has been argued that fairy tales can play a vital role in child development (Bettelheim, 1975).

or

Bettelheim (1975) argued that fairy tales can play a vital role in child
development.

or

In 1975 Bruno Bettelheim argued that fairy tales can play a vital role in
child development.

If the reference is to a specific chapter or page, that information
should also be included. For example:

(Bettelheim, 1975, p. 126)
(Bettelheim, 1975, chap. 6)

Note that the abbreviations for page and chapter emphasize the
distinction between the year of publication and the part of the work
being referred to.

B. A Work with Two or More Authors

If a work has two authors, you should mention the names of both
authors every time a reference is made to this work:

In a recent study of children (Walker & Emory, 1983) it was argued
that . . .

or

More recently, Walker and Emory (1983) have argued that . . .

Note that the ampersand (&) is used only within parentheses.

Scientific papers often have multiple authors because of the amount
of research involved. In the first reference to a work with up to six
authors, you should identify each of the authors:

Hodges, McKnew, Cytryn, Stern, and Kline (1982) have shown . . .

Subsequent references to the same work should use an abbreviated
form:

Hodges et al. (1982) also questioned . . .

If a work has six authors or more, this abbreviated form should be
used even in the first reference. If confusion is possible because you
refer to more than one work by the first author, list as many authors
as necessary to distinguish between the two works.

C. A Work with a Corporate Author

When a work has a corporate author, your first reference should include the full name of the corporation, committee, agency, or institution involved. For example:

(United States Fish and Wildlife Service [USFWS], 1984)

Subsequent references to the same source can be abbreviated:

(USFWS, 1984)

D. A Reference to More Than One Work

When the same citation refers to two or more sources, the works should be listed alphabetically according to the author's name and separated with semicolons:

(Pepler & Rubin, 1982; Schesinger, 1982; Young, 1984)

If you are referring to more than one work by the same author(s), list the works in the order in which they were published.

The validity of this type of testing has been established during the last three years (Collins, 1986, 1988).

If you refer to more than one work by the same author published in the same year, distinguish individual works by identifying them as "a," "b," "c," etc.:

These findings have been questioned by Walker (1983a, 1983b).

ORGANIZING A BIBLIOGRAPHY

Documenting your sources parenthetically or with notes allows you to reveal exactly which parts of a paper are supported by or owed to the works you have consulted. But a bibliography, which is a list of the sources consulted, is also essential so that readers can evaluate your research and possibly draw upon your sources for work of their own.

Works Cited in MLA Style

In an MLA style bibliography, the works cited are arranged in alphabetical order determined by the author's last name. MLA style requires that the author's first name be given. Every important word in the titles of books, articles, and journals is capitalized. The titles of books, journals, and news-papers are all underlined (italicized). The titles of articles, stories, and poems appear within quotation marks. Second and subsequent lines are indented five spaces (leave five spaces blank). Here are some examples:

A. A Book with One Author

> Marcus, Steven. <u>Engels, Manchester, and the Working Class</u>. New York:
>   Random, 1974.

Although it is important to give the author's full name, the book's full title, and the place of publication, you should use a shortened form of the publisher's name (Random House in this case) by cit-ing one key term.

B. A Book with Two or Three Authors

> Gilbert, Sandra M., and Susan Gubar. <u>The Madwoman in the Attic: The Woman</u>
>   <u>Writer and the Nineteenth-Century Literary Imagination</u>. New
>   Haven: Yale UP, 1979.

Note that the subtitle is included, set off from the main title by a colon. The second author's name is not inverted, and abbreviations are used for "University Press" to provide a shortened form of the publisher's name. For books with three authors, put commas after the names of the first two authors; separate the second two au-thors with a comma followed by "and."

C. An Edited Book

> Garner, Helen, ed. <u>A Book of Religious Verse</u>. New York: Oxford UP,
>   1972.

D. A Book with More Than Three Authors or Editors

> Clark, Donald, et al., eds. <u>English Literature</u>. New York: Macmillan,
>   1960.

Give the name of the first author or editor only and add the ab-breviation "et al."

E. A Revised Edition

> Smart, William. <u>Eight Modern Essayists</u>. 4th ed. New York: St. Martin's,
>   1985.

F. A Work in an Anthology

Bentley, Louise. "Why I Can't Swim." <u>The Resourceful Writer</u>. Ed. Suzanne
S. Webb. San Diego: Harcourt, 1986. 64–66.

Note that a period comes after the title of the selection but before the second quotation marks. A period is also used to separate the date of publication from the pages between which the selection can be found. No abbreviation is used before the page reference. (For a variation on this example, see the editor's note on p. 444.)

G. A Translated Book

Camus, Albert. <u>Notebooks 1935–1942</u>. Trans. Philip Thody. New York:
Knopf, 1963.

H. A Work in More Than One Volume

Daiches, David. <u>A Critical History of English Literature</u>. 2 vols. New
York: Ronald, 1960.

If the work has been published over several years, give the inclusive dates.

I. An Introduction, Preface, Foreward, or Afterward

Schorer, Mark. Afterword. <u>Babbitt</u>. By Sinclair Lewis. New York: Signet–
NAL, 1961. 320–327.

J. An Article in an Encyclopedia

Hunt, Roberta M. "Child Welfare." <u>Encyclopedia Americana</u>. 1985 ed.

For citing material from well-known encyclopedias, give the author's name first, then the article title. If material is arranged alphabetically within the source, which is usually the case, there is no need to include volume and page numbers. You should give the full title of the encyclopedia, the edition if it is stated, and the year of publication (e.g., "15th ed. 1986"). When no edition number is stated, identify the edition by the year of publication (e.g., "1985 ed."). If the author of the article is identified only by initials, look elsewhere within the encyclopedia for a list identifying the names these initials stand for. If the article is unsigned, give the title first. (Note: This same form can be used for other reference books, such as dictionaries and the various editions of *Who's Who.*)

K. A Government Publication

> United States. Bureau of the Census. <u>State and Metropolitan Data Book</u>
> <u>1986</u>. Washington: GPO, 1986.

For many government publications, the author is unknown. When this is the case, the agency that issued the publication should be listed as the author. State the name of the government (e.g., "United States," "Florida," "United Nations") followed by a period. Then give the name of the agency that issued the work, using abbreviations only if you can do so clearly (e.g., "Bureau of the Census," "National Institute on Drug Abuse," "Dept. of Labor") followed by a period. The underlined title of the work comes next followed by another period. Then give place of publication, publisher, and date. Most federal publications are printed in Washington by the Government Printing Office (GPO), but you should be alert for exceptions. (Note: Treat pamphlets just as you would a book.)

L. A Journal Article with One Author

> Beidler, Peter G. "What Can You Do with an English Major?" <u>College En-</u>
> <u>glish</u> 47 (1985): 39–42.

The volume number comes after the journal title without any intervening punctuation. The year of publication is included within parentheses after the volume number. A colon separates the year of publication and the page reference.

M. A Journal Article Paginated Anew in Each Issue

> Aronson, Arnold. "American Scenography." <u>Drama Review</u> 28.2 (1984):
> 2–22.

In this case, the issue number is included immediately after the volume number, and the two are separated by a period without any intervening space.

N. An Article from a Magazine Published Monthly

> Owen, David. "I Spied on the Twelfth Grade." <u>Esquire</u> Mar. 1981: 72–78.

Instead of citing the volume number, give the month and year of the issue. Abbreviate the month.

O. An Article from a Magazine Issued Weekly

Gallant, Mavis. "Overhead in a Balloon." <u>New Yorker</u> 2 July 1984:
    34–44.

The form is the same as for an article in a magazine that is issued monthly, but you add the date immediately before the month. Although months are usually abbreviated, an exception is made for May, June, and July.

P. An Article from a Daily Newspaper

Robinson, Karen. "The Line to Privacy Is Unlisted." <u>Milwaukee Journal</u> 26
    Mar. 1985, sunrise ed., sec. 2: 2.

If more than one edition is available on the date in question, specify the edition immediately after the date. If the city of publication is not part of the newspaper's name, identify the city in brackets after the newspaper title. Since newspapers often consist of separate sections, you should cite the section number if each section has separate pagination. If a newspaper consists of only one section, or if the pagination is continuous from one section to the next, then you do not need to include the section number. If separately paginated sections are identified by letters, omit the section reference but include the letter of the section with the page number (e.g., 7B or D19). If the article is unsigned, begin the citation with the title of the article; alphabetize the article under its title, passing over small words like "a" and "the."

Q. An Editorial

Lewis, Anthony. "The Wasted Country." Editorial. <u>New York Times</u> 21 Mar.
    1985, natl. ed.: 27.

Editorials are identified as such between the title of the article and the title of the newspaper or magazine.

R. An Interview

Fox, Cynthia. Personal interview. 16 Jan. 1982.

If you interview someone, alphabetize the interview under the name of the person interviewed.

References in APA Style

In APA style, the reference list is arranged alphabetically, the order being determined by the author's last name. The date of publication is emphasized by placing it within parentheses immediately after the author's name. If a second or third line is necessary, such lines should be indented three spaces (leave three spaces blank).

A. Book with One Author

Gardner, H. (1975). <u>The shattered mine</u>. New York: Knopf.

Note that the author's first name is indicated only by an initial. Only the first letter of the first word in the title is capitalized. The name of the publisher, Alfred A. Knopf, is given in shortened form. A period comes after the parenthesis surrounding the date of publication, and also after the title and publisher.

B. Book with Two or More Authors

Jencks, C., & Riesman, D. (1968). <u>The academic revolution</u>. Garden City: Doubleday.

An ampersand is used to separate the names of two authors. When there are three or more authors, separate their names with commas and put an ampersand immediately before the last author's name.

C. Edited Book

Bottomore, T., & Nisbet, R. (Eds.). (1978). <u>A history of sociological analysis</u>. New York: Basic.

Give the names of all editors, no matter how many there are. The abbreviation for editors is "Eds."; it should be included within parentheses between the names of the editors and the date of publication. A single editor is identified as such by "Ed." in parentheses.

D. Article or Chapter in an Edited Book

Rickman, J. (1940). On the nature of ugliness and the creative impulse. In H. Ruitenbeek (Ed.), <u>The creative imagination</u> (pp. 97–121). Chicago: Quadrangle.

Do not invert the editor's name when it is not in the author's position. Do not put the title of the article or chapter in quotation marks. Use a comma to separate the editor from the title of the edited book. The pages between which the material can be found appear within parentheses immediately after the book title. Use "p." for page and "pp." for pages.

E. Translated Book

```
Beauvoir, S. de. (1972). The coming of age (P. O'Brian, Trans.). New
    York: Putnam's. (Original work published 1970)
```

Within parentheses immediately after the book title, give the translator's name followed by a comma and the abbreviation "Trans." If the original work was published earlier, include this information at the end.

F. Revised Edition of a Book

```
Samuelson, P.A. (1980). Economics (11th ed.). New York: McGraw.
```

The edition is identified immediately after the title. Note that edition is abbreviated "ed." and should not be confused with "Ed." for editor.

G. Book with a Corporate Author

```
American Medical Association. (1982). Family medical guide. New York:
    Random.
```

H. Multivolume Book

```
Jones, E. (1953–57). The life and work of Sigmund Freud (Vol. 2). New
    York: Basic.
```

The volume number is included within parentheses immediately after the title. When a multivolume book is published over a number of years, list the years between which it was published.

I. Journal Article with One Author

```
Cornell, S. (1985). Crisis and response in Indian–White relations:
    1960–1984. Social Problems, 32, 44–59.
```

Do not use quotation marks around the article title. Capitalize all important words in the journal title and underline. Put a comma after the journal title and then give the volume and page numbers. Abbreviations are not used for "volume" and "page." To distinguish between the numbers, underline the volume number and put a comma between it and the page numbers.

J. Journal Article with Up to Six Authors

Korner, A., Zeanah, C.H., Linden, J., Berkowitz, R., Kraemer, H., &
   Agras, W.S. (1985). The relations between neonatal and later activity and temperament. Child Development, 56, 38–52.

K. Journal Article Paginated Anew in Each Issue

Kupfer, D.J., & Reynolds, C.F. (1983). Sleep disorders. Hospital Practice, 28 (2), 101–119.

When each issue of a journal begins with page 1, you need to include the issue number in parentheses immediately after the
underlined volume number.

L. Article from a Magazine Issued Monthly

McDermott, J. (1983, November). Robots are taking a hand in our affairs.
   Smithsonian, pp. 60–69.

Within parentheses immediately after the author, include the month
of issue after the year of publication. Use "p." or "pp." in front of
the page number(s). Do not include the volume number. Follow
the same form for an article in a magazine issued on a specific day,
but add the date after the month:

Greenfield, M. (1984, June 11). The whole world is listening. Newsweek,
   p. 88.

M. Article from a Newspaper

Alsop, R. (1988, May 13). Advertisers put consumers on the couch. Wall
   Street Journal, p. 17.

Place the exact date of issue within parentheses immediately after
the author. After the newspaper title, specify the page number(s).

N. Government Document

National Institute of Alcohol Abuse and Alcoholism. (1980). Facts about
   alcohol and alcoholism (DHHS Publication No. ADM 80–31). Washington
   DC: U.S. Government Printing Office.

List the agency that produced the document as the author if no
author is identified. Within parentheses immediately after the document title, give the publication number which the government
assigned to the document; it can usually be found on or near the
title page and should not be confused with the call number which
a library may have assigned to the document.

The Numbered System

In a numbered system the bibliography may be arranged in alphabetical order (determined by the authors' last names) or in the order in which the works are cited within the paper itself. Once this sequence is established, the items are assigned numbers in consecutive order beginning with 1, and these numbers are used as citations within the paper. There are many variations on the particular form of the bibliographical entries; authors of scientific papers should adopt the style recommended by the journal for which they are writing. But here are examples of two frequently used forms:

A. *Biology*

1. Ferris, F.G.; Beveridge, T. J. Functions of bacterial cell surface structures. Bioscience. 35:172–177; 1985.
2. Lewis, A. E. Biostatistics. New York: Reinhold; 1966.

Note that neither journal nor book titles are underlined. Quotation marks are not used for article titles. The year of publication appears at the end of the citation, and it is preceded by a semicolon.

B. *Chemistry*

(1) Silverman, M. P. <u>J. Chem. Ed</u>. 1984, <u>62</u>, pp. 112–114.
(2) Bard, A. J. <u>Chemical Equilibrium</u>; Harper & Row: New York, 1966; pp. 17–28.

Note that journal titles are abbreviated, and article titles are not included.

For an example of a numbered system in use, see the essay by Timothy Paetsch (pp. 351–54).

RULES TO REMEMBER

Whether you document your sources by using footnotes or one of the recommended systems for parenthetical references, you should remember the following rules:

1. Every source cited in a reference should have a corresponding entry in the bibliography.
2. Be consistent. Don't shift from the author/year system to the author/work system in the middle of your paper.
3. Try to vary the introductions you use for quotations and paraphrases and make sure that the material in question has been incorporated smoothly into your text. Read your first draft aloud to be better able to judge its readability.
4. When you mention authorities by name, try to identify who they are

so that your audience can evaluate the source. (For example, "According to Ira Glasser, executive director of the American Civil Liberties Union, recent congressional legislation violates. . . .") But do not insult the intelligence of your audience by identifying well-known figures.

5. If in doubt about whether to document a source, you would probably be wise to go ahead and document it. But be careful not to over-document your paper. A paper that is composed of one reference after another usually lacks synthesis and interpretation.

EVALUATING YOUR READING

By reading several selections in each of the following nine units, you should begin to recognize that some writers make stronger arguments than others. You will find that some essays make sense to you and others do not. But when you find yourself inclined to reject a particular selection, ask yourself why you want to do so. Is it because your own point of view is prejudiced? Is it because the style is more difficult than you are used to? Or is it because you have carefully analyzed the piece in question and identified a faulty premise, an overly large inductive leap, or one or more of the logical fallacies described earlier in this introduction? If you are reading attentively and working toward improving your own ability in argumentation, then you should always have specific reasons for criticizing anything you read. The flaws you cite should be on the page, not in your mind.

Moreover, the readings that follow should help you to clarify your own thinking on several major issues. By analyzing, summarizing, and comparing the arguments of others, you should become better able to formulate an argument of your own. You may find yourself siding with one writer and rejecting another. You may find that every writer makes at least one good point and that you want to draw these points together in a single essay. Or you may discover that none of the essays are persuasive and that you want to argue an entirely different thesis.

Whatever the case, the readings collected in this book are meant to provide you only with a starting point. Part 3 of the book discusses ways to do further research, not only on the issues in Part 2 but on almost any subject that would bring you to draw upon the resources of a library. But whether you are evaluating selected essays on gun control or researching a term paper on Aztec courting rituals, the process will require the skills that you will be perfecting in the weeks ahead. The quality of your writing will depend upon the quality of your reading and, most importantly, how carefully you think about what you read.

PART 2

The Arguments

Section 1
Mandatory Drug Testing: A Question of Privacy

JOHN J. BURT
Drugs and the Modern Athlete

John J. Burt is Dean of the College of Physical Education, Recreation, and Health at the University of Maryland. His belief in the importance of good health is evident in his books, which include Education for Sexuality *(1970) and* Toward a Healthy Life Style *(1980), and in the following article which was first published in* **1987.**

Beset by a rapidly spreading moral malignancy, darkness has now fallen 1 on the road to intercollegiate athletics, a road that has in recent times been potholed by behaviors that are dishonest, illegal, exploitative, and unhealthy. Because these are values that colleges and universities were created to discourage, intercollegiate athletics are now endangered. Either these potholes must be filled or the roads to athletics must be closed down. Indeed, we have come to a time in history when young people are reporting that being an athlete—even a very good one—is no longer something to be proud of.

Hence, there is a great need today for athletes who can restore to athletics 2 its powerful tradition—athletes who are honest and drug free and law abiding and healthy. This higher type of athletics needs its champions as it never did before, and there is no more essential and nobler task for the modern athlete—high school, college or professional—than to be seen and recognized as a star against the darkness of contemporary athletics.

One of the potholes requiring immediate attention is drug abuse among   3
athletes—a problem that can only be solved by athletes helping athletes. To head this discussion in the right direction, let me begin with two observations. First, it should be noted that most athletes don't have a drug problem. In fact, 80 percent don't even use drugs ("The Substance," 1985). Second, the use of drugs among athletes does not appear to be greater than the use among students in general or society at large. The problem, then, reduces to the question: what's to be done for the small number of athletes who use drugs?

One option is to look the other way—consoling one's self with the knowl-   4
edge that athletes are no worse than anyone else. This widespread attitude relieves the modern athlete of any responsibility toward those who use drugs. Going a step further, some drug-free athletes have assisted their drug-using friends in cheating on drug tests. Even worse, there have been reports of drug-free athletes treating other athletes by buying drugs for them.

A second attitude is one that compels athletes to help other athletes with   5
their drug problems. In recommending this attitude, I ask you to consider the following cases. At one large and athletically powerful university, the team physician conducted exit interviews with all graduating athletes. Among these was a sub-group of drug users, all of whom had tested positive at some time during their college careers. Interestingly, these students, without exception, strongly supported the drug testing option. When an athlete at another university refused to be drug tested, the coach called him and his parents to a conference where it was explained that drug testing was a necessary condition for continuing on the team. This athlete transferred to another university, but both the athlete and his parents highly recommended the drug-testing university to a younger brother athlete.

Further, we have reports from a number of athletes who say that they   6
strongly support drug testing for the reason that it permits them to say: no thank you, I can't use drugs; I am in a drug testing program for athletes. These examples point to some seldom recognized facts about drug-using athletes: (1) they understand that drug use is not in the best interest of either health or their athletic performance; (2) they need assistance in saying no to drugs; (3) they respect and appreciate those who help them to break away from drugs, but usually only after the fact; (4) they endorse drug testing as an effective option for dealing with the drug problem.

So let's discuss the drug testing option in more detail—beginning with the   7
assumption that properly designed and properly conducted drug testing programs, while a nuisance for the drug-free athlete, can be of great assistance to the drug-using athlete. Such programs, however, can only work when they have the support of well-informed athletes.

With respect to drug testing, there are at least two important questions   8
facing the modern athlete: (1) What are my rights? and (2) What are my responsibilities?

The Rights of Athletes

Off the athletic field or outside the gymnasium, athletes have been too   9
passive in the protection of their rights, and it is my hope that they will
correct this situation and also that they won't put rights ahead of responsibilities. For example, athletes certainly have the right not to help each other
with the drug problem; nevertheless, one would hope that they would feel
some sense of responsibility to do so. If athletics are to be restored to a high
level of public respect, a blending of rights and responsibilities will be required.

Regarding rights, the fourth amendment promises to athletes, like every-   10
one else, that they will be left alone unless they raise suspicions of guilt. It
forbids any intrusions on human dignity and privacy on the mere chance that
incriminating evidence might be obtained. Since medical procedures—including urinalysis screening—may be regarded as a personal search capable of
revealing incriminating evidence, the modern athlete should understand what
the Fourth Amendment does and does not permit relative to personal searches.

The Fourth Amendment protects against *unreasonable* searches and sei-   11
zures. Hence, the central issues regarding the legality of random drug testing
of athletes evolves around the question: Is it reasonable? Since there can be
no precise definition or mechanical application of "reasonableness," this becomes a complicated issue involving a balancing of the need for the search
against the invasion of personal rights.

With reference to the reasonableness criteria, two types of searches have   12
been allowed: (1) a search conducted pursuant to a warrant authorized by a
detached magistrate and based on probable cause that a violation of law has
occurred, and (2) a warrantless search conducted pursuant to public interest
and safety. Random drug testing falls in the warrantless search category.

One type of warrantless search (called an administrative search) permits   13
the personal searching of people at airports, the borders of our country, and
at the entrance to courthouses and prisons. The Supreme Court has also
ruled that administrative searches are reasonable in the sport of horse racing.
For example, the State of New Jersey conducts an administrative search in
which jockeys are required to submit to daily breathalyzer and random urine
tests. In this case, the courts ruled that public interest in maintaining
the integrity of a highly regulated sport outweighed the right of individual privacy.

In order for colleges and universities to make good on the claim that ran-   14
dom drug testing of athletes is reasonable, at least three requirements pursuant to an administrative search would have to be met:

- The testing college or university would be required to justify the claim
  that intercollegiate sports—by their nature, conduct, and regulation—
  result in reduced privacy expectations for the athlete.
- The testing college or university would be required to identify a strong
  public interest in making testing imperative and to justify drug testing
  as a necessary condition for participation in sport.

• The testing college or university would be required to make good on the claim that they were unable to identify a less intrusive alternative mechanism by which its objective(s) might be achieved.

Regarding these requirements, the modern athlete should be familiar with   15
at least four arguments that are currently offered in favor of random drug testing of athletes as an administrative search.

Argument One: the random drug testing of athletes is "reasonable"   16
because there is a strong public interest in whether athletes are perform-
ing in full health. If the outcome of intercollegiate athletic contests were of no interest to anyone other than the players, if these contests were con-ducted in private, if no tickets or television rights were sold, if the behavior of athletes did not reflect upon the institutions that they represent, if these institutions were not held responsible for the health and safety of athletes, then drug testing clearly would be a violation of Fourth Amendment prom-ises. A good argument can be made for a strong public interest in how hard athletes try and whether they perform in full health.

Argument Two: The random drug testing of athletes is "reasonable"   17
because intercollegiate sports are pervasively regulated and participa-
tion is a privileged choice. As an athlete, one receives, among other special considerations, immediate and first rate health care; special academic advis-ing and tutelage; room and board; public visibility and travel opportunities; and for a small number, the chance to go on to professional sports. These are privileges not available to nonathletes. However, in company with these privileges, the athlete should clearly expect a reduction in privacy. This is because intercollegiate sports are pervasively regulated: e.g., training rules, including bed checks; training tables; frequent medical examinations; grade checks to determine eligibility; conference regulations; NCAA regulations; and a set of rules that govern the conduct of athletic contests.

Argument Three: The random drug testing of athletes is "reasonable"   18
because the aim of drug testing is to return the athlete to health rather
than to collect evidence that is legally incriminating. Obviously this ar-gument does not apply for those drug testing programs that specify punitive actions against athletes. However, a good argument can be made for an ex-ception to privacy when the sole aim of drug testing is to return the athlete to health. In such programs, colleges and universities must agree to not vol-untarily supply personally identifiable test results to any agency or person not connected with the health of the athlete. The results of a search legiti-mized for health reasons should not thereafter be used for punitive reasons.

Argument Four: The random drug testing of athletes is "reasonable"   19
because colleges and universities must reserve the right to conduct upon
their athletes whatever test it deems necessary to the protection of health
and safety. Good athletic programs require that all athletes be medically certified as fit for competition, be appropriately conditioned for competition, be outfitted with the appropriate safety equipment, and be provided medical supervision. Moreover, good athletic programs demand that athletes be dis-

qualified from competition whenever in the judgment of health authorities their continued participation would constitute a threat to health.

To ensure informed judgments regarding the welfare of athletes, health [20] officials must not be denied the use of any important diagnostic test, no matter how intrusive it might seem. And drug testing should be viewed and treated like other medical procedures. The argument reduces to this: to prohibit the use of an effective screening test could clearly hamper the efforts of health officials to protect the health and safety of athletes.

References

"The Substance Use and Abuse Habits of College Student-Athletes." (1985). College of Human Medicine, Michigan State University.

QUESTIONS FOR MEANING

1. According to Burt, why do college athletes support drug testing programs?
2. What criteria need to be met if a drug testing program is to be considered "reasonable"?
3. Why does Burt believe that athletes have special responsibilities that offset their right to privacy?
4. What should be the purpose of drug testing?

QUESTIONS ABOUT STRATEGY

1. Consider Burt's use of figurative language in paragraphs 1–3. Is it effective?
2. Why does Burt acknowledge that "most athletes don't have a drug problem" before beginning his discussion of drug testing?
3. Should Burt have identified the universities he cites in paragraph 5?
4. Italics in print are the equivalent of underlining. Why does Burt put the four arguments on behalf of drug testing in italics? What does this show about his relationship to his audience?

SANDY PADWE
Symptoms of a Deeper Malaise

Throughout the 1970s and 1980s an increasing number of stories were re-
ported concerning drug abuse involving professional athletes. Responding to
growing public concern about drugs, Pete Rozelle, the commissioner of the Na-
tional Football League, and Peter Ueberroth, the commissioner of baseball, both
ordered drug testing programs in the mid-1980s. The following essay by Sandy
adwe, a senior editor at Sports Illustrated, *argues that testing athletes for drug*
use is hypocritical. It was first published in **1985.**

For pure hypocrisy, there is little that can match the statement Pete Roz-   1
elle, the commissioner of the National Football League, made at a press conference he called July 7 to announce the details of the N.F.L.'s drug testing
program. "Our concern," he said, "is the health and welfare of the players—
those taking drugs and those injured by those taking drugs."

When novelist Pat Toomay, a former defensive end for several N.F.L. teams,   2
including the Dallas Cowboys and the Oakland Raiders, heard what Rozelle
had said, he laughed. "All of a sudden he's worried," said Toomay, who retired in 1980 after a ten-year career. "Why wasn't he worried twenty years
ago? Fifteen years ago? Five? It's been going on forever. What about all those
guys running around on amphetamines? Painkillers? Steroids? They just didn't
start hurting people last season, you know."

The timing of Rozelle's press conference seemed cynical coming as it did   3
when stories about the death of Len Bias, the Maryland University basketball
star, and of Don Rogers, the Cleveland Browns safety, were blanketing the
front page, the sports page and the nightly national news telecasts. The league
said that the timing was a coincidence and that it had been working on a
drug testing program ever since revelations of drug use by six players on the
New England Patriots soured the aftermath of Super Bowl XX.

Rozelle is no newcomer to the problems of drugs in the N.F.L. Former St.   4
Louis Cardinals linebacker Dave Meggyesy, now the western director of the
N.F.L. Players Association, wrote about it in *Out of Their League* in 1970.
North Dallas Forty, a novel by Pete Gent, a former receiver for the Cowboys
and the New York Giants, remains the quintessential work on the subject of
football and drugs.

In 1973, George Burman, a Washington Redskins center, was one of sev-   5
eral players who detailed drug abuse, especially amphetamine usage, on the
team, only to have his coach, George Allen, say: "I know we don't have a drug
problem. I'm not worried about it." (Allen now chairs the President's Council
on Physical Fitness.) Later that same year, Representative Harley Staggers
and Senator Birch Bayh presided over hearings in Washington on drug abuse
in sports. Professional football received plenty of attention, and in 1974 the
N.F.L. found its flagship case with the San Diego Chargers. Rozelle fined the

team's owners, general manager Harland Svare and eight players a total of $40,000 for violations of league rules on drugs. (Cocaine was not involved.) For years after, whenever someone suggested that the N.F.L. wasn't doing all it could about the problem, league officials would point to the Chargers' fines as proof of how tough they could be. But the fines had little effect on the players, who understood that the league's drug policy was basically cosmetic, aimed at placating public opinion. Drug use hardly changed, according to Toomay and several other players active at the time.

As long as the drugs involved in sports were only amphetamines, steroids, 6 painkillers and a little marijuana here and there, and as long as the books being written about the subject were by dissidents such as Meggyesy and Gent—or, in baseball, Jim Bouton—the commissioners felt no discomfort. The same could be said of the directors of athletics at colleges and universities.

Stories of cocaine abuse moved the drug issue to another level. They out- 7 raged the public, made TV advertisers nervous and caught the interest of the sporting press. To a lot of editors, coke was a hotter, trendier drug than amphetamines or anabolic steroids. The use of the latter was limited to enhancing one's performance, and in the anything-goes world of athletic competition no one cares about how players excel, as long as they excel.

For years cocaine had been creeping into the sports world. Warren Jabali, 8 who played for Denver in the old American Basketball Association, told *Newsday* in 1973 that he had heard of cocaine dealers on professional basketball teams. In 1978, Bob Hayes, the former Olympic gold medalist who had earned the title of "the world's fastest human," was arrested for selling cocaine. Hayes had been a wide receiver for "America's team," the Dallas Cowboys, so the shock was even greater when Hayes was imprisoned a year later. After that there seemed to be a new drug scandal on the wires every week, often involving cocaine. Some of the athletes were little-known subs and second-stringers, or solid though obscure starters. But others had plenty of headline value.

By 1985 the question preoccupying the press and the commissioners of 9 professional sports was, Can the integrity of the various games be protected? Rozelle ordered a handful of highly publicized suspensions for cocaine use. But his public relations blitz was nothing compared to the one launched that year by Peter Ueberroth, the commissioner of baseball, who held a series of press conferences on cocaine and granted selective interviews to journalists from prominent newspapers, magazines and television networks.

Ueberroth's initial strategy was to win public support for a drug testing 10 program, and the public bought it after a parade of big-name players such as Keith Hernandez and Dave Parker testified in a Pittsburgh trial that summer that they had used drugs. When Ueberroth finally announced his testing plan, which basically called for players, general managers, secretaries, mail clerks and minor leaguers to pee into a bottle, there was even more backing for his position. With public opinion favoring testing, a number of major league players allowed testing clauses to be written into their contracts. That left the Major League Baseball Players Association—which opposes any testing that isn't negotiated under the collective bargaining agreement—to explain why it was trying to protect those players who hadn't signed their civil liberties away in the rush to judgment by the fans and the sporting press, which, by and large, had the rope and noose ready.

Then, one day last spring, Ueberroth simply waved his Olympic torch and proclaimed that baseball was drug-free. Apparently all those clean-cut young men who appeared in the Pittsburgh courtroom had been aberrations.   11

The deaths of Bias and Rogers were hardly aberrations, though. That's when sports and the streets really met, leaving the fans genuinely shocked at the demise, within such a short period, of two seemingly indestructible athletes. If only the fans had been as concerned through the years about the lives wasted by drug use in cities and on campuses. But athletes are perceived as different, special. In the first wave of news stories about Bias and Rogers, both were portrayed by coaches, family and friends as near-saints, people who would never touch a drug. If Bias and Rogers had died in car accidents, it would have been more understandable—a one- or two-day story. Instead, with the press leading the mourning, the deaths became a rallying point for all those groups who see the issue of drug testing in simplistic yes-or-no terms, the Constitution be damned.   12

The sports media played a major role in stoking the mob mentality. For the first time athletes had died as a result of cocaine abuse, and that focused the issue for the editors and news directors, who felt the public's anger through mail, polls and telephone calls. If sportswriters and broadcasters and their editors know anything, it's how to get a bet down quickly on a good horse. The Bias/Rogers story was a sure thing.   13

There was no murkiness now for the sports news managers, no departmental generation gap to bridge. Most of the older editors and writers neither understood nor cared about drugs, while the younger generation had been exposed to drug use since college. But both were happy to ignore the warning signals around them. In fact, some young sportswriters had exchanged good weed and good coke during interviews with athletes. It proved the reporter was one of the guys and could be trusted not to write about sensitive subjects, just as the older guys had proved it for all those years by not writing about boozing and whoring. Why spoil a good thing and cut off a source by getting into the real touchy stuff?   14

If you want to know what's really happening in sports, the place to find out is not usually on the printed page or on the evening telecasts. It's in the press room before and after games, where, over the free food and booze, the writers talk about who's drugged out and whose groin pull is really the clap. Of course, the gossip is off-the-record stuff, passed on by some coach, general manager or agent, or even a player. Quite often it's leaked as part of a whispering campaign by someone who wants to harm the victim for any of a variety of reasons. The best way to get rid of a malcontent or a hypochondriac or a druggie is to plant some gossip with a writer and have the writer pass it on along the grapevine. Pretty soon your problem vanishes to some other team or right out of the league.   15

There's a culture within a culture operating in sports. On one side, you   16
have a predominantly white power structure, consisting of management and
the press, which is serviced by management's powerful public relations machine. On the other side are the athletes, many of whom come from racial,
ethnic and youth cultures with values and peer pressures completely antithetical to those of the people in control. You won't get a clear understanding
of the inner workings of this culture from the press because most sports
departments have an aversion to sociological issues and the abstractions they
spawn. So all those competing forces just fester, bothering the daylights out
of the fans, who don't quite comprehend what's going on and don't quite
want to know.

From management's point of view, until Bias and Rogers died the real   17
issues had been contained beautifully. The sports press—with a few troublesome exceptions—had been numbed. It sat there nodding off in front of the
fire, feet up, full-bellied and belching like some Dickensian character in a
country inn. So when the two men died, the press reacted predictably and
hypocritically, with horror and wonder, as if it had just discovered that there
is a real world out there which wasn't created by the P.R. people. Drugs?
Right here in River City? Could it be?

Moral indignation oozed from nearly every VDT and microphone. The pub-   18
lic expected indignation, but it didn't want the front page transferred to the
sports page. As Wilfrid Sheed wrote in *Harper's* in 1984: "Sports continues
its rounds as the Magnificent Evasion, since it also keeps us away from the
bad news at home and in one's psyche. Many men, and a spattering of women,
talk about sports from morning to night for fear something else might get
in." The last thing the public wants to read about on the sports page is drugs,
politics, antitrust suits, or questions about racism and sexism and colliding
cultures. The more drug stories that appear in the papers or on TV, the
angrier the public gets. Fans regard such stories as a personal affront, an
invasion of sacred territory, a defilement of the temple. They cling to the
concept of the athlete as role model, and there are plenty of politicians, commissioners, sportswriters and broadcasters to tell them that's the way it should
be.

Why is the public so outraged when some quarterback or third baseman   19
is picked up on a cocaine charge? When a John Belushi self-destructs, there
is no outcry for the drug testing of actors. Outrage, it seems, is reserved for
sports. When *Sports Illustrated* polled 2,000 adults about their views on sports
last spring, it was no surprise that 73 percent of the respondents favored
drug testing. A wonderful follow-up question to anyone who favors testing
for athletes is whether that person would accept such examinations as a
condition for employment. It also would be interesting to poll the members
of the baseball, basketball, football and hockey writers associations to see if
their members would submit to random drug testing.

Testing is not the simple answer in sports. There are questions about the   20
testing procedures themselves that have not been answered. The tests are
hardly infallible. And, then, do you test just for hard drugs or for the perfor-

mance-enhancing drugs too? Rozelle's plan does not call for steroid testing, which is laughable given the evidence available about steroid use throughout the league. The N.F.L. says it is still working on the testing methodology. The questions over testing will deeply affect the players' future, not to mention their civil liberties as well as those of every other American. Civil libertarians are finally learning how powerful sport is in the United States and how law-enforcement officials and politicians can take advantage of the emotion of the moment to swing the debate over drug testing in their favor, if not in the Constitution's.

The public must realize that athletes are not heroes. Simply putting on a   21
uniform does not make them better people or give them a greater standard of behavior to uphold. Too many athletes are overpampered individuals who have been told all their life that they are special because they can throw a ball or run swiftly. They are eased through colleges and universities when they should be learning to read and write. Not only do they accept it, they expect it. They are the recipients of money, clothes, cars, women and drugs from all manner of people, while teachers, coaches, administrators and even some parents look the other way. Many athletes fully understand sport's amorality and don't even try to distinguish right from wrong.

If college and pro teams look away while the players pump themselves full   22
of steroids, painkillers and amphetamines so they can play when they are hurt, why should athletes think there is anything wrong with doing coke with friends to relax? To be consistent, the press and the fans should be as con-cerned about athletes' use of painkillers or performance-enhancing drugs as they are about cocaine. Does the reason they aren't have anything to do with America's love affair with winning? Athletes are revered for scoring touch-downs, runs and baskets by a group of individuals to whom winning—or cov-ering the point spread—has become an end in itself. Players get the message: Use whatever means it takes to get the score in your team's favor. Such an attitude skews values completely and bleeds all the beauty from our games.

For their part, the teams and schools expect the athletes to be paragons   23
of virtue and role models. They make the players live this hypocrisy in order to receive financial benefits. As the system unravels—and it is unraveling faster than Roger Clemens can throw a baseball—the impulse will be to reach for a panacea like drug testing rather than to deal with much deeper, much more complex problems, which go to the very core of sport in America. In-stead of calling for testing, the people with the nooses should be checking the foundation. It's about to collapse.

QUESTIONS FOR MEANING

1. Why does Padwe believe that the N.F.L. drug testing program is hypocrit-ical?
2. How does Padwe define drug use? How does his definition differ from the sort of drug use that the media usually focus upon?
3. What was the effect of the deaths of Len Bias and Don Rogers?

4. What does Padwe mean when he writes, "There's a culture within a culture operating in sports"?
5. How does Padwe view most sports reporting? Why is it that sports writers often ignore difficult or troubling topics?
6. Vocabulary: blitz (9), aberrations (11), demise (12), aversion (16), amorality (21), skews (22), paragons (23).

QUESTIONS ABOUT STRATEGY

1. Can you find any evidence of irony in this essay? Does it ever degenerate into sarcasm?
2. Why does Padwe associate Peter Ueberroth with the Olympic torch? Why is this an appropriate metaphor?
3. Consider the allusion to Dickens in paragraph 17. Do you understand it? Could Padwe expect his original audience to understand it?
4. What is the purpose of the reference to John Belushi in paragraph 19? What point is Padwe making?

AMERICAN SOCIETY FOR INDUSTRIAL SECURITY
Why Drug Testing Is Needed

*One of the many forms of argument is the "policy statement" with which an organization, institution, corporation, or government body outlines its stand on a particular issue and provides a rationale for that policy. The following statement was adopted in **1987** by the American Society for Industrial Security, a professional organization of men and women who do security work in private and public industry.*

The illicit drug trade in America has fast become a $110 billion annual business.[1] According to the Research Triangle Institute, a North Carolina-based research organization, drug abuse cost the US economy $60 billion in 1983, nearly a 30 percent increase from the more than $47 billion estimated for 1980.[2]

No one seriously disputes that drug abuse in the workplace is a serious and growing problem for both public and private employers. Increasingly, the problem continues to contribute to the high rate of employee absenteeism, rising health care costs, a high rate of accidents, and the low productivity of our work force. It has been aptly called an American tragedy.

As a result, ASIS—and its Standing Committee on Substance Abuse—is in   3
favor of drug testing efforts by both business and government. We believe a
comprehensive drug testing program puts drug abusers on notice that they
will be held strictly accountable for their actions.

There Is Basis for Concern

Let there be no doubt that drug abuse in the workplace carries a heavy   4
price tag for our society—one that translates not only into dollars but also
into pain and suffering for innocent members of the public. The following are
some examples of that price tag:

• Since 1975, more than fifty train accidents have been attributed to drug-   5
impaired employees. In these mishaps, more than eighty people were injured,
thirty-seven lost their lives, and property valued at more than $34 million
was destroyed.[3]

• In 1979, a Conrail employee, while under the influence of drugs, lost   6
control of his locomotive and crashed into the rear of another train. Two
people lost their lives and damages exceeded $400,000.[4] The same scenario
repeated itself only recently.

• A recent study by the US Department of Justice found that more than   7
50 percent of all persons arrested in New York and Washington, DC, for serious crimes were found to be using one or more illegal drugs. Cocaine seemed
to be the drug of choice among those who were arrested.[5]

• Cocaine, once the drug of the rich and famous, now has a clientele of   8
more than 4 million regulars, reaching from the assembly line to the board-
room of many of our major corporations.[6]

• Employees who use drugs are at least three times as likely to be in-   9
volved in an accident, seven times as likely to be the target of garnishment
proceedings, and often function at only 65 percent of their work potential.[7]

Presently, some 20 percent of all federal agencies and more than 25 per-   10
cent of all Fortune 500 companies conduct some type of drug screening or
testing program.[8] The utility, petroleum, and chemical industries—the first
private employers to use drug testing—are now being joined by a multitude
of other industries, including state and local governments, in screening or
testing their employees for drugs.

Because of the sensitive nature of their work, airlines and railroads are   11
also turning to drug testing programs as a way of filtering out employees who
pose a danger to the public. Recently, they were joined by such corporate
giants as AT&T, IBM, and DuPont. Drug testing, like going through metal
detectors at today's airports, has become an unfortunate necessity.

ASIS views drug testing, when properly and lawfully applied, as a positive   12
step towards combating drug abuse both at the workplace and in our society
at large. ASIS also thinks that utimately it is the public who stands to gain.

ASIS is cognizant that, if abused, drug testing can prove detrimental. But,   13
in those few cases involving abuses, the courts have demonstrated both a
willingness and an ability to intervene.

ASIS is also cognizant that drug testing by itself cannot rid the workplace   14
or our society of drugs. Rather, it must be carried out in conjunction with
educational and related programs, for our growing dependence on drugs poses
a direct long-term threat to our society.

Need for Drug Prevention Programs

For drug testing to prove both meaningful and useful, it must be con-   15
ducted in conjunction with educational, counseling, and treatment programs.
Among other things, we recommend the following:
* *An active antidrug program.* Employers should establish clear, com-   16
prehensive, and well-documented policies concerning the use, possession, and
sale of drugs at the workplace. The antidrug program should be publicized
and include sanctions. It should encompass all strata of the work force.
* *Judicious use of screening and testing.* Both federal and local courts   17
have upheld the validity of drug testing provided it is carried out at the
preemployment stage; conducted for cause; or, within certain confines, conducted at random.
The courts have also made it amply clear they will allow drug testing where   18
it is not discriminatory or abusive, has been published well in advance, is not
used as a subterfuge to discourage union activities, is not clearly in violation
of public policy, and is in compliance with any collective bargaining agreement or other contractual arrangement between an employer and his or her
employees.
* *Use of employee assistance programs.* Attempts to rehabilitate other-   19
wise good employees make both economic and political sense. Not only can
it prove time-consuming to recruit, hire, and train a new employee, it
can also prove costly in terms of dollars. Counseling and treatment can go a
long way in helping employees who are addicted to drugs—provided
employees also want to help themselves. A concerted effort should be made
to assist them.
* *Education and training.* The ultimate goal should be to obtain a work   20
environment that is 100 percent drug-free. In addition to the aforementioned
programs, this goal can be achieved through a continuous educational process involving films, free literature, training seminars, community involvement, counseling, incentives, etc. Keeping in mind that a drug-free workplace
is a healthier and happier environment, a continuing drug education program
results in better morale as well as financial benefits.

Conclusion

A drug-free workplace, though ideal, should be the goal of every business   21
and government agency in America. However, drug testing is only one of
several steps that must be taken to achieve this objective. When incorporated
into a comprehensive antidrug effort, drug testing can go a long way in combating drug abuse at the workplace.

Notes

1. "The Plague Among Us," *Newsweek,* June 16, 1986, p. 15.

2. "Battling the Enemy Within," *Time,* March 17, 1986, p. 53.

3. "Battling the Enemy Within," p. 53.

4. "Battling the Enemy Within," p. 53.

5. "Wide Drug Use Found in People Held in Crimes," *New York Times,* June 4, 1986, p. 1.

6. "The Plague Among Us," p. 15.

7. "Drug Abuse in the Workplace," *DEA/Registrant Facts,* 1985, p. 6.

8. Nell Henderson. "Drug-Testing Industry Flourishes," *Washington Business,* June 30, 1986, p. 1.

QUESTIONS FOR MEANING

1. What are some of the problems that occur in the workplace as a result of drug abuse?
2. Under what circumstances is drug testing legally feasible?
3. According to this policy statement, how has drug abuse changed during the past decade?
4. Vocabulary: scenario (6), cognizant (13), conjunction (14), sanctions (16), strata (16), subterfuge (18).

QUESTIONS ABOUT STRATEGY

1. What type of organization is employed in this policy statement?
2. Does this statement include any concessions?
3. How credible are the sources cited in this statement? Are there any claims that require additional support?
4. Is this statement more likely to appeal to management or to employees? To what sort of audience is it directed?

JOHN HOERR
Winning the Drug Wars

Although drug testing has been used in professional sports, and also in some school systems, it is most frequently used in the workplace. In 1986, a presidential commission recommended that public and private employers consider the possibility of drug testing programs as part of the war on drugs. Many large companies now screen both applicants and employees for traces of illegal drugs in their urine. John Hoerr is a senior writer for Business Week, *which published the following argument in* **1986.**

Something akin to public hysteria over drug abuse is producing the typical   1
American search for a quick cure to a complex problem. The panacea in this case—mandatory testing of employees for drug use—raises serious issues about worker privacy that will eventually be settled in legislatures and the courts. Equally important, merely testing people for drugs is not likely to solve drug abuse in the workplace.

No one would argue that the U.S. doesn't have a serious drug problem—   2
and has had one for some time. Employers are becoming more aware of the personal and economic damage caused by drug—and alcohol—abuse. Research Triangle Institute, a nonprofit research firm in North Carolina, says that significant drug and alcohol addiction afflicted 13% to 15% of the work force in 1983 and cost employers $99 billion in lost productivity. That helps account for the growth in drug testing in the private sector: Almost 30% of the nation's largest corporations screen job applicants, current employees, or both—up from 3% in 1982.

Strong Action

There are other reasons for the increasing reliance on urine tests to detect   3
drug users on the job. In a report issued last March, the President's Commission on Organized Crime called on all public and private employers to institute drug-testing programs. And opinion polls show that the public wants strong action taken against drug trafficking, partly because of media coverage of drug-related problems. In cities such as New York, local studies show growing use of "fad drugs" such as crack, a form of cocaine. The heavily publicized deaths of young athletes have added to the perception that drug abuse is spreading.

Alan F. Westin, an authority on privacy rights at Columbia University, notes   4
also that many companies are worried about liability suits brought against them for accidents caused by employees on drugs and alcohol. "The corporate world acts through a herd instinct," he adds. "The leaders are moving, and so all the other animals are beginning to move."

But a backlash is developing against testing in the workplace. In Washing-   5
ton, government unions are contesting President Reagan's recent executive
order that calls for the testing of all federal employees in "sensitive" jobs.
Across the nation, the American Civil Liberties Union has filed suits on behalf
of police officers, firefighters, and teachers who either have been fired as a
result of drug screening or face mandatory tests.

Several federal district courts have ruled that government employees are   6
protected from random, mandatory urine tests because of the Fourth
Amendment's ban on "unreasonable searches and seizures." But the Reagan
Administration argues strongly against this interpretation and is intervening
as a "friend of the court" in a key case in Boston. The Justice Dept. supports
a Boston Police Dept. testing plan that's being challenged by a police union.

But the Fourth Amendment applies only to government action, and pri-   7
vate employers so far face no such restraints. They've been free to deny jobs
to applicants who test positively and to fire employees for the use of drugs.

There haven't been any broad court decisions involving private-sector   8
workers. But experts such as Westin believe city and state governments will
pass laws prohibiting random testing, though the screening of employees
holding such safety-related jobs as pilot, bus driver, and nuclear plant oper-
ator will be allowed. Evidence of impairment also may be a guideline for
permitting testing.

A more immediate problem faces employers who are instituting drug   9
screening. Those administering the tests often don't know what they ought
to do with the results. Firing someone on the basis of one "positive" urinalysis—a test that's not wholly reliable—is not a satisfactory answer. "I see a
lot of executives who are seduced by the notion that simple drug testing will
weed out undesirable employees," says Los Angeles management attorney
Alfred Klein. "But it will also weed out some desirable employees if you evaluate the test results and not the person." Such tests, Klein says, should be
part of a comprehensive employee assistance program with the ultimate goal
of rehabilitation.

Mixed Up

The testing procedures present many problems. Some controls on testing   10
seem required partly because the least expensive and most common urine
test can't always distinguish between cough syrups, decongestants, or painkillers and illegal drugs. A person who merely inhales someone else's marijuana smoke might test positive. And samples can easily get mixed up.

For these reasons, the experts say, employees should not be fired based   11
on the results of one test. Companies with good assistance programs usually
follow up with a more sophisticated test. If that shows positive, the employee
can be given the choice of entering a treatment program or being discharged.
Urine tests should be an integral part of an assistance program, not a separate procedure. Also, testing is not a substitute for management diligence in

identifying workers who are performing poorly or displaying unusual behavior: They should be referred to a treatment program.

Studies show the recovery rate for alcohol and drug abusers is 35% to 60% of treated employees. Moreover, a good assistance program returns $5 for each $1 invested. This is why treatment for drug abuse—not testing—should be the focus for employers. 12

QUESTIONS FOR MEANING

1. What reasons are cited by Hoerr to account for the increasing number of companies that use drug testing?
2. What difference is there between testing government employees and testing employees in the private sector?
3. Why should business go to the trouble and expense of establishing programs to help employees overcome drug abuse?
4. Vocabulary: panacea (1), liability (4), intervening (6), impairment (8), integral (11), diligence (11).

QUESTIONS ABOUT STRATEGY

1. At what point in this essay does the author first reveal his opinion of mandatory drug testing?
2. What does this essay reveal about Hoerr's sense of audience?
3. This short essay is divided into three sections. Could these divisions be eliminated?

NAT HENTOFF
Presumption of Guilt

A staff writer for The New Yorker *and* The Village Voice, *Nat Hentoff is the author of more than twenty books on subjects ranging from the history of jazz to the need for educational reform. Much of his work is devoted to chronicling political and social problems. As a member of the board of the American Civil Liberties Union, he has been especially concerned with potential violations of the rights guaranteed to Americans by the Constitution. His belief in the importance of civil liberties is apparent in the following essay, which was first published in* **1986.**

> "I don't take drugs and I don't believe I have to piss in a bottle to prove I don't."
> —Bob Stanley, pitcher, Boston Red Sox

> "If you hang all the people, you'll get all the guilty."
> —Tom T. Hall, country singer

In March, Ira Glasser, executive director of the American Civil Liberties   1
Union, sent a letter to twenty of the nation's largest labor unions inviting
them to take part in a series of seminars this fall to work out a strategy for
the unions and the ACLU to protect the privacy of Americans where
they work.

"Government employees and employees of private industry, railway work-   2
ers and baseball players," Glasser wrote, "are being required in ever greater
numbers to prove their innocence by submitting to intrusive and humiliating
urine and blood tests." The seminars, he said, would deal not only with "random drug testing of people not suspected of using drugs" but also with "other
violations of the right to privacy of the workplace."

As many workers can testify, privacy rights in the workplace have been   3
eroding for a long time by means that range from management eavesdrop-
ping on employee telephone calls to placement of hidden microphones in
employee washrooms in order to pick up intelligence concerning "trouble-
makers." What prompted Glasser's rallying cry, however, was the proclama-
tion of an unprecedented massive and official attack on workers' privacy.

On March 2, the President's Commission on Organized Crime strongly rec-   4
ommended—in the name of "national security"—that all Federal employees
be tested for drug use. Not particular individuals about whom some reasonable suspicion of drug abuse exists, but *all* employees. Furthermore, the
Commission urged all private employers who have Federal contracts to begin
dragnet testing of their workers. If the contractors refuse, they should be
denied any further Government business.

The Commission went on to recommend that all private employers, not   5
just those with Federal contracts, start collecting urine samples and otherwise screen their workers from drug use. Peter Rodino, chairman of the House
Judiciary Committee and a member of the President's Commission on Orga-

nized Crime, objected strenuously, noting that such wholesale testing "raises civil-liberties concerns." Nonsense, said Attorney General Edwin Meese, a mail-order scholar of the Framers' intentions on these matters. No unlawful search and seizure is involved, Meese explained, because, "by definition, it's not an unreasonable seizure because it's something the employee consents to as a condition of employment."

In other words, when the boss tells you to pee in a bottle if you want to keep your job, you consent to that condition if you don't want to lose your job.   6

At the press conference with the Attorney General was the chairman of the President's Commission, Judge Irving Kaufman of the Second Circuit Court of Appeals. Kaufman was the judge who sent Ethel and Julius Rosenberg to the electric chair after praying earnestly for guidance, thus making God an accomplice in the execution. As the years went on, Kaufman, extremely sensitive to charges that he was the prosecutor's judge in the Rosenberg case, has developed an exceptional reputation as a defender of First Amendment rights of defendants, especially the press, against the Government. But now, in the twilight of his career, Kaufman has again become the prosecutor's judge by supporting dragnet drug testing of millions of Americans.   7

The testing he and the majority of the Commission advocate, says Kaufman, is no more an invasion of privacy than requiring any American to walk through metal detectors at an airport. However, as Tom Wicker noted in *The New York Times*, "Having one's bodily fluids forcibly and randomly inspected is substantially different from putting one's luggage through an electronic device."   8

What's more, the drug tests aren't even accurate. "The most commonly used urine test is notoriously unreliable," Ira Glasser noted in an ACLU statement. "It cannot identify specific drugs and it cannot distinguish between common cold medicine and illegal substances like marijuana and cocaine. The test cannot determine when someone used a particular drug, or to what extent. And it cannot measure impairment of the ability to function on the job."   9

There are also blood tests for drugs, and they reveal much more than the Government or a private employer claims to be testing for. Charles Seabrook, an unusually probing science writer, pointed out in the *Atlanta Journal & Constitution* last year that "from a single ounce of a person's blood, sophisticated computerized tests can determine, or at least strongly suggest, whether a person is predisposed to heart attacks, whether he smokes, drinks to excess, has had a venereal disease, or is epileptic, schizophrenic, or subject to depression. . . . 'Given enough blood and enough lab technicians, I could find out hundreds of things about you—what you eat, what drugs you take, even the kind of booze you drink,' says Dr. James Woodford, a forensic chemist in Atlanta, who is frequently consulted in drug-related cases."   10

Judge Kaufman and the Attorney General may have unwittingly rendered a considerable service to the nation because their proposal has begun to   11 focus attention on routine invasions of privacy in the workplace. A growing number of large corporations have been doing just what the President's Commission on Organized Crime is pushing.

As an index of the dragnet testing that is already in place, everyone who   12
applies for work at United Airlines, IBM, Exxon, Du Pont, Federal Express, Lockheed, Shearson Lehman, TWA, and a good many other companies has to undergo urinalysis. Indeed, at least a quarter of the *Fortune* 500 companies test all applicants for drugs. Even without prodding from the President's Commission, many other firms, large and small, would have joined the list. Any time management has a chance to control its work force more firmly, it seizes on that chance. Now, the notion that every worker is guilty until proven innocent also has the imprimatur of a blue-ribbon Government commission that insists on regarding urinalysis and other forms of testing workers—before and after they're hired—as essential for national security.

At the ACLU seminars with labor unions to be held in the months ahead,   13
the first distinction to be drawn will be between the Government and private employers. Although Kaufman and Meese claim there are no constitutional problems with regard to testing public employees, case law indicates otherwise. When the State is the employer, the Fourth Amendment prohibition against unreasonable search and seizure comes into play. The Fourth Amendment requires that there be probable cause—or, in some instances, the lower standard of reasonable suspicion—that *particular* individuals may be doing or holding something illegal.

In 1984, for example, the Eighth Circuit Court of Appeals affirmed a de-   14
cision granting prison guards an injunction against random urinalysis even though they certainly perform crucial security functions. The court ruled that for the bodily fluids of public employees to be seized there has to be an *individualized,* reasonable basis for the search.

In East Rutherford, New Jersey, last year, the school board ordered all   15
students to undergo urine and blood testing for drugs and alcohol as part of an annual physical examination. Any student who tested positive would be suspended or expelled from school. The ACLU of New Jersey, representing five of the students, took the case to court and the rule was struck down because, said the judge, it violated each student's "legitimate expectation of privacy and personal security" under the Fourth Amendment.

Also in 1985, the school board of the Patchogue-Medford School District   16
on Long Island decided that to be given tenure, a teacher would have to submit to a urine test to determine the presence or absence of illegal drugs. In Suffolk County Supreme Court, Justice Thomas Stark could not have been more clear in his decision declaring that the school board had acted unconstitutionally:

"The Fourth Amendment of the United States Constitution, applicable to   17
state action through the Fourteenth . . . protects individuals from unreasonable searches of the person. The compulsory extraction of bodily fluids is a search and seizure within the meaning of the Fourth Amendment." Such a

search is permissible, he added, only when there is particularized, reasonable suspicion "based on objective supportable facts."

Workers in private employment, however, do not have Fourth Amendment [18] protections because the order to give up bodily fluids does not come from the State. Alternative sources of protection are available, however. Union contracts can include, through collective bargaining, provisions extending to workers the equivalent of First Amendment, Fourth Amendment, and other constitutional rights. Some United Auto Workers locals, for example, have won contracts with clauses that make it difficult to fire an employee for anything he says or puts on a bulletin board or wears on a T-shirt.

Until now, most workers and their unions have been slow to recognize the [19] importance of battling for such contract clauses. It may well be that the Meese-Kaufman assault on workers' privacy may spur more collective-bargaining strategy to get language that will give workers the same rights on the job as they have on the streets and at home. As bus driver Randy Kemp of Seattle put it in *Time*, "You've got to have a search warrant to search my house. Well, my body is a lot more sacred than my home."

Another route to protecting privacy is through state constitutions and lo- [20] cal statutes. Some state constitutions have stronger privacy provisions than the U.S. Constitution, and if the language covers private employees, dragnet and random searches can be banned. Richard Emery, a Fourth Amendment specialist with the New York Civil Liberties Union, also points out that under some local human-rights statutes, it is illegal to fire anyone who has a disability if that disability does not affect his job performance. Drug use can be a disability, but not necessarily one that interferes with worker competence. Accordingly, if a local statute includes drug dependence as a disability, and if the worker is doing his job efficiently, he can't be fired if he fails a drug test.

More directly specific is a San Francisco ordinance—the first in the coun- [21] try—that prohibits employers from administering random, dragnet blood and urine tests. And state legislatures in California, Maine, Oregon, and Maryland are considering bills that would limit or regulate testing of employees.

Clearly, there is potential for a natural alliance between workers and civil [22] libertarians to educate local and state legislators and to lobby for protective statutes. Invasion-of-privacy horror stories and realistic remedies ought to be covered in union newspapers, general publications, and—never to be underestimated—letters to the editors of all kinds of papers and magazines.

For many workers, civil liberties have long seemed to be a class issue. If [23] you look at the composition of most ACLU affiliates and chapters, the overwhelming majority of members are lawyers, academics, enlightened businessmen, and a very few union officials. Blue-collar workers are seldom represented. The rights that have appealed most to workers are economic rights, and they don't see the ACLU and other civil liberties organizations as being particularly concerned with take-home pay and benefits. But when a worker can lose his job if he won't piss into a bottle, the Fourth Amendment, at least, becomes much less abstract, and that's why a coalition between the usual civil-liberties activists and workers is not only plausible but potentially effective.

The possibility of protests within certain shops also exists. Job actions not   24
for more pay but to be a free citizen at work could put some heat on certain company officials.

Take the *Los Angeles Times*. Its editorial page has been among the most   25
forceful and lucid in the nation in fighting to keep the Bill of Rights in work-ing order. Yet, according to Daniel Jussim, writing in the ACLU's *Civil Lib-erties* newsletter, "The *Los Angeles Times*, though its director of employee relations says there's no particular drug problem at his newspaper, recently adopted a mandatory urinalysis program 'to stay current with what other employers are doing.' "

Imagine the impact in Los Angeles if Anthony Day, the civil libertarian   26
who is editor of the *Los Angeles Times*'s editorial page, were to lead a picket line outside the paper with such signs as:

JAMES OTIS, FATHER OF THE FOURTH AMENDMENT, FOUGHT BRITISH GENERAL   27
SEARCH WARRANTS ON BEHALF OF WORKING PEOPLE—NOT JUST PUBLISHERS.

The need for alliances to preserve what's left of privacy grows greater by   28
the day. Charles Seabrook writes of new tests that can "detect the presence of the abnormal levels of chemicals found in patients with severe depression, schizophrenia, and manic-depression . . . that can detect chemical 'markers' that may mean a person is at high risk of developing diabetes, arthritis, or cancer . . . that can screen for more than 150 genetic diseases, including sickle cell anemia . . . and cystic fibrosis."

Would an employer hire someone who is at risk of developing cancer?   29
Should an employer have access to such private information?

On a more modest level, a new test developed by Werner Baumgartner, a   30
Los Angeles chemist, bypasses such old-time procedures as requiring the random suspect to urinate into a cup or bottle. The new test uses radiation on hair and discloses not only what drugs have been taken but when they were taken, something urinalysis can't do.

As for coming attractions that verify the prescience of George Orwell, *The*   31
Washington Post reported in mid-1984, "Researchers in academia and in-dustry say it is now possible to envision a product that could instantaneously assess whether employees are concentrating on their jobs by analyzing their brain waves as they work."

There isn't much time left to create, in law, the best possible defenses   32
against Government and employer intrusions into privacy, including intru-sions that now seem inconceivable.

QUESTIONS FOR MEANING

1. What does Hentoff mean by "privacy rights in the workplace" and "drag-net testing"?
2. What motive does Hentoff attribute to corporations that require drug test-ing of applicants and employees?

3. What information can be learned from blood tests for drugs? How could such tests be abused?
4. What kind of tests does Hentoff imagine being used in the future?
5. According to Hentoff, under what circumstances would a mandatory drug test be permissible without violating the Fourth Amendment?
6. How can the right to privacy be protected?
7. Vocabulary: intrusive (2), unprecedented (3), forensic (10), imprimatur (12), coalition (23), prescience (31).

QUESTIONS ABOUT STRATEGY

1. Does Hentoff make any ad hominem arguments?
2. Why does Hentoff focus attention on tests that are more sophisticated than urinalysis?
3. Can you explain the allusion to George Orwell in paragraph 31? Is it appropriate for this context?

ANNE MARIE O'KEEFE
The Case Against Drug Testing

As both a psychologist and a lawyer who specializes in health issues, Anne Marie O'Keefe is concerned not only with the problem of drug abuse but also with the legality of drug-testing programs. Her argument against mandatory drug testing was first published by Psychology Today *in* **1987.**

During 1986, the nation's concern over illegal drug use reached almost   1
hysterical proportions. The U.S. House of Representatives passed legislation that, had the Senate agreed, would have suspended certain Constitutional protections and required the death penalty for some drug offenses. The President issued an executive order calling for the mass drug testing of federal employees in "sensitive" positions. Federal courts have deemed such testing to be illegal for some classes of federal workers; however, these decisions are still being appealed, and the administration is determined to forge ahead with its drug-testing program. And private employers have turned increasingly to chemical laboratories to determine who is fit for hiring, promotion and continuing employment. Between 1982 and 1985, the estimated proportion of Fortune-500 companies conducting routine urinalysis rose from 3 to nearly 30 percent—a figure expected to reach 50 percent by this year or next year.

While there are issues of legitimate concern about drug use and public   2
safety, the speed and enthusiasm with which many of our elected represen-

tatives and business leaders have embraced drug testing as a panacea has left many questions unanswered. Why did our national drug problem so rapidly become the focus of political and business decisions? Did this change reflect a sudden, serious worsening of the problem? Why did mass drug testing suddenly gain favor? Was it shown to be particularly effective in detecting and deterring illegal drug use? And finally, what are the costs of making employees and job applicants take urine tests?

Our country has a serious drug problem. The National Institute on Drug   3
Abuse (NIDA) estimates that nearly two-thirds of those now entering the work force have used illegal drugs—44 percent within the past year. But ironically, the drug-testing craze has come just when most types of drug use are beginning to wane. NIDA reports that for all drugs except cocaine, current rates are below those of 1979, our peak year of drug use.

Why the furor now? The drug-testing fad might be viewed as the product   4
of both election-year posturing and well-timed and well-financed marketing efforts by test manufacturers. During the 1970s, the relatively low-cost chemical assay (called EMIT) that promised to detect drugs in urine was first manufactured. In the beginning, these tests were used only by crime laboratories, drug-treatment programs and the military. By the early 1980s, a handful of private employers were also using them. But more recently, sales of drug tests have gotten a big boost from the attitudes and edicts of the Reagan administration. On March 3, 1986, the President's Commission on Organized Crime recommended that all employees of private companies contracting with the federal government be regularly subjected to urine testing for drugs as a condition of employment. Then came the President's executive order on September 15, requiring the head of each executive agency to "establish a program to test for the use of illegal drugs by employees in sensitive positions." It remains unclear how many millions of federal workers will be subject to such testing if the President gets his way.

Strangely, drug testing is becoming widespread despite general agreement   5
that the results of mass tests are often highly inaccurate. Error rates reflect both inherent deficiencies in the technology and mistakes in handling and interpreting test results. In a series of studies conducted by the federal Centers for Disease Control (CDC) and NIDA, urine samples spiked with drugs were sent periodically to laboratories across the country serving methadone treatment centers. Tests on these samples, which the labs knew had come from CDC, revealed drug-detection error rates averaging below 10 percent. However, when identical samples subsequently were sent to the same laboratories, but not identified as coming from CDC, error rates increased to an average of 31 percent, with a high of 100 percent. These errors were "false negatives," cases in which "dirty" urine samples were identified as "clean."

Independent studies of laboratory accuracy have also confirmed high error   6
rates. One group of researchers reported a 66.5 percent rate of "false positives" among 160 urine samples from participants in a methadone treatment center. False-positive mistakes, identifying a "clean" urine sample as containing an illegal drug, are far more serious in the context of worker screening

than are false-negative mistakes. This is because false positives can result in innocent people losing their jobs. Ironically, since the error rates inherent in the drug tests are higher than the actual rate of illegal drug use in the general working population, as reported by NIDA, the tests are more likely to label innocent people as illegal drug users than to identify real users.

Many of the false-positive results stem from a phenomenon known as "cross-   7
reactivity." This refers to the fact that both over-the-counter and prescription drugs, and even some foods, can produce false-positive results on the tests. For example, Contac, Sudafed, certain diet pills, decongestants and heart and asthma medications can register as amphetamines on the tests. Cough syrups containing dextromethorphan can cross-react as opiates, and some antibiotics show up as cocaine. Anti-inflammatory drugs and common painkillers, including Datril, Advil and Nuprin, mimic marijuana. Even poppy seeds, which actually contain traces of morphine, and some herbal teas containing traces of cocaine can cause positive test results for these drugs.

Commercial testing companies almost always claim very high accuracy and   8
reliability. But because these laboratories are not uniformly regulated, employers who buy their services may find it hard to confirm these claims or even to conduct informed comparative shopping. Companies that mass-market field-testing kits such as EMITs (which cost an estimated $15 to $25 per test) usually recommend that positive test results be confirmed with other laboratory procedures, which can run from $100 to $200 per test. But relatively few employers seem to be using the expensive back-up procedures before firing employees who test positive. Even when employers do verify positive results, employees who turn out to be drug-free upon retesting will already be stigmatized.

The tests have other critical failings, particularly their limited sensitivity   9
to certain drugs, a shortcoming the drug-test manufacturers readily admit. Consider cocaine, for example. Despite great concern in the 1980s over the use of cocaine, the only illicit drug whose use is on the rise, this is the drug to which the tests are least sensitive since its chemical traces dissipate in a few days. Alcohol, which is legal but potentially detrimental to job performance, is also hard to detect, since traces disappear from within 12 to 24 hours. By contrast, urine testing is, if anything, overly sensitive to marijuana; it can detect the drug's chemical byproducts (not its active ingredient) for weeks after its use and can even pick up the residue of passive inhalation. Drug testing does not indicate the recency of use, nor does it distinguish between chronic and one-time use. Most important, though urinalysis can reveal a lot about off-the-job activities, it tells nothing about job performance.

Mass drug testing is expensive, but its greatest costs are not financial and   10
cannot be neatly quantified. The greatest costs involve violations of workers' rights and the poor employee morale and fractured trust that result when workers must prove their innocence against the presumption of guilt.

The most important cost of drug testing, however, may be the invasion of   11
workers' privacy. Urinalysis may be highly inaccurate in detecting the use of illegal drugs, but it can reveal who is pregnant, who has asthma and who is

being treated for heart disease, manic-depression, epilepsy, diabetes and a host of other physical and mental conditions.

In colonial times, King George III justified having his soldiers break into 12
homes and search many innocent people indiscriminately on the grounds that the procedure might reveal the few who were guilty of crimes against the Crown. But the founders of our nation chose to balance things quite differently. An important purpose and accomplishment of the Constitution is to protect us from government intrusion. The Fourth Amendment is clear that "the right of the people to be secure in their persons . . . against unreasonable searches and seizures, shall not be violated. . . ." Searches are permitted only "upon probable cause, supported by Oath or affirmation, and particularly describing the place to be searched, and the persons or things to be seized."

The U.S. Supreme Court has ruled that extracting bodily fluids constitutes 13
a search within the meaning of this Amendment. Therefore, except under extraordinary circumstances, when the government seeks to test an employee's urine, it must comply with due process and must first provide plausible evidence of illegal activity. People accused of heinous crimes are assured of this minimum protection from government intrusion. Because employees in our government work force deserve no less, most courts reviewing proposals to conduct mass tests on such employees have found these programs to be illegal.

Unfortunately, workers in the private sector are not as well protected. The 14
Constitution protects citizens only from intrusions by government (county, state and federal); it does not restrict nongovernmental employers from invading workers' privacy, although employers in the private sector are subject to some limitations. The constitutions of nine states have provisions specifically protecting citizens' rights to privacy and prohibiting unreasonable searches and seizures. Several private lawsuits against employers are now testing the applicability of these shields. Local governments, can, if they wish, pass legislation to protect private employees from unwarranted drug tests; in fact, San Francisco has done so. In addition, union contracts and grievance procedures may give some workers protection from mass drug testing, and civil-rights laws could block the disproportionate testing of minorities. Nonetheless, private employees have relatively little legal protection against mandatory drug testing and arbitrary dismissal.

Civil libertarians claim that as long as employees do their work well, in- 15
quiries into their off-duty drug use are no more legitimate than inquiries into their sex lives. Then why has drug testing become so popular? Perhaps because it is simple and "objective"—a litmus test. It is not easily challenged because, like the use of lie detectors, it relies on technology that few understand. It is quicker and cheaper than serious and sustained efforts to reduce illegal drug use, such as the mass educational efforts that have successfully reduced cigarette smoking. And finally, while drug testing may do little to address the real problem of drug use in our society, it reinforces the employer's illusion of doing something.

Apparently some employers would rather test their employees for drugs   16
than build a relationship with them based on confidence and loyalty. Fortunately, there are employers, such as the Drexelbrook Engineering Company
in Pennsylvania, who have decided against drug testing because of its human
costs. As Drexelbrook's vice president put it, a relationship "doesn't just come
from a paycheck. When you say to an employee, 'you're doing a great job;
just the same, I want you to pee in this jar and I'm sending someone to watch
you,' you've undermined that trust."

QUESTIONS FOR MEANING

1. What is meant by "false negatives," "false positives," and "cross-reactiv-
   ity"?
2. What is revealed by the study conducted by the Centers for Disease Control which is discussed in paragraph 5?
3. What drug is urinalysis most likely to detect? What type of drug use is it
   likely to overlook?
4. How does O'Keefe account for the rise in drug-testing? Why does O'Keefe
   believe the popularity of drug-testing is "ironic" and "strange"?
5. Vocabulary: furor (4), posturing (4), assay (4), stigmatized (8), quantified
   (10), morale (10), arbitrary (14).

QUESTIONS ABOUT STRATEGY

1. What concessions does O'Keefe make regarding drug abuse?
2. Why does O'Keefe provide the initials for the National Institute on Drug
   Abuse and the Centers for Disease Control within parentheses immediately after first using these names in paragraphs 3 and 5?
3. Why does O'Keefe report the price of widely used field-testing kits and
   the cost of laboratory procedures that are recommended for back-up testing?
4. Consider the quotation with which this essay ends. Is this an effective
   conclusion?

IRVING R. KAUFMAN
The Battle over Drug Testing

The recipient of many awards for distinguished service to the judiciary, Irving R. Kaufman has been a member of the New York bar since 1932 and a judge since 1949. He first came to national prominence as the judge who presided over the espionage trial of Julius and Ethel Rosenberg in the early 1950s. More recently, he was appointed chairman of the President's Commission on Organized Crime by Ronald Reagan in 1983. In the following essay, originally written for the New York Times *in **1986,** Kaufman defends the Commission's recommendation that the use of drug testing be considered when appropriate.*

All over America, the scenario is being acted out with increasing frequency. The players are remarkably diverse—an office manager in San Francisco, a police officer in Boston, even a Cabinet officer in the White House. Each of these individuals, and thousands more, has been asked to take a drug test at work. Some have acquiesced; others have refused. Those who have not yet confronted the issue personally would be well advised to consider it, for drug testing is shaping up as the premier issue in labor relations for the next decade. 1

"Scarcely any political question arises in the United States which is not resolved sooner or later into a judicial question," said Alexis de Tocqueville. Drug testing, for better or worse, is once again proving the veracity of the axiom. Opponents of drug testing in the workplace have pleaded their case not only on editorial pages but in the courtroom, where, typically, they denounce the practice as an invasion of privacy. The legal verdict remains uncertain, but it should be evident that drug testing is not a clear-cut issue; it may assume a multiplicity of forms in a variety of contexts, and nothing is served by reducing the debate to a series of slogans. 2

On Sept. 15, President Reagan signed an executive order calling for drug testing of a broad range of the Federal Government's 2.8 million civilian employees, earmarking about $56 million for the undertaking in the first year. The increased use of drug testing by governmental agencies and private employers—more than a quarter of the Fortune 500 companies test job applicants—is part of a larger trend in society's war on drug abuse, with a pronounced shift of emphasis to the drug user. But to inquire whether someone is for or against drug testing in the workplace is really to pose a question without content, the variables are so great. Is the drug test to be administered to Government workers—in which case the Fourth Amendment's protection from unreasonable searches and seizures must be satisfied—or to employees in private industry? Does a given company intend to test its employees at random or will a worker be asked to submit to urinalysis only when he exhibits some sign of drug abuse? Are employees to be included in the screening or only job applicants? 3

These important distinctions, however, have not prevented some employ- 4
ers and civil liberties groups from adopting blanket positions on drug testing.
Those in favor insist that an employer has the right to demand a drug-free
work force, and point to diminished productivity, increased accidents and
absenteeism as the effects of drug abuse. Opponents of "jar wars"—the columnist William Safire's appellation—challenge its constitutionality in the case
of public employees and its reliability in any context. More fundamentally,
they claim that employers are not simply concerned with performance, but
with enforcing a brand of morality; if an employee smokes a joint on the
weekend, they reason, it is no concern to management as long as he performs
competently come Monday.

The President first hinted that a major policy shift was in the works on 5
July 30, when he announced that he was considering widespread testing of
Government employees, extending the existing testing procedures of such
agencies as the Federal Bureau of Investigation, the Immigration and Naturalization Service, the Federal Aviation Administration, the Postal Service,
the Drug Enforcement Administration and the military services. At a press
conference, the President said he and his Cabinet had "pretty much agreed
that mandatory testing is justified where the employees have the health of
others and the safety of others in their hands." He also urged that "voluntary"
drug testing be considered inside and outside the Government. As if to set
an example, President Reagan and Vice President Bush underwent urinalysis,
and 78 members of the White House senior staff were asked to participate in
a "voluntary testing."

My experience as chairman of the President's Commission on Organized 6
Crime, which fulfilled its mandate and disbanded last March, taught me just
how sensitive a topic drug testing is with the public, and how quick the
media can be to jump to conclusions. The commission examined every activity of organized crime, including money laundering, labor racketeering and
misconduct by lawyers. But one conclusion stood out from the rest: drug
trafficking is the lifeblood of organized crime, bringing in billions of dollars of
revenues annually. Accordingly, the commission was determined to bring before the public proposals to combat drug abuse. The report we issued recommended that Federal agencies implement policies aimed at reducing drug
use among their employees and consider including suitable drug-testing programs where appropriate. It was also suggested that Government contracts
not be awarded to companies that make no effort to detect and eliminate
drug abuse among their workers.

For the next few days, the press reported that the commission had come 7
out in favor of mandatory drug testing for all Federal employees, and that it
had asked the Government not to award contracts to private companies that
do not administer across-the-board drug screening under any circumstances.
The fact is the commission never intended to call for anything so severe.
Above all, our recommendations were intended to launch a national debate.
With that debate now full-blown, it would be inappropriate for me, as an
active Federal judge, to express my conclusions about the legality of various

drug-testing practices. Rather, my purpose here is to inform and to delineate the framework of the current debate.

Drug abuse has become an epidemic in America, so it should come as no surprise that the problem has spilled over into the workplace. The National Institute on Drug Abuse reports that 65 percent of those entering the work force have used illegal drugs, 44 percent in the last year. In its study on drug trafficking, the President's Commission on Organized Crime reported that 20 million Americans use marijuana at least once a month and that 6 million use cocaine as often. A study by the Research Triangle Institute, a North Carolina business-sponsored research organization, found that drug use drained $60 billion from the nation's economy in 1983.   8

In justifying drug testing, employers may cite the need for reliable performance from those who hold the public safety in their hands, such as airline pilots and nuclear power plant operators. Less dramatic rationales are offered when lives do not hang in the balance. Employers may claim an interest in the health and safety of employees, for instance, and the right to be free from the expense of workers who are not doing their jobs properly.   9

But is this really all that is behind the increasing popularity of drug testing? Some, like the columnist Charles Krauthammer, have suggested that this screening is an attempt to improve behavior rather than production. Krauthammer labels testing an "extraordinary experiment in law enforcement," and regards it as a "sinister" form of "disguised and benign" social control. "It carries the threat of a real, material sanction, a sanction that hits you where it hurts, but doesn't quite put you in jail," he writes. "It jeopardizes your job, but not your liberty. And is administered not by guys in blue suits with guns, but in white coats and gloves—on orders not from a judge but from your boss." Ira Glasser, executive director of the American Civil Liberties Union, echoes that view.   10

The protests, however, have not dampened the enthusiasm of government and business for drug testing. The precursor of all drug-detection programs was the Department of Defense's move in the 1970's to identify and treat returning Vietnam veterans addicted to heroin. Today, each branch of the military services administers drug tests. Where the nation's defense is deemed at stake, the courts have been most deferential. In the private sector, some of the most prestigious companies in the country require job applicants to undergo urinalysis—including Exxon, the International Business Machines Corporation, Lockheed, Shearson Lehman Brothers, Federal Express, United Airlines, Trans World Airlines, Hoffman-La Roche, Du Pont, the American Telephone and Telegraph Company and The New York Times. Peter Ueberroth, commissioner of baseball, has made drug testing mandatory for players in the professional leagues, and the National Football League recently announced plans to test players for drug use three times a year.   11

The number of businesses that test not just applicants, but employees, is also on the rise. Two Wall Street firms, Kidder, Peabody & Company, and Smith Barney, Harris Upham & Company, recently became the first brokerage houses to check employees for use of illegal drugs.   12

In the public sector, too, testing is catching on, not only in Federal agencies but in a growing number of local police and fire departments. Last April, Francis M. Roache, the Boston Police Commissioner, announced that he would require the department's 2,400 employees to be tested for drugs at least once a year. Police chiefs in Houston and Los Angeles are also pressing for authority to conduct random drug tests.   13

Can the test results be trusted? A plethora of charges have been leveled against the reliability of urinalysis, ranging from speculation that nasal sprays cause positive results to allegations of built-in racial bias because of the similarity between the chemical composition of the pigment melanin, found in high levels in blacks and Hispanic people, and the active ingredient in marijuana. Others claim that positive tests may result from passive inhalation of marijuana smoke. But these assertions are spurious, according to J. Michael Walsh and Richard L. Hawks of the National Institute on Drug Abuse. Drug screening through urinalysis can be extremely accurate, they say, but much depends on the quality-control procedures followed by the laboratory and on the commitment to follow-up tests for all positive results.   14

The manufacturer of the most popular screening test, known as EMIT (Enzyme Multiplied Immunoassay Technique) claims an accuracy rate of better than 95 percent under ideal circumstances. But opponents of testing maintain that even the slimmest margin of error is unacceptable. They also fear that standards will be lowered as laboratories compete for business and employers balk at expensive confirmation assays.   15

The accuracy issue is far from settled. Apparently, there is truth to the assertion that certain kinds of widely available medications react in the same way as marijuana when analyzed. Syva, the manufacturer of the EMIT assay, warns that certain anti-inflammatory drugs can cause a false positive for marijuana, specifically the painkiller ibuprofen, found in Advil and other over-the-counter products. In addition, a person who eats enough food containing poppy seeds, which naturally contain morphine, could be surprised to find people asking questions about his heroin habit. Dr. Walsh of the National Institute on Drug Abuse, however, maintains that false positives can be virtually eliminated through proper confirmation and quality-control procedures. Unconfirmed positives, he emphasizes, should always be reported as negatives.   16

My expertise, however, is not as a scientist but as a judge. I turn, then, to some of the emerging legal questions raised by drug testing, especially when it is performed by the Government. The lawsuits have begun to reach the courts, but it is still too early to say how the constitutional arguments will ultimately fare.   17

Most of the legal issues surrounding drug screening in the workplace are in flux, but participants in the current debate seem to agree on a few general propositions. The first is that, unlike workers in private industry, Government employees may claim the protection of the Fourth Amendment's prohibition against unreasonable searches and seizures. The second is that private employers are not subject to the Fourth Amendment's strictures (although they   18 may be subject to other legal constraints) because the Bill of Rights restrains only the actions of Government officials or those acting closely in concert with them. Any discussion of the constitutionality of testing public employees for drugs, therefore, should begin with an examination of the historical roots of the amendment.

The Fourth Amendment to the Constitution had its genesis in abuses suf-   19
fered by the colonists at the hands of Mother England. To protect its mer-cantile empire, Parliament restricted trade between the colonies and areas outside the empire by imposing prohibitive import duties on goods entering the colonies from outside the empire. As a result, smuggling became wide-spread and was practiced by even the most respectable colonists. John Han-cock, for example, was accused of smuggling in 1768. He defended himself on the ground that the import duty was a form of taxation without representation.

The notorious Writ of Assistance was the principal enforcement mecha-   20
nism for collection of duty fees. The writ was essentially a general warrant for the King's custom inspectors indiscriminately to search homes and ware-houses in order to insure that the Crown received all of the tribute to which it was entitled. Today, the general search—its end, to ferret out evidence of a crime; its means, virtually unrestricted—remains the paradigm of the kind of governmental intrusion most reviled by the Fourth Amendment. The Fourth Amendment teaches, then, that no matter how compelling the Government's need to pursue a given policy, the individual's right to privacy must serve as a check. As drug-testing programs begin to resemble the general search, their legitimacy grows increasingly suspect.

The Fourth Amendment provides that the "right of the people to be se-   21
cure in their persons, houses, papers, and effects, against unreasonable searches and seizures, shall not be violated, and no Warrants shall issue, but upon probable cause, supported by Oath, or affirmation, and particularly describing the place to be searched, and the persons or things to be seized." By its terms, the amendment covers much more than the wholesale warehouse searches of the 18th century. All searches pursuant to a warrant must be supported by probable cause, and there is an independent requirement of reasonableness.

The landmark case of Boyd v. United States, decided in 1886, leaves no   22
doubt that a search may sometimes be reasonable even though conducted without a validly issued warrant. For example, a police officer may search the area immediately surrounding a lawfully arrested suspect for a weapon. Sim-ilarly, an officer who observes suspicious conduct may stop and frisk a sus-pect if he has reasonable grounds to believe the suspect is armed. But wholesale drug testing of employees falls into a different category, for the tests are often administered without suspicion of any particular individual, and the odds are that any given person will be found free of drugs.

Under the emerging doctrine of the "administrative search," however, courts   23
sometimes allow broad-scale searches to be conducted without a warrant or individualized suspicion. Anyone who has flown on a commercial airline in

the last 15 years has been subjected to an administrative search in the form of a cursory check of his person and belongings before boarding. These searches, instituted by the Federal Aviation Administration pursuant to Presidential order, fall within the ambit of the Fourth Amendment, but have been held reasonable by the courts. The reasonableness inquiry turns on a balancing test by the judge, who must weigh the urgency of the Government's reasons for conducting the search against the constitutionally protected interest in "the sanctities of a man's home and the privacies of life."

The United States Supreme Court first authorized an administrative search   24
in 1967, in a case involving housing inspection. The Court found that inspectors could assure compliance with the minimum standards of municipal codes only by conducting periodic inspections of all structures. But, significantly, the Court did require the inspectors to obtain inspection warrants before nonconsensual entry of a building.

In 1972, in a case involving the inspection of gun dealers, the Court dis-   25
pensed completely with the warrant requirement because of the highly regulated nature of the firearms industry, where pervasive Government regulations and licensing reduced the dealers' legitimate expectation of privacy. Unannounced periodic inspections were essential if the law was to serve as a credible deterrent, the Court said. Clearly, though, it would contradict our constitutional history to conclude that any search of commercial property where the Government has a regulatory interest satisfies the Fourth Amendment. After all, the dreaded Writs of Assistance, which supplied the stimulus to enact the Fourth Amendment, involved searches of commercial warehouses. The Court has acknowledged this by distinguishing between searches of highly regulated industries, such as firearms, liquor and mining, on the one hand, and ordinary businesses, on the other. Searches of the latter must be accompanied by a warrant unless the proprietor gives his consent.

In some instances, the Court has extended the administrative search doc-   26
trine to inspections of the individual. Administrative searches of persons who have exhibited no behavior that would give rise to suspicion of illegal activity have been approved at United States border areas, at entrances to courthouses and, as mentioned, at airport departure gates. In addition, the highly regulated nature of the horse-racing industry was the basis for upholding random, mandatory drug testing of jockeys by the United States Court of Appeals for the Third Circuit last July. The lawsuit, filed by five famous jockeys, including William Shoemaker and Angel Cordero, contested the New Jersey Racing Commission's policy of drawing the names of several jockeys from an envelope each day and requiring them to furnish urine samples after the last race that day. The court rejected the jockeys' insistence on individualized suspicion before testing, instead embracing the racing commission's contention that searches in the highly regulated racing industry are reasonable.

It must be noted that a search of the person is more akin to a search of   27
the home than to inspection of a commercial enterprise, for the Fourth Amendment applies with its greatest vigor to intrusions upon the human body. Still, a Federal Court of Appeals in California upheld preboarding

screening of all airplane passengers and their carry-on luggage because of
the indisputable need to prevent the hijacking of airliners. The court acknowledged the danger of airport searches being subverted into constitutionally prohibited general searches for evidence of a crime, but was satisfied
that the inspections were to prevent hijacking rather than to prosecute individuals for illegally possessing firearms.

The constitutional status of a drug-testing program, similarly, may hinge   28
in part on the purpose to which the program is put. If designed merely to
identify and rehabilitate drug users, as the President recently maintained, the
danger of a general search for evidence of crime is avoided. If criminal investigations or prosecutions were the primary purpose of the tests, one could
argue that the searches would be subject to the warrant and probable-cause
requirements of the Fourth Amendment. (It is further worth pointing out
that unlike possession and distribution of illegal drugs, use alone is not generally an indictable offense.) In the airport search case, the United States
Court of Appeals for the Ninth Circuit noted that authorities searched all
passengers and had no power to single out travelers. By analogy, a drug-
testing program may appear more reasonable when it applies to all employees within a given group, not just those who stir the boss's whimsy.

Some critics argue that it is a cramped notion of "consent" that deems an   29
employee's decision to submit to drug testing on pain of losing his job "con-
sensual," but the question of consent will invariably enter into the legal calculus. In the airport case, the court emphasized the voluntary nature of the
search: only passengers who choose to board a plane are searched. In another case, in which welfare benefits were conditioned on a case worker's
periodic visits to the home, the Supreme Court held that the visitation was
voluntary because the recipient was free to reject the conditions and forfeit
the payments. Whether the same logic will apply to permit a Government
employer to require workers to either submit to drug testing or find another
job remains to be seen.

Courts will also make inquiries into the intrusiveness of the method of   30
drug testing. When Fourth Amendment rights are implicated, the Government is frequently required to employ the least restrictive means available to
achieve its interest. Civil libertarians point out that to insure authenticity,
workers must be observed while giving urine samples, creating embarrassment and humiliation. Furthermore, if grounds for individualized suspicion
do exist, the basic rationale for the administrative search becomes atten-
uated. The Court approved administrative searches in housing inspections
because it was impossible to tell from the outside whether any given house
was in violation. But if a problem presents observable suspicious activity,
counsel will surely argue that a blanket search subjecting everyone to governmental intrusion runs afoul of the Fourth Amendment's reasonableness
requirement.

Few generalizations can be made from the small but growing body of legal   31
precedent in drug testing cases. One observation that can be made, however,

is that courts are extremely sensitive to the factual context surrounding the testing. Last year, for example, a United States District Court in Atlanta ruled that employees of a public utility who worked on high-voltage electric wires could be forced to submit to urinalysis. The tests were administered after an undercover agent planted among the workers by management reported that some of the employees had been smoking marijuana at work. The court found the tests reasonable in light of the extremely dangerous nature of the work and the careful nature of the investigation.

Similar considerations were present in one of the earliest drug testing   32
cases to reach the courts. In 1976, a union representing 5,500 bus drivers challenged the constitutionality of the Chicago Transit Authority's requirement that bus operators submit to blood or urine tests following their involvement in a serious accident, or upon suspicion of drug or alcohol impairment. Here, again, the court found the intrusions reasonable, considering the transit authority's "paramount" interest in insuring that drivers are unimpaired. In the parlance of the Fourth Amendment, the interest in safety negated any "reasonable expectation of privacy." Several cases have upheld the testing of police and correction officers, whether conducted at random or "for cause." Last August, the New York State Supreme Court rejected a challenge to the testing of correction officers who drive prison vans and buses for New York City, citing the strong security and safety considerations involved in transporting prisoners.

But there have been dissenting voices, and notably articulate ones at that.   33
On Sept. 18, Judge H. Lee Sarokin of Federal District Court in Newark ruled that mandatory urine testing of government employees, such as policemen and firefighters in Plainfield, N.J., violated the Fourth Amendment. Only a strong suspicion that a certain individual was using illegal drugs could justify testing a worker, the court held. And last year, Harold D. Vietor, chief judge of the United States District Court in Des Moines, reinstated a prison guard's pay, lost when he was temporarily discharged after refusing to take a urine test. Although prison officials had received an anonymous tip that the guard was using drugs, Judge Vietor determined that an individual's urine may not be tested unless the same kind of cause that is needed to search his house is present. Although the state pressed its need to identify drug smugglers and keep its correctional staff drug-free, the court reasoned that the same logic could be used to support searching the guards' homes, or tapping their telephones. "There is no doubt about it," Judge Vietor wrote, "searches and seizures can yield a wealth of information useful to the searcher. (That is why King George III's men so frequently searched the colonists.) That potential, however, does not make a governmental employer's search of an employee a constitutionally reasonable one."

In another well publicized case, the Appellate Division of the New York   34
State Supreme Court ruled last summer that probationary teachers in a Long Island school district could not be compelled to submit to urinalysis. Without reasonable suspicion of drug abuse, the court said, the tests would be an

unconstitutional invasion of privacy. "Strikingly absent from the record is even a scintilla of suspicion, much less a reasonable suspicion," the court noted.

Employers in the private sector are not subject to the Fourth Amendment, but drug testing in this area will hardly go unchallenged. Workers may be able to raise privacy claims pursuant to local statutes, union agreements or even state constitutional provisions. For example, a computer programmer sued the Southern Pacific Railroad in San Francisco in 1985 after she was discharged for refusing to submit to a drug test. Though her case is still unresolved, she has the benefit of an explicit right-to-privacy provision in the California Constitution.   35

Workers in private industry may also be able to challenge the accuracy of test results in certain circumstances, aided by recently enacted ordinances, such as one passed in San Francisco. In another suit filed against Southern Pacific, an office manager was required to enroll in a rehabilitation program after urinalysis indicated the presence of cocaine. The manager contends that the test was a "false positive." For 28 days, according to his lawyer, he was isolated from his family at a drug clinic, although all follow-up tests were negative and doctors said there was no need for rehabilitation. For weeks after, the manager was required to attend drug-therapy meetings and to undergo regular testing. He obtained an injunction against further testing under a local ordinance, but was demoted the next day, prompting a second suit, which is being litigated.   36

Unfortunately, the debate on drug screening has been rich in emotion and hyperbole. Not all proposals for drug testing are the brainchild of Big Brother or a knee-jerk reaction to saturation media coverage of drug abuse. Some screening programs may genuinely represent an effort to keep the workplace drug-free in order to insure safety and improve performance. But, though good intentions are reassuring, heightened sensitivity to concerns about privacy, accuracy and legality are indispensable.   37

QUESTIONS FOR MEANING

1. What does Kaufman mean when he describes drug testing as "part of a larger trend in society's war on drug abuse, with a pronounced shift of emphasis to the drug user"? Where has the emphasis usually been?
2. Why did the President's Commission on Organized Crime decide to focus attention on drug abuse? What were its recommendations?
3. What does "money laundering" mean in paragraph 6?
4. What was the Writ of Assistance, and how was it used against American colonists before the revolution? Why did the British use it? What effect did this writ eventually have on the American Constitution?
5. Can you explain what is meant by "probable cause" in paragraph 21?
6. Which businesses have the courts held it reasonable to search without a warrant?
7. Why did the courts hold that bus drivers can be required to submit to drug testing?

8. Vocabulary: acquiesced (1), veracity (2), axiom (2), contexts (2), appellation (4), delineate (7), sanction (10), deferential (11), plethora (14), spurious (14), flux (18), mercantile (19), notorious (20), ferret (20), paradigm (20), reviled (20).

QUESTIONS ABOUT STRATEGY

1. At what points in his essay does Kaufman recognize the views of people who oppose drug testing?
2. Why does Kaufman discuss airline baggage checks (in paragraphs 23 and 27)? Is he making an analogy between such searches and mandatory drug testing?
3. Where in this long essay does Kaufman most clearly summarize his own position?
4. Why does Kaufman devote so much space to reviewing various court cases? What effect did this review have upon your own view of mandatory drug testing?
5. How does Kaufman characterize the debate over drug testing? Why is it useful for him to present the debate from this point of view?

ONE STUDENT'S ASSIGNMENT

Summarize "The Battle over Drug Testing" by Irving Kaufman in approximately 500 words. Be sure to include each of the most important points made in this essay, and be careful to avoid letting your own opinion interfere with objectively summarizing what Kaufman has written.

A Summary of
Irving Kaufman's "The Battle over Drug Testing"
James A. McClain

Due to the increasing prevalency of drug abuse among work‐   1
ers, drug testing is on the rise and is becoming a major issue
in labor relations. Knowing that this judicially controver‐
sial issue is complex, it would be well to outline and ex‐
plain the current debate.

Those in favor of drug testing promote a workplace free of   2
drug abuse because of the decreases in production and the in‐
creases in injuries and unexcused absences that accompany
it. Advocates also say that testing for drugs by urinalysis

produces reliable results and that false positives are minimized by proper laboratory procedures. Opponents of drug
testing question its legality for public employees. They
also say testing programs are affecting employees' personal
lifestyles and argue that even the smallest percent error in
test results is too much. However, these objections have not
deterred more and more private businesses, federal agencies, and police and fire departments from testing employees
and, in some cases, applicants also.

This increase in drug testing has spurred many legal ques-   3
tions. One involves public employees who claim immunity from
testing under the Fourth Amendment's teaching "that no matter how compelling the Government's need to pursue a given
policy, the individual's right to privacy must serve as a
check" against unreasonable searches and seizures. But any
conclusion about the legality of testing public employees
needs to begin with a look at the amendment's history. The
British precipitated it by using a general warrant prior to
the American revolution to enter homes in random search of
lawbreakers. If drug testing programs likewise end up being
searches without suspecting a certain individual, their legality will come into question and public employees may be
able to obtain immunity.

Even so, under some circumstances courts do allow searches   4
(like the inspecting of airline passengers and their baggage) to proceed without a warrant or individualized suspicion. The courts realize that a search of the person as at
airports is explicitly addressed by the Fourth Amendment but
are convinced the screenings are to locate hijackers and not
to incriminate persons who may be doing something illegal
such as smuggling cocaine. "The constitutional status of a
drug–testing program, similarly, may hinge in part on the
purpose to which the program is put. If designed merely to
identify and rehabilitate drug users . . . the danger of a
general search for evidence of crime is avoided."

The question of consent is another legal controversy. Is   5
it right to request that workers either bow to drug testing
or look for other employment? Courts are also concerned
about safety, which they feel overrides the right for privacy in some cases, as with bus drivers and airplane pilots.
But in non–life–threatening situations the courts say that
testing can be warranted only when it is almost certain that
an individual is using drugs.

A final question concerns non-government employees. 6
They're not able to find shelter under the Fourth Amendment
but may be able to claim a right to privacy against drug testing because of state, local, or union provisions. These
workers may also be able to oppose testing on the grounds of
its accuracy.

Thus, although testing programs are designed to improve 7
the workplace by keeping drugs out, their intrusiveness, reliability, and constitutionality also need to be carefully
considered.

SUGGESTIONS FOR WRITING

1. When you were in high school, did you know any students who used drugs? If so, write an essay for or against the drug testing of students that incor- porates your own experience or observations.
2. Write an argument against testing athletes for drug use that will respond to each of John Burt's four arguments on behalf of drug testing.
3. Write an argument for or against drug testing in the workplace.
4. Both Nat Hentoff and Anne Marie O'Keefe oppose mandatory drug testing. Compare their arguments and determine which is stronger.
5. Write an essay defining the meaning of the Fourth Amendment. Draw your information from Hoerr, Kaufman, and O'Keefe.
6. Is there any alternative to drug testing? Write an argument on behalf of some other method besides testing for fighting drug abuse.
7. Anne Marie O'Keefe claims that drug use was beginning to decline by the mid-1980s. Do a research paper to determine if this is so and what factors could be responsible for the decline.
8. Synthesize the major arguments for and against mandatory drug testing.
9. Do a research paper on what sophisticated tests can reveal about people besides whether or not they have used illegal drugs.

Section 2

Gun Control: Triggering a National Controversy

JEANNE SHIELDS
Why Nick?

When people discuss controversial issues, they sometimes lose sight of how these issues affect individual lives. Gun control has been the subject of national debate for so many years that it may seem of interest only to men and women who are directly involved with guns: those who either own them, sell them, or work with them. But the abstract can become painfully real to anyone who becomes the victim of handgun violence, as this essay by Jeanne Shields reveals. After her son was murdered, Shields became active in the movement to control handguns. Her essay, which originally appeared in Newsweek *in* **1978,** *is both a tribute to the memory of her son and an argument on behalf of stricter laws regulating the sale and possession of guns.*

1   If the telephone rings late at night, I always mentally check off where each child is, and at the same time get an awful sinking feeling in the pit of my stomach.

2   Four years ago, April 16, we had a telephone call very late. As my husband answered, I checked off Pam in Long Beach (California), Nick in San Francisco, David in New Brunswick (New Jersey) and Leslie outside Boston. The less my husband spoke, the tighter the knot got in my stomach. Instinctively, I knew it was bad news, but I wasn't prepared for what he had to tell me. Our eldest son, Nick, 23, had been shot dead on a street in San Francisco.

3   Nick was murdered at about 9:30 p.m. He and a friend, Jon, had come from lacrosse practice and were on their way home. They stopped to pick up a rug at the home of a friend. While Jon went in to get the rug, Nick rearranged the lacrosse gear in the back of their borrowed Vega. He was shot three times in the back and died instantly, holding a lacrosse stick.

4   Nick was the fourteenth victim of what came to be called the "Zebra killers." Between the fall of 1973 and April 16, 1974, they had randomly killed fourteen people and wounded seven others—crippling one for life. Four men were subsequently convicted of murder in a trial that lasted thirteen months.

My son was tall, dark and handsome, and a good athlete. He was particularly good at lacrosse and an expert skier. Nick was an ardent photographer and wrote some lovely poetry. He was a gentle and sensitive man with an infectious grin and the capacity to make friends easily. It was hard for me to believe he was gone.

The generous support and love of our friends gave us the strength to go on during those days. The calls and letters that poured in from those who knew Nick were overwhelming. In his short life, Nick had touched so many people in so many ways. It was both heartwarming and very humbling.

But always, running through those blurred days was the question. Why? Why Nick? My deep faith in God was really put to the test. Yet, nothing that I could do or think of, or pray for, was ever going to bring Nick back.

Because Nick was shot two days after Easter, the funeral service was filled with Easter prayers and hymns. Spring flowers came from the gardens of friends. The day was mild, clear and beautiful, and a kind of peace and understanding seeped into my aching heart.

No matter how many children you have, the death of one leaves a void that cannot be filled. Life seems to include a new awareness, and one's philosophy and values come under sharper scrutiny. Were we just to pick up the pieces and continue as before? That choice became impossible, because a meaning had to be given to this vicious, senseless death.

That summer of 1974, the newspapers, magazines and television were full of Watergate. But I couldn't concentrate on it or anything else. Instead I dug hard in the garden for short periods of time, or smashed at tennis balls.

On the other hand, my husband, Pete, immersed himself in a study of the gun-control issue. Very near to where Nick had died, in a vacant lot, two small children found a gun—*the* gun. It was a .32-caliber Beretta. Police, in tracing it, found that initially it had been bought legally, but then went through the hands of seven different owners—most of whom had police records. Its final bullets, fired at close range, had killed my son—and then it was thrown carelessly away.

Pete's readings of Presidential commission recommendations, FBI crime statistics and books on the handgun issue showed him that our Federal laws were indeed weak and ineffective. He went to Washington to talk to politicians and to see what, if anything, was being done about it. I watched him wrestle with his thoughts and spend long hours writing them down on paper—the pros and cons of handgun control and what could logically be done about the proliferation of handguns in this nation.

Through friends, Pete had been introduced in Washington to the National Council to Control Handguns, a citizens' lobby seeking stricter Federal controls over handguns. As Pete became more closely associated with the NCCH as a volunteer, it became increasingly obvious that he was leaning toward a greater involvement.

Consequently, with strong encouragement from me and the children, Pete took a year's leave of absence from his job as a marketing executive so that he could join NCCH full time. A full year and a half later, he finally resigned and became the NCCH chairman.

The main adversaries of handgun control are members of the powerful   15
and financially entrenched National Rifle Association, macho men who don't understand the definition of a civilized society. They are aided by an apathetic government which in reality is us, because we citizens don't make ourselves heard loud and clear enough. How many people are in the silent majority, who want to see something done about unregulated sale and possession of handguns? Why do we register cars and license drivers, and not do the same for handguns? Why are the production and sale of firecrackers severely restricted—and not handguns?

I now work in the NCCH office as a volunteer. One of my jobs is to read   16
and make appropriate card files each day from a flood of clippings describing handgun incidents. The daily newspapers across the country recount the grim litany of shootings, killings, rapes and robberies at gun point. Some of it's tough going, because I am poignantly aware of what a family is going through. Some of it's so appalling it makes me literally sick.

Some people can no longer absorb this kind of news. They have almost   17
become immune to it, because there is so much violence. To others, it is too impersonal; it's always something that happens to somebody else—not to you.

But anybody can be shot. We are all in a lottery, where the likelihood of   18
your facing handgun violence grows every day. Today there are 50 million handguns in civilian hands. By the year 2000, there will be more than 100 million.

So many families have given up so much to the deadly handgun. It will   19
take the women of this country—the mothers, wives, sisters and daughters— to do something about it. But when will they stand up to be counted and to be heard? Or will they wait only to hear the telephone ringing late at night?

QUESTIONS FOR MEANING

1. Why is Shields especially interested in working for stronger *federal* controls in handguns? Does she present any evidence that such controls would save lives? Would gun control have saved the life of her son?
2. Describe the Shields family as they are presented in this essay. What sort of marriage do the parents seem to have? What are the children like? What type of home do you think they live in? How can you tell?
3. What is the National Council to Control Handguns, and what sort of work does the author of this essay do there? What is the object of this work?
4. Why does Shields believe that it will take "the women of this country— the mothers, wives, sisters and daughters" to control handgun violence? Is this a reasonable observation on the nature of violence in America? Or is it a simple case of sexual stereotyping? Does Shields support her conclusion, or does she contradict herself?
5. Vocabulary: ardent (5), proliferation (12), apathetic (15), litany (16), poignantly (16), and appalling (16).

QUESTIONS ABOUT STRATEGY

1. Why does Shields begin her essay with a description of her son's murder? And why does she repeat such small details as the specific car he was driving, and what he was holding in his hand when he died?
2. Shields writes lovingly of her son in paragraph 5, describing him as athletic, gentle, sensitive, friendly, and "tall, dark and handsome." How do you respond to this description when you read it? Does the description make Nick come alive for you? Does it make you more or less sympathetic to a mother's grief?
3. Shields acknowledges in paragraph 11 that the gun that killed her son was originally bought legally. What effect does this have upon her argument?
4. Does Shields ever say anything likely to offend the people she most needs to convince? Is this essay really designed to make an audience come to favor gun control, or does it have some other purpose?
5. How would you characterize the tone of this essay? Is there any evidence to suggest that Shields may have been too close to her subject to write about it effectively?

ADAM SMITH
Fifty Million Handguns

Adam Smith is the pseudonym of George J. Goodman. A magna cum laude graduate of Harvard and a former Rhodes Scholar, Goodman has written several novels and screenplays. He is best known for the work he has published as "Adam Smith," the name he borrowed from a great eighteenth century economist. A well-respected journalist, "Adam Smith" writes about business and finance for magazines like Esquire, Fortune, *and* New York. *He is also the author of several bestselling books on money management:* The Money Game *(1968),* Supermoney *(1972), and* Paper Money *(1980). He was moved to write about gun control in* **1981,** *after a good friend was murdered. Smith alludes to this murder, and also to the death of John Lennon, which occurred only a few days later. But he does not dwell upon these deaths, preferring to show how they are part of a large and complex problem.*

"You people," said my Texas host, "do not understand guns or gun people." By "you people" he meant not just me, whom he happened to be addressing, but anyone from a large eastern or midwestern city. My Texas host is a very successful businessman, an intelligent man. "There are two cultures," he said, "and the nongun culture looks down on the gun culture."

My Texas host had assumed—correctly—that I do not spend a lot of time with guns. The last one I knew intimately was a semi-automatic M-14, and, as any veteran knows, the Army bids you call it a weapon, not a gun. I once had to take that weapon apart and reassemble it blindfolded, and I liked it better than the heavy old M-1. We were also given a passing introduction to the Russian Kalashnikov and the AK-47, the Chinese copy of that automatic weapon, presumably so we could use these products of our Russian and Chinese enemies if the need arose. I remember that you could drop a Kalashnikov in the mud and pick it up and it would still fire. I also remember blowing up a section of railroad track using only an alarm clock, a primer cord, and a plastic called C-4. The day our little class blew up the track at Fort Bragg was rather fun. These experiences gave me some credibility with friends from the "gun culture." (Otherwise, they have no lasting social utility whatsoever.) And I do not share the fear of guns—at least of "long guns," rifles and shotguns—that some of my college-educated city-dweller friends have, perhaps because of my onetime intimacy with that Army rifle, whose serial number I still know.

In the gun culture, said my Texas host, a boy is given a .22 rifle around   3
the age of twelve, a shotgun at fourteen, and a .30-caliber rifle at sixteen. The young man is taught to use and respect these instruments. My Texas host showed me a paragraph in a book by Herman Kahn in which Kahn describes the presentation of the .22 as a rite of passage, like a confirmation or a bar mitzvah. "Young persons who are given guns," he wrote, "go through an immediate maturing experience because they are thereby given a genuine and significant responsibility." Any adult from the gun culture, whether or not he is a relative, can admonish any young person who appears to be careless with his weapon. Thus, says Kahn, the gun-culture children take on "enlarging and maturing responsibilities" that their coddled upper-middleclass counterparts from the nongun culture do not share. The children of my Texas host said "sir" to their father and "ma'am" to their mother.

I do not mean to argue with the rite-of-passage theory. I am quite willing   4
to grant it. I bring it up because the subjects of guns and gun control are very emotional ones, and if we are to solve the problems associated with them, we need to arrive at a consensus within and between guns and nongun cultures in our country.

Please note that the rite-of-passage gifts are shotguns and rifles. Long guns   5
having sporting uses. Nobody gives a child a handgun, and nobody shoots a flying duck with a .38 revolver. Handguns have only one purpose.

Some months ago, a college friend of mine surprised a burglar in his home   6
in Washington, D.C. Michael Halberstam was a cardiologist, a writer, and a contributor to this magazine. The burglar shot Halberstam, but Halberstam ran him down with his car on the street outside before he died, and the case received widespread press. I began to work on this column, in high anger, right after his death. A few days later, John Lennon was killed in New York. These two dreadful murders produced an outpouring of grief, followed immediately by intense anger and the demand that something be done, that Congress pass a gun-control law. The National Rifle Association was quick to point out that a gun-control law would not have prevented either death; Halberstam's killer had already violated a whole slew of existing laws, and Lennon's was clearly sufficiently deranged or determined to kill him under any gun law. The National Rifle Association claims a million members, and it is a

highly organized lobby. Its Political Victory Fund "works for the defeat of antigun candidates and for the support and election of progun office seekers." Let us grant the National Rifle Association position that the accused killers in these two recent spectacular shootings might not have been deterred even by severe gun restrictions.

In the course of researching this column, I talked to representatives of   7 both the progun and the antigun lobbies. Anomalies abound. Sam Fields, a spokesman for the National Coalition to Ban Handguns, is an expert rifleman who was given a gun at age thirteen by his father, a New York City policeman. The progun banner is frequently carried by Don Kates Jr., who describes himself as a liberal, a former civil rights worker, and a professor of constitutional law. Fields and Kates have debated each other frequently. Given their backgrounds, one might expect their positions to be reversed.

Some of the progun arguments run as follows: 8

Guns don't kill people, people kill people. Gun laws do not deter criminals.   9 (A 1976 University of Wisconsin study of gun laws concluded that "gun control laws have no individual or collective effect in reducing the rate of violent crime.") A mandatory sentence for carrying an unlicensed gun, says Kates, would punish the "ordinary decent citizens in high-crime areas who carry guns illegally because police protection is inadequate and they don't have the special influence necessary to get a 'carry' permit." There are fifty million handguns out there in the United States already; unless you were to use a giant magnet, there is no way to retrieve them. The majority of people do not want guns banned. A ban on handguns would be like Prohibition—widely disregarded, unenforceable, and corrosive to the nation's sense of moral order. Federal registration is the beginning of federal tyranny; we might someday need to use those guns against the government.

Some of the antigun arguments go as follows: 10

People kill people, but handguns make it easier. When other weapons   11 (knives, for instance) are used, the consequences are not so often deadly. Strangling or stabbing someone takes a different degree of energy and intent than pulling a trigger. Registration will not interfere with hunting and other rifle sports but will simply exercise control over who can carry handguns. Ordinary people do not carry handguns. If a burglar has a gun in his hand, it is quite insane for you to shoot it out with him, as if you were in a quick-draw contest in the Wild West. Half of all the guns used in crimes are stolen; 70 percent of the stolen guns are handguns. In other words, the supply of handguns used by criminals already comes to a great extent from the households these guns were supposed to protect.

"I'll tell you one thing," said a lieutenant on the local police force in my   12 town. "You should never put that decal in your window, the one that says THIS HOUSE IS PROTECTED BY AN ARMED CITIZEN. The gun owners love them, but that sign is just an invitation that says 'Come and rob my guns.' Television sets and stereos are fenced at a discount; guns can actually be fenced at a premium. The burglar doesn't want to meet you. I have had a burglar tell me, 'If I wanted to meet people, I would have been a mugger.'"

After a recent wave of burglaries, the weekly newspaper in my town pub-   13 lished a front-page story. "Do not buy a gun—you're more likely to shoot yourself than a burglar," it said. At first the police agreed with that sentiment. Later, they took a slightly different line. "There is more danger from people having accidents or their kids getting hold of those guns than any service in defending their houses; but there was a flap when the paper printed that, so now we don't say anything," said my local police lieutenant. "If you want to own a gun legally, okay. Just be careful and know the laws."

What police departments tell inquiring citizens seems to depend not only   14
on the local laws but also on whether or not that particular police department belongs to the gun culture.

Some of the crime statistics underlying the gun arguments are surprising.   15
Is crime-ridden New York City the toughest place in the country? No: your chances of being murdered are higher in Columbus, Georgia, in Pine Bluff, Arkansas, and in Houston, Texas, among others. Some of the statistics are merely appalling: we had roughly ten thousand handgun deaths last year. The British had forty. In 1978, there were 18,714 Americans murdered. Sixty-four percent were killed with handguns. In that same year, *we had more killings with handguns by children ten years old and younger than the British had by killers of all ages.* The Canadians had 579 homicides last year; we had more than twenty thousand.

H. Rap Brown, the Sixties activist, once said, "Violence is as American as   16
apple pie." I guess it is. We think fondly of Butch Cassidy and the Sundance Kid; we do not remember the names of the trainmen and the bank clerks they shot. Four of our Presidents have died violently; the British have never had a prime minister assassinated. *Life* magazine paid $8,000 to Halberstam's accused killer for photos of his boyhood. Now he will be famous, like Son of Sam. The list could go on and on.

I am willing to grant to the gunners a shotgun in every closet. Shotguns   17
are not used much in armed robberies, or even by citizens in arguments with each other. A shotgun is a better home-defense item anyway, say my police friends, if only because you have to be very accurate with a handgun to knock a man down with one. But the arguments over which kinds of guns are best only demonstrate how dangerously bankrupt our whole society is in ideas on personal safety.

Our First Lady has a handgun.   18

Would registry of handguns stop the criminal from carrying the unregis-   19
tered gun? No, and it might afflict the householder with some extra red tape. However, there is a valid argument for registry. Such a law might have no immediate effect, but we have to begin somewhere. We license automobiles and drivers. That does not stop automobile deaths, but surely the highways would be even more dangerous if populated with unlicensed drivers and un-inspected cars. The fifty million handguns outstanding have not caused the crime rate to go down. Another two million handguns will be sold this year, and I will bet that the crime rate still does not go down.

Our national behavior is considered close to insane by some of the other   20
advanced industrial nations. We have gotten so accustomed to crime and violence that we have begun to take them for granted; thus we are surprised

to learn that the taxi drivers in Tokyo carry far more than five dollars in cash, that you can walk safely around the streets of Japan's cities, and that Japan's crime rate is going *down.* I know there are cultural differences; I am told that in Japan the criminal is expected to turn himself in so as not to shame his parents. Can we imagine that as a solution to crime here?

In a way, the tragic killings of Michael Halberstam and John Lennon have   21
distracted us from a larger and more complex problem. There is a wave of grief, a wave of anger—and then things go right on as they did before. We become inured to the violence and dulled to the outrage. Perhaps, indeed, no legislation could stop murders like these, and perhaps national gun legislation would not produce overnight change. The hard work is not just to get the gunners to join in; the hard work is to do something about our ragged system of criminal justice, to shore up our declining faith in the institutions that are supposed to protect us, and to promote the notion that people should take responsibility for their own actions.

What makes us so different from the Japanese and the British and the   22
Canadians? They are not armed, as we are, yet their streets and houses are far safer. Should we not be asking ourselves some sober questions about whether we are living the way we want to?

QUESTIONS FOR MEANING

1. In his opening paragraph, Smith introduces the idea that there are two separate cultures in the United States—the "gun culture" and the "nongun culture." Describe these different cultures in your own words. What sort of people belong to the gun culture? How can you identify them? How do they differ from people who have nothing to do with guns?
2. Smith tells us that the army wants its soldiers to use the word "weapon" rather than "gun." What's the difference? Do the words we use to describe objects affect how we see them—and therefore how we use them? What reason is there for teaching men and women that guns are "weapons"?
3. What are the "anomalies" that Smith reports in paragraph 7?
4. Why has gun culture remained so strong in the United States—compared to England, Canada, and Japan? Does Smith provide any explanation why our country is so much more violent than other industrial nations?
5. According to a lieutenant on the police force in Smith's home town, "Television sets and stereos are fenced at a discount; guns can actually be fenced at a premium." What does this mean?
6. What is Smith saying about Nancy Reagan (who was First Lady when this essay was written)? "Our First Lady has a handgun" seems like a simple observation. But what is its implication when set in a separate paragraph and juxtaposed against the paragraph that immediately precedes it?
7. Many people who oppose gun control also believe that it's important to "support your local police." Although he recognizes that some police departments belong to the gun culture and others do not, Smith emphasizes reasons why police do not like private citizens to own guns. Explain why the police may feel this way.

8. How committed is Smith to the importance of gun control? Does he see gun control as a way to insure public safety, or does he see it only as a first step in working toward that goal? Is there anything else that he wants?

QUESTIONS ABOUT STRATEGY

1. At what point in the essay does it first become clear that Adam Smith is in favor of gun control?
2. What is the importance of paragraph 2? Why does Smith devote so much space to describing his experience with a variety of weapons when he was in the army? What is this supposed to prove about him?
3. In paragraphs 9 and 11, Smith summarizes the leading arguments of both sides. Is he fair to each or does he allow his own opinion to influence his summaries in any way?
4. Comment on the use of italics in paragraph 15. Is this sentence worth emphasizing? Why this sentence and not another? Is this a genuinely disturbing sentence, or does putting it in italics give it prominence artificially, making it seem more disturbing than it really is?
5. Smith argues that "we need to arrive at a consensus between gun and nongun cultures in our country." How has he tried to do this? What concessions has he offered, and what sort of compromise has he proposed?

ROBERT J. SPITZER
Shooting Down Gun Myths

*Much of the debate over gun control has involved the Second Amendment: "A well regulated militia being necessary to the security of a free state, the right of the people to keep and bear arms shall not be infringed." The following essay by Robert J. Spitzer argues that the amendment does not guarantee every individual the right to own a gun. Spitzer teaches political science at the State University of New York, College at Cortland. His essay was first published in **1985.***

The media event that began on Dec. 22, 1984, when subway rider Bernhard Hugo Goetz responded to a demand for $5 from four youths with bullets from a .38-caliber revolver serves as a recent reminder that what historian Richard Hofstadter once labeled the "gun culture" is still tightly woven into the fabric of the American psyche. Much has been written about the political and criminological consequences of gun control, including the proliferation of weapons (especially cheap handguns), the effectiveness or ineffectiveness of various gun control measures and the almost staggering influence of the National Rifle Association in preventing stricter gun laws.

Yet there has been surprisingly little public examination of the central 2
constitutional question pertaining to guns—namely, the meaning of the Second Amendment: "A well regulated militia being necessary to the security of a free state, the right of the people to keep and bear arms shall not be infringed." The oft-repeated cry of gun control opponents extolling the so-called individual "right to keep and bear arms" has been accepted by most of the public (a 1978 survey reported that 88 percent of Americans believe they have an individual right to bear arms) in large part because it has often and stridently been repeated. A simple examination of how the courts have interpreted the Second Amendment shows, however, that those who think the Constitution gives them a right to tote a gun have not got a leg to stand on.

The Second Amendment admittedly has not received as much of the Su- 3
preme Court's attention over the years as have other Bill of Rights issues, like free speech, free press and the right to counsel. But four cases provide the basis for understanding the Supreme Court's thinking on the matter over the last century.

The first Supreme Court ruling on the Second Amendment occurred in a 4
case called U.S. v. Cruikshank (1876). Speaking for the Court, Chief Justice Morrison R. Waite said the right "of bearing arms for a lawful purpose is not a right granted by the Constitution, nor is it in any manner dependent upon that instrument for its existence." The Cruikshank case established two principles: First, the Second Amendment does not afford an individual right to bear arms (as distinct from an individual's participation in a collective body or militia); second, the Second Amendment is not legally "incorporated"— that is, does not apply to the states through the due process and equal protection clauses of the 14th Amendment. The concept of "incorporation" is highly important in understanding the scope of the Second Amendment and the Bill of Rights as a whole. The process of incorporation has been the means by which the courts have extended constitutional protections to individuals in non-Federal cases. In 1876, none of the Bill of Rights had been incorporated; today, however, most of the constitutional protections we take for granted, like protection from unreasonable searches and seizures and the rights of free assembly and free exercise of religion, protect us because the Supreme Court "incorporated" them. The Court has never, however, "incorporated" the Second Amendment.

The second important court case was Presser v. Illinois (1886). In that 5
case, the Court reaffirmed Cruikshank, and stated that the Second Amendment does not apply to the states (is not "incorporated") and affirmed that though the states have the right to form militias, they are also free to regulate the circumstances under which citizens bear arms, within the parameters of state constitutions.

In an 1894 case, Miller v. Texas, the Supreme Court upheld the right of 6
states to regulate arms and said again that the Second Amendment did not apply to the states. The fourth and most important case came in 1939. U.S. v. Miller involved a challenge to Federal gun regulations stemming from the National Firearms Act of 1934. Speaking for a unanimous Court, Justice James

C. McReynolds affirmed the right of the Federal Government to regulate fire-arms (in particular, transport and possession) and stated unambiguously that citizens possess a constitutional right to bear arms only in connection with service in a militia. Justice Miller also cited the Cruikshank and Presser cases as precedent, affirming the principles articulated in those cases.

The continued pertinence of the Miller case is indicated by two other re-   7
cent Supreme Court cases. In a 1972 case, Adams v. Williams, Justices William O. Douglas and Thurgood Marshall issued a joint dissent in which they cited Miller and affirmed their view that the state could regulate firearms as it saw fit. The case itself, however, did not deal with the Second Amendment. In 1980, Justice Harry A. Blackmun commented in a footnote to his majority opinion (Lewis v. U.S.) that the Miller case represented the Court's thinking on gun control.

One final case warrants mention, though it was not reviewed by the Su-   8
preme Court. On June 8, 1981, the village of Morton Grove, Ill., enacted an ordinance that banned the possession of handguns, except for police, prison officials, the military, collectors and others needing guns for their work. Residents who owned guns could keep and use them in licensed gun clubs, however. The ordinance was challenged by the National Rifle Association and their sympathizers. Both the Federal District Court and the Federal Court of Appeals rejected the arguments of the ordinance opponents. Both Federal courts said that the Second Amendment did not apply to the states, that there was no individual right to bear arms, that the Morton Grove ordinance was a reasonable exercise of authority and that the right to bear arms applies only to the maintenance of a well regulated militia (as was said in Miller).

The case of Quilici v. Village of Morton Grove was appealed to the Su-   9
preme Court, but it declined to hear the case, leaving the lower Federal court ruling as the operative interpretation.

This recitation of cases demonstrates the Court's long recognition of the   10
right of the Government to regulate the ownership and use of firearms as it sees fit. The fact that sweeping national regulations have not been enacted is not due to a lack of constitutional authority, but rather to the political clout of gun control opponents and a gun "mythology" perpetuated in large part by gun enthusiasts.

Even if we examine the intentions of the founding fathers, it is clear that   11
their considerations in authorizing the Second Amendment lay with national defense. The citizen militia was considered the military force least threatening to democratic values and institutions. They feared the baneful consequences of a regular standing army, as European and earlier American history were replete with examples of tyrannies extended by such armies. Despite these fears, the founding fathers were also well aware of the military limitations of an army composed of part-time soldiers, and provision was made in the Constitution (Article I, Section 8) for both a militia and a standing army. The role of the citizen militia was formally supplanted in 1916 by the National Defense Act, which recognized the National Guard as the militia. And,

of course, early fears of a standing army that would overthrow American democratic institutions never materialized.

Thus, the Second Amendment protects a "right to keep and bear arms" only for service in a "well regulated militia" that has not been called up since the beginning of the 19th century. As Bill of Rights scholar Irving Brant observed, the Second Amendment "comes to life chiefly on the parade floats of rifle associations and in the propaganda of mail-order houses selling pistols to teen-age gangsters."   12

Many have applauded the actions of Bernhard Goetz as legitimate self-defense, or as justifiable vigilantism. But even if we accept the propriety of his actions, how do we disentangle his "right" to carry and use a gun from the less ambiguous case of James Alan Kearbey, a 14-year-old junior high school student who, on Jan. 21, entered his Goddard, Kan., school with an M-1 rifle and a .357 magnum pistol (popularized in Clint Eastwood's film "Dirty Harry"). Kearbey shot and killed the school principal and wounded three others. Goddard English teacher Darlene Criss ironically described the town as "the safest place in America."   13

The Goetz case and the Kearbey case both argue for Government to exercise its right to regulate the possession and use of firearms. But as the merits of gun control are debated, it is time that we once and for all excised erroneous references to an individual, constitutionally based "right" to bear arms.   14

QUESTIONS FOR MEANING

1. Why does Spitzer believe that the Second Amendment does not guarantee an individual right to bear arms?
2. What is now recognized as the "well regulated militia" referred to in the Second Amendment?
3. What does Spitzer mean by "incorporation" in paragraph 4?
4. Of the various cases involving gun control that have been heard by the Supreme Court, which was the most important?
5. In paragraph 13, Spitzer asks how the "right" of Bernard Goetz to carry a gun can be separated from the right of James Alan Kearbey to do the same? Can you answer this question?
6. Vocabulary: psyche (1), stridently (2), articulated (6), baneful (11), replete (11), vigilantism (13), propriety (13), erroneous (14), excised (14).

QUESTIONS ABOUT STRATEGY

1. To what extent does Spitzer's argument rest upon his discussion of Supreme Court rulings?
2. Why does Spitzer discuss the case of Quilici v. Village of Morton Grove even though it was not heard by the Supreme Court?
3. How effective is the quotation from Irving Brant in paragraph 12?
4. What advantage is there to including the case of James Alan Kearbey in this argument? Why is this case "less ambiguous" than the Goetz case?

EDWARD ABBEY
The Right to Arms

Edward Abbey lives in Wolf Hole, Arizona. A former ranger for the National Park Service, Abbey now describes himself as an "Agrarian anarchist." He writes frequently about the beauty of the American west and the ways in which that beauty has been spoiled by government, business, and tourism. His many books include such novels as Fire on the Mountain *(1963),* The Monkey Wrench Gang *(1975), and* Good News *(1980), and several collections of essays, such as* Desert Solitaire *(1968),* Abbey's Road *(1979), and, most recently,* Beyond the Wall: Essays from the Outside *(1984). As the following* **1979** *essay reveals, Abbey values the importance of the individual in a world in which individuals are at risk.*

If guns are outlawed
Only outlaws will have guns
(True? False? Maybe?)

Meaning weapons. The right to own, keep, and bear arms. A sword and a   1
lance, or a bow and a quiverful of arrows. A crossbow and darts. Or in our time, a rifle and a handgun and a cache of ammunition. Firearms.

In medieval England a peasant caught with a sword in his possession would   2
be strung up on a gibbet and left there for the crows. Swords were for gentlemen only. *(Gentlemen!)* Only members of the ruling class were entitled to own and bear weapons. For obvious reasons. Even bows and arrows were outlawed—see Robin Hood. When the peasants attempted to rebel, as they did in England and Germany and other European countries from time to time, they had to fight with sickles, bog hoes, clubs—no match for the sword-wielding armored cavalry of the nobility.

In Nazi Germany the possession of firearms by a private citizen of the   3
Third Reich was considered a crime against the state; the statutory penalty was death—by hanging. Or beheading. In the Soviet Union, as in Czarist Russia, the manufacture, distribution, and ownership of firearms have always been monopolies of the state, strictly controlled and supervised. Any unauthorized citizen found with guns in his home by the OGPU or the KGB is automatically suspected of subversive intentions and subject to severe penalties. Except for the landowning aristocracy, who alone among the population were allowed the privilege of owning firearms, for only they were privileged to hunt, the ownership of weapons never did become a widespread tradition in Russia. And Russia has always been an autocracy—or at best, as today, an oligarchy.

In Uganda, Brazil, Iran, Paraguay, South Africa—wherever a few rule many—   4
the possession of weapons is restricted to the ruling class and to their supporting apparatus: the military, the police, the secret police. In Chile and

Argentina at this very hour men and women are being tortured by the most up-to-date CIA methods in the effort to force them to reveal the location of their hidden weapons. Their guns, their rifles. Their arms. And we can be certain that the Communist masters of modern China will never pass out firearms to *their* 800 million subjects. Only in Cuba, among dictatorships, where Fidel's revolution apparently still enjoys popular support, does there seem to exist a true citizen's militia.

There must be a moral in all this. When I try to think of a nation that has   5
maintained its independence over centuries, and where the citizens still retain their rights as free and independent people, not many come to mind. I think of Switzerland. Of Norway, Sweden, Denmark, Finland. The British Commonwealth. France, Italy. And of our United States.

When Tell shot the apple from his son's head, he reserved in hand a second   6
arrow, it may be remembered, for the Austrian tyrant Gessler. And got him too, shortly afterward. Switzerland has been a free country since 1390. In Switzerland basic national decisions are made by initiative and referendum—direct democracy—and in some cantons by open-air meetings in which all voters participate. Every Swiss male serves a year in the Swiss Army and at the end of the year takes his government rifle home with him—where he keeps it for the rest of his life. One of my father's grandfathers came from Canton Bern.

There must be a meaning in this. I don't think I'm a gun fanatic. I own a   7
couple of small-caliber weapons, but seldom take them off the wall. I gave up deer hunting fifteen years ago, when the hunters began to outnumber the deer. I am a member of the National Rifle Association, but certainly no John Bircher. I'm a liberal—and proud of it. Nevertheless, I am opposed, absolutely, to every move the state makes to restrict my right to buy, own, possess, and carry a firearm. Whether shotgun, rifle, or handgun.

Of course, we can agree to a few commonsense limitations. Guns should   8
not be sold to children, to the certifiably insane, or to convicted criminals. Other than that, we must regard with extreme suspicion any effort by the government—local, state, or national—to control our right to arms. The registration of firearms is the first step toward confiscation. The confiscation of weapons would be a major and probably fatal step into authoritarian rule—the domination of most of us by a new order of "gentlemen." By a new and harder oligarchy.

The tank, the B-52, the fighter-bomber, the state-controlled police and   9
military are the weapons of dictatorship. The rifle is the weapon of democracy. Not for nothing was the revolver called an "equalizer." *Egalité* implies *liberté*. And always will. Let us hope our weapons are never needed—but do not forget what the common people of this nation knew when they demanded the Bill of Rights: An armed citizenry is the first defense, the best defense, and the final defense against tyranny.

If guns are outlawed, only the government will have guns. Only the police,   10
the secret police, the military. The hired servants of our rules. Only the government—and a few outlaws. I intend to be among the outlaws.

QUESTIONS FOR MEANING

1. Do you recognize the italicized lines with which the essay opens? If so, where have you seen them?
2. In paragraph 4, Abbey moves from "weapons," to "guns" to "rifles" and finally, in a separate sentence, to "arms." Is he playing with the meaning of the word "arms"? What are the connotations and denotations of this particular word?
3. What allusion is implicit in Abbey's mention of "egalité and liberté"?
4. How does Abbey seem to feel about "gentlemen"? In what particular sense does he use this term? How does the question of differences in social class relate to the question of gun control?
5. Vocabulary: autocracy (3), oligarchy (3), and referendum (6).

QUESTIONS ABOUT STRATEGY

1. Abbey uses numerous sentence fragments. Why does he do so? How do they affect the rhythm of his essay if you read it out loud? Is there any particular pattern that determines what ideas are conveyed in fragments? Is Abbey's style suitable for the subject he is writing about?
2. In paragraph 7 Abbey claims that he's not "a gun fanatic." Can you identify any other concessions Abbey offers to make his case seem reasonable?
3. Abbey describes himself as a "liberal." What advantage is there in making this claim? What does his essay reveal about his political beliefs beyond the issue of gun control?
4. Why does Abbey introduce into his argument references to Robin Hood, William Tell, Nazi Germany, and the B52? How do these allusions help to advance the point of this argument?

JAMES MOORE
Looking for Good Guys

*Although the need for gun control continues to be debated, we have had a limited form of federal gun control in this country since 1968. The following essay offers an inside view of what it is like trying to enforce this law. The former head of the Bureau of Alcohol, Tobacco and Firearms in Portland, Maine, James Moore first published this argument in **1988**, three years after his retirement.*

As a special agent with the Bureau of Alcohol, Tobacco and Firearms, I   1
spent 25 years using federal gun laws to take bad guys off the street. I didn't mind facing hit men, hate groups and racketeers—that's what I signed up for and that's what the Treasury Department trained me to do. But I never got used to the sniping and sabotage from the so-called "good guys." People who'd never seen an ATF agent before refused to cooperate because gun groups had convinced them we were out to disarm the nation. In fact, a juror once told me he'd voted to acquit a defendant charged with possession of a pistol by a felon. His reason: "The government uses them gun laws to harass people." The man he freed was reputedly one of Missouri's most notorious mafia executioners.

Another good guy sold 300 pistols off the books from his Missouri gun   2
shop and sabotaged the ATF's ability to trace guns used in a crime. Federal law requires firearms dealers to keep a listing of weapons in stock—when each is received, sold and to whom. This enables the ATF to trace 30,000 guns each year for local police departments. With good records, it was able to trace the revolver that John W. Hinckley Jr. used in 1981 to shoot President Reagan within 16 minutes of the time the serial number was turned over to an ATF agent. Without any records, the Missouri dealer that I helped convict made a higher profit because the firearms couldn't be traced, as did an ex-convict who resold some of the guns in local taverns. Eleven of the weapons, we later learned, turned up in violent crimes, including three murders.

In 1982 ATF inspectors found that 20 percent of the dealers they visited   3
had operated in violation of the law. Admittedly, most offenses were matters of sloppy record keeping; yet that year, 8,755 traces of guns used in a crime failed primarily because of faulty records. Nonetheless, in 1986 gun groups were able to convince Congress to restrict the bureau's already limited supervision of gun dealers.

The ATF can't require fingerprints on an application. Unless it can prove   4
that a person is an ex-convict, a fugitive or a court-certified mental case, it must issue a license to anyone who sends in the congressionally approved price of $10 a year. And with 600 inspectors, it can't possibly keep tabs on all 250,000 license holders—12,500 of whom, according to our best estimates, are full-time dealers. Most license holders, in fact, are collectors and traders

who like to buy and sell guns when they're away from home. And they don't want to be inconvenienced by having the paperwork done at their local gun shops. But the rules—a one-line ledger entry for an acquisition, another entry and a form for a sale—were too burdensome for these hobbyists, gun groups said. And in 1986 Congress reduced recordkeeping crimes to misdemeanors, prohibited unannounced visits by ATF agents and restricted inspections to one a year. Which still leaves us with the problem of unscrupulous dealers who have been caught selling machine guns, fencing hot goods, dealing drugs and marketing "assassins' kits"—briefcases containing pistols that are equipped with silencers and triggered at the handle.

I'm retired now, but I keep wondering why those who love to collect and   5
trade guns don't seem too concerned about illegal gun sales—why they don't root the renegades from their ranks and act like good guys. In the 10 years ending in 1985, more than 3 million Americans were assaulted, robbed or murdered with guns. In this century alone, firearms homicides have exceeded the 437,796 battlefield deaths Americans have suffered in all wars, except the Civil War. Does anyone really think there is no connection between guns and crime?

Don't tell me that any gun law is the first step toward national confiscation   6
and a police state. I heard that line almost every day for 25 years. The first step toward a police state is the formation of a police department; and the first step toward killing your neighbor is buying a gun. First steps don't mean much.

Which is why I also have to laugh at the archenemy of gun lovers, that   7
group of people who want to ban the private ownership of firearms. It's an impossible idea—the right to bear arms is deeply ingrained in America even if ardent abolitionists scoff at the tradition. Gun opponents ought to realize that the entire United States Army can't sweep one small state or even a single city with the hope of seizing all weapons. Nor could federal and state governments lock up everyone who has the elementary skill to assemble a zip gun. In practical terms, these people serve an unintended purpose: they give form and substance to the ominous specter gun organizations use to frighten their followers. By trying to ban guns they make it easier for those who own them to believe there is a sinister plot to disarm America.

Rabid gun lovers and radical gun haters are caught in a symbiotic relation-   8
ship that leaves the rest of us with no champion, no voice. They perpetuate one another's worst fears. Yet polls show that a majority of Americans reject universal confiscation but accept reasonable controls.

Since 1968 we've had a federal law that allows us to trace guns and to   9
lock up felons and adjudicated mentally ill people when we catch them armed and before they kill someone. It lets the rest of us own all the guns we want. We just have to buy handguns in our home state so there will be a record, accessible to local police, in case they need to prove who bought it.

The law works, but if you want aggressive and effective enforcement you'll   10
have to stand up and say so. Congressmen don't act on the results of national

polls—they react to the demands of constituents who express their wishes in letters and in the voting booth. The issue of gun crimes really comes down to this: should Americans support the convenience of the gun traders' hobby at the expense of public safety? The time has come for the good guys to be heard.

QUESTIONS FOR MEANING

1. What does Moore mean by "good guys"? Does his meaning remain constant throughout the essay?
2. Why is it impossible for agents of the Bureau of Alcohol, Tobacco and Firearms to monitor every American gun dealer?
3. What evidence does Moore provide to support his claim that federal gun control law works?
4. How did federal gun control law change in 1986?
5. Vocabulary: misdemeanors (4), renegades (5), scoff (7), rabid (8), symbiotic (8), adjudicated (9).

QUESTIONS ABOUT STRATEGY

1. Where does Moore incorporate personal experience in this essay? Where does he depart from personal experience, and why was it important for him to do so?
2. Does Moore ever seem to contradict himself?
3. Where does Moore anticipate opposition? How well does he respond to it?
4. In his conclusion Moore writes, "The issue of gun crimes really comes down to this: should Americans support the convenience of the gun traders' hobby at the expense of public safety?" Is this a false dilemma? Are there any circumstances under which it would be possible to support both "convenience" and "safety"?

DON B. KATES, JR.
Against Civil Disarmament

A graduate of Yale Law School, Don B. Kates, Jr., has worked as an Office of Educational Opportunity poverty lawyer and taught both criminal and constitutional law. During the last ten years, he has emerged as one of the most articulate opponents of gun control, a subject on which he has written for numerous magazines. In the following essay, which originally appeared in Harper's *in* **1978,** *Kates argues that conventional attitudes toward gun control need to be rethought. He tries to show that the controversy over gun control has confused the traditional distinction between liberal and conservative views.*

Despite almost 100 years of often bitter debate, federal policy and that of   1
44 states continues to allow handguns to any sane adult who is without felony convictions. Over the past twenty years, as some of our most progressive citizens have embraced the notion that handgun confiscation would reduce violent crime, the idea of closely restricting handgun possession to police and those with police permits has been stereotyped as "liberal." Yet when the notion of sharply restricting pistol ownership first gained popularity, in the late nineteenth century, it was under distinctly conservative auspices.

In 1902, South Carolina banned all pistol purchases, the first and only state   2
ever to do so. (This was nine years before New York began requiring what was then an easily acquired police permit.) Tennessee had already enacted the first ban on "Saturday Night Specials," disarming blacks and the laboring poor while leaving weapons for the Ku Klux Klan and company goons. In 1906, Mississippi enacted the first mandatory registration law for all firearms. In short order, permit requirements were enacted in North Carolina, Missouri, Michigan, and Hawaii. In 1922, a national campaign of conservative business interests for handgun confiscation was endorsed by the (then) archconservative American Bar Association.

Liberals at that time were not necessarily opposed in principle to a ban   3
on handguns, but they considered such a move irrelevant and distracting from a more important issue—the prohibition of alcohol. To Jane Addams, William Jennings Bryan, and Eleanor Roosevelt (herself a pistol carrier), liquor was the cause of violent crime. (Before dismissing this out of hand, remember that homicide studies uniformly find liquor a more prevalent factor than handguns in killings.) Besides, liberals were not likely to support the argument advanced by conservatives for gun confiscation: that certain racial and immigrant groups were so congenitally criminal (and/or politically dangerous) that they could not be trusted with arms. But when liberalism finally embraced handgun confiscation, it was by applying this conservative viewpoint to the entire populace. Now it is all Americans (not just Italians, Jews, or blacks) who must be considered so innately violent and unstable that they cannot be trusted with arms. For, we are told, it is not robbers or burglars who commit most murders, but average citizens killing relatives or friends.

It is certainly true that only a little more than 30 percent of murders are   4
committed by robbers, rapists, or burglars, while 45 percent are committed
among relatives or between lovers. (The rest are a miscellany of contract
killings, drug wars, and "circumstances unknown.") But it is highly misleading
to conclude from this that the murderer is, in any sense, an average gun
owner. For the most part, murderers are disturbed, aberrant individuals with
long records of criminal violence that often include several felony convictions. In terms of endangering his fellow citizen, the irresponsible drinker is
far more representative of all drinkers than is the irresponsible handgunner
of all handgunners. It is not my intention here to defend the character of the
average American handgun owner against, say, that of the average Swiss whose
government not only allows, but requires, him to keep a machine gun at
home. Rather it is to show how unrealistic it is to think that we could radically decrease homicide by radically reducing the number of civilian firearms.
Study after study has shown that even if the *average* gun owner complied
with a ban, the one handgun owner out of 3,000 who murders (much less the
one in 500 who steals) is not going to give up his guns. Nor would taking
guns away from the murderer make much difference in murder rates, since
a sociopath with a long history of murderous assault is not too squeamish to
kill with a butcher knife, ice pick, razor, or bottle. As for the extraordinary
murders—assassins, terrorists, hit men—proponents of gun bans themselves
concede that the law cannot disarm such people any more than it can disarm
professional robbers.

The repeated appearance of these facts in studies of violent crime has   5
eroded liberal and intellectual support for banning handguns. There is a growing
consensus among even the most liberal students of criminal law and criminology that handgun confiscation is just another plausible theory that doesn't
work when tried. An article written in 1968 by Mark K. Benenson, longtime
American chairman of Amnesty International, concludes that the arguments
for gun bans are based upon selective misleading statistics, simple-minded
non sequiturs, and basic misconceptions about the nature of murder as well
as of other violent crimes.

A 1971 study at England's Cambridge University confounds one of the   6
most widely believed non sequiturs: "Banning handguns must work, because
England does and look at its crime rate!" (It is difficult to see how those who
believe this can resist the equally simple-minded pro-gun argument that gun
possession deters crime: "Everybody ought to have a machine gun in his
house because the Swiss and the Israelis do, and look how low their crime
rates are!")

The Cambridge report concludes that social and cultural factors (not gun   7
control) account for Britain's low violence rates. It points out that "the use
of firearms in crime was very much less" before 1920 when Britain had "no
controls of any sort." Corroborating this is the comment of a former head of
Scotland Yard that in the mid-1950s there were enough illegal handguns to
supply any British criminal who wanted one. But, he continued, the social
milieu was such that if a criminal killed anyone, particularly a policeman, his
own confederates would turn him in. When this violence-dampening social

milieu began to dissipate between 1960 and 1975, the British homicide rate doubled (as did the American rate), while British robbery rates accelerated even faster than those in America. As the report notes, the vaunted handgun ban proved completely ineffective against rising violence in Britain, although the government frantically intensified enforcement and extended controls to long guns as well. Thus, the Cambridge study—the only in-depth study ever done of English gun laws—recommends "abolishing or substantially reducing controls" because their administration involves an immense, unproductive expense and diverts police resources from programs that might reduce violent crime.

The latest American study of gun controls was conducted with federal   8
funding at the University of Wisconsin. Advanced computerized techniques allowed a comprehensive analysis of the effect of every form of state handgun restriction, including complete prohibition, on violence in America. Published in 1975, it concludes that "gun-control laws have no individual or collective effect in reducing the rate of violent crime."

Many previous studies reaching the same conclusion had been discounted   9
by proponents of a federal ban, who argued that existing state bans cannot be effective because handguns are illegally imported from free-sale states. The Wisconsin study compared rates of handgun ownership with rates of violence in various localities, but it could find *no correlation.* If areas where handgun ownership rate are high have no higher per capita rates of homicide and other violence than areas where such rates are low, the utility of laws designed to lower the rates of handgun ownership seems dubious. Again, the problem is not the "proliferation of handguns" among the law-abiding citizenry, it is the existence of a tiny fraction of irresponsible and criminal owners whom the law cannot possibly disarm of these or other weapons.

Far from refuting the Wisconsin study, the sheer unenforceability of hand-   10
gun bans is the main reason why most experts regard them as not worth thinking about. Even in Britain, a country that, before handguns were banned, had less than 1 percent of the per capita handgun ownership we have, the Cambridge study reports that "fifty years of very strict controls has left a vast pool of illegal weapons."

It should be emphasized that liberal defectors from gun confiscation are   11
no more urging people to arm themselves than are those who oppose banning pot or liquor necessarily urging people to indulge in them. They are only saying that national handgun confiscation would bring the federal government into a confrontation with millions of responsible citizens in order to enforce a program that would have no effect upon violence, except the negative one of diverting resources that otherwise might be utilized to some effective purpose. While many criminologists have doubts about the wisdom of citizens trying to defend themselves with handguns, the lack of evidence to justify confiscation requires that this remain a matter of individual choice rather than government fiat.

Nor can advocates of gun bans duck the evidence adverse to their position   12
by posing such questions as: Why should people have handguns; what good

do they do; why *shouldn't* we ban them? In a free country, the burden is not upon the people to show why they should have freedom of choice. It is upon those who wish to restrict that freedom to show good reason for doing so. And when the freedom is as deeply valued by as many as is handgun ownership, the evidence for infringing upon it must be very strong indeed.

If the likely benefits of handgun confiscation have been greatly exagger-   13
ated, the financial and constitutional costs have been largely ignored. Consider the various costs of any attempt to enforce confiscation upon a citizenry that believes (whether rightly or not) that they urgently need handguns for self-defense and that the right to keep them is constitutionally guaranteed. Most confiscationists have never gotten beyond the idea that banning handguns will make them magically disappear somehow. Because they loathe handguns and consider them useless, the prohibitionists assume that those who disagree will readily turn in their guns once a national confiscation law is passed. But the leaders of the national handgun prohibition movement have become more realistic. They recognize that defiance will, if anything, exceed the defiance of Prohibition and marijuana laws. After all, not even those who viewed drinking or pot smoking as a blow against tyranny thought, as many gun owners do, that violating the law is necessary to the protection of themselves and their families. Moreover, fear of detection is a lot more likely to keep citizens from constant purchases of liquor or pot than from a single purchase of a handgun, which, properly maintained, will last years.

To counter the expected defiance, the leaders of the national confiscation   14
drive propose that handgun ownership be punished by a nonsuspendable mandatory year in prison. The mandatory feature is necessary, for otherwise prosecutors would not prosecute, and judges would not sentence, gun ownership with sufficient severity. The judge of a special Chicago court trying only gun violations recently explained why he generally levied only small fines: The overwhelming majority of the "criminals" who come before him are respectable, decent citizens who illegally carry guns because the police can't protect them and they have no other way of protecting themselves. He does not even impose probation because this would prevent the defendants, whose guns have been confiscated, from buying new ones, which, the judge believes, they need to live and work where they do.

These views are shared by judges and prosecutors nationwide; studies find   15
that gun-carrying charges are among the most sympathetically dealt with of all felonies. To understand why, consider a typical case that would have come before this Chicago court if the D.A. had not dropped charges. An intruder raped a woman and threw her out of a fifteenth-floor window. Police arrived too late to arrest him, so they got her roommate for carrying the gun with which she scared him off when he attacked her.

Maybe it is not a good idea for this woman to keep a handgun for self-   16
defense. But do we really want to send her to federal prison for doing so? And is a mandatory year in prison reasonable or just for an ordinary citizen who has done nothing more hurtful than keeping a gun to defend herself—

when the minimum mandatory sentence for murder is only seven years and most murderers serve little more?

Moreover, the kind of nationwide resistance movement that a federal handgun ban would provoke could not be broken by imprisoning a few impecunious black women in Chicago. Only by severely punishing a large number of respectable citizens of every race and social class would resisters eventually be made to fear the law more than the prospect of living without handguns in a violent society. At a very conservative estimate, at least half of our present handgun owners would be expected to defy a federal ban.* To imprison just 1 percent of these 25 million people would require several times as many cells as the entire federal prison now has. The combined federal, state, and local jail systems could barely manage. Of course, so massive an enforcement campaign would also require doubling expenditure for police, prosecutors, courts, and all the other sectors of criminal justice administration. The Wisconsin study closes with the pertinent query: "Are we willing to make sociological and economic investments of such a tremendous nature in a social experiment for which there is no empirical support?" 17

The argument against a federal handgun ban is much like the argument against marijuana bans. It is by no means clear that marijuana is the harmless substance that its proponents claim. But it would take evidence far stronger than we now have to justify the enormous financial, human, institutional, and constitutional costs of continuing to ferret out, try, and imprison even a small percentage of the otherwise law-abiding citizens who insist on having pot. Sophisticated analysis of the criminalization decision takes into account not only the harms alleged to result from public possession of things like pot or guns, but the capacity of the criminal law to reduce those harms and the costs of trying to do so. Unfortunately most of the gun-control debate never gets beyond the abstract merits of guns—a subject on which those who view them with undifferentiated loathing are no more rational than those who love them. The position of all too many gun-banning liberals is indistinguishable from Archie Bunker's views on legalizing pot and homosexuality: "I don't like it and I don't like those who do—so it ought to be illegal." 18

The emotionalism with which many liberals (and conservatives as well) react against the handgun reflects not its reality but its symbolism to people who are largely ignorant of that reality. A 1975 national survey found a direct correlation between support for more stringent controls and the inability to answer simple questions about present federal gun laws. In other words, the less the respondent knew about the subject, the more likely he was to support national confiscation. Liberals advocate severely punishing those who 19

---

*I reach this estimate in this fashion: Surveys uniformly find a majority of gun owners support gun registration—in theory. In practice, however, they refuse to register because they believe this will identify their guns for confiscation if and when a national handgun ban eventually passes. In 1968, Chicago police estimated that two-thirds of the city's gun owners had not complied with the new state registration law; statewide noncompliance was estimated at 75 percent. In Cleveland, police estimate that almost 90 percent of handgun owners are in violation of a 1976 registration requirement. My estimate that one out of two handgun owners would defy national confiscation is conservative indeed when between two out of three and nine out of ten of them are already defying registration laws because they believe such laws presage confiscation.

will defy confiscation only because the liberal image of a gun owner is a criminal or right-wing fanatic rather than a poor black woman in Chicago defending herself against a rapist or a murderer. Contrary to this stereotype, most "gun nuts" are peaceful hobbyists whose violence is exclusively of the Walter Mitty type. Gun owners' views are all too often expressed in right-wing terms (which does nothing for the rationality of the debate) because twenty years of liberal vilification has given them nowhere else to look for support. If only liberals knew it, handgun ownership is disproportionately high among the underprivileged for whom liberals traditionally have had most sympathy. As the most recent (1975) national demographic survey reports: "The top subgroups who own a gun *only* for self-defense include blacks (almost half own one for this reason alone), lowest income group, senior citizens." The average liberal has no understanding of why people have guns because he has no idea what it is like to live in a ghetto where police have given up on crime control. Minority and disadvantaged citizens are not about to give up their families' protection because middle-class white liberals living and working in high-security buildings and/or well-policed suburbs tell them it's safer that way.

A final cost of national gun confiscation would be the vast accretion of [20] enforcement powers to the police at the expense of individual liberty. The Police Foundation, which ardently endorses confiscation, recently suggested that federal agencies and local police look to how drug laws are enforced as a model of how to enforce firearms laws. Coincidentally, the chief topic of conversation at the 1977 national conference of supporters of federal confiscation was enforcement through house searches of everyone whom sales records indicate may ever have owned a handgun. In fact, indiscriminate search, complemented by electronic surveillance and vast armies of snoopers and informers, is how handgun restrictions are enforced in countries like Holland and Jamaica, and in states like Missouri and Michigan.* Even in England, as the Cambridge report notes, each new Firearms Act has been accompanied by new, unheard-of powers of search and arrest for the police.

These, then, are the costs of banning handguns: even attempting an effec- [21] tive ban would involve enormous expenditures (roughly equal to the present cost of enforcing all our other criminal laws combined) to ferret out and jail hundreds of thousands of decent, responsible citizens who believe that they vitally need handguns to protect their families. If this does not terrorize the rest of the responsible handgun owners into compliance, the effort will have to be expanded until millions are jailed and the annual gun-banning budget closely seconds defense spending. And all of this could be accomplished only by abandoning many restraints our Constitution places upon police activity.

What would we have to show for all this in terms of crime reduction? [22] Terrorists, hit men, and other hardened criminals who are not deterred by

---

*According to the ACLU, St. Louis police have conducted 25,000 illegal searches in the past few years under the theory that any black man driving a late-model car possesses a handgun.

Michigan court records indicate that almost 70 percent of all firearms charges presented are thrown out because the evidence was obtained through unconstitutional search.

the penalties for murder, robbery, rape, burglary, et cetera are not about to be terrified by the penalties for gun ownership—nor is the more ordinary murderer, the disturbed, aberrant individual who kills out of rage rather than cupidity.

What we should have learned from our experience of Prohibition, and England's with gun banning, is that violence can be radically reduced only through long-term fundamental change in the institutions and mores that produce so many violent people in our society. It is much easier to use as scapegoats a commonly vilified group (drinkers or gun owners) and convince ourselves that legislation against them is an easy short-term answer. But violence will never be contained or reduced until we give up the gimmicky programs, the scapegoating, the hypocritical hand-wringing, and frankly ask ourselves whether we are willing to make the painful, disturbing, far-reaching institutional and cultural changes that are necessary.   23

QUESTIONS FOR MEANING

1. What states were the first to initiate gun control legislation, and what motivated them to do so? Who were the supporters of these early laws, and who were they trying to control? Why does Kates believe that it is important to remember the history of the movement for gun control as we argue about the possibility of additional legislation?
2. What does Kates mean by "company goons" in paragraph 2?
3. In paragraph 6, Kates summarizes two simple arguments and describes them as non sequiturs. Explain why the reasoning is faulty in both the examples he cites.
4. What types of people are the most likely to own handguns? Why do these people feel that they need guns? Why is it, according to Kates, that the average liberal cannot understand this?
5. According to this essay, what is the main reason why gun control cannot work?
6. Proponents of gun control have frequently advocated a mandatory year in prison for anyone illegally possessing a handgun. Why do such people insist that the penalty be mandatory? Why does Kates oppose this idea in particular?
7. Vocabulary: congenitally (3), aberrant (4), felony (4), milieu (7), dissipate (7), loathe (13), impecunious (17), pertinent (17), empirical (17), vilification (19), demographic (19), and cupidity (22).

QUESTIONS ABOUT STRATEGY

1. Why does Kates quote a chairman of Amnesty International in paragraph 5? Why is this more effective than quoting the president of the National Rifle Association? Similarly, why does he describe the poor black woman in Chicago? What does this tell us about his audience? What type of people is Kates trying to convince, and what is his basic strategy in doing so?

2. What basic values does Kates assume in making this argument? What does he think of "law"—what it can and cannot do?

3. Why does Kates compare gun legislation with laws designed to control marijuana? Why is he then able to argue that gun laws are even harder to enforce?

4. Does Kates ever resort to ridiculing his opponents, or does he consistently treat them with respect?

5. Does Kates offer any alternatives to gun control as a way of making America less violent? Is it his responsibility to do so in order to make a good argument?

WILLIAM R. TONSO
White Man's Law

A professor of sociology at the University of Evansville, William R. Tonso is the author of Gun and Society *(1982). Drawing upon the work of Don B. Kates and other sources, he argues that the demand for gun control is the result of prejudice against minorities and the poor. The following essay provides an example of his views. It was first published in* **1985.**

Chances are that you've never heard of General Laney. He hasn't had a brilliant military career, at least as far as I know. In fact, I'm not certain that he's even served in the military. General, you see, isn't Laney's rank. General is Laney's first name. General Laney does, however, have a claim to fame, unrecognized though it may be. 1

Detroit resident General Laney is the founder and prime mover behind a little-publicized organization known as the National Black Sportsman's Association, often referred to as "the black gun lobby." Laney pulls no punches when asked his opinion of gun control: "Gun control is really race control. People who embrace gun control are really racists in nature. All gun laws have been enacted to control certain classes of people, mainly black people, but the same laws used to control blacks are being used to disarm white people as well." 2

Laney is not the first to make this observation. Indeed, allied with sportsmen in vocal opposition to gun controls in the 1960s were the militant Black Panthers. Panther Minister of Information Eldridge Cleaver noted in 1968: "Some very interesting laws are being passed. They don't name me; they don't say, take the guns away from the niggers. They say that people will no longer be allowed to have (guns). They don't pass these rules and these regulations specifically for black people, they have to pass them in a way that will take in everybody." 3

Some white liberals have said essentially the same thing. Investigative re-   4
porter Robert Sherrill, himself no lover of guns, concluded in his book *The
Saturday Night Special* that the object of the Gun Control Act of 1968 was
black control rather than gun control. According to Sherrill, Congress was so
panicked by the ghetto riots of 1967 and 1968 that it passed the act to "shut
off weapons access to blacks, and since they (Congress) probably associated
cheap guns with ghetto blacks and thought cheapness was peculiarly the
characteristic of imported military surplus and the mail-order traffic, they
decided to cut off these sources while leaving over-the-counter purchases
open to the affluent." Congressional motivation may have been more complex
than Sherrill suggests, but keeping blacks from acquiring guns was certainly
a large part of that motivation. . . .

There is little doubt that the earliest gun controls in the United States   5
were blatantly racist and elitist in their intent. San Francisco civil-liberties
attorney Don B. Kates, Jr., an opponent of gun prohibitions with impeccable
liberal credentials (he has been a clerk for radical lawyer William Kunstler, a
civil-rights activist in the South, and an Office of Economic Opportunity lawyer), describes early gun control efforts in his book *Restricting Handguns:
The Liberal Skeptics Speak Out.* As Kates documents, prohibitions against
the sale of cheap handguns originated in the post-Civil War South. Small
pistols selling for as little as 50 or 60 cents became available in the 1870s
and '80s, and since they could be afforded by recently emancipated blacks
and poor whites (whom agrarian agitators of the time were encouraging to
ally for economic and political purposes), these guns constituted a significant
threat to a southern establishment interested in maintaining the traditional
class structure.

Consequently, Kates notes, in 1870 Tennessee banned "selling all but 'the   6
Army and Navy model' handgun, i.e., the most expensive one, which was
beyond the means of most blacks and laboring people." In 1881, Arkansas
enacted an almost identical ban on the sale of cheap revolvers, while in 1902,
South Carolina banned the sale of handguns to all but "sheriffs and their
special deputies—i.e., company goons and the KKK." In 1893 and 1907, respectively, Alabama and Texas attempted to put handguns out of the reach
of blacks and poor whites through "extremely heavy business and/or trans-
actional taxes" on the sale of such weapons. In the other Deep South states,
slavery-era bans on arms possession by blacks continued to be enforced by
hook or by crook.

The cheap revolvers of the late 19th and early 20th centuries were re-   7
ferred to as "Suicide Specials," the "Saturday Night Special" label not becoming widespread until reformers and politicians took up the gun control cause
during the 1960s. The source of this recent concern about cheap revolvers,
as their new label suggests, has much in common with the concerns of the
gun-law initiators of the post-Civil War South. As B. Bruce-Briggs has written
in the *Public Interest,* "It is difficult to escape the conclusion that the 'Saturday Night Special' is emphasized because it is cheap and is being sold to a
particular class of people. . . .

Those who argue that the concern about cheap handguns is justified be-   8
cause these guns are used in most crimes should take note of *Under the
Gun: Weapons, Crime, and Violence in America*, by sociologists James D.
Wright, Peter H. Rossi, and Kathleen Daly. The authors, who undertook an
exhaustive, federally funded, critical review of gun issue research, found *no
conclusive proof that cheap handguns are used in crime more often than
expensive handguns.* (Interestingly, the makers of quality arms, trying to
stifle competition, have sometimes supported bans on cheap handguns and
on the importation of cheap military surplus weapons. Kates observes that
the Gun Control Act of 1968, which banned mail-order gun sales and the
importation of military surplus firearms, "was something domestic manufacturers had been impotently urging for decades.") But the evidence leads one
to the conclusion that cheap handguns are considered threatening primarily
because minorities and poor whites can afford them.

Attempts to regulate the possession of firearms began in the northern   9
states during the early part of the 20th century, and although these regulations had a different focus from those that had been concocted in the South,
they were no less racist and elitist in effect or intent. Rather than trying to
keep handguns out of the price range that blacks and the poor could afford,
New York's trend-setting Sullivan Law, enacted in 1911, required a police
permit for legal possession of a handgun. This law made it possible for the
police to screen applicants for permits to possess handguns, and while such
a requirement may seem reasonable, it can be and has been abused.

Members of groups not in favor with the political establishment or the   10
police are automatically suspect and can easily be denied permits. For instance, when the Sullivan Law was enacted, southern and eastern European
immigrants were considered racially inferior and religiously and ideologically
suspect. (Many were Catholics or Jews, and a disproportionate number were
anarchists or socialists.) Professor L. Kennett, coauthor of the authoritative
history *The Gun in America*, has noted that the measure was designed to
"strike hardest at the foreign-born element," particularly Italians. Southern
and eastern European immigrants found it almost impossible to obtain gun
permits.

Over the years, application of the Sullivan Law has become increasingly   11
elitist as the police seldom grant handgun permits to any but the wealthy or
the politically influential. A beautiful example of this hypocritical elitism is
the fact that while the *New York Times* often editorializes against the private possession of handguns, the publisher of that newspaper, Arthur Ochs
Sulzberger, has a hard-to-get permit to own and carry a handgun. Another
such permit is held by the husband of Dr. Joyce Brothers, the pop psychologist who has claimed that firearms ownership is indicative of male sexual
inadequacy.

Gun-control efforts through the centuries have been propelled by racist   12
and elitist sentiments. Even though European aristocrats were members of a
weapons-loving warrior caste, they did their best to keep the gun from becoming a weapon of war. It was certainly all right to kill with civilized weap-

ons such as the sword, the battle ax, or the lance; these were weapons that the armored knights were trained to use and which gave them a tremendous advantage over commoners who didn't have the knights' training or possess their expensive weapons and armor. But guns, by virtue of being able to pierce armor, democratized warfare and made common soldiers more than a match for the armored and aristocratic knights, thereby threatening the existence of the feudal aristocracy.

As early as 1541, England enacted a law that limited legal possession of   13 handguns and crossbows (weapons that were considered criminally dangerous) to those with incomes exceeding 100 pounds a year, though long-gun possession wasn't restricted—except for Catholics, a potentially rebellious minority after the English Reformation. Catholics couldn't legally keep militia-like weapons in their homes, as other Englishmen were encouraged to do, but they could legally possess defensive weapons—except, as Bill of Rights authority Joyce Lee Malcolm has noted in her essay "The Right to Keep and Bear Arms: The Common Law Tradition," during times "of extreme religious tension."

According to Malcolm, when William and Mary came to the English throne,   14 they were presented with a list of rights, one of which was aimed at staving off any future attempt at arms confiscation—"all Protestant citizens had a right to keep arms for their defence." England then remained free of restrictive gun legislation until 1920 when, even though the crime rate was very low, concern about the rebellious Irish and various political radicals ushered in today's draconian gun laws. (Colin Greenwood, former superintendent of the West Yorkshire Metropolitan Police, has discovered in his research at Cambridge University that the English gun crime rate is significantly *higher* now than it was before that nation's strict gun laws were enacted.)

Alas, the European aristocracy wasn't able to control gun use, and at least   15 in part, the spread of effective firearms helped to bring down aristocracy and feudalism. By contrast, in 17th-century Japan the ruling Tokugawa Shogunate was able to establish a rigidly stratified society that deemphasized the development of guns and restricted arms possession to a warrior aristocracy, the *samurai*. When Commodore Perry "reopened" Japan to the rest of the world in the middle of the 19th century, few Japanese were familiar with guns (the sword was the most honored weapon of the samuari) and the most common guns were primitive matchlocks similar to those introduced to Japan by the Portuguese in the middle of the 16th century. As post-Perry Japan modernized and acquired a modern military, it also quickly developed modern weaponry. But a citizenry without a gun-owning tradition was easily kept in place in a collectivist society where individuals were more susceptible to formal and informal social controls than are westerners.

The preceding are just samples of the political uses to which gun controls   16 have been put throughout the world. Nazi Germany, the Soviet Union, and South Africa are modern examples of repressive governments that use gun control as a means of social control. Raymond G. Kessler, a lawyer-sociologist who has provided some of the most sociologically sophisticated insights into the gun control issue, suggests in a *Law and Policy Quarterly* article that attempts tc regulate the civilian possession of firearms have five political functions. They "(1) increase citizen reliance on government and tolerance of increased police powers and abuse; (2) help prevent opposition to government; (3) facilitate repressive action by government and its allies; (4) lessen the pressure for major or radical reform; and (5) can be selectively enforced against those perceived to be a threat to government."

Of course, while many gun control proponents might acknowledge that such measures have been used in the ways Kessler lists, they would deny that the controls that they support are either racist or elitist, since they would apply to everybody and are aimed at reducing violence for everybody. Yet the controls that they advocate are in fact racist and classist in *effect*, and only the naive or the dishonest can deny their elitist *intent.*   17

Kessler has also written that while liberals are likely to sympathize with the poor and minorities responsible for much of this nation's violent crime, when they are victimized themselves, "or when they hear of an especially heinous crime, liberals, like most people, feel anger and hostility toward the offender. The discomfort of having incompatible feelings can be alleviated by transferring the anger away from the offender to an inanimate object—the weapon."   18

A perfect example of this transference is provided by Pete Shields, the chairman of the lobbying group Handgun Control Inc., whose son was tragically murdered with a handgun by one of San Francisco's Zebra killers—blacks who were killing whites at random in the early 1970s. This killing was carried out by a black man who was after whites—his own skin color and that of his victim were important to the killer—but in his grief, the white liberal father couldn't blame the criminal for this racist crime. So the gun was the culprit. The upshot is that we now have Handgun Control Inc., with its emphasis on the *weapon* used to commit a crime rather than the criminal. Yet blacks and minorities, who would be prevented from defending themselves, are likely to be harmed most by legislation proposed by Handgun Control Inc., the National Coalition to Ban Handguns, and other proponents of strict handgun controls.   19

Since the illegal possession of a handgun (or of any gun) is a crime that doesn't produce a victim and is unlikely to be reported to the police, handgun permit requirements or outright handgun prohibitions aren't easily enforced. And as civil liberties attorney Kates has observed, when laws are difficult to enforce, "enforcement becomes progressively more haphazard until at last the laws are used only against those who are unpopular with the police." Of course minorities, especially minorities who don't "know their place," aren't likely to be popular with the police, and these very minorities, in the face of police indifference or perhaps even antagonism, may be the most inclined to look to guns for protection—guns that they can't acquire legally and that place them in jeopardy if possessed illegally. While the intent of such laws may not be racist, their effect most certainly is.   20

Today's gun-control battle, like those of days gone by, largely breaks down along class lines. Though there are exceptions to the rule, the most dedicated and vociferous proponents of strict gun controls are urban, upper-middle-   21 class or aspiring upper-middle-class, pro-big-government liberals, many of whom are part of the New Class (establishment intellectuals and the media), and most of whom know little or nothing about guns and the wide range of legitimate uses to which they are regularly put. Many of these elitists make no secret of their disdain for gun-owners. For instance, Gov. Mario Cuomo of New York recently dismissed those who are opposed to the Empire State's mandatory seat-belt law as "NRA hunters who drink beer, don't vote, and lie to their wives about where they were all weekend."

On the other hand, the most dedicated opponents of gun control are often   22
rural- or small-town-oriented, working- or middle-class men and women, few of whom possess the means to publicize their views, but many of whom know a great deal about the safe and lawful uses of guns. To these Americans, guns mean freedom, security, and wholesome recreation. The battle over gun controls, therefore, has come about as affluent America has attempted to impose its anti-gun prejudices on a working-class America that is comfortable with guns (including handguns), seldom misuses them (most gun crime is urban), and sees them as protection against criminal threats and government oppression.

How right you are, General Laney. "All gun laws have been enacted to   23
control certain classes of people. . . ."

QUESTIONS FOR MEANING
1. Why does Tonso object to New York State's Sullivan Law?
2. What led England to adopt gun control in the 1920s?
3. According to this essay, what are the political motives that lead to gun control?
4. What does Tonso mean by "transference" in paragraph 19?
5. What is wrong with a law that is selectively enforced?
6. Vocabulary: impeccable (5), emancipated (5), agrarian (5), impotently (8), authoritative (10), collectivist (15), vociferous (21).

QUESTIONS ABOUT STRATEGY
1. Why do you think Tonso chose to begin this essay with a reference to General Laney when he realized that his audience was probably unfamiliar with this man?
2. Consider Tonso's use of sources in this essay. How well are they incorporated into Tonso's own argument? Which is the most effective?
3. Why does Tonso discuss both English and Japanese history?
4. How does Tonso characterize his opponents? Does he treat them fairly? What is the quotation from Mario Cuomo meant to illustrate?

JOSH SUGARMANN
The NRA Is Right

*Most of the debate over gun control has focused on whether there's a need to restrict handgun ownership. In the following essay, first published in **1987**, Josh Sugarmann argues on behalf of banning handguns altogether. A freelance writer living in New York, Sugarmann was communications director of the National Coalition to Ban Handguns from 1984 to 1986.*

One tenet of the National Rifle Association's faith has always been that   1
handgun controls do little to stop criminals from obtaining handguns. For once, the NRA is right and America's leading handgun control organization is wrong. Criminals don't buy handguns in gun stores. That's why they're criminals. But it isn't criminals who are killing most of the 20,000 to 22,000 people who die from handguns each year. We are.

This is an ugly truth for a country that thinks of handgun violence as a
"crime" issue and believes that it's somehow possible to separate "good"   2
handguns (those in our hands for self-defense) from "bad" handguns (those in the hands of criminals).

Contrary to popular perception, the most prevalent form of handgun death   3
in America isn't murder but suicide. Of the handgun deaths that occur each year, approximately 12,000 are suicides. An additional 1,000 fatalities are accidents. And of the 9,000 handgun deaths classified as murders, most are not caused by predatory strangers. Handgun violence is usually the result of people being angry, drunk, careless, or depressed—who just happen to have a handgun around. In all, fewer than 10 percent of handgun deaths are felony-related.

Though handgun availability is not a crime issue, it does represent a major   4
public health threat. Handguns are the number one weapon for both murder and suicide and are second only to auto accidents as the leading cause of death due to injury. Of course there are other ways of committing suicide or crimes of passion. But no means is more lethal, effective, or handy. That's why the NRA is ultimately wrong. As several public health organizations have noted, the best way to curb a public health problem is through prevention—in this case, the banning of all handguns from civilian hands.

The Enemy Is Us

For most who attempt suicide, the will to die lasts only briefly. Only one   5
out of every ten people attempting suicide is going to kill himself no matter what. The success or failure of an attempt depends primarily on the lethality of the means. Pills, razor blades, and gas aren't guaranteed killers, and they take time. Handguns, however, lend themselves well to spontaneity. Consider that although women try to kill themselves four times as often as men, men

succeed three to four times as often. For one reason: women use pills or less lethal means; men use handguns. This balance is shifting, however, as more women own or have access to handguns. Between 1970 and 1978 the suicide rate for young women rose 50 percent, primarily due to increased use of handguns.

Of course, there is no way to lock society's cupboard and prevent every   6
distraught soul from injuring him or herself. Still, there are ways we can promote public safety without becoming a nation of nannies. England, for instance, curbed suicide by replacing its most common means of committing suicide—coal stove gas—with less toxic natural gas. Fifteen years after the switch, studies found that suicide rates had dropped and remained low, even though the number of suicide *attempts* had increased. "High suicide rates seem to occur where highly lethal suicidal methods are not only available, but also where they are culturally acceptable," writes Dr. Robert Markush of the University of Alabama, who has studied the use of handguns in suicide.

Most murders aren't crime-related, but are the result of arguments be-   7
tween friends and among families. In 1985, 59 percent of all murders were committed by people known to the victim. Only 15 percent were committed by strangers, and only 18 percent were the result of felonious activity. As the FBI admits every year in its *Uniform Crime Reports,* "murder is a societal problem over which law enforcement has little or no control." The FBI doesn't publish separate statistics on who's killing whom with handguns, but it is assumed that what is true of all murders is true of handgun murders.

Controlling the Vector

Recognizing that eliminating a disease requires prevention, not treatment,   8
health professionals have been in the forefront of those calling for a national ban on handguns. In 1981, the Surgeon General's Select Panel for the Promotion of Child Health traced the "epidemic of deaths and injuries among children and youth" to handguns, and called for "nothing short of a total ban." It is estimated that on average, one child dies from handgun wounds each day. Between 1961 and 1981, according to the American Association of Suicidology, the suicide rate for 15- to 24-year-olds increased 150 percent. The report linked the rise in murders and suicides among the young to the increased use of firearms—primarily handguns. In a 1985 report, the Surgeon General's Workshop on Violence and Public Health recommended "a complete and universal ban on the sale, manufacture, importation, and possession of handguns (except for authorized police and military personnel)."

Not surprisingly, the American Public Health Association, the American   9
Association of Suicidology, and the American Psychiatric Association, are three of the 31 national organizations that are members of National Coalition to Ban Handguns (NCBH).

Comparing the relationship between handguns and violence to mosquitos   10
and malaria, Stephen P. Teret, co-director of the Johns Hopkins Injury Pre-

vention Center, says, "As public health professionals, if we are faced with a disease that is carried by some type of vehicle/vector like a mosquito, our initial response would be to control the vector. There's no reason why if the vehicle/vector is a handgun, we should not be interested in controlling the handgun."

The NRA refers to handgun suicides, accidental killings, and murders by   11
acquaintances as "the price of freedom." It believes that handguns right enough wrongs, stop enough crimes, and kill enough criminals to justify these deaths. But even the NRA has admitted that there is no "adequate measure that more lives are saved by arms in good hands than are lost by arms in evil hands." Again, the NRA is right.

A 1985 NCBH study found that a handgun is 118 times more likely to be   12
used in a suicide, murder, or fatal accident than to kill a criminal. Between 1981 and 1983, nearly 69,000 Americans lost their lives to handguns. During that same period there were only 583 justifiable homicides reported to the FBI, in which someone used a handgun to kill a stranger—a burglar, rapist, or other criminal. In 1982, 19 states reported to the FBI that not once did a private citizen use a handgun to kill a criminal. Five states reported that more than 130 citizens were murdered with handguns for each time a handgun was justifiably used to kill a criminal. In no state did the number of self-defense homicides approach the murder toll. Last year, a study published in the *New England Journal of Medicine* analyzing gun use in the home over a six-year period in the Seattle, Washington area, found that for every time a firearm was used to kill an intruder in self-defense, 198 lives ended in murders, suicides, or accidents. Handguns were used in more than 70 percent of those deaths.

Although handguns are rarely used to kill criminals, an obvious question   13
remains: How often are they used merely to wound or scare away intruders? No reliable statistics are available, but most police officials agree that in a criminal confrontation on the street, the handgun-toting civilian is far more likely to be killed or lose his handgun to a criminal than successfully use the weapon in self-defense. "Beyond any doubt, thousands more lives are lost every year because of the proliferation of handguns than are saved," says Joseph McNamara, chief of police of San Jose, who has also been police chief in Kansas City, a beat cop in Harlem, and is the author of a book on defense against violent crime. Moreover, most burglaries occur when homes are vacant, so the handgun in the drawer is no deterrent. (It would also probably be the first item stolen.)

Faced with facts like these, anti-control advocates often turn to the argu-   14
ment of last resort: the Second Amendment. But the historic 1981 Morton Grove, Illinois, ban on handgun sale and possession exploded that rationale. In 1983, the U.S. Supreme Court let stand a lower court ruling that stated, "Because the possession of handguns is not part of the right to keep and bear arms, [the Morton Grove ordinance] does not violate the Second Amendment."

Criminal Equivocation

Unfortunately, powerful as the NRA is, it has received additional help from   15
the leading handgun control group. Handgun Control Inc. (HCI) has helped
the handgun lobby by setting up the perfect strawman for the NRA to shoot
down. "Keep handguns out of the wrong hands," HCI says. "By making it
more difficult for criminals, drug addicts, etc., to get handguns, and by ensuring that law-abiding citizens know how to maintain their handguns, we can
reduce handgun violence," it promises. Like those in the NRA, HCI chairman
Nelson T. "Pete" Shields "firmly believe(s) in the right of law-abiding citizens
to possess handguns . . . for legitimate purposes."

In its attempt to paint handgun violence solely as a crime issue, HCI goes   16
so far as to sometimes ignore the weapon's non-crime death tally. In its most
recent poster comparing the handgun murder toll in the U.S. with that of
nations with strict handgun laws, HCI states: "In 1983, handguns killed 35
people in Japan, 8 in Great Britain, 27 in Switzerland, 6 in Canada, 7 in Sweden, 10 in Australia, and 9,014 in the United States." Handguns *killed* a lot
more than that in the United States. About 13,000 suicides and accidents
more.

HCI endorses a ban only on short-barrelled handguns (the preferred weapon   17
of criminals). It advocates mandatory safety training, a waiting period during
which a background check can be run on a purchaser, and a license to carry
a handgun, with mandatory sentencing for violators. It also endorses mandatory sentencing for the use of a handgun in a crime. According to HCI communications director Barbara Lautman, together these measures would "attack
pretty much the heart of the problem."

HCI appears to have arrived at its crime focus by taking polls. In his 1981   18
book, *Guns Don't Die—People Do,* Shields points out that the majority of
Americans don't favor a ban on handguns. "What they do want, however, is a
set of strict laws to control the easy access to handguns by the criminal and
the violence prone—*as long as those controls don't jeopardize the perceived right of law-abiding citizens to buy and own handguns for self
defense* [italics his]." Shields admits "this is not based on any naive hope that
criminals will obey such laws. Rather, it is based on the willingness of the
rest of us to be responsible and accountable citizens, and the knowledge that
to the degree we are, we make it more difficult for the criminal to get a
handgun." This wasn't always HCI's stand. Founded in 1974 as the National
Council to Control Handguns, HCI originally called a ban on private handgun
possession the "most effective" solution to reducing violent crime rapidly and
was at one time a member of NCBH. Michael Beard, president of NCBH,
maintains the HCI's focus on crime "started with a public relations concern.
Some people in the movement felt Americans were worried about crime, and
that was one way to approach the problem. That's the problem when you use
public opinion polls to tell you what your position's going to be. And I think
a lot of the handgun control movement has looked at whatever's hot at the
time and tried to latch onto that, rather than sticking to the basic message

that there is a relationship between the availability of handguns and the handgun violence in our society. . . . Ultimately, nothing short of taking the product off the market is really going to have an effect on the problem."

HCI's cops and robbers emphasis has been endlessly frustrating to many   19
in the anti-handgun movement. HCI would offer handgun control as a solution to crime, and the NRA would effectively rebut their arguments with the commonsensical observation that criminals are not likely to obey such laws. I can't help but think that HCI's refusal to abandon the crime argument has harmed the longterm progress of the movement.

Saturated Dresser Drawers

In a nation with 40 million handguns—where anyone who wants one can   20
get one—it's time to face a chilling fact. We're way past the point where registration, licensing, safety training, waiting periods, or mandatory sentencing are going to have much effect. Each of these measures may save some lives or help catch a few criminals, but none—by itself or taken together—will stop the vast majority of handgun suicides or murders. A "controlled" handgun kills just as effectively as an "uncontrolled" one.

Most control recommendations merely perpetuate the myth that with proper   21
care a handgun can be as safe a tool as any other. Nothing could be further from the truth. A handgun is not a blender.

Those advocating a step-by-step process insist that a ban would be too   22
radical and therefore unacceptable to Congress and the public. A hardcore 40 percent of the American public has always endorsed banning handguns. Many will also undoubtedly argue that any control measure—no matter how ill-conceived or ineffective—would be a good first step. But after more than a decade, the other foot hasn't followed.

In other areas of firearms control there has been increasing recognition   23
that bans are the most effective solution. The only two federal measures passed since the Gun Control Act of 1968 have been bans. In each case, the reasoning was simple: the harm done by these objects outweighed any possible benefit they brought to society. In 1986, Congress banned certain types of armor-piercing "cop-killer" bullets. There was also a silver lining to last year's NRA-McClure-Volkmer handgun "decontrol" bill, which weakened the already lax Gun Control Act of 1968, making it legal, for instance, for people to transport unloaded, "not readily accessible" handguns interstate. A last-minute amendment added by pro-control forces banned the future production and sale of machine guns for civilian use.

Unfortunately, no law has addressed the major public health problem. Few   24
suicides, accidental killings, or acquaintance murders are the result of cop-killer bullets or machine guns.

Outlawing handguns would in no way be a panacea. Even if handgun pro-   25
duction stopped tomorrow, millions would remain in the dresser drawers of America's bedrooms—and many of them would probably stay there. Contrary to NRA fantasies, black-booted fascists would not be kicking down doors

searching for handguns. Moreover, the absolute last segment of society to be affected by any measure would be criminals. The black market that has fed off the legal sale of handguns would continue for a long while. But by ending new handgun production, the availability of illegal handguns can only decrease.

Of course, someone who truly wants to kill himself can find another way.   26
A handgun ban would not affect millions of rifles and shotguns. But experience shows that no weapon provides the combination of lethality and convenience that a handgun does. Handguns represent only 30 percent of all the guns out there but are responsible for 90 percent of firearms misuse. Most people who commit suicide with a firearm use a handgun. At minimum, a handgun ban would prevent the escalation of killings in segments of society that have not yet been saturated by handgun manufacturers. Further increases in suicides among women, for example, might be curtailed.

But the final solution lies in changing the way handguns and handgun   27
violence are viewed by society. Public health campaigns have changed the way Americans look at cigarette smoking and drunk driving and can do the same for handguns.

For the past 12 years, many in the handgun control movement have con-   28
fined their debate to what the public supposedly wants and expects to hear—not to reality. The handgun must be seen for what it is, not what we'd like it to be.

QUESTIONS FOR MEANING

1. Why does Sugarmann believe that gun control would reduce the number of handgun deaths that occur each year in the United States?
2. What causes of handgun violence are identified by Sugarmann?
3. What does Sugarmann mean by "strawman" in paragraph 15?
4. How does Sugarmann's position differ from the policy of Handgun Control Inc.?
5. Why is it that men kill themselves more often than women do even though women attempt suicide more frequently?
6. Vocabulary: tenet (1), prevalent (3), predatory (3), nannies (6), rationale (14), fascists (25), curtailed (26).

QUESTIONS ABOUT STRATEGY

1. Consider the title of this essay. Why do you think Sugarmann chose it?
2. Does Sugarmann make any concessions to opponents of gun control?
3. Why does Sugarmann link gun control with public health campaigns?
4. Sugarmann devotes five paragraphs to attacking an organization that is working to control handguns, an organization with which he might have forged an alliance. Was this wise? Did he have any choice?

ONE STUDENT'S ASSIGNMENT

Read all the essays on gun control in The Informed Argument *and draw them together by determining what are the major arguments for and against control. Try to show how the arguments of different writers relate to one another by making comparisons whenever possible. Limit your essay to between 750 and 1,000 words.*

A Synthesis of Arguments on Gun Control
Pam Schmidt

Do you want to live in another Nazi Germany where the government has total control, or do you want your child accidentally shot by a handgun originally purchased for your protection? These questions may seem farfetched, but questions like them come up when people argue about gun control. They haven't made it easier for me to decide exactly where I stand on the issue. I think there are valid arguments supporting each side.

Many people in favor of gun control use startling statistics to try to gain the public's support. For example, Jeanne Shields, who became active in the movement to control handguns after her son was killed in 1974, writes that "Today there are 50 million handguns in civilian hands. By the year 2000, there will be more than 100 million" (104). Adam Smith, a well-respected journalist, adds that "70% of . . . stolen guns are handguns. In other words, the supply of handguns used by criminals already comes to a great extent from the households these guns were supposed to protect" (107). A retired special agent for the Bureau of Alcohol, Tobacco and Firearms, James Moore, shocks us by saying that "In this century alone, firearms homicides have exceeded the 437,796 battlefield deaths Americans have suffered in all wars, except the Civil War" (118). One of the main reasons people buy handguns is to protect their family from criminals, but I'm sure many people would be surprised to know that "a handgun is 118 times more likely to be used in a suicide, murder, or fatal accident than to kill a criminal" (Sugarmann 135).

Much of the public seems to think that gun control means the banning of all guns, but Smith and Sugarmann don't want to interfere with the recreational use of shotguns. "I am

willing to grant the gunners a shotgun in every closet"
(Smith 108); on the other hand, "nobody shoots a flying duck
with a .38 revolver. Handguns have only one purpose" (Smith
106). Sugarmann agrees, "A handgun ban would not affect millions of rifles and shotguns" (138). They also both agree
that other weapons, such as knives, are not as deadly as
handguns (Smith 107; Sugarmann 133).

A key argument of people against gun control is that the   4
American people have a constitutional right to keep and bear
arms as declared in the Second Amendment. Edward Abbey, a
former ranger for the National Park Service, asks his readers to "not forget what the common people of this nation knew
when they demanded the Bill of Rights: An armed citizenry is
. . . the best defense . . . against tyranny" (115). However, there have been many cases which say that the Second
Amendment doesn't apply to the banning or restricting of
handguns. For example, Robert J. Spitzer cited three rulings
by the Supreme Court that said, in effect, "the Second Amendment did not apply to the states" (112). This view was also
taken by Sugarmann, who quotes a recent Supreme Court ruling: "Because the possession of handguns is not part of the
right to bear arms, [the Morton Grove Ordinance] does not violate the Second Amendment" (135).

A major question about gun control is simply, does it work?   5
One study that was done by the University of Wisconsin in
1976 concluded that "gun-control laws have no individual or
collective effect in reducing the rate of violent crime"
(Kates 122). This study is referred to by many opponents of
gun control, and it is also mentioned by Adam Smith. James
Moore, on the other hand, says that "With good records, [the
ATF] was able to trace the revolver that John W. Hinckley,
Jr., used in 1981 to shoot President Reagan within sixteen
minutes of the time the serial number was turned over to an
ATF agent" (117). That obviously says something for the gun
control laws that are already in effect.

Many opponents of gun control are afraid of America becom-   6
ing a police state. Edward Abbey compares gun control laws to
Nazi Germany. He feels that the rights of the American people
can be taken away if they have no way to protect themselves
from the government. Kates believes that the "final cost of
national gun confiscation would be the vast accretion of enforcement powers to the police at the expense of individual

liberty" (125). William Tonso, a professor of sociology at the University of Evansville, also implies this by writing "Nazi Germany, the Soviet Union, and South Africa are modern examples of repressive governments that use gun control as a means of social control" (130). Moore, however, doesn't be-lieve this. His response to the familiar line that "any gun law is the first step toward national confiscation and a po-lice state" is: "The first step toward a police state is the formation of a police department" (118).

Another issue that is brought up when debating gun control 7 is racism. William Tonso and Don Kates both feel that gun control laws are to keep handguns away from blacks. Kates cited that the first states to create gun control laws were South Carolina, Mississippi, Tennessee, North Carolina, and Missouri, all being southern states containing many poor blacks (120). Robert Sherrill, who is cited by Tonso, "con-cluded in his book The Saturday Night Special that the object of the Gun Control Act of 1968 was black control rather than gun control" (128). Some people argue that the banning of cheap handguns is justified because they are used in most crimes, however, a study done by sociologists James D. Wright, Peter H. Rossi, and Kathleen Daly, found "no conclu-sive proof that cheap handguns are used in crime more often than expensive handguns [emphasis deleted]" (Tonso 129).

Whether someone opposes or supports gun control, just 8 about everyone can agree on a couple of points. For instance, "Guns should not be sold to children, to the certifiably in-sane, or to convicted criminals" (Abbey 115). Both support-ers and opponents of gun control also agree that violence is a problem in this country. The one thing they don't agree on is whether or not the restricting or banning of handguns would help solve this problem.

SUGGESTIONS FOR WRITING

1. Shields, Smith, Abbey, and Kates all describe members of what Smith calls "the gun culture." Summarize and compare these descriptions de-termining which, if any, seem fair and accurate.
2. Shields, Smith, Abbey, and Moore all draw upon personal experience in making their arguments. If you have ever used a gun, write an essay on gun control that begins with an account of your experience.
3. Kates argues that "liberals" should oppose gun control but recognize that

many liberals are in favor of it. Addressing yourself to a liberal, college-educated audience, write a deductive argument for or against control. Your premise should define either the rights of citizens or the responsibilities of government.

4. What is your own opinion of gun control? Were you influenced by your reading in this unit? Summarize at least two of the arguments you have read and use these summaries as the foundation for a short essay of your own. Be sure to summarize the argument of at least one writer with whom you disagree—carefully explaining why the "opposition" did not convince you.

5. Regardless of your own opinion on gun control, which essay in this unit is the most persuasive? Write an essay in defense of this writer, evaluating the techniques he or she has used.

6. Regardless of your own opinion on gun control, which essay in this unit is the weakest? Reveal the flaws you perceive in the essay, and do not indulge in ad hominem attacks.

7. Write an essay explaining why advocates of gun control object especially to handguns. Draw support from Adam Smith and Josh Sugarmann.

8. Both Kates and Tonso charge that gun control is racist. Do you agree? Write an essay in support of the position you take on this aspect of the controversy over gun control.

9. Do a research paper comparing the rate of violent crime in two states with significantly different gun laws.

10. Define the meaning of the Second Amendment, drawing upon the essay by Robert Spitzer and your own research.

Section 3
Capital Punishment: Justice or Vengeance?

H. L. MENCKEN
The Penalty of Death

Henry Louis Mencken (1880–1956) was a journalist who enjoyed a national reputation throughout the first half of the twentieth century, especially during the 1920s. Although he worked for the Baltimore Sun *for over forty years, Mencken was no ordinary journalist. Fascinated by words, he wrote one of the best books ever written on the way we write and speak,* The American Language, *first published in 1919 and revised and enlarged in several subsequent editions. But it was as an essayist that Mencken won his largest audience. As co-editor of* The Smart Set *from 1914–1923, he was in a position to encourage writers such as James Joyce, D. H. Lawrence, and Sinclair Lewis. As founder and editor of* The American Mercury *in 1924, Mencken found a forum from which he could speak out on almost any subject that interested him. At a time in our history when many Americans were feeling complacent about life in a country that seemed the richest and strongest in the world, Mencken made a specialty of exposing fools and ridiculing popular notions. The following essay on capital punishment, from* Prejudices, Fifth Series (**1926**), *is characteristic of both his thought and style.*

Of the arguments against capital punishment that issue from uplifters, two 1
are commonly heard most often, to wit:

1. That hanging a man (or frying him or gassing him) is a dreadful business, degrading to those who have to do it and revolting to those who have to witness it.
2. That it is useless, for it does not deter others from the same crime.

The first of these arguments, it seems to me, is plainly too weak to need 2
serious refutation. All it says, in brief, is that the work of the hangman is
unpleasant. Granted. But suppose it is? It may be quite necessary to society
for all that. There are, indeed, many other jobs that are unpleasant, and yet
no one thinks of abolishing them—that of the plumber, that of the soldier,

that of the garbage-man, that of the priest hearing confessions, that of the sand-hog, and so on. Moreover, what evidence is there that any actual hang-man complains of his work? I have heard none. On the contrary, I have known many who delighted in their ancient art, and practised it proudly.

In the second argument of the abolitionists there is rather more force, but even here, I believe, the ground under them is shaky. Their fundamental error consists in assuming that the whole aim of punishing criminals is to deter other (potential) criminals—that we hang or electrocute A simply in order to so alarm B that he will not kill C. This, I believe, is an assumption which confuses a part with the whole. Deterrence, obviously, is *one* of the aims of punishment, but it is surely not the only one. On the contrary, there are at least half a dozen, and some are probably quite as important. At least one of them, practically considered, is *more* important. Commonly, it is de-scribed as revenge, but revenge is really not the word for it. I borrow a better term from the late Aristotle: *katharsis. Katharsis,* so used, means a salu-brious discharge of emotions, a healthy letting off of steam. A school-boy, disliking his teacher, deposits a tack under the pedagogical chair; the teacher jumps and the boy laughs. This is *katharsis.* What I contend is that one of the prime objects of all judicial punishments is to afford the same grateful relief (*a*) to the immediate victims of the criminal punished, and (*b*) to the general body of moral and timorous men. 3

These persons, and particularly the first group, are concerned only indi-rectly with deterring other criminals. The thing they crave primarily is the satisfaction of seeing the criminal actually before them suffer as he made them suffer. What they want is the peace of mind that goes with the feeling that accounts are squared. Until they get that satisfaction they are in a state of emotional tension, and hence unhappy. The instant they get it they are comfortable. I do not argue that this yearning is noble; I simply argue that it is almost universal among human beings. In the face of injuries that are un-important and can be borne without damage it may yield to higher impulses; that is to say, it may yield to what is called Christian charity. But when the injury is serious Christianity is adjourned, and even saints reach for their sidearms. It is plainly asking too much of human nature to expect it to con-quer so natural an impulse. A keeps a store and has a bookkeeper, B. B steals $700, employs it in playing at dice or bingo, and is cleaned out. What is A to do? Let B go? If he does he will be unable to sleep at night. The sense of injury, of injustice, of frustration will haunt him like pruritus. So he turns B over to the police, and they hustle B to prison. Thereafter A can sleep. More, he has pleasant dreams. He pictures B chained to the wall of a dungeon a hundred feet underground, devoured by rats and scorpions. It is so agreeable that it makes him forget his $700. He has got his *katharsis.* 4

The same thing precisely takes place on a larger scale when there is a crime which destroys a whole community's sense of security. Every law-abid-ing citizen feels menaced and frustrated until the criminals have been struck down—until the communal capacity to get even with them, and more than even, has been dramatically demonstrated. Here, manifestly, the business of 5 deterring others is no more than an afterthought. The main thing is to destroy the concrete scoundrels whose act has alarmed everyone, and thus made everyone unhappy. Until they are brought to book that unhappiness continues; when the law has been executed upon them there is a sigh of relief. In other words, there is *katharsis*.

I know of no public demand for the death penalty for ordinary crimes,   6 even for ordinary homicides. Its infliction would shock all men of normal decency of feeling. But for crimes involving the deliberate and inexcusable taking of human life, by men openly defiant of all civilized order—for such crimes it seems, to nine men out of ten, a just and proper punishment. Any lesser penalty leaves them feeling that the criminal has got the better of society—that he is free to add insult to injury by laughing. That feeling can be dissipated only by a recourse to *katharsis*, the invention of the aforesaid Aristotle. It is more effectively and economically achieved, as human nature now is, by wafting the criminal to realms of bliss.

The real objection to capital punishment doesn't lie against the actual ex-   7 termination of the condemned, but against our brutal American habit of putting it off so long. After all, every one of us must die soon or late, and a murderer, it must be assumed, is one who makes that sad fact the cornerstone of his metaphysic. But it is one thing to die, and quite another thing to lie for long months and even years under the shadow of death. No sane man would choose such a finish. All of us, despite the Prayer Book, long for a swift and unexpected end. Unhappily, a murderer, under the irrational American system, is tortured for what, to him, must seem a whole series of eternities. For months on end he sits in prison while his lawyers carry on their idiotic buffoonery with writs, injunctions, mandamuses, and appeals. In order to get his money (or that of his friends) they have to feed him with hope. Now and then, by the imbecility of a judge or some trick of juridic science, they actually justify it. But let us say that, his money all gone, they finally throw up their hands. Their client is now ready for the rope or the chair. But he must still wait for months before it fetches him.

That wait, I believe, is horribly cruel. I have seen more than one man   8 sitting in the death-house, and I don't want to see any more. Worse, it is wholly useless. Why should he wait at all? Why not hang him the day after the last court dissipates his last hope? Why torture him as not even cannibals would torture their victims? The common answer is that he must have time to make his peace with God. But how long does that take? It may be accomplished, I believe, in two hours quite as comfortably as in two years. There are, indeed, no temporal limitations upon God. He could forgive a whole herd of murderers in a millionth of a second. More, it has been done.

QUESTIONS FOR MEANING

1. Why does Mencken believe that capital punishment is justifiable?
2. Do you understand the meaning of *katharsis*? Can you think of examples from your own experience to illustrate this principle?

3. How absolute is Mencken's proposal? Does he want all murderers to be executed or does he recognize that circumstances make some murders worse than others?
4. What flaws does Mencken see in the American judicial system?
5. Vocabulary: refutation (2), salubrious (3), pedagogical (3), timorous (3), manifestly (5), dissipated (6), and buffoonery (7).

QUESTIONS ABOUT STRATEGY

1. How would you describe Mencken's style? Consider his diction in particular. What kind of effect does a word like "uplifters" have in paragraph 1? Why does Mencken write about *frying* a man rather than "electrocuting" him? Does language of this sort belong in an essay that moves on to discuss Aristotle? Is this shift strange and exciting—or is it a sign of sloppy writing?
2. Mencken begins his essay with a summary of what he believes to be the two principal arguments against capital punishment. Is this a fair summary? Are there any important arguments that he overlooks?
3. Do you think Mencken really knew many hangmen who "delighted in their ancient art?" If not, why do you think he says so?
4. Comment on Mencken's use of illustration, especially his example of the school boy with a tack in paragraph 3 and the storekeeper in paragraph 4. Are these examples useful in explaining *katharsis*? Are you persuaded that capital punishment is analogous to them?

CLARENCE DARROW
The Futility of the Death Penalty

Specializing in labor and political cases, Clarence Darrow (1857–1938) was one of the most famous lawyers in American history. He was especially prominent in the 1920s, a decade that witnessed his two most celebrated cases. In 1925, he was the defense attorney for John L. Scopes, a high school biology teacher who was charged with violating a Tennessee law that prohibited teaching any theory that suggested man may have evolved from a lower species. Although Charles Darwin had published The Origin of Species *more than a half century earlier, evolution was still regarded as a dangerous doctrine that would undermine the moral authority of the Bible. The Scopes trial attracted worldwide attention as a major test of civil liberties, especially freedom of thought. Darrow lost the case, but his forceful defense of Scopes almost certainly saved teachers in other states from being prosecuted under similar laws.*

A year earlier, Darrow had undertaken an even more difficult case when he defended Nathan Leopold and Richard Loeb in a notorious murder case. Although his clients had confessed to an unusually cold-blooded murder and popular feeling demanded that they be executed, Darrow managed to win prison terms for them by arguing persuasively against the death penalty. His objections to capital punishment are best summarized in the following essay, first published in **1928.**

Little more than a century ago, in England, there were over two hundred 1 offenses that were punishable with death. The death sentence was passed upon children under ten years old. And every time the sentimentalist sought to lessen the number of crimes punishable by death, the self-righteous said no, that it would be the destruction of the state; that it would be better to kill for more transgressions rather than for less.

Today, both in England and America, the number of capital offenses has 2 been reduced to a very few, and capital punishment would doubtless be abolished altogether were it not for the self-righteous, who still defend it with the same old arguments. Their major claim is that capital punishment decreases the number of murders, and hence, that the state must retain the institution as its last defense against the criminal.

It is my purpose in this article to prove, first, that capital punishment is 3 no deterrent to crime; and second, that the state continues to kill its victims, not so much to defend society against them—for it could do that equally well by imprisonment—but to appease the mob's emotions of hatred and revenge.

Behind the idea of capital punishment lie false training and crude views 4 of human conduct. People do evil things, say the judges, lawyers, and preachers, because of depraved hearts. Human conduct is not determined by the causes which determine the conduct of other animal and plant life in the universe. For some mysterious reason human beings act as they please; and if they do not please to act in a certain way, it is because, having the power of choice, they deliberately choose to act wrongly. The world once applied this doctrine to disease and insanity in men. It was also applied to animals, and even inanimate things were once tried and condemned to destruction. The world knows better now, but the rule has not yet been extended to human beings.

The simple fact is that every person starts life with a certain physical   5
structure, more or less sensitive, stronger or weaker. He is played upon by everything that reaches him from without, and in this he is like everything else in the universe, inorganic matter as well as organic. How a man will act depends upon the character of his human machine, and the strength of the various stimuli that affect it. Everyone knows that this is so in disease and insanity. Most investigators know that it applies to crime. But the great mass of people still sit in judgment, robed with self-righteousness, and determine the fate of their less fortunate fellows. When this question is studied like any other, we shall then know how to get rid of most of the conduct that we call "criminal," just as we are now getting rid of much of the disease that once afflicted mankind.

If crime were really the result of wilful depravity, we should be ready to   6
concede that capital punishment may serve as a deterrent to the criminally inclined. But it is hardly probable that the great majority of people refrain from killing their neighbors because they are afraid; they refrain because they never had the inclination. Human beings are creatures of habit; and, as a rule, they are not in the habit of killing. The circumstances that lead to killings are manifold, but in a particular individual the inducing cause is not easily found. In one case, homicide may have been induced by indigestion in the killer; in another, it may be traceable to some weakness inherited from a remote ancestor; but that it results from *something* tangible and understandable, if all the facts were known, must be plain to everyone who believes in cause and effect.

Of course, no one will be converted to this point of view by statistics of   7
crime. In the first place, it is impossible to obtain reliable ones; and in the second place, the conditions to which they apply are never the same. But if one cares to analyze the figures, such as we have, it is easy to trace the more frequent causes of homicide. The greatest number of killings occur during attempted burglaries and robberies. The robber knows that penalties for burglary do not average more than five years in prison. He also knows that the penalty for murder is death or life imprisonment. Faced with this alternative, what does the burglar do when he is detected and threatened with arrest? He shoots to kill. He deliberately takes the chance of death to save himself from a five-year term in prison. It is therefore as obvious as anything can be that fear of death has no effect in diminishing homicides of this kind, which are more numerous than any other type.

The next largest number of homicides may be classed as "sex murders."   8
Quarrels between husbands and wives, disappointed love, or love too much requited cause many killings. They are the result of primal emotions so deep

that the fear of death has not the slightest effect in preventing them. Spontaneous feelings overflow in criminal acts, and consequences do not count.

Then there are cases of sudden anger, uncontrollable rage. The fear of   9
death never enters into such cases; if the anger is strong enough, consequences are not considered until too late. The old-fashioned stories of men deliberately plotting and committing murder in cold blood have little foundation in real life. Such killings are so rare that they need not concern us here. The point to be emphasized is that practically all homicides are manifestations of well-recognized human emotions, and it is perfectly plain that the fear of excessive punishment does not enter into them.

In addition to these personal forces which overwhelm weak men and lead   10
them to commit murder, there are also many social and economic forces which must be listed among the causes of homicides, and human beings have even less control over these than over their own emotions. It is often said that in America there are more homicides in proportion to population than in England. This is true. There are likewise more in the United States than in Canada. But such comparisons are meaningless until one takes into consideration the social and economic differences in the countries compared. Then it becomes apparent why the homicide rate in the United States is higher. Canada's population is largely rural; that of the United States is crowded into cities whose slums are the natural breeding places of crime. Moreover, the population of England and Canada is homogeneous, while the United States has gathered together people of every color from every nation in the world. Racial differences intensify social, religious, and industrial problems, and the confusion which attends this indiscriminate mixing of races and nationalities is one of the most fertile sources of crime.

Will capital punishment remedy these conditions? Of course it won't; but   11
its advocates argue that the fear of this extreme penalty will hold the victims of adverse conditions in check. To this piece of sophistry the continuance and increase of crime in our large cities is a sufficient answer. No, the plea that capital punishment acts as a deterrent to crime will not stand. The real reason why this barbarous practice persists in a so-called civilized world is that people still hold the primitive belief that the taking of one human life can be atoned for by taking another. It is the age-old obsession with punishment that keeps the official headsman busy plying his trade.

And it is precisely upon this point that I would build my case against   12
capital punishment. Even if one grants that the idea of punishment is sound, crime calls for something more—for careful study, for an understanding of causes, for proper remedies. To attempt to abolish crime by killing the criminal is the easy and foolish way out of a serious situation. Unless a remedy deals with the conditions which foster crime, criminals will breed faster than the hangman can spring his trap. Capital punishment ignores the causes of crime just as completely as the primitive witch doctor ignored the causes of disease; and, like the methods of the witch doctor, it is not only ineffective as a remedy, but is positively vicious in at least two ways. In the first place,

the spectacle of state executions feeds the basest passions of the mob. And in the second place, so long as the state rests content to deal with crime in this barbaric and futile manner, society will be lulled by a false sense of security, and effective methods of dealing with crime will be discouraged.

It seems to be a general impression that there are fewer homicides in   13 Great Britain than in America because in England punishment is more certain, more prompt, and more severe. As a matter of fact, the reverse is true. In England the average term for burglary is eighteen months; with us it is probably four or five years. In England, imprisonment for life means twenty years. Prison sentences in the United States are harder than in any country in the world that could be classed as civilized. This is true largely because, with us, practically no official dares to act on his own judgment. The mob is all-powerful and demands blood for blood. That intangible body of people called "the public" vents its hatred upon the criminal and enjoys the sensation of having him put to death by the state—this without any definite idea that it is really necessary.

For the last five or six years, in England and Wales, the homicides re-   14 ported by the police range from sixty-five to seventy a year. Death sentences meted out by jurors have averaged about thirty-five, and hangings, fifteen. More than half of those convicted by juries were saved by appeals to the Home Office. But in America there is no such percentage of lives saved after conviction. Governors are afraid to grant clemency. If they did, the newspapers and the populace would refuse to re-elect them.

It is true that trials are somewhat prompter in England than America, but   15 there no newspaper dares publish the details of any case until after the trial. In America the accused is often convicted by the public within twenty-four hours of the time a homicide occurs. The courts sidetrack all other business so that a homicide that is widely discussed may receive prompt attention. The road to the gallows is not only opened but greased for the opportunity of killing another victim.

Thus, while capital punishment panders to the passions of the mob, no   16 one takes the pains to understand the meaning of crime. People speak of crime or criminals as if the world were divided into the good and the bad. This is not true. All of us have the same emotions, but since the balance of emotions is never the same, nor the inducing causes identical, human conduct presents a wide range of differences, shading by almost imperceptible degrees from that of the saint to that of the murderer. Of those kinds of conduct which are classed as dangerous, by no means all are made criminal offenses. Who can clearly define the difference between certain legal offenses and many kinds of dangerous conduct not singled out by criminal statute? Why are many cases of cheating entirely omitted from the criminal code, such as false and misleading advertisements, selling watered stock, forestalling the market, and all the different ways in which great fortunes are accumulated to the envy and despair of those who would like to have money but do not know how to get it? Why do we kill people for the crime of homicide

and administer a lesser penalty for burglary, robbery, and cheating? Can anyone tell which is the greater crime and which is the lesser?

Human conduct is by no means so simple as our moralists have led us to   17
believe. There is no sharp line separating good actions from bad. The greed
for money, the display of wealth, the despair of those who witness the display, the poverty, oppression, and hopelessness of the unfortunate—all these
are factors which enter into human conduct and of which the world takes no
account. Many people have learned no other profession but robbery and burglary. The processions moving steadily through our prisons to the gallows are
in the main made up of these unfortunates. And how do we dare to consider
ourselves civilized creatures when, ignoring the causes of crime, we rest content to mete out harsh punishments to the victims of conditions over which
they have no control?

Even now, are not all imaginative and humane people shocked at the spec-   18
tacle of a killing by the state? How many men and women would be willing
to act as executioners? How many fathers and mothers would want their
children to witness an official killing? What kind of people read the sensational reports of an execution? If all right-thinking men and women were not
ashamed of it, why would it be needful that judges and lawyers and preachers apologize for the barbarity? How can the state censure the cruelty of the
man who—moved by strong passions, or acting to save his freedom, or influenced by weakness or fear—takes human life, when everyone knows that the
state itself, after long premeditation and settled hatred, not only kills, but
first tortures and bedevils its victims for weeks with the impending doom?

For the last hundred years the world has shown a gradual tendency to   19
mitigate punishment. We are slowly learning that this way of controlling human beings is both cruel and ineffective. In England the criminal code has
consistently grown more humane, until now the offenses punishable by death
are reduced to practically one. There is no doubt whatever that the world is
growing more humane and more sensitive and more understanding. The time
will come when all people will view with horror the light way in which society
and its courts of law now take human life; and when that time comes, the
way will be clear to devise some better method of dealing with poverty and
ignorance and their frequent byproducts, which we call crime.

QUESTIONS FOR MEANING

1. In his opening paragraphs, Darrow claims that capital punishment is supported by "the self-righteous." What kind of people is he referring to? Do
   you agree with him?
2. Why does Darrow believe that capital punishment does not deter crime?
   Why does he believe it is still carried out?
3. Darrow argues that "Capital punishment ignores the causes of crime." At
   what points in his essay does he try to reveal what these causes are?
4. How would you describe Darrow's opinion of human nature?

5. Toward the end of his essay Darrow asks, "Why do we kill people for the crime of homicide and administer a lesser penalty for burglary, robbery, and cheating? Can anyone tell which is the greater crime and which is the lesser?" Can you?

QUESTIONS ABOUT STRATEGY

1. For what sort of audience do you think this essay was originally written? Is there any evidence in it that Darrow was not addressing "the great mass of people" or the "mob" to which he refers in paragraphs 5 and 13?
2. In paragraph 9, Darrow argues, "The old fashioned stories of men deliberately plotting and committing murder in cold blood have little foundation in real life." Consider whether you agree with him, and consider also his purpose in making this claim.
3. How useful is the comparison between England and the United States?
4. Why does Darrow introduce "fathers," "mothers," and "children" into his second to last paragraph?
5. This essay was written more than fifty years ago. Do you think its argument is still valid, or does it seem out of date?

EDWARD I. KOCH
Death and Justice

A former Congressman, Edward I. Koch has been mayor of New York City since 1978. Despite several scandals involving corruption in his administration, he himself has remained widely respected as an effective mayor and a politician who is unafraid to speak his mind. He is also the author of two books: Mayor *(1985), an autobiography he wrote with William Rauch, and* Politics *(1986). The following essay originally appeared in* The New Republic *in **1985.***

Last December a man named Robert Lee Willie, who had been convicted   1
of raping and murdering an 18-year-old woman, was executed in the Louisiana state prison. In a statement issued several minutes before his death, Mr. Willie said: "Killing people is wrong. . . . It makes no difference whether it's citizens, countries, or governments. Killing is wrong." Two weeks later in South Carolina, an admitted killer named Joseph Carl Shaw was put to death for murdering two teenagers. In an appeal to the governor for clemency, Mr. Shaw wrote: "Killing is wrong when I did it. Killing is wrong when you do it. I hope you have the courage and moral strength to stop the killing."

It is a curiosity of modern life that we find ourselves being lectured on   2
morality by cold-blooded killers. Mr. Willie previously had been convicted of

aggravated rape, aggravated kidnapping, and the murders of a Louisiana deputy and a man from Missouri. Mr. Shaw committed another murder a week before the two for which he was executed, and admitted mutilating the body of the 14-year-old girl he killed. I can't help wondering what prompted these murderers to speak out against killing as they entered the death-house door. Did their newfound reverence for life stem from the realization that they were about to lose their own?

Life is indeed precious, and I believe the death penalty helps to affirm this   3
fact. Had the death penalty been a real possibility in the minds of these murderers, they might well have stayed their hand. They might have shown moral awareness before their victims died, and not after. Consider the tragic death of Rosa Velez, who happened to be home when a man named Luis Vera burglarized her apartment in Brooklyn. "Yeah, I shot her," Vera admitted. "She knew me, and I knew I wouldn't go to the chair."

During my 22 years in public service, I have heard the pros and cons of   4
capital punishment expressed with special intensity. As a district leader, councilman, congressman, and mayor, I have represented constituencies generally thought of as liberal. Because I support the death penalty for heinous crimes of murder, I have sometimes been the subject of emotional and outraged attacks by voters who find my position reprehensible or worse. I have listened to their ideas. I have weighed their objections carefully. I still support the death penalty. The reasons I maintain my position can be best understood by examining the arguments most frequently heard in opposition.

(1) *The death penalty is "barbaric."* Sometimes opponents of capital   5
punishment horrify with tales of lingering death on the gallows, of faulty electric chairs, or of agony in the gas chamber. Partly in response to such protests, several states such as North Carolina and Texas switched to execution by lethal injection. The condemned person is put to death painlessly, without ropes, voltage, bullets, or gas. Did this answer the objections of death penalty opponents. Of course not. On June 22, 1984, *The New York Times* published an editorial that sarcastically attacked the new "hygienic" method of death by injection, and stated that "execution can never be made humane through science." So it's not the method that really troubles opponents. It's the death itself they consider barbaric.

Admittedly, capital punishment is not a pleasant topic. However, one does   6
not have to like the death penalty in order to support it any more than one must like radical surgery, radiation, or chemotherapy in order to find necessary these attempts at curing cancer. Ultimately we may learn how to cure cancer with a simple pill. Unfortunately, that day has not yet arrived. Today we are faced with the choice of letting the cancer spread or trying to cure it with the methods available, methods that one day will almost certainly be considered barbaric. But to give up and do nothing would be far more barbaric and would certainly delay the discovery of an eventual cure. The analogy between cancer and murder is imperfect, because murder is not the "disease" we are trying to cure. The disease is injustice. We may not like the death penalty, but it must be available to punish crimes of cold-blooded mur-

der, cases in which any other form of punishment would be inadequate and, therefore, unjust. If we create a society in which injustice is not tolerated, incidents of murder—the most flagrant form of injustice—will diminish.

(2) *No other major democracy uses the death penalty.* No other major   7
democracy—in fact, few other countries of any description—are plagued by a murder rate such as that in the United States. Fewer and fewer Americans can remember the days when unlocked doors were the norm and murder was a rare and terrible offense. In America the murder rate climbed 122 percent between 1963 and 1980. During that same period, the murder rate in New York City increased by almost 400 percent, and the statistics are even worse in many other cities. A study at M.I.T. showed that based on 1970 homicide rates a person who lived in a large American city ran a greater risk of being murdered than an American soldier in World War II ran of being killed in combat. It is not surprising that the laws of each country differ according to differing conditions and traditions. If other countries had our murder problem, the cry for capital punishment would be just as loud as it is here. And I daresay that any other major democracy where 75 percent of the people supported the death penalty would soon enact it into law.

(3) *An innocent person might be executed by mistake.* Consider the   8
work of Adam Bedau, one of the most implacable foes of capital punishment in this country. According to Mr. Bedau, it is "false sentimentality to argue that the death penalty should be abolished because of the abstract possibility that an innocent person might be executed." He cites a study of the 7,000 executions in this country from 1893 to 1971, and concludes that the record fails to show that such cases occur. The main point, however, is this. If government functioned only when the possibility of error didn't exist, government wouldn't function at all. Human life deserves special protection, and one of the best ways to guarantee that protection is to assure that convicted murderers do not kill again. Only the death penalty can accomplish this end. In a recent case in New Jersey, a man named Richard Biegenwald was freed from prison after serving 18 years for murder; since his release he has been convicted of committing four murders. A prisoner named Lemuel Smith, who, while serving four life sentences for murder (plus two life sentences for kidnapping and robbery) in New York's Green Haven Prison, lured a woman corrections officer into the chaplain's office and strangled her. He then mutilated and dismembered her body. An additional life sentence for Smith is meaningless. Because New York has no death penalty statute, Smith has effectively been given a license to kill.

But the problem of multiple murder is not confined to the nation's peni-   9
tentiaries. In 1981, 91 police officers were killed in the line of duty in this country. Seven percent of those arrested in the cases that have been solved had a previous arrest for murder. In New York City in 1976 and 1977, 85 persons arrested for homicide had a previous arrest for murder. Six of these individuals had two previous arrests for murder, and one had four previous murder arrests. During those two years the New York police were arresting for murder persons with a previous arrest for murder on the average of one

every 8.5 days. This is not surprising when we learn that in 1975, for example, the median time served in Massachusetts for homicide was less than two-and-a-half years. In 1976 a study sponsored by the Twentieth Century Fund found that the average time served in the United States for first-degree murder is ten years. The median time served may be considerably lower.

(4) *Capital punishment cheapens the value of human life.* On the con-   10
trary, it can be easily demonstrated that the death penalty strengthens the value of human life. If the penalty for rape were lowered, clearly it would signal a lessened regard for the victims' suffering, humiliation, and personal integrity. It would cheapen their horrible experience, and expose them to an increased danger of recurrence. When we lower the penalty for murder, it signals a lessened regard for the value of the victim's life. Some critics of capital punishment, such as columnist Jimmy Breslin, have suggested that a life sentence is actually a harsher penalty for murder than death. This is sophistic nonsense. A few killers may decide not to appeal a death sentence, but the overwhelming majority make every effort to stay alive. It is by exacting the highest penalty for the taking of human life that we affirm the highest value of human life.

(5) *The death penalty is applied in a discriminatory manner.* This   11
factor no longer seems to be the problem it once was. The appeals process for a condemned prisoner is lengthy and painstaking. Every effort is made to see that the verdict and sentence were fairly arrived at. However, assertions of discrimination are not an argument for ending the death penalty but for extending it. It is not justice to exclude everyone from the penalty of the law if a few are found to be so favored. Justice requires that the law be applied equally to all.

(6) *Thou Shalt Not Kill.* The Bible is our greatest source of moral inspi-   12
ration. Opponents of the death penalty frequently cite the sixth of the Ten Commandments in an attempt to prove that capital punishment is divinely proscribed. In the original Hebrew, however, the Sixth Commandment reads, "Thou Shalt Not Commit Murder," and the Torah specifies capital punishment for a variety of offenses. The biblical viewpoint has been upheld by philosophers throughout history. The greatest thinkers of the 19th century— Kant, Locke, Hobbes, Rousseau, Montesquieu, and Mill—agreed that natural law properly authorizes the sovereign to take life in order to vindicate justice. Only Jeremy Bentham was ambivalent. Washington, Jefferson, and Franklin endorsed it. Abraham Lincoln authorized executions for deserters in wartime. Alexis de Tocqueville, who expressed profound respect for American institutions, believed that the death penalty was indispensable to the support of social order. The United States Constitution, widely admired as one of the seminal achievements in the history of humanity, condemns cruel and inhuman punishment, but does not condemn capital punishment.

(7) *The death penalty is state-sanctioned murder.* This is the defense   13
with which Messrs. Willie and Shaw hoped to soften the resolve of those who sentenced them to death. By saying in effect, "You're no better than I am," the murderer seeks to bring his accusers down to his own level. It is also a

popular argument among opponents of capital punishment, but a transparently false one. Simply put, the state has rights that the private individual does not. In a democracy, those rights are given to the state by the electorate. The execution of a lawfully condemned killer is no more an act of murder than is legal imprisonment an act of kidnapping. If an individual forces a neighbor to pay him money under threat of punishment, it's called extortion. If the state does it, it's called taxation. Rights and responsibilities surrendered by the individual are what give the sate its power to govern. This contract is the foundation of civilization itself.

Everyone wants his or her rights, and will defend them jealously. Not   14
everyone, however, wants responsibilities, especially the painful responsibilities that come with law enforcement. Twenty-one years ago a woman named Kitty Genovese was assaulted and murdered on a street in New York. Dozens of neighbors heard her cries for help but did nothing to assist her. They didn't even call the police. In such a climate the criminal understandably grows bolder. In the presence of moral cowardice, he lectures us on our supposed failings and tries to equate his crimes with our quest for justice.

The death of anyone—even a convicted killer—diminishes us all. But we   15
are diminished even more by a justice system that fails to function. It is an illusion to let ourselves believe that doing away with capital punishment removes the murderer's deed from our conscience. The rights of society are paramount. When we protect guilty lives, we give up innocent lives in exchange. When opponents of capital punishment say to the state: "I will not let you kill in my name," they are also saying to murderers: "You can kill in your *own* name as long as I have an excuse for not getting involved."

It is hard to imagine anything worse than being murdered while neighbors   16
do nothing. But something worse exists. When those same neighbors shrink back from justly punishing the murderer, the victim dies twice.

QUESTIONS FOR MEANING

1. What does Koch mean by "natural law" in paragraph 12 and "moral cowardice" in paragraph 14?
2. According to Koch, how is it possible for a murder victim to die twice?
3. Why does Koch believe that the Sixth Commandment, "Thou shalt not kill," does not apply to capital punishment?
4. On what grounds does Koch make a distinction between "murder" and "capital punishment"?
5. Vocabulary: heinous (4), reprehensible (4), sophistic (10), ambivalent (12), seminal (12), extortion (13), paramount (15).

QUESTIONS ABOUT STRATEGY

1. Why does Koch begin his argument by citing the views of two murderers who were sentenced to death?
2. Why does Koch reveal that he has spent twenty-two years in public service? Is this information relevant to his argument?

3. How effective is the analogy between capital punishment and treatment for cancer in paragraph 6?
4. Koch devotes much of his argument to responding to the views of people who oppose capital punishment. Are there any arguments against capital punishment that he has overlooked?
5. Why does Koch refer to Kitty Genovese toward the end of his essay?
6. How effective is Koch's use of statistics?

ANNA QUINDLEN
Death Penalty's False Promise

Even though they may be horrified by reports of murder and feel the need for revenge, there are many people who are nevertheless opposed to capital punishment because they believe it is "inherently immoral"—as Anna Quindlen explains in the following essay. Quindlen is a columnist for the New York Times, *where this essay was published in **1986**.*

Ted Bundy and I go back a long way, to a time when there was a series of   1
unsolved murders in Washington State known only as the Ted murders. Like a lot of reporters, I'm something of a crime buff. But the Washington Ted murders—and the ones that followed in Utah, Colorado and finally in Florida, where Ted Bundy was convicted and sentenced to die—fascinated me because I could see myself as one of the victims. I looked at the studio photographs of young women with long hair, pierced ears, easy smiles, and I read the descriptions: polite, friendly, quick to help, eager to please. I thought about being approached by a handsome young man asking for help, and I knew if I had been in the wrong place at the wrong time I would have been a goner.

By the time Ted finished up in Florida, law enforcement authorities sus-   2
pected he had murdered dozens of young women. He and the death penalty seemed made for each other.

The death penalty and I, on the other hand, seem to have nothing in com-   3
mon. But Ted Bundy has made me think about it all over again, now that the outlines of my 60s liberalism have been filled in with a decade as a reporter covering some of the worst back alleys in New York City and three years as a mother who, like most, would lay down her life for her kids.

Simply put, I am opposed to the death penalty. I would tell that to any   4
judge or lawyer undertaking the voir dire of jury candidates in a state in which the death penalty can be imposed. That is why I would be excused from such a jury. In a rational, completely cerebral way, I think the killing of one human being as punishment for the killing of another makes no sense and is inherently immoral.

But whenever my response to an important subject is rational and com-   5
pletely cerebral, I know there is something wrong with it—and so it is here.
I have always been governed by my gut, and my gut says I am hypocritical
about the death penalty. That is, I do not in theory think that Ted Bundy, or
others like him, should be put to death. But if my daughter had been the one
clubbed to death as she slept in a Tallahassee sorority house, and if the bite
mark left in her buttocks had been one of the prime pieces of evidence against
the young man charged with her murder, I would with the greatest pleasure
kill him myself.

The State of Florida will not permit the parents of Bundy's victims to do   6
that, and, in a way, that is the problem with an emotional response to capital
punishment. The only reason for a death penalty is to exact retribution. Is
there anyone who really thinks that it is a deterrent, that there are considerable numbers of criminals out there who think twice about committing
crimes because of the sentence involved? The ones I have met in the course
of my professional duties have either sneered at the justice system, where
they can exchange one charge for another with more ease than they could
return a shirt to clothing store, or they have simply believed that it is the
other guy who will get caught, get convicted, get the stiffest sentence. Of
course, the death penalty would act as a deterrent by eliminating recidivism,
but then so would life without parole, albeit at greater taxpayer expense.

I don't believe deterrence is what most proponents seek from the death   7
penalty anyhow. Our most profound emotional response is to want criminals
to suffer as their victims did. When a man is accused of throwing a child
from a high-rise terrace, my emotional—some might say hysterical—response is that he should be given an opportunity to see how endless the
seconds are from the 31st story to the ground. In a civilized society that will
never happen. And so what many people want from the death penalty, they
will never get.

Death is death, you may say, and you would be right. But anyone who has   8
seen someone die suddenly of a heart attack and someone else slip slowly
into the clutches of cancer knows that there are gradations of dying.

I watched a television re-enactment one night of an execution by lethal   9
injection. It was well done; it was horrible. The methodical approach, people
standing around the gurney waiting, made it more awful. One moment there
was a man in a prone position; the next moment that man was gone. On
another night I watched a television movie about a little boy named Adam
Walsh, who disappeared from a shopping center in Florida. There was a re-
enactment of Adam's parents coming to New York, where they appeared on
morning talk shows begging for their son's return, and in their hotel room,
where they received a call from the police saying that Adam had been found:
not all of Adam, actually, just his severed head, discovered in the waters of a
Florida canal. There is nothing anyone could do that is bad enough for an
adult who took a 6-year-old boy away from his parents, perhaps tortured,
then murdered, him and cut off his head. Nothing at all. Lethal injection? The
electric chair? Bah.

And so I come back to the position that the death penalty is wrong, not   10
only because it consists of stooping to the level of the killers, but also because it is not what it seems. Just before Ted Bundy's most recent execution
date was postponed, pending further appeals, the father of his last known
victim, a 12-year-old girl, said what almost every father in his situation must
feel. "I wish they'd bring him back to Lake City," said Tom Leach of the town
where Kimberly Leach lived and died, "and let us all have at him." But the
death penalty does not let us all have at him in the way Mr. Leach seems to
mean. What he wants is for something as horrifying as what happened to his
child to happen to Ted Bundy. And that is impossible.

QUESTIONS FOR MEANING

1. What does Quindlen mean by "60s liberalism" in paragraph 3?
2. If you never heard of Ted Bundy, what have you learned about him from
   this essay?
3. What does this essay reveal about its author? What information about herself does Quindlen include within her argument?
4. In paragraph 6, Quindlen claims, "The only reason for a death penalty is
   to exact retribution." Is this true?
5. Explain what Quindlen means by "gradations of dying" in paragraph 8.
6. Why does Quindlen believe that the death penalty "is not what it seems"?
7. Vocabulary: voir dire (4), cerebral (4), albeit (6), recidivism (6), gurney
   (9), prone (9).

QUESTIONS ABOUT STRATEGY

1. Why does Quindlen begin her essay by identifying herself with the victims
   of Ted Bundy?
2. Where does Quindlen use specific details to convey the brutality of murder?
3. What does Quindlen gain from revealing that she has mixed feelings about
   capital punishment? Does this admission help or hurt her argument?
4. Quindlen claims that the death penalty is wrong because "it consists of
   stooping to the level of the killers" and because it does not make criminals
   "suffer as their victims did." In citing these two reasons, has Quindlen
   contradicted herself?

MARGARET MEAD
A Life for a Life: What That Means Today

*Margaret Mead (1901–1978) was one of the first women to earn an interna-
tional reputation in anthropology, a field that had been previously dominated
by men—with the notable exception of Ruth Benedict, under whom Mead studied at Columbia University. She was still in her twenties when she published
her most famous book,* Coming of Age in Samoa *(1928). Presenting an idyllic
view of life in the South Pacific, Mead explored the relationship between child
rearing and group cultures, arguing that Americans could learn much from
cultures entirely different from our own. Although modern anthropologists now
question the validity of Mead's early research, she is still respected as one of the
most accomplished women of her generation.*

*Mead's interests were not confined to anthropology but extended to psychol-
ogy, economics, and a wide variety of social problems. She was opposed to capital punishment, and welcomed the 1972 Supreme Court decision that struck
down all existing laws under which men and women could be sentenced to
death. In this historic ruling, referred to as* Furman v. Georgia *after the case
which inspired it, the Court declared that the death penalty was unfair because
it was applied haphazardly. However, the Court allowed states the opportunity
to reestablish capital punishment by writing new laws that would be clear and
nondiscriminatory. Many states began to do so, and the long national debate on
capital punishment gathered new force. Mead contributed to that debate with
the following essay, published in* **1978** *shortly before her death.*

As Americans we have declared ourselves to be champions of human rights   1
in the world at large. But at home . . .

At home the Congress and the majority of our state legislatures have been   2
hurrying to pass new laws to ensure that persons convicted of various violent
crimes (but not the same ones in all states) may be—or must be—executed.

In my view, it is a sorry spectacle to see a great nation publicly proclaim-   3
ing efforts to modify violence and to protect human rights in distant parts of
the world and at the same time devoting an inordinate amount of time and
energy at every level of government to ensure that those men and women
convicted of capital offenses will be condemned to death and executed. Decisions to carry out such vengeful, punitive measures against our own people
would reverberate around the world, making a cold mockery of our very real
concern for human rights and our serious efforts to bring about peace and
controlled disarmament among nations.

If we do in fact take seriously our chosen role as champions of human   4
rights, then certainly we must also reinterpret drastically the very ancient
law of "a life for a life" as it affects human beings in our own society today.
I see this as a major challenge, especially for modern women.

But first we must understand where we are now.   5

In the late 1960s we lived through a kind of twilight period when without   6
any changes in our laws, men and women were condemned to death but the
sentences were not carried out. Those who had been condemned were left
to sit and wait—often for years.

In 1972 there was a brief period when it seemed that capital punishment   7
had finally been abolished in the whole United States, as it has been in most
of the modern countries of western Europe and in many other countries. For
then, in the case of *Furman v. Georgia,* the Supreme Court of the United
States ruled that existing laws whereby certain convicted criminals were condemned to death were haphazard and arbitrary in their application and constituted cruel and unusual punishment, which is prohibited by the Eighth
Amendment to the Constitution. True, the Court was divided; even the five
justices who supported the ruling were quite sharply divided in their reasoning. Nevertheless, *Furman v. Georgia* saved the lives of 631 persons in prisons across the country who were under sentence of death.

It seemed that we had passed a watershed.   8

But we were quickly disillusioned. The Supreme Court had not yet abol-   9
ished capital punishment; the justices merely had ruled out the discriminatory manner in which the current laws were applied. As Justice William O.
Douglas pointed out in his concurring opinion, the existing system allowed
"the penalty to be discriminatorily and disproportionately applied to the poor,
the Blacks and the members of unpopular groups."

In response, lawmakers in many states—often pushed by their constitu-   10
ents and by law-enforcement agencies—tried to meet the objections by means
of new and contrasting laws. Some of these laws made the death penalty
mandatory; no exceptions or mitigating circumstances were possible. Others
made the death penalty discretionary, that is, they provided very specific
guidelines for defining mitigating circumstances that should be taken into
account. The reason was that experts differed radically in their opinions as
to what the justices of the Supreme Court would find acceptable in revised
laws.

In their haste, these lawmakers missed their chance to think in quite other   11
terms.

Meanwhile, of course, cases were tried and a few women and many men   12
were once more condemned. In July, 1976, the principles underlying the new
laws were tested as the Supreme Court of the United States announced rulings in five of these cases, upholding three discretionary death-penalty statutes and ruling against two that imposed mandatory capital punishment. As
a result, the death sentences of 389 persons in 19 states were later reduced
to life imprisonment.

But the lawmaking and the convictions have continued. At the end of 1977,   13
the number of condemned prisoners in the death rows of penitentiaries in
the 33 states that then had capital punishment laws amounted to 407—five
women and 402 men—divided almost evenly between white Americans and
Black or Hispanic Americans. Two were Native Americans—Indians—and

concerning six, even this meager background information was lacking. Most were poor and ill educated, too unimportant to be permitted to enter into plea bargaining and too poor to hire the expensive legal talent that makes possible very different treatment in the courts for more affluent and protected individuals.

In early 1977 one man, Gary Gilmore, whose two attempts at suicide were given extravagant publicity, finally was executed in the midst of glaring national publicity in the mass media. Looking back at this one sordidly exploited event, can anyone picture how we would react if, without discussion, it were suddenly decided to execute *all* the death row prisoners who were without resources to prolong their lives?   14

What we are much more likely to do, I think, is to seesaw between the old, old demand for drastic retribution for crimes against human beings that very rightly rouse us to anger, fear and disgust and our rather special American belief that almost everyone (except the suspected criminal we catch on the run and kill forthwith) is entitled to a second chance. So we make harsh laws, convict some of the people who break them—and then hesitate. What next?   15

Every month the number of those convicted, sentenced and waiting grows. Violent criminals, they become the victims of our very ambiguous attitudes toward violence and our unwillingness to face the true issues.   16

The struggle for and against the abolition of capital punishment has been going on in our country and among enlightened peoples everywhere for well over a century. In the years before the Civil War the fight to end the death penalty was led in America by men like Horace Greeley, who also was fighting strongly to abolish slavery, and by a tiny handful of active women like New England's Dorothea Dix, who was fighting for prison reform. In those years three states—Michigan in 1847, Rhode Island in 1852 and Wisconsin in 1853—renounced the use of capital punishment, the first jurisdictions in the modern world to do so.   17

Both sides claim a primary concern for human rights. Those who demand that we keep—and carry out—the death penalty speak for the victims of capital crimes, holding that it is only just that murderers, kidnapers, rapists, hijackers and other violent criminals should suffer for the harm they have done and so deter others from committing atrocious crimes.   18

In contrast, those who demand that we abolish capital punishment altogether are convinced that violence breeds violence—that the death penalty carried out by the State against its own citizens in effect legitimizes willful killing. Over time, their concern has been part of a much more inclusive struggle for human rights and human dignity. They were among those who fought against slavery and they have been among those who have fought for the civil rights of Black Americans, of immigrants and of ethnic minorities and Native Americans, for the rights of prisoners of war as well as for the prisoners in penitentiaries, for the rights of the poor, the unemployed and the unemployable, for women's rights and for the rights of the elderly and of children.   19

Now, I believe, we can—if we will—put this all together and realize that   20
in our kind of civilization "a life for a life" need not mean destructive retribution, but instead the development of new forms of community in which,
because all lives are valuable, what is emphasized is the prevention of crime
and the protection of all those who are vulnerable.

The first step is to realize that in our society we have permitted the kinds   21
of vulnerability that characterize the victims of violent crime and have ignored, where we could, the hostility and alienation that enter into the making
of violent criminals. No rational person condones violent crime, and I have
no patience with sentimental attitudes toward violent criminals. But it is time
that we open our eyes to the conditions that foster violence and that ensure
the existence of easily recognizable victims.

Americans respond generously—if not always wisely—to the occurrence   22
of natural catastrophes. But except where we are brought face to face with
an unhappy individual or a family in trouble, we are turned off by the hu-
manly far more desperate social catastrophes of children who are trashed by
the schools—and the local community—where they should be learning for
themselves what it means and how it feels to be a valued human being. We
demean the men and women who are overwhelmed by their inability to meet
their responsibilities to one another or even to go it alone, and we shut out
awareness of the fate of the unskilled, the handicapped and the barely tolerated elderly. As our own lives have become so much more complex and
our social ties extraordinarily fragile, we have lost any sense of community
with others whose problems and difficulties and catastrophes are not our
own.

We do know that human lives are being violated—and not only by crimi-   23
nals. But at least we can punish criminals. That is a stopgap way. But it is
not the way out of our dilemma.

We also know that in any society, however organized, security rests on   24
accepted participation—on what I have called here a sense of community in
which everyone shares.

Up to the present, the responsibility for working out and maintaining the   25
principles on which any code of law must depend and for the practical administration of justice has been primarily a male preoccupation. At best, women
working within this framework have been able sometimes to modify and
sometimes to mitigate the working of the system of law.

Now, however, if the way out is for us to place the occurrence of crime   26
and the fate of the victim and of the criminal consciously within the context
of our way of living and our view of human values, then I believe liberated
women have a major part to play and a wholly new place to create for themselves in public life as professional women, as volunteers and as private citizens concerned with the quality of life in our nation. For it is women who
have constantly had to visualize in personal, human terms the relationships
between the intimate details of living and the setting in which living takes
place. And it is this kind of experience that we shall need in creating new
kinds of community.

Women working in new kinds of partnership with men should be able to   27
bring fresh thinking into law and the administration of justice with a greater
awareness of the needs of individuals at different stages of life and the po-
tentialities of social institutions in meeting those needs. What we shall be
working toward is a form of deterrence based not on fear of punishment—
which we know is ineffective, even when the punishment is the threat of
death—but on a shared way of living.

It will be a slow process at best to convince our fellow citizens that justice   28
and a decline in violence can be attained only by the development of communities in which the elderly and children, families and single persons, the
gifted, the slow and the handicapped can have a meaningful place and live
with dignity and in which rights and responsibilities are aspects of each other.
And I believe that we can make a start only if we have a long view, but know
very well that what we can do today and tomorrow and next year will not
bring us to utopia. We cannot establish instant security; we can only build
for it step by step.

We must also face the reality that as far as we can foresee there will   29
always be a need for places of confinement—prisons of different kinds, to be
frank—where individuals will have to be segregated for short periods, for
longer periods or even, for some, for a whole lifetime. The fear that the violent person will be set free in our communities (as we all know happens all
too often under our present system of law) is an important component in
the drive to strengthen—certainly not to abolish—the death penalty. For their
own protection as well as that of others, the few who cannot control their
violent impulses and, for the time being, the larger number who have become
hopelessly violent must be sequestered.

But we shall have to reconsider the whole question of what it means to   30
be confined under some form of restraint, whether for a short period or for
a lifetime. Clearly, prisons can no longer be set apart from the world. Prisoners must have some real and enduring relationship to a wider community
if they are to have and exercise human rights. Whether as a way station or
as a permanent way of living for a few persons, prison life must in some way
be meaningful.

There is today a Prisoners Union, organized by former prisoners as well   31
as a variety of local unions within many prisons. We shall have to draw on
the knowledge and experience of groups of this kind. Here again I believe
that women, who have not been regularly and professionally involved in traditional prison practices, may be freer to think and construct new practices
than male experts working alone.

The tasks are urgent and difficult. Realistically we know we cannot abolish   32
crime. But we can abolish crude and vengeful treatment of crime. We can
abolish—as a nation, not just state by state—capital punishment. We can
accept the fact that prisoners, convicted criminals, are hostages to our own
human failures to develop and support a decent way of living. And we can
accept the fact that we are responsible to them, as to all living beings, for
the protection of society, and especially responsible for those among us who
need protection for the sake of society.

QUESTIONS FOR MEANING

1. In paragraph 3, Mead refers to "human rights" and implies that capital punishment is a form of violence that violates these rights. What does she mean by this? Define "human rights" in your own words.
2. Why does Mead believe that women should be especially important in the movement to reform American justice?
3. Mead argues that "human lives are being violated—and not only by criminals." What does it mean to violate human life? Who does it besides criminals?
4. In her concluding paragraph, Mead argues that convicted criminals "are hostages to our own human failures to develop and support a decent way of living." Do you agree with this? If so, how would you define the "new forms of community" that Mead calls for?
5. Vocabulary: arbitrary (7), constituents (10), mitigating (10), discretionary (10), ambiguous (16), utopia (28), and sequestered (29).

QUESTIONS ABOUT STRATEGY

1. Is this essay addressed primarily to an audience of women? Does Mead's sense of audience limit the effectiveness of her argument?
2. Why does Mead devote paragraphs 6–17 to summarizing the history of capital punishment in America? Did you find this summary useful in understanding her argument?
3. In paragraphs 18 and 19, Mead contrasts people who favor capital punishment with people who oppose it. Does this comparison help or hurt her case?
4. Why does Mead link the rights of prisoners to "the rights of the poor, the unemployed and the unemployable?"
5. At what points in her essay does Mead claim to be writing objectively and realistically? Why does she feel it was necessary to reassure her audience in this way?

ERNEST VAN DEN HAAG
Death and Deterrence

Born in the Netherlands, Ernest van den Haag came to the United States in
1940. A practicing psychoanalyst, he has taught sociology and criminal justice
at Harvard, Yale, and the New School for Social Research. Through numerous
articles and many books, he has established himself as a conservative ideologue
who is willing to take unpopular stands and argue articulately for them. His
books include Passion and Social Restraint *(1963),* The Jewish Mystique *(1969),*
Political Violence and Civil Disobedience *(1972), and* Punishing Criminals: Concerning a Very Old and Painful Question *(1975). The following essay originally ap-*
peared in **1986** *in the* National Review, *a conservative magazine to which van*
den Haag is a regular contributor.

Professor Stephen K. Layson, an economist at the University of North Car-   1
olina at Greensboro, has published in the *Southern Economic Journal* (July
1985) a statistical study of the effects of executions on the murder rate. He
concluded that every execution of a murderer deters, on the average, 18
murders that would have occurred without it.

Layson also inquired into the effects of the arrest and conviction of mur-   2
derers on the murder rate. His correlations indicate that a 1 per cent increase in the clearance (arrest) rate for murder would lead to 250 fewer
murders per year. Currently the clearance rate is 75 per cent. Further, a 1
per cent increase in murder convictions would deter about 105 murders. Currently 38 per cent of all murders result in a conviction; 0.1 per cent of murders result in an execution.

Attempts to correlate murder to punishment rates have been made for a   3
long time. Most had flagrant defects. Some correlated murder rates to the
presence or absence of capital-punishment statutes—not to executions, which
alone matter. Others failed properly to isolate murder rates from variables
other than punishment, even when these variables were known to influence
murder rates. For instance, changes in the proportion of young males in the
population do influence murder rates regardless of executions, since most
murders are committed by young males. The first major statistical analysis
that properly handled all variables was published by Isaac Ehrlich in the
American Economic Review (June 1975). Ehrlich found that from 1933 to
1969 "an additional execution per year . . . may have resulted on the average
in seven or eight fewer murders."

Ehrlich's study went against the cherished beliefs of most social scientists   4
(after all, it confirmed what common sense tells us). A whole cottage industry arose to refute him. In turn he refuted the refuters. The verdict is inconclusive. As is often the case in statistical matters, if a different period is
analyzed, or some technical assumptions are changed, a different result is
produced. Thus the testimony of Professor Thorsten Sellin, given in 1953—

long before Ehrlich wrote—to the Royal Commission on Capital Punishment in Great Britain, still stands. Asked whether he could "conclude . . . that capital punishment has no deterrent effect," Sellin, an ardent but honest opponent of capital punishment, replied, "No, there is no such conclusion." Despite considerable advances in methods of analysis I think that, as yet, it has not been proved conclusively that capital punishment deters more than life imprisonment, or that it does not. However, the preponderance of evidence now does tend to show that capital punishment deters more than alternative punishments. Professor Layson's paper will add to that preponderance. But many attempts will be made to refute it, and, in all likelihood, the verdict will still be that the statistics are not conclusive.

What are we to deduce? Obviously people fear death more than life im-   5 prisonment. Only death is final. Where there is life there is hope. Actual murderers feel that way: 99.9 per cent prefer life imprisonment to death. So will prospective murderers. What is feared most deters most. Possibly, statistics do not show this clearly, because there are so few executions compared to the number of murders. It is even possible that the uncertain prospect of execution deters so few not already deterred by the prospect of life imprisonment that there is no statistical trace. Yet, if by executing convicted murderers there is any chance, even a mere possibility, of deterring future murderers, I think we should execute them. The life even of a few victims who may be spared seems infinitely precious to me. The life of the convicted murderer has but negative value. His crime has forfeited it.

Opponents of capital punishment usually admit that their opposition has   6 little to do with statistical data. When asked whether they would favor the death penalty if it were shown conclusively that each execution deters, say, one hundred murders, such opponents as Ramsey Clark (former U.S. attorney general) or Henry Schwarzschild (ACLU) resoundingly say no. But neither likes the inference that must be drawn: that he is more interested in keeping murderers alive than in sparing their victims, that he values the life of a convicted murderer more than the life of innocent victims. Those who do not share this bizarre valuation will favor capital punishment.

For beyond deterrence, or possible deterrence, there is justice. The thought   7 that the man who cruelly and deliberately slaughtered your child for fun or profit is entitled peacefully to live out his days at taxpayers' expense, playing tennis or baseball or enjoying the prison library, is hard to stomach. Wherefore about 75 per cent of Americans favor the death penalty, for the sake of justice, and to save innocent lives. I think they are right.

On occasion I have been presented with a hypothetical. Suppose, I have   8 been asked, that each execution were shown to raise rather than reduce the murder rate. Of course this is quite unlikely (wherefore there is no serious evidence): The more severe and certain the punishment, the less often the crime occurs, all other things being equal. The higher the price of anything, the less is bought. But, if one accepts, *arguendo,* the hypothetical, the answer depends on whether one prefers justice—which demands the execution of the murderer—or saving the lives that, by this hypothesis, could be saved by not executing him. I love justice, but I love innocent lives more. I would prefer to save them.

Fortunately we do not face this dilemma. On the contrary. Capital punish-   9
ment not only satisfies justice but is also more likely to save innocent lives than life imprisonment.

QUESTIONS FOR MEANING

1. According to van den Haag, has it ever been clearly established that capital punishment does not deter crime? Is he certain that it does?
2. Would van den Haag favor capital punishment even if it would not deter murder? Under what circumstances would he oppose the death penalty?
3. Can you explain what van den Haag means by "variables" in paragraph 3?
4. Why does van den Haag believe that the lives of convicted murderers have only "negative value"? Do you agree?
5. Vocabulary: correlations (2), flagrant (3), ardent (4), preponderance (4), resoundingly (6).

QUESTIONS ABOUT STRATEGY

1. Does van den Haag ever weaken his case through exaggeration?
2. Does van den Haag make any claims that he fails to support?
3. How would you describe the tone of this essay? Is it appropriate for the topic?

DAVID BRUCK
Decisions of Death

When the Supreme Court ruled against capital punishment in 1972, it did so because it believed that a penalty that is selectively applied amounts to "cruel and unusual punishment" which is prohibited by the Eighth Amendment. As Justice William O. Douglas wrote in his concurring opinion, "In a Nation committed to Equal Protection of the laws there is no permissible 'caste' aspect of law enforcement. Yet we know that the discretion of judges and juries in imposing the death penalty enables the penalty to be selectively applied, feeding prejudices against the accused if he is poor and despised, poor and lacking political clout, or if he is a member of a suspect or unpopular minority, and saving those who by social position may be in a more protected position." Although states that allow capital punishment have rewritten their laws since then, South Carolina attorney David Bruck has compiled evidence that suggests the death penalty is still unfair because it is still applied selectively. In his essay, which was first published in **1983,** *Bruck argues that capital punishment is a lottery rigged by race.*

There are 1,150 men and 13 women awaiting execution in the United States. It's not easy to imagine how many people 1,163 is. If death row were really a row, it would stretch for 1.3 miles, cell after six-foot-wide cell. In each cell, one person, sitting, pacing, watching TV, sleeping, writing letters. Locked in their cells nearly twenty-four hours a day, the condemned communicate with each other by shouts, notes, and hand-held mirrors, all with a casual dexterity that handicapped people acquire over time. Occasionally there is a break in the din of shouted conversations—a silent cell, its inhabitant withdrawn into a cocoon of madness. That's what death row would look like. That's what, divided up among the prisons of thirty-four states, it does look like.

This concentration of condemned people is unique among the democratic countries of the world. It is also nearly double the number of prisoners who were on death row in 1972 when the Supreme Court, in *Furman* v. *Georgia,* averted a massive surge of executions by striking down all the nation's capital punishment laws.

But in another sense, death row is very small. If every one of these 1,163 inmates were to be taken out of his or her cell tomorrow and gassed, electrocuted, hanged, shot, or injected, the total of convicted murderers imprisoned in this country would decline from some 33,526 (at last count) to 32,363—a reduction of a little over 3 percent. Huge as this country's death row population has become, it does not include—and has never included—more than a tiny fraction of those who are convicted of murder.

It falls to the judicial system of each of the thirty-eight states that retain capital punishment to cull the few who are to die from the many who are convicted of murder. This selection begins with the crime itself, as the community and the press react with outrage or with indifference, depending on the nature of the murder and the identity of the victim. With the arrest of a suspect, police and prosecutors must decide what charges to file, whether to seek the death penalty, and whether the defendant should be allowed to plea-bargain for his life. Most of these decisions can later be changed, so that at any point from arrest to trial the defendant's chances of slipping through the death penalty net depend on chance: the inclinations and ambitions of the local prosecutor, the legal and political pressures which impel him to one course of action or another, and the skill or incompetence of the court-appointed defense counsel.

In the courtroom, the defendant may be spared or condemned by the countless vagaries of the trial by jury. There are counties in each state where the juries almost always impose death, and counties where they almost never do. There are hanging judges and lenient judges, and judges who go one way or the other depending on who the victim's family happens to be, or the defendant's family, or who is prosecuting the case, or who is defending it.

Thus at each stage between arrest and sentence, more and more defendants are winnowed out from the ranks of those facing possible execution: in 1979, a year which saw more than eighteen thousand arrests for intentional homicides and nearly four thousand murder convictions throughout the United States, only 159 defendants were added to death row. And even for those few who are condemned to die, there lies ahead a series of appeals which whittle down the number of condemned still further, sparing some and consigning others to death on the basis of appellate courts' judgments of the nuances of a trial judge's instructions to the jury, of whether the court-appointed defense lawyer had made the proper objections at the proper moments during the trial, and so on. By the time the appeals process has run its course, almost every murder defendant who faced the possibility of execution when he was first arrested has by luck, justice, or favor evaded execution, and a mere handful are left to die.

This process of selection is the least understood feature of capital punishment. Because the media focus on the cases where death has been imposed and where the executions are imminent, the public sees capital punishment not as the maze-like system that it is, but only in terms of this or that individual criminal, about to suffer just retribution for a particular crime. What we don't see in any of this now-familiar drama are hundreds of others whose crimes were as repugnant, but who are jailed for life or less instead of condemned to death. So the issues appear simple. The prisoner's guilt is certain. His crime is horrendous. Little knots of "supporters" light candles and hold vigils. His lawyers rush from court to court raising arcane new appeals.

The condemned man himself remembers the many points of his procession through the judicial system at which he might have been spared, but was not. He knows, too, from his years of waiting in prison, that most of those who committed crimes like his have evaded the execution that awaits him. So do the prosecutors who have pursued him through the court system, and the judges who have upheld his sentence. And so do the defense lawyers, the ones glimpsed on the TV news in the last hours, exhausted and overwrought for reasons that, given their client's crimes, must be hard for most people to fathom.

I am one of those lawyers, and I know the sense of horror that propels   9
those last-minute appeals. It is closely related to the horror that violent crime awakens in all of us—the random kind of crime, the sniper in the tower or the gunman in the grocery store. The horror derives not from death, which comes to us all, but from death that is inflicted *at random,* for no reason, for being on the wrong subway platform or the wrong side of the street. Up close, that is what capital punishment is like. And that is what makes the state's inexorable, stalking pursuit of this or that particular person's life so chilling.

The lawyers who bring those eleventh-hour appeals know from their work   10
how many murderers are spared, how few are sentenced to die, and how chance and race decide which will be which. In South Carolina, where I practice law, murders committed during robberies may be punished by death. According to police reports, there were 286 defendants arrested for such murders from the time that South Carolina's death penalty law went into effect in 1977 until the end of 1981. (About a third of those arrests were of blacks charged with killing whites.) Out of all of those 286 defendants, the prosecution had sought the death penalty and obtained final convictions by the end of 1981 against 37. And of those 37 defendants, death sentences were imposed and affirmed on only 4; the rest received prison sentences. What distinguished those 4 defendants' cases was this: 3 were black, had killed white storeowners, and were tried by all-white juries; the fourth, a white, was represented at his trial by a lawyer who had never read the state's murder statute, had no case file and no office, and had refused to talk to his client for the last two months prior to the trial because he'd been insulted by the client's unsuccessful attempt to fire him.

If these four men are ultimately executed, the newspapers will report and   11
the law will record that they went to their deaths because they committed murder and robbery. But when so many others who committed the same crime were spared, it can truthfully be said only that these four men were *convicted* because they committed murder; they were *executed* because of race, or bad luck, or both.

If one believes, as many do, that murderers deserve whatever punishment   12
they get, then none of this should matter. But if the 1,163 now on death row throughout the United States had actually been selected by means of a lottery from the roughly 33,500 inmates now serving sentences for murder, most Americans, whatever their views on capital punishment as an abstract matter, would surely be appalled. This revulsion would be all the stronger if we limited the pool of those murderers facing execution by restricting it to blacks. Or if we sentenced people to die on the basis of the race of the *victim,* consigning to death only those—whatever their race—who have killed whites, and sparing all those who have killed blacks.

The reason why our sense of justice rebels at such ideas is not hard to   13
identify. Violent crime undermines the sense of order and shared moral val-

ues without which no society could exist. We punish people who commit such crimes in order to reaffirm our standards of right and wrong, and our belief that life in society can be orderly and trusting rather than fearful and chaotic. But if the punishment itself is administered chaotically or arbitrarily, it fails in its purpose and becomes, like the crime which triggered it, just another spectacle of the random infliction of suffering—all the more terrifying and demoralizing because this time the random killer is organized society itself, the same society on which we depend for stability and security in our daily lives. No matter how much the individual criminal thus selected for death may "deserve" his punishment, the manner of its imposition robs it of any possible value, and leaves us ashamed instead of reassured.

It was on precisely this basis, just eleven years ago, that the Supreme   14
Court in *Furman* v. *Georgia* struck down every death penalty law in the United States, and set aside the death sentences of more than six hundred death row inmates. *Furman* was decided by a single vote (all four Nixon appointees voting to uphold the death penalty laws), and though the five majority justices varied in their rationales, the dominant theme of their opinions was that the Constitution did not permit the execution of a capriciously selected handful out of all those convicted of capital crimes. For Justice Byron White and the rest of the *Furman* majority, years of reading the petitions of the condemned had simply revealed "no meaningful basis for distinguishing the few cases in which [death] is imposed from the many in which it is not." Justice Potter Stewart compared the country's capital sentencing methods to being struck by lightning, adding that "if any basis can be discerned for the selection of these few to be sentenced to die, it is on the constitutionally impermissible basis of race." Justice William O. Douglas summarized the issue by observing that the Constitution would never permit any law which stated

> that anyone making more than $50,000 would be exempt from the death penalty . . . [nor] a law that in terms said that blacks, those that never went beyond the fifth grade in school, those who made less than $3,000 a year, or those who were unpopular or unstable would be the only people executed. *A law which in the overall view reaches that result in practice has no more sanctity than a law which in terms provides the same.* [Emphasis added.]

On the basis of these views, the Supreme Court in *Furman* set aside   15
every death sentence before it, and effectively cleared off death row. Though *Furman* v. *Georgia* did not outlaw the death penalty as such, the Court's action came at a time when America appeared to have turned against capital punishment, and *Furman* seemed to climax a long and inexorable progression toward abolition. After *Furman*, Chief Justice Warren E. Burger, who had dissented from the Court's decision, predicted privately that there would never be another execution in the United States.

What happened instead was that the majority of state legislatures passed   16
new death sentencing laws designed to satisfy the Supreme Court. By this
year, eleven years after *Furman*, there are roughly as many states with capital punishment laws on the books as there were in 1972.

In theory the capital sentencing statutes under which the 1,163 prisoners   17
now on death row were condemned are very different from the death penalty
laws in effect prior to 1972. Under the pre-*Furman* laws, the process of
selection was simple: the jury decided whether the accused was guilty of
murder, and if so, whether he should live or die. In most states, no separate
sentencing hearing was held: jurors were supposed to determine both guilt
and punishment at the same time, often without benefit of any information
about the background or circumstances of the defendant whose life was in
their hands. Jurors were also given no guidelines or standards with which to
assess the relative gravity of the case before them, but were free to base
their life-or-death decision on whatever attitudes or biases they happened to
have carried with them into the jury room. These statutes provided few grounds
for appeal and worked fast: as late as the 1950s, many prisoners were executed within a few weeks of their trials, and delays of more than a year or
two were rare.

In contrast, the current crop of capital statutes have created complex,   18
multitiered sentencing schemes based on lists of specified "aggravating" and
"mitigating" factors which the jury is to consider in passing sentence. Sentencing now occurs at a separate hearing after guilt has been determined.
The new statutes also provide for automatic appeal to the state supreme
courts, usually with a requirement that the court determine whether each
death sentence is excessive considering the defendant and the crime.

The first of these new statutes—from Georgia, Florida, and Texas—came   19
before the Supreme Court for review in 1976. The new laws were different
from one another in several respects—only Georgia's provided for case-by-
case review of the appropriateness of each death sentence by the state supreme court; Florida's permitted the judge to sentence a defendant to death
even where the jury had recommended a life sentence; and the Texas statute
determined who was to be executed on the basis of the jury's answer to the
semantically perplexing question of whether the evidence established "beyond a reasonable doubt" a "probability" that the defendant would commit
acts of violence in the future. What these statutes all had in common, however, was some sort of criteria, however vague, to guide juries and judges in
their life-or-death decisions, while permitting capital defendants a chance to
present evidence to show why they should be spared. Henceforth—or so
went the theory behind these new laws—death sentences could not be imposed randomly or on the basis of the race or social status of the defendant
and the victim, but only on the basis of specific facts about the crime, such
as whether the murder had been committed during a rape or a robbery, or
whether it had been "especially heinous, atrocious and cruel" (in Florida), or
"outrageously or wantonly vile, horrible or inhuman" (in Georgia).

After considering these statutes during the spring of 1976, the Supreme   20
Court announced in *Gregg* v. *Georgia* and two other cases that the new laws
satisfied its concern, expressed in *Furman,* about the randomness and un-
fairness of the previous death sentencing systems. Of course, the Court had
no actual evidence that these new laws were being applied any more equally
or consistently than the ones struck down in *Furman.* But for that matter,
the Court had not relied on factual evidence in *Furman,* either. Although
social science research over the previous thirty years had consistently found
the nation's use of capital punishment to be characterized by arbitrariness
and racial discrimination, the decisive opinions of Justices White and Stewart
in *Furman* cited none of this statistical evidence, but relied instead on the
justices' own conclusions derived from years of experience with the appeals
of the condemned. The *Furman* decision left the Court free to declare the
problem solved later on. And four years later, in *Gregg* v. *Georgia,* that is
what it did.

It may be, of course, that the Court's prediction in *Gregg* of a new era of   21
fairness in capital sentencing was a sham, window dressing for what was in
reality nothing more than a capitulation to the mounting public clamor for a
resumption of executions. But if the justices sincerely believed that new legal
guidelines and jury instructions would really solve the problems of arbitrariness and racial discrimination in death penalty cases, they were wrong.

Before John Spenkelink—a white murderer of a white victim—was exe-   22
cuted by the state of Florida in May 1979, his lawyers tried to present to the
state and federal courts a study which showed that the "new" Florida death
penalty laws, much like the ones which they had replaced, were being applied far more frequently against persons who killed whites than against those
who killed blacks. The appeals courts responded that the Supreme Court had
settled all of these arguments in 1976 when it upheld the new sentencing
statutes: the laws were fair because the Supreme Court had said they were
fair; mere evidence to the contrary was irrelevant.

After Spenkelink was electrocuted, the evidence continued to mount. In   23
1980 two Northeastern University criminologists, William Bowers and Glenn
Pierce, published a study of homicide sentencing in Georgia, Florida, and
Texas, the three states whose new death penalty statutes were the first to
be approved by the Supreme Court after *Furman.* Bowers and Pierce tested
the Supreme Court's prediction that these new statutes would achieve consistent and evenhanded sentencing by comparing the lists of which convicted
murderers had been condemned and which spared with the facts of their
crimes as reported by the police. What they found was that in cases where
white victims had been killed, black defendants in all three states were from
four to six times more likely to be sentenced to death than were white defendants. Both whites and blacks, moreover, faced a much greater danger of
being executed where the murder victims were white than where the victims
were black. A black defendant in Florida was thirty-seven times more likely
to be sentenced to death if his victim was white than if his victim was black;
in Georgia, black-on-white killings were punished by death thirty-three times

more often than were black-on-black killings; and in Texas, the ratio climbed to an astounding 84 to 1. Even when Bowers and Pierce examined only those cases which the police had reported as "felony-circumstance" murders (i.e., cases involving kidnapping or rape, and thus excluding mere domestic and barroom homicides), they found that both the race of the defendant and the race of the victim appeared to produce enormous disparities in death sentences in each state.

A more detailed analysis of charging decisions in several Florida counties even suggested that prosecutors tended to "upgrade" murders of white victims by alleging that they were more legally aggravated than had been apparent to the police who had written up the initial report, while "downgrading" murders of black victims in a corresponding manner, apparently to avoid the expensive and time-consuming process of trying such murders of blacks as capital cases. Their overall findings, Bowers and Pierce concluded, 24

> are consistent with a single underlying racist tenet: that white lives are worth more than black lives. From this tenet it follows that death as punishment is more appropriate for the killers of whites than for the killers of blacks and more appropriate for black than for white killers.

Such stark evidence of discrimination by race of offender and by race of victim, they wrote, is "a direct challenge to the constitutionality of the post-*Furman* capital statutes . . . [and] may represent a two-edged sword of racism in capital punishment which is beyond statutory control."

This new data was presented to the federal courts by attorneys for a Georgia death row inmate named John Eldon Smith in 1981. The court of appeals replied that the studies were too crude to have any legal significance, since they did not look at all the dozens of circumstances of each case, other than race, that might have accounted for the unequal sentencing patterns that Bowers and Pierce had detected. 25

The matter might have ended there, since the court's criticism implied that only a gargantuan (and extremely expensive) research project encompassing the most minute details of many hundreds of homicide cases would be worthy of its consideration. But as it happened, such a study was already under way, supported by a foundation grant and directed by University of Iowa law professor David Baldus. Using a staff of law students and relying primarily on official Georgia state records, Baldus gathered and coded more than 230 factual circumstances surrounding each of more than a thousand homicides, including 253 death penalty sentencing proceedings conducted under Georgia's current death penalty law. Baldus's results, presented in an Atlanta federal court hearing late last summer, confirmed that among defendants convicted of murdering whites, blacks are substantially more likely to go to death row than are whites. Although blacks account for some 60 percent of Georgia homicide victims, Baldus found that killers of black victims are punished by death less than one-tenth as often as are killers of white 26 victims. With the scientific precision of an epidemiologist seeking to pinpoint the cause of a new disease, Baldus analyzed and reanalyzed his mountain of data on Georgia homicides, controlling for the hundreds of factual variables in each case, in search of any explanation other than race which might account for the stark inequalities in the operation of Georgia's capital sentencing system. He could find none. And when the state of Georgia's turn came to defend its capital sentencing record at the Atlanta federal court hearing, it soon emerged that the statisticians hired by the state to help it refute Baldus's research had had no better success in *their* search for an alternative explanation. (In a telephone interview after the Atlanta hearing, the attorney general of Georgia, Michael Bowers, assured me that "the bottom line is that Georgia does not discriminate on the basis of race," but referred all specific questions to his assistant, who declined to answer on the grounds that the court proceeding was pending.)

The findings of research efforts like Baldus's document what anyone who   27
has worked in the death-sentencing system will have sensed all along: the Supreme Court notwithstanding, there is no set of courtroom procedures set out in lawbooks which can change the prosecution practices of local district attorneys. Nor will even the most elaborate jury instructions ever ensure that an all-white jury will weigh a black life as heavily as a white life.

At bottom, the determination of whether or not a particular defendant   28
should die for his crime is simply not a rational decision. Requiring that the jury first determine whether his murder was "outrageously or wantonly vile, horrible, or inhuman," as Georgia juries are invited to do, provides little assurance that death will be imposed fairly and consistently. Indeed, Baldus's research revealed that Georgia juries are more likely to find that a given murder was "outrageously or wantonly vile, horrible, or inhuman" when the victim was white, and likelier still when the murderer is black—hardly a vindication of the Supreme Court's confidence in *Gregg* v. *Georgia* that such guidelines would serve to eliminate racial discrimination in sentencing.

At present, 51 percent of the inhabitants of death row across the country   29
are white, as were seven of the eight men executed since the Supreme Court's *Gregg* decision. Five percent of the condemned are Hispanic, and almost all of the remaining 44 percent are black. Since roughly half the people arrested and charged with intentional homicide each year in the United States are white, it would appear at first glance that the proportions of blacks and whites now on Death Row are about those that would be expected from a fair system of capital sentencing. But what studies like Baldus's now reveal is how such seemingly equitable racial distribution can actually be the product of racial discrimination, rather than proof that discrimination has been overcome.

The explanation for this seeming paradox is that the judicial system dis-   30
criminates on the basis of the race of the *victim* as well as the race of the defendant. Each year, according to the F.B.I.'s crime report, about the same numbers of blacks as whites are arrested for murder throughout the United States, and the totals of black and white murder victims are also roughly

equal. But like many other aspects of American life, our murders are segregated: white murderers almost always kill whites, and the large majority of black killers kill blacks. While blacks who kill whites tend to be singled out for harsher treatment—and more death sentences—than other murderers, there are relatively few of them, and so the absolute effect on the numbers of blacks sent to death row is limited. On the other hand, the far more numerous black murderers whose victims were also black are treated relatively leniently in the courts, and are only rarely sent to death row. Because these dual systems of discrimination operate simultaneously, they have the overall effect of keeping the numbers of blacks on death row roughly proportionate to the numbers of blacks convicted of murder—even while individual defendants are being condemned, and others spared, on the basis of race. In short, like the man who, with one foot in ice and the other in boiling water, describes his situation as "comfortable on average," the death sentencing system has created an illusion of fairness.

In theory, law being based on precedent, the Supreme Court might be   31
expected to apply the principles of the *Furman* decision as it did in 1972 and strike down death penalty laws which have produced results as seemingly racist as these. But that's not going to happen. *Furman* was a product of its time: in 1972 public support for the death penalty had been dropping fairly steadily over several decades, and capital punishment appeared to be going the way of the stocks, the whipping post, the White and Colored drinking fountains. The resurgence of support for capital punishment in the country over the last decade has changed that, at least for now. Last summer the Supreme Court upheld every one of the four death sentences it had taken under consideration during its 1982–83 session, and in November the Court heard arguments by California in support of its claim that the states should not be required to compare murder sentences on a statewide basis in order to assure fairness in capital sentencing. The justices may have given an indication of their eventual decision on California's appeal when, just three hours before they heard that case, they lifted a stay of execution in a Louisiana case where a condemned prisoner named Robert Wayne Williams had been attempting to challenge the very limited method of comparison used by the Louisiana courts: as a result, Williams may well be dead by the time the California decision is handed down this spring. When in 1972 the Supreme Court was faced with a choice between fairness and the death penalty, it chose fairness. This time the odds are all with the death penalty.*

Even with the Court's increasingly hard-line stance on capital appeals, there   32
will probably not be any sudden surge of executions in the next year or two. One of the unreckoned costs of the death penalty is the strain it places on the state and federal judicial systems. Any large number of imminent executions would overload those systems to the point of breakdown. A great deal

---

*In late 1986, the Supreme Court considered an argument against capital punishment based on the Baldus study cited on pp. 175–76. This case *(McCleskey v. Kemp)* was decided April 22, 1987, with the Court ruling to uphold capital punishment as administered in the state of Georgia [editor's note].

is being said nowadays about the need to speed up capital appeals: Justice Lewis Powell even added his voice to the chorus last spring at the very moment that the Supreme Court had the question of stays of execution under consideration in a pending case. But this attitude tends to moderate the closer one gets to a specific case. No judge wants to discover after it's too late that he permitted someone to be executed on the basis of factual or legal error, and for that reason alone the backlog of death row prisoners can be expected to persist.

Still, the pace of executions is going to pick up to a more or less steady   33 trickle: possibly one a month, possibly two, maybe more. In September Mississippi's William Winter became the first governor since Ronald Reagan to permit an execution by lethal gas: Jimmy Lee Gray died banging his head against a steel pole in the gas chamber while the reporters counted his moans (eleven, according to the Associated Press). A month later, J. D. Autry came within minutes of dying by lethal injection in Texas, only to have Supreme Court Justice Byron White reverse his decision of the day before and stay the execution. Now Autry is reprieved until the Supreme Court decides whether California (and by implication Texas) must compare capital sentences to ensure some measure of fairness: if the Court rules that they don't have to, Autry will in all likelihood be executed next year.

So far, the power of the death penalty as a social symbol has shielded   34 from scrutiny the huge demands in money and resources which the death sentencing process makes on the criminal justice system as a whole. Whatever the abstract merits of capital punishment, there is no denying that a successful death penalty prosecution costs a fortune. A 1982 study in New York state concluded that just the trial and first stage of appeal in a death penalty case under that state's proposed death penalty bill would cost the taxpayers of New York over $1.8 million—more than twice as much as imprisoning the defendant for life. And even that estimate does not include the social costs of diverting an already overburdened criminal justice system from its job of handling large numbers of criminal cases to a preoccupation with the relative handful of capital ones. But the question of just how many laid-off police officers one execution is worth won't come up so long as the death penalty remains for most Americans a way of expressing feelings rather than a practical response to the problem of violent crime.

It is impossible to predict how long the executions will continue. The rise   35 in violent crime in this country has already begun to abate somewhat, probably as a result of demographic changes as the baby boom generation matures beyond its crime-prone teenage and early adult years. But it may well turn out that even a marked reduction in the crime rate won't produce any sharp decrease in public pressure for capital punishment: the shift in public opinion on the death penalty seems to have far deeper roots than that. The death penalty has become a potent social symbol of national resolve, another way of saying that we're not going to be pushed around anymore, that we've got the willpower and self-confidence to stand up to anyone, whether muggers or Cubans or Islamic fanatics, that we're not the flaccid weaklings that "they" have been taking us for. The death penalty can only be understood as one of the so-called "social issues" of the Reagan era: it bears no more relationship to the problem of crime than school prayer bears to the improvement of public education. Over the past half-century, executions were at their peak during the Depression of the 1930s, and almost disappeared during the boom years of the 1950s and early 1960s. The re-emergence of the death penalty in the 1970s coincided with the advent of chronic inflation and recession, and with military defeat abroad and the decline of the civil rights movement at home. Given this historical record, it's a safe bet that whether the crime rates go up or down over the next several years, public support for executions will start to wane only as the country finds more substantial foundations for a renewal of confidence in its future.

In the meantime we will be the only country among all the Western industrial democracies which still executes its own citizens. Canada abolished capital punishment in 1976, as did France in 1981; England declined to bring back hanging just this summer. By contrast, our leading companions in the use of the death penalty as a judicial punishment for crime will be the governments of the Soviet Union, South Africa, Saudi Arabia, and Iran—a rogues' gallery of the most repressive and backward-looking regimes in the world. Just last week Christopher Wren reported in *The New York Times* that the total number of executions in the People's Republic of China may reach five thousand or more this year alone.   36

It's no accident that democracies tend to abolish the death penalty while autocracies and totalitarian regimes tend to retain it. In his new book, *The Death Penalty: A Debate*, John Conrad credits Tocqueville with the explanation for this, quoting from *Democracy in America:*   37

> When all the ranks of a community are nearly equal, as all men think and feel in nearly the same manner, each of them may judge in a moment the sensations of all the others; he casts a rapid glance upon himself, and that is enough. There is no wretchedness into which he cannot readily enter, and a secret instinct reveals to him its extent . . . In democratic ages, men rarely sacrifice themselves for one another, but they display general compassion for the members of the human race. They inflict no useless ills, and they are happy to relieve the griefs of others when they can do so without much hurting themselves; they are not disinterested, but they are humane. . . .

Tocqueville went on to explain that his identification of America's democratic political culture as the root of the "singular mildness" of American penal practices was susceptible of an ironic proof: the cruelty with which Americans treated their black slaves. Restraint in punishment, he wrote, extends as far as our sense of social equality, and no further: "the same man who is full of humanity toward his fellow creatures when they are at the same time his equals becomes insensible to their affliction as soon as that equality ceases."   38

In that passage, written 150 years ago, Tocqueville reveals to us why it is   39
that the death penalty—the practice of slowly bringing a fully conscious human face to face with the prospect of his own extinction and then killing
him—should characterize the judicial systems of the least democratic and
most repressive nations of the world. And it reveals too why the vestiges of
this institution in America should be so inextricably entangled with the question of race. The gradual disappearance of the death penalty throughout most
of the democratic world certainly suggests that Tocqueville was right. The
day when Americans stop condemning people to death on the basis of race
and inequality will be the day when we stop condemning anyone to death
at all.

QUESTIONS FOR MEANING

1. Why does Bruck believe that capital punishment is like a lottery? In which
   paragraphs does he develop his argument that executions are determined
   by chance?
2. Explain the difference between capital punishment laws before and after
   1972. Where does Bruck summarize the difference for you?
3. What does Bruck mean when he writes that capital punishment "has become a potent social symbol of national resolve"?
4. Bruck makes the unusual argument that the death penalty is expensive, a
   charge that is often raised against sentencing men and women to life imprisonment. What evidence does he offer to support his claim?
5. Vocabulary: vagaries (5), winnowed (6), imminent (7), repugnant (7), arcane (7), inexorable (9), disparities (23), gargantuan (26), epidemiologist
   (26), abate (35), flaccid (35), and inextricably (39).

QUESTIONS ABOUT STRATEGY

1. Bruck begins his essay with a description of "death row." Is this an effective opening? Why?
2. Why does Bruck pause to tell us that Jimmy Lee Gray was reported to
   have moaned eleven times before dying in a Mississippi gas chamber? Do
   details of this sort help us to understand the reality of capital punishment
   or is Bruck simply playing on our feelings? Consider his use of detail
   throughout the essay.
3. In paragraph 9, Bruck reveals that he is a lawyer. Why do you think he
   makes this revelation? Does it lead you to take what he says more seriously? If so, why?
4. Bruck uses many statistics in the course of his essay. How much do they
   add to his argument?
5. At the conclusion of paragraph 31, Bruck writes, "When in 1972 the Supreme Court was faced with a choice between fairness and the death pen-

alty, it chose fairness." Is it fair to imply that capital punishment cannot be fair? Does Bruck succeed in persuading you of this?

6. How effective is the comparison Bruck draws between American penal laws and those of other countries?

WALTER BERNS
For Capital Punishment

Walter Berns is a well-known political scientist. He did graduate work at Reed College and the London School of Economics before receiving his Ph.D. from the University of Chicago in 1953. He has been the recipient of Carnegie, Fulbright, and Guggenheim fellowships and taught at Yale, Cornell, Georgetown, and the University of Toronto. A contributor to numerous anthologies and scholarly journals, he is the author of several books, including Freedom, Virtue, and the First Amendment *(1957),* Constitutional Cases in American Government *(1963), and* The First Amendment and the Future of American Government *(1976). The following essay is drawn from his book* For Capital Punishment: Crime and the Morality of the Death Penalty (*1979*).

Until recently, my business did not require me to think about the punish- 1
ment of criminals in general or the legitimacy and efficacy of capital punishment in particular. In a vague way, I was aware of the disagreement among professionals concerning the purpose of punishment—whether it was intended to deter others, to rehabilitate the criminal, or to pay him back—but like most laymen I had no particular reason to decide which purpose was right or to what extent they may all have been right. I did know that retribution was held in ill repute among criminologists and jurists—to them, retribution was a fancy name for revenge, and revenge was barbaric—and, of course, I knew that capital punishment had the support only of policemen, prison guards and some local politicians, the sort of people Arthur Koestler calls "hang hards" (Philadelphia's Mayor Rizzo comes to mind). The intellectual community denounced it as both unnecessary and immoral. It was the phenomenon of Simon Wiesenthal that allowed me to understand why the intellectuals were wrong and why the police, the politicians, and the majority of the voters were right: we punish criminals principally in order to pay them back, and we execute the worst of them out of moral necessity. Anyone who respects Wiesenthal's mission will be driven to the same conclusion.

Of course, not everyone will respect that mission. It will strike the busy 2
man—I mean the sort of man who sees things only in the light cast by a concern for his own interests—as somewhat bizarre. Why should anyone de-

vote his life—more than thirty years of it!—exclusively to the task of hunting down the Nazi war criminals who survived World War II and escaped punishment? Wiesenthal says his conscience forces him "to bring the guilty ones to trial." But why punish them? What do we hope to accomplish now by punishing SS Obersturmbannführer Adolph Eichmann or SS Obersturmführer Franz Stangl or someday—who knows?—Reichsleiter Martin Bormann? We surely don't expect to rehabilitate them, and it would be foolish to think that by punishing them we might thereby deter others. The answer, I think, is clear: We want to punish them in order *to pay them back.* We think they must be made to pay for their crimes with their lives, and we think that we, the survivors of the world they violated, may legitimately exact that payment because we, too, are their victims. By punishing them, we demonstrate that there are laws that bind men across generations as well as across (and within) nations, that we are not simply isolated individuals, each pursuing his selfish interests and connected with others by a mere contract to live and let live. To state it simply, Wiesenthal allows us to see that it is right, morally right, to be angry with criminals and to express that anger publicly, officially, and in an appropriate manner, which may require the worst of them to be executed.

Modern civil-libertarian opponents of capital punishment do not understand this. They say that to execute a criminal is to deny his human dignity; they also say that the death penalty is not useful, that nothing useful is accomplished by executing anyone. Being utilitarians, they are essentially selfish men, distrustful of passion, who do not understand the connection between anger and justice, and between anger and human dignity.   3

Anger is expressed or manifested on those occasions when someone has acted in a manner that is thought to be unjust, and one of its origins is the opinion that men are responsible, and should be held responsible, for what they do. Thus, as Aristotle teaches us, anger is accompanied not only by the pain caused by the one who is the object of anger, but by the pleasure arising from the expectation of inflicting revenge on someone who is thought to deserve it. We can become angry with an inanimate object (the door we run into and then kick in return) only by foolishly attributing responsibility to it, and we cannot do that for long, which is why we do not think of returning later to revenge ourselves on the door. For the same reason, we cannot be more than momentarily angry with any one creature other than man; only a fool or worse would dream of taking revenge on a dog. And, finally, we tend to pity rather than to be angry with men who—because they are insane, for example—are not responsible for their acts. Anger, then, is a very human passion not only because only a human being can be angry, but also because anger acknowledges the humanity of its objects: it holds them accountable for what they do. And in holding particular men responsible, it pays them the respect that is due them as men. Anger recognizes that only men have the capacity to be moral beings and, in so doing, acknowledges the dignity of human beings. Anger is somehow connected with justice, and it is this that   4 modern penology has not understood; it tends, on the whole, to regard anger as a selfish indulgence.

Anger can, of course, be that; and if someone does not become angry with an insult or an injury suffered unjustly, we tend to think he does not think much of himself. But it need not be selfish, not in the sense of being provoked only by an injury suffered by onself. There were many angry men in America when President Kennedy was killed; one of them—Jack Ruby—took it upon himself to exact the punishment that, if indeed deserved, ought to have been exacted by the law. There were perhaps even angrier men when Martin Luther King, Jr., was killed, for King, more than anyone else at the time, embodied a people's quest for justice; the anger—more, the "black rage"—expressed on that occasion was simply a manifestation of the great change that had occurred among black men in America, a change wrought in large part by King and his associates in the civil-rights movement: the servility and fear of the past had been replaced by pride and anger, and the treatment that had formerly been accepted as a matter of course or as if it were deserved was now seen for what it was, unjust and unacceptable. King preached love, but the movement he led depended on anger as well as love, and that anger was not despicable, being neither selfish nor unjustified. On the contrary, it was a reflection of what was called solidarity and may more accurately be called a profound caring for others, black for other blacks, white for blacks, and, in the world King was trying to build, American for other Americans. If men are not saddened when someone else suffers, or angry when someone else suffers unjustly, the implication is that they do not care for anyone other than themselves or that they lack some quality that befits a man. When we criticize them for this, we acknowledge that they ought to care for others. If men are not angry when a neighbor suffers at the hands of a criminal, the implication is that their moral faculties have been corrupted, that they are not good citizens.

Criminals are properly the objects of anger, and the perpetrators of terrible crimes—for example, Lee Harvey Oswald and James Earl Ray—are properly the objects of great anger. They have done more than inflict an injury on an isolated individual; they have violated the foundations of trust and friendship, the necessary elements of a moral community, the only community worth living in. A moral community, unlike a hive of bees or a hill of ants, is one whose members are expected freely to obey the laws and, unlike those in a tyranny, are trusted to obey the laws. The criminal has violated that trust, and in so doing has injured not merely his immediate victim but the community as such. He has called into question the very possibility of that community by suggesting that men cannot be trusted to respect freely the property, the person, and the dignity of those with whom they are associated. If then, men are not angry when someone else is robbed, raped, or murdered, the implication is that no moral community exists, because those men do not care for anyone other than themselves. Anger is an expression of that caring, and society needs men who care for one another, who share their pleasures and their pains, and do so for the sake of the others. It is the passion that can cause us to act for reasons having nothing to do with selfish or mean calculation; indeed, when educated, it can become a generous passion, the passion that protects the community or country by demanding punishment for its enemies. It is the stuff from which heroes are made.

A moral community is not possible without anger and the moral indigna-   7
tion that accompanies it. Thus the most powerful attack on capital punishment was written by a man, Albert Camus, who denied the legitimacy of anger and moral indignation by denying the very possibility of a moral community in our time. The anger expressed in our world, he said, is nothing but hypocrisy. His novel *L'Etranger* (variously translated as *The Stranger* or *The Outsider*) is a brilliant portrayal of what Camus insisted is our world, a world deprived of God, as he put it. It is a world we would not choose to live in and one that Camus, the hero of the French Resistance, disdained. Nevertheless, the novel is a modern masterpiece, and Meursault, its antihero (for a world without anger can have no heroes), is a murderer.

He is a murderer whose crime is excused, even as his lack of hypocrisy is   8
praised, because the universe, we are told, is "benignly indifferent" to how we live or what we do. Of course, the law is not indifferent; the law punished Meursault and it threatens to punish us if we do as he did. But Camus the novelist teaches us that the law is simply a collection of arbitrary conceits. The people around Meursault apparently were not indifferent; they expressed dismay at his lack of attachment to his mother and disapprobation of his crime. But Camus the novelist teaches us that other people are hypocrites. They pretend not to know what Camus the opponent of capital punishment tells us: namely, that "our civilization has lost the only values that, in a certain way, can justify that penalty . . . [the existence of] a truth or a principle that is superior to man." There is no basis for friendship and no moral law; therefore, no one, not even a murderer, can violate the terms of friendship or break that law; and there is no basis for the anger that we express when someone breaks that law. The only thing we share as men, the only thing that connects us one to another, is a "solidarity against death," and a judgment of capital punishment "upsets" that solidarity. The purpose of human life is to stay alive.

Like Meursault, Macbeth was a murderer, and like *L'Etranger*, Shake-   9
speare's *Macbeth* is the story of a murder; but there the similarity ends. As Lincoln said, "Nothing equals Macbeth." He was comparing it with the other Shakespearean plays he knew, the plays he had "gone over perhaps as frequently as any unprofessional reader . . . *Lear, Richard Third, Henry Eighth, Hamlet*"; but I think he meant to say more than that none of these equals *Macbeth.* I think he meant that no other literary work equals it. "It is wonderful," he said. *Macbeth* is wonderful because, to say nothing more here, it teaches us the awesomeness of the commandment "Thou shalt not kill."

What can a dramatic poet tell us about murder? More, probably, than any-   10
one else, if he is a poet worthy of consideration, and yet nothing that does not inhere in the act itself. In *Macbeth*, Shakespeare shows us murders com-

mitted in a political world by a man so driven by ambition to rule that world that he becomes a tyrant. He shows us also the consequences, which were terrible, worse even than Macbeth feared. The cosmos rebelled, turned into chaos by his deeds. He shows a world that was not "benignly indifferent" to what we call crimes and especially to murder, a world constituted by laws divine as well as human, and Macbeth violated the most awful of those laws. Because the world was so constituted, Macbeth suffered the torments of the great and the damned, torments far beyond the "practice" of any physician. He had known glory and had deserved the respect and affection of king, countrymen, army, friends, and wife; and he lost it all. At the end he was reduced to saying that life "is a tale told by an idiot, full of sound and fury, signifying nothing"; yet, in spite of the horrors provoked in us by his acts, he excites no anger in us. We pity him; even so, we understand the anger of his countrymen and the dramatic necessity of his death. *Macbeth* is a play about ambition, murder, tyranny; about horror, anger, vengeance, and, perhaps more than any other of Shakespeare's plays, justice. Because of justice, Macbeth has to die, not by his own hand—he will not "play the Roman fool, and die on [his] own sword"—but at the hand of the avenging Macduff. The dramatic necessity of his death would appear to rest on its *moral* necessity. Is that right? Does this play conform to our sense of what a murder means? Lincoln thought it was "wonderful."

Surely Shakespeare's is a truer account of murder than the one provided   11
by Camus, and by truer I mean truer to our moral sense of what a murder is and what the consequences that attend it must be. Shakespeare shows us vengeful men because there is something in the souls of men—then and now—that requires such crimes to be revenged. Can we imagine a world that does not take its revenge on the man who kills Macduff's wife and children? (Can we imagine the play in which Macbeth does not die?) Can we imagine a people that does not hate murderers? (Can we imagine a world where Meursault is an outsider only because he does not *pretend* to be outraged by murder?) Shakespeare's poetry could not have been written out of the moral sense that the death penalty's opponents insist we ought to have. Indeed, the issue of capital punishment can be said to turn on whether Shakespeare's or Camus' is the more telling account of murder.

There is a sense in which punishment may be likened to dramatic poetry.   12
Dramatic poetry depicts men's actions because men are revealed in, or make themselves known through, their actions; and the essence of a human action, according to Aristotle, consists in its being virtuous or vicious. Only a ruler or a contender for rule can act with the freedom and on a scale that allows the virtuousness or viciousness of human deeds to be fully displayed. Macbeth was such a man, and in his fall, brought about by his own acts, and in the consequent suffering he endured, is revealed the meaning of morality. In *Macbeth* the majesty of the moral law is demonstrated to us; as I said, it teaches us the awesomeness of the commandment "Thou shalt not kill." In a similar fashion, the punishments imposed by the legal order remind us of the reign of the moral order; not only do they remind us of it, but by enforcing

its prescriptions, they enhance the dignity of the legal order in the eyes of moral men, in the eyes of those decent citizens who cry out "for gods who will avenge injustice." That is especially important in a self-governing community, a community that gives laws to itself.

If the laws were understood to be divinely inspired or, in the extreme case, divinely given, they would enjoy all the dignity that the opinions of men can grant and all the dignity they require to ensure their being obeyed by most of the men living under them. Like Duncan in the opinion of Macduff, the laws would be "the Lord's anointed," and would be obeyed even as Macduff obeyed the laws of the Scottish kingdom. Only a Macbeth would challenge them, and only a Meursault would ignore them. But the laws of the United States are not of this description; in fact, among the proposed amendments that became the Bill of Rights was one declaring, not that all power comes from God, but rather "that all power is originally vested in, and consequently derives from the people"; and this proposal was dropped only because it was thought to be redundant: the Constitution's preamble said essentially the same thing, and what we know as the Tenth Amendment reiterated it. So Madison proposed to make the Constitution venerable in the minds of the people, and Lincoln, in an early speech, went so far as to say that a "political religion" should be made of it. They did not doubt that the Constitution and the laws made pursuant to it would be supported by "enlightened reason," but fearing that enlightened reason would be in short supply, they sought to augment it. The laws of the United States would be obeyed by some men because they could hear and understand "the voice of enlightened reason," and by other men because they would regard the laws with that "veneration which time bestows on everything."

Supreme Court justices have occasionally complained of our habit of making "constitutionality synonymous with wisdom." But the extent to which the Constitution is venerated and its authority accepted depends on the compatibility of its rules with our moral sensibilities; despite its venerable character, the Constitution is not the only source of these moral sensibilities. There was even a period, before slavery was abolished by the Thirteenth Amendment, when the Constitution was regarded by some very moral men as an abomination: Garrison called it "a covenant with death and an agreement with Hell," and there were honorable men holding important political offices and judicial appointments who refused to enforce the Fugitive Slave Law even though its constitutionality had been affirmed. In time this opinion spread far beyond the ranks of the original abolitionists until those who held it composed a constitutional majority of the people, and slavery was abolished.

But Lincoln knew that more than amendments were required to make the Constitution once more worthy of the veneration of moral men. This is why, in the Gettysburg Address, he made the principle of the Constitution an inheritance from "our fathers." That it should be so esteemed is especially important in a self-governing nation that gives laws to itself, because it is only a short step from the principle that the laws are merely a product of one's own will to the opinion that the only consideration that informs the law is self-interest; and this opinion is only one remove from lawlessness. A nation of simply self-interested men will soon enough perish from the earth.

It was not an accident that Lincoln spoke as he did at Gettysburg or that   16
he chose as the occasion for his words the dedication of a cemetery built on a portion of the most significant battlefield of the Civil War. Two-and-a-half years earlier, in his First Inaugural Address, he had said that Americans, north and south, were not and must not be enemies, but friends. Passion had strained but must not be allowed to break the bonds of affection that tied them one to another. He closed by saying this: "The mystic chords of memory, stretching from every battlefield, and patriot grave, to every living heart and hearthstone, all over this broad land, will yet swell the chorus of the Union, when again touched, as surely they will be, by the better angels of our nature." The chords of memory that would swell the chorus of the Union could be touched, even by a man of Lincoln's stature, only on the most solemn occasions, and in the life of a nation no occasion is more solemn than the burial of the patriots who have died defending it on the field of battle. War is surely an evil but as Hegel said, it is not an "absolute evil." It exacts the supreme sacrifice, but precisely because of that it can call forth such sublime rhetoric as Lincoln's. His words at Gettysburg serve to remind Americans in particular of what Hegel said people in general needed to know, and could be made to know by means of war and the sacrifices demanded of them in wars: namely, that their country is something more than a "civil society" the purpose of which is simply the protection of individual and selfish interests.

Capital punishment, like Shakespeare's dramatic and Lincoln's political po-   17
etry (and it is surely that, and was understood by him to be that), serves to remind us of the majesty of the moral order that is embodied in our law, and of the terrible consequences of its breach. The law must not be understood to be merely a statute that we enact or repeal at our will, and obey or disobey at our convenience—especially not the criminal law. Wherever law is regarded as merely statutory, men will soon enough disobey it, and will learn how to do so without any inconvenience to themselves. The criminal law must possess a dignity far beyond that possessed by mere statutory enactment or utilitarian and self-interested calculations. The most powerful means we have to give it that dignity is to authorize it to impose the ultimate penalty. The criminal law must be made awful, by which I mean awe-inspiring, or commanding "profound respect or reverential fear." It must remind us of the moral order by which alone we can live as *human* beings, and in America, now that the Supreme Court has outlawed banishment, the only punishment that can do this is capital punishment.

The founder of modern criminology, the eighteenth century Italian, Cesare   18
Beccaria, opposed both banishment and capital punishment because he understood that both were inconsistent with the principle of self-interest, and self-interest was the basis of the political order he favored. If a man's first or only duty is to himself, of course he will prefer his money to his country; he will also prefer his money to his brother. In fact, he will prefer his brother's money to his brother, and a people of this description, or a

country that understands itself in this Beccarian manner, can put the mark of Cain on no one. For the same reason, such a country can have no legitimate reason to execute its criminals, or, indeed, to punish them in any manner. What would be accomplished by punishment in such a place? Punishment arises out of the demand for justice, and justice is demanded by angry, morally indignant men; its purpose is to satisfy that moral indignation and thereby promote the lawabidingness that, it is assumed, accompanies it. But the principle of self-interest denies the moral basis of that indignation.

Not only will a country based solely on self-interest have no legitimate reason to punish; it may have no need to punish. It may be able to solve what we call the crime problem by substituting a law of contracts for law of crimes. According to Beccaria's social contract, men agree to yield their natural freedom to the "sovereign" in exchange for his promise to keep the peace. As it becomes more difficult for the sovereign to fulfill his part of the contract, there is a demand that he be made to pay for his nonperformance. From this comes compensation or insurance schemes embodied in statues whereby the sovereign (or state), being unable to keep the peace by punishing criminals, agrees to compensate its contractual partners for injuries suffered at the hands of criminals, injuries the police are unable to prevent. The insurance policy takes the place of law enforcement and the *posse comitatus,* and John Wayne and Gary Cooper, give way to Mutual of Omaha. There is no anger in this kind of law, and none (or no reason for any) in the society.

The principle can be carried further still. If we ignore the victim (and nothing we do can restore his life anyway), there would appear to be no reason why—the worth of a man being his price, as Beccaria's teacher, Thomas Hobbes, put it—coverage should not be extended to the losses incurred in a murder. If we ignore the victim's sensibilities (and what are they but absurd vanities?), there would appear to be no reason why—the worth of a woman being *her* price—coverage should not be extended to the losses incurred in a rape. Other examples will no doubt suggest themselves.

This might appear to be an almost perfect solution to what we persist in calling the crime problem, achieved without risking the terrible things sometimes done by an angry people. A people that is not angry with criminals will not be able to deter crime, but a people fully covered by insurance has no need to deter crime: they will be insured against all the losses they can, in principle, suffer. What is now called crime can be expected to increase in volume, of course, and this will cause an increase in the premiums paid, directly or in the form of taxes. But it will no longer be necessary to apprehend try, and punish criminals, which now costs Americans more than $1.5 billion a month (and is increasing at an annual rate of about 15 percent), and one can buy a lot of insurance for $1.5 billion. There is this difficulty, as Rousseau put it: To exclude anger from the human community is to concentrate all the passions in a "self-interest of the meanest sort," and such a place would not be fit for human habitation.

When, in 1976, the Supreme Court declared death to be a constitutional penalty, it decided that the United States was not that sort of country; most

19

20

21

22

of us, I think, can appreciate that judgment. We want to live among people who do not value their possessions more than their citizenship, who do not think exclusively or even primarily of their own rights, people whom we can depend on even as they exercise their rights, and whom we can trust, which is to say, people who, even in the absence of a policeman, will not assault our bodies or steal our possessions, and might even come to our assistance when we need it, and who stand ready, when the occasion demands it, to risk their lives in defense of their country. If we are of the opinion that the United States may rightly ask of its citizens this awful sacrifice, then we are also of the opinion that it may rightly impose the most awful penalty; if it may rightly honor its heroes, it may rightly execute the worst of its criminals. By doing so, it will remind its citizens that it is a country worthy of heroes.

QUESTIONS FOR MEANING

1. According to Berns, what causes anger? Is anger an honorable emotion? If so, why?
2. Berns defines "the busy man" as "the sort of man who sees things only in the light cast by a concern for his own interests." What other words might he have used besides "busy" to describe such men?
3. Why does Berns believe that the United States is in danger of becoming dominated by self-interest? Why does he believe the death penalty represents a commitment to the lives and needs of others?
4. What does Berns mean by "enlightened reason" in paragraph 13?
5. Do you understand Berns's summary of *The Stranger* and *Macbeth?* If you have read neither of these two works, which would you be most interested in reading as the result of the discussion in this essay?
6. Do you recognize the allusion with which paragraph 15 concludes?
7. Paraphrase what Berns says about the relationship between crime and insurance.
8. Why does Berns believe that "criminal law must be made awful"?
9. Berns concludes his argument by declaring that the United States is "a country worthy of heroes." What does this mean?

QUESTIONS ABOUT STRATEGY

1. What kind of audience do you think this essay was originally written for?
2. Why does Berns introduce the names of Simon Wiesenthal, President Kennedy, and Martin Luther King into his essay?
3. Where does Berns characterize his opponents? Does Berns make any attempt to appease them?
4. Berns presents himself as someone who is well-read in both literature and history. Does his analysis of Camus, Shakespeare, and the Civil War add force to his argument? Or is he just showing off how much he knows?
5. Berns begins his essay by acknowledging that he is a "layman" who had only recently begun to think seriously about capital punishment. Is this a

good way to prepare an audience for a lengthy argument? Are there any risks to this approach?

6. Berns refers repeatedly to Lincoln throughout his essay. Did this strike you as strange in an argument on behalf of capital punishment? Does Berns succeed in convincing you that Lincoln would have agreed with him? Is this a type of argument or persuasion?

ONE STUDENT'S ASSIGNMENT

Write an argument for or against capital punishment based upon a fundamental value which you hold. Include material from at least three essays in The Informed Argument, *but do not use any other sources beyond your personal experience—which you may include if you wish to do so. Use MLA style parenthetical documentation. Since all of your sources will come from the textbook we are using for this class, you do not need to include a list of works cited for this particular assignment.*

A Matter of Life or Death
Suzanne Wright

I come from a small town where it was a major news story   1
when the Lion's Club decided to reseed the baseball diamond
in our only public park. People seldom locked their doors,
and I was never afraid to walk home at night after choir practice. During my junior and senior years in high school, I
often wished that I lived someplace that was more exciting,
and I looked forward to being able to go to college away from
home. But growing up in a small town, where I knew my neighbors and my neighbors knew me, helped me to understand the
value of individual life. It is for this reason that I am in
favor of capital punishment.

It might seem strange that I believe in the value of life   2
and also support the death penalty. This could almost seem
like a contradiction, since opponents of capital punishment
often cite the sanctity of human life as a reason for abolishing the death penalty. They believe that if it is wrong
for someone to kill someone else, it is also wrong for the
state to take away someone's life. I believe that the death
penalty affirms the value of human life by showing that murder is the most serious of all crimes. If we value human life,

and want to make this clear, then murder has to receive a punishment which is more severe than that given for any
other crime.

One common argument against capital punishment is that it   3
does not deter other violent crimes. According to Clarence
Darrow, one of the most famous lawyers in American history,
"The old-fashioned stories of men deliberately plotting and
committing murder in cold blood have little foundation in
real life" (149). Darrow goes on to argue that the death penalty is inappropriate for a crime which is seldom premeditated. I agree that the death penalty should not be imposed
on someone who has killed someone else in a moment of panic or
confusion, but the law already makes a distinction between
murder in the second and first degree. A murder which has
been planned cannot be excused. It is only for this type of
murder, murder in the first degree, that I favor the death
penalty.

Whether or not capital punishment deters any murders may   4
never be settled, but like H. L. Mencken and Walter Berns, I
don't think deterrence is really the point of the death penalty. Capital punishment enables the average person to see
that justice has been done. If deprived of this sense, people
feel frustrated. Mencken uses the term katharsis, which he
defines as "a healthy letting off of steam" (144), to justify
the death penalty as a type of relief mechanism for society
as a whole. When people are made to feel that criminals are
"getting away with murder," then it's very hard for them to
take the law seriously. When the average person begins to
think that laws don't work, everyone is bound to suffer.

Even though I favor capital punishment, I must admit that   5
the courts are often unfair. A study by David Baldus, a law
professor at the University of Iowa, showed that "killers of
black victims are punished by death less than one-tenth as
often as are killers of white victims" (Bruck 175-76). This
certainly seems to show that racism is often a factor in deciding which murderers will live and which will die. The
color of someone's skin should not affect the punishment
which is given for a crime, and prejudice must be eliminated
from our courts. But this doesn't mean that convicted first-
degree murderers should never be executed; it only means
that a greater effort must be made to apply the law consistently (Koch 155).

I realize that capital punishment will not solve the prob-   6

lem of violent crime and that big cities like Miami, Los Angeles, and New York will never be as peaceful as a small town
in the middle of Wisconsin. It is important, however, for
people to feel safe wherever they live. This sense of security cannot exist if the law seems to treat murder lightly.
Imposing capital punishment upon first-degree murderers who
have been found guilty "beyond a reasonable doubt" is an essential way of demonstrating that crimes of this sort cannot
be tolerated in a civilized society.

SUGGESTIONS FOR WRITING

1. Opponents of capital punishment traditionally argue that it does not deter crime. If you favor capital punishment, respond to this argument by
   drawing upon the work of Ernest van den Haag.
2. Both H. L. Mencken and Walter Berns defend capital punishment on the
   grounds that it psychologically satisfies the victims of violent crime. Summarize and compare their views. Then write an essay questioning whether
   the death penalty can be justified on these grounds.
3. If executions allow for a "healthy letting off of steam," as Mencken puts
   it, should they be made public? Write an essay for or against televising
   executions. Whatever your position, make sure you consider all of the
   consequences of letting people watch someone die.
4. Margaret Mead and Clarence Darrow both suggest that capital punishment does nothing to resolve the causes of violent crime. Identify a social
   problem which you believe to be a cause of violence and argue on behalf
   of a specific reform.
5. Write a summary of David Bruck's argument against capital punishment.
   Limit your summary to approximately 500 words.
6. If you yourself oppose capital punishment, do you take an absolute position or are there any crimes for which you would make an exception?
   If you would allow capital punishment for special cases, write an essay
   explaining why the death penalty would be appropriate for the special
   case or cases you have in mind.
7. If you are absolutely opposed to capital punishment, what penalty would
   you impose upon someone who has committed premeditated murder? Be
   specific in working out the details of how your alternative punishment
   would be carried out.
8. According to H. L. Mencken, "The real objection to capital punishment
   doesn't lie against the actual extermination of the condemned, but against
   our brutal American habit of putting if off so long." Do you agree? Write
   an essay for or against capital punishment that will focus on the advantages or disadvantages of lengthy appeals. Can our system of extended

appeals be defended as a necessary safeguard against executing the innocent? Or is it a subtle form of torture—both for the criminal and his victims?

9. If you believe that capital punishment is unconstitutional, write an essay of definition that will establish what the framers of the Constitution meant by "cruel and unusual punishment."

10. What is the history of capital punishment in your state? If there is no death penalty, do a research paper on how and when it came to be abolished. If your state has reintroduced capital punishment since 1972, explain the new law and either defend it or attack it.

11. Research the case of someone executed within the last ten years, and then argue whether or not the death penalty was appropriate in this case.

12. Darrow and Bruck both compare American justice to laws in other countries. Do a research paper on a country that has abolished capital punishment, revealing what the consequences have been.

Section 4

Censorship in Schools: Who Controls Education?

FRANK TRIPPETT

The Growing Battle of the Books

Born in Mississippi, Frank Trippett attended Duke University and the University of Mississippi before becoming a reporter and editor. From 1955 to 1961, he was state capital bureau chief for the St. Petersburg Times, *an experience that led to his first book,* The States: United they Fall *(1967), a study of American state legislatures. His political writing about state and local governments earned Trippett a special citation from the American Political Science Association. An associate editor at* Newsweek *from 1961 to 1968, and a senior editor at* Look *from 1968 to 1971, Trippett is now a senior writer for* Time *magazine, which published the following essay in* **1981.**

Written words running loose have always presented a challenge to people   1
bent on ruling others. In times past, religious zealots burned heretical ideas
and heretics with impartiality. Modern tyrannies promote the contentment
and obedience of their subjects by ruthlessly keeping troubling ideas out of
their books and minds. Censorship can place people in bondage more efficiently than chains.

Thanks to the First Amendment, the U.S. has been remarkably, if not en-   2
tirely, free of such official monitoring. Still, the nation has always had more
than it needs of voluntary censors, vigilantes eager to protect everybody from
hazards like ugly words, sedition, blasphemy, unwelcome ideas and, perhaps
worst of all, reality. Lately, however, it has been easy to assume that when
the everything-goes New Permissiveness gusted forth in the 1960s, it blew
the old book-banning spirit out of action for good.

Quite the contrary. In fact, censorship has been on the rise in the U.S. for   3
the past ten years. Every region of the country and almost every state has
felt the flaring of the censorial spirit. Efforts to ban or squelch books in public libraries and schools doubled in number, to 116 a year, in the first five
years of the 1970s over the last five of the 1960s—as Author L. B. Woods
documents in *A Decade of Censorship in America—The Threat to Class-*

rooms and Libraries, 1966–1975. The upsurge in book banning has not since let up, one reason being that some 200 local, state and national organizations now take part in skirmishes over the contents of books circulating under public auspices. The American Library Association, which has been reporting an almost yearly increase in censorial pressures on public libraries, has just totted up the score for 1980. It found, without surprise, yet another upsurge: from three to five episodes a week to just as many in a day. Says Judith Krug, director of the A.L.A.'s Office for Intellectual Freedom: "This sort of thing has a chilling effect."

That, of course, is precisely the effect that censorship always intends. And   4 the chill, whether intellectual, political, moral or artistic, is invariably hazardous to the open traffic in ideas that not only nourishes a free society but defines its essence. The resurgence of a populist censorial spirit has, in a sense, sneaked up on the nation. National attention has focused on a few notorious censorship cases, such as the book-banning crusade that exploded into life-threatening violence in Kanawha County, W. Va., in 1974. But most kindred episodes that have been cropping up all over have remained localized and obscure. The Idaho Falls, Idaho, school book review committee did not make a big splash when it voted, 21 to 1, to ban *One Flew Over the Cuckoo's Nest*—in response to one parent's objection to some of the language. It was not much bigger news when Anaheim, Calif., school officials authorized a list of *approved* books that effectively banned many previously studied books, including Richard Wright's classic *Black Boy.* And who recalls the Kanawha, Iowa, school board's banning *The Grapes of Wrath* because some scenes involved prostitutes?

Such cases, numbering in the hundreds, have now been thoroughly tracked   5 down and sorted out by English Education Professor Edward B. Jenkinson of Indiana University in a study, *Censors in the Classroom—The Mind Benders.* He began digging into the subject after he became chairman of the Committee Against Censorship of the National Council of Teachers of English. His 184-page report reviews hundreds of cases (notorious and obscure), suggests the scope of censorship activity (it is ubiquitous), discusses the main censorial tactics (usually pure power politics) and points to some of the subtler ill effects. Popular censorship, for one thing, induces fearful teachers and librarians to practice what Jenkinson calls "closet censorship." The targets of the book banners? Jenkinson answers the question tersely: "Nothing is safe."

Case histories make that easy to believe. The books that are most often   6 attacked would make a nice library for anybody with broad-gauged taste. Among them: *Catcher in the Rye, Brave New World, Grapes of Wrath, Of Mice and Men, Catch-22, Soul on Ice,* and *To Kill a Mockingbird. Little Black Sambo* and *Merchant of Venice* run into recurring protests based on suspicions that the former is anti-black, the latter anti-Semitic. One school board banned *Making It with Mademoiselle,* but reversed the decision after finding out it was a how-to pattern book for youngsters hoping to learn dressmaking. Authorities in several school districts have banned the *American*

Heritage Dictionary not only because it contains unacceptable words but because some organizations, the Texas Daughters of the American Revolution among them, have objected to the sexual intimations of the definition of the word bed as a transitive verb.

Censorship can, and often does, lead into absurdity, though not often slap-   7
stick absurdity like the New Jersey legislature achieved in the 1960s when it enacted a subsequently vetoed antiobscenity bill so explicit that it was deemed too dirty to be read in the legislative chambers without clearing out the public first. The mother in Whiteville, N.C., who demanded that the Columbus County library keep adult books out of the hands of children later discovered that her own daughter had thereby been made ineligible to check out the Bible. One group, a Florida organization called Save Our Children, has simplified its censorship goals by proposing to purge from libraries all books by such reputed homosexuals as Emily Dickinson, Willa Cather, Virginia Woolf, Tennessee Williams, Walt Whitman and John Milton.

Most often, censors wind up at the ridiculous only by going a very danger-   8
ous route. The board of the Island Trees Union Free School District on Long Island, N.Y., in a case still being contested by former students in court, banned eleven books as "anti-American, anti-Christian, anti-Semitic and just plain filthy." Later they discovered that the banished included two Pulitzer prizewinners: Bernard Malamud's *The Fixer* and Oliver La Farge's *Laughing Boy.* For censors to ban books they have never read is commonplace. For them to deny that they are censoring is even more so. Said Attorney George W. Lipp Jr., announcing plans to continue the legal fight for the Island Trees board: "This is not book burning or book banning but a rational effort to transmit community values."

Few censors, if any, tend to see that censorship itself runs counter to   9
certain basic American values. But why have so many people with such an outlook begun lurching forth so aggressively in recent years? They quite likely have always suffered the censorial impulse. But they have been recently emboldened by the same resurgent moralistic mood that has enspirited evangelical fundamentalists and given form to the increasingly outspoken constituency of the Moral Majority. At another level, they probably hunger for some power over something, just as everybody supposedly does these days. Thus they are moved, as American Library Association President Peggy Sullivan says, "by a desperation to feel some control over what is close to their lives."

Americans are in no danger of being pushed back to the prudery of the   10
19th century. The typical U.S. newsstand, with its sappy pornutopian reek, is proof enough of that, without even considering prime-time TV. But the latter-day inflamed censor is no laughing matter. One unsettling feature of the current censorial vigilantism is its signs of ugly inflammation. There is, for instance, the cheerily incendiary attitude expressed by the Rev. George A. Zarris, chairman of the Moral Majority in Illinois. Says Zarris: "I would think moral-minded people might object to books that are philosophically alien to what they believe. If they have the books and feel like burning them, fine." The

notion of book burning is unthinkable to many and appalling to others, if only because it brings to mind the rise of Adolf Hitler's Germany—an event marked by widespread bonfires fed by the works of scores of writers including Marcel Proust, Thomas Mann, H. G. Wells and Jack London.

Unthinkable? In fact, the current wave of censorship has precipitated two   11
of the most outrageous episodes of book burning in the U.S. since 1927, when Chicago Mayor William ("Big Bill") Thompson, an anglophobe miffed by a view sympathetic to the British, had a flunky put the torch on the city hall steps to one of Historian Arthur Schlesinger Sr.'s books. In Drake, N. Dak., the five-member school board in 1973 ordered the confiscation and burning of three books that, according to Professor Jenkinson, none of the members had read: Kurt Vonnegut's *Slaughterhouse Five*, James Dickey's *Deliverance* and an anthology of short stories by writers like Joseph Conrad, John Steinbeck and William Faulkner. Said the school superintendent later: "I don't regret it one bit, and we'd do it again. I'm just sorry about all the publicity that we got." In Warsaw, Ind., a gaggle of citizens in 1977 publicly burned 40 copies of *Values Clarifications*, a textbook, as a show of support for a school board that decided to ban both written matter and independent-minded teachers from its system. Said William I. Chapel, a member of that board: "The bottom line is: Who will control the minds of the students?"

An interesting question. It baldly reveals the ultimate purpose of all cen-   12
sorship—mind control—just as surely as the burning of books dramatizes a yearning latent in every consecrated censor. The time could not be better for recalling something Henry Seidel Canby wrote after Big Bill Thompson put Arthur Schlesinger to the flame. Said Canby: "There will always be a mob with a torch ready when someone cries, 'Burn those books!' " The real bottom line is: How many more times is he going to be proved right?

QUESTIONS FOR MEANING

1. Can you define "the chilling effect" that censorship has according to this essay?
2. How many of the banned books referred to in this essay have you yourself read? Knowing that they have been censored, would you be more or less inclined to read them?
3. In paragraph 6, Trippett mentions that there are "sexual intimations" in the *American Heritage Dictionary*'s "definition of the word *bed* as a transitive verb." Show that you understand what he means by using the word in this sense in a sentence.
4. What causes people to feel "a desperation to feel some control over what is close to their lives"? Why might parents be especially anxious to censor books in the 1980s? What do they fear? Are their fears legitimate?
5. A schoolboard member quoted by Trippett argues that censorship amounts to a question of who will control the minds of students. Should anyone control the minds of students? If so, who?

QUESTIONS ABOUT STRATEGY

1. Do you detect any bias in Trippett's essay? How fair is he to his opponents?
2. Trippett argues that censorship is dangerous, and yet in paragraph 7 he cites several comic examples. Why does he do this?
3. How impressed are you by the individual cases of censorship that Trippett describes? Does he persuade you that censorship is a growing problem?
4. Comment on Trippett's use of the verb "lurching" in paragraph 9. What are the connotations of this word? What makes it an interesting word choice?
5. In a lively piece of phrasing, Trippett associates a "typical U.S. newsstand" with "sappy pornutopian reek." What kind of magazines is he referring to? How would you define "pornutopian reek," and why is it "sappy"?

IVAN B. GLUCKMAN
Separating Myth from Reality

*When arguing about "censorship," many people are unclear about what they mean. Does the word mean preventing the publication of something or could it also apply to actions that restrict public access to something already published? Ivan B. Gluckman is director of legal services and government relations for the National Association of Secondary School Principals. In the following essay, which was first published in **1985,** Gluckman demonstrates the importance of definition in argumentation.*

Individuals and organized groups have expressed concern not only about   1
the skills being developed in public school students, but also about the ethical and moral values—or lack of them—presented to them.

Most of the criticism has been directed toward books, films, and other   2
instructional materials used in the school. Although some of the critics are affiliated with a religious group or have an orientation to religious issues, criticism has also come from groups and individuals more concerned with political or racial issues unrelated to any religious organization or belief.

Undoubtedly some school boards and administrators, seeking to placate   3
these critics, may avoid the use of certain instructional materials or even remove them from the schools. Concerned at this reaction, a number of lawsuits have been initiated by persons and groups who see such actions not only as detrimental to public education, but as a violation of the basic constitutional rights of students under the First Amendment.

Usually, these actions by school boards and administrators, and sometimes   4
even the demands of the citizens themselves, are deplored as "censorship."

To assess these charges and the implications that this increasingly emotional situation has for American public education, it is necessary to examine the concept of "censorship" and separate myth from reality regarding this emotionally charged word.

Censorship: What It Is and What It Isn't

The dictionary says "censorship" is the examination of written or printed   5
matter by a public official in order to forbid its publication, circulation, or representation if it contains anything objectionable. (Webster's Third New International Dictionary, 1976).

Under this definition, criticism of books or other instructional materials by   6
anyone who is not in an official position is not censorship. Indeed, criticism or other objection raised by a parent or other private citizen of a school district to the local school board or one of the district's administrators is a proper exercise of First Amendment rights by these citizens. It is somewhat paradoxical that anyone concerned about constitutional rights and freedoms would attack those seeking to exercise such a right even if they disagree with the basis of their objections.

In any event, there should be no question about a citizen's legitimate right   7
to present objections to books or other instructional materials to the governing body of the school district, the board, or to those employees to whom the board has assigned its authority over these materials. Such action, however, should never be termed "censorship" because the private citizen has no authority to remove the material from the schools.

The removal of material by a board on the basis of citizen objection is, of   8
course, a different matter. Because members of school boards are public officials, their actions could possibly be regarded as "censorship." Even a moment's reflection should make it apparent, however, that no reasonable interpretation of the term would assume that all actions by a board to control instructional materials in its district could be so regarded.

Historically, censorship was the work of an official appointed for the spe-   9
cific purpose of reviewing material that would not have been of interest or concern to that official except for political reasons, namely to suppress ideas or expressions believed to be inimical to the state or its leaders. Clearly, this is not the situation with members of a public school board.

Its duties include making decisions regarding the approval of textbooks,   10
school library books, and all other materials related to the educational process; but so long as the exercise of this authority is grounded in educational rather than political criteria, it would appear that decisions of a school board in this area are not to be regarded as "censorship" in the pejorative sense in which the word is so often used.

One of the bases of current civil libertarian concern is that the exercise of   11
discretion by a school board member or administrator may be the fear of criticism by some group in the community rather than any personal conclu-

sion of his or her own. But while such a motivation may not be desirable, it does not make the action any less permissible under the law.

Indeed, it can certainly be argued that response to any serious concern   12
expressed by citizens of a school district is an appropriate basis for consideration of action by a member of a publicly elected or appointed school board.

While all this should seem obvious, the source of information upon which   13
a board member bases decisions or actions concerning instructional materials continues to be criticized as some kind of impropriety by those concerned about actions taken by the school boards. This was certainly true in the case of *Pico* v. *Island Trees School District*[1] involving removal by a board of books from the school library.

In this case, the plaintiff student alleged that the source of the school   14
board's actions was information provided to board members who had attended a meeting of "a politically conservative organization of parents concerned about education legislation in the state of New York." Part of this concern extended to the presence of certain books in school libraries. None of the courts which considered the *Pico* case considered these allegations relevant, however, since everyone depends on outside information as the basis for reaching decisions.

Another implication in the criticism of board actions in alleged censorship   15
of school instructional materials is that the board is acting in some improper manner if it makes decisions on matters of this kind itself rather than delegating the decision to someone it employs. While there can be no question that routine decisions on the selection of textbooks, other curricular materials, and books for the school library are normally assigned to various members of the professional staff, there is no legal basis to contend that the board cannot retain such authority for itself, or intervene in specific situations brought to its attention by citizens of the district.

Only those decisions that are arbitrary, capricious, or based on some illegal   16
motivation or purpose are subject to legitimate objection. The courts are slow to interfere with the usual exercise of authority by school boards, which are, after all, executive agencies of the state. Even in the decision most often cited as the source of student rights, *Tinker* v. *Des Moines Independent Community School District,*[2] the U.S. Supreme Court noted that federal courts should not ordinarily "intervene in the resolution of conflicts which arise in the daily operation of public school systems."

Certainly the selection and control of instructional materials must be regarded as matters reasonably within the normal control of school boards, and   17
therefore, all actions taken under that authority cannot be regarded as "censorship."

The Real Issue

When should courts examine instances of alleged impropriety by boards   18
or administrators in regard to selection and control of public school instructional materials?

This is the question with which the federal courts have been grappling in recent years, and their failure to provide clear and complete answers is not necessarily proof of their disloyalty to the cause of individual freedom. It may instead be evidence only of the difficulty of the problem.   19

Generally speaking, the answer is that the courts will question a board's authority only when there is evidence that its action has interfered with the constitutional rights of a complainant. This was the basis of the Supreme Court's decision in *West Virginia State Bd. of Educ.* v. *Barnette* in 1943, when it held that even in the midst of a great war, a school board could not compel a public school student to salute the nation's flag.[3]   20

In the celebrated *Tinker* case, the Court had to first find that the plaintiff's wearing of a black armband was a kind of "silent speech" before any investigation could properly be made of the board's order that it not be worn in the school.   21

In the *Pico* case, therefore, the Supreme Court had first to determine whether the specific interest asserted by the student plaintiff was one protected by the constitution, in particular the First Amendment. While it was unwilling to recognize a student's "right to know" any specific information, or a "right to read" any particular books, a plurality of the Court conceded that there is some kind of "right to receive information and ideas," which is "an inherent corollary of the rights of free speech and press."[4]   22

On this basis, and following the lead of several lower federal courts, the plurality concluded that removal of books from a school library by the board could be regarded as an interference with the First Amendment rights of students.[5]   23

Noting that school boards generally have almost unlimited discretion in curricular matters, the court, however, distinguished the school library from the classroom on the ground that the latter was in the nature of a "compulsory environment" as contrasted to the "regime of voluntary inquiry" that exists in the school library.   24

Because of this distinction, it is unlikely that the exercise of discretion in the selection of curricular materials by the school board, and presumably by its administrators or other employees to whom it assigns its authority, would be regarded as being as potentially violative of student First Amendment rights as would the removal of books from the school library.   25

Even in the latter case, the Court made clear that the mere removal of books from the library should not automatically be regarded as constitutionally impermissible. This would only be true if it could be shown that the board's motivation for taking its action was inappropriate. It was on the definition of what kinds of motivation were and were not appropriate that the Court found its greatest disagreements. While there was general agreement that racial or religious bias would be inappropriate motives for removing books, there was equal agreement that removal of materials on the grounds of obscenity, vulgarity, or mere "educational unsuitability" was permissible.   26

The plurality also indicated that it would not sustain action based on a desire by the board to impose upon the students "a political orthodoxy" to   27 which the board members adhered; but it recognized the authority of local school boards "to establish and apply their curriculum in such a way as to transmit community values," and that "there is a legitimate and substantial community interest in promoting respect for authority and traditional values, be they social, moral or political."[6]

It is this important subject that is the basis of much of the criticism of   28
many critics of school textbooks and other instructional material. How legitimate is this criticism and can the demands based upon it be squared with
the concerns of civil libertarians for the nurturing of individual freedom and
creative thought?

The Place of Values

Much of the current dispute between those concerned with the ethical   29
shortcomings of public school curriculum and instructional materials and the
civil libertarians seems to be caused by a lack of communication between the
two groups based perhaps on some suspicion of the other's motives. Each
group thinks the other has a hidden agenda that is its real concern.

The civil libertarians seem to believe that the real purpose of those ex-   30
pressing a need for the inculcation of "community values" is to inject some
kind of sectarian religion into the public schools. On the other side, some of
those talking about the need for values seem to believe that the real motivation of civil libertarians is to create a value-neutral environment in public
schools that will leave youngsters adrift in a state of "amorality"
and confusion.

While there undoubtedly are partisans of such extreme views in both camps,   31
it seems equally certain that there are many citizens, and probably a majority
of those concerned with public schools who do not harbor any such ideas.
These people should be able to recognize the reasonable fears of their fellow
citizens and be willing to find an area of agreement in which school boards
and their employees are permitted to exercise discretion in the selection of
instructional materials that are not only factually accurate, but are also designed to inculcate in students some common denominator of wholesome,
nonsectarian moral and ethical values.

One can indeed argue with some persuasiveness that the objectives of   32
inculcating moral values and the preservation of free intellectual inquiry are
not just compatible, but complementary. Look, for example, at the preamble
to the constitution of the first state in which public schools were established,
the Commonwealth of Massachusetts. Written by John Adams and ratified in
1780, and speaking of the purpose of the public schools, it states:

> Wisdom and knowledge, as well as virtue . . . being necessary for the preser-
> vation of their [i.e., the people's] rights and liberties . . . it shall be the duty of
> legislatures to cherish the interests of literature and the sciences . . . to
> countenance and inculcate the principles of humanity and general benevolence,
> public and private charity, industry and frugality, honesty and punctuality in
> their dealings, sincerity, good humor, and all social affections [and] generous
> sentiments among the people.[7]

The state statutes spell out these goals in further detail, charging instruc-   33
tors to impress on the minds of children and youth:

> . . . principles of piety and justice, and a sacred regard for truth, love of
> their country, humanity, and universal benevolence, sobriety, industry and fru-
> gality, chastity, moderation and temperance, and those other virtues which are
> the ornament of human society and the basis upon which a republican consti-
> tution is founded. . . .[8]

These constitutional and statutory mandates derive from the very nature   34
of the public school system, which was established for the public purpose of
preparing all youth to participate in, and assume the burdens of citizenship.
As Newton Edwards, one of the most respected authorities on school
law, said:

> The state finds its right to tax for the maintenance of a system of public
> schools in its duty to promote the public welfare, the good order and peace of
> society. The primary function of the public school, in legal theory at least, is
> not to confer benefits upon the individual as such. The school exists as a state
> institution because the very existence of civil society demands it.[9]

Conclusion

Civil libertarians certainly have a legitimate concern that the habit of free   35
inquiry be nurtured in youngsters while they are in public schools. At the
same time, those concerned with the preservation of some common ethical
heritage in society have an equally legitimate interest and concern.

Unfortunately, many in the latter camp have removed their children from   36
public schools in recent years in the belief that their concerns are no longer
being given adequate attention. Such actions can only harm the public schools
which libertarians desire to protect and preserve.

Happily, there seems to be no reason that the goals and desires of a large   37
majority of concerned citizens on both sides can be met if neither makes
unreasonable demands upon the other or sounds exaggerated alarms about
their motives. Claims of rampant "secular humanism" and "preventive censorship" in the schools would both seem to fall into this latter category.

What is needed is for both sides to listen more openly to what others are   38
saying, and then to think more carefully about the purposes which the public
school must serve. The result should be more light and less heat which, as in
most situations, will usually help to find a better way.

Notes

1. 457 U.S. 853, 102 S.Ct. 2799 (1982).

2. 393 U.S. 503, 89 S.Ct. 733 (1969).

3. 319 U.S. 624, 63 S.Ct. 1178 (1943).

4. Four judges dissented on this point, finding no basis for a student constitutional right to specific materials being made available in the school library.

5. The Court did not conclude that the exercise of discretion by a board in the *selection* of books for the school library could constitute such an interference, and this has created a somewhat anomalous situation. As one judge put it in another school library case, it is "unsupportable under any theory of constitutional law we can discover for a book to acquire tenure," Mulligan J., President's Council, Dist. 25 v. Community School Bd. 457 F.2d 289, 293; (2d Cir. 1972).

6. The Pico case was remanded by the Supreme Court to the Federal District Court to determine what the actual motivation of the school board had been in ordering the removal of books from its library. Rather than be subjected to a jury trial on this issue, however, the board agreed to return the books to the library shelves.

7. Mass. Constitution, Chapter 5, Section 2.

8. Mass. General Statutes, Chapter 71, Section 30.

9. *The Courts and the Public Schools,* 3rd ed. (Chicago, Ill.: University of Chicago Press, 1971) pp. 23–24.

QUESTIONS FOR MEANING

1. How does Gluckman define censorship? What does he mean by describing it as an "emotionally charged word"?
2. Why does Gluckman believe citizens have the right to present complaints about the books being used in public schools?
3. Why does Gluckman believe that the removal of printed material by a school board is not the equivalent of censorship?
4. What distinction did the Supreme Court make between books assigned as part of the curriculum and books found in a school library? Which type of book is more likely to be protected by the First Amendment?
5. According to Gluckman, when should courts examine allegations that a school board is exerting improper control over instructional material?
6. Why can schools be expected to convey "respect for authority and traditional values, be they social, moral, or political"?
7. Vocabulary: affiliated (2), placate (3), paradoxical (6), inimical (9), pejorative (10), capricious (16), corollary (22), partisans (31), inculcate (31), mandates (34).

QUESTIONS ABOUT STRATEGY

1. Why does Gluckman begin his essay with a four paragraph long summary of the problem of censorship? Why does he define censorship before presenting his own views?
2. How clear are Gluckman's references to various court cases?
3. Why does Gluckman quote the Massachusetts Constitution?
4. What sort of role does Gluckman seek to play through this essay?

TOM WICKER
The Wrong Lesson

*In May 1983, Dr. Robert E. Reynolds, the principal of Hazelwood East High School near St. Louis, Missouri, deleted articles on divorce and teenage pregnancy from the school newspaper. "The students and families in the articles were described in such an accurate way that readers could tell who they were," Dr. Reynolds explained. "When it became clear that the articles were going to tread on the right of privacy of students and their parents, I stepped in to stop the process." Three of the student journalists involved sued on the grounds that the principal had interfered with the newspaper's function as "a public forum." The principal's decision was initially upheld in court, but when the lower court's decision was appealed, a three-judge panel for the Court of Appeals for the Eighth Circuit ruled in favor of the students. The case subsequently made its way to the Supreme Court, which in January **1988** ruled 5 to 3 that school officials had acted within their rights.*

The following editorial appeared in the New York Times *shortly after the Supreme Court decision was announced. Educated at the University of North Carolina and a former Nieman Fellow at Harvard, Tom Wicker has written for the* New York Times *since 1960.*

The Supreme Court, as Justice William J. Brennan Jr. wrote in dissent, taught "young men and women" the wrong civics lesson when it upheld the right of a principal to impose prior restraint on a student newspaper. So it did, and that damaging lesson may well be absorbed far beyond the corridors of high school.

Most specifically, the Court's 5-to-3 decision in the Hazelwood school case may now be invoked in efforts to limit freedom of expression in student publications, theatrical presentations and the like at state universities. Despite the differences in high schools and colleges, it's hard to see why the rationale of the decision—that public education officials may censor an activity "reasonably related to legitimate pedagogical concerns"—could not be cited by university administrators.

What, moreover, are "legitimate pedagogical concerns"? Justice Byron R. White's opinion for the majority went so far as to say that schools could legitimately censor expression that might "associate the school with any position other than neutrality on matters of public controversy." What kind of support is that for the supposedly American values of robust debate and the "marketplace" of ideas?

Besides, the Hazelwood principal did far more than dissociate his school from articles to which he objected in its student newspaper. He quashed the printing of two pages of the paper, effectively silencing speech—not just in the two articles to which he objected, but in four others on the pages. The

Court found this action "not unreasonable," owing to the nature of his objections to the two articles, to the fact that the student publication, in the Court's view, was not a "public forum" and that its contents were a "legitimate pedagogical" matter over which the principal had jurisdiction.

In so finding, the Court nevertheless upheld a "prior restraint"—the pre-   5
vention of publication of something someone finds offensive. In the Pentagon Papers case and others, prior restraints have been held unconstitutional except in the most exceptional cases. Now the Court not only holds that prior restraint may be imposed almost routinely on student publications; but it adds substance to the view that in some cases, for some forms of expression, prior restraint is constitutional after all.

A high school newspaper partially financed by the school board, and which   6
is published as part of the curriculum, may not be technically, as Justice White insisted, a "public forum." But it may be the only forum the students have; if school officials can censor it, student rights of expression previously established by the Supreme Court have been limited. If student speech is not fully protected by the First Amendment, are there other classes of citizens who might be so limited?

The decision well may drive some students to "underground" publica-   7
tions—and to the logical conclusion that what schools teach about free speech is not what schools practice. Isn't *that* a legitimate pedagogical concern?

The Hazelwood principal's reasons for objecting to the articles in question   8
seem reasonable—he thought one might violate some students' privacy and that the other was unfair to a person mentioned in it. But whatever his good intentions, he had open to him other remedies than prior restraint.

It's not even clear why he couldn't have insisted upon changes he thought   9
necessary. Page proofs were shown to him on May 10; publication was not scheduled until May 13.

But if there really was no time for editing, the principal could have speci-   10
fied his objections and warned against future violations. In addition, to prevent future problems, he could have ordered a change in procedure to make sure he had adequate time to read page proofs and work out agreed-upon changes with the student editors. Perhaps a stronger, or a better understood, set of rules for publication could have been worked out to prevent future conflicts.

All of these possible courses of action, it will be objected, would have   11
resulted in publication of the articles to which the principal objected. But some expressions will always be found offensive or unjustifiable or incorrect by some in the audience; and it is inherent in a free press that privacy will sometimes be violated, not always necessarily, and that some stories may be unfair.

If such excesses could be prevented by authority, the press, in the nature   12
of the case, would not be free. The Hazelwood lesson is that some authorities can prevent some publications. As Justice Brennan observed, that's the wrong lesson.

QUESTIONS FOR MEANING

1. Why does Wicker believe that the Hazelwood case may have damaging effects "far beyond the corridors of high school"?
2. Can you explain what Wicker means in paragraph 3 by "the 'marketplace' of ideas"?
3. What is the meaning of the legal phrase "prior restraint"?
4. According to Wicker, what else could the Hazelwood principal have done instead of removing two pages from the school paper?

QUESTIONS ABOUT STRATEGY

1. Why does Wicker put quotation marks around "young men and women" in paragraph 1? Is he making a point?
2. Consider Wicker's use of quotations in paragraphs 2–4. Why were these phrases worth quoting? Would paraphrase have worked as well?
3. Does Wicker make any concessions?

FLANNERY O'CONNOR
Total Effect and the Eighth Grade

Flannery O'Connor (1925–1964) ranks as one of the best American writers in this century. During her relatively short life she published only two novels, Wise Blood *(1952) and* The Violent Bear it Away *(1960), and a collection of short stories,* A Good Man is Hard to Find *(1955). A second collection of stories,* Everything That Rises Must Converge *(1965) was published posthumously. In the years since her death, increasing numbers of readers have come to discover the strangely wonderful combination of grotesque humor and religious mystery that characterizes the best of O'Connor's fiction. She has been the subject of many critical studies, and her* Complete Stories *won the National Book Award when published in 1972. "Total Effect and the Eighth Grade" was written in* **1963;** *it is drawn from* Mystery and Manners, *a collection of O'Connor's essays and occasional prose edited by Sally and Robert Fitzgerald.*

In two recent instances in Georgia, parents have objected to their eighth- and ninth-grade children's reading assignments in modern fiction. This seems to happen with some regularity in cases throughout the country. The unwitting parent picks up his child's book, glances through it, comes upon passages of erotic detail or profanity, and takes off at once to complain to the school board. Sometimes, as in one of the Georgia cases, the teacher is dismissed and hackles rise in liberal circles everywhere.

The two cases in Georgia, which involved Steinbeck's *East of Eden* and John Hersey's *A Bell for Adano,* provoked considerable newspaper comment.

One columnist, in commending the enterprise of the teachers, announced that students do not like to read the fusty works of the nineteenth century, that their attention can best be held by novels dealing with the realities of our own time, and that the Bible, too, is full of racy stories.

Mr. Hersey himself addressed a letter to the State School Superintendent in behalf of the teacher who had been dismissed. He pointed out that his book is not scandalous, that it attempts to convey an earnest message about the nature of democracy, and that it falls well within the limits of the principle of "total effect," that principle followed in legal cases by which a book is judged not for isolated parts but by the final effect of the whole book upon the general reader. 3

I do not want to comment on the merits of these particular cases. What concerns me is what novels ought to be assigned in the eighth and ninth grades as a matter of course, for if these cases indicate anything, they indicate the haphazard way in which fiction is approached in our high schools. Presumably there is a state reading list which contains "safe" books for teachers to assign; after that it is up to the teacher. 4

English teachers come in Good, Bad, and Indifferent, but too frequently in high schools anyone who can speak English is allowed to teach it. Since several novels can't easily be gathered into one textbook, the fiction that students are assigned depends upon their teacher's knowledge, ability, and taste: variable factors at best. More often than not, the teacher assigns what he thinks will hold the attention and interest of the students. Modern fiction will certainly hold it. 5

Ours is the first age in history which has asked the child what he would tolerate learning, but that is a part of the problem with which I am not equipped to deal. The devil of Educationism that possesses us is the kind that can be "cast out only by prayer and fasting." No one has yet come along strong enough to do it. In other ages the attention of children was held by Homer and Virgil, among others, but, by the reverse evolutionary process, that is no longer possible; our children are too stupid now to enter the past imaginatively. No one asks the student if algebra pleases him or if he finds it satisfactory that some French verbs are irregular, but if he prefers Hersey to Hawthorne, his taste must prevail. 6

I would like to put forward the proposition, repugnant to most English teachers, that fiction, if it is going to be taught in the high schools, should be taught as a subject and as a subject with a history. The total effect of a novel depends not only on its innate impact, but upon the experience, literary and otherwise, with which it is approached. No child needs to be assigned Hersey or Steinbeck until he is familiar with a certain amount of the best work of Cooper, Hawthorne, Melville, the early James, and Crane, and he does not need to be assigned these until he has been introduced to some of the better English novelists of the eighteenth and nineteenth centuries. 7

The fact that these works do not present him with the realities of his own time is all to the good. He is surrounded by the realities of his own time, and 8 he has no perspective whatever from which to view them. Like the college student who wrote in her paper on Lincoln that he went to the movies and got shot, many students go to college unaware that the world was not made yesterday; their studies began with the present and dipped backward occasionally when it seemed necessary or unavoidable.

There is much to be enjoyed in the great British novels of the nineteenth   9
century, much that a good teacher can open up in them for the young student. There is no reason why these novels should be either too simple or too difficult for the eighth grade. For the simple, they offer simple pleasures; for the more precocious, they can be made to yield subtler ones if the teacher is up to it. Let the student discover, after reading the nineteenth-century British novel, that the nineteenth-century American novel is quite different as to its literary characteristics, and he will thereby learn something not only about these individual works but about the sea-change which a new historical situation can effect in a literary form. Let him come to modern fiction with this experience behind him, and he will be better able to see and to deal with the more complicated demands of the best twentieth-century fiction.

Modern fiction often looks simpler than the fiction that preceded it, but in   10
reality it is more complex. A natural evolution has taken place. The author has for the most part absented himself from direct participation in the work and has left the reader to make his own way amid experiences dramatically rendered and symbolically ordered. The modern novelist merges the reader in the experience; he tends to raise the passions he touches upon. If he is a good novelist, he raises them to effect by their order and clarity a new experience—the total effect—which is not in itself sensuous or simply of the moment. Unless the child has had some literary experience before, he is not going to be able to resolve the immediate passions the book arouses into any true, total picture.

It is here the moral problem will arise. It is one thing for a child to read   11
about adultery in the Bible or in *Anna Karenina*, and quite another for him to read about it in most modern fiction. This is not only because in both the former instances adultery is considered a sin, and in the latter, at most, an inconvenience, but because modern writing involves the reader in the action with a new degree of intensity, and literary mores now permit him to be involved in any action a human being can perform.

In our fractured culture, we cannot agree on morals; we cannot even agree   12
that moral matters should come before literary ones when there is a conflict between them. All this is another reason why the high schools would do well to return to their proper business of preparing foundations. Whether in the senior year students should be assigned modern novelists should depend both on their parents' consent and on what they have already read and understood.

The high-school English teacher will be fulfilling his responsibility if he   13
furnishes the student a guided opportunity, through the best writing of the past, to come, in time, to an understanding of the best writing of the present.

He will teach literature, not social studies or little lessons in democracy or the customs of many lands.

And if the student finds that this is not to his taste? Well, that is regret-   14
table. Most regrettable. His taste should not be consulted; it is being formed.

QUESTIONS FOR MEANING

1. Where does the title of this essay come from? Explain what "total effect" means.
2. What does O'Connor think of high school English teachers? Do you agree with her?
3. According to O'Connor, what is the proper function of a high school education, and how much say should students have in defining their own needs?
4. Does O'Connor really believe that "our children are too stupid now to enter the past imaginatively"? If she doesn't mean it, why did she write it?
5. What does O'Connor mean by the "devil of Educationism"?
6. Why does O'Connor believe that modern fiction is often more difficult than it looks?
7. Does O'Connor believe that teachers should be restricted to a list of approved books? If so, does she indicate who should do the approving? Should this responsibility rest primarily upon teachers or parents?

QUESTIONS ABOUT STRATEGY

1. A good summary should be clear and objective. How would you describe the tone of paragraphs 2–3, where O'Connor summarizes two censorship cases that were in the news when she wrote? Does she give any indication what her own thesis will be? Or is she perfectly neutral?
2. Can you detect the use of irony anywhere in this essay? If so, where? What function does it serve?
3. In paragraph 6, O'Connor compares the teaching of English to the teaching of Algebra. Is this a valid comparison? Or is she confusing the issue by comparing subjects that are fundamentally different?
4. Is a college student really capable of thinking Lincoln could have gone to the movies, or is this an exaggeration that weakens O'Connor's case?
5. To what extent is O'Connor's argument likely to displease both parents and teachers? Is this a thoughtful argument balanced between those who favor censorship and those who oppose it? Does O'Connor go beneath the surface of controversy and reveal an underlying problem of serious importance? Or does she miss the point about what this controversy is all about?

SUSAN B. NEUMAN
Rethinking the Censorship Issue

Underlying much of the debate over censorship in schools is the belief that students are easily influenced by what they read. But research on the nature of reading has indicated that "reading" is a complex activity—and that different readers will perceive the same text in different ways. Susan B. Neuman, who teaches English at Eastern Connecticut State University, argues against censorship by discussing the various factors that determine how we respond to what we read. Her essay was first published in **1986.**

The right to read is considered sacred. It is based on an ideology of literacy which associates reading with progress, with competence, serving the interests of social and political stability. There is an unspoken assumption that given the opportunity, people will read something of value, making reading a social good instead of a social evil. 1

But reading can be a double-edged sword. Even early reformers of the late eighteenth and early nineteenth century recognized that literacy might be counterproductive. Some scholars were concerned that the extension of reading to the masses might cheapen and debase reading. Pressures from church organizations and local citizen groups demanded careful selection of reading materials suitable to common perceptions of proper socialization. As a result, the Sedition Act of 1798 imposed severe restraints upon the freedom of citizens to read, followed by cultural censorship of books on charges of obscenity as evidenced in the court battles in Pennsylvania, *Commonwealth vs. Sharpless,* 1815, and in Massachusetts, *Commonwealth vs. Holmes,* 1821 (Haney 1974). 2

Controversies related to censorship are based on two contradictory theories of freedom (Gelhorn 1960). Advocates of censorship regard it as a means to prevent the debasement of individual virtues and protect cultural standards and democracy. Opponents see it as a danger to the freedom of choice, without which democracy can not survive. 3

But there is another issue in the censorship debate which has not significantly been addressed. Underlying these controversies are three implicit theories regarding the power of print and the effect of reading. One assumption is that reading influences the opinions and beliefs of the reader—especially children—the significant measure (Beach 1976). Fundamental cultural values, beliefs and attitudes are transmitted, and these materials affect our views toward the world and ourselves. The second is that the effect of a book, article, or passage is universal, implying that there's one *correct meaning* for a particular work and that all who are exposed will respond in a uniform manner (Purves and Beach 1972). A book, accordingly, is a stimulus that causes a specific effect. The third posits that the effects of reading are context independent. Here, the assumption focuses attention narrowly on the 4 interaction between the reader and the content of the passage without re-gard to the cultural, social, and historical context.

Rather than focus on the propriety of censorship in general or the condi-   5
tion under which it might be justified, I will review the censorship debate in light of these three underlying assumptions. This review will question these assumptions, focusing primarily on existing theories and methodological studies in reading and in the broader field of mass communication research.

Does Reading Significantly Influence the Opinions and Beliefs of the Reader?

Reading enters into a pattern of influences that already exist. Personality   6
styles, developed by important factors such as heredity and home environ-ment, are relatively stable. The influence of personality on responses toward reading, therefore, may be stronger than any short-term changes in person-ality as a result of reading (Beach 1976).

Klapper formulated the principle of selected attention, selective percep-   7
tion, and selective retention as a fundamental theory to describe the way people use media (1960). It suggests that from a multiplicity of available content individuals will selectively attend to reading materials, particularly if they are related to their interests, consistent with already existing attitudes, congruent with their beliefs, and supportive of their values. Rather than change opinions, reading most often promotes reinforcement.

Beach's (1973) study of college students tends to verify this hypothesis.   8
Among the subjects studied, these common reading traits were noted: the tendency to be absorbed in the familiar rather than to obtain new informa-tion; to remember figures mentioned but to comprehend them inaccurately; and to relate facts in such a way as to make a consistent interpretation sat-isfying to the individual. Responses to written material were influenced by readers' prejudices and personal experiences.

In the event they are exposed to unsympathetic material, people tend not   9
to perceive it, to recast it, or to reinterpret it to satisfy already existing views (Lesser 1957; Holland 1975; Strang 1942). Any form of new information con-trary to deep-seated conviction tends to confuse and perplex readers. Read-ers will transform material into a synthesis or unity which is integrative and satisfying. Holland, in a psychoanalytic study of five readers, described this pattern in terms of "identity theme" where readers recreate the message of a work to reflect their life styles. "The moralist will find a reinforcement of his ethical views; the scientifically minded man will see verifiable reality" (Holland, 125). If the dissonance becomes too great, readers will likely turn to other activities to satisfy their needs.

Conversion to new attitudes or beliefs through reading, while rare, might   10
occur under conditions when the reader is confronted with new information (Klapper 1960; Krugman 1965; McGuire, 1969; Tyler and Voss 1982). Waples et al. (1940), in their analysis of the social effects of reading, found that the less readers knew about the complexity of and objections to issues, the greater

the change in public opinion. But attitudes that were particularly salient and committing were most resistant to change. Tyler and Voss's research on knowledge and attitudinal effects suggests a model in which knowledge processing dominates when readers are confronted with new information while attitudes dominate when passage contents are of low informational value (1982).

It is natural to assume that ideas and issues presented in books signifi-   11
cantly affect readers. However, it appears that personality characteristics of individuals act as a filtering device, influencing the interpretations of the content and, ultimately, the power of the effect. Rather than changing opinions, reading tends to confirm our knowledge of issues and reinforces already established beliefs. Whatever conditions might occur to discontinue the spiral of reinforcement of predispositions, authorities agree, will not result from the reading material alone (Burress 1979; Steffensen, Joag-Dev, and Anderson 1979; Klapper 1960).

Does a Book Have One Universal Meaning?

Evidence suggests that there is no one *correct meaning* for a book (Purves   12
and Beach 1972; Purves 1973; Rosenblatt 1978). The meaning of a work evolves from an interplay of reader and material. Rather than being uniform, the manner in which people are exposed to content varies from person to person because of individual psychological differences. This, in turn, leads to varying effects (Beach 1976; De Fleur and Ball-Rokeach 1975).

Readers tend to impose an interpretation dependent upon their own per-   13
ceptions (Squire 1964). The more closely people can identify with material being read, the more intense will be their interest and involvement (Beach and Neuman, in preparation). It is *then* that a text becomes a "poem" as Rosenblatt describes, a personal experience capable of influencing readers' attitudes and actions (1978). It is the convergence of the text and the reader that brings the literary work into existence. In this respect, Iser (1974) refers to the act of reading as a "sense-making activity." Variations among readers account for different realizations of a given text. Reading, then, should be seen as constructive. Something new, something personal is created in each reading act. The power of the text is released through energies exerted by readers (Chaplin 1982).

Studies in schema theory represent one of the more promising new direc-   14
tions in our understanding of how information is acquired and retained. Knowledge units, or schemata, describe how information is represented in the mind and how that representation aids its use (Rumelhart 1980). These units reflect one's background knowledge as well as the universe of possible meanings to be constructed from a given text. Different people, reading a similar text, will take away different meanings (Anderson, Reynolds, Goetz, and Schallert 1977; Read and Rosen 1981; Reynolds, Taylor, Steffensen, Shirey, and Anderson 1982). Steffensen, Joag-Dev, and Anderson (1979), in their study of readers from India and America, found that schemata pro-

foundly influenced the manner in which a story was comprehended, learned, and remembered.

The impact of reading might be further effected by the perceived pur-   15
poses and needs of readers. Several researchers have theorized that it is the strength of a particular need that determines the effect (Blumer and Katz 1974; Holmlov 1982; Levy 1977). Thus, for example, the person more strongly and more exclusively moved to read materials from certain information will most likely acquire knowledge from it. In a study of over 100 high school students, Holmlov (1982) reported that the perceived need for information was a better predictor of knowledge gained than other factors including reading interests, amount of reading, or other background variables.

A book, then, is not simply a stimulus that causes a special effect. Reading   16
materials contain particular attributes that appear to have a differential effect according to the information needs and the personality characteristics of readers. Since there are individual differences in personality characteristics, there will be variations in effect. One work creates different meanings for different people. In this respect, there is a complexity or uniqueness in each person's reading pattern.

Are the Effects of Reading Context-Independent?

Some evidence in research literature suggests that the environment as   17
well as informal social relationships play a significant role in determining the effects of communication content (Carey, Harste, and Smith 1981; Delain, Pearson, and Anderson 1985; Gray 1946; Rogers 1973). People not only pass on information but also interpretations of content. In doing so, this personal influence factor becomes an important intervening variable between the content of what is read and the response to that message (Katz 1960).

Mass communications researchers have attempted to analyze the role of   18
social relations in the diffusion of ideas, behaviors, and attitudes through the mass media (Berelson et al. 1954; Lazarsfeld et al. 1948; Merton 1949). As the result of several independent studies analyzing voter behavior in the 1940s, Lazarsfeld formulated the two-step flow hypothesis to describe the effect of interpersonal relations in terms of communications effects. His theory suggests that information flowed through two basic stages. First, information moved from the media (primarily radio and newspapers) to well-informed individuals or "opinion leaders" who frequently attended to mass communications. Second, it moved from those people through interpersonal channels to individuals who had less direct exposure and who depended on others for their information.

The two-step flow theory is suggestive for reading research. A reading   19
experience is typically described as the involvement of author and reader in a contractual relationship which makes every reading event a personal interaction. Beyond the individual experience, however, lies a sociological response, one assuming that despite the heterogeneity of our society, certain types of behavior are predictive of certain social groups. What the two-step

flow hypothesis emphasizes is that reading is a mass media *and* a social process. The act of reading relates the individual to the environment and conditions that relationship.

One of the more distinct examples of the interplay between social envi-   20 ronment and communications content occurred before the Civil War. *Uncle Tom's Cabin* by Harriet Beecher Stowe has been considered one of the major forces leading to the eventual outbreak of the War by arousing the national conscience and crystallizing opinion on both sides of the issues. Its effect, however, did not altogether lie in the number of people who read the book. *Uncle Tom's Cabin* had a tremendous influence in the South where it was banned. Ironically, the principal effect of these restrictions was to spread the fame of the book. Today, the book is rarely read or assigned in classes. Any mention of it brings to mind a sensational, highly sentimental polemic. The power of the book was reflected in the emotional climate of its age (Neuman 1985).

Neither the text nor the reader, therefore, can be studied in isolation.   21 These contextual factors may modify possible meanings to be constructed from an encounter with a given text. Carey, Harste, and Smith (1981), for example, studied the effects of context on the interpretation of reading material. Undergraduates were presented with ambiguously worded written passages into two social settings. Physical education and music students, in context related settings, tended to exhibit greater background knowledge scores, suggesting the strong effects of situational context. The importance of the social context is further extended by literary critic Stanley Fish who suggests that the interpretation of a text is controlled in interpretive communities. Interpretation is never totally free but always constrained by prior acquisitions such as language, generic norms, social patterns, and beliefs (Fish 1982).

Katz suggests that the effects of communication content are related to   22 who one is, to what one knows, to whom one knows (1960). The effects of reading then are not simply responses to various stimuli but in fact depend on a convergence of influences including psychological characteristics, the content of the book, and social category similarities which people bring to their reading and which, moreover, will be further influenced by members of their norm group and the social context. In this respect, reading is regarded as a mass medium, capable of reaching large and diverse audiences, thus affecting levels of knowledge, attitudes and ideologies.

Conclusions

The assumptions that underlie the censorship debate represent complex   23 issues in reading research. But there are several tentative conclusions which directly relate to the continuing challenge of censorship. First, people tend to read for reinforcement of ideas and beliefs already held. Readers' prejudices and personal experiences color their responses to their reading. Advocates of censorship have claimed that, given certain materials, students' attitudes will change. Based on the studies surveyed here, it appears that little short-term change in values or behavior occurs through reading. Second, there is a complexity and uniqueness in individual reading patterns. What readers get out of a passage depends to a large extent on what they bring to the passage. Readers' responses vary considerably. Predictions about the nature of these responses to certain materials are highly questionable. Third, the effects of reading tend to be influenced by interpersonal relationships and the social context. Readers' opinions are more likely to be determined by their environment, family, peers, and schooling than by reading alone. Claims by censorship advocates that reading certain books will result in anti-social behavior are not supported by research. Books do not appear to have the functions attributed by censors who present them as major contributing factors to sexual immorality, juvenile delinquency, and political unrest.

Living in a pluralistic society, we will always experience tension and disagreements about where to draw the line. Pressures to censor materials will continue, and schools and communities need to be prepared by developing a well-articulated rationale for selecting literature in school programs. Such guidelines might include the age appropriateness of certain materials, the context in which a book is presented, and the instructional strategies to be used. In addition, there might also be times and valid reasons for using potentially offensive materials. A study of World War II, for example, might well include pro-Nazi materials. But the purpose and the objectives must be openly communicated to the public.   24

Censorship is negative because it eliminates choice and discourages reading. It does not encourage or create opportunities for positive reading experiences. Further education, rather than censorship, can lead to an informed citizenry. That is the goal that educators must emphasize.   25

We must also continue to develop more integrative and sophisticated theoretical models to understand the complex relationship not only between readers and texts but also the social conditions that influence public opinion. By doing so, we will begin to specify not what we *think* we know about how people are affected by reading, but with rigorous research designs, how these events *actually* take place. That will be our best response to the continuing challenge of censorship.   26

References*

Anderson, Richard C., Ralph E. Reynolds, Diane L. Schallert, and Ernest T. Goetz. "Frameworks for Comprehending Discourse." *American Educational Research Journal* 14 (Winter 1977): 367–382.

*This essay uses the author/date system for documentation recommended by *The Chicago Manual of Style*. It is very similar to the APA author/year system. The only difference is that there is no comma separating the author and the date in *Chicago Manual* style parenthetical documentation. The *Chicago Manual* recognizes two different forms for the reference list, one of which places the year of publication (without parentheses) immediately after the author's name, while the other places the date of publication at the end of the entry. For her reference list, Neuman used the latter of these two possibilities; it is the form appropriate for writing in the humanities. For additional information, see *The Chicago Manual of Style* [editor's note].

Beach, Richard. *The Literary Response Process of College Students while Reading and Discussing Three Poems.* Doctoral diss., University of Illinois, 1973.

———."Issues of Censorship and Research on Effects and Response to Reading." *Journal of Research and Development in Education* 9 (1976): 3–21.

Beach, Richard, and Susan B. Neuman. "The Role of Readers' Prototypical Assumptions in Response to Reading Two Short Stories." Submitted for publication.

Berelson, Bernard, Paul Lazarsfeld, and William MePhee. *Voting: A Study of Opinion Formation in a Presidential Campaign.* Chicago: University of Chicago Press, 1954.

Blumer, Jay, and Elihu Katz, eds. *The Uses of Mass Communications: Current Perspectives on Gratifications Research.* Beverly Hills, California: Sage Press, 1974.

Burress, Lee. "A Brief Report of the 1977 NCTE Censorship Report." In *Dealing with Censorship,* edited by James E. David. Urbana: NCTE, 1979.

Carey, Robert, Jerome C. Harste, and S. L. Smith, "Contextual Constraints and Discourse Processes: A Replication Study," *Reading Research Quarterly* 16 (1981): 201–212.

Chaplin, Miriam. "Rosenblatt Revisited: The Transaction Between Reader and Text." *Journal of Reading* 26 (November 1982): 150–155.

De Fleur, Melvin, and Sandra Ball-Rokeach. *Theories of Mass Communication,* 3rd ed. New York: McKay, 1975.

DeLain, Marsha T., P. David Pearson, and Richard Anderson. "Reading Comprehension and Creativity in Black Language Use: You Stand to Gain by Playing the Sounding Game!" *American Educational Research Journal* 22 (Summer 1985): 155–174.

Fish, Stanley. "Working on the Chain Gang: Interpretation in the Law and in Literary Criticism." *Critical Inquiry* 9 (September 1982): 201–216.

Gelhorn, Walter. "Restraints on Book Reading." In *The First Freedom.* Chicago: American Library Association, 1960.

Gray, William S. "The Social Effects of Reading." *School Review* 55 (May 1947): 269–277.

Haney, Robert. *Comstockery in America.* Boston: Beacon Press, 1960.

Holland, Norman. *Five Readers Reading.* New Haven: Yale University Press, 1975.

Holmlov, P. G. "Motivation for Reading Different Content Domains." *Communication Research* 9 (April 1982): 314–320.

Iser, Wolfgang. "The Interaction Between Text and Reader." In *The Reader in the Text,* edited by Susan R. Suleiman and Inge Crosman. Princeton: Princeton University Press, 1980.

Katz, Elihu. "The Two-Step Flow of Communication." In *Mass Communications,* edited by Wilbur Schramm. Urbana: University of Illinois Press, 1960.

Klapper, Joseph T. *The Effects of Mass Communication.* New York: Free Press, 1960.

Krugman, Herbert. "The Impact of Television Advertising: Learning without Involvement." *Public Opinion Quarterly* 29 (Summer 1965): 349–358.

Lazarsfeld, Paul, Bernard Berelson, and H. Gaudet. *The People's Choice.* New York: Columbia University Press, 1948.

Lesser, Simon. *Fiction and the Unconscious.* Chicago: University of Chicago Press, 1954.

Levy, M. R. "The Uses and Gratifications of Television News," Ph.D. diss., Columbia University, 1977.

McGuire, William J. "The Nature of Attitudes and Attitude Change." In *The Handbook of Social Psychology,* edited by G. Lindzey and E. Aronson, Vol. 3, *The Individual in a Social Context,* 2nd ed. Reading, Massachusetts: Addison-Wesley, 1969.

Merton, Robert K. "Patterns of Influence: A Study of Interpersonal Influence and Communications Behavior in a Local Community. In *Communication Research,* edited by Paul Lazarsfeld and Frank Stanton. New York: Harper and Brothers, 1949.

Neuman, Susan B. "The Legacy of Uncle Tom's Cabin: A Case Study in Book History." Paper presented to the American Association of Public Opinion Research, Great Gorge, New Jersey, 1985.

Purves, Alan and Richard Beach. *Literature and the Reader.* Urbana: NCTE, 1972.

Read, Simon J. and Mary Rosson. "Rewriting History. The Biasing Effect of Beliefs on Memory." *Social Cognition* 1 (1982): 240–255.

Reynolds, Richard, Marsha Taylor, Margaret Steffensen, Larry Shirey, and Richard Anderson. "Cultural Schemata and Reading Comprehension." *Reading Research Quarterly* 17 (1982): 353–366.

Rogers, Everett M. "Mass Media and Interpersonal Communication. In *Handbook of Communication,* edited by Ithiel de Sola Poot et al. Chicago: Rand McNally, 1973.

Rosenblatt, Louise. *The Reader the Text the Poem.* Carbondale: Southern Illinois University Press, 1978.

Rumelhart, David. "Schemata: The Building Blocks of Cognition." In *Theoretical Issues in Reading Comprehension,* edited by Rand J. Spiro et al. Hillsdale: Lawrence Erlbaum Associates, 1980.

Squire, James. *The Responses of Adolescents while Reading Four Short Stories.* Urbana: NCTE, 1964.

Steffensen, Margaret, Chitra Joag-Dev, and Richard Anderson. "A Cross-Cultural Perspective on Reading Comprehension." *Reading Research Quarterly* 15 (1979): 10–29.

Strang, Ruth. *Explorations in Reading Patterns.* Chicago: University of Chicago Press, 1942.

Tyler, Sherman, and James Voss. "Attitude and Knowledge Effects in Prose Processing." *Journal of Learning and Verbal Behavior* 21 (1982): 524–538.

Waples, Douglas, Bernard Berelson, and Franklin Bradshaw. *What Reading Does to People.* Chicago: University of Chicago Press, 1940.

QUESTIONS FOR MEANING

1. Why is the right to read considered "sacred" according to Neuman?
2. What are the two contradictory theories of freedom that underlie controversies about censorship?
3. What are the three assumptions about reading that Neuman challenges in this essay?
4. What is the effect of personality upon the way we read? What happens when readers are confronted with new information? Under what circumstances is this new information most likely to change an opinion already held by the reader?
5. Explain what Neuman means when she writes that there is no one "correct meaning" of a book. Why does she believe that reading is constructive?

6. Why does Neuman believe it is important for schools to develop guidelines for selecting school reading material?
7. Vocabulary: congruent (7), salient (10), convergence (13), differential (16), diffusion (18), polemic (20), tentative (23).

QUESTIONS ABOUT STRATEGY

1. How would you describe Neuman's writing style?
2. What is the example of *Uncle Tom's Cabin* meant to illustrate?
3. At what points in her essay does Neuman use summary?
4. What assumptions has Neuman made about her audience in writing this essay?

FRANCES FITZGERALD
Rewriting History

Frances FitzGerald comes from a family with a strong interest in politics and international affairs. Her father was a deputy director of the CIA, and her mother is a former American ambassador to the United Nations. A magna cum laude graduate of Radcliffe, FitzGerald went to Vietnam as a free-lance writer in 1966. She stayed for over a year gathering the material for Fire in the Lake *(1972). One of the first serious books on the American involvement in Vietnam, it won the 1973 Pulitzer Prize for writing about contemporary affairs. "Rewriting History" is an editor's title for an excerpt from FitzGerald's much respected second book,* America Revised *(**1979**), a study of the ways in which American history books have changed over the years, presenting significantly different views of the past in response to various types of pressure.*

To the uninitiated, the very thought of what goes on in a textbook house   1
must inspire a good deal of vertigo. Way up in some office building sit people—ordinary mortals with red and blue pencils—deciding all the issues of American history, not to mention those of literature and biology. What shall we think of the Vietnam War? Of the American Revolution? What is the nature of American society and what are its values? The responsibility of these people seems awesome, for, as is not true of trade publishers, the audiences for their products are huge, impressionable, and captive. Children have to read textbooks; they usually have to read all of each textbook and are rarely asked to criticize it for style or point of view. A textbook is there, much like Mt. Everest awaiting George Mallory, and it leaves no alternative. The textbook editors, therefore, must appear to be the arbiters of American values, and the publishing companies the Ministries of Truth for children. With such power over the past and the future, textbook people—or so the uninitiated

assume—should all be philosophers. Oddly, however, few people in the textbook business seem to reflect on their role as truth givers. And most of them are reluctant to discuss the content of their books. Occasionally, a young editor full of injured idealism will "leak" a piece of information about house policy. In one publishing house, a young woman pulled me inside her office conspiratorially to show me a newspaper article attacking a literary anthology that her company had published a few years before. The article expressed outrage about the profanity in the book, pointing to the use of the word "damn" in one short story. "Don't tell anyone I showed you this, or I'll lose my job," the young woman whispered. She went on to say that she had had to revise the anthology—a task that consisted of removing the offending selection and finding stories by two American women and a Puerto Rican man to replace three short stories by Anglo-Saxon men.

"Isn't that a bit arbitrary?" I asked.   2

"Oh, yes," she said. "But, you see, we're under such great pressure. We'd   3
never sell the book without a Hispanic-American."

The reticence of the textbook people derives, one soon discovers, from   4
the essential ambiguity of their position. On one hand, they are running what amount to Ministries of Truth for children, and, on the other, they are simply trying to make money in one of the freest of free enterprises in the United States, where companies often go under. The market sets limits to the publishers' truth-giving powers. These limits are invisible to outsiders, and they shift like sandbars over time, but the textbook people have a fairly good sense of where they are likely to run aground—and for the rest they feel their way along. Under the circumstances, there is no point in discussing final, or even intermediate, principles, since these would merely upset the navigation. It takes someone used to operating under the norms of trade publishing to demonstrate where principles conflict with market realities.

Robert Bernstein, the president of Random House, runs a large book-pub-   5
lishing complex. In 1974, the head of Pantheon, a Random House division, showed Bernstein the manuscript of what Bernstein thought was an excellent new ninth-grade history of Mississippi. The product of a collaboration between students and faculty of Tougaloo and Millsaps Colleges, the book, unlike the old textbook in use in Mississippi schools, discussed racial conflict frankly and pointed out the contributions that black people had made to the state. The manuscript had been turned down by several textbook houses, but Bernstein—against the advice of some of his own textbook people—backed its publication as a textbook. Pantheon published it as both a trade book and a textbook, under the title *Mississippi: Conflict and Change*. Most of the books never left the warehouse, because the one customer for them, the Mississippi State Textbook Purchasing Board, refused to approve the text for use in state schools at state expense, even though the one textbook in use had gone largely unchanged for ten years and the board was authorized to approve as many as five state histories. As an activist in civil-rights and civil-liberties causes, Bernstein was outraged. So were the authors of the book, and so were some parents, students, and local school officials in Mississippi,

and they retained the N.A.A.C.P. Legal Defense and Educational Fund to file suit against the Mississippi State Textbook Purchasing Board on the ground that its one approved history deprecated black Mississippians and championed white supremacy. "This business is shockingly political," Bernstein told me. "Especially in the South it's shocking."

Shocking as it might be, though, Random House did not join the Legal   6
Defense Fund in bringing suit. Historically, textbook houses do not bring such actions, and rarely, if ever, do they protest when their books are banned by school authorities or burned by outraged citizens. Unlike many trade publishers in similar circumstances (and unlike Pantheon in this case), they acquiesce, give way to pressure, and often cut out the offending passages. In the fall of 1974, a group of parents and other citizens in Kanawha County, West Virginia, demonstrated and finally shut down schools throughout the county in protest against some books newly acquired for classroom use or for the school libraries. Among the objects of their wrath were a number of stories by black writers (the protesters claimed that these were critical of whites), an anti-war poem, and a Mark Twain satire on the Book of Genesis. The incident made national news for weeks and created a good deal of consternation among publishers, teachers, and civil-liberties groups. The Teacher Rights Division of the National Education Association studied the controversy and concluded, not surprisingly, that it was basically a cultural conflict between liberal values and the fundamentalist beliefs of the community. No national organization found anything objectionable in the books, and yet at least one publishing house revised its literary anthology to meet Kanawha County standards.

Trade-book publishers tend to look upon such incidents as First Amend-   7
ment issues, and to see the acquiescence of textbook publishers as pure cowardice—as a betrayal of civil-liberties principles for commercial ends. But there is a sense in which they are wrong. For it is one thing to defend the right to publish a book and quite another to insist that schools must use the book. Why should the editors of Random House, Rand McNally, or Ginn & Company act as the arbiters of the classroom? Who are they to insist that children read Langston Hughes instead of Henry Wadsworth Longfellow, or works by three Anglo-Saxon men instead of works by two American women and one Hispanic-American man? A group like the National Education Association or the Legal Defense Fund can bring a case against a school board for censorship. But textbook publishers are only the servants of the schools, the providers of what they require. And yet textbook publishers rarely make this argument, since, taken to its logical conclusion, it implies that they have— and should have—no standards; that truth is a market commodity, determined by what will sell. Naturally, the publishers do not want to make this admission; hence the swampiness of their public statements, and their strangely unfocussed anxiety when they're asked about their editorial decisions.

To look further into the question of textbook selection and rejection is to   8
see that there is some matter of principle involved. In most countries, national authorities—academies or Ministries of Education—more or less dic-

tate educational policy and the content of textbooks. But the American educational system has always been highly decentralized, and resistant to national authority of any sort. From the publishers' point of view, the educational system is a market, but from the point of view of the schools it is a rough kind of democracy. If a state or a school district wants a certain kind of textbook—a certain kind of truth—should it not have it? The truth is everywhere political, and this system is in principle no less reasonable and no more oppressive of the individual than the alternative of a national authority. In fact, it might be argued that it is less oppressive—that, given the size of the United States, the texts reflect the values and attitudes of society at large much more accurately than they would without decentralization. At least to some degree, they reflect the society itself.

The texts represent the society imperfectly, because the democracy of the   9
educational system is not perfect. In the first place, texts are chosen by adults, and not by the children who must read them. An alternative system is difficult to conceive, but the fact remains that the texts do not represent children. In the second place, not all adults, or even all teachers, have a voice in the selection of schoolbooks. The system of selection is far from uniform across the country, and depends upon a variety of institutions analogous to the Electoral College or to the Senate as it was conceived by the Founding Fathers. About half of the states, for instance, have some form of state-level control over the selection of elementary-school textbooks; slightly fewer states have that control over the choice of secondary-school textbooks. In most of these states, a board of education, a superintendent of schools, or a special textbook committee reviews all texts submitted by the publishers and lists or adopts a certain number of them in each category for use in the public   •
schools. The practices of these review boards vary widely, as does their membership. Some boards, for instance, can by law adopt only a few books in each category, and in practice they may, as the one in Mississippi did, adopt only one. Others simply weed out a few books they judge substandard and leave the real power of decision to the schools. In the so-called non-adoption states, the school districts usually have committees to examine the texts, and the practices of the committees differ more than those of the state boards. The system is, in fact, so complicated nationwide that publishers employ people to spend most of their time figuring out how it works.

The theory behind the practice of state- or districtwide adoptions is that   10
some educational authority should stand between the world of commerce and the hard-pressed teachers to insure that the books meet certain educational standards. The standards are not, however, entirely academic. The guidelines for most state boards include dicta on the subject matter of the books and on the attitudes they display. The 1976 guidelines of the State Instructional Materials Councils for Florida, for instance, note, "Instructional materials should accurately portray man's place in ecological systems, including the necessity for the protection of our environment and conservation of our natural resources. [They] should encourage thrift and humane treatment of people and should not contain any material reflecting unfairly upon per-

sons because of their race, color, creed, national origin, ancestry, sex, or occupation." The State of Oregon has traditionally prohibited its schools from
using texts that speak slightingly of the Founding Fathers. In some cases,
the unwritten criteria of state boards are more specific and more important
to the selection of books; in certain instances, they contradict the written guidelines.

Then, too, the whole system is less than democratic, because it is biassed   11
toward the large adoption units—the large adoption states and the big-city
school districts—and particularly biassed toward the ones that make a narrow selection of books. For example, the recommendation of a social-studies
book by the Texas State Textbook Committee can make a difference of
hundreds of thousands of dollars to a publisher. Consequently, that committee has traditionally had a strong influence on the content of texts. In certain
periods, the committee has made it worthwhile for publishers to print a special Lone Star edition of American history, for use in Texas alone. Much more
important, it has from time to time exercised veto power over the content of
texts used nationwide. For example, in 1961 a right-wing fringe group called
Texans for America intimidated the committee, and it pressed several publishers to make substantial changes in their American-history and geography
texts. Macmillan, for one, deleted a passage saying that the Second World
War might have been averted if the United States had joined the League of
Nations. The Silver Burdett Company took out two passages concerning the
need for the United States to maintain friendly relations with other countries
and the possibility that some countries would occasionally disagree with us
and substituted passages saying that some countries were less free than the
United States. Various publishers deleted references to Pete Seeger, Langston Hughes, and several other offenders against the sensibilities of Texans
for America. Not only the largest states but combinations of smaller ones
have often exerted an influence disproportionate to the size of their school
populations. The fact that most of the former Confederate states have state-
level adoptions has meant that until recently conservative white school boards
have imposed their racial prejudices not only on the children in their states
but on children throughout the nation.

In sum, the system of adoptions has a significant impact on the way Amer-   12
icans are taught their own history. Because of the Texas State Textbook
Committee, New England children, whose ancestors heartily disapproved of
the Mexican War, have grown up with heroic tales of Davy Crockett and Sam
Houston. Because of actions taken by the Detroit school board and the Newark Textbook Council in the early sixties, textbooks began for the first time
to treat the United States as a multiracial society.

The school establishment is not the only group that shapes American his-   13
tory in the textbooks. It is often private-interest groups or citizens' organizations that bring about the most important political changes in the texts.
The voices of these outside pressure groups have risen and fallen almost
rhythmically in the course of the past fifty years. Sometimes there seems to
be a great deal of public interest in textbooks, sometimes very little. What is

noteworthy is that until 1960 the voices were pretty much alike; after that, they became much more varied, and the public debate over texts altered dramatically.

The history of public protests against textbooks goes back at least to the   14
middle of the nineteenth century, but these protests grew in size and intensity with the establishment of universal secondary education, in the twentieth. The first important outbreak of them occurred in the years following the First World War. In that period, the mayor of Chicago and the Hearst newspapers, using adjectives such as "unpatriotic" and "un-American," created an uproar over what they said was the pro-British bias of certain texts. (According to Henry Steele Commager, one of the objects of their rage was an account of the battle of Bunker Hill in a text by Andrew C. McLaughlin. That being a simpler era in the history of textbook publishing, McLaughlin himself answered the charges. According to Commager, he volunteered to change a sentence that read, "Three times the British returned courageously to the attack" to one reading, "Three times the cowardly British returned to the attack.") Simultaneously, the Daughters of the American Revolution attacked some of the texts for not putting enough stress on American military history. The Ku Klux Klan got into the act by complaining of pro-Jewish and pro-Catholic sentiments. Then a number of fundamentalist groups protested against the teaching of evolutionary theory, and eventually succeeded in purging some biology texts of references to evolution. Finally, and with no publicity at all, several utilities associations, including the National Electric Light Association, the American Gas Association, and the American Railway Association, put pressure on the publishers and school officials to doctor the texts in their favor. They got results until their efforts were discovered by the Federal Trade Commission. This wave of right-wing indignation receded as the Depression hit, and for the next ten years such groups remained silent. During the thirties, the peace was broken only by the Women's Christian Temperance Union and the liquor interests, whose debate seems to have ended in a draw.

Then, in 1939, there erupted the most furious of all textbook controversies   15
to date, the subject of which was a series on American civilization by Dr. Harold Rugg. A professor at Columbia University Teachers College, Dr. Rugg had written his series (intended for pupils in elementary and junior high school) in the twenties and had begun publishing it in 1930. His aim in writing it had been to bring some realism into the schoolbook description of American society, and to a great extent he succeeded. In one volume, *An Introduction to Problems of American Culture,* he discussed unemployment, the problems faced by new immigrants, class structure, consumerism, and the speedup of life in an industrial society. These questions had never before been dealt with extensively in any school text, and the frankness of his approach remains startling even today. Rugg is probably still the only text writer who has advocated national economic planning and who has used the word "Socialist" on the first page of a book. His series does not, however, advocate Socialism. The books are full of pieties about the need for American

children to become "tolerant, understanding and cooperating citizens." The series sold very well in the thirties. It was used in school systems containing nearly half of all American children, and for almost a decade there were no complaints about it. In 1939, a chorus of protests suddenly broke out. The first was from the Advertising Federation of America, which was offended by Rugg's disparaging remarks about advertising; then the National Association of Manufacturers, the American Legion, and a columnist for the Hearst press joined in, calling the series Socialist or Communist propaganda. The charges caught on and spread to community groups across the country. Dr. Rugg went on an extensive lecture tour to defend the series, during which he announced publicly that he was neither a Communist nor a Socialist. But in vain. A number of school boards banned the books, and others simply took them out of circulation. In 1938, the Rugg books sold 289,000 copies; in 1944, they sold only 21,000 copies; not long afterward, they disappeared from the market altogether.

During the forties, business associations and right-wing citizens' groups   16
attacked a number of other liberal textbooks and maintained a high level of pressure on the publishers. By 1950 or so, the merely conservative groups had been so successful that they had nothing more to complain about: the texts had become reflections of the National Association of Manufacturers viewpoint. This surrender by the publishers did not, however, end the war; it merely moved the battle lines farther to the right. In the mid-fifties, the anti-fluoridation lobby went on the offensive, followed a few years later by the John Birch Society, which—quite imaginatively—blamed the textbooks for the North Koreans' success in "brainwashing" a handful of American pris-oners of war. The textbook publishers took this seriously, for by that time they were so sensitive to right-wing pressure that they were checking their books before publication with a member of the Indiana State Textbook Com-mission named Ada White. Mrs. White believed, among other things, that Ro-bin Hood was a Communist, and she urged that books that told the Robin Hood story be banned from Indiana schools. The publishers were no less mindful of the Texas State House of Representatives, which—in a state that already required a loyalty oath from all textbook writers—approved a reso-lution urging that "the American history courses in the public schools em-phasize in the textbooks our glowing and throbbing history of hearts and souls inspired by wonderful American principles and traditions."

The mid-sixties must have been a bewildering period for the textbook   17
companies. In the space of a year or two, the political wind veered a hundred and eighty degrees. For the first time in publishing history, large-scale pro-tests came from the left and from non-white people, and for the first time such protests were listened to. The turnaround began with a decision made by the Detroit Board of Education. In 1962, the local branch of the N.A.A.C.P. charged that one history text, published by Laidlaw Brothers, depicted slav-ery in a favorable light, and called on the Detroit board to withdraw it from the city school system. The N.A.A.C.P. and other civil-rights organizations had denounced racial prejudice in the textbooks a number of times in prior years

with no real effect. This time, however, the Detroit board withdrew the text, and subsequently began to examine for racial bias all the history texts used in the school system. The Newark Textbook Council soon followed suit. The movement then spread to other big-city school systems and was taken up by organizations representing other racial and ethnic minority groups—Mexican-Americans, Puerto Ricans, American Indians, Asian-Americans, Armenian-Americans, and so on—all of whom claimed, with justice, to have been ignored or abused by the textbooks. Within a few years, a dozen organizations, from the B'nai B'rith's Anti-Defamation League to a new Council on Interracial Books, were studying texts for racial, ethnic, and religious bias and making recommendations for a new generation of texts. What began as a series of discreet protests against individual books became a general proposition: all texts had treated the United States as a white, middle-class society when it was in fact multiracial and multicultural. And this proposition, never so much as suggested before 1962, had by the late sixties come to be a truism for the educational establishment.

The causes of this sudden upsurge of protest and the equally sudden change 18 of perspective among educators are easy to understand in retrospect. As a result of the migrations from South to North during and after the Second World War, black Americans had become by the sixties a strong minority of the population in many Northern cities. In Detroit and Newark, they had become a majority. At the same time, the civil-rights movement had begun to focus national attention on the ugly facts of racial discrimination and prejudice in all areas of American life. A need for a change in the depiction of blacks and other minorities in textbooks, on television, and in advertising was merely one of the themes of the civil-rights movement, but it was the one that was the easiest to deal with. White Americans could resist racial integration in employment, in housing, and in the schools, but no one could deny the minorities at least a token place in the picture of American society. There was no principle to support a counter-argument, and, more important, no reason to make one. An alteration in the symbols could be made without any change in the reality.

The abrupt reversal of perspective in the schools created some panic in 19 the textbook houses. Three or four years—the time it usually takes to produce a new basic text—seemed like an aeon relative to the change in consciousness. A single year was enough to outdate any given picture of America, and nobody could know what the next change would be. (On the evidence of one elementary-school social-studies text, the panic must have reached an all-time high at Noble & Noble. As late as 1964, *New York: Past and Present* made only fleeting reference to blacks. Two years later, another Noble & Noble book, *The New York Story,* included five chapters on blacks.) No sooner had the editors begun to paste in pictures of Ralph Bunche and write reports on the civil-rights movement than along came the women's movement, sending them quite literally back to the drawing board—this time to change their representation of half the human species.

Only in the mid-seventies did the rate of change slow and the positions   20
harden enough for the publishers to write guidelines for authors and editors
on the treatment of racial and other minorities in the textbooks. These guidelines—which have since been published and thus set fast, at least for a while—
give instructions on such things as the percentage of illustrations to be devoted
to the various groups, and ways to avoid stereotyping in text or pictures. The
most interesting thing about them is the rather substantial modifications they
make in the English language. The Holt, Rinehart & Winston guidelines on
gender, for instance, include such strictures as "Avoid 'the founding fathers,'
use 'the founders.'" (Holt also says, "Men are to be shown participating in a
variety of domestic chores, such as cooking, sewing, housework, child-rearing,
etc. Care should be taken to avoid implying that they are inept at these
activities.") Houghton Mifflin advises its editors to make sparing use of quoted
material with male references, such as "These are the times that try men's
souls"; it has discouraged the use of "the fatherland" and female pronouns
referring to boats. To avoid ethnic stereotyping, its guidelines warn against
the overuse of names like "Mary" and "John" and the use of only one ethnic
name in lists of arbitrarily chosen names. Macmillan, for its part, urges its
editors not to transform ordinary words into negative concepts by adding
"black" to them, as in "black market," and it gives "native Americans" as an
alternative term for American Indians. There is, as the editors recognize, a
certain arbitrariness about these decisions on usage. Allyn & Bacon, for instance, subscribes to "native Americans" but not to "Hispanic-Americans."
"We won't use the term Hispanic-Americans," one editor told me, "unless, of
course, that becomes the way to go."

As the sixties ended, the publishers may have thought they had found   21
some peace. But it was not to be. Just as soon as their guidelines were issued
and pictures of female mechanics and native-American chairpersons began
to appear in the books, the reaction set in. The demonstrations in Kanawha
County were followed by a spate of smaller-scale protests in communities
across the country. Then the John Birch Society emerged from a decade of
near-silence to direct or help along (it was difficult to tell which) demonstrations in Washington against one of the new federally funded social-studies
programs. Some of the protesters were merely registering conservative objections to what they saw as the excesses of the sixties; others went further,
and attacked the whole drive for racial equality and women's rights.

More than automobile manufacturers or toothpaste executives, textbook   22
publishers see themselves as beleaguered, even persecuted, people. And there
is some justice in this view, for textbooks have become the lightning rods of
American society. In the past, public protest over textbooks occurred only in
times of rapid political or social change. Now a great number of organizations
and informal groups take an interest in the content of texts. In addition to
the racial and ethnic organizations, many of which disagree on what constitutes a "fair and accurate representation" of any given group, a multitude of
educational and civil-rights groups have research departments devoted ex-

clusively to the analysis of textbooks. Many of these departments—on the right and on the left—have with experience become sophisticated both in their analyses of text materials and in their methods of approaching publishers, school boards, and the federal bureaucracy. The public battle over texts is thus more intense and more complicated than it has ever been before. At the same time, the publishers have become much more sensitive to the market. Having availed themselves of many of the new market-research techniques, they can now register not just the great upheavals in society but also the slight tremors. They find this a mixed blessing. On the one hand, there are fewer surprises; on the other hand, they have had to become horrendously self-conscious. Does this math text have enough Polish-sounding people buying oranges? Does that third-grade reader show a woman fireperson? What will play in New York that will not offend the sensibilities of Peoria? As the publishers well know, it is impossible to satisfy everyone—or anyone for a long period.

There is perhaps only one group left in the country which does not bother   23
the publishers—or anyway not very often—and that is the academic community. True, scholars do help "develop" textbooks, and occasionally they are permitted to have a significant role in determining their content. In the nineteen-sixties, the federal government was spending large sums for the development of new teaching materials, and groups of scholars selected by the learned societies developed a new generation of textbooks in the natural and social sciences. (The history texts, however, were not affected, for the American Historical Association did not take part.) But most scholars do not take secondary-school (or even college) textbooks seriously—not even when they have a hand in writing them. They do not make a practice of reading textbooks in their field, and no academic journal reviews textbooks on a regular basis. One consequence is that new scholarship trickles down extremely slowly into the school texts; as it proceeds, usually by way of the college texts, the elapsed time between the moment an idea or an approach gains currency in the academic community and the moment it reaches the school texts may be fifteen years or more. Another consequence is that there is no real check on the intellectual quality—or even the factual accuracy—of school textbooks. The result is that on the scale of publishing priorities the pursuit of truth appears somewhere near the bottom.

In a perfectly democratic, or custom-designed, world, every teacher would   24
be allowed to choose his or her own history textbook—which is to say that the publishing houses would publish books in a variety large enough to suit all tastes. But this has somehow never happened, in spite of all the structural changes the textbook business has undergone in the United States over the past hundred years. The late nineteenth century ought to have been the period for a great diversity of books, because scores of publishers were competing then in a burgeoning school market. At the time, however, the content of texts was the least of a publisher's worries, for—particularly in the West, where the competition was the most intense—the sale of books depended largely on which company could most successfully bribe or otherwise corrupt

the whiskey dealers, preachers, and political-party hacks who sat on the school boards. This degree of free enterprise proved uneconomical in the long run. In the eighteen-nineties, three of the major companies banded together to form the American Book Company, which acquired a seventy-five- to eighty-per-cent monopoly of the textbook market. Yet this streamlining of the industry did not make for a wider selection of books. Indeed, when the American Book Company acquired a total monopoly in geography publishing, it produced no new books in that field for many years. Competition was eventually reëstablished, and there was some greater variety in the texts until the ideological freeze of the Cold War. In recent years, the industry has been a model of American free enterprise: four hundred companies (forty of them major ones) have competed fiercely, but with a fairly high degree of probity, to sell more or less the same product to the same people.

In the mid-sixties, there were high hopes in the publishing industry that this situation would change. Sitting at the feet of Marshall McLuhan, the publishers decided that the era of mass production was over—along with the era of literacy and linear reasoning—and that they should at once prepare to deliver instant all-around audiovisual programming with individualized feedback for every child. The era of software had come—the era of total communication and perfect customization. Not only—or even principally—the textbook publishers but a lot of high-rolling communications-industry executives dreamed of equipping every classroom in America with television sets, video cameras, holography sets, and computer terminals. As a first step toward this post-industrial future, the executives built conglomerates designed to put all kinds of software components and communications capability under one roof. Xerox acquired Ginn & Company; RCA bought Random House; C.B.S. acquired Holt, Rinehart & Winston; Raytheon bought D.C. Heath; and Time Inc. acquired Little, Brown and Company and Silver Burdett and, with General Electric, formed the General Learning Corporation.

The problem was that all the new theories about education, information, and business in the future rested on the availability of large-scale government funding, a growing student population, and a ballooning economy. And none of these conditions held for very long. As soon as the costs of the Vietnam War came home, the schools drastically curtailed their multimedia programs, the government cut back funding of research projects to develop new teaching methods and materials, and the conglomerates began to look like no more than the sum of their parts. And then, with great speed, fashions changed, and educational theory turned conservative. Parents and school boards complained that children couldn't read or write anymore—that what they needed was textbook drill. Publishers, up to their ears in machinery, began to look on textbooks as the basic winter coat. While they continued to produce some of the cheapest of the new materials—such things as magazines and filmstrips—they put their money back into books: both the hardbacks and a new generation of paperbacks, which allowed teachers a choice of supplementary material. "It began to dawn on them," one trade-book editor says, "that the book is finally the most efficient retrieval system we possess."

The big basic history textbook thus seems here to stay, at least for a bit,   27
and to stay just about what it has always been in this century—a kind of
lowest common denominator of American tastes. The books of the seventies
are somewhat more diverse than those of the fifties, but still they differ from
one another not much more than one year's crop of Detroit sedans. This is
hardly surprising, since, like cars, textbooks are expensive to design and relatively cheap to duplicate. The development of a new eleventh-grade history
text can cost five hundred thousand dollars (more this year, perhaps), with
an additional hundred thousand in marketing costs. Since the public schools
across the country now spend less than one per cent of their budgets on
buying books (textbook publishing is only a seven-hundred-million-dollar-a-
year business), publishers cannot afford to have more than one or two basic
histories on the market at the same time. Consequently, all of them try to
compete for the center of the market, designing their books not to please
anyone in particular but to be acceptable to as many people as possible. The
word "controversial" is as deeply feared by textbook publishers as it is cov-
eted by trade-book publishers. What a textbook reflects is thus a compromise, an America sculpted and sanded down by the pressures of diverse
constituents and interest groups.

QUESTIONS FOR MEANING

1. Why does FitzGerald believe that publishers have "power over the past
   and the future?" Is this an exaggeration? Can you think of anything besides textbooks that shapes our understanding of past and future?
2. If you have never heard of George Mallory, can you figure out who he
   was from the way he's mentioned in paragraph 1?
3. When FitzGerald writes about "Ministries of Truth," she is alluding to
   what famous twentieth century novel?
4. Who chooses textbooks? What sort of guidelines do they follow in choosing books for adoption? Who gets left out of the selection process?
5. Why has the state of Texas been able to have so much influence with
   publishers?
6. Why did the 1960s bring a great change in the demands that publishers
   try to satisfy? Why did a reaction eventually set in during the 1970s?
7. What does FitzGerald mean by "scholars," and why do they have little
   interest in textbooks?
8. Why don't textbook publishers protest censorship? Why do they respond
   to public criticism by cutting offending passages from their books?
9. Does FitzGerald justify her claim that "on the scale of publishing priorities the pursuit of truth appears somewhere near the bottom"?
10. Vocabulary: vertigo (1), reticence (4), acquiesce (6), consternation (6),
    arbiters (7), disparaging (15), truism (17), horrendously (22), and ideo-
    logical (24).

QUESTIONS ABOUT STRATEGY

1. What sort of tone does FitzGerald adopt toward the publishing industry? Is she critical, ironic, or sympathetic? Is her tone consistent throughout her argument?
2. Good writers know that changing a word or two can entirely change an idea. Consider the words of Andrew C. McLaughlin quoted in paragraph 14. Is this a good example of the type of censorship that concerns Fitz-Gerald? This was sixty years ago. Do you think any writer or publisher would be this crude today?
3. What does the story of Dr. Harold Rugg illustrate?
4. Consider FitzGerald's diction in paragraphs 25 and 26 where she writes about "all-around audiovisual programming with individualized feedback" and quotes an editor describing books as "the most efficient retrieval system we possess." Is this use of jargon deliberate or accidental? How does it compare with FitzGerald's prevailing style?
5. This argument is only a selection from the introductory chapter of a book FitzGerald has written on the subject of American history textbooks. If you were to read the rest of the book, what points would you most want FitzGerald to pursue in more detail?

WARREN BURGER

Board of Education, Island Trees v. Pico

*Warren Burger was the fifteenth chief justice of the United States. He studied at the University of Minnesota and practiced law in St. Paul until 1953 when Dwight Eisenhower appointed him an assistant attorney general in charge of the civil division of the Justice Department. Burger was named to the U.S. Court of Appeals for the District of Columbia in 1956 and acquired a reputation as a strict constructionist in criminal law. Conservatives were pleased when Richard Nixon appointed Burger chief justice in May 1969, but Burger showed himself to be independent minded. An advocate of judicial reform, Burger called for streamlining court procedures and requiring better training for judges and lawyers. But he was reluctant to expand the power of the courts, as the following opinion reveals. It is an unabridged transcript of Burger's dissenting opinion from an important **1982** Court decision on censorship in public schools. Following the custom of the Court, Burger uses* ante *(Latin for "before") to direct readers to specific pages in the majority opinion from which he is dissenting.*

SUPREME COURT OF THE UNITED STATES

No. 80-2043

BOARD OF EDUCATION, ISLAND TREES UNION FREE SCHOOL DISTRICT NO. 26 ET AL., PETITIONERS *v.* STEVEN A PICO, BY HIS NEXT FRIEND, FRANCES PICO ET AL.

ON WRIT OF CERTIORARI TO THE UNITED STATES COURT OF APPEALS FOR THE SECOND CIRCUIT

[June 25, 1982]

CHIEF JUSTICE BURGER, with whom JUSTICE POWELL, JUSTICE REHNQUIST, and JUSTICE O'CONNOR join, dissenting.   1

The First Amendment, as with other parts of the Constitution, must deal   2 with new problems in a changing world. In an attempt to deal with a problem in an area traditionally left to the states, a plurality of the Court, in a lavish expansion going beyond any prior holding under the First Amendment, expresses its view that a school board's decision concerning what books are to be in the school library is subject to federal court review.[1] Were this to become the law, this Court would come perilously close to becoming a "super censor" of school board library decisions. Stripped to its essentials, the issue comes down to two important propositions: *first,* whether local schools are to be administered by elected school boards, or by federal judges and teenage pupils; and *second,* whether the values of morality, good taste, and relevance to education are valid reasons for school board decisions concerning the contents of a school library. In an attempt to place this case within the protection of the First Amendment, the plurality suggests a new "right" that, when shorn of the plurality's rhetoric, allows this Court to impose its own views about what books must be made available to students.[2]

I

A

I agree with the fundamental proposition that "students do not 'shed their rights to freedom of speech or expression at the schoolhouse gate.'" *Ante,* at 11. For example, the Court has held that a school board cannot compel a student to participate in a flag salute ceremony. *West Virginia Bd. of Education* v. *Barnette,* 319 U.S. 624 (1943), or *prohibit* a student from expressing certain views, so long as that expression does not disrupt the educational process. *Tinker* v. *Des Moines School Dist.,* 393 U.S. 503 (1969). Here, however, no restraints of any kind are placed on the students. They are free to read the books in question, which are available at public libraries and bookstores; they are free to discuss them in the classroom or elsewhere. Despite this absence of any direct external control on the students' ability to express

3

---

[1]At the outset, the plurality notes that certain school board members found the books in question "objectionable" and "improper" for junior and senior high school students. What the plurality apparently finds objectionable is that the inquiry as to the challenged books was initially stimulated by what is characterized as "a politically conservative organization of parents concerned about education," which had concluded that the books in question were "improper fare for school students." *Ante,* at 2. As noted by the District Court, however, and in the plurality opinion, *ante,* at 5, both parties substantially agreed about the motivation of the school board in removing the books:

"[T]he board acted not on religious principles but on its conservative educational philosophy, and on its belief that the nine books removed from the school library and curriculum were irrelevant, vulgar, immoral, and in bad taste, making them educationally unsuitable for the district's junior and senior high school students." 474 F. Supp. 387, 392 (1979).

[2]In oral argument counsel advised the Court that of the original plaintiffs, only "[o]ne of them is still in school . . . until this June, and will assumedly graduate in June. *There is a potential question of mootness.*" Transcripts of Oral Argument 4-5 (Emphasis added.) The sole surviving plaintiff has therefore either recently been graduated from high school or is within days or even hours of graduation. Yet the plurality expresses views on a very important constitutional issue. Fortunately, there is no binding holding of the Court on the critical constitutional issue presented.

We do well to remember the admonition of Justice Frankfurter that "the most fundamental principle of constitutional adjudication is not to face constitutional questions but to avoid them, if at all possible." *United States* v. *Lovett,* 328 U.S. 303, 320 (1946) (Frankfurter, J., concurring.) In the same vein, Justice Stone warned that "the only check upon our own exercise of power is our own sense of self-restraint." *United States* v. *Butler,* 297 U.S. 1, 79 (1936) (Stone, J., dissenting.)

themselves, the plurality suggests that there is a new First Amendment "entitlement" to have access to particular books in a school library.

The plurality cites *Meyer* v. *Nebraska,* 262 U.S. 390 (1923), which struck   4
down a state law that restricted the teaching of modern foreign languages in
public and private schools, and *Epperson* v. *Arkansas,* 393 U.S. 97 (1968),
which declared unconstitutional under the Establishment Clause a law banning the teaching of Darwinian evolution, to establish the validity of federal
court interference with the functioning of schools. The plurality finds it unnecessary "to re-enter this difficult terrain," *ante,* at 7, yet in the next breath
relies on these very cases and others to establish the previously unheard of
"right" of access to particular books in the public school library.[3] The apparent underlying basis of the plurality's view seems to be that students have
an enforceable "right" to receive the information and ideas that are contained
in junior and senior high school library books. *Ante,* at 12. This "right" purportedly follows "ineluctably" from the sender's First Amendment right to
freedom of speech and as a "necessary predicate" to the recipient's meaningful exercise of his own rights of speech, press, and political freedom. *Ante,* at
12–13. No such right, however, has previously been recognized.

It is true that where there is a willing distributor of materials, the govern-   5
ment may not impose unreasonable obstacles to dissemination by the third
party. *Virginia State Board of Pharmacy* v. *Virginia Citizens Consumer
Council, Inc.,* 425 U.S. 748 (1976). And where the speaker desires to express
certain ideas, the government may not impose unreasonable restraints. *Tinker*
v. *Des Moines School Dist., supra.* It does not follow, however, that a school
board must affirmatively aid the speaker in its communication with the recipient. In short the plurality suggests today that if a writer has something to
say, the government through its schools must be the courier. None of the
cases cited by the plurality establish this broad-based proposition.

First, the plurality argues that the right to receive ideas is derived in part   6
from the sender's first amendment rights to send them. Yet we have previously held that a sender's rights are not absolute. *Rowan* v. *Post Office Dept.,*
397 U.S. 728 (1970).[4] Never before today has the Court indicated that the
government has an *obligation* to aid a speaker or author in reaching an
audience.

Second, the plurality concludes that "the right to receive ideas is a nec-   7
essary predicate to the *recipient's* meaningful exercise of his own rights of
speech, press, and political freedom." *Ante,* at 13 (emphasis in original). However, the "right to receive information and ideas," *Stanley* v. *Georgia,* 394
U.S. 557, 564 (1969), cited *ante,* at 12, does not carry with it the concomitant
right to have those ideas affirmatively provided at a particular place by the
government. The plurality cites James Madison to emphasize the importance

---

[3]Of course, it is perfectly clear that, unwise as it would be, the board could wholly dispense with the school library, so far as the First Amendment is concerned.

[4]In *Rowan* a unanimous Court upheld the right of a homeowner to direct the local post office to stop delivery of unwanted materials that the householder viewed as "erotically arousing or sexually provocative."

of having an informed citizenry. *Ante,* at 13. We all agree with Madison of course, that knowledge is necessary for effective government. Madison's view, however, does not establish a *right* to have particular books retained on the school library shelves if the school board decides that they are inappropriate or irrelevant to the school's mission. Indeed, if the need to have an informed citizenry creates a "right," why is the government not also required to provide ready access to a variety of information? This same need would support a constitutional "right" of the people to have public libraries as part of a new constitutional "right" to continuing adult education.

The plurality also cites *Tinker, supra,* to establish that the recipient's   8
right to free speech encompasses a right to have particular books retained in the school library shelf. *Ante,* at 14. But the cited passage of *Tinker* notes only that school officials may not *prohibit* a student from expressing his or her view on a subject unless that expression interferes with the legitimate operations of the school. The government does not "contract the spectrum of available knowledge." *Griswold* v. *Connecticut,* 381 U.S. 479, 482 (1965), cited *ante,* at 12, by choosing not to retain certain books on the school library shelf; it simply chooses not to be the conduit for that particular information. In short, even assuming the desirability of the policy expressed by the plurality, there is not a hint in the First Amendment, or in any holding of this Court, of a "right" to have the government provide continuing access to certain books.

B

Whatever role the government might play as a conduit of information, schools   9
in particular ought not be made a slavish courier of the material of third parties. The plurality pays homage to the ancient verity that in the administration of the public schools " 'there is a legitimate and substantial community interest in promoting respect for authority and traditional values be they social, moral, or political.' " *Ante,* at 10. If, as we have held, schools may legitimately be used as vehicles for "inculcating fundamental values necessary to the maintenance of a democratic political system," *Ambach* v. *Norwick,* 441 U.S. 68, 77 (1979), school authorities must have broad discretion to fulfill that obligation. Presumably all activity within a primary or secondary school involves the conveyance of information and at least an implied approval of the worth of that information. How are "fundamental values" to be inculcated except by having school boards make content-based decisions about the appropriateness of retaining materials in the school library and curriculum? In order to fulfill its function, an elected school board *must* express its views on the subjects which are taught to its students. In doing so those elected officials express the views of their community; they may err, of course, and the voters may remove them. It is a startling erosion of the very idea of democratic government to have this Court arrogate to itself the power the plurality asserts today.

The plurality concludes that under the Constitution school boards cannot   10
choose to retain or dispense with books if their discretion is exercised in a
"narrowly partisan or political manner." *Ante,* at 16. The plurality concedes
that permissible factors are whether the books are "pervasively vulgar," *ante,*
at 17, or educationally unsuitable. *Ibid.* "Educational suitability," however, is
a standardless phrase. This conclusion will undoubtedly be drawn in many—
if not most—instances because of the decisionmaker's content-based judgment that the ideas contained in the book or the idea expressed from the
author's method of communication are inappropriate for teenage pupils.

The plurality also tells us that a book may be removed from a school   11
library if it is "pervasively vulgar." But why must the vulgarity be "pervasive"
to be offensive? Vulgarity might be concentrated in a single poem or a single
chapter or a single page, yet still be inappropriate. Or a school board might
reasonably conclude that even "random" vulgarity is inappropriate for teenage school students. A school board might also reasonably conclude that the
school board's retention of such books gives those volumes an implicit endorsement. Cf. *FCC* v. *Pacifica Foundation,* 438 U.S. 726 (1978).

Further, there is no guidance whatsoever as to what constitutes "political"   12
factors. This Court has previously recognized that public education involves
an area of broad public policy and "'go[es] to the heart of representative
government.'" *Ambach* v. *Norwick,* 441 U.S. 68, 74 (1979). As such, virtually
all educational decisions necessarily involve "political" determinations.

What the plurality views as valid reasons for removing a book at their core   13
involve partisan judgments. Ultimately the federal courts will be the judge of
whether the motivation for book removal was "valid" or "reasonable." Undoubtedly the validity of many book removals will ultimately turn on a judge's
evaluation of the books. Discretion must be used, and the appropriate body
to exercise that discretion is the local elected school board, not judges.[5]

We can all agree that as a matter of *educational policy* students should   14
have wide access to information and ideas. But the people elect school boards,
who in turn select administrators, who select the teachers, and these are the
individuals best able to determine the substance of that policy. The plurality
fails to recognize the fact that local control of education involves democracy
in a microcosm. In most public schools in the United States the *parents* have
a large voice in running the school.[6] Through participation in the election of

[5]Indeed, this case is illustrative of how essentially all decisions concerning the retention of school library
books will become the responsibility of federal courts. As noted above, *supra,* n. 1, the parties agreed that the
school board in this case acted not on religious principles but "on its belief that the nine books removed from
the school library and curriculum were irrelevant, vulgar, immoral, and in bad taste, making them educationally
unsuitable for the district's junior and senior high school students."
Despite this agreement as to motivation, the case is to be remanded for a determination of whether removal
was in violation of the standard adopted by the plurality. The school board's error appears to be that they
made their own determination rather than relying on experts. *Ante,* at 20.

[6]*Epperson* v. *Arkansas, supra,* at 104. There are approximately 15,000 school districts in the country. U.S.
Bureau of Census, Statistical Abstract of the United States (102 ed. 1981) (Table 495: Number of Local
Governments, by Taxing Power and Type, and Public School Systems—States: 1971 and 1977). See also Diamond, The First Amendment and Public Schools: The Case Against Judicial Intervention, 59 TX L. Rev. 477,
506–507, n. 130 (1981).

school board members, the parents influence, if not control, the direction of their children's education. A school board is not a giant bureaucracy far removed from accountability for its actions; it is truly "of the people and by the people." A school board reflects its constituency in a very real sense and thus could not long exercise unchecked discretion in its choice to acquire or remove books. If the parents disagree with the educational decisions of the school board, they can take steps to remove the board members from office. Finally, even if parents and students cannot convince the school board that book removal is inappropriate, they have alternative sources to the same end. Books may be acquired from book stores, public libraries, or other alternative sources unconnected with the unique environment of the local public schools.[7]

II

No amount of "limiting" language could rein in the sweeping "right" the plurality would create. The plurality distinguishes library books from textbooks because library books "by their nature are optional rather than required reading." *Ante,* at 8. It is not clear, however, why this distinction requires *greater* scrutiny before "optional" reading materials may be removed. It would appear that required reading and textbooks have a greater likelihood of imposing a "'pall of orthodoxy'" over the educational process than do optional reading. *Ante,* at 16. In essence, the plurality's view transforms the availability of this "optional" reading into a "right" to have this "optional" reading maintained at the demand of teenagers.   15

The plurality also limits the new right by finding it applicable only to the *removal* of books once acquired. Yet if the First Amendment commands that certain books cannot be *removed,* does it not equally require that the same books be *acquired?* Why does the coincidence of timing become the basis of a constitutional holding? According to the plurality, the evil to be avoided is the "official suppression of ideas." *Ante,* at 17. It does not follow that the decision to *remove* a book is less "official suppression" than the decision not to acquire a book desired by someone.[8] Similarly, a decision to eliminate certain material from the curriculum, history for example, would carry an equal—probably greater—prospect of "official suppression." Would the decision be subject to our review?   16

---

[7]Other provisions of the Constitution, such as the Establishment Clause, *Epperson* v. *Arkansas, supra,* and the Equal Protection Clause, also limit the discretion of the school board.

[8]The formless nature of the "right" found by the plurality in this case is exemplified by this purported distinction. Presumably a school district could, for any reason, choose not to purchase a book for its library. Once it purchases that book, however, it is "locked in" to retaining it on the school shelf until it can justify a reason for its removal. This anomalous result of "book tenure" was pointed out by the District Court in this case. 474 F. Supp. 387, 395–396. See also *Presidents Council* v. *Community School Board,* 457 F. 2d 289, 293 (CA2 1972). Under the plurality view, if a school board wants to be assured that it maintains control over the education of its students, every page of every book sought to be acquired must be read before a purchase decision is made.

III

Through use of bits and pieces of prior opinions unrelated to the issue of   17
this case, the plurality demeans our function of constitutional adjudication.
Today the plurality suggests that the *Constitution* distinguishes between school
libraries and school classrooms, between *removing* unwanted books and *acquiring* books. Even more extreme, the plurality concludes that the Constitution *requires* school boards to justify to its teenage pupils the decision to
remove a particular book from a school library. I categorically reject this
notion that the Constitution dictates that judges, rather than parents, teachers, and local school boards, must determine how the standards of morality
and vulgarity are to be treated in the classroom.

QUESTIONS FOR MEANING

1. Why does Burger believe that federal courts should not be involved in
   choosing books for school libraries? What flaws does he perceive in the
   reasoning of colleagues on the Supreme Court who disagreed with him?
2. What basic principles does Burger share with his opponents on the Court?
   What concessions does he make to them?
3. To what extent does this argument amount to an interpretation of how to
   read the Constitution? What worries Burger beyond the question of what
   books should be in school libraries?
4. Burger argues that a local school board is a "democracy in a microcosm."
   What does this mean? Does Burger support this claim? What do you know
   about school boards and how they are elected? How representative are
   they? What sort of people are usually elected? Are there any people who
   are not represented on school boards?
5. Why does Burger see a difference between school libraries and public libraries? How do their functions differ?
6. Vocabulary: lavish (2), plurality (2), ineluctably (4), concomitant (7),
   conduit (9), verity (9), inculcated (9), arrogate (9), implicit (11), and
   adjudication (17).

QUESTIONS ABOUT STRATEGY

1. Does Burger advance his argument inductively or deductively?
2. Is Burger's argument inhibited in any way by legal jargon? How would you
   characterize his style as a writer?
3. Why does Burger repeatedly put quotation marks around "right"?
4. Much of Burger's argument depends upon the analysis of language. He
   questions a number of words and phrases used by other justices: "pervasively vulgar," "educational suitability," and "necessary predicate." He also
   explores the relationship between the right to *send* ideas and the right to
   receive them, as well as censorship by *removal* and censorship by *non-
   acquisition.* Are you persuaded that his concern with language is valid,

or do you think he perceives difficulties where none exist? What is the relationship between language and the law? Why is it important for judges and lawyers to write well?

5. Is there any point where Burger weakens his case by pushing his argument further than it had to go? Does he ever go out on a legal limb and seem to take an unnecessarily extreme position?

A TEST CASE

Although "censorship" is often associated with opposition to sexually explicit material, books have been objected to for many different reasons—as the selections in this section have shown. To help you to better understand the controversy over what should or should not be taught in American schools, here is a short story that has inspired considerable debate when taught in high school English courses. As you read "The Lottery," try to discover why parents might object to it. It is followed by an essay by a high school teacher providing background on the story and the debate surrounding it.

SHIRLEY JACKSON
The Lottery

Born in San Francisco, Shirley Jackson (1919–1965) moved to a rural community in Vermont after her marriage in 1940. Her novels include The Road through the Wall *(1948),* Hangsman *(1949),* The Bird Nest *(1954),* The Sundial *(1958), and* We Have Always Lived in the Castle *(1962) But Jackson is best known for "The Lottery," a short story that was first published in* The New Yorker *in* **1948.**

The morning of June 27th was clear and sunny, with the fresh warmth of   1
a full-summer day; the flowers were blossoming profusely and the grass was richly green. The people of the village began to gather in the square, between the post office and the bank, around ten o'clock; in some towns there were so many people that the lottery took two days and had to be started on June 26th, but in this village, where there were only about three hundred people, the whole lottery took less than two hours, so it could begin at ten o'clock in the morning and still be through in time to allow the villagers to get home for noon dinner.

The children assembled first, of course. School was recently over for the   2
summer, and the feeling of liberty sat uneasily on most of them; they tended to gather together quietly for a while before they broke into boisterous play, and their talk was still of the classroom and the teacher, of books and repri-

mands. Bobby Martin had already stuffed his pockets full of stones, and the other boys soon followed his example, selecting the smoothest and roundest stones; Bobby and Harry Jones and Dickie Delacroix—the villagers pronounced this name "Dellacroy"—eventually made a great pile of stones in one corner of the square and guarded it against the raids of the other boys. The girls stood aside, talking among themselves, looking over their shoulders at the boys, and the very small children rolled in the dust or clung to the hands of their older brothers or sisters.

Soon the men began to gather, surveying their own children, speaking of   3
planting and rain, tractors and taxes. They stood together, away from the pile of stones in the corner, and their jokes were quiet and they smiled rather than laughed. The women, wearing faded house dresses and sweaters, came shortly after their menfolk. They greeted one another and exchanged bits of gossip as they went to join their husbands. Soon the women, standing by their husbands, began to call to their children, and the children came reluctantly, having to be called four or five times. Bobby Martin ducked under his mother's grasping hand and ran, laughing, back to the pile of stones. His father spoke up sharply, and Bobby came quickly and took his place between his father and his oldest brother.

The lottery was conducted—as were the square dances, the teen-age club,   4
the Halloween program—by Mr. Summers, who had time and energy to devote to civic activities. He was a round-faced, jovial man and he ran the coal business, and people were sorry for him, because he had no children and his wife was a scold. When he arrived in the square, carrying the black wooden box, there was a murmur of conversation among the villagers, and he waved and called, "Little late today, folks." The postmaster, Mr. Graves, followed him, carrying a three-legged stool, and the stool was put in the center of the square and Mr. Summers set the black box down on it. The villagers kept their distance, leaving a space between themselves and the stool, and when Mr. Summers said, "Some of you fellows want to give me a hand?" there was a hesitation before two men, Mr. Martin and his oldest son, Baxter, came forward to hold the box steady on the stool while Mr. Summers stirred up the papers inside it.

The original paraphernalia for the lottery had been lost long ago, and the   5
black box now resting on the stool had been put into use even before Old Man Warner, the oldest man in town, was born. Mr. Summers spoke frequently to the villagers about making a new box, but no one liked to upset even as much tradition as was represented by the black box. There was a story that the present box had been made with some pieces of the box that had preceded it, the one that had been constructed when the first people settled down to make a village here. Every year, after the lottery, Mr. Summers began talking again about a new box, but every year the subject was allowed to fade off without anything's being done. The black box grew shabbier each year; by now it was no longer completely black but splintered badly along one side to show the original wood color, and in some places faded or stained.

Mr. Martin and his oldest son, Baxter, held the black box securely on the   6
stool until Mr. Summers had stirred the papers thoroughly with his hand.
Because so much of the ritual had been forgotten or discarded, Mr. Summers
had been successful in having slips of paper substituted for the chips of wood
that had been used for generations. Chips of wood, Mr. Summers had argued,
had been all very well when the village was tiny, but now that the population
was more than three hundred and likely to keep on growing, it was necessary
to use something that would fit more easily into the black box. The night
before the lottery, Mr. Summers and Mr. Graves made up the slips of paper
and put them in the box, and it was then taken to the safe of Mr. Summers's
coal company and locked up until Mr. Summers was ready to take it to the
square next morning. The rest of the year, the box was put away, sometimes
one place, sometimes another; it had spent one year in Mr. Graves's barn and
another year underfoot in the post office, and sometimes it was set on a shelf
in the Martin grocery and left there

There was a great deal of fussing to be done before Mr. Summers declared   7
the lottery open. There were the lists to make up—of heads of families, heads
of households in each family, members of each household in each family.
There was the proper swearing-in of Mr. Summers by the postmaster, as the
official of the lottery; at one time, some people remembered, there had been
a recital of some sort, performed by the official of the lottery, a perfunctory,
tuneless chant that had been rattled off duly each year; some people believed
that the official of the lottery used to stand just so when he said or sang it,
others believed that he was supposed to walk among the people, but years
and years ago this part of the ritual had been allowed to lapse. There had
been, also, a ritual salute, which the official of the lottery had had to use in
addressing each person who came up to draw from the box, but this also had
changed with time, until now it was felt necessary only for the official to
speak to each person approaching. Mr. Summers was very good at all this; in
his clean white shirt and blue jeans, with one hand resting carelessly on the
black box, he seemed very proper and important as he talked interminably
to Mr. Graves and the Martins.

Just as Mr. Summers finally left off talking and turned to the assembled   8
villagers, Mrs. Hutchinson came hurriedly along the path to the square, her
sweater thrown over her shoulders, and slid into place in the back of the
crowd. "Clean forgot what day it was," she said to Mrs. Delacroix, who stood
next to her, and they both laughed softly. "Thought my old man was out back
stacking wood," Mrs. Hutchinson went on, "and then I looked out the window
and the kids were gone, and then I remembered it was the twenty-seventh
and came a-running." She dried her hands on her apron, and Mrs. Delacroix
said, "You're in time, though. They're still talking away up there."

Mrs. Hutchinson craned her neck to see through the crowd and found her   9
husband and children standing near the front. She tapped Mrs. Delacroix on
the arm as a farewell and began to make her way through the crowd. The
people separated good-humoredly to let her through; two or three people
said, in voices just loud enough to be heard across the crowd, "Here comes

your Missus, Hutchinson," and "Bill, she made it after all." Mrs. Hutchinson reached her husband, and Mr. Summers, who had been waiting, said cheerfully, "Thought we were going to have to get on without you, Tessie." Mrs. Hutchinson said, grinning, "Wouldn't have me leave m'dishes in the sink, now, would you, Joe?" and soft laughter ran through the crowd as the people stirred back into position after Mrs. Hutchinson's arrival.

"Well, now," Mr. Summers said soberly, "guess we better get started, get   10
this over with, so's we can go back to work. Anybody ain't here?"

"Dunbar," several people said. "Dunbar, Dunbar."   11

Mr. Summers consulted his list. "Clyde Dunbar," he said. "That's right. He's   12
broke his leg, hasn't he? Who's drawing for him?"

"Me, I guess," a woman said, and Mr. Summers turned to look at her. "Wife   13
draws for her husband," Mr. Summers said. "Don't you have a grown boy to do it for you, Janey?" Although Mr. Summers and everyone else in the village knew the answer perfectly well, it was the business of the official of the lottery to ask such questions formally. Mr. Summers waited with an expression of polite interest while Mrs. Dunbar answered.

"Horace's not but sixteen yet," Mrs. Dunbar said regretfully. "Guess I gotta   14
fill in for the old man this year."

"Right," Mr. Summers said. He made a note on the list he was holding.   15
Then he asked, "Watson boy drawing this year?"

A tall boy in the crowd raised his hand. "Here," he said. "I'm drawing for   16
m'mother and me." He blinked his eyes nervously and ducked his head as several voices in the crowd said things like "Good fellow, Jack," and "Glad to see your mother's got a man to do it."

"Well," Mr. Summers said, "guess that's everyone. Old Man Warner   17
make it?"

"Here," a voice said, and Mr. Summers nodded.   18

A sudden hush fell on the crowd as Mr. Summers cleared his throat and   19
looked at the list. "All ready?" he called, "Now, I'll read the names—heads of families first—and the men come up and take a paper out of the box. Keep the paper folded in your hand without looking at it until everyone has had a turn. Everything clear?"

The people had done it so many times that they only half listened to the   20
directions; most of them were quiet, wetting their lips, not looking around. Then Mr. Summers raised one hand high and said, "Adams." A man disengaged himself from the crowd and came forward. "Hi, Steve," Mr. Summers said, and Mr. Adams said, "Hi, Joe." They grinned at one another humorlessly and nervously. Then Mr. Adams reached into the black box and took out a folded paper. He held it firmly by one corner as he turned and went hastily back to his place in the crowd, where he stood a little apart from his family, not looking down at his hand.

"Allen," Mr. Summers said. "Anderson . . . Bentham."   21

"Seems like there's no time at all between lotteries any more," Mrs. Dela-   22
croix said to Mrs. Graves in the back row. "Seems like we got through with the last one only last week."

"Time sure goes fast," Mrs. Graves said.   23

"Clark . . . Delacroix."   24

"There goes my old man," Mrs. Delacroix said. She held her breath while   25
her husband went forward.

"Dunbar," Mr. Summers said, and Mrs. Dunbar went steadily to the box   26
while one of the women said, "Go on, Janey," and another said, "There
she goes."

"We're next," Mrs. Graves said. She watched while Mr. Graves came around 27
from the side of the box, greeted Mr. Summers gravely, and selected a slip
of paper from the box. By now, all through the crowd there were men holding
the small folded papers in their large hands, turning them over and over
nervously. Mrs. Dunbar and her two sons stood together, Mrs. Dunbar holding
the slip of paper.

"Harburt . . . Hutchinson."   28

"Get up there, Bill," Mrs. Hutchinson said, and the people near her laughed. 29

"Jones."

"They do say," Mr. Adams said to Old Man Warner, who stood next to him,   30
"that over in the north village they're talking of giving up the lottery."

Old Man Warner snorted. "Pack of crazy fools," he said. "Listening to the   31
young folks, nothing's good enough for *them.* Next thing you know, they'll be
wanting to go back to living in caves, nobody work any more, live *that* way
for a while. Used to be a saying about 'Lottery in June, corn be heavy soon.'
First thing you know, we'd all be eating stewed chickweed and acorns. There's
always been a lottery," he added petulantly. "Bad enough to see young Joe
Summers up there joking with everybody."

"Some places have already quit lotteries," Mrs. Adams said.   32

"Nothing but trouble in *that,*" Old Man Warner said stoutly. "Pack of young 33
fools."

"Martin." And Bobby Martin watched his father go forward. "Overdyke . . .   34
Percy."

"I wish they'd hurry," Mrs. Dunbar said to her older son. "I wish they'd   35
hurry."

"They're almost through," her son said.   36

"You get ready to run tell Dad," Mrs. Dunbar said.   37

Mr. Summers called his own name and then stepped forward precisely and   38
selected a slip from the box. Then he called, "Warner."

"Seventy-seventh year I been in the lottery," Old Man Warner said as he   39
went through the crowd. "Seventy-seventh time."

"Watson." The tall boy came awkwardly through the crowd. Someone said,   40
"Don't be nervous, Jack," and Mr. Summers said, "Take your time, son."

"Zanini."   41

After that, there was a long pause, a breathless pause, until Mr. Summers,   42
holding his slip of paper in the air, said, "All right, fellows." For a minute, no
one moved, and then all the slips of paper were opened. Suddenly, all the
women began to speak at once, saying, "Who is it?" "Who's got it?" "Is it the
Dunbars?" "Is it the Watsons?" Then the voices began to say, "It's Hutchinson. It's Bill," "Bill Hutchinson's got it."

"Go tell your father," Mrs. Dunbar said to her older son.   43

People began to look around to see the Hutchinsons. Bill Hutchinson was   44
standing quiet, staring down at the paper in his hand. Suddenly, Tessie
Hutchinson shouted to Mr. Summers. "You didn't give him time enough to
take any paper he wanted. I saw you. It wasn't fair."

"Be a good sport, Tessie," Mrs. Delacroix called, and Mrs. Graves said, "All   45
of us took the same chance."

"Shut up, Tessie," Bill Hutchinson said.   46

"Well, everyone," Mr. Summers said, "that was done pretty fast, and now   47
we've got to be hurrying a little more to get done in time." He consulted his
next list. "Bill," he said, "you drew for the Hutchinson family. You got any
other households in the Hutchinsons?"

"There's Don and Eva," Mrs. Hutchinson yelled. "Make *them* take their   48
chance?"

"Daughters draw with their husband's families, Tessie," Mr. Summers said   49
gently. "You know that as well as anyone else."

"It wasn't *fair*," Tessie said.   50

"I guess not, Joe," Bill Hutchinson said regretfully. "My daughter draws   51
with her husband's family, that's only fair. And I've got no other family except
the kids."

"Then, as far as drawing for families is concerned, it's you," Mr. Summers   52
said in explanation, "and as far as drawing for households is concerned, that's
you, too. Right?"

"Right," Bill Hutchinson said.   53

"How many kids, Bill?" Mr. Summers asked formally.   54

"Three," Bill Hutchinson said. "There's Bill, Jr., and Nancy, and little Dave.   55
And Tessie and me."

"All right, then," Mr. Summers said. "Harry, you got their tickets back?"   56

Mr. Graves nodded and held up the slips of paper. "Put them in the box,   57
then," Mr. Summers directed. "Take Bill's and put it in."

"I think we ought to start over," Mrs. Hutchinson said, as quietly as she   58
could. "I tell you it wasn't *fair.* You didn't give him time enough to choose.
*Every*body saw that."

Mr. Graves had selected the five slips and put them in the box, and he   59
dropped all the papers but those onto the ground, where the breeze caught
them and lifted them off.

"Listen, everybody," Mrs. Hutchinson was saying to the people around her.   60

"Ready, Bill?" Mr. Summers asked, and Bill Hutchinson, with one quick   61
glance around at his wife and children, nodded.

"Remember," Mr. Summers said, "take the slips and keep them folded until   62
each person has taken one. Harry, you help little Dave." Mr .Graves took the
hand of the little boy, who came willingly with him up to the box. "Take a
paper out of the box, Davy," Mr. Summers said. Davy put his hand into the
box and laughed. "Take just *one* paper," Mr. Summers said. "Harry, you hold
it for him." Mr. Graves took the child's hand and removed the folded paper
from the tight fist and held it while little Dave stood next to him and looked
up at him wonderingly.

"Nancy next," Mr. Summers said. Nancy was twelve, and her school friends   63 breathed heavily as she went forward, switching her skirt, and took a slip daintily from the box. "Bill, Jr.," Mr. Summers said, and Billy, his face red and his feet over-large, nearly knocked the box over as he got a paper out. "Tessie," Mr. Summers said. She hesitated for a minute, looking around defiantly, and then set her lips and went up to the box. She snatched a paper out and held it behind her.

"Bill," Mr. Summers said, and Bill Hutchinson reached into the box and   64 felt around, bringing his hand out at last with the slip of paper in it.

The crowd was quiet. A girl whispered, "I hope it's not Nancy," and the   65 sound of the whisper reached the edges of the crowd.

"It's not the way it used to be," Old Man Warner said clearly. "People ain't   66 the way they used to be."

"All right," Mr. Summers said. "Open the papers. Harry, you open little   67 Dave's."

Mr. Graves opened the slip of paper and there was a general sigh through   68 the crowd as he held it up and everyone could see that it was blank. Nancy and Bill, Jr., opened theirs at the same time, and both beamed and laughed, turning around to the crowd and holding their slips of paper above their heads.

"Tessie," Mr. Summers said. There was a pause, and then Mr. Summers   69 looked at Bill Hutchinson, and Bill unfolded his paper and showed it. It was blank.

"It's Tessie," Mr. Summers said, and his voice was hushed. "Show us her   70 paper, Bill."

Bill Hutchinson went over to his wife and forced the slip of paper out of   71 her hand. It had a black spot on it, the black spot Mr. Summers had made the night before with the heavy pencil in the coal-company office. Bill Hutchinson held it up, and there was a stir in the crowd.

"All right, folks," Mr. Summers said. "Let's finish quickly."   72

Although the villagers had forgotten the ritual and lost the original black   73 box, they still remembered to use stones. The pile of stones the boys had made earlier was ready; there were stones on the ground with the blowing scraps of paper that had come out of the box. Mrs. Delacroix selected a stone so large she had to pick it up with both hands and turned to Mrs. Dunbar. "Come on," she said. "Hurry up."

Mrs. Dunbar had small stones in both hands, and she said, gasping   74 for breath, "I can't run at all. You'll have to go ahead and I'll catch up with you."

The children had stones already, and someone gave little Davy Hutchinson   75 a few pebbles.

Tessie Hutchinson was in the center of a cleared space by now, and she   76 held her hands out desperately as the villagers moved in on her. "It isn't fair," she said. A stone hit her on the side of the head.

Old Man Warner was saying, "Come on, come on, everyone." Steve Adams   77 was in the front of the crowd of villagers, with Mrs. Graves beside him.

"It isn't fair, it isn't right," Mrs. Hutchinson screamed, and then they were   78 upon her. ■

EDNA BOGERT
Censorship and "The Lottery"

*Most readers agree that "The Lottery" is a disturbing story. But attempts to keep
students from reading it raise a number of interesting questions: Why would
parents object to their children reading this story? To what extent should students be protected from potentially disturbing ideas? Can anyone be well educated without being confronted by material that challenges conventional
values? The following essay by Edna Bogert, a high school English teacher in
New Castle, Delaware, discusses "The Lottery" in an attempt to understand parental objections to it. Her essay was first published in* **1985.**

For over two generations, high school and college students have been   1
reading Shirley Jackson's short story "The Lottery." This deceptively simple
horror tale, first published thirty-five years ago, has been included in anthologies at least since 1950. Its initial publication in *The New Yorker* magazine
on June 28, 1948, precipitated more responses from readers than any other
fiction ever before published by that magazine. Of the three-hundred letters
that were received by the author herself that summer, only thirteen of them
could have been considered kind.[1] Most letter writers had taken the story
literally. They thought that the fiction was based on fact and wanted to know
the details of where, when, and to whom the events described had happened.

While the letters were almost wholly negative, none suggested that the   2
story should not be available to the public. Up until 1982 it was only a character in fiction who suggested "The Lottery" be removed from a school's
curriculum, a candidate for school board in Elizabeth Peter's 1977 novel, *Devil
May Care*, who says people do not "want their children to read a book that
shows kids stoning their mothers to death."

Although in six separate nation-wide surveys conducted between 1965 and   3
1981 "The Lottery" was *not* among the most frequently challenged works in
American high schools, a 1982 survey sponsored by the National Council of
Teachers of English and the Wisconsin Council of Teachers of English found
"The Lottery" to be among the forty-eight works most frequently challenged
by local censorship groups as unsuitable for high school students.[2] This could,
of course, be partially due to the increase in the number of groups currently
trying to limit the choice of materials available in high schools. However,
since "The Lottery" has remained almost unchallenged for over a third of a
century, it may not be just the increased number of would-be censors but
what the story actually says.

On the literal level, "The Lottery" is almost pastoral in its simplicity, at   4
least until the last few paragraphs. The setting is a small farming village of
about 300 people. It's a clear June morning, and the people of the village
gradually leave their farms, kitchens, and shops for an important civic event,
a lottery which has taken place annually for as long as any of them can

remember. The children feel restless, only recently out of school for the summer. Neighbors greet each other, chat, and joke quietly while preparations for the lottery are made by Mr. Summers, the town's most civic-minded citizen. Just as it is about to begin, the last resident to arrive, Mrs. Hutchinson, comes running to join her husband and three children. Mr. Summers calls the names in alphabetical order, and heads of families go forward to receive a piece of paper, exchanging small pleasantries with Mr. Summers on the way. When all of the family heads have received their slips, they look to see who has the slip with the black mark. It is the Hutchinson family. Tessie Hutchinson complains that the drawing was not conducted fairly. A second drawing takes place, and we learn that it is she who has the black mark.

The ritualistic end follows. Children and grownups pick up pebbles, stones, and rocks and begin to stone Mrs. Hutchinson who screams, "It isn't fair, it isn't right."   5

Critic Robert Heilman suggests that readers have been tricked.[3] We have been led to expect that a story which began realistically will end that way. Heilman says that the switch from realism to symbolism leaves readers "shaken up," but that such a shocking ending detracts from the realization of the author's intent in telling the story.   6

Seymour Lainoff, on the other hand, sees the story as an example of the scapegoat rite of primitive cultures, an annual event which often took place at the time of the summer solstice.[4] Although he says that the theme of Jackson's story is the savagery that lies beneath our civilized surface, Lainoff believes that the story shows that the author is optimistic about the future, giving as evidence that fact that some towns have given up their lotteries.   7

Perhaps the real core of the story might better be seen through the use of semiotic analysis to examine some of its significant codes. According to semiotician Robert Scholes, readers use narrativity when they read fiction.[5] Readers, both visualize the scenes of the narrative and predict the coming events of the plot based on prior events. In doing so, readers subordinate their own beliefs and their own freedom of thought to the narrative. Some writers, such as Bertold Brecht, have deplored this abandonment of the reader's self to the narrative and have used various means to prevent it. Brecht, for example, used time-lapse devices that interrupt the narrative. The concluding paragraphs of "The Lottery" have a similar effect. They interrupt the narrativity of readers, making them stop to say, "What's happening here?" Then readers begin to predict again, this time more slowly, suspiciously, wondering how this trick came to be played and what it can mean. It becomes evident to readers that the surface structure of the story does not convey its whole meaning. Readers must look below the surface to find the deep structure or underlying meaning of the story.   8

Going back to the beginning of the story, we read again the description of an idyllic day of "fresh warmth," "clear and sunny" with flowers "blossoming profusely," the "grass richly green"—in short, perfect weather for a picnic. But now that we know that the morning is not going to culminate in a picnic, but in ritual murder, the irony of the beauty of the day becomes clear. Show-   9 ing the peaceful, pastoral setting, of happy children and friendly villagers assembling for what we had supposed to be a happy event makes the shock of the violent ending more profound.

In re-examining the story we want to discover the reason that this lottery,   10 this annual murder, takes place. The village is said to have a population of about 300 and "likely to keep on growing." Could the lottery be a form of population control? But one less villager a year wouldn't be very effective, so that can't be the reason. Is entertainment the purpose? No—no one seems to enjoy the stoning. We might wonder whether the purpose is for excitement, to feel more alive in having escaped being chosen, except that the villagers obviously just want to get it over with. They are getting bored with the ritual. There *is* no reason for the lottery, except that of tradition. The village is a traditional community. Men and women fill traditional roles, the women working in the kitchens, the men in the fields. Tradition dictates that the male head of the family choose the slip from the traditional black box. The lottery is held, year after year, only because it has always been done that way. For as long as Old Man Warner can remember, "There's always been a lottery." When Mr. Adams remarks that a neighboring village is thinking of giving up the lottery, Warner quotes an old saying which implies a cause-effect relationship between the lottery and the harvest: "Lottery in June, corn be heavy soon." Without the lottery, he says, "We'd all be eating stewed chickweed and acorns." None of the younger citizens challenge the logic of this remark, which strongly suggests the relationship of sacrifice to the harvest, like that practiced by primitive people and documented by anthropologist Sir James Frazer in *the Golden Bough.*

Frazer, besides giving examples of the relationship of sacrifice to the har-   11 vest, also cites incidents of the sacrifice of innocent human beings to ward off evil:

> . . . whether the evils are conceived of as invisible or as embodied in a material form is a circumstance entirely subordinate to the main object of the ceremony, which is simply to effect a total clearance of all the ills that have been infesting a people. (p. 665)

Tessie Hutchinson, who almost arrived too late for the drawing because   12 she would not leave her sinkful of dirty dishes, can be characterized an innocent. However, the village depicted in this story can hardly be termed primitive. Judging by the surnames of its inhabitants and by the description of the town, it is probably a fairly typical New England village.[6] But people in modern New England villages don't put innocent women to death, although such was not always the case, as Shirley Jackson wrote in her *The Witchcraft of Salem Village* (1956).

Witchcraft may no longer be practiced in Salem, but our modern world   13 still has its scapegoats. Barely three years before the appearance of "The Lottery," the world was horrified to learn of the extent to which Hitler and his followers had gone in their persecution of Europe's Jews, Gypsies, and other victims, the scapegoats for what some perceived to be the evils of Europe. By their deaths Germany was to be purified. It was against this background that "The Lottery" was written. The theme of mindless and unchallenged tradition has as its corollary the theme of control. The children, out of school for summer, are described as not quite knowing what to do without someone to tell them. They still talk "of books and reprimands." There were no teachers to control their behavior and "the feeling of liberty set uneasily on them."

The adherence of people to unconsidered traditions and unchallenged controls is held up to examination in "The Lottery" in such a way as to suggest that traditions *ought* to be re-examined from time to time. The story establishes that a group of ordinary people has the ability to commit extraordinarily horrible deeds, *if* people in the group are unable or unwilling to think for themselves.

What the villagers in Shirley Jackson's story did was to go along with a tradition that required the murder of a member of the community each year. What the citizens of Germany did a few decades ago was to go along with a leader whose expressed goal was the extermination of a group of people. What the voters of South Africa are doing now and were doing when "The Lottery" first appeared is to allow a government policy to continue which drastically limits the freedom of millions of its black inhabitants. The Union of South Africa banned Shirley Jackson's story when it appeared. Her husband said that she was always proud of that fact. She felt that they, at least, understood it. They apparently could not allow in that country a story which might persuade people to reconsider long-standing policies.

The United States is currently undergoing a wave of conservatism and attempts by some groups to forcibly preserve traditions that seem to be changing (for example, the traditional roles of men and women). In their efforts, some groups try to control the curricula and values taught in public schools. "The Lottery" would have us reconsider traditions. Perhaps, as in South Africa, the would-be censors understand its deep meaning very well.

Notes

1. Shirley Jackson, "Biography of a Story," *Come Along With Me,* ed. Stanley Hyman (New York: Viking, 1968), pp. 211–24.

2. "Study Notes . . . Increase in Challenges to School Library Books," Alex Heard, in *Education Week,* December 8, 1982. The book, *The Lottery,* is according to this study being challenged. However, it is the volume's culminating short story, "The Lottery," which is by far the best known part of the book and, I assume, the reason for using the book. (This is not to say that Shirley Jackson's uniquely ironic view of human nature depicted in some of the other stories might not bring forth censors' ire if they read them.)

3. *Modern Short Stories,* ed. Robert B. Heilman (New York: Harcourt, Brace, 1950), pp. 384–85.

4. Seymour Lainoff, "Jackson's The Lottery," *Explicator* 12 (1954): Item 34.

5. Robert Scholes, *Semiotics and Interpretation,* (Brown University, 1982).

6. It is interesting to note that, at the time she wrote "The Lottery," Shirley Jackson was a resident of the small New England village of North Bennington,Vermont.

QUESTIONS FOR MEANING

1. How does Bogert account for the fact that although "The Lottery" has been frequently anthologized for over thirty years, attempts to restrict high school students from reading it rose significantly in the 1980s?
2. Explain what Bogert means by "narrativity" in paragraph 8.
3. According to Bogert's reading of "The Lottery," what is the only reason for the stoning that takes place in the story?
4. What connection does Bogert make between "The Lottery" and Hitler's Germany?
5. Vocabulary: pastoral (4), scapegoat (7), semiotic (8), corollary (13).

QUESTIONS ABOUT STRATEGY

1. Why does Bogert include a summary of "The Lottery" in her essay?
2. Consider the statement with which paragraph 3 concludes. Can you follow Bogert's reasoning?
3. Why does Bogert discuss racism in South Africa at the end of this essay? How is she able to do so without seeming to lose track of her topic?

One Student's Assignment

Write an argument for or against allowing high school students to read "The Lottery" by Shirley Jackson. Include a paragraph long summary of the story for the benefit of anyone in your audience who has not read it. Also include references to at least two other sources on censorship in The Informed Argument, at least one of which should represent a viewpoint different from your own. Use MLA style parenthetical documentation.

A Student's Right to Read
Connie J. Thompson

Adolescence is a time of changing awareness. Young adults   1
begin to view critically the ideas and values of the same authority figures they had previously held as infallible. One
of the consequences of this increasing skepticism is that

students often feel apathetic about their education. School is considered unimportant when learning becomes nothing more than satisfying requirements set by others. This creates a dilemma for educators. They are challenged not only to teach the information necessary for a thorough education, but also to motivate students to want to learn on their own.

I believe this challenge can be met with imagination and enthusiasm. With their knowledge and love of literature, English teachers can often get students to see that the characters of the past were not so different from themselves in their struggles with life. This is most likely to be accomplished when both teachers and students are able to make use of thought-provoking material.

Censorship is often defended under the guise of protecting the public from the influence of unsettling or unpopular ideas. This is faulty reasoning, since values are usually established early in life by the significant people surrounding us. It seems unlikely then that reading would dramatically alter a person's beliefs, values, or direction in life (Neuman 216). Nevertheless, many people are afraid of unpopular ideas or any views which seem to violate the norms of our society.

Such collective uneasiness would certainly contribute towards understanding the dispute over Shirley Jackson's "The Lottery." This deceptively simple short story leads the reader easily into the rural setting of a seemingly innocent village to witness the annual lottery. The reader is left unprepared for the dramatic ending of the story, in which the woman chosen by the lottery is stoned to death by the other citizens present, making its impact abrupt and unsettling. This unanticipated turn of events could serve to elicit a strong emotional response in readers, forcing them to examine their feelings about the importance of tradition (Bogert 249).

Unsettling as it may be, Jackson's story does not allow for apathy on the part of the reader, nor does it stand alone in its attempt to challenge traditional views. It is only one of many works which have been banned for introducing unconventional views. But giving students the opportunity to read and discuss this story could provide teachers with an ideal opportunity to help students think about their values instead of accepting them unconditionally.

I suggest that those who want to censor material because it

includes disturbing or unpopular ideas rethink their motives. Perhaps we have rested too long on unchallenged ideas
of right and wrong. Perhaps we need to fuel the fires of
thought, step outside ourselves, and learn from literature
that is unsettling. It has been argued that modern fiction is
too complex for high school students, that by involving the
reader so intensely in the action of the story, the author
gives rise to moral problems which the students may not easily resolve (O'Connor 209). I would cite this as all the more
reason to offer these experiences in combination with a
teacher's guidance and interpretation. Presented in the appropriate educational context, a story like "The Lottery"
will not corrupt the minds of students. It may spur them on to
affirm their existing values, or it may spark their curiosity and open their minds to new possibilities. This type of
material offers students the chance to take an interest in
their own education, and this, in turn, helps teachers to
teach effectively.

SUGGESTIONS FOR WRITING

1. What is censorship? Write an essay of definition making clear the meaning
   of this much used word.
2. Drawing upon the work of Susan Neuman, write an essay for or against
   the claim that what students read can change their values and beliefs.
3. Have you ever been upset by a book you were required to read in school?
   If so, write an essay explaining what bothered you about this book. Would
   you prevent your teacher from using this book with other students? Try
   to base your case upon some fundamental principle and not just your
   personal taste.
4. What are the rights of parents in determining what their children are taught?
   When teachers and parents differ about the desirability of a particular
   book, who should have the final word—and why? Write an essay arguing
   on behalf of either parents or teachers.
5. Flannery O'Connor and Warren Burger both address the issue of censorship in public schools. What about college? Should a college teacher have
   absolute authority in choosing what books to teach? Or should he or she
   be subject to some restraint? Write an essay defining the responsibilities
   of college teachers and the extent to which the college classroom should
   be free of censorship.
6. According to the National Council of Teachers of English, the most fre-

quently censored books in American schools include: *Catcher in the Rye, The Grapes of Wrath, Nineteen Eighty-Four, Lord of the Flies, The Adventures of Huckleberry Finn, Brave New World, The Scarlet Letter, A Farewell to Arms, One Flew Over the Cuckoo's Nest,* and *One Day in the Life of Ivan Denisovich.* Choose any one of these books that you have not previously read. Read it. And then argue for or against its use in a senior high school English class.

7. Go to a public library and interview the librarian in charge of circulation. Ask if the library has ever been pressured into withdrawing a book from circulation. Ask also if the library keeps a record of complaints made against the books in its collection. If so, ask if you can see this record and use it for evidence in determining the extent to which censorship is an issue in your own community.

8. All of the material in this section concerns censorship in education. Do a research paper on censorship in the performing arts. To what extent is film, music, or drama subject to censorship in the United States?

Section 5

Animal Experimentation: Do Rats Have Rights?

TERESA K. RYE

How I Benefited from Animal Research

*For many readers, the controversy over animal experimentation may seem re-
mote and abstract. But as Teresa K. Rye suggests in the following essay, the nature of medical research can suddenly become of great personal concern. A
registered nurse, Rye offered the following comments at a national symposium
on the use of animals in research, sponsored by the U.S. Department of Health
and Human Services in **1984.***

As I am listening to these proceedings and talking to you today, my emo- 1
tions are of deep gratitude for the work that has been done by medical researchers and practitioners. Had I been born 20 years earlier I would not be
alive now. Had the research not been performed to develop the knowledge
base and sophisticated techniques to support the surgery that I had, I would
have only a short life to look forward to.

I was asked to come and speak at this symposium as I have directly re- 2
ceived the benefits of animal research. A year-and-a-half ago I had open-
heart surgery at the Brigham and Women's Hospital in Boston performed by
Doctor Cohn. I am 28 years old. I am a registered nurse and an instructor for
nursing education and research at University Hospital at Boston University
Medical Center. In October 1982 I underwent surgery for repair of a very
rare congenital heart defect called the scimitar syndrome. In spite of my
education as a nurse, I had never heard of this syndrome. The name is derived from the appearance of the chest X-ray which shows the veins connecting the lungs to the heart in a semi-curved pattern around the right side
of the heart.

The very name "scimitar syndrome" frightened me. I felt doomed. My car- 3
diologist said this defect is so rare, he would be surprised if he saw three or
four more cases of this type in his entire career. I was told I would need
open-heart surgery. The alternative would have been to develop pulmonary
artery hypertension and almost certain death around age 35.

My operation was unique. Part of my surgery required the heart-lung by-   4
pass machine to be turned off. It was a chilling experience for me to learn
my body was frozen to 15° centigrade and that I had been clinically dead for
30 minutes during the operation. I hope that legislators, lobbyists, and research agencies appreciate that these kinds of procedures would be impossible to perform had there not been an animal research model. No number
of mathematical, statistical, analytical, and engineering techniques could replace the animal model in my case. I am deeply fortunate to have the opportunity of a normal life expectancy now. Death at 35 seems much too close
for me.

I was admitted for surgery and stayed in the hospital for 11 days. I recu-   5
perated at home and returned to work 6 weeks after my surgery, working 4
hours a day. Two weeks later, just 2 months after the operation, I was working full-time.

Not only was my successful surgery due to the techniques developed from   6
animal research, but also the diagnostic testing was possible because of animal modeling. I required a cardiac catheterization as well as a nuclear scan
with injections of dye to diagnose my abnormality.

It was by chance that this problem was discovered. I had begun a new job   7
and had a routine chest X-ray as a pre-employment screen to rule out tuberculosis. I was called to the employee health department to discuss the findings of my film. The physician told me my right heart was enlarged and the
blood vessels over my right lung were quite prominent. He said the film suggested that I had a congenital heart defect with signs of an abnormal left to
right shunting of blood. He urged me to see a cardiologist.

I was shocked, confused, and scared. At the time I was working as a sur-   8
gical intensive care unit nurse. I felt absolutely fine and lead a physically
active life. I had no other symptoms of cardiac disease aside from what had
been described as a benign heart murmur that I had known about since age
12. As a surgical intensive care unit nurse I was familiar with the battery of
tests I would have to undergo. I was aware of the life-threatening risks that
could arise during a cardiac catheterization as well as from open-heart surgery. As a nurse I was caring for patients who did, indeed, develop serious—
sometimes fatal—complications. I found myself experiencing maximum stress.

Once again, animal research had a direct benefit for me. I was able to use   9
medication to ease my anxiety and continue to be productive at work while
I waited 6 weeks between my cardiac catheterization and my open-heart
surgery.

The first day after my surgery I developed a life-threatening complication.   10
My left lung collapsed from positive pressure on the mechanical ventilator. I
needed a chest tube emergently inserted into my lung to re-expand it. This
procedure also could not have been performed without prior animal testing.

At times I experienced intense pain. One of my friends, also a nurse, came   11
to visit me in the intensive care unit and asked me "How is the pain?" I did
not remember this, but later she told me I said "It's killing me. I don't want
to move." She asked, "Does the medication help?" I said, "Yes, it does." I am

thankful for the amnesia of some of my experience. I sincerely hope and have to believe that animals are given the same kind of relief.

Six years ago I adopted a kitten from the Boston Animal Shelter. She has   12
grown into a beautiful affectionate cat. She has given me much happiness and feelings of love. Her picture was on my bedside table at the hospital. Even though I am a pet owner and animal lover, there is no question in my mind that animal research must be continued.

I have tremendous appreciation for the advances in science, the skill and   13
care from my doctors and nurses and the gift of life from animals that allow my continued good health.

Ten years ago, Lane Potter, in the *Proceedings of the Royal Society of*   14
Medicine, posed five questions for animal researchers: Is the animal the best experimental system for the problem? Must the animal be conscious at any time throughout the experiment? Can pain or discomfort associated with the experiment be lessened or eliminated? Could the number of animals be reduced? Is the problem worth solving anyhow?

For me, it is clear that some research involving the use of animals similar   15
to man must continue if mankind is to continue to advance and survive. For me, it is clear that these animals deserve the utmost respect and care that we can give them. They give so much to us. Antivivisectionist legislation which, in some cases, would absolutely prohibit animal research, would cause irreparable damage to the advancement of medical science. If these measures were in place 20 years ago, surgery involving an open chest and heart would not be possible. I would probably be experiencing the beginning signs and symptoms of chronic pulmonary artery hypertension. I would be unable to work in my early thirties. I would have high medical care costs and would be facing almost certain death at age 35.

But today I am looking forward to turning 29 next week and intend to   16
have a big celebration when I turn 35. I hope that research using animals continues so that children who are presently in life-threatening situations will also have a chance to look forward to birthdays, anniversaries and a healthy, productive life.

QUESTIONS FOR MEANING

1. How was Rye's heart defect discovered?
2. Why does Rye believe that animal experimentation probably saved her life?
3. How did Rye's experience as a nurse affect her feelings during her own treatment?

QUESTIONS ABOUT STRATEGY

1. Does Rye clearly explain the condition from which she suffered? Should she have included more detail?
2. Rye limits her testimony almost entirely to her own experience. Was this a wise decision?

3. Why does Rye mention her cat and describe herself as "a pet owner and animal lover"?
4. Does Rye show any awareness of animal rights?

DAVID P. RALL
Testing the Effects of Chemicals

The Director of the National Institute of Environmental Health Sciences and the National Toxicology Program, David P. Rall has an M.D. and a Ph.D. from Northwestern University. In addition to his work as a scientist and an administrator, he also teaches pharmacology at the University of North Carolina. The following essay was written for EPA Journal, *the journal of the Environmental Protection Agency. It was first published in* **1984,** *alongside of the essay by George Roush which begins on page 260.*

Modern civilization has learned to develop methods and to use the products of these methods to provide for human sustenance and comfort. This technology has created tremendous benefits as well as rapid changes in our environment. The lifespan of the average U.S. citizen has increased dramatically in the last century. While curative medicine and preventive vaccines played an important role, the results of technological innovation have been critical factors—improved nutrition, sanitation, shelter, and water supply. However, this increasingly rapid rate of innovation and our inability to anticipate the consequences of these changes should continue to be cause for concern.

One of the most innovative areas has been in the chemical process industry, leading to inexpensive plastics, agricultural chemicals, etc. These have contributed to a better, longer life for all of us. We have come to learn, however, that some chemicals can act like a double-edged sword: while most offer real benefits to mankind, a few can also pose a threat. Society obviously needs the fruits of the chemical industry, but at the same time it needs protection from those few chemicals that can adversely affect human health.

The hazards of some of these chemicals have been well studied. It is known that many human diseases can be traced to chemical exposure: male sterility to Kepone and dibromochloropropane; neurologic disease to Kepone, methyl, mercury, lead, and methyl butyl ketone; lung cancer to asbestos, arsenic, bis(chloromethyl)ether and others; liver hemangiosarcoma to vinyl chloride; mesothelioma to asbestos, etc.

Fortunately, most chemicals are relatively non-toxic and require few if any controls to protect human health. It appears that only a small fraction of chemicals are highly toxic. Thus, to protect the public health and to prevent disease, this fraction should be accurately identified so that appropriate methods of control can be considered.

The mainstay of this hazard identification process is the laboratory animal   5 toxicity study. A lifetime toxicity study of experimental animals, usually rats and mice—beginning at weaning, ending at death, using multiple dose levels of the chemical being tested—provides information on the kinds of toxic effects caused by the chemical and the doses or concentrations causing these toxic effects. This standard test determines if a chemical causes cancer and produces damaging effects on certain organ systems in animals—liver, lung, kidney, and endocrine systems. In the absence of relevant epidemiological/clinical data, these data typically constitute the primary basis for human hazard identification.

Historically, laboratory animal investigations have provided the basis for   6 understanding disease processes and for developing new and better medicines. It should not be surprising that the results of toxicological testing in laboratory animals predict reasonably well the effects of chemical exposure in humans.

The molecular, cellular, tissue and organ functions are strikingly similar in   7 all animal species; processes such as Na^- and K^+ transport, ion regulation, energy metabolism, and DNA replication vary little as one moves along the phylogenetic ladder. The classic work or the transmission of neural impulses in the squid axon is directly relevant to man. Extensive studies of renal function in fish, rodents, and dogs provide the basis for current understanding of renal function and the treatment of hypertension in man.

As long ago as 1966, *Cancer Chemotherapy Report* in Volume 50 de-   8 scribed the testing of a series of 18 anti-cancer drugs in laboratory animals after the toxicity of these compounds had been determined in clinical trials with cancer patients. The animal tests mimicked the dose schedule and route of administration. The results in mice and rats showed that the toxicity— essentially the maximum tolerated dose in laboratory animals and patients when expressed on a chemical doses per unit body surface area basis—was quite close, generally within a two- to three-fold range. The greatest differences were about ten-fold.

The relevance of laboratory animal toxicity studies as well as carcinogen-   9 icity studies has been extensively considered and was reaffirmed in the 1977 National Academy of Science-National Research Council report on *Drinking Water and Health*. Almost all of the known human carcinogens as defined by the International Agency for Research on Cancer (IARC) are carcinogenic in appropriate laboratory animal studies. In fact, animal data showing a carcinogenic response to a chemical have even preceded human case reports or epidemiological findings in a number of instances. Examples of chemicals for which initial indication of carcinogenic potential occurred in animal studies include aflatoxin, 4-aminobiphenyl, Cis(chloromethyl)ether, diethylstilbestrol, melphalan, mustard gas, and vinyl chloride.

It is certainly true that not all animal carcinogens have been shown to   10 cause cancer in humans. This may be because we have not yet developed the epidemiologic or clinical tools we need to relate disease to a specific chemical which has been shown to be toxic in animal experiments. However, most scientists recognize the importance of animal data as an indicator of human carcinogenic potential. For instance, the IARC has long taken the position, as stated in its most recent monograph on the evaluation of the carcinogenic risk of chemicals to humans, that:

> In the absence of adequate data on humans, it is reasonable, for practical purposes, to regard chemicals for which there is sufficient evidence of carcinogenicity in animals as if they presented a carcinogenic risk to humans. The use of the expressions 'for practical purposes' and 'as if they presented a carcinogenic risk' indicates that at the present time a correlation between carcinogenicity in animals and possible human risk cannot be made on a purely scientific basis, but only pragmatically. Such a pragmatical correlation may be useful to regulatory agencies in making decisions related to the primary prevention of cancer.

In conclusion, it seems clear that laboratory animal data will continue to play an essential part in identifying the potentially toxic effects of chemical exposures and in protecting the human population from them. In addition, such data will often be used to confirm the identification of hazards and support the findings from epidemiological investigations. Further, as increasing emphasis is placed on the question of biological relevance in assessing possible human health hazards, laboratory animal data may provide essential scientific insight into issues such as mechanisms of action and effective target dose. Data emanating from clinical or epidemiological studies remain the best indicators of toxicity. However, when adverse health effects are observed in humans, it indicates that we have failed to prevent human exposure, which is the goal of public health.   11

Finally, in the absence of relevant epidemiological data, laboratory animal studies will continue to offer the primary means for determining and perhaps preventing the likelihood of adverse effects on human health. It is this critical first step which provides the basis for effective regulation of hazardous chemicals and can help to prevent unnecessary regulation.   12

QUESTIONS FOR MEANING

1. What does Rall mean when he writes, "some chemicals can act like a double-edged sword"?
2. What similarities exist among all animal species? How do these similarities affect the rationale for animal experimentation?
3. According to Rall, what is the objective of animal testing?
4. Vocabulary: sustenance (1), sterility (3), epidemiological (5), renal (7), carcinogenic (9), monograph (10), emanating (11).

QUESTIONS ABOUT STRATEGY

1. What is the premise of this argument?
2. Does Rall make any concessions?
3. Why does Rall limit his focus to the role of animal experimentation in identifying carcinogens?

GEORGE ROUSH, JR.
Is Animal Testing Overrated?

While recognizing that animal experimentation can be important, some scientists believe that research procedures need to be improved. George Roush, Jr, is Director of Medicine and Environmental Health for Monsato—a large chemical manufacturing company that is subject to the regulations of the Environmental Protection Agency (EPA). Roush wrote the following essay for The EPA Journal *in **1984.***

Few recent scientific endeavors have been subjected to more criticism than the use of mice and rats in determining whether certain chemicals may pose a cancer risk to people. This criticism has ranged from the highly technical to the simply ludicrous—cartoons of bloated rats guzzling hundreds of cans of diet soft drinks. 1

All of this attention indicates the importance of the issue, namely whether feeding large amounts of a suspect substance to several hundred test animals for two years, then probing their organs for cancer, can tell us anything valuable about the potential effects of the same substance on ourselves. And while animal studies of this sort may be an easy target for the satirist, their importance to human health decisions and to the fate of everyday products merits a more thoughtful discussion. 2

To begin with, there is almost no aspect of the animal-to-people translation not beset with uncertainty and embroiled in intense scientific debate. Points of contention include the extent to which human versus animal cells are able to combat potentially carcinogenic molecules, how human organ systems may differ from those of animals in the way they handle or metabolize various substances, and how actual human exposure to these substances compares with that of laboratory animals under test conditions. 3

All of these factors come together in a fundamental dilemma of animal testing for potential cancer agents. This is that many of the 20 or so known carcinogens, such as asbestos and vinyl chloride, also cause cancer in rats or mice, but the vast majority of the more than 1,000 compounds that cause 4 cancer in one or more animal species do not do so in people, to the best of our collective scientific knowledge. Substances in this category include saccharin, lead and phenobarbital.

So, while there are apparently some similarities between people and animals in reacting to some cancer agents, this relationship is hardly simple, direct or consistent. If it were, the past few decades of our exposure to substances that have caused cancer in rodents should have steadily driven up the occurrence of the disease among ourselves. But they haven't. Too many Americans now die of cancer (about one in four), but the age-adjusted death rate from cancer among the population as a whole has remained nearly constant since the 1930s. Further, the rate of occurrence of most types of cancer has remained stable or declined. One notable exception is lung cancer which has been increasing, due mostly, the experts feel, to the effects of smoking tobacco.

Despite the tentative nature of its usefulness, animal testing remains the best experimental tool now available for detecting substances with a carcinogenic potential.

Obviously, we cannot deliberately expose people to questionable materials in order to judge the outcome. Further, despite the arguments of the proponents of such short-term, test-tube screens as the Ames test, most experts agree that not enough research yet exists to support their use in place of animal studies.

In addition, our collective experience with animal tests has taught us a number of things to bear in mind as we both design these studies and attempt to interpret their results. For example, we know that some substances will cause cancer in some animal species but not in others. Thus, the dye intermediate, beta-naphthylamine, causes tumors in dogs and hamsters but not in mice and rats. In fact, we know that for some species and some substances, sex differences exist in the development of tumors. To control for problems of species differences, all reputable researchers in government, industry and academia now use more than one species in testing a substance.

We also know that considerable caution must be used in drawing conclusions about the potential carcinogenicity of a substance based upon studies in mice. These animals are particularly prone to spontaneous development of tumors, especially liver and lung tumors. As a result, some researchers avoid using mice, and others again compensate for this problem by employing a second animal species. But the knowledge of these and other caveats still does not give us much confidence in drawing conclusions about cancer for people from animals. To improve this process, we must do more basic research in the area of pharmacokinetics. This means we must learn more about the similarities and differences between people and specific experimental animals regarding:

- how test substances behave in the bodies of each;
- how these substances are transformed or metabolized in the bodies of each, and what breakdown products or metabolites are formed;

- how long these materials remain in the bodies of people versus animals;
- which organ systems they affect;
- and whether the metabolites, rather than the parent compound, may be carcinogenic.

The recognition of the importance of these questions is growing among all   10
of those involved in the animal-testing debate. Experts in and out of government are starting to focus on the need for answers. Provided the right research is undertaken, we will be able in the near future to make more meaningful use of animal test results than we are now.

No discussion of animal testing would be complete without touching upon   11
that issue which has sparked so much of the human versus rodent debate: the use of the "maximum tolerated dose" or MTD. This is the highest dose that won't reduce an animal's lifespan due to effects other than tumors.

Critics of the MTD approach point out the absurdity of its size in relation   12
to human exposure. For example, they might cite two studies on trichloroethylene (used to decaffeinate coffee and for many other purposes) which involved the human equivalent of millions of cups of coffee a day.

The scientific critics also make a more technical objection: that tumors   13
produced in animals under high-dose conditions may reflect not the inherent toxicity of the test substance but the effects of bodily stress caused by organ systems attempting to metabolize the high doses in unusual ways.

Advocates of the MTD approach contend that because so few animals (rel-   14
ative to the human population) are used in these studies, they must be exposed to extremely high doses to determine if the chemical has any cancerous effect at all, particularly if it is thought to be a weak carcinogen.

Fortunately, the debate is not at a standstill. For product registration pur-   15
poses, regulatory agencies such as EPA sometimes recommend the use of three doses in chronic animal feeding studies—the MTD, a low dose aimed at a no-effect level, and a dose somewhere between these two. Similarly, the National Toxicology Program, the federal government's principal animal-testing arm for chronic effects, now has begun to employ three doses in its studies.

These procedural changes are a commendable attempt on the part of fed-   16
eral agencies to obtain a more complete and realistic picture of the carcinogenic potency, if any, of test substances. For example, the variety of data yielded by several dosing levels can help regulatory agencies construct better "dose-response curves" against which human exposure levels can be measured and from which estimates of human risk can be drawn.

Of course, this will only happen if regulatory agencies use the data in this   17
way. But their record in this regard has been spotty at best. Too often, we in industry still see risk assessments consisting mainly of mathematical calculations based upon high-dose levels in single animal species. These are of limited use. They are only one piece in what ought to be a more fully devel-

oped picture of potential human hazard. To get this picture, the full complement of information on a substance must be considered, including its
biochemistry and pharmacokinetic aspects.

I would offer two other thoughts regarding risk assessment. They concern   18
both how regulatory agencies, such as EPA, use animal tests in this work,
and how they don't use other, equally (or perhaps more) valid information.

Single positive animal studies have been sufficient to put the agency's   19
rulemaking wheels in motion. But no number of negative animal tests seems
adequate to keep these wheels from spinning. A single negative study ought
not neutralize a positive, but several negative findings contrasted with one
positive ought to cause regulators to consider whether the appropriate next
step should be further research as opposed to precipitate regulatory action.

A more troubling aspect of the agency's risk assessment process is its   20
apparent lack of respect for well conducted human epidemiological studies.
Now women and men seem to count less than rodents in the decision-making
process. This despite the fact that numerous scientific bodies have stressed
the importance of epidemiology in determining human risk. As recently as
last, August, an interdisciplinary panel convened by Oxford University's Dr.
Phillipe Shubik reported that: "Human data provide the only direct evidence
that a chemical produces cancer in man. . . . Because of their central role in
the identification of human risk, epidemiological studies are indispensable
and require substantial expansion."

I'm not arguing for the use of human evidence to the exclusion of animal   21
data. Instead, I'm urging that EPA take into account as much quality information as is available on a particular substance: animal test results, human
mortality and morbidity, the route and extent of human exposure, and studies that elucidate species' similarities and differences.

The Roman poet Horace wrote that "the mountains will be in labor, and   22
the birth will be an absurd little mouse." The controversy over animal testing
has turned this couplet on its head: the mouse has produced a mountain of
scientific debate. But as we scale up and down this mountain, we need to
keep in sight the common destination—animal testing systems that will allow
us to do what is right and reasonable in protecting both our health and our
economic well-being.

QUESTIONS FOR MEANING

1. What points of disagreement in the debate over animal experimentation
   are identified by Roush?
2. Is the death rate from cancer increasing in the United States?
3. How do researchers try to compensate for species differences when experimenting upon animals? Does Roush believe that this is sufficient?
4. Why has MTD, or "maximum tolerated dose" been controversial? How has
   testing begun to change in response to this criticism?
5. Vocabulary: ludicrous (1), beset (3), caveats (9), elucidate (21).

QUESTIONS ABOUT STRATEGY

1. Does Roush provide adequate examples to illustrate the claims he makes?
2. How would you describe the tone of this essay?
3. Where in his essay does Roush make specific recommendations for procedural reform? How has he prepared his audience for these recommendations?

C. R. GALLISTEL

Bell, Magendie, and the Proposals to Restrict the Use of Animals in Neurobehavioral Research

Charles Ransom Gallistel was born in Indianapolis. He received his B.A. from Stanford University in 1963 and his Ph.D. from Yale in 1966. He is a professor of psychology at the University of Pennsylvania, where he is also chairperson of the psychology department. Since 1972, he has been a consulting editor of the Journal of Comparative and Physiological Psychology. *Gallistel is the coauthor of* The Child's Understanding of Number *(1978) and a contributor to numerous scholarly journals. His unequivocal defense of animal experimentation in "Bell, Magendie, and the Proposals to Restrict the Use of Animals in Neurobehavioral Research" provoked considerable discussion upon its* **1981** *publication in the* American Psychologist.

ABSTRACT: The discovery by Magendie of the sensory and motor functions of the dorsal and ventral roots of the spinal nerves provides an illuminating case study of the scientific and ethical considerations that arise when one contem-plates restricting neurobehavioral research on animals because of the suffering it causes them. Such restrictions reduce the number of worthless experiments only at the cost of reducing the number of worthwhile experiments—experi-ments that shed new light on the sources of behavior and provide the knowl-edge that enables us to alleviate human suffering. Therefore, one should urge the abandonment of animal research in part or in toto only if one believes that the moral value attached to the avoidance of animal suffering is greater than the moral value attached to the enrichment of human understanding and the alleviation of human suffering.

A bill called the "Research Modernization Act" is now before Congress,   1
where it is picking up influential support. The bill would ban most surgical
experiments using live animals, on the theory that the same knowledge may
usually be gained by computer simulations, experiments on bacteria, and so

on (see Broad, 1980). The bill would establish a review committee that would allow *at most* one experiment of a given type to be done on live animals. The proponents of this legislation claim that the law is a moral imperative and that it would not cause serious harm to research in the life sciences. I wish to argue that this bill would devastate behavioral neurobiology and that it is an affront to moral sensibility.

Behavioral neurobiology tries to establish the manner in which the nervous system mediates behavioral phenomena. It does so by studying the behavioral consequences of one or more of the following procedures: (a) destruction of a part of the nervous system, (b) stimulation of a part, and (c) administration of drugs that alter neural functioning. These three techniques are as old as the discipline. A recent addition is (d) the recording of electrical activity. All four procedures cause the animal at least some temporary distress. In the past they have frequently caused intense pain, and they occasionally do so now. Also, they often impair the animal's proper functioning, sometimes transiently, sometimes permanently.   2

From the beginning, this enterprise has provoked moral censure, to which the experimentalists have often reacted defensively. The terms of this debate have changed hardly at all in 200 years. Consider the following passage, written shortly after 1800 (Le Gallois, 1813, pp. 19–21):   3

Before I close this introduction, I wish in some degree to exculpate the physiologists who make experiments upon living animals, from the reproaches of cruelty, so frequently uttered against them. I do not pretend wholly to justify them. I would only remark, the most part of those who utter these reproaches may be deserving of the same. For example, do they not go, or have they never gone a hunting? How can the sportsman, who for his own pleasure mutilates so many animals, and often in so cruel a manner, be more humane than the physiologist who is forced to make them perish for his instruction? Whether the rights we assume over those animals be lawful or not, it is certain that few people scruple to destroy, in a variety of ways, such of those animals as cause them the least inconvenience, though ever so trifling; and that we only feed the most part of those that surround us, to sacrifice them to our wants. I can scarcely comprehend that we should be wrong in killing them for our instruction, when we think we are right in destroying them for our food.

I own that it would be barbarous to make animals suffer in vain, if the object of the experiment could be obtained without it. But it is impossible. Experiments upon living animals are one of the greatest lights of physiology. The difference between the dead and the living animal is infinite. If the ablest mechanician is unable to discover all the effect of a machine after having seen it work, how could the most learned anatomist devise, by the study only of the organs, the effect of a machine as prodigiously complicated as the body of an animal. To find out its secrets, it is not enough to observe the simultaneous exercise of all the functions in the animal, while in health; it is above all important to study the effect of the derangement, or the cessation of such or such a function. It is in determining by this analysis what the function of such or such an organ is, as well as its relation with the other functions, that the art of

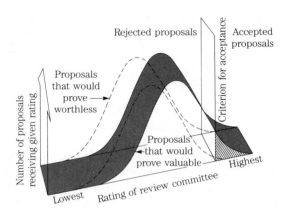

FIGURE 1. Rating of Review Committee

The dilemma faced by review committees that are determined to eliminate worthless experiments. The shaded area represents the proposals that are allowed to be carried out. Even though the criterion for acceptance has been set so high as to eliminate most of the research that if carried out would have proved valuable, some research projects that in fact prove worthless are still done. Before the fact, many worthless experiments (e.g., Bell, 1811) look as good as or better than many very valuable experiments (e.g., Magendie, 1822). The number of worthless experiments permitted becomes negligible only when the criteria is so high that nearly all the valuable experiments are rejected.

experiments upon living animals consists. But to be able to do it with some degree of precision, it is indispensably necessary to multiply the victims, on account of the variety of circumstances and accidents which may render that result uncertain or inconclusive. I should be tempted to say of physiological experiments, what has been said of charities: *perdenda sunt multa; ut semel ponas bene.* SENECA. [Translation: Many are a waste, that one may come out well.]

The passage just quoted seems to me to contain most of the basic facts   4
and positions in the debate between behavioral neurobiologists and antivivi-sectionists. Let me first summarize what I take to be matters of fact:

1. Experimental surgery causes pain and distress to animals.
2. Researchers are well aware of this pain. Since the discovery of ether in 1847, they have used anesthetics to reduce or prevent the pain, wherever such reduction or prevention does not affect the conclusions that can be drawn from the experiment.
3. There is no way to establish the relation between the nervous system and behavior without some experimental surgery.
4. Most experiments conducted by behavioral neurobiologists, *like scientific experiments in general,* may be seen in retrospect to have been a waste of time, in the sense that they did not prove anything or yield any new insight.

5. There is no way of discriminating in advance the waste-of-time experiments from the illuminating ones with anything approaching certainty. Such judgments are necessarily made under conditions of high
uncertainty. As shown by the theory of signal detection, a necessary
consequence of this uncertainty is that any attempt to reduce the
number of neurobehavioral experiments by prior evaluation of their
possible significance will necessarily give rise to many "false negatives" without eliminating "false positives." That is, prior restraints
on neurobehavioral experiments will lead to rejection of experiments
whose results would in fact have been important and allowance of
experiments whose results will prove unimportant. This will be true
no matter how stringent and cumbersome the a priori evaluation
(see Figure 1).

These five statements must be taken as facts. Any attempt to advance a   5
pro- or antivivisectionist position by denying one or another of these statements evades the ethical question by denying the very circumstances that
give it force. The force of these circumstances can best be appreciated by
the study of specific historical cases. One case that should be analyzed at
length by anyone contemplating restricting neurobehavioral experiments is
the discovery that the dorsal and ventral roots of the spinal cord are sensory
and motor, respectively.

In 1822 François Magendie discovered that in young puppies the dorsal   6
and ventral roots of the peripheral nerves come together outside the spinal
column, so that they can be separately severed with relative ease. Magendie
had been wondering for some time what would be the effect of cutting one
or another root on the behavior of the limb or body segment served by the
nerve. In the other animals he was familiar with, the roots fused before exit-
ing from the spine. They could only be cut individually after breaking open
the spine, which, in the days before anesthesia, was all but impossible to do
without damaging the spinal cord. Soon after discovering the favorable anatomical disposition of the roots in young puppies, Magendie began exposing
the spines of 6–8-week-old puppies and cutting either the dorsal or the ventral roots of one or more nerves. After several such experiments he was able
to publish his famous three-page communication in which he concluded that
the dorsal roots carried sensory signals while the ventral roots carried motor
signals (Magendie, 1822).

Magendie's experiments place the ethical problems posed by neurobehav-   7
ioral research in sharp relief for the following reasons: (a) The results were
of the utmost importance. (b) The animals used were puppies and the pain
of the necessary surgical procedure was both intense and unalleviated by
anesthetics, whose discovery lay 25 years in the future. (c) Other very similar
experiments had been conducted by some of the leading neuroscientists of
the day—most notably the English anatomist Charles Bell—without yielding
the decisive, all-important insight. (d) The experiments, because they rapidly
became well-known and because they were sometimes performed in public,

incurred widespread moral censure and helped fuel the antivivisection movement in 19th century England.

Let me elaborate on these points. First, as regards the significance of the   8
results, I can do no better than quote from the introduction to a recent book
by Cranefield (1974,p.xiii) on the history of the Bell-Magendie precedence
dispute:

> The discovery that the dorsal and ventral roots are the sensory and motor roots
> is one of the most important in the history of biology. The importance of the
> discovery has never been doubted; as E.H. Ackerknecht has recently written to
> me, "it is, after Harvey, probably the most momentous *single* discovery in phys-
> iology, and it had a more immediate influence on practical medicine than Harv-
> ey's discovery. Romberg's book on neurology, the first of its kind, is unthinkable
> without it."
>
> A comparison with Harvey is by no means idle, since just as no rational
> physiology of the cardiovascular system was possible before Harvey's discovery,
> so no rational physiology of the nervous system was possible before the discov-
> ery of the separate functions of the roots of the spinal nerves. It was the first
> unequivocal localization of function in the nervous system and it made possible
> and led directly to the study of the spinal reflex. The study of the spinal reflex
> culminated in the work of Sherrington, work that led to our modern concepts
> of the physiology of the entire central nervous system.

As regards the pain caused the animals—the other horn of the dilemma,   9
so to speak—little elaboration is necessary, except to note that the pain was
hideous, that there was no way known to the science of the day of mitigating
it, and last, for the reasons already explained, that the animal of choice was
the one most likely to arouse human sympathy—the puppy.

The third point, the similar but inconclusive experiments conducted by   10
other leading neuroscientists of that time, requires considerable elaboration.
The elaboration is rich both in its irony and in its implications for the question of whether antivivisectionist sentiment may be appeased without doing
serious damage to the progress of neuroscience. In 1811, in a privately circulated pamphlet, Charles Bell reported the results of experiments on rabbits
involving the sectioning of dorsal and/or ventral roots. The report of these
experiments is sketchy, and the wording of the conclusions is diffuse and
obscure; but, in essence, Bell concluded erroneously that the ventral roots
subserved voluntary behavior while the dorsal roots subserved involuntary
behavior. Bell's conclusions were steered in the direction of error by a theory
of nervous system function that he had derived from his anatomical studies.
In subsequent publications Bell made brief allusions to these results and to
related results from experiments involving the sectioning of cranial nerves in
donkeys; but he did not give any clear statement of their implications, nor
did he attach much importance to them *until* Magendie published his paper
in 1822. Immediately thereafter Bell and his students began a clamorous,

unprincipled, but largely successful campaign to claim priority for what was properly Magendie's discovery.

In the course of this campaign, Bell advanced more or less self-contradic- 11
tory claims. He repeatedly reproached Magendie for the cruelty of the experiments, claiming that the experiments were unnecessary and counterproductive
and that the correct conclusion could be reached by anatomical observation
alone. On the other hand, he argued that he, himself, had performed the
crucial experiment first in 1811 and that Magendie had been inspired to "rep-
licate" it by one of Bell's pupils, who demonstrated the related cranial nerve
experiment to Magendie in late 1821. Bell even reissued "improved" versions
of his earlier publications, in which crucial passages were reworded so as to
appear to anticipate Magendie's conclusions.

Bell's reproaches and his claims that experiments were unnecessary were 12
picked up by antivivisectionists and helped to get passed the laws that to
this day make neurobehavioral work more difficult in England than in America or on the Continent. The claim that experiments on living animals are
unnecessary finds its echo today in the claim made by antivivisectionists that
it is possible to do neurobehavioral research by computer simulation, without
ever cutting into a living animal.

These claims are absurd and nothing illustrates their absurdity better than 13
the case at hand. There is nothing in anatomical observation per se that can
do more than faintly suggest the functions of the roots. Bell himself knew
that the results from the experiments on living animals were central to his
claim of priority. Without them he had no claim, which is why—after 1822—
he repeatedly emphasized his experiments on rabbits and donkeys. The irony
is that Bell's erroneous inferences from anatomical observation played no
small role in misleading his interpretation of his vivisection experiments. If
anatomical observations are of little use, computer simulation is of still less
use. What is there to simulate? You can make a computer whose input and
output wires are segregated; you can make one in which they are inter-
twined; you can even make one in which the same wires are used for both
functions. None of this modeling will tell you what the case is with the dorsal
and ventral roots of mammalian nerves.

The sorry story of Bell's attempt to claim priority also illustrates the un- 14
desirability of setting up committees to pass in advance on whether the
results to be obtained from a given experiment performed by a given experimenter are sufficiently important to outweigh the pain to be inflicted.
Bell was one of the most important neuroscientists of his day. Furthermore,
his vivisection experiments were inspired by a very general if vague and murky
(in retrospect!) theory. Magendie was also a scientist of great stature, but he
had no theory; indeed, he mistrusted and eschewed the system building that
Bell was addicted to. Magendie just wanted to see what would happen. In
Bell's hands, the crucial experiment led only to vague conclusions, to which
Bell himself attributed little importance. In Magendie's hands, the experiment
led to a clear conclusion whose importance was immediately obvious to all
of the leading neuroscientists of his time.

Had Bell and Magendie simultaneously submitted proposals for the exper-   15
iment to a Humane-Vivisection Committee for its permission, it is hard not
to believe that they would have given the nod to Bell rather than to Magendie, assuming they gave either permission. If Magendie in 1822 had asked
permission of a committee that happened to be aware of Bell's 1811 work—
which is to assume an unusually well-informed committee—they would no
doubt have refused permission on the grounds that the experiment had already been done by a first-rate researcher with meaningless results.

In summary, the debate over the ethics of surgical experiments on ani-   16
mals in behavioral neurobiology must come to grips with the following two
dilemmas:

1. While it is true that these experiments cause pain and/or distress to
   the animals, it is equally true that the science cannot progress without them.
2. While it is true that most of the animals which suffer in the course
   of neurobehavioral research suffer in vain, it is equally true that there
   is no way to restrict experimentation only to those experiments that
   will yield meaningful data.

A consideration of the Bell-Magendie case makes it clear why restricting   17
research on living animals is certain to restrict the progress in our understanding of the relation between the nervous system and behavior. Therefore,
one should advocate such restrictions only if one believes that the moral
value of this scientific knowledge and of the many human and humane benefits that flow from it cannot outweigh the suffering of a rat.

It is an affront to my own ethical sensibility to hear arguments that the   18
suffering of animals is of greater moral weight than are the advancement of
human understanding and the consequent alleviation of human suffering. Like
Le Gallois, I can scarcely comprehend how it can be right to use animals to
provide food for our bodies but wrong to use them to provide food for thought.
But, of course, I place a very high moral value on the advancement of human
understanding. Those for whom science has no moral value will find my argument without force, assuming that they are also unmoved by the prospect
that such understanding will alleviate human suffering.

References*

Bell, C. (1811). *Idea of a new anatomy of the brain.* London: Strahan.

Broad, W.J. (1980). Legislating an end to animals in the lab. *Science, 208,* 575–576.

Cranefield, P.F. (1974). *The way in and the way out: François Magendie, Charles Bell and the roots of the spinal nerves.* Mount Kisco: Futura.

* This essay uses the APA author/year style of documentation. The following essay by Deborah Mayo uses the
same system. For a discussion of this system see Part 1 (pp. 51–53, 58–60).

Le Gallois, M. (1813). *Experiments on the principle of life* (N.C. Nancrede & J.C. Nancrede, Trans.). Philadelphia: Thomas.

Magendie, F. (1822). Expériences sur les fonctions des racines des nerfs rachidien. *Journal de Physiologie Expérimentale et Pathologique, 2,* 276–279.

QUESTIONS FOR MEANING

1. What is behavioral neurobiology and what does it do to animals?
2. Who was François Magendie and what did he discover? Describe his experiments and explain why they were significant.
3. Why are many scientific experiments a waste of time? How does Gallistel justify this?
4. Because he could assume that his audience understood the difference between "sensory signals" and "motor signals," Gallistel does not explain the distinction. Do you understand these functions? If you know nothing about biology or psychology, where could you go to learn basic scientific vocabulary?
5. Why is Gallistel critical of Charles Bell? What does the Bell/Magendie conflict illustrate?
6. Vocabulary: simulations (1), imperative (1), affront (1), transiently (2), censure (3), exculpate (3), prodigiously (3), and erroneously (10).

QUESTIONS ABOUT STRATEGY

1. Gallistel makes no attempt to hide the fact that animal experimentation involves animal suffering. Was he wise to admit this? Does this admission strengthen or weaken his argument?
2. The quotation included in paragraph 3 is unusually long. Was it worth including? What is it meant to illustrate? Could Gallistel have paraphrased it in fewer words without losing anything important?
3. Consider the tone of this essay—and the last paragraph in particular. Is Gallistel unnecessarily combative? Should he show more tolerance for his opponents? Or is his attitude understandable when seen within the context of what has been written on the other side?
4. What does the graph (Figure 1) add to this essay? Could it have been left out?

DEBORAH G. MAYO
Against a Scientific Justification of Animal Experiments

*A magna cum laude graduate of Clark University, where she had a double ma-
jor in philosophy and mathematics, Deborah Mayo has done extensive research
on the use of statistics in science, economics, and philosophy. She received her
Ph.D. from the University of Pennsylvania in 1979 and currently teaches philosophy at Virginia Polytechnic Institute and State University. She has received
several fellowships from the National Endowment for the Humanities and published essays in numerous scholarly journals. "Against a Scientific Justification
of Animal Experiments" was first published in **1983.** Drawing upon her training in logic and statistical testing, Mayo questions the scientific validity of experiments involving laboratory animals—thus moving the debate over animal
experimentation beyond the questions of ethics and morality most often focused
upon by other writers. As you read her essay, you will find that she has
amassed an impressive amount of evidence to support her point of view.*

Introduction

Discussions of the treatment of animals typically focus on their use as food   1
and clothing, omitting the widespread use of animals in laboratory research.
Animals serve as experimental subjects in teaching surgical operations; in
testing the efficiency and safety of drugs, food, cars, household cleaners, and
makeup; in psychological studies of pain, stress, and depression; and in satisfying the curiosity and desire of humans to learn more about biological
processes. In so doing they are subjected to shocks, burns, lesions, crashes,
stresses, diseases, mutilations, and the general array of slings and arrows of
the laboratory environment.

If it is agreed that killing and torturing animals is prima facie wrong, then   2
additional justification is necessary in order to defend the sacrifice of millions
of animals each year to research. The justification most frequently offered is
that animal research provides increases both in scientific knowledge and in
the health, safety, and comfort of humans. As Lowrance (1976) remarks:

> For most people, any qualms over jeopardizing the animals are more than offset
> by the desire to gain knowledge useful in alleviating human suffering (p. 52).
> . . . Few people would engage in such work were it not so essential (p. 54).

So closely is scientific experimentation associated with animal experimentation that those who oppose or criticize animal experiments are often taken
to be opposing or critizing science. One finds advocates of humane experimental methods labeled as anti-science and referred to as "those whose love
of animals leads them into a hatred of science and even humanity . . ." (Lane-

Petter, 1963, p. 472). The classic volume, *Experimental Surgery* (Markowitz et al., 1959) introduces the student to the Antivivisection Movement with the following remarks (emphasis added):

> It must be apparent . . . that ordinary antivivisectionists are immune to the usual methods of exposition by reasoned argument. *They strain at a dog and swallow a baby. . . .* They are an unfortunate evil in our midst, and we must accustom ourselves to their presence as we do to bad weather, and to disease.

The error in depicting critics of animal experiments as anti-science becomes clear when one begins to question the extent to which the purported scientific aims of these experiments are actually accomplished. For then it turns out that the experiments and not their critics are unscientific. However, humanists concerned with the treatment of animals too rarely question the scientific basis of animal experiments and fail to uncover dissent within the scientific community itself. To the philosopher's arguments that animal experimentation is morally indefensible, the animal researcher responds that they benefit humanity. But if the most common uses of animals in research can be shown to be neither significantly beneficial to humans nor scientifically sound, then any appeal to such benefits in justifying these uses is undermined. It is the purpose of this paper to undermine the justification of common types of animal experiments by questioning their practical and scientific relevance and validity. Those experiments that cannot be justified on scientific grounds can be no more justified than the frivolous killing and torturing of animals. In fact they are even less capable of justification, since such experiments block more fruitful uses of scientific resources.

Irrelevant Experiments

I shall first consider the relevance of animal experiments and then discuss various problems leading to their invalidity. In an important sense, invalidity is not separate from irrelevance, since invalid experiments are surely irrelevant ones. However, in this section I shall focus on experiments that are irrelevant because of the triviality or obviousness of the question they ask. Indeed, many experiments do not even have a specific question in mind at the outset. They are often carried out simply to see what will happen and after the results are in some sort of hypothesis is formulated. Whether the hypothesis has been formulated before or after the experiment is not reported in the description of the experiment. Yet, formulating the hypothesis on the basis of the experiment can be shown to lead researchers to conclude, wrongly, that something of relevance has been observed (see Mayo, 1981).

I must emphasize that the examples I here consider are not at all exceptional or unusual. On the contrary, each represents a basic type of experiment that is performed with minor variations on millions of animals each year. An examination of the *Psychopharmaceutical Abstracts,* in which summaries of published experimental results are reported, will attest to the triviality and repetitiveness of the great majority of inquiries. What is particularly disturbing about the irrelevant experiments mentioned here is the amount of pain and suffering they involve. That such irrelevant painful experiments are not rare even at present is made plain in Jeff Diner's (1979) *Physical and Mental Suffering of Experimental Animals,* in which research from 1975–1978 is reviewed. It must also be kept in mind that these experiments are examples of ones considered important enough to publish. It is fair to assume that, in reality, many more experiments with even less relevance are performed. I limit myself to considering only recent experiments, to make it clear that these are not atrocities of the past.

(i) Infant monkeys were blinded at the University of Chicago in order to   5
assess whether blindness inhibited social interactions as measured by facial expressions. The result: blind monkeys showed all normal facial expressions, except threat (Berkson & Becker, 1975).

(ii) Pigeons were starved to 70% of their weight in the City University of   6
New York. It was concluded that following starvation pigeons ate more than usual (*Journal of Comparative and Physiological Psychology,* Sept., 1971).

(iii) The Department of Psychology at the University of Iowa studied the   7
effects of brain lesions on the grooming behavior of cats. Cats underwent surgery to produce various types of brain lesions and films were taken of their subsequent grooming behavior. It was reported that:

> Statistical analyses of the grooming behavior shown on the films indicated that cats with pontile lesions and cats with tectal lesions spent less time grooming. . . . Other studies revealed that cats with pontile or tectal lesions were deficient in removing tapes stuck on their fur (Swenson & Randall, 1977).

(iv) At the Downstate Medical Center rats were surgically brain damaged   8
and then stimulated by pinching their tails. They were then offered substances to drink. It was reported that (Mufson et al., 1976):

> Brain-damaged animals during tail pinch-induced drinking trials are responsive to the sensory properties of the test liquid. Chocolate milk is consumed, but tap water is actively rejected. Tail pinch to sham-operated control rats failed to induce such behavior; instead, it induced rage behavior towards the hand that pinched the tail.

(Is it to be concluded from this that brain damage decreases rage at painful stimuli and increases the desire for chocolate milk?)

(v) The following experiment carried out at the George Washington University Medical Center is a typical example of radiation research. Non-anesthetized rabbits had their heads irradiated while being restrained in "a Lucite restraining device." It is reported that "The developing skin, mucosal and eye   9 lesions were recorded and often photographed, but no treatment was offered" (Bradley et al., 1977). The report continues to describe in detail the monstrous radiation-induced damage without drawing any conclusions.

(vi) An extremely widespread sort of experiment involves assessing the effects of various drugs on "punished responding." Punished responding typically involves first teaching an animal to perform some task such as pressing a key by rewarding it with food, and later changing these rewards to punishments such as electric shocks. A number of such experiments have been carried out by Dr. J.E. Barrett using pigeons. Here, the "punishments" consist of electric shocks administered through electrodes implanted around the pubis bone. The results are rather inconclusive. It is reported that (Barrett & Witkin, 1976):

> The broad range of effects obtained in the present experiment make it difficult to readily characterize the effects of drug interactions on behavior.

(vii) At Emory University cats were used to study how two different kinds of painful stimuli, foot shock and tooth shock, influence behavior. To administer tooth shock, electrodes were implanted in the upper canine teeth of the cats. Foot shock was administered by means of stainless steel rods that formed the grid floor of the shuttle box in which the cats were placed. The cats were trained to escape the shocks by jumping across a barrier. However, when the cats were also subjected to the tooth shock, they were unable to escape the foot shock. It was concluded that tooth shock exerted a stronger influence than foot shock on behavior. The report regrets that (Anderson et al., 1976):

> Since 14 mA was the maximum amount of current that could be generated by our apparatus, it was not possible to determine if foot shock levels greater than that would have led to escape responding.

(viii) The *British Journal of Ophthalmology* published the experiments of Dr. Zauberman, which measured the number of grams of force needed to strip the retinas from the eyes of cats. There was nothing said about how this or similar experiments that were carried out could be relevant to the problem of detached retinas in humans.

(ix) A good deal of research has as its goal the determination of the effects of various operations on the sexual behavior of animals. For example, for a number of years the American Museum of Natural History in New York has conducted research on the effect of surgical mutilation on the sexual behavior of cats. In 1969 cats raised in isolation had penis nerves severed. The results of years of sex testing on these cats were overwhelmingly unsurprising: genital desensitization together with sexual inexperience inhibits the normal sexual behavior in cats (cited in Pratt, 1976, p. 72).

Numerous other experiments by the same researchers were conducted to   14
determine the effect of surgically destroying the olfactory area on the brain
on sexual behavior in cats, monkeys, hamsters, rats, and mice. The conclusions from all of these experiments were reported to be "contradictory."

(x) Some experiments are rendered trivial or useless because they do no   15
more than repeat an experiment already performed numerous times. Even
worse is the continuous repetition of experiments whose relevance is dubious in the first place. For example, there is the experiment that has been
carried out since the time of Claude Bernard, one of the founders of modern
vivisection methods. This experiment involves sewing up the ends of the in-
testines of dogs rendering them unable to defecate. Death has been observed
to follow in some cases between 5 and 11 days, in other cases between 8 and
34 days. To what use is such information to be put?

One of the reasons for continually repeating an experiment that has al-   16
ready produced a result is that by using enough animals a result that is of a
sufficient degree of statistical significance can be obtained. It is thought that
the more observations the greater the evidence. However, this is based upon
a statistical fallacy. The more experiments needed in order to observe an
effect that is statistically significant, the smaller and more trivial the effect
is. With enough experiments, even a chance occurrence is rendered overwhelmingly significant, statistically speaking.

Invalidity of Experiments

Experimental investigations are multi-staged affairs involving a host of   17
background variables, the gathering, modeling, and analyses of data and inferences based upon the data. At each stage a variety of flaws can arise to
render the experiment and inferences based upon it invalid. I shall consider
some of the most pronounced flaws that arise in carrying out animal experiments and making inferences from them in medical and pharmacological research. These flaws stem from the disparity between experimentally induced
conditions and conditions in humans, from within- and between-species differences, and from confounding variables before, during, and after experimental treatment. I consider each of these in turn.

Artificial Induction of Disease

One type of medical research involves ascertaining whether certain patho-   18
logical conditions in humans can be alleviated or cured by certain drugs.
Animals are used as "models" upon which to test these treatments. To do
this it is necessary for the animal subject to have the condition in question,
and in order to bring this about healthy animals are made sick. To this end
they surgically have organs removed or damaged; they are injected with
pathogenic organisms and cancer cells; they have irritants applied to their
eyes and shaved skins; are forced to inhale various substances, and consume
deficient diets. To produce such conditions as fear, anxiety, ulcers, heart dis-

eases, and shock, animals are stressed by electric shocks or subjected to specially made pain devices, such as the Blalock Press and the Noble-Collip Drum.

It turns out, however, that the conditions artificially induced have little in common with the naturally occurring diseases in animals (when these exist) and much less in common with the diseases in man. This renders any conclusions drawn on the basis of treating these induced conditions of little relevance for treating humans (or even animals in cases where the condition naturally occurs). Extrapolating results from animal research to humans also frequently fails because of an absence of comparative examples of diseases in animals (particularly with hereditary diseases). For example, ulcers do not occur naturally in animals, and cancer in animals is quite different from cancer in man.   19

It is for this reason that the usefulness of animals in cancer research has been questioned. Most of the anticancer agents in use today have been tested in animals, most commonly rodents who have had tumors transplanted into them. This method, however, is of questionable validity. As noted in a review of testing anticancer drugs (*The Lancet*, April 15, 1972):   20

> Since no animal tumor is closely related to a cancer in human beings, an agent which is active in the laboratory may well prove to be useless clinically.

The situation would not be so serious if these agents were merely useless. In fact they are quite harmful, often causing side effects that may themselves precipitate further ills or even death. When researchers announce that a substance has been found to be effective in treating animal cancers, it is not revealed that the cell kinetics in animal cancers are vastly different than in humans. As the review above states:

> Animal tumours favored as test models have short doubling-times and a large proportion of cells in cycle with short generation-times. Probably, in many human cancers, intermitotic times are much longer and many cells are out of cycle. . . .

Since all anticancer agents in use have had their effectiveness assessed by animal tests, virtually all of them act only on rapidly dividing cells. This is one reason that treating human cancers (which typically do not divide rapidly) with these agents fails. The possibility of transplanting actual human cancers to animals is a suggestion which has been tried, but with poor results. As *The Lancet* review remarks, "This is hardly surprising, in view of the vastly different biochemical make-up of the animal model and of the human tumour which responds."

Hence, people are given drug after drug in the hope of arresting cancer when in fact these drugs have been evaluated upon cancers and organisms   21 "vastly different" from their own. It may be argued that no better method is available for treating cancer, and so for the time being it is the best that can be done. Such, however, is not the case. In the last 30 years or so new techniques have been developed which hold much promise. These new techniques involve testing anticancer agents on cultures of human cancer cells. This has the advantage of permitting the sensitivity of individual cancers to chemotherapy to be estimated, providing each patient with treatment custom-tailored to the type of cancer involved. This would prevent individuals from having to suffer the agonies of numerous trial agents that may be entirely ill-suited for treating their particular strain of cancer. If these newer techniques are to be developed sufficiently, some of the attention presently given to animal testing will have to be channeled into these alternatives. Unfortunately, researchers have been reluctant to do so.

22   The need to induce pathological conditions in animals in order to test some treatment upon them gives rise to an additional area of medical research. This area involves experiments that have as their sole aim the determination of how various pathological conditions can best be brought about in animals. Although such research has provided means for inducing a number of conditions, cures for these conditions have not been forthcoming.

23   For instance, research has repeatedly been carried out in order to find ways of inducing peritonitis in dogs. Peritonitis is the painful condition suffered by humans after rupturing their appendices. Even after a standard method for producing this disease in dogs was available (i.e., surgically tying off the appendix and feeding the dog castor oil), further experiments to find improved methods were made. One such experiment is reported by Hans Ruesch in *Slaughter of the Innocent* (Ruesch, 1978, pp. 105–106):

> With each dog strapped down and his belly laid open, the 'surgeons'—subsidized by the American taxpayers who of course had never been asked for their consent—tied off and crushed the appendix, then cut out part of the intestinal tract and the spleen. With the intestinal system thus multilated and unable to function normally, the dog was made to swallow a large dose of castor oil. The authors stated that thus 'a fatal, fulminating, diffuse peritonitis of appendical origin may be uniformly produced in dogs.'

There was no attempt to cure peritonitis, the aim having been merely to cause it. It was reported that the average survival time of the agonized dogs in this experiment was 39 hours.

24   Arguments to the effect that it is wrong to cause pain and suffering to animals are often rejected by claiming that animals simply do not suffer. Descartes, for example, asserted that the cries of an animal are no more significant than the creaking of a wheel. Ironically, it is precisely upon the assumption that animals *do* suffer from stress, fear, and pain in a manner similar to humans that the validity of much of animal experimentation rests. Few, if any, conditions are studied as widely in animals are are pain, stress,

ulcers, fear, and anxiety. An enormous amount of data has been compiled about how to produce such conditions, a good deal of which arose from the research of Hans Selye (1956). To obtain this data, millions of animals, primarily rats, mice, rabbits, and cats were and continue to be subjected to burns, poisons, shocks, frustrations, muscle and bone crushing, exposure, and gland removal. However, as is generally the case with artificially induced conditions in animals, laboratory-induced stress and stress-related conditions have little in common with stress and stress-related diseases in humans. To support this claim, it is necessary to consider something about how these conditions are induced in the laboratory animal.

One of the tools developed in 1942 to aid Selye in his research on stress, is the stress producing Noble-Collip Drum, named after its inventors, R.L. Noble and J.B. Collip. The animals, locked and strapped (paws taped) inside the revolving metal drum, are tossed about and in so doing are thrust against iron projections in the drum. This treatment (often involving thousands of tosses at a rate of 40 tosses a minute) crushes bones, tissues, and teeth, and ruptures and scrambles organs. In assessing the considerable work of Selye, the *British Medical Journal* (May 22, 1954, p. 1195) concluded that experimentally induced stress had little in common with conditions that humans develop. Ulcers brought about in animals subjected to a rotating drum differ from ulcers in humans, not only because of a difference in species, but because ulcers in humans stem from rather different origins (e.g., long-term psychological stresses) than do those created in the laboratory through physical torture. Unsurprisingly, treatments developed from Selye's stress research (e.g., administering a hormone excreted by tortured animals, ACTH) are of very dubious value. As one surgeon points out (Ogilvie, 1935): 25

> They [gastric and duodenal ulcers] never occur naturally in animals, and they are hard to reproduce experimentally. They have been so produced, but usually by methods of gross damage that have no relation to any possible causative factor in man; moreover, these experimental ulcers are superficial and heal rapidly, and bear little resemblance to the indurated chronic ulcers we see in our patients.

The Noble-Collip Drum has been criticized not only as being inhumane, but as being too crude to be scientifically useful. In what is considered a definitive review of experimentally produced shock, H.B. Stoner made this remark about it. "It is impossible to describe the effect of the injury and study the injured tissue quantitatively. . . . The method seems altogether too crude for modern purposes" (Stoner, 1961). Despite this, the Noble-Collip Drum is still used in experiments on stress and shock. Typically, these experiments attempt to test the effect of various drugs on the ability of unanesthetized animals to withstand the trauma of the drum.

The most widely used means for bringing about stress, terror, anxiety, and shock is administering electric shocks. A number of researchers are fond of 26 experiments in which animals are trained to avoid electric shocks by performing some task, such as pressing a lever, and thousands of such experiments are performed yearly. After the animal has learned this "shock avoidance," frequently the experimental condition will be changed so that what previously permitted the animal to avoid shock now delivers shock. When such an experiment was performed on rhesus monkeys, it was found to produce "conflict" followed by gastroduodenal lesions. Countless experiments of this sort are repeatedly performed simply to bring about stressful conditions—without any attempt to treat these. When there is an attempt to treat the induced stress-related condition, the results are often useless or meaningless because of the disparity between natural and artificially induced conditions.

Electric shocks are also commonly used to induce aggression in animals, 27 mainly rats. When the restrained animals are given a sufficient number of shocks, they will bite, box, or strike each other. Then the effects of a number of drugs on shock-induced aggression are assessed. In one case, which is typical of such research, the effect of mescaline on rats in a shock-induced aggression situation was tested (Sbordone & Garcia, 1977). Although in some cases the drug appeared to increase aggression, it was also found that the same aggression was shown by some nontreated rats. Hence, attributing the increased aggression to the drug is of questionable validity. Pratt (1976) describes the work of a prominent researcher in aggression studies, Dr. Roger Ulrich:

> Ulrich's work since 1962 . . . has consisted largely in causing pain to rats and observing the resulting aggressive behavior. This investigator would give painful foot-shocks to the rats through an electrified grid floor . . . (p. 61). Ulrich then introduced other distressing stimuli. . . . Bursts of intense noise (135 db, sustained for more than 1 min.) were introduced. The effects of castration were tried; . . . and, finally one pair had their whiskers cut off and were blinded by removal of their eyes (pp. 61–62)).

All of this aggression research has done little to control human aggression, which is rather different from the shock-induced aggression in rats. Ulrich himself has very recently come to question the usefulness of his past research. In a letter appearing in the *Monitor* he confesses (Ulrich, 1978):

> Initially my research was prompted by the desire to understand and help solve the problem of human aggression but I later discovered that the results of my work did not seem to justify its continuance. Instead I began to wonder if perhaps financial rewards, professional prestige, the opportunity to travel, etc. were the maintaining factors.

Another condition that electric shocks are employed to induce is epilepsy. Monkeys are given electric shocks that produce convulsions similar to those caused by epilepsy and eventually drive them insane. The insane monkey is then given a variety of drugs with the hope of curing or controlling epilepsy. However, while the monkeys display behavior that appears similar to epilepsy in man, their shock-induced fits have little bearing on human epilepsy, which has rather different origins. Hence, inferences from such experiments to treating human epilepsy are of very questionable validity. Unsurprisingly, the animal-tested drugs have failed to cure or control epilepsy.

The development of drugs to prevent brain hemorrhages proceeds in a   28
similar manner. To evaluate the efficacy of drugs on animals, it is first required to create blood clots in the brains of test animals. To this end, their skulls are cracked by hammer blows, causing the brain to form blood clots. Drugs are then given to the animals to determine which seem to improve their wretched state. But blood clots from hammer blows are rather different from those arising in humans, which are a gradual result of circulation problems or from long-term unhealthy eating and living habits.

In the interest of studying the effects of certain drugs on overeating (hy-   29
perphagia) researchers tested the drugs on rats that had overeaten (Wallach et al., 1977). However, in order to induce overeating in these rats they were forced to eat by painfully pinching their tails. The procedure was described as follows: "Tail pinch was applied for 10 minutes. Pressure was gradually increased until the animal either ate or became frantic." However, humans do not overeat because they are under pain of torture to do so. As such, the effects of drugs on the overeating of animals forced to overeat are irrelevant for assessing their effect on humans who overeat.

Underlying all these cases of induction of diseases is the assumption that   30
by artificially creating a condition in animals that appears to resemble a pathological state in man, one can make inferences about the latter on the basis of treating the former. This assumption is often false because of the disparity between experimentally induced conditions in animals and the corresponding conditions in humans. Indeed, there is also likely to be a disparity between artifically produced disease in animals and its natural occurrence (if it exists) in that animal. An example of this is seen in the case of inducing a deficiency of vitamin E in mice. Because this deficiency brought about a syndrome similar to muscular dystrophy, it was theorized that vitamin E would be effective in treating muscular dystrophy in man. In 1961, researchers showed (Loosli, 1967) that hereditary muscular dystrophy in mice and the dystrophy brought about by a vitamin E deficiency in mice were fundamentally different. Hence, the inference that vitamin E is useful in treating muscular dystrophy (as opposed to vitamin E deficiency) is invalid not only for humans, but for mice as well. The researchers concluded that it is never certain that experimentally induced disease sufficiently copies an inborn error.

In addition to producing misleading inferences, the techniques of animal   31
research are seen to be detrimental in that they take attention away from more fruitful methods, such as clinical observation of humans. In a 1978 address, Dr. Alice Heim, chairperson of the psychological section of the British Association for the Advancement of Science, remarked (*The Times,* September, 1978):

Surely it is more valuable to work with disturbed human beings who seek help than to render cats and other animals 'experimentally neurotic'; then try to 'cure' them; and then try to draw an analogy between these animals and the immensely more complex *homo sapiens.*

Differences Between and Within Species

In addition to using animals as "models" for disease, animals are widely   32 used to test the efficiency and safety of drugs and environmental substances by toxicologists and pharmacologists. The problem of differences between species is perhaps greatest in toxicological research. This problem often prevents the valid extrapolation of the results of animal tests to humans.

In experiments carried out to determine how poisonous various chemicals   33 are, the classic measure of toxicity used is called the *median lethal dose,* abbreviated as LD_{50}. It is defined as the dose of a substance needed to kill 50% of a given species of animals. Each year, millions of animals, usually mice, are force-fed drugs, insecticides, floor polishes, food additives, lipsticks, and other chemical substances, and the dosage required to kill about half of them (within 14 days) is calculated. But the significance of the LD_{50} measure is far from clear.

The purpose of the LD_{50} test is to determine the degree to which sub-   34 stances are poisonous to humans. However, for a number of reasons it fails to provide such a determination. For one thing, many of the test substances are relatively innocuous and hence enormous quantities must be forced down the animals' throats to cause them to die. In such cases, the death is often caused simply by the damage done by the massive quantities and not the test substance itself. The calculated LD_{50}s for these substances have no bearing on the manner in which the substance is to be used by humans.

Having found the LD_{50}, experiments with increasingly lower dosages are   35 made to ascertain the supposedly safe dosage of the drug (the LD_0). The next step is to extrapolate this safe dosage to humans. This extrapolation is made simply by multiplying the weight of the animal proportionately to the weight of humans. However, this safe level applies only to the test animal and it may differ radically for humans. This is particularly true when, as is often the case, the animal's death is attributable to the sheer volume of the substance. Extrapolating in this manner is also based on the assumption that the drug acts in a linear fashion—that twice the dosage means twice the effect. In fact, there is typically a threshold below which substances may have no real effect.

It might be thought that despite the differences between test animals and   36 humans, that the LD_{50} may still provide a rank order of the degree of toxicity of substances. Such is not the case. One problem is that a substance with a low LD_{50} may be extremely poisonous over a long period of time, such as lead and asbestos. Hence, the LD_{50} is not useful for ascertaining the result of chronic exposure. In addition, it has been found that in different laboratories not only do the LD_{50} values differ, but the orderings differ as well. This arises from interspecies differences and a number of environmental factors that I shall take up later.

Scientists themselves have come to see the LD_{50} tests as clumsy and crude   37
and lacking in reliability. In one study on four widely used household chemicals, it was found that the LD_{50}s in six laboratories differed both absolutely and relatively. It was concluded that "neither a particular method nor a single value may be regarded as a correct one" (Loosli, 1967, p. 120). Still, in the US, as in most countries, health agencies require that the LD_{50} be calculated for each of the thousands of new substances introduced each year.

Another test promoted by the FDA involves the use of rabbits' eyes to   38
determine how dangerous various substances are to human eyes. In addition to cosmetics, detergents and pesticides are also tested in this way. In 1973, Revlon alone used 1500 rabbits for eye and skin irritancy tests. As is usual for toxicity tests, no anesthesia is used since it is claimed to interfere with the results of the tests. The rabbits are immobilized in restraining devices for weeks, their eyes (which lack tear glands) being held open with clamps. In assessing the severity of eye irritants, the measure is not numerical, as with the LD_{50}. Rather, the eyes of the restrained rabbits are observed after several hours of having the irritant applied, and are described in terms of such categories as ulcerated cornea, inflamed iris, and gross destruction. Such crude determinations yield results that are unreliable and unmeaningful. In 1971, 25 of the best known laboratories jointly conducted a comprehensive evaluation of irritancy tests on rabbits. It was noted that "extreme variation" existed in the way the laboratories assessed the effects of irritants on rabbits.

The study (Weil & Scala, 1971) concluded that: 39

> The rabbit eye and skin procedure currently recommended by the Federal agencies . . . should not be recommended as standard procedures in any new regulations. Without careful reeducation these tests result in unreliable results.

As this was reported by the very laboratories that carry out such tests, it may be regarded as an understatement. Despite the acknowledged crudity and unreliability of these toxicity tests and measures, they are still routinely carried out, primarily as a means by which manufacturers can protect themselves and obtain the right to market new substances.

Underlying the use of animal models for pharmacological tests is the pre-   40
sumption that it will be possible to extrapolate to humans. However, the vast differences that exist between species make the results from one species an unreliable indicator for another. There are a number of ways that substances can produce different effects in different animals. Chemicals act upon living things in five main stages: absorption, distribution, excretion, metabolism, and mechanism of action, and interspecies differences may arise during any of these. Even if the difference is quite small at each stage, they may accumulate to yield a large total interspecies discrepancy. These interspecies differ-

ences make inferences from animal experiments very much dependent upon which animal is used as the research model.

Richard Ryder (1975, p. 150) illustrates the gross differences between species in the effectiveness of drugs by citing the following results. The effect of a 'Product X' was found to vary as follows: 41

Species	Body weight, mg/kg
Man	1
Sheep	10
Rabbit	200
Monkey	15.2

From these results it is clear that testing the substance on rabbits will be a poor indicator of its effectiveness in humans. Still, rabbits are a popular animal for this sort of testing.

Interspecies differences may lead to concluding that substances that are innocuous or beneficial in humans are harmful, and that substances that have insidious effects on humans are harmless. For example, penicillin is extremely poisonous to guinea pigs. Had penicillin been subjected to the routine animal tests, as new drugs presently are, it would never have been tried on humans. On the other hand, what is a deadly poison to humans, strychnine, may be safely consumed by guinea pigs. Similarly, a dose of belladonna that is fatal to humans is harmless for a rabbit, the often used laboratory animal. Morphine, while sedating most species, incites frantic excitement in cats, dogs, and mice. Arsenic, deadly for humans, can be safely consumed in enormous quantities by sheep. Still, foxes and chickens die from almonds, and parrots are poisoned by parsley. Tuberculin, which, because it cured TB in guinea pigs, was thought to also be a cure in humans, turned out to cause TB in humans. Digitalis, which because it was seen to produce severely high blood pressure in dogs was thought to be dangerous for humans, turned out to be a major treatment for humans with heart disease.   42

In certain species, aspirin is highly toxic and it has been seen to produce malformations in the fetuses of rats (*Newsweek,* Nov. 20, 1972). Other substances that are not teratogenic for humans, but are known to cause malformations in the offspring of laboratory animals, are adrenaline, insulin, and certain antibiotics. The converse is the case with drugs such as thalidomide, which was tested extensively in animals (e.g., the popular laboratory Wistar rat) without any adverse effects to the fetus, but which turned out to produce monstrous human babies. The thalidomide tragedy drove people to conclude that more animal testing was needed to protect the safety of humans, when, ironically, the tragedy was a product of animal testing. More specifically, it resulted from the invalidating factor of interspecies differences. After thalidomide was found to produce deformed humans, researchers tried re-   43 peatedly to produce similar effects on animals. One hundred fifty different strains and substrains of rabbits were tested, but with no malformations. Finally, it was found that such malformations could be produced in New Zealand white rabbits. One might ask what the point was in carrying out these experiments after thalidomide was already seen to produce malformed human fetuses. The teratogenic effects of a number of other drugs have also been shown not only to vary with species, but also with different strains of the same species.

It is interesting to note that the German drug company that marketed   44
thalidomide, was, after being tried for two and a half years, acquitted on charges of having marketed a dangerous drug. The acquittal was based on the testimonies of numerous medical authorities who claimed that animal tests are never conclusive for making inferences about humans. Despite the failure of animal tests to reveal the danger of thalidomide, Turkish professor S.T. Aygun was able to discover its teratogenic properties through the use of chick embryos, and prevented its being marketed in Turkey. Thalidomide's dangers have also been revealed by testing it on sea-urchin eggs (Krieg, 1964). Much more on alternatives to animal testing may be found in Ruesch, 1978. Unfortunately, even those medical authorities who have come to see animal testing as scientifically unsound are reluctant to voice their views. The following remarks made by two doctors in 1976 express this point (Stiller & Stiller, 1976):

> In praxis all animal experiments are scientifically indefensible, as they lack any scientific validity and reliability in regard to humans. They only serve as an alibi for the drug manufacturers, who hope to protect themselves thereby. . . . But who dares to express doubts of our much-vaunted technological medicine, or even just to ask questions, without meeting the solid opposition from the vested interests of science, business, and also of politics and news media?

Confusion of Background Variables

Invalid inferences arise when what is attributed to the experimental treat-   45
ment actually arises from the influences of nontreatment variables. Animals even of the same species react differently under the same treatment as a result of nontreatment variables, both of the genetic and environmental kind. Different responses result from differences in the health of the animal, its age, sex, litter, and strain, its living conditions, stressful or painful stimuli, and even odors and the time of day. These variables arise before, during, and after the experimental treatment. I will now consider some ways in which these nontreatment variables may be confused with treatment variables and hence give rise to faulty inferences.

Animals that ultimately become subjects for research may start out with   46
very different characteristics. An experimental response may be the effect not of the experimental treatment in question, but of some former condition of the animal quite unrelated to the treatment. Hence, the background of

experimental animals is of major relevance to the reliability of conclusions based upon them—a fact that is often ignored. How are research animals obtained, and how does their background influence the reliability of experiments made upon them?

Animals that find themselves in research laboratories may be of the "specially bred" variety, or they may have arisen from a "random source," that is, from dealers or pounds. In the case of dogs and cats, the great majority come from random sources and are typically stray, unwanted, or stolen pets. For example, of the over 300,000 dogs used in biomedical research in the US in 1969, only about 40,000 were bred specially for the laboratory. By the time a random-source animal reaches the laboratory, an average of one month has been spent either in pounds, with dealers, in transport, or in the wild. Within this period the animal is subjected to poor diet and shelter, and a variety of stressful, unhygienic conditions. In an article in *Life* (February 4, 1966), the outrageous conditions maintained by dog dealers were exposed. The article reports: 47

> Unscrupulous dog 'dealers' taking advantage of the growing demand for dogs for vital medical research, are running a lucrative and unsavory business. Laboratories now need almost two million dogs a year . . . Some dealers keep big inventories of dogs in unspeakably filthy compounds that seem scarcely less appalling than the concentration camps of World War II. Many do not sell directly to labs but simply dispose of their packs at auction where the going rate is 30¢ a pound. Puppies, often drenched in their own vomit, sell for 10¢ apiece.

Unsurprisingly, as one researcher testified, 40% of the dogs obtained this way die before they can even be used for research.

Hence, when such animals get sick or die upon receiving some treatment there is little reason to suppose the treatment was to blame. One researcher, testifying at a congressional hearing following the exposition in *Life*, told of the following case. A drug had been condemned on the basis of an experiment in which all the dogs receiving it died, but it turned out to be distemper and not the drug that was responsible for the deaths (U.S. House, 1966). Nor have conditions improved much since the passage of the Laboratory Animals Welfare Act of 1966, which requires licensing and inspections. The rate of animal deaths prior to experimentation is still high. A more detailed discussion of the human animal laws may be found in Pratt, 1976 and Ruesch, 1978.   48

Animals that arrive at the laboratory with infections often render results equivocal. Experiments that are particularly vulnerable to the existence of intercurrent infections are immunology, radiation, and carcinogenesis studies. Carcinogenesis, for example, is affected by the efficiency of immunological responses and rate of cell turnover, and both of these are affected by indigenous pathogens.   49

To avoid the problem that the variability of the health of research animals presents, means by which animals are bred uniformly free of disease have   50 been developed. Strains of bacteriologically sterile animals, most often rodents, are bred especially for use in the laboratory. These germ-free animals are born by cesarean section, raised in sterile surroundings, and fed sterile foods. The germ-free condition of specially bred animals is advertised as a major selling point in advertisements by suppliers of research animals. One recent ad (*Laboratory Animal Science*, February, 1977) boasts *"New* Cesarean derived, Barrier reared CAMM RATS-Certified Pathogen Free."

However, the resulting "uniform biological material" as these animals are   51
often called, differs radically form normal animals. Animals raised in totally sterile conditions fail to develop immunologies that provide a natural defense mechanism against disease. Hence, they are likely to be far more susceptible to disease than their naturally bred counterparts.

By using specially bred animals that are biologically uniform there is less   52
variability in response, and as such, the results are claimed to be more reliable. It is true that there will be more reliability in the sense of more agreement among successive experiments with uniform as opposed to non-uniform animals. However, there will not be more reliability in the sense of accurately representing natural, random-bred, heterogeneous animal and human populations. For this, uniformly bred animals provide extremely unreliable models. It is true that uniform research animals yield less variability in response, and hence an effect may be detected with fewer animals. However, the effect detected is not a reliable indicator of the effect that would arise in animals found in nature, much less in humans.

The demand for uniformity in research animals, is, according to a prominent researcher, M.W. Fox, often a "pseudo-sophistication." According to Fox,   53
"Few investigators inquire or are aware of how the prior life history and environmental experiences of the animal may influence his experiment" (Fox, 1974, pp. 96–97). However, a knowledge of how the background of the animal influences the experimental results is necessary to ensure the validity of the experiment. Even when not bred to be germ-free, the laboratory animal may fail to develop the resistance to various stresses that it would in its natural habitat where it would normally be faced with a number of stresses. An example of such a natural stress is brought about when baby animals are left alone while their mothers go in search of food. Hence, the laboratory animal is apt to be less hearty than its natural counterpart.

For the most part, research animals are chosen not on the basis of how   54
appropriate they are for a given experiment—even when such information is available. Rather, they are selected for processing such characteristics as taking up little space, being inexpensive, being nocturnal, being docile and adaptable to laboratory environments. An advertisement for Marshall beagles (*Laboratory Animal Science*, February, 1977) boasts of having designed their research animal as one might design a car model. The ad reads:

TRY OUT 1977 MODELS. Large selection of COMPACTS, MID SIZE & FULL SIZE MODELS. The Marshall Beagle is built with you in mind. All models feature sturdy unitized body construction and Easy Handling.

As a result, inappropriate animals are often used for detecting the effect of an experimental treatment. One way in which an animal may be inappropriate is if it tends to spontaneously generate the effect in question even when the experimental treatment is absent (i.e., in control animals).

Rats and mice, for example, tend spontaneously to develop a high inci-   55
dence of tumors. This renders them unsuitable for detecting tumors. Still, no animals are used as often as rats and mice for assessing the effect of numerous experimental treatments upon the production of tumors. The reason is that they are inexpensive and take up little room. Examples of recent experimental treatments tested this way are saccharin and oral contraceptives. The *British Medical Journal* (October 28, 1972, p. 190) made the following remark concerning the report of the Council on Safety of Medicines on tests of oral contraceptives:

> The tables in the report show incidences of 25% of lung tumours and 17% of liver tumours in *control mice* and 26% adrenal tumours, 30% pituitary tumours, and 99% mammary tumours in *control rats*. It is difficult to see how experiments on strains of animals so exceedingly liable to develop tumours of these various kinds can throw useful light on the carcinogenicity of any compound for man.

In this experiment, rats exposed to high dosages (up to 400 times the   56
human use) of contraceptives were found to have more tumors than those not exposed. But this does not mean that the additional tumors were caused by the contraceptives, particularly given the high rate of tumors in untreated controls. The question of how many more tumors must be observed to conclude that treated rats differ significantly from untreated rats poses an important statistical problem. Given the high rate of tumors in controls, a rather high rate of tumors in a large sample of treated rats should be required. The report, however, does not indicate how many more tumors were observed. The Commitee's report itself (Committee on Safety of Medicines, 1972) concludes that:

> . . . although a carcinogenic effect can be produced when some of the preparations are used in high doses throughout the life-span in certain strains of rat and mouse, this evidence cannot be interpreted as constituting a carcinogenic hazard to women when these preparations are used as oral contraceptives.

The report also notes that many animals died from the high dosage of the compound given.

The conclusion of this committee contrasts with the conclusions of the   57
FDA with respect to the banning of DDT and the recently proposed banning of saccharin. In both cases the evidence consists of an increase of tumors observed in rats given extremely high doses of the substance in question.

Without additional evidence, conclusions about the danger of these substances are ill-grounded, both because of the high doses and the high spontaneous rate of tumors in rats.

Even if the experimental effect observed does not result from a condition 58 already present in the animal before entering the lab, it may arise from non-treatment factors introduced after entering the lab. Claude Bernard, the founder of modern animal experimentation, himself admitted that "The experimental animal is never in a normal state. The normal state is merely a supposition, an assumption." The animal is placed in an abnormal state because of the host of stressors it is confronted with.

Animals in the lab are deprived of their natural habitat, and often are 59 terrorized by what they see even before they themselves are experimented upon. It is not uncommon for animals, particularly dogs, to be subject to devocalization prior to experimentation (sometimes referred to as "the anesthesia of the public."), which is itself a trauma. Also common is for an animal to be used for additional research after it has already undergone one or more experiments. (This practice, illegal in Britain, is legal in the US.)

When an animal is in fear or pain, all its organs and biochemical systems 60 are affected. Measurement parameters such as blood pressure, temperature, metabolic rate, and enzyme reactions have been found to vary up to three times their normal value as a result of pain and stress (Hillman, 1970). Hence the value of any of these parameters measured following an experimental treatment may result not from the treatment, but from unrelated pain and stress to which the experimental animal has been subjected. As such, any experiment attempting to detect variations smaller than those already known to be attributable to experimental stress is invalidated. As one physiologist studying the effects of fear and pain notes, "It [experimental stress] is almost certainly the main reason for the wide variation reported among animals upon whom painful experiments have been done" (Hillman, 1970).

Animals may be stressed simply by being handled by the experimenter, or 61 by the order in which they are taken to the experimental room from the cage. When animals are taken one by one from a cage or pen, the last animals taken differ markedly from the first few taken because of the stress brought about from the changing composition of the cage or pen. As one researcher (Magalhaes, 1974, p. 103) states:

> Even apparently minor procedures such as successively removing rats from their colony cage for decapitation and subsequent biochemical analysis can have a marked influence on the results. One experimenter found that the corticosteroid measures obtained from the first few rats taken out of their cage were very much lower compared to those from the last few to be taken.

To avoid this problem, animals are sometimes experimented upon in their usual animal facility instead of removing them to the laboratory. But this gives rise to a number of other variables that tend to bias the experimental result, as the following notes (Magalhaes, 1974), p. 104):

> . . . the distress vocalizations, struggling and release of alarm odors during restraint (while taking blood samples, for example) may affect other animals that are to be sampled later, and from such animals 'later down the line' the samples might be qualitatively very different.

Experimental effects are also influenced by the manner in which the experimental treatment is administered. For example, different results are likely to be obtained if a substance is forced-fed to an animal by a stomach tube as opposed to having it be eaten naturally. As we have already noted, the response may arise not from the substance administered, but from the large quantity the animal is forced to consume. As the toxicologist Dr. Leo Friedman points out: "We know that administration of *enough* of any substance in high enough dosage will produce some adverse effect" (Friedman, 1970). For example, massive amounts of common table salt cause birth defects in pregnant rats. However, there is no evidence that low doses of salt cause birth defects in humans.   62

There are a number of less obvious background variables that can arise to confuse the effect of the experimental treatment, and hence lead to invalid inferences. Such variables include the time of day, the temperature of the room, and even the color of the clothing worn by the experimenter. Drug toxicity, for example, has been found to vary with the time of day at which animals are given the drug. Other time-dependent reactions are susceptibility to seizures and irradiation. Animals apparently have certain 24-hour rhythms, including periods of maximum activity and periods of minimum activity (Ader, 1974). Animals react differently to test treatments according to whether they occur during their period of maximum or minimum activity.   63

For example, it is known that restraining rats causes them to suffer gastric lesions. However, when restraint occurs during the rats' periods of maximum activity, the rats are significantly more susceptible to the development of gastric lesions than those restrained during periods of minimum activity (Ader, 1974, p. 111). Presumably, being restrained during a period of maximum activity is perceived by the rat as being more stressful than being restrained during a period of minimum activity. It would seem likely, then, that rats restrained (as they are) for the introduction of some experimental treatment may show disturbances that are largely the result not of the treatment, but of the time of day. The influence of time also serves to explain some of the variation found between labs. After observing the significant effects of time, one researcher (Ader, 1974, p. 120, emphasis added) was led to conclude: 64

> . . . it does not seem facetious to ask how many discrepancies in the literature are attributable not to who is right and who is wrong, but to *when* the behavior was sampled.

Conclusion

The considerations I have discussed provide a strong argument against a   65
scientific justification of a great deal of animal experimentation; for they have
identified numerous sources that often prevent such experiments from being
scientifically relevant or valid. Often, an animal experiment is rendered irrelevant because the question it seeks to answer is trivial or obvious, or has
already been answered countless times. Invalid experiments frequently arise
from the disparity between artificially induced conditions in the laboratory
and natural ones, from differences within and among species, and from a
number of background variables whose effects are confused with experimental variables.

A few of these problems can be avoided to some extent, for example, by   66
being careful to control a large number of background variables. For the most
part, however, these problems exist as limitations in principle to the beneficial use of animals in research. For instance, animals will never be able to
produce tumors, ulcers, or a number of other pathological conditions in a
manner that is similar to humans. The complex psychological problems humans face are not the sort of things that can be induced in laboratory animals. The differences in drug toxicity in animals cannot be overcome,
and accounting for the vast number of background variables is practically
impossible.

Admittedly, it is possible to claim that animal experimentation is justifiable   67
despite the fact that it is of no practical value. Ruesch (1978, p. 144) cites
one such attempt made by Professor Leon Asher. According to Asher:

> . . . one might ask oneself whether it isn't a sacred case of conscience to follow
> the call toward the solution of the mysteries of life, and whether man shouldn't
> consider it a *religious duty* to satisfy the desire for exploration that Provi-
> dence has placed in our hearts, without asking whether our research on life has
> any value for medical science or any other practical value.

However, not all actions that satisfy a "desire for exploration" may be considered permissible (much less a religious duty). Experimenting on humans
may also satisfy such a desire, and one is likely to learn much more from
humans than from animals. Surely, pointless inquisitiveness does not justify
the infliction of pain and suffering, and both humans and animals have the
capacity to suffer.

Increasing emphasis on research has also done harm to patient care. As   68
Ryder notes (1975, p. 75):

> A doctor's merit is no longer rated on how many patients he cures but on how
> many papers he publishes in learned journals. This has encouraged a great deal
> of trivial research and often there has been a decline in the standards of clini-
> cal care.

The employment of human data (which is available in great abundance) is one way to replace a good deal of medical, psychological, and toxicological research on animals with a more scientifically sound alternative.

Other promising alternatives to animal experiments are the use of tissue cultures and mathematical models. Tissue culture involves cultivating living cells outside the organism, and has the advantage of permitting the growth of human as opposed to animal cells. Mathematical models, derived from theory or from past experiments, may be used to predict responses or effects from a variety of experimental conditions that are formulated mathematically. The strongest argument in favor of developing these alternatives is that much of animal experimentation is scientifically, and hence morally, indefensible.

69

References

Ader, R. (1974). Environmental variables in animal experimentation: the relevance of 24-hour rhythms in the study of animal behavior. In H. Magalhaes (Ed.), *Environmental variables in animal experimentation.* Lewisburg, Pennsylvania: Bucknell University Press.

Anderson, K.V., Pear, G.S., & Honeycut, C. (1976). Behavioral evidence showing the predominance of diffuse pain stimuli over discrete stimuli in influencing perception. *Journal of Neuroscience Research, 2,* 283–289.

Barrett, J.E., & Witkin, J.M. (1976). Interaction of D-Amphetamine with Pentobarbital and Chlordiazeopoxide: effects on punished and unpunished behavior of pigeons. *Pharmacology, Biochemistry, and Behavior, 5,* 285–292.

Berkson, G. & Becker, J.D. (1975). Facial expressions and social responsiveness of blind monkeys. *Journal of Abnormal Psychology, 84,* 519–523.

Bradley, E.W., Zook, B.C., Casarett, G.W., Bondelid, R.O., Maier, J.G., & Rogers, C.C. (1977). Effects of fast neutrons on rabbits. *International Journal of Radiation, Oncology, Biology and Physics, 2,* 1133–1139.

Committee on Safety of Medicines. (1972). *Carcinogenicity tests of oral contraceptives.* London: H.M.S.O.

Diner, J. (1979). *Physical and mental suffering of experimental animals: a review of scientific literature 1975–1978.* Washington: Animal Welfare Institute.

Fox, M.W. (1974). Space and social distance in the ecology of laboratory animals. In H. Magalhaes (Ed.), *Environmental variables in animal experimentation* (pp. 96–105). Lewisburg, Pennsylvania: Bucknell University Press.

Friedman, L. (1970). Symposium on the evaluation of the safety of food additives and chemical residues: II the role of the laboratory animal study of intermediate duration for evaluation of safety. *Toxicology and Applied Pharmacology, 16,* 498–506.

Hillman, H. (1970). *Scientific undesirability of painful experiments.* Zurich: WFPA.

Krieg, M.B. (1964). *Green medicine.* Chicago: Rand McNally.

Lane-Petter, E. (1963). Humane vivisection. *Laboratory Animal Care, 13,* 469–473.

Loosli, R. (1967). Duplicate testing and reproducibility. In R.H. Regamey et. al. (Eds.), *International symposium on laboratory animals* (pp. 117–123). Basel: Karger.

Lowrance, M. (1976). *Of acceptable risk.* Los Altos, California: Kaufmann.

Magalhaes, H. (Ed.). (1974). *Environmental variables in animal experimentation.* Lewisburg, Pennsylvania: Bucknell University Press.

Markowitz, J., Archibald, J., & Downie, H.G. (1959). *Experimental surgery* (4th ed.). Baltimore: Williams & Wilkins.

Mayo, D. (1981). Testing statistical testing. In J.C. Pitt (Ed.), *Philosophy in economics* (pp. 175–203). Dordrecht: Reidel.

Mufson, E.J., Balagura, S., & Riss, W. (1976). Tail pinch-induced arousal and stimulus-bound behavior in rats with lateral hypothalamic lesions. *Brain, Behavior and Evolution, 13,* 154–164.

Ogilvie, W.H. (1935, February 23). [Letter to the Editor]. *Lancet,* p. 419.

Pratt, D. (1976). *Painful experiments on animals.* New York: Argus.

Ragemey, R.H., Hennessen, W., Ikic, D., & Ungar, J. (Eds.). (1967). *International symposium on laboratory animals.* Basel: Karger.

Ruesch, H. (1978). *Slaughter of the innocent.* New York: Bantam.

Ryder, R. (1975). *Victims of science.* London: Davis-Poynter.

Sbordone, R.J., & Garcia, J. (1977). Untreated rats develop 'pathological' aggression when paired with a mescaline-treated rat in shock-elicited aggression situation. *Behavioral Biology, 21,* 451–461.

Selye, H. (1956). *The stress of life.* New York: McGraw.

Stiller, H., & Stiller, M. (1976). *Tierversuch und Tierexperimentator.* Munich: Hirthammer.

Stoner, H.B. (1961). Critical analysis of traumatic shock models. *Federation Procedings, 20,* Supplement 9, pp. 38–48.

Swenson, R.M., & Randall, W. (1977). Grooming behavior in cats with pontile lesions and cats with tectal lesions. *Journal of Comparative and Physiological Psychology, 91,* 313–326.

Ulrich, R.E. (1978, March). [Letter to the Editor]. *American Psychological Association Monitor,* p. 16.

Wallach, M.B., Dawber, M., McMahon, M., & Rogers, C. (1977). A new anorexigen assay: stress-induced hyperphagia in rats. *Pharmacology, Biochemistry and Behavior, 6,* 529–531.

Weil, M., & Scala, R. (1971). Study of intra-and inter-laboratory variability in the results of rabbit eye and skin irritations tests. *Toxicology and Applied Pharmacology, 19,* 276–360.

QUESTIONS FOR MEANING

1. Is Deborah Mayo entirely opposed to animal experimentation? Would she ban all tests on animals?
2. What is Mayo's principal objection to the peritonitis experiment described in paragraph 23?
3. What's wrong with the eye tests described in paragraph 38?
4. Explain what LD_{50} means.

5. Does Mayo offer any explanation why scientists may be tempted to do trivial and even useless research?
6. Why is it important to know the background of any animal being experimented upon? What's wrong with using animals that have been specially bred for use in laboratories? What other variables can affect the results of an experiment?
7. What alternatives are there to animal experimentation? Does Mayo offer any specific evidence to suggest that such alternatives are feasible?
8. Vocabulary: purported (2), disparity (17), confounding (17), ascertaining (18), pathological (18), extrapolating (19), precipitate (20), kinetics (20), induce (22), toxicological (32), innocuous (34), linear (35), insidious (42), teratogenic (43), carcinogenesis (49), and indigenous (49).

QUESTIONS ABOUT STRATEGY

1. Mayo argues that animal experimentation is bad science. Does she convince you that this is so? How "scientific" is her own argument? Does she sound as if she knows what she's talking about?
2. Does this essay ever seem emotional? In presenting detailed descriptions of experiments in which the suffering of animals is vividly portrayed, does Mayo ever advance her argument by playing upon the feelings of her audience?
3. Does Mayo ever repeat herself? Is so, where? Is repetition justifiable in an essay of this length?
4. Why does Mayo break her essay into individually titled subsections?
5. Where in her essay does Mayo recognize the premise that supports arguments on behalf of animal experimentation? Are there any other points in the essay where Mayo represents her opponents' point of view?

PETER SINGER
All Animals Are Equal¹

Born in Melbourne, Peter Singer taught philosophy at University College, Ox-
ford, and at New York University before returning to Australia, where he is
now Professor of Philosophy and Director of the Centre of Human Bioethics at
Monash University. His books include Democracy and Disobedience *(1974),* Practical Ethics *(1979),* Marx *(1980),* The Expanding Circle *(1981), and* The Reproduction Revolution: New Ways of Making Babies *(1982). He is best known for his*
work on behalf of animal rights. If the rise of the animal liberation movement
*can be traced to any single work it would be Singer's **1973** essay "All Animals*
Are Equal." Singer subsequently expanded his essay into a book, Animal Liberation: A New Ethic for Our Treatment of Animals *(1975), and coedited an anthol-*
ogy of essays on this subject, Animal Rights and Human Obligations *(1975). As you*
read the original essay and consider its careful reasoning, you should be able
to recognize that Singer's argument deserves to be taken seriously.

In recent years a number of oppressed groups have campaigned vigorously   1
for equality. The classic instance is the Black Liberation movement, which
demands an end to the prejudice and discrimination that has made blacks
second-class citizens. The immediate appeal of the black liberation movement and its initial, if limited success made it a model for other oppressed
groups to follow. We became familiar with liberation movements for Spanish-
Americans, gay people, and a variety of other minorities. When a majority
group—women—began their campaign, some thought we had come to the
end of the road. Discrimination on the basis of sex, it has been said, is the
last universally accepted form of discrimination, practiced without secrecy or
pretense even in those liberal circles that have long prided themselves on
their freedom from prejudice against racial minorities.

One should always be wary of talking of "the last remaining form of dis-   2
crimination." If we have learnt anything from the liberation movements, we
should have learnt how difficult it is to be aware of latent prejudice in our
attitudes to particular groups until this prejudice is forcefully pointed out.

A liberation movement demands an expansion of our moral horizons and   3
an extension or reinterpretation of the basic moral principle of equality. Practices that were previously regarded as natural and inevitable come to be seen
as the result of an unjustifiable prejudice. Who can say with confidence that
all his or her attitudes and practices are beyond criticism? If we wish to avoid
being numbered amongst the oppressors, we must be prepared to re-think
even our most fundamental attitudes. We need to consider them from the
point of view of those most disadvantaged by our attitudes, and the practices
that follow from these attitudes. If we can make this unaccustomed mental
switch we may discover a pattern in our attitudes and practices that consistently operates so as to benefit one group—usually the one to which we

ourselves belong——at the expense of another. In this way we may come to see that there is a case for a new liberation movement. My aim is to advocate that we make this mental switch in respect of our attitudes and practices towards a very large group of beings: members of species other than our own—or, as we popularly though misleadingly call them, animals. In other words, I am urging that we extend to other species the basic principle of equality that most of us recognize should be extended to all members of our own species.

All this may sound a little far-fetched, more like a parody of other libera-   4
tion movements than a serious objective. In fact, in the past the idea of "The Rights of Animals" really has been used to parody the case for women's rights. When Mary Wollstonecroft, a forerunner of later feminists, published her *Vindication of the Rights of Women* in 1792, her ideas were widely re-garded as absurd, and they were satirized in an anonymous publication enti-tled *A Vindication of the Rights of Brutes.* The author of this satire (actually Thomas Taylor, a distinguished Cambridge philosopher) tried to refute Woll-stonecroft's reasonings by showing that they could be carried one stage fur-ther. If sound when applied to women, why should the arguments not be applied to dogs, cats and horses? They seemed to hold equally well for these "brutes"; yet to hold that brutes had rights was manifestly absurd; therefore the reasoning by which this conclusion had been reached must be unsound, and if unsound when applied to brutes, it must also be unsound when applied to women, since the very same arguments had been used in each case.

One way in which we might reply to this argument is by saying that the   5
case for equality between men and women cannot validly be extended to non-human animals. Women have a right to vote, for instance, because they are just as capable of making rational decisions as men are; dogs, on the other hand, are incapable of understanding the significance of voting, so they cannot have the right to vote. There are many other obvious ways in which men and women resemble each other closely, while humans and other ani-mals differ greatly. So, it might be said, men and women are similar beings, and should have equal rights, while humans and non-humans are different and should not have equal rights.

The thought behind this reply to Taylor's analogy is correct up to a point,   6
but it does not go far enough. There *are* important differences between hu-mans and other animals, and these differences must give rise to *some* differ-ences in the rights that each have. Recognizing this obvious fact, however, is no barrier to the case for extending the basic principle of equality to non-human animals. The differences that exist between men and women are equally undeniable, and the supporters of Women's Liberation are aware that these differences may give rise to different rights. Many feminists hold that women have the right to an abortion on request. It does not follow that since these same people are campaigning for equality between men and women they must support the right of men to have abortions too. Since a man cannot have an abortion, it is meaningless to talk of his right to have one. Since a pig can't vote, it is meaningless to talk of its right to vote. There is no reason

why either Women's Liberation or Animal Liberation should get involved in such nonsense. The extension of the basic principle of equality from one group to another does not imply that we must treat both groups in exactly the same way, or grant exactly the same rights to both groups. Whether we should do so will depend on the nature of the members of the two groups. The basic principle of equality, I shall argue, is equality of consideration; and equal consideration for different beings may lead to different treatment and different rights.

So there is a different way of replying to Taylor's attempt to parody Woll- 7
stonecroft's arguments, a way which does not deny the differences between humans and non-humans, but goes more deeply into the question of equality, and concludes by finding nothing absurd in the idea that the basic principle of equality applies to so-called "brutes". I believe that we reach this conclusion if we examine the basis on which our opposition to discrimination on grounds of race or sex ultimately rests. We will then see that we would be on shaky ground if we were to demand equality for blacks, women, and other groups of oppressed humans while denying equal consideration to non-humans.

When we say that all human beings, whatever their race, creed or sex, are 8
equal, what is it that we are asserting? Those who wish to defend a hierarchical, inegalitarian society have often pointed out that by whatever test we choose, it simply is not true that all humans are equal. Like it or not, we must face the fact that humans come in different shapes and sizes; they come with differing moral capacities, differing intellectual abilities, differing amounts of benevolent feeling and sensitivity to the needs of others, differing abilities to communicate effectively, and differing capacities to experience pleasure and pain. In short, if the demand for equality were based on the actual equality of all human beings, we would have to stop demanding equality. It would be an unjustifiable demand.

Still, one might cling to the view that the demand for equality among hu- 9
man beings is based on the actual equality of the different races and sexes. Although humans differ as individuals in various ways, there are no differences between the races and sexes *as such.* From the mere fact that a person is black, or a woman, we cannot infer anything else about that person. This, it may be said, is what is wrong with racism and sexism. The white racist claims that whites are superior to blacks, but this is false—although there are differences between individuals, some blacks are superior to some whites in all of the capacities and abilities that could conceivably be relevant. The opponent of sexism would say the same: a person's sex is no guide to his or her abilities, and this is why it is unjustifiable to discriminate on the basis of sex.

This is a possible line of objection to racial and sexual discrimination. It is 10
not, however, the way that someone really concerned about equality would choose, because taking this line could, in some circumstances, force one to accept a most inegalitarian society. The fact that humans differ as individuals, rather than as races or sexes, is a valid reply to someone who defends a

hierarchical society like, say, South Africa, in which all whites are superior in status to all blacks. The existence of individual variations that cut across the lines of race or sex, however, provides us with no defence at all against a more sophisticated opponent of equality, one who proposes that, say, the interests of those with I.Q. ratings above 100 be preferred to the interests of those I.Q.s below 100. Would a hierarchical society of this sort really be so much better than one based on race or sex? I think not. But if we tie the moral principle of equality to the factual equality of the different races or sexes, taken as a whole, our opposition to racism and sexism does not provide us with any basis for objecting to this kind of inegalitarianism.

There is a second important reason why we ought not to base our opposition to racism and sexism on any kind of factual equality, even the limited kind asserts that variations in capacities and abilities are spread evenly between the different races and sexes: we can have no absolute guarantee that these abilities and capacities really are distributed evenly, without regard to race or sex, among human beings. So far as actual abilities are concerned, there do seem to be certain measurable differences between both races and sexes. These differences do not, of course, appear in each case, but only when averages are taken. More important still, we do not yet know how much of these differences is really due to the different genetic endowments of the various races and sexes, and how much is due to environmental differences that are the result of past and continuing discrimination. Perhaps all of the important differences will eventually prove to be environmental rather than genetic. Anyone opposed to racism and sexism will certainly hope that this will be so, for it will make the task of ending discrimination a lot easier; nevertheless it would be dangerous to rest the case against racism and sexism on the belief that all significant differences are environmental in origin. The opponent of, say, racism who takes this line will be unable to avoid conceding that if differences in ability did after all prove to have some genetic connection with race, racism would in some way be defensible.   11

It would be folly for the opponent of racism to stake his whole case on a dogmatic commitment to one particular outcome of a difficult scientific issue which is still a long way from being settled. While attempts to prove that differences in certain selected abilities between races and sexes are primarily genetic in origin have certainly not been conclusive, the same must be said of attempts to prove that these differences are largely the result of environment. At this stage of the investigation we cannot be certain which view is correct, however much we may hope it is the latter.   12

Fortunately, there is no need to pin the case for equality to one particular outcome of this scientific investigation. The appropriate response to those who claim to have found evidence of genetically-based differences in ability between the races or sexes is not to stick to the belief that the genetic explanation must be wrong, whatever evidence to the contrary may turn up: instead we should make it quite clear that the claim to equality does not depend on intelligence, moral capacity, physical strength, or similar matters of fact. Equality is a moral ideal, not a simple assertion of fact. There is no   13 logically compelling reason for assuming that a factual difference in ability between two people justifies any difference in the amount of consideration we give to satisfying their needs and interests. The principle of the equality of human beings is not a description of an alleged actual equality among humans: it is a prescription of how we should treat humans.

Jeremy Bentham incorporated the essential basis of moral equality into   14 his utilitarian system of ethics in the formula: "Each to count for one and none for more than one." In other words, the interests of every being affected by an action are to be taken into account and given the same weight as the like interests of any other being. A later utilitarian, Henry Sidgwick, put the point in this way: "The good of any one individual is of no more importance, from the point of view (if I may say so) of the Universe, than the good of any other."[2] More recently, the leading figures in contemporary moral philosophy have shown a great deal of agreement in specifying as a fundamental presupposition of their moral theories some similar requirement which operates so as to give everyone's interests equal consideration—although they cannot agree on how this requirement is best formulated.[3]

It is an implication of this principle of equality that our concern for others   15 ought not to depend on what they are like, or what abilities they possess— although precisely what this concern requires us to do may vary according to the characteristics of those affected by what we do. It is on this basis that the case against racism and the case against sexism must both ultimately rest; and it is in accordance with this principle that speciesism is also to be condemned. If possessing a higher degree of intelligence does not entitle one human to use another for his own ends, how can it entitle humans to exploit non-humans?

Many philosophers have proposed the principle of equal consideration of   16 interests, in some form or other, as a basic moral principle; but, as we shall see in more detail shortly, not many of them have recognised that this principle applies to members of other species as well as to our own. Bentham was one of the few who did realize this. In a forward-looking passage, written at a time when black slaves in the British dominions were still being treated much as we now treat non-human animals, Bentham wrote:

The day *may* come when the rest of the animal creation may acquire those rights which never could have been witholden from them but by the hand of tyranny. The French have already discovered that the blackness of the skin is no reason why a human being should be abandoned without redress to the caprice of a tormentor. It may one day come to be recognised that the number of the legs, the villosity of the skin, or the termination of the *os sacrum*, are reasons equally insufficient for abandoning a sensitive being to the same fate. What else is it that should trace the insuperable line? Is it the faculty of reason, or perhaps the faculty of discourse? But a full-grown horse or dog is beyond comparison a more rational, as well as a more conversable animal, than an infant of a day, or a week, or even a month, old. But suppose they were otherwise, what would it avail? The question is not, Can they reason? nor Can they *talk?* but, *Can they suffer?*[4]

In this passage Bentham points to the capacity for suffering as the vital   17
characteristic that gives a being the right to equal consideration. The capacity for suffering—or more strictly, for suffering and/or enjoyment or happiness—is not just another characteristic like the capacity for language, or for
higher mathematics. Bentham is not saying that those who try to mark "the
insuperable line" that determines whether the interests of a being should be
considered happen to have selected the wrong characteristic. The capacity
for suffering and enjoying things is a pre-requisite for having interests at all,
a condition that must be satisfied before we can speak of interests in any
meaningful way. It would be nonsense to say that it was not in the interests
of a stone to be kicked along the road by a schoolboy. A stone does not have
interests because it cannot suffer. Nothing that we can do to it could possibly
make any difference to its welfare. A mouse, on the other hand, does have
an interest in not being tormented, because it will suffer if it is.

If a being suffers, there can be no moral justification for refusing to take   18
that suffering into consideration. No matter what the nature of the being, the
principle of equality requires that its suffering be counted equally with the
like suffering—in so far as rough comparisons can be made—of any other
being. If a being is not capable of suffering, or of experiencing enjoyment or
happiness, there is nothing to be taken into account. This is why the limit of
sentience (using the term as a convenient, if not strictly accurate, shorthand
for the capacity to suffer or experience enjoyment or happiness) is the only
defensible boundary of concern for the interests of others. To mark this
boundary by some characteristic like intelligence or rationality would be to
mark it in an arbitrary way. Why not choose some other characteristic, like
skin color?

The racist violates the principle of equality by giving greater weight to the   19
interests of members of his own race, when there is a clash between their
interests and the interests of those of another race. Similarly the speciesist
allows the interests of his own species to override the greater interests of
members of other species.[5] The pattern is the same in each case. Most human beings are speciesists. I shall now very briefly describe some of the
practices that show this.

For the great majority of human beings, especially in urban, industrialized   20
societies, the most direct form of contact with members of other species is
at meal-times: we eat them. In doing so we treat them purely as means to
our ends. We regard their life and well-being as subordinate to our taste for
a particular kind of dish. I say "taste" deliberately—this is purely a matter of
pleasing our palate. There can be no defense of eating flesh in terms of satisfying nutritional needs, since it has been established beyond doubt that we
could satisfy our need for protein and other essential nutrients far more efficiently with a diet that replaced animal flesh by soy beans, or products
derived from soy beans, and other high-protein vegetable products.[6]

It is not merely the act of killing that indicates what we are ready to do   21
to other species in order to gratify our tastes. The suffering we inflict on the
animals while they are alive is perhaps an even clearer indication of our
speciesism than the fact that we are prepared to kill them.[7] In order to have

meat on the table at a price that people can afford, our society tolerates methods of meat production that confine sentient animals in cramped, unsuitable conditions for the entire durations of their lives. Animals are treated like machines that convert fodder into flesh, and any innovation that results in a higher "conversion ratio" is liable to be adopted. As one authority on the subject has said, "cruelty is acknowledged only when profitability ceases".[8] So hens are crowded four or five to a cage with a floor area of twenty inches by eighteen inches, or around the size of a single page of the *New York Times*. The cages have wire floors, since this reduces cleaning costs, though wire is unsuitable for the hens' feet; the floors slope, since this makes the eggs roll down for easy collection, although this makes it difficult for the hens to rest comfortably. In these conditions all the birds' natural instincts are thwarted: they cannot stretch their wings fully, walk freely, dust-bathe, scratch the ground, or build a nest. Although they have never known other conditions, observers have noticed that the birds vainly try to perform these actions. Frustrated at their inability to do so, they often develop what farmers call "vices," and peck each other to death. To prevent this, the beaks of young birds are often cut off.

This kind of treatment is not limited to poultry. Pigs are now also being reared in cages inside sheds. These animals are comparable to dogs in intelligence, and need a varied, stimulating environment if they are not to suffer from stress and boredom. Anyone who kept a dog in the way in which pigs are frequently kept would be liable to prosecution, in England at least, but because our interest in exploiting pigs is greater than our interest in exploiting dogs, we object to cruelty to dogs while consuming the produce of cruelty to pigs. Of the other animals, the condition of veal calves is perhaps worst of all, since these animals are so closely confined that they cannot even turn around or get up and lie down freely. In this way they do not develop unpalatable muscle. They are also made anaemic and kept short of roughage, to keep their flesh pale, since white veal fetches a higher price; as a result they develop a craving for iron and roughage, and have been observed to gnaw wood off the sides of their stalls, and lick greedily at any rusty hinge that is within reach. 22

Since, as I have said, none of these practices cater for anything more than our pleasures of taste, our practice of rearing and killing other animals in order to eat them is a clear instance of the sacrifice of the most important interests of other beings in order to satisfy trivial interests of our own. To avoid speciesism we must stop this practice, and each of us has a moral obligation to cease supporting the practice. Our custom is all the support that the meat-industry needs. The decision to cease giving it that support may be difficult, but it is no more difficult than it would have been for a white Southerner to go against the traditions of his society and free his slaves; if we do not change our dietary habits, how can we censure those slaveholders who would not change their own way of living? 23

The same form of discrimination may be observed in the widespread practice of experimenting on other species in order to see if certain substances are safe for human beings, or to test some psychological theory about the 24 effect of severe punishment on learning, or to try out various new compounds just in case something turns up. People sometimes think that all this experimentation is for vital medical purposes, and so will reduce suffering overall. This comfortable belief is very wide of the mark. Drug companies test new shampoos and cosmetics that they are intending to put on the market by dropping them into the eyes of rabbits, held open by metal clips, in order to observe what damage results. Food additives, like artificial colorings and preservatives, are tested by what is known as the "LD_{50}"—a test designed to find the level of consumption at which 50% of a group of animals will die. In the process, nearly all of the animals are made very sick before some finally die, and others pull through. If the substance is relatively harmless, as it often is, huge doses have to be forcefed to the animals, until in some cases sheer volume or concentration of the substance causes death.

Much of this pointless cruelty goes on in the universities. In many areas of science, non-human animals are regarded as an item of laboratory equipment, to be used and expended as desired. In psychology laboratories experimenters devise endless variations and repetitions of experiments that were of little value in the first place. To quote just one example, from the experimenter's own account in a psychology journal: at the University of Pennsylvania, Perrin S. Cohen hung six dogs in hammocks with electrodes taped to their hind feet. Electric shock of varying intensity was then administered through the electrodes. If the dog learnt to press its head against a panel on the left, the shock was turned off, but otherwise it remained on indefinitely. Three of the dogs, however, were required to wait periods varying from 2 to 7 seconds while being shocked before making the response that turned off the current. If they failed to wait, they received further shocks. Each dog was given from 26 to 46 "sessions" in the hammock, each session consisting of 80 "trials" or shocks, administered at intervals of one minute. The experimenter reported that the dogs, who were unable to move in the hammock, barked or bobbed their heads when the current was applied. The reported findings of the experiment were that there was a delay in the dogs' responses that increased proportionately to the time the dogs were required to endure the shock, but a gradual increase in the intensity of shock had no systematic effect in the timing of the response. The experiment was funded by the National Institutes of Health, and the United States Public Health Service.[9]

In this example, and countless cases like it, the possible benefits to mankind are either non-existent or fantastically remote; while the certain losses to members of other species are very real. This is, again, a clear indication of speciesism.

In the past, argument about vivisection has often missed this point, because it has been put in absolutist terms: would the abolitionist be prepared to let thousands die if they could be saved by experimenting on a single animal? The way to reply to this purely hypothetical question is to pose another: would the experimenter be prepared to perform his experiment on an orphaned human infant, if that were the only way to save many lives? (I say "orphan" to avoid the complication of parental feelings, although in doing

25

26

27

so I am being overfair to the experimenter, since the nonhuman subjects of experiments are not orphans.) If the experimenter is not prepared to use an orphaned human infant, then his readiness to use nonhumans is simple discrimination, since adult apes, cats, mice and other mammals are more aware of what is happening to them, more self-directing and, so far as we can tell, at least as sensitive to pain, as any human infant. There seems to be no relevant characteristic that human infants possess that adult mammals do not have to the same or a higher degree. (Someone might try to argue that what makes it wrong to experiment on a human infant is that the infant will, in time and if left alone, develop into more than the nonhuman, but one would then, to be consistent, have to oppose abortion, since the fetus has the same potential as the infant—indeed, even contraception and abstinence might be wrong on this ground, since the egg and sperm, considered jointly, also have the same potential. In any case, this argument still gives us no reason for selecting a nonhuman, rather than a human with severe and irreversible brain damage, as the subject for our experiments.)

The experimenter, then, shows a bias in favor of his own species whenever 28 he carries out an experiment on a nonhuman for a purpose that he would not think justified him in using a human being at an equal or lower level of sentience, awareness, ability to be self-directing, etc. No one familiar with the kind of results yielded by most experiments on animals can have the slightest doubt that if this bias were eliminated the number of experiments performed would be a minute fraction of the number performed today.

Experimenting on animals, and eating their flesh, are perhaps the two ma- 29 jor forms of speciesism in our society. By comparison, the third and last form of speciesism is so minor as to be insignificant, but it is perhaps of some special interest to those for whom this paper was written. I am referring to speciesism in contemporary philosophy.

Philosophy ought to question the basic assumptions of the age. Thinking 30 through, critically and carefully, what most people take for granted is, I believe, the chief task of philosophy, and it is this task that makes philosophy a worthwhile activity. Regrettably, philosophy does not always live up to its historic role. Philosophers are human beings and they are subject to all the preconceptions of the society to which they belong. Sometimes they succeed in breaking free of the prevailing ideology: more often they become its most sophisticated defenders. So, in this case, philosophy as practiced in the universities today does not challenge anyone's preconceptions about our relations with other species. By their writings, those philosophers who tackle problems that touch upon the issue reveal that they make the same unquestioned assumptions as most other humans, and what they say tends to confirm the reader in his or her comfortable speciesist habits.

I could illustrate this claim by referring to the writings of philosophers in 31 various fields—for instance, the attempts that have been made by those interested in rights to draw the boundary of the sphere of rights so that it runs parallel to the biological boundaries of the species *homo sapiens*, including infants and even mental defectives, but excluding those other beings of equal

or greater capacity who are so useful to us at mealtimes and in our laboratories. I think it would be a more appropriate conclusion to this paper, however, if I concentrated on the problem with which we have been centrally
concerned, the problem of equality.

It is significant that the problem of equality, in moral and political philos-   32
ophy, is invariably formulated in terms of human equality. The effect of this
is that the question of the equality of other animals does not confront the
philosopher, or student, as an issue in itself—and this is already an indication
of the failure of philosophy to challenge accepted beliefs. Still, philosophers
have found it difficult to discuss the issue of human equality without raising,
in a paragraph or two, the question of the status of other animals. The reason
for this, which should be apparent from what I have said already, is that if
humans are to be regarded as equal to one another, we need some sense of
"equal" that does not require any actual, descriptive equality of capacities,
talents or other qualities. If equality is to be related to any actual characteristics of humans, these characteristics must be some lowest common denominator, pitched so low that no human lacks them—but then the philosopher
comes up against the catch that any such set of characteristics which covers
all humans will not be possessed *only by humans.* In other words, it turns
out that in the only sense in which we can truly say, as an assertion of fact,
that all humans are equal, at least some members of other species are also
equal—equal, that is, to each other and to humans. If, on the other hand, we
regard the statement "All humans are equal" in some non-factual way, perhaps as a prescription, then, as I have already argued, it is even more difficult
to exclude non-humans from the sphere of equality.

This result is not what the egalitarian philosopher originally intended to   33
assert. Instead of accepting the radical outcome to which their own reasonings naturally point, however, most philosophers try to reconcile their beliefs
in human equality and animal inequality by arguments that can only be described as devious.

As a first example, I take William Frankena's well-known article "The Con-   34
cept of Social Justice."[10] Frankena opposes the idea of basing justice on merit,
because he sees that this could lead to highly inegalitarian results. Instead
he proposes the principle that:

> . . . all men are to be treated as equals, not because they are equal, in any
> respect but simply because they are human. They are human because they have
> emotions and desires, and are able to think, and hence are capable of enjoying
> a good life in a sense in which other animals are not.

But what is this capacity to enjoy the good life which all humans have, but   35
no other animals? Other animals have emotions and desires, and appear to
be capable of enjoying a good life. We may doubt that they can think—although the behavior of some apes, dolphins and even dogs suggest that some
of them can—but what is the relevance of thinking? Frankena goes on to

admit that by "the good life" he means "not so much the morally good life as the happy or satisfactory life," so thought would appear to be unnecessary for enjoying the good life; in fact to emphasise the need for thought would make difficulties for the egalitarian since only some people are capable of leading intellectually satisfying lives, or morally good lives. This makes it difficult to see what Frankena's principle of equality has to do with simply being *human*. Surely every sentient being is capable of leading a life that is happier or less miserable than some alternative life, and hence has a claim to be taken into account. In this respect the distinction between humans and non-humans is not a sharp division, but rather a continuum along which we move gradually, and with overlaps between the species, from simple capacities for enjoyment and satisfaction, or pain and suffering, to more complex ones.

Faced with a situation in which they see a need for some basis for the moral gulf that is commonly thought to separate humans and animals, but can find no concrete difference that will do the job without undermining the equality of humans, philosophers tend to waffle. They resort to high-sounding phrases like "the intrinsic dignity of the human individual;"[11] They talk of the "intrinsic worth of all men" as if men (humans?) had some worth that other beings did not,[12] or they say that humans, and only humans, are "ends in themselves" while "everything other than a person can only have value for a person."[13]   36

This idea of a distinctive human dignity and worth has a long history; it can be traced back directly to the Renaissance humanists, for instance to Pico della Mirandola's *Oration on the Dignity of Man*. Pico and other humanists based their estimate of human dignity on the idea that man possessed the central, pivotal position in the "Great Chain of Being" that led from the lowliest forms of matter to God himself; this view of the universe, in turn, goes back to both classical and Judeo-Christian doctrines. Contemporary philosophers have cast off these metaphysical and religious shackles and freely invoke the dignity of mankind without needing to justify the idea at all. Why should we not attribute "intrinsic dignity" or "intrinsic worth" to ourselves? Fellow-humans are unlikely to reject the accolades we so generously bestow on them, and those to whom we deny the honor are unable to object. Indeed, when one thinks only of humans, it can be very liberal, very progressive, to talk of the dignity of all human beings. In so doing, we implicitly condemn slavery, racism, and other violations of human rights. We admit that we ourselves are in some fundamental sense on a par with the poorest, most ignorant members of our own species. It is only when we think of humans as no more than a small sub-group of all the beings that inhabit our planet that we may realize that in elevating our own species we are at the same time lowering the relative status of all other species.   37

The truth is that the appeal to the intrinsic dignity of human beings appears to solve the egalitarian's problems only as long as it goes unchallenged. Once we ask *why* it should be that all humans—including infants, mental defectives, psychopaths, Hitler, Stalin and the rest—have some kind of dignity or worth that no elephant, pig or chimpanzee can ever achieve, we see   38 that this question is as difficult to answer as our original request for some relevant fact that justifies the inequality of humans and other animals. In fact, these two questions are really one: talk of intrinsic dignity or moral worth only takes the problem back one step, because any satisfactory defence of the claim that all and only humans have intrinsic dignity would need to refer to some relevant capacities or characteristics that all and only humans possess. Philosophers frequently introduce ideas of dignity, respect and worth at the point at which other reasons appear to be lacking, but this is hardly good enough. Fine phrases are the last resource of those who have run out of arguments.

In case there are those who still think it may be possible to find some   39
some relevant characteristic that distinguishes all humans from all members of other species, I shall refer again, before I conclude, to the existence of some humans who quite clearly are below the level of awareness, self-consciousness, intelligence, and sentience, of many non-humans. I am thinking of humans with severe and irreparable brain damage, and also of infant humans. To avoid the complication of the relevance of a being's potential, however, I shall henceforth concentrate on permanently retarded humans.

Philosophers who set out to find a characteristic that will distinguish hu-   40
mans from other animals rarely take the course of abandoning these groups of humans by lumping them in with the other animals. It is easy to see why they do not. To take this line without re-thinking our attitudes to other animals would entail that we have the right to perform painful experiments on retarded humans for trivial reasons; similarly it would follow that we had the right to rear and kill these humans for food. To most philosophers these consequences are as unacceptable as the view that we should stop treating non-humans in this way.

Of course, when discussing the problem of equality it is possible to ignore   41
the problem of mental defectives, or brush it aside as if somehow insignificant.[14] This is the easiest way out. What else remains? My final example of speciesism in contemporary philosophy has been selected to show what happens when a writer is prepared to face the question of human equality and animal inequality without ignoring the existence of mental defectives, and without resorting to obscurantist mumbo-jumbo. Stanley Benn's clear and honest article "Egalitariansim and Equal Consideration of Interests"[15] fits this description.

Benn, after noting the usual "evident human inequalities" argues, correctly   42
I think, for equality of consideration as the only possible basis for egalitarianism. Yet Benn, like other writers, is thinking only of "equal consideration of human interests." Benn is quite open in his defence of this restriction of equal consideration:

> . . . not to possess human shape *is* a disqualifying condition. However faithful or intelligent a dog may be, it would be a monstrous sentimentality to attribute to him interests that could be weighed in an equal balance with those of human

beings . . . if, for instance, one had to decide between feeding a hungry baby or a hungry dog, anyone who chose the dog would generally be reckoned morally defective, unable to recognize a fundamental inequality of claims.

This is what distinguishes our attitude to animals from our attitude to imbeciles. It would be odd to say that we ought to respect equally the dignity or personality of the imbecile and of the rational man . . . but there is nothing odd about saying that we should respect their interests equally, that is, that we should give to the interests of each the same serious consideration as claims to considerations necessary for some standard of well-being that we can recognize and endorse.

Benn's statement of the basis of the consideration we should have for   43
imbeciles seems to me correct, but why should there be any fundamental inequality of claims between a dog and a human imbecile? Benn sees that if equal consideration depended on rationality, no reason could be given against using imbeciles for research purposes, as we now use dogs and guinea pigs. This will not do: "But of course we do distinguish imbeciles from animals in this regard," he says. That the common distinction is justifiable is something Benn does not question; his problem is how it is to be justified. The answer he gives is this:

> . . . we respect the interests of men and give them priority over dogs not *in-sofar* as they are rational, but because rationality is the human norm. We say it is *unfair* to exploit the deficiencies of the imbecile who falls short of the norm, just as it would be unfair, and not just ordinarily dishonest, to steal from a blind man. If we do not think in this way about dogs, it is because we do not see the irrationality of the dog as a deficiency or a handicap, but as normal for the species. The characteristics, therefore, that distinguish the normal man from the normal dog make it intelligible for us to talk of other men having interests and capacities, and therefore claims, of precisely the same kind as we make on our own behalf. But although these characteristics may provide the point of the distinction between men and other species, they are not in fact the qualifying conditions for membership, or the distinguishing criteria of the class of morally considerable persons; and this is precisely because a man does not become a member of a different species, with its own standards of normality, by reason of not possessing these characteristics.

The final sentence of this passage gives the argument away. An imbecile,   44
Benn concedes, may have no characteristics superior to those of a dog; nevertheless this does not make the imbecile a member of "a different species" as the dog is. *Therefore* it would be "unfair" to use the imbecile for medical research as we use the dog. But why? That the imbecile is not rational is just the way things have worked out, and the same is true of the dog—neither is any more responsible for their mental level. If it is unfair to take advantage of an isolated defect, why is it fair to take advantage of a more general limitation? I find it hard to see anything in this argument ex-

cept a defence of preferring the interests of members of our own species because they are members of our own species. To those who think there might be more to it, I suggest the following mental exercise. Assume that it has been proven that there is a difference in the average, or normal, intelligence quotient for two different races, say whites and blacks. Then substitute the term "white" for every occurrence of "men" and "black" for every occurrence of "dog" in the passage quoted; and substitute "high I.Q." for "rationality" and when Benn talks of "imbeciles" replace this term by "dumb whites"— that is, whites who fall well below the normal white I.Q. score. Finally, change "species" to "race". Now re-read the passage. It has become a defence of a rigid, no exceptions division between whites and blacks, based on I.Q. scores, *not withstanding an admitted overlap* between whites and blacks in this respect. The revised passage is, of course, outrageous, and this is not only because we have made fictitious assumptions in our substitutions. The point is that in the original passage Benn was defending a rigid division in the amount of consideration due to members of different species, despite admitted cases of overlap. If the original did not, at first reading strike us as being as outrageous as the revised version does, this is largely because although we are not racists ourselves, most of us are speciesists. Like the other articles, Benn's stands as a warning of the ease with which the best minds can fall victim to a prevailing ideology.

Notes

1. Passages of this article appeared in a review of *Animals, Men and Morals,* edited by S. and R. Godlovitch and J. Harris (Gollancz and Taplinger, London 1972) in *The New York Review of Books,* April 5, 1973. The whole direction of my thinking on this subject I owe to talks with a number of friends in Oxford in 1970–71, especially Richard Keshen, Stanley Godlovitch, and, above all, Roslind Godlovitch.

2. *The Methods of Ethics* (7th Ed.) p. 382.

3. For example, R. M. Hare, *Freedom and Reason* (Oxford, 1963) and J. Rawls. *A Theory of Justice* (Harvard, 1972); for a brief account of the essential agreement on this issue between these and other positions, see R. M. Hare, "Rules of War and Moral Reasoning," *Philosophy and Public Affairs,* vol. 1, no. 2 (1972).

4. *Introduction to the Principles of Morals and Legislation,* ch. XVII.

5. I owe the term "speciesism" to Dr. Richard Ryder.

6. In order to produce 1 lb. of protein in the form of beef or veal, we must feed 21 lbs. of protein to the animal. Other forms of livestock are slightly less inefficient, but the average ratio in the U.S. is still 1:8. It has been estimated that the amount of protein lost to humans in this way is equivalent to 90% of the annual world protein deficit. For a brief account, see Frances Moore Lappe, *Diet for a Small Planet* (Friends of The Earth/Ballantine, New York 1971) pp. 4–11.

7. Although one might think that killing a being is obviously the ultimate wrong one can do to it, I think that the infliction of suffering is a clearer indication of speciesism because it might be argued that at least part of what is wrong with killing a human is that most humans are

conscious of their existence over time, and have desires and purposes that extend into the future—see, for instance, M. Tooley, "Abortion and Infanticide," *Philosophy and Public Affairs*, vol. 2, no. 1 (1972). Of course, if one took this view one would have to hold—as Tooley does—that killing a human infant or mental defective is not in itself wrong, and is less serious than killing certain higher mammals that probably do have a sense of their own existence over time.

8. Ruth Harrison, *Animal Machines* (Stuart, London, 1964). This book provides an eye-opening account of intensive farming methods for those unfamiliar with the subject.

9. *Journal of the Experimental Analysis of Behavior*, vol. 13, no. 1 (1970). Any recent volume of this journal, or of other journals in the field, like the *Journal of Comparative and Physiological Psychology*, will contain reports of equally cruel and trivial experiments. For a fuller account, see Richard Ryder, "Experiments on Animals" in *Animals, Men and Morals*.

10. In R. Brandt (ed.) *Social Justice* (Prentice Hall, Englewood Cliffs, 1962); the passage quoted appears on p. 19.

11. Frankena, *op. cit.* p. 23.

12. H. A. Bedau, "Egalitarianism and the Idea of Equality" in *Nomos IX. Equality,* ed. J. R. Pennock and J. W. Chapman, New York 1967.

13. G. Vlastos, "Justice and Equality" in Brandt, *Social Justice,* p. 48.

14. E. G. Bernard Williams, "The Idea of Equality," in *Philosophy, Politics and Society* (second series) ed. P. Laslett and W. Runciman (Blackwell, Oxford, 1962) p. 118; J. Rawls, *A Theory of Justice*, pp. 509–10.

15. *Nomos IX: Equality;* the passages quoted are on pp. 62ff.

QUESTIONS FOR MEANING

1. What is Singer's premise in arguing that animals deserve equal consideration with humans? Why can animals be said to have "interests"? Explain what Singer means by "equality."

2. What is "speciesism," and what two forms does it most commonly take?

3. Why have philosophers traditionally argued on behalf of "human dignity"? If you reject Singer's argument that "all animals are equal," explain why human beings have more "dignity" or "worth" than nonhuman animals. Try to answer the question that Singer poses in paragraph 38: Why can "infants, mental defectives, psychopaths, Hitler, Stalin, and the rest—have some kind of dignity or worth that no elephant, pig or chimpanzee can ever achieve"?

4. Singer challenges the argument (represented by William Frankena in paragraph 34) that the ability to think distinguishes humans from other animals. Have you ever had experience with an animal that seemed to think?

5. Singer asks, "What is the relevance of thinking?" Is this a strange question for a philosopher to ask? How important is thinking to Singer himself? Is he contradicting himself?

6. What is the role of philosophy in the modern world? What are the respon-

sibilities of philosophers, and how should they write? What is Singer's opinion of philosophy as practiced in most universities? Do you agree? If you have ever taken a course in philosophy, what did you learn from it? Would Singer have respected your teacher?

7. Judging from this essay, what philosopher seems to have had an especially strong influence on Singer in shaping his position regarding the rights of animals?

8. Vocabulary: latent (2), advocate (3), parody (4), refute (4), hierarchical (8), folly (12), insuperable (16), waffle (36), and intrinsic (37).

QUESTIONS ABOUT STRATEGY

1. What is the function of paragraphs 1 and 2? Why does Singer wait until the end of the third paragraph before introducing the subject of "members of species other than our own—or, as we popularly though misleadingly call them, animals"? Explain why it can be misleading to call animals "animals." Why does Singer want us to reconsider our use of this term?

2. Explain the analogy that Thomas Taylor made between the rights of women and the rights of "brutes." Why does Singer go to the trouble of describing a work in which the idea of equality for women was ridiculed?

3. Singer was very much aware that he was arguing a point of view with which many people would disagree. At what points in his essay does he anticipate and respond to opposition?

4. What is the basic strategy of this argument? Where does Singer place the responsibility for assuming the burden of proof? To what extent does Singer's argument depend upon exposing the shortcomings of his opponents? If his opponents can be shown to reason badly, would it necessarily follow that Singer argues well? Distinguish between those paragraphs in which Singer analyzes the work of other philosophers and those in which he advances his own case.

5. What does this essay tell you about the type of audience Singer was writing for? What sort of political principle does Singer assume his audience shares with him? Is the logic of this argument strong enough to convince someone who did not share Singer's politics?

6. If you were to take Singer's argument and put it into the form of a syllogism, how would it read?

EDWARD C. MELBY, JR.

A Statement from the Association for Biomedical Research

Edward C. Melby, Jr., is a veterinarian who received his D.V.M. from Cornell University in 1954. He was in private practice for several years before devoting himself to teaching and research. He taught laboratory animal medicine at the Johns Hopkins School of Medicine from 1962 to 1974, when he returned to Cornell as Professor of Medicine and Dean of the College of Veterinary Medicine. He is the author of the Handbook of Laboratory Animal Science, Volumes 1–3 *(1974–1976). As President of the Association for Biomedical Research, he offered the following testimony before a congressional committee in* **1981,** *when several laws that would restrict animal-based research were under serious consideration.*

1   Mr. Chairman, Members of the Subcommittee, I am Edward C. Melby, Jr., President of the Association for Biomedical Research. I am also Dean of the Faculty and Professor of Medicine of the College of Veterinary Medicine at Cornell University. Prior to accepting that appointment in 1974, I served 12 years as a Professor and Director of the Division of Comparative Medicine of the Johns Hopkins University School of Medicine.

2   The Association for Biomedical Research (ABR), established in 1979, represents nearly 200 universities, hospitals, medical schools, veterinary schools, research institutes, animal producers and suppliers, pharmaceutical, chemical, petroleum and contract testing companies. ABR's primary objective is to help assure the continuation of responsible biomedical research.

3   It is our understanding that we are here today to discuss the use of live animals in medical research and laboratory testing. Perhaps one of the most significant steps taken in the past few years was the passage of the Laboratory Animal Welfare Act, Public Law 89–544, in 1966, for it marked a new era in research regulation. Amendments in 1970 as well as subsequently have broadened the Act to its present form known as the "Animal Welfare Act" and it now protects show horses, zoo and aquarium species, and other categories of animals as well as those used in laboratories. Ironically, the two largest categories of animals in the United States—largest by far—are not covered by the present Act; pet dogs and cats, and farm animals. It is important to understand this dichotomy perhaps best expressed through citing the numbers of animals involved. In FY 1980, 188,700 dogs were studied in research in the United States according to official U.S. Department of Agriculture figures. This can be compared to the over three billion—that is three billion—chickens raised for food each year in the United States or the thirteen million—that is thirteen million—dogs killed each year by public pounds, municipal animal shelters, and "humane" societies, according to reliable estimates. There are believed to be about 35 million pet dogs in the United

States at any moment, yet the Animal Welfare Act does not cover them. We will return to this point in a moment. But think about those numbers because it is important to put these data into proper perspective; 188,700 dogs studied in medicine and science compared to over thirteen million killed as unclaimed, unwanted dogs each year by towns and cities across America.

ABR was established precisely because no private, non-profit, non-governmental organization seemed to exist which would interact in *a positive way* with scientists, animal welfare organizations, science-based industries in medicine and health, universities and research institutions, and government regulators. ABR has, therefore, in its mere two years of existence, established lines of communication among these varied organizations and, in a more formal way, met with USDA officials to hold serious discussions on improving the Animal Welfare Act. These efforts are ongoing and have been very useful, we believe.   4

ABR here wishes to emphasize that it welcomes proposals, questions, and discussions with representatives of any interest in the field of animal use in biomedical research. Surprisingly, no animal welfare organization or "humane" society has presented any written proposal to us, nor has any legislator sought the views of the constituency ABR represents through contacting ABR. We hope such representations will be made in the future and assure the Subcommittee that ABR will respond thoughtfully and reliably to any consultation requested. We offer our services as a sounding board to all concerned with biomedical research.   5

The Subcommittee has expressed an interest in whether laboratory animals are studied unnecessarily or inappropriately. ABR has no reason to believe that in science as in politics or law, there is perfection. The difficulty with words like "unnecessary" or "inappropriate" is that what seems unnecessary to one person from one vantage point, may seem absolutely necessary to another from a different vantage point. Had a Pasteur or a Madam Curie in France, or a Fleming or a Lister in England, or a Salk or a DeBakey in the United States been prevented from following their studies on vaccines, X-rays, penicillin, antiseptics, polio or heart surgery because they were judged "unnecessary," these advances and concepts so taken for granted would not have been developed as they were. Verification of their results by a certain amount of replication was and is an essential part of the scientific process.   6

Having said that, it is clear to us that endless repetition and duplication without purpose is to be avoided. It is our opinion that the peer review system of the major granting agencies, such as the National Institute of Health, the editorial review process for originality of thought by scientific journals, and the cost effectiveness of private industry, prevent most so-called "unnecessary" animal experiments. Those persons and organizations opposed to *all* studies of animals will, of course, consider all such studies as "unnecessary"—a view far from that of mainstream America, we believe. Nevertheless, any improvements which would prevent unnecessary experiments without preventing those which turn out, sometimes unexpectedly, to have been very necessary, would be welcome. The Association for Biomedical Research be-   7 lieves that none of the legislative proposals now in the Congress succeed in making this distinction, but ABR is anxious to work toward this goal.

The use of techniques labelled by some as "alternatives" to animals is as old as chemistry, physics, astronomy and modern science itself. Recent NIH studies have shown that roughly one third of its current budget is spent on research using mammals and about one fourth on research using humans themselves, the remainder being in research which studies neither people nor mammals directly. In other words, NIH's average yearly support over the last three fiscal years for projects which do not involve laboratory mammals constitutes 55% of total research dollars expended. Further in FY 1980, approximately 28% of NIH funds were committed to projects using neither humans or mammals. In dollars this translates into $704.8 million. This, combined with the finding that animal use declined by 40% in the decade 1968 through 1978 in the United States by a National Research Council–Institute of Laboratory Animal Resources survey published in 1980, must be taken by any reasonable person as stong evidence of science incorporating non-animal techniques as soon as they become scientifically reliable. So-called "alternatives" are consistently incorporated into research, education and testing requirements as the particular medical or scientific field warrants. In addition, the significant pressures of inflation on scientific endeavors have made acquisition and use of animals increasingly expensive. As a result, universities and private industry have experienced considerable motivation to replace animals with less expensive, non-animal techniques wherever possible. A significant percentage of industry's research and development budget is dedicated to the search for in vitro techniques as standard procedures. It must be emphasized, however, that the criterion of scientific excellence must remain the principal determinant of any research method. Where appropriate alternatives to the use of living animals have and will continue to be developed; the benefits obtained through their precision and reproducibility certainly make alternatives a most attractive choice. Several of the present legislative proposals before the Congress in respect to these so-called "alternatives" are therefore redundant and, in our view, dangerous to the conduct of science by the time-tested, scientific peer review process in this country. The Soviet Union, it should be recalled, has still not recovered in medicine and biology from the period of "Lysenkoism" when the government dictated false biological information as a mandated approach to science.

The appropriate care, acquisition and maintenance of laboratory animals is of continuing interest and concern to all responsible scientists. ABR therefore supports efforts to amend those components of the Animal Welfare Act in need of improvement, to which I referred earlier. Indeed, ABR would recommend expansion of the present Act's coverage to pet dogs and cats, and those in municipal pounds or animal shelters, whose municipalities or owning organizations receive federal funds. ABR would be pleased to interact with Congressional sponsors of bills related to animal welfare to insure participation of the larger biomedical community, including the major research and teaching organizations and research-based industries of America.

We would be pleased to respond to any questions or comments you may
have, and hope that members of the Congress or their staff will contact our
office at any time information from the biomedical perspective is required.   10

As part of these hearings, we wish to offer specific comment on four bills   11
(HR 556, HR 4406, HR 930 and HR 220) now under consideration by the
Subcommittee on Science, Research and Technology. For purposes of clarity
I list these according to the specific points identified by the Committee for
review:

1. Excessive, unnecessary, uneconomic or inappropriate use of animals in cur-   12
   rent practice:

   Biomedical research institutions in this country operate under a peer re-   13
   view system comprised of before-the-fact reviews of applications and subsequent reviews of data and results in scientific meetings as well as by
   reviewers and editors of scientific journals. In 1966 the Animal Welfare Act
   (Public Law 89-547) was enacted. At about the same time, the scientific
   community sponsored an independent, peer review accreditation program
   under the auspices of the American Association for Accreditation of Laboratory Animal Care which now accredits some 440 institutions. Institutions
   now follow guidelines prescribed by the NIH Office of Protection of Research
   Risks, and a signed statement by each investigator is prepared in making
   application for research funds that principles for the proper use of animals
   are being followed.

   According to studies carried out under the auspices of the National Acad-   14
   emy of Sciences–National Research Council, reported in 1980, there was a
   40% decrease in total animal use in the decade 1968 through 1978. Although
   the reasons are varied, there is good evidence to indicate that the supply
   and use of healthier animals has reduced loss as well as variation in results
   and hence, reduced the need for confirmation through repetitive studies.
   Additionally, there has been the ongoing process of incorporating "new technologies" including tissue culture, computer modeling, in vitro diagnostic and
   assay instrumentation and, most recently, the advent of recombinant DNA
   techniques. This has been an ongoing process. For example, records of the
   College I head indicate that tissue culture techniques were introduced on
   this campus in the mid-1940's. The very nature of science requires that such
   new technologies be implemented as soon as they are demonstrated to be
   the equal or superior to existing techniques. Furthermore, economic pressures require that more effective substitutions be introduced wherever
   possible.

2. Ways to promote more humane and appropriate use of animals, including   15
   alternatives to animal use:

   Concurrent with the enormous expansion of biomedical research follow-   16
   ing World War II, the scientific community has made a major commitment to
   the improvement of laboratory animal science. Indeed, an entirely new area
   of scientific specialization and the infrastructure to support it, has evolved
   to meet that need. Training programs have evolved in both the two and four
   year colleges to train animal technicians and technologists; a new specialty
   board recognized by the American Veterinary Medical Association, the Amer-

ican College of Laboratory Animal Medicine, certifies veterinarians with advanced training and experience in that specialty; and most institutions provide
in-house training programs for animal technicians and graduate students,
many following the programs fostered by the American Association for Laboratory Animal Science. Through these and related efforts the personnel directly involved in the care and use of laboratory animals have gained significant
understanding of the humane care and specialized requirements of the various animal species used.

I believe it is important to repeat observations made earlier in this testi-   17
mony. So-called "alternatives" are consistently incorporated into research,
education and testing requirements as the particular medical or scientific
field warrants. In recent years, the significant pressures of inflation on scientific endeavors have made acquisition and use of animals increasingly expensive. As a result, universities and private industry have experienced
considerable motivation to replace animals with less expensive, non-animal
techniques wherever possible. It must be emphasized, however, that the criterion of scientific excellence must remain the principle determinant of any
research method. Where appropriate alternatives to the use of living animals
have been developed; the benefits obtained through their precision and reproducibility certainly make alternatives a most attractive choice. Both HR
930 and HR 220 have been written in such a manner as to be a constructive
force and we generally support that approach.

3. Incentives for development of more and improved alternatives to animal use: 18

The object of all research must be that of uncovering facts and truths,   19
regardless of the approach. In science there are enumerable "incentives for
excellence and accuracy," including various awards, recognition by learned
societies, research grant support, authorship of books and scientific papers
and perhaps most importantly, the acceptance and recognition of one's peers.
As mentioned previously, alternatives to animal use have continually been
developed, accepted and implemented based upon scientific validity, improvement of effectiveness, cost reduction and efficiency. It is questionable
whether or not additional "incentives" can really be granted to stimulate the
development of meaningful alternatives to animal use, especially if this is
carried out without reference to whether or not such methods are scientifically useful in the understanding of human or animal disease or for predicting safety of drugs. If the approach necessitates the use of animals, the scientist
must be sensitive to the animal's requirements. It is our belief that the continuing progress of scientific knowledge will continue, as it has in the
past, to recognize, develop and implement such alternatives without artificial stimulants.

4. Responses from academic, private and public research institutions to prob-   20
lems raised by pending legislative proposals:

In reviewing the several bills now before the Congress, two are particu-   21
larly worthy of comment. HR 556 is, in our opinion, an intrusion into the
scientist's ability to use a wide variety of approaches based upon experience,
experimental design and intended objectives. To artificially require deviation
from accepted scientific principles would create a situation not unlike the
Lysenko era in the Soviet Union. As presented, the bill would mandate a
wholesale diversion of 30% to 50% of *all* federal research funds from existing, peer reviewed projects, thus jeopardizing the entire scientific research

program of the nation. As objectionable as that mandate might be, the fundamental issue with the approach taken by the bill is that it fails to recognize innovative and creative scientific inquiry, mandating restrictions on what have proven to be the most fruitful approaches to biological and medical research since the advancement of the germ theory of disease.

HR 4406 proposes to amend the existing animal welfare act in a number of ways. Perhaps of greatest concern is the attempt to modify section 3(a) which would attempt to define "pain" in animals. It has been clearly demonstrated that the concept and interpretation of pain is exceptionally complex and clarification is not amenable by the sort of definition proposed. In section 10, we object strongly to the recommendation that inspectors be given authority to "confiscate or destroy" animals which, in the sole judgment of the inspector are "suffering as a result of failure to comply with any provision—" unless the institution's animal care committee is convened. In the day to day working situation of a complex institution such as the University I serve, such a provision for the convening of a committee for immediate action is clearly fraught with impossible problems. Furthermore, the scientific qualifications of individual "inspectors" is and will probably always remain a questionable aspect.

5. Areas in which animal-based research or testing remains crucial to protection or enhancement of human health:

This topic must be addressed in a variety of ways and to adequately respond to the question would require a voluminous amount of data. I will, therefore, limit my observations but would be pleased to provide members of the Committee with additional information should that be helpful.

In the area of infectious disease, prior to advances in chemotherapy and vaccines, such diseases were the cause of most deaths in the industrialized world. Today, many have been reduced to the point where infectious disease ranks among the lowest causes of death. Biologic production and testing has always been dependent on animal use since only the complex, biologically interrelated systems of the whole animal can respond in a fashion indicative to that of man. Certain aspects of testing have been delegated to "alternatives" and where proven efficacious, these practices will continue and expand. Similarly, the toxic effects of many antibiotics and other chemotherapeutic agents have first been recognized through their application in animals. This method of testing is the only one endorsed by the FDA for human use and the USDA for animal use, for no accpetable alternatives currently exist which embody the total host response provided by animals. Relatively recent examples of the importance of such testings and the use of a variety of systems are found in the development of polio vaccine and the identification of thalidomide as a teratogen.

In the underdeveloped countries, many infectious diseases still account for tremendous morbidity and mortality. According to the 1980 World Health Organization Summary Reports, 200,000,000 people are affected by schistosomiasis; 100,000,000 by leishumaniasis with 400,000 new cases developing annually; 300–400,000,000 cases of malaria which kills in excess of 1,000,000 children each year, and, 100,000,000 humans are affected by trypanosomiasis. It is estimated that the morbidity from these four diseases alone is four times the entire population of the United States. At the present time, there are no alternatives to the use of animals in demonstrating the host response to these infectious agents. Any severe reduction in the use of animals to continue important studies on the these diseases, aimed at treatment and prevention, would severely impede the progress being made by many U.S. research institutions, including Cornell, thus prolonging the suffering and death of millions of humans throughout the world.

In the United States, hepatitis B infection remains an important cause of   27
death and illness. Recent evidence indicates that infected individuals demonstrate a very high rate of developing cancer of the liver in later life. Outside of the United States, hepatitis is a major contributor to human suffering. At the present time, Cornell University, under contract from NIH, is developing an important animal model for hepatitis B virus research and vaccine testing using the feral woodchuck, *Marmota monax*. Should attempts be made to eliminate the use of this or other valuable animal models for hepatitis B research, it will severely impact the ability to develop a protective vaccine for man.

In spite of significant progress in treatment and control, leprosy remains   28
a major world-wide disease with many cases occurring here in the United States. To date, the only method for studying the growth and establishment of infection of the causative agent is through the use of the armadillo. Continued research in this disease will be dependent on the use of this animal model.

The above examples are directed to human disease, yet it is important to   29
recognize that millions of domestic animals are saved in the United States each year through the use of prophylactic vaccination. Recent United States Department of Agriculture figures show that in 1970, for every 10,000 poultry sent to slaughter, 158 poultry had Marek's Disease. In 1979, as the result of the development of a new vaccine, the incidence of Marek's Disease was reduced to 11 cases per 10,000 poultry. As an example of other control measures, in 1950, there were 1.4 cases of hog cholera per 10,000 animals. In 1979, this figure was reduced to zero. Hog cholera has been virtually eliminated. In 1950, there were .86 cases of cattle tuberculosis per 10,000 animals slaughtered. This disease is transmissible to man. In 1979, cattle tuberculosis was reduced to .008 cases per 10,000, thus decreasing the prevalence of this disease by 1000-fold. A significant number of vaccines used in control of diseases of animals were developed and tested at Cornell University, the most recent being the canine parvovirus vaccine to protect against a new disease which simultaneously occurred in several parts of the world in 1978. Recognizing the tremendous number of dogs lost to this disease since 1978, and the significant distress this brought to animal owners, we question the wisdom of mandating discontinuing the use of living animals in such research.

In the area of non-infectious disease, the major cause of mortality in the   30
United States is that of diseases associated with the cardiovascular system. During the past three decades, animals have played an instrumental role in the development of new surgical, therapeutic and electronic devices which have played an enormous role in decreasing both mortality and morbidity. As an example, it is estimated that 50,000 coronary bypass operations take place

annually in this country, thus relieving thousands suffering from pain and for many, prolonging their lives.

Cancer ranks second, after cardiovascular disease, as a cause of death in America. Tremendous advances have been made in cancer chemotherapy and the public is just recognizing that permanent cures are now possible for many forms of cancer. Granted, much remains to be done in solving the ravages of this disease, but I must point out that all chemotherapeutic agents have first been tested in animals for signs of toxicity. Indeed, animals remain the key for further progress in our conquest of cancer. 31

Other diseases of significance in the United States have likewise benefited from animal experimentation. Animal "models," or those animals in which similar if not identical disease syndromes exist, obviously represent a fertile source of investigation. In many instances, the information gained can be of direct benefit to the animal populations involved, thus preventing death or improving the quality of their lives. As examples, one can cite spontaneous systemic lupus erythematosus, rheumatoid arthritis, and hemolytic anemia. In the field of endocrinology we have benefited immensely from the use of animals to delineate the growth changes and bodily responses altered through disorders of the endocrine system. Such studies have shed new light on diseases such as thyroiditis, pituitary giantism, Cushing's syndrome, Addison's disease, and many others. The isolation, purification, testing and synthesis of a number of hormones have significantly influenced the lives of millions. Again, because of the complexities of the systems involved, only living animals manifest the full range of physiologic changes needed to develop, test and produce such compounds. 32

In diseases of the central nervous system, significant advances have been made in products such as lithium for patients with manic depression. At the present time, investigators at Cornell are testing several new synthetic lithium compounds in animals which promise to bring beneficial therapeutic effects without the severe toxicity currently encountered with the parent compound. 33

Chronic debilitating diseases, such as rheumatoid and osteoarthritis, have benefited greatly from animal research. During the past two decades, surgical procedures developed in animals have led to the production and implantation of total hip joint prosthetic devices, knees, and other bone replacements in man. Such devices have provided pain-free locomotion in thousands of Americans who were previously immobile. 34

The examples cited above are chosen merely to illustrate the importance of animal experimentation to relieve pain, suffering and death in both man and animals. The listing is representative of only a small portion of those diseases and disorders in which animals have made useful contributions to human medicine; most were selected because they are currently used or are under study at Cornell University; thus, I have personal knowledge concerning this work. 35

The Subcommittee should also be aware of the fact that, since World War II, there have been 52 Nobel Prize winners in medicine and physiology. Thirty-seven of these awards were achieved with NIH grant awards. We have had 36

21 Nobel Prize winners in chemistry; twelve of these received NIH support. Within the past few days, this year's Nobel Prize recipients were announced. Their scientific observations and discoveries were made by utilizing animal models—non-human primates. The science being conducted in this country is perhaps the finest in the world. Congress must strive to preserve the right of scientific freedom to insure continued creativity and excellence.

In this correspondence I have intended to be informative, yet to construc-   37
tively criticize the various bills currently before the Subcommittee on Science, Research and Technology. We are aware that under certain conditions our research animals are subjected to painful procedures, yet we do everything possible to minimize the number of such procedures and to use drugs to abrogate pain. Rest assured that we agree that alternatives to living animals should be employed whenever appropriate and that science will continue, as it has in the past, the development of new alternative methods. It is our opinion that enactment of HR 930 or HR 220 would promote such alternatives without disrupting biomedical research. We wish to emphasize to the Committee the significant past achievements in biomedical science, many of which have been accomplished through the use of living animals, and stress the importance of their use in ongoing and future studies. Attempts to reduce the use of animals through restrictive legislation or through the imposition of unnecessary bureaucratic authority which extends beyond the time-tested, peer review system, would seriously impede efforts to improve the lives of both man and animals.

On behalf of the Association for Biomedical Research, thank you for per-   38
mitting me to comment on these issues.

QUESTIONS FOR MEANING

1. Why does Melby believe that animal experimentation is already subject to sufficient control? Explain what he means by "peer review."
2. What pressures outside the research community affect the number of animals used in testing? How, in particular, does the economy affect animal experimentation?
3. What is the Association for Biomedical Research? What is its purpose, and what exactly does it do? Does it seem like a reputable organization?
4. What specific accomplishments is Melby able to cite in support of animal experiments? How seriously do you take these achievements? Does Melby persuade you that American science is worthy of respect?
5. Vocabulary: dichotomy (3), verification (6), redundant (8), auspices (13), implemented (14), infrastructure (16), innovative (21), amenable (22), and delineate (32).

QUESTIONS ABOUT STRATEGY

1. Why does Melby begin by explaining who he is? Was this an appropriate way to begin? Under what circumstances might you begin an essay this way?

2. How does Melby present himself to the Committee? At what points in his testimony does he try to emphasize that he is a reasonable man?
3. How does Melby go about appealing to the animal lovers in his audience? Does he make any argument that would appeal to people who have pets? Why does he do this?
4. Does Melby present any information that caused you to reconsider your own position on this subject? If so, what was it? Try to explain why you found this point or points effective.

ONE STUDENT'S ASSIGNMENT

Using APA style documentation, write an argument for or against animal-based research. Include material from at least two sources in The Informed Argument *and at least one source that you have located on your own. Because your paper will include material from outside the textbook we are using, remember to supply readers with an APA style reference list at the end of your essay.*

A Plea for Animal Justice
Travis Knopf

For many years, scientists have been using various species   1
of animals in laboratory research. Much of this research is
vital to the promotion of human health and welfare. Through
the use of animals, scientists have made many positive discoveries in the fields of infectious disease, chronic debilitating diseases, and cardiovascular functions (Melby,
1981). The problem that has developed is the mistreatment of
the animals and the poor conditions they are kept in across
the country. My interest in this topic is magnified because
of my love for animals. I am opposed to the vast majority of
animal experiments, but I can justify some aspects of this
research method if the animals being used are treated with
care. There can be no suffering, malnutrition, abuse, or
torture in the experimentation I support.

Criticism of animal experimentation is often taken as a   2
direct assault against science itself (Mayo, 1983, p. 272).
But one can value science and still oppose animal experimentation. In fact, many current experiments are themselves
scientifically irrelevant, as well as being cruel. These

tests require the use, abuse, and even torture of animals in some extreme cases. One example mentioned by Mayo (1983) was New York University's deliberate starvation of pigeons to seventy percent of their weight. It was concluded after the experiment that, following starvation, the pigeons ate more (p. 274). This obvious result required the deaths of many pigeons. Why? Is it necessary for animals to be sacrificed for such irrelevant experiments?

Another form of animal experimentation is multi-staged, disease investigation. In these experiments various diseases, including cancer cells, are injected into healthy animals and the results are recorded. As one might expect, the results of a disease like cancer on a non-human animal are just as severe as the effects on a cancer-plagued human. From the early stages of injection, all the way to the last few minutes of suffering life, animals often suffer through a barrage of death-inducing experiments. Ultimately, however, the conditions prevalent during the animal's disease have little in common with the actual conditions humans encounter. This discrepancy raises serious questions about the need for animals in disease experimentation.

In addition to disease testing, there is cosmetic safety testing. This form of animal experimentation, in most cases, has little human life or death implications. This is due to the relatively low amount of toxin in most products. Unfortunately, these experiments have a deadly effect on the animal subjects which are given life-threatening dosages of the toxin. In an experiment conducted by Revlon, Inc., rabbits were used to test cosmetic products. Samples of various cosmetics were placed into the rabbits' eyes to see what cosmetics cause irritation and which ones do not. This whole process is called the Draize Test, and it is used by cosmetic companies to meet regulations. The sad, yet obvious effect of this experiment is blindness in the rabbits. Most animal rights supporters are totally opposed to such experimentation because it not only hurts the rabbits, but it is used in testing non-essential substances. Perhaps it is time to reconsider the danger that cosmetic products create. An alternative to using animals is needed (Mayo, 1983, p. 283).

One of the most brutal forms of animal experimentation is the "LD_{50}" test. This is a test designed to find the level of poison consumption at which fifty percent of a control group

of animals will die. In this experiment, almost all of the
animals are made very ill before some actually die (Singer,
1973, p. 302). Even our government is guilty of violent misuse of animals. At the Armed Forces Biology Research Institute in Maryland, monkeys were starved for eighteen hours.
They were then electrically prodded to run a treadmill and
subjected to gamma-radiation. The monkeys were retested for
six hours each day until death. The ultimate purpose of this
experiment was to study the effect of radiation on endurance
(Curtis, 1980).

Some alternatives to the use of animals are being explored   6
and tried by a growing number of scientists who are searching
for simpler and more cost-efficient ways to achieve their
goals. As reported in <u>Scientific American</u> ("Three R's,"
1986), feasible alternatives are termed the "three R's:" replacement with non-animals, reduction in the number of animals required, and refinement of techniques in order to
reduce their pain and distress. Currently, computer models
and simulation seem to be the best and most likely animal replacement in labs throughout our country. Other promising
alternatives to animal experiments are the use of tissue
cultures and mathematical models. "The strongest argument
in favor of developing these alternatives is that much of animal experimentation is scientifically, and hence morally,
indefensible" (Mayo, 1983, p. 292).

In spite of the fact that animal experimentation is still   7
widespread and abuses are still certainly occurring, animal
rights supporters have done a great deal of good; their accomplishments over the last few years has been substantial.
They have launched an ethical debate and created a public
awareness of this issue. Legislation has been enacted to
control animal suffering and abuse; enforcement of regulations is evident; and alternatives to animal use are being
explored, funded, and attempted. All of this seems to imply
that animal experimentation is becoming less of a problem
and that the future is rapidly improving.

Unfortunately, animal experimentation will not disap-   8
pear. It will continue as long as the scientific and medical
need is there. If this experimentation is to continue, however, conditions for the animals being used must be carefully considered. All of the controversy this topic stirs up
is going to continue to bounce between scientific and medi-

cal knowledge and animal misuse. Where the boundary lies
will be solely up to the individuals involved in animal experimentation.

References*

Curtis, P. (1980, February). The case against animal experi-
    ments. Reader's Digest. pp. 181–186.
Mayo, D. (1983). Against a scientific justification of animal
    experiments. In R. Miller (Ed.), The informed argument (pp.
    272–293). San Diego: Harcourt.
Melby, E. (1981). A statement from the Association for
    Biomedical Research. In R. Miller (Ed.), The informed ar-
    gument (pp. 311–319). San Diego: Harcourt.
Singer, P. (1973). All animals are equal. In R. Miller (Ed.),
    The informed argument (pp. 295–309). San Diego: Harcourt.
Three r's (1986, April). Scientific American. pp. 68–70.

SUGGESTIONS FOR WRITING

1. Drawing upon Rye, Gallistel, and Melby, write an essay defending the use
   of animals in medical research.
2. Is all research equally valid? Can some experiments on animals be justified
   even if others cannot, or must one take an absolute position on this issue?
   If you think that some types of research are acceptable, write an essay
   that will define what is and what isn't permissible.
3. Is an elephant equal to a pig? Write an essay with the thesis that all animals are *not* equal. Make sure that you take the views of Peter Singer into
   account and respond directly to them.
4. Interview someone who uses animals in either teaching or research, and
   then write a paper defending or attacking the way animals are used in
   your own school or community.
5. Can you oppose the use of animals in scientific research and still eat meat?
   Or is this a contradiction in your own values? Write an essay on the relationship between eating animals and experimenting upon them. Is there a

*This reference list illustrates how to include a magazine article with no author. The work is alphabetized under the first important word in the title. (In this case, the source happens to come last because of the word "Three"; the source is *not* listed last because of missing information.) When Travis included parenthetical documentation to this source within his essay, he correctly provided the title in place of the unidentified author. "Three R's" is an unusually short title; for longer titles, a shortened version should be included within the parenthetical reference in the text. Thus, if no author had been identified for the article in *Reader's Digest*, that article could have been referred to as "The Case" [editor's note].

difference between these two activities that makes one defensible and the other not? Are you opposed to both? Or do you see nothing wrong with the way humans make use of animals? What is your position?

6. Thousands of cats and dogs are abandoned each year by owners who no longer wish to care for them. Some die slow deaths from starvation and disease. Others are rescued by humane societies which house and feed them and try to find new homes for them. If a new home cannot be found, the abandoned animal is either destroyed or sold to a research facility. Should unwanted pets be used for animal experiments? Are former pets entitled to special protection?

7. What do religions teach regarding the relationships between human beings and animals? Write a paper defending or attacking animal experimentation according to Buddhist, Christian, Hindu, Jewish or Moslem beliefs.

8. Gallistel and Mayo both observe that animal experimentation in Great Britain is more restricted than it is the United States. Do a research paper on the nature of the laws that protect animals in Britain and argue whether or not such laws would be desirable in our own country. Your argument is likely to be especially convincing if you are able to determine what effect British laws have had upon the practice of science. Is major research still being done in Great Britain, or has British law crippled the practice of science there?

9. Synthesize the arguments by David P. Rall and George Roush, Jr.

Section 6

Competition:
Is It Good for You?

ROSS WETZSTEON
The Winner Instinct

One of the issues on which men and women have often disagreed is the extent to which competition is healthy and productive. An editor and writer at The Village Voice *in New York City, Ross Wetzsteon argues that men are naturally competitive and that competition is fun—implying that women may not under-stand the pleasure that comes from competing. He wrote the following essay for* Redbook *in* **1984.**

My wife used to hate playing cards with me. "You're too competitive," she 1
kept saying. "You get so intense, you can't just have fun—you always have to
win."

That didn't have anything to do with the way I felt, but try telling her that. 2
All I could do was deny that I'm competitive.

Then one rainy weekend in the country we played a vicious, back-and- 3
forth game of rummy, and when Kay finally edged me by three points, I could
see that her pleasure in winning was jeopardized by her fear that I'd sulk.

"Now, don't get mad just because you lost," she said. 4

"Mad? That was the closest game I've ever played!" 5

"You're just trying to prove you're not competitive." 6

"Not competitive? Then why was the game so much fun?"

She smiled cautiously as she gathered in the cards. "Now you're just trying 7
to pretend you don't care whether you won or lost."

"Of course I care, damn it, but don't you see? It's not winning or losing 8
that matters—it's the competition itself!"

I suddenly realized that when the subject had come up before, the only 9
reason I'd always denied being competitive was that Kay had made it seem
like such a dirty word. "Sure, women are just as ambitious and aggressive as
men," she had said once, "but we've been inhibited from expressing competitiveness. We were told when we were young that the only way we could
compete was for the attention of men—to compete in any other way was
'unfeminine.' But society defines competitiveness as a brutal, winning-is-

325

everything attitude. So if by competition you mean imitating the macho way men behave—no, thanks."

My wife just couldn't see that competitiveness means a lot more to men   10
than that win-at-any-cost ethic. Listen to New York Mets' pitcher Tom Seaver, one of the most thoughtful athletes in America: "When we finally won the World Series, I realized I'd been wrong since boyhood. I'd always believed the thrill was in celebrating the victory. Now I saw that the thrill was in competition for its own sake." So I finally decided to admit that, yes, I'm very competitive, and what's more, I'm proud of it.

Now, I'm not going to deny that there are elements of adolescent insecu-   11
rity or latent hostility or sexual rivalry in a lot of competition between men— all I'm saying is that there's another side to the story. Take male kidding around, for instance. I always tell my friend Arthur that he exaggerates so compulsively, he'll even tell people his summer house is at Six-Mile Harbor instead of Three-Mile Harbor. He comes right back at me: "You're putting on so much weight, pretty soon they'll have to give you your own zip code."

We indulge in so much of this typically male insulting humor that our   12
wives can be forgiven for thinking that beneath our surface joking there must be bitter rivalry. Believe me, we see the "oh-you-men" way they roll their eyes, but what we actually hear when we insult each other like this is one of the most reassuring things a friend can say: "I know all your faults—you can't hide a thing from me—but I like you anyway. I accept you the way you are." Still skeptical? Just let some guy who's not a close friend try to get away with that kind of one-upmanship.

Male competitiveness in our professional lives is often a way to show our   13
mutual respect. Sure, no one needs to be told that many men adopt a to-hell-with-the-bastards attitude in business; but far more often men also experience rivalry as a spur to achievement, as a means of being drawn to perform at the top of our abilities. I testified in a lawsuit a couple of years ago, and you would have thought the opposing attorneys would kill rather than let the other get the upper hand. But I overheard them talking after the decision. "I enjoy trying a case against you," one of them said. "You really keep me on my toes."

"Going up against you isn't any picnic," the other one answered. "I know   14
I've got to do my best just to stand a chance."

Can you tell which one won the case?   15

I've heard other men express the same feelings in any number of highly   16
competitive professions. "It's really sad," the owner of a newspaper where I once worked told me when a competing publication suddenly folded. "I ran a much better paper because of them. Now I'm afraid I'll get lazy." And while I'm not going to argue that men regret pulling off a deal against a competitor, their gratification is often less if they don't feel they were seriously challenged.

In sports the image of "winning is everything" is even more misleading.   17
Most men I know get their real kick in sports not from winning but from the

fact that the playing field is one of the few places where companionship and challenge come together. In bowling or touch football or softball, stiff competition not only brings men closer together; it also encourages them to do their best. This paradox at the heart of sports allows men to feel both friendship and self-satisfaction, to share moments of pride. Of course, there are nonstop competitors like John McEnroe, but there are also competitors like my friends Josh and Michael—anyone watching them play tennis would think their lives were riding on the outcome. But after the match is over, you can't tell who won—they both feel great. Competition has pushed them to the limits of their abilities; they've done as well as they possibly could; they've done something well together.

Still think winning is everything to men? Take my friend Fred, who finally   18
managed to beat his weekly tennis partner after losing something like ten sets in a row. "You must feel terrific," I said.

"Yeah, I suppose so," he said offhandedly.   19

"What's wrong?" I asked.   20

"Well, to tell the truth," Fred said, "he was so far off his game, it wasn't   21
much fun."

I knew exactly how he felt—I play tennis so competitively that my friends   22
call my game "Death in the Afternoon," but I'd much rather play way over my head and lose 2–6 than hack around and win 6–love.

So when my wife says that men can't relate to one another except com-   23
petitively, that it's a way to disguise their animosity or assert their superiority—no more apologies from me. I now argue that there's much more going on, that men just as often use competition as a means of expressing acceptance or respect or sharing.

Take it from me—busting your butt to win has its own rewards, whether   24
you win or not. I came home from a tennis match one day absolutely glowing. "You must have won," Kay remarked.

"Why do you say that?"   25

"You look so happy."   26

"Well, actually I lost," I said. "But he was so good, he made me play better   27
than I've ever played in my life."

QUESTIONS FOR MEANING

1. Why has competition become a "dirty word"? Why does Wetzsteon not only admit that he's competitive but also claim that he's "proud of it"?
2. Why does Wetzsteon believe that competition itself can be more rewarding than simply winning? Do you agree?
3. What does Wetzsteon mean when he writes of "the paradox at the heart of sports"?
4. Can you identify the allusion in the joking reference to the author's tennis game as "Death in the Afternoon"?

QUESTIONS ABOUT STRATEGY

1. What role does Wetzsteon's wife play in this essay?
2. In contrasting the way he and his wife feel about competition, does Wetzsteon ever use sexual stereotypes?
3. Where in his essay does Wetzsteon reveal he is aware that competition is not entirely admirable?
4. How effective is Wetzsteon's use of dialogue?

KATHERINE MARTIN
Is Winning Everything?

Athletics is one of the areas in which competition is most encouraged. But what happens when adults organize athletic competition for their children and pressure them to excel? The following essay written for Parents *magazine by Katherine Martin considers the potentially harmful effects of athletic competition on children. It was first published in* **1986.** *Martin's work has also appeared in such magazines as* Esquire, Ms, *and* Cosmopolitan. *The author of* Non-Impact Aerobics *(1987), she is now working as a screen writer in southern California.*

In the thick of a heated baseball game a young umpire is verbally harassed   1
by two vehement coaches. The boy tries his best on the next play but gets more abuse from a parent restrained only by a hurricane fence. Exasperated, he flops down on the ground while the coaches and a referee go at it with each other.

A young boy afraid of batting is forced to stand at home plate while his   2
father deliberately throws pitches that hit him.

During a Little League game a mother storms down to the dugout and   3
belts her son across the head for being tagged out.

A football coach grabs the face mask of a youngster, yanks him spit-close   4
and screams obscenities at him.

A father beats his exhausted son to keep him running laps around a track.   5

Twenty million children between the ages of eight and sixteen play orga-   6
nized sports outside of school, and their experience in ballparks and on playing fields has enormous impact on their physical, emotional, and social development. Most of us believe that there's nothing more basic to the American way of rearing young people than sports, but many have come to realize that the world of sports for youth is not an entirely innocent or happy one. In recent years adults have imposed unchildlike standards on children's sports. In our zeal, we've overorganized, overregimented, overstructured, and overtrained our kids. We've claimed their games for the serious business of adult competition.

"That wasn't the case when there was a lot more spontaneous play," says   7
Barry Goldberg, M.D., associate clinical professor of pediatrics at Yale University and pediatric consultant at the Institute of Sports Medicine and Athletic Trauma at Lenox Hill Hospital in New York City. "Our society has changed a great deal in the last twenty years. The small community is vanishing and there's less open space. People have to trek to playing fields. As a result, organized teams have become a way to get kids together and, often, they're patterned after professional and college sports.

"As adults intervene in children's games," warns Goldberg, echoing a grow-   8
ing concern among youth sports experts, "we have to accept the responsibility for the end product."

That end product isn't always pretty. Over the past ten years, there have   9
been reports of children paralyzed and killed from "spearing" during football games, and passing out from dehydration. One coach reportedly injected oranges with amphetamines to get his ten- to twelve-year-old football players "up" for a game.

Many parents are transformed—and often not for the better—when they   10
see their youngsters in the thick of athletic competition. "When you first go out to watch your child play sports, you see this biological extension of yourself on the field and you feel some powerful emotions," says Rainer Martens, Ph.D., founder of the American Coaching Effectiveness Program (ACEP) and author of *Joy and Sadness in Children's Sports* (Human Kinetics Publishers). "Parents just aren't prepared for that. Suddenly, they find themselves acting in ways they'd never think of at home—standing up and screaming, 'You dummy! Catch the ball!' Behavior like this has a potentially severe effect on children."

Speaking of these effects, psychologist Thomas Tutko, a leading authority   11
on youth sports and coauthor of the sobering book, *Winning Is Everything And Other American Myths* (Macmillan), comments, "I'm concerned about how many good athletes are scarred by injury or burned out psychologically by the time they are fifteen because they are unable to meet the insatiable needs of their parents, their coach, their fans, or their own personal obsession. And I am concerned, too, about those kids who feel rejected because of their limited athletic prowess.

"The effects may not be physically evident," continues Tutko, "but failure   12
in sports, or heavy-handed approaches by parents and coaches can destroy a child's self-esteem, turn him away from a lifelong involvement in physical activity, foster negative attitudes toward authority figures, and encourage hostile, aggressive behavior."

Our unfettered responses to our children as athletes can create insidious   13
pressures. In her twelve years of extensive research on the socio-psychological aspects of competitive youth sports, Tara Scanlan, Ph.D., associate professor of kinesiology at the University of California, Los Angeles, found that children experience intense stress when they perceive they're being pressured to participate in an activity and when they worry about the performance expectations and evaluations of their parents and coaches. "Kids are

very dependent on adults for feelings of their own competence and sense of self," says Scanlan. "It may not always seem so, since they may try to be stoic, tough little athletes who don't cry, but they process everything."

The implications for parents are clear. "As parents, we all have to walk a   14
very fine line between caring and creating pressure, between enthusiasm and going overboard," comments Bob Chandler, former all-pro football player, in the recent film, *The Winning Trap: Sports and Our Kids.* "We have to answer the question, What's in it for us? as honestly as we can, because unless we know what we want out of kids' sports we can't be truly effective in helping our children get what they want."

Before involving our children in team sports we need to look at our own   15
feelings about winning and losing, which may be colored by frustrations we feel in other areas of our lives, in our careers, or marital relationships. Our attitudes about sports may be charged, moreover, with memories of our own experiences as children, of our early successes or humiliations on the playing field.

"Before involving your child," says pediatrician Nathan Smith, a sports   16
medicine specialist at the University of Washington in Seattle and coauthor of *Kidsports* (Addison-Wesley), "ask yourself whether you're ready to be the parent of a loser, of a bench warmer. How would your responses differ if your child struck out or made a home run in a tie game? Would you be embarrassed if your child broke into tears after a tough loss or after making a mistake? Can you tolerate becoming a target for your child's displaced anger and frustration when there is no other outlet for disappointment and hurt?"

Or how would you feel if your child was benched during an important   17
game so that a child with less ability would have a chance to play? How would you react if an official made a questionable call against your child?

If we understand our own expectations and motivations, we can help our   18
children explore theirs. We will be ready to hear what they are saying, rather than what we want them to say. Why do they want to play? What do they expect the sport they have chosen to be like?

Although children learn very early the high value placed on sports by so-   19
ciety, when they play on their own, they tend to have a different perspective on sports than adults. They want to win, but winning is not their exclusive goal. In a ten-year study of more than a thousand children, sports psychologist Terry Orlick discovered that 90 percent of his young respondents would rather play on a losing team than warm a bench on a winning team. In fact, winning was at the bottom of their list. They wanted fun and excitement, and they wanted to improve their skills and be with friends.

"If sides are unequal, if rules give an advantage to one team, children will   20
negotiate to make it possible for either side to win," says another youth-sport expert, Vern Seefeldt, Ph.D., director of the Youth Sports Institute at Michigan State University. "That thrill of the unexpected is a major part of why children play sports. As adults we try to set up a distinct advantage for our team. We want to remove the element of uncertainty.

"When we were kids," Seefeldt continues, "we used to make up all kinds   21
of modifications to games, because we didn't always have the right number
of people for a team, or the use of a baseball diamond or a basketball court.
Now, as adults, we organize our children's games right down to the letter of
the rule, leaving them very little opportunity for innovation and creativity, and depriving them of the process of arbitrating, negotiating, finding so-
lutions."

According to Tutko, "We actually cripple children psychologically when we   22
set up all the plays. They feel like machines. Sport can be a medium to train
children to be more responsible, but we have made winning take precedence
over learning. That's so shortsighted. We could be teaching them leadership
skills by having them take turns running the team's calisthenics and drills.
We could teach them how to set up and run their own plays by alternating
team captains every practice."

To guide our children's involvement with sports, we must recognize that   23
they have different needs at different ages and that, at each stage, success
should be seen as an ongoing process of achieving potential.

QUESTIONS FOR MEANING

1. Why have sports for children become increasingly organized by adults?
2. When children play on their own, how do their games differ from those
   that are organized and supervised by adults?
3. Why do adults sometimes treat children unkindly when they fail to excel
   at sports?
4. What effects on children can result from an overemphasis on sports?
5. What should parents do before involving their children in organized sports?
6. Vocabulary: harassed (1), vehement (1), zeal (6), insatiable (11), unfettered (13), kinesiology (13), stoic (13), marital (15), innovation (21),
   precedence (22).

QUESTIONS ABOUT STRATEGY

1. What type of reasoning does Martin use to organize her material?
2. This essay originally appeared in *Parents* magazine. What evidence can
   you point to in the essay that shows Martin had her audience clearly in
   mind as she wrote?
3. Consider Martin's use of quotations. Do they help her to make her case?
   Could she afford to cut any of them?
4. Why does Martin identify Barry Goldberg, Rainer Martens, Thomas
   Tutko, Tara Scanlan, Bob Chandler, Nathan Smith, Terry Orlick, and
   Vern Seefeldt?

ALFIE KOHN
Why Competition?

In recent years, Alfie Kohn has emerged as a leading critic of competition. His book on this subject, No Contest: The Case Against Competition, *was published by Houghton Mifflin in 1986. His views on competition have also appeared in* Change, Psychology Today, The Los Angeles Times—*and* The Humanist, *which published the following essay in* **1980,** *when Kohn was a graduate student at the University of Chicago.*

W-H-I-T-E! White Team is the team for me!" The cheer is repeated, be- 1
coming increasingly frenzied as scores of campers, bedecked in the appropriate color, try to outshout their Blue opponents. The rope stretched over
the lake is taut now, as determined tuggers give it their all. It looks as if a
few will be yanked into the cold water, but a whistle pierces the air. "All
right, we'll call this a draw." Sighs of disappointment follow, but children are
soon scrambling off to the Marathon. Here, competitors will try to win for
their side by completing such tasks as standing upside-down in a bucket of
shampoo or forcing down great quantities of food in a few seconds before
tagging a teammate.

As a counselor in this camp over a period of several years, I witnessed a 2
number of Color Wars, and what constantly amazed me was the abrupt and
total transformation that took place each time one began. As campers are
read their assignments, children who not ten minutes before were known as
"David" or "Margie" suddenly have a new identity; they have been arbitrarily
designated as members of a team. The unspoken command is understood by
even the youngest among them: Do everything possible to win for your side.
Strain every muscle to prove how superior *we* are to the hostile Blues.

And so they will. Children who had wandered aimlessly about the camp 3
are suddenly driven with a Purpose. Children who had tired of the regular
routine are instantly provided with Adventure. Children who had trouble making
friends are unexpectedly part of a new Crowd. In the dining hall, every camper
sits with his or her team. Strategy is planned for the next battle; troops are
taught the next cheer. There is a coldness bordering on suspicion when passing someone with a blue T-shirt—irrespective of any friendship B.C. (Before
Colors). If anyone has reservations about participating in an activity, he needs
only to be reminded that the other team is just a few points behind.

I

Why Sport?" asks Ed Cowan (*The Humanist,* November/December 1979). 4
When the sports are competitive ones, I cannot find a single reason to answer
his rhetorical query. Mr. Cowan's discussion of the pure—almost mystical—

aesthetic pleasure that is derived from athletics only directs attention away from what is, in actuality, the primary impetus of any competitive activity: winning.

I would not make such a fuss over Color War, or even complain about the absurd spectacle of grown men shrieking and cursing on Sunday afternoons were it not for the significance of the role played by competition in our culture. It is bad enough that Americans actually regard fighting as a sport: it is worse that the outcome of even the gentlest of competitions—baseball—can induce fans to hysteria and outright violence. But sports is only the tip of the proverbial iceberg. Our entire society is affected by—even structured upon—the need to be "better than." 5

My thesis is admittedly extreme; it is, simply put, that *competition by its very nature is always unhealthy.* This is true, to begin with, because competition and cooperation are mutually exclusive orientations. I say this fully aware of the famed camaraderie that is supposed to develop among players—or soldiers—on the same side. First, I have doubts, based on personal experience, concerning the depth and fullness of relationships that result from the need to become more effective against a common enemy. 6

Second, the "realm of the interhuman," to use Martin Buber's phrase, is severely curtailed when those on the other side are excluded from any possible community. Worse, they are generally regarded with suspicion and contempt in any competitive enterprise. (This is not to say that we cannot remain on good terms with, say, tennis opponents, but that whatever cooperation and meaningful relationship is in evidence exists in spite of the competitiveness.) Finally, the sweaty fellowship of the lockerroom (or, to draw the inescapable parallel again, the trenches) simply does not compensate for the inherent evils of competition. 7

The desire to win has a not very surprising (but too rarely remarked upon) characteristic: it tends to edge out other goals and values in the context of any given competitive activity. When I was in high school, I was a very successful debater for a school that boasted one of the country's better teams. After hundreds and hundreds of rounds of competition over three years, I can assert in no uncertain terms that the purpose of debate is not to seek the truth or resolve an issue. No argument, however compelling, is ever conceded; veracity is never attributed to the other side. The only reason debaters sacrifice their free time collecting thousands of pieces of evidence, analyzing arguments, and practicing speeches, is to win. Truth thereby suffers in at least two ways. 8

In any debate, neither team is concerned with arriving at a fuller understanding of the topic. The debaters concentrate on "covering" arguments, tying logical knots, and, above all, sounding convincing. Beyond this, though, there exists a tremendous temptation to fabricate and distort evidence. Words are left out, phrases added, sources modified in order to lend credibility to the position. One extremely successful debater on my team used to invent names of magazines which ostensibly printed substantiation for crucial arguments he wanted to use. 9

With respect to this last phenomenon, it is fruitless—and a kind of self-   10
deception, ultimately—to shake our heads and deplore this sort of thing. Similarly, we have no business condemning "overly rough" football players or the
excesses of "overzealous" campaign aides or even, perhaps, violations of the
Geneva Convention in time of war (which is essentially a treatise on How to
Kill Human Beings Without Doing Anything *Really* Unethical). We are engag-
ing in a massive (albeit implicit) exercise of hypocrisy to decry these activities while continuing to condone, and even encourage, the competitive
orientation of which they are only the logical conclusion.

II

The cost of any kind of competition in human terms is incalculable. When   11
my success depends on other people's failure, the prospects for a real human
community are considerably diminished. This consequence speaks to the profoundly antihumanistic quality of competitive activity, and it is abundantly
evident in American society. Moreover, when my success depends on my
being *better than*, I am caught on a treadmill, destined never to enjoy real
satisfaction. Someone is always one step higher, and even the summit is a
precarious position in light of the hordes waiting to occupy it in my stead. I
am thus perpetually insecure and, as psychologist Rollo May points out, perpetually anxious.

> . . . individual competitive success is both the dominant goal in our culture and
> the most pervasive occasion for anxiety . . . [This] anxiety arises out of the
> interpersonal isolation and alienation from others that inheres in a pattern in
> which self-validation depends on triumphing over others (*The Meaning of
> Anxiety*, rev. ed.)

I begin to see my self-worth as conditional—that is to say, my goodness   12
or value becomes contingent on how much better I am than so many others
in so many activities. If you believe, as I do, that unconditional self-esteem is
a singularly important requirement for (and indicator of) mental health, then
the destructiveness of competition will clearly outweigh any putative benefit, whether it be a greater effort at tug-of-war or a higher gross national
product.

From the time we are quite small, the ethic of competitiveness is drummed   13
into us. The goal in school is not to grow as a human being or even, in
practice, to reach a satisfactory level of intellectual competence. We are pushed
instead to become brighter than, quicker than, better achievers than our
classmates, and the endless array of scores and grades lets us know at any
given instant how we stand on that ladder of academic success.

If our schools are failing at their explicit tasks, we may rest assured of   14
their overwhelming success regarding this hidden agenda. We are well-trained
to enter the marketplace and compete frantically for more money, more pres-

tige, more of all the "good things" in life. An economy such as ours, understand, does not merely permit competition: *it demands it.* Ever greater profits becomes the watchword of private enterprise, and an inequitable distribution of wealth (a polite codeword for human suffering) follows naturally from such an arrangement.

Moreover, one must be constantly vigilant lest one's competitors attract   15
more customers or conceive some innovation that gives them the edge. To become outraged at deceptive and unethical business practices is folly; it is the competitiveness of the system that promotes these phenomena. Whenever people are defined as opponents, doing everything possible to triumph must be seen not as an aberration from the structure but as its very consummation. (I recognize, of course, that I have raised a plethora of difficult issues across many disciplines that cry out for a more detailed consideration. I hope, however, to at least have opened up some provocative, and largely neglected, lines of inquiry.)

This orientation finds its way into our personal relationships as well. We   16
bring our yardstick along to judge potential candidates for lover, trying to determine who is most attractive, most intelligent, and . . . the best lover. At the same time, of course, *we* are being similarly reduced to the status of competitor. The human costs are immense.

"Why Sport?", then, is a good question to begin with. It leads us to inquire,   17
"Why Miss Universe contests?" "Why the arms race?" and—dare we say it— "Why capitalism?" Whether a competition-free society can actually be constructed is another issue altogether, and I readily concede that this mentality has so permeated out lives that we find it difficult even to imagine alternatives in many settings. The first step, though, consists in understanding that rivalry of any kind is both psychologically disastrous and philosophically unjustifiable, that the phrase, "healthy competition" is a contradiction in terms. Only then can we begin to develop saner, richer lifestyles for ourselves as individuals, and explore more humanistic possibilities for our society.

QUESTIONS FOR MEANING

1. Why does Kohn believe that competition is "always unhealthy"?
2. Can you explain the reference to the Geneva Convention in paragraph 10?
3. Why does Kohn believe that it is foolish to criticize violence in sports and unethical business activities?
4. Does Kohn offer any alternative to competitive behavior?
5. Vocabulary: impetus (4), proverbial (5), curtailed (7), veracity (8), precarious (11), contingent (12), plethora (15), permeated (17).

QUESTIONS ABOUT STRATEGY

1. Why does Kohn open his essay with a three-paragraph description of children competing at camp? Where else does Kohn draw upon personal experience to support his thesis?

2. In paragraphs 7 and 10, Kohn links competitive sports with warfare. What does this reveal about the purpose of this essay?
3. Does Kohn offer any concessions likely to appeal to people who believe that competition is beneficial?
4. How effective is the conclusion of this essay?

RICHARD W. EGGERMAN
Competition as a Mixed Good

*Richard W. Eggerman is an associate professor of philosophy at Oklahoma State University. He is also a runner who competes in numerous marathons. His interest in running, together with his interest in ethics, led him to respond to Alfie Kohn's argument against competition. The following essay was first published in **1982** by* The Humanist, *the same magazine that had published Kohn's essay two years earlier.*

"Competition by its very nature is always unhealthy. Rivalry of any kind is   1
both psychologically disastrous and philosophically unjustifiable." These claims
made by Alfie Kohn in "Why Competition?" (*The Humanist*, January/February 1980) are too strong to be defensible. Although competition has certain negative features, there are positive aspects which should be noted. Competition is neither an unqualified evil, as Kohn would claim, nor an unqualified good, as a Vince Lombardi would have it. But it is on balance more likely to be a good than an evil.

The competitive person is one who, through his or her actions, indicates a   2
keen concern for succeeding in situations that measure relative worth or excellence in an area. This usually involves attempting to beat another person, although it is possible to speak of persons competing against standards rather than persons. Furthermore, not every attempt at beating another person counts as competition in the sense at issue here. We are interested in assessing the merits of rivalry when the rivalry is more for its own sake than for the sake of some essential good, such as one's life or the lives of loved ones. When two soldiers fight to the death in hand-to-hand combat, there is clearly rivalry, but it would unnecessarily obscure issues to regard this as competition in the same sense that rivalry for its own sake is competition.

It may be unwise to assess in one category competition for children and   3
competition for adults. It is reasonable to suppose that children may be peculiarly liable to dangers of comparisons of relative worth in a way that adults are not, just as it is reasonable to suppose that children should not be exposed to pornography, violence, and so forth. One cannot presume that, if competition is a healthy activity on balance for the normal adult, it will also

be a healthy activity for the child. In order to avoid blurring what may be significantly different categories, I shall restrict this assessment of competition to only adults.

Some claims against competition are valid. It can lead to cheating, whether by tempting one to fabricate sources in the course of a debate or to improve one's lie on the golf course. This does not, of course, show that it must or even usually does lead to cheating, nor does it show that cheating, in the context of sport makes a person more apt to cheat in noncompetitive areas, as in filing an income tax return. Nonetheless, cheating, even when done only occasionally and in the context of a sport, is still morally wrong. If competitive pressure tends to incite people to commit such a wrong, then this is a mark against competition.   4

A particularly insidious aspect of cheating is the tendency of competition to obscure the very wrongness of certain actions as long as everyone is doing them. For instance, dishonest practices in college athletic recruiting have gone on for so long as the result of pressures to win that the ability of the persons involved to recognize the difference between right and wrong seems largely to have withered. It is now perceived by some schools as a part of the game to entice would-be players with cars, female companionship, no-work jobs, and even altered high school transcripts. Cheating when one is aware of the wrongness of it is bad enough, but cheating to such an extent that one's moral sensibilities become anesthetized is surely worse.   5

Some suggest that competition leads one to regard opponents with suspicion and contempt. This happens often enough to be noteworthy. The tactic of "psyching up" by developing an artificial contempt or hatred has been publicized in some notable cases; Muhammed Ali in his earlier years, the "Mad Hungarian" relief pitcher, Al Hrabosky, and tennis stars John MacEnro and Ilie Nastase come immediately to mind. The situation is surely out of hand when the contempt becomes contagious and causes fans also to treat rivals with contempt, leading to incidents of violence. Competition sometimes leads persons to such behavior; whether such attitudes in fact make victory more likely is debatable.   6

Another questionable aspect of competition is its tendency to lead persons to perform under conditions which threaten long-term impairment to their health. "Playing while injured" is seen as meritorious rather than silly. It is an indictment of competition that it could tempt persons to risk permanent disability for the sake of the big game.   7

Closely allied is the phenomenon of using drugs to improve one's performance artificially, whether it be by blocking pain, increasing endurance beyond nature's limits, or increasing aggressiveness. Such chemical stimulation risks long-term injuries, but the pressures of competition cause persons to disregard this.   8

Other claims made against competition are without serious merit. Kohn, for example, suggests that competition is anti-humanistic because in it one person's success depends upon another person's failure. But it is not always true that A's succeeding must involve B's failing. And, even when this is the   9 case, it does not follow that the situation is antihumanistic (if one assumes this word to mean something like "at odds with the development of one's desirable human potential").

In competition, losing should not necessarily be seen as failing. If a runner finishes behind Bill Rogers in the marathon but runs the race twenty minutes faster than he has ever before, one cannot say that he has failed. If a person enters a city tennis tournament and is eliminated in the third round, he cannot be said to have failed if neither he nor anyone else expected him to survive the first round. The point is simple: failure in competition is not to be identified with losing *per se* but rather with performing below reasonable expectations. Only when one could reasonably have expected to win does losing mean failing. In most competition someone wins and someone or many lose, but this does not mean that many (or even *any*) have performed below reasonable expectations and have, therefore, failed.   10

Even when two persons of equal ability, both with strong expectations of winning, are competing in an important contest, it does not follow that the situation is anti-humanistic. In some cases, loss (when seen as failure) may lead to a deterioration of the personality in some important way, but it is flagrantly wrong to imply that it must do so. Psychological studies indicate that competitive persons are apt to be self-assertive, tough-minded, self-sufficient, forthright, emotionally detached, and cheerfully optimistic with an absence of severe mood swings. Failures simply do not lead in a consistent way to deleterious effects upon the psyche of the competitor, for he or she realizes that competition (perhaps unlike real life) will provide him or her with another day and a second chance. Failure will cause short-term disappointment, but only a hedonist of a very simplistic sort would equate short-term disappointment with anti-humanism.   11

Kohn suggests that the competitor is caught on a treadmill, never able to enjoy real satisfaction because there are always others who are, or soon will be, better than he or she. But this also ignores the matter of reasonable expectations. The awareness that others are better is not *per se* a source of dissatisfaction unless the competitor can reasonably expect to be the very best; the awareness that others may become better is surely not a source of dissatisfaction, since no one can reasonably expect to remain the best forever. Such a claim would come closer to being defensible if it were to suggest that competitors seldom enjoy real satisfaction because they seldom are realistic in their expectations. But even this is quite dubious, for competitors, in spite of brief periods of heady and unreasonable expectations, usually do entertain fairly realistic impressions of what they are capable and usually realize that even if they are "the best" they are not going to win all the time.   12

The "agony of defeat" approach to sport may give the opposite impression, but it probably has more to do with television's attempt to hype than with a genuine feature of competition. This is not to suggest that there are no keen disappointments involved in competition but rather that the view of the competitor as *perpetually* insecure or unsatisfied is generally quite fictional.   13

What are the virtues of competition? Frequently persons attempt to defend it by pointing to various good results that allegedly follow from it, such   14 as character building, cooperation, and catharsis of anti-social tendencies. Most psychological studies, however, indicate that these consequentialist approaches to defending competition are doubtful if not simply false.

The virtue of competition is more likely to be intrinsic in character. Competition is enjoyable to most persons who participate in it. This is confirmed by the increasing numbers of persons who participate in city softball, tennis, and golf leagues. Such hedonistic reasons should not be considered alone but should be considered.   15

More importantly, competition offers an opportunity for deep pride to those who move beyond the level of casual involvement. The serious competitor who has worked to master his or her sport feels real accomplishment at what he or she can do. Competitors find that it is the competitive situation which routinely leads them to new levels of performance, often feats they did not know they were capable of. Runners frequently discover that a tough race leads them to performances they never dreamed possible, performances far superior to anything they can push themselves to in training. In such situations, one feels completely invigorated, very much in contrast to much of the humdrum routine of daily life. Perhaps under harsher conditions persons would not feel the pride which is generated from excelling at artificial challenges presented by competition, for the necessities of survival would provide sufficient feelings of accomplishment. But for many persons today the task of providing shelter and food has become too easy to provide feelings of real accomplishment. In the absence of such natural sources of pride, persons seek substitutes, and competition fits the bill excellently.   16

This is not, of course, to suggest that competition is the only way in which one can obtain a sense of pride in accomplishment today, nor that everyone who so competes will receive such benefits. But it is a plausible source, and this recommends it highly. Nor am I claiming that the virtues of competition in this regard should take priority over other activities which have more fundamental claims upon the person. It would be wrong for a person to neglect his children while "fulfilling" himself continuously on the golf course. Competitive rewards are basically self-centered, a fact which places them behind most moral *obligations* in any reasonable ranking of priorities. But they are still valuable, personal rewards—a fact too often overlooked by critics of competition.   17

Do competition's liabilities outweigh its assets, or vice versa? I am inclined to claim that *most* persons who engage in competition benefit from the experience and, further, that, if a minimal amount of consideration were given to the true nature of competitive activity, almost everyone who tried it would benefit. Let us imagine the case of enlightened competitors—persons who take a bit of time to assess what they want from competition and how best to achieve it.   18

Enlightened competitors have reasonable expectations about their performances. They are not frustrated at the mere perception that others are better, as long as they can see themselves as making reasonable improvement. They are not terribly upset by an occasional lapse in performance, for they know that it is unreasonable to expect to play one's best game every time   19 out. They will upon reflection see that cheating is antithetical to their goals of deep pride, rather than a means to it, for cheating vitiates their reward. It destroys the possibility of pride at performing well and thwarts the goal at drawing out maximal levels of performance. With a bit more reflection, they see that playing while injured or drugged is at odds with the most effective pursuit of their goals of maximal long-term development, for victories purchased today at the expense of risking permanent damage are too much of a risk. And, finally, they regard worthy rivals with gratitude and respect, rather than contempt, for they realize that it is only through their pushing themselves to the limit that they discover what those limits are.

The enlightened competitor may seem a rather utopian character, espe- 20
cially against the backdrop of competition as usually witnessed in professional or major college sports. This fact has more to do with the corruption of genuine competition at such levels of sport than with intrinsic problems of competition. When persons perform for a paycheck or scholarship rather than for intrinsic pride and achievement, cheating, intimidation, risk of debilitating injury, and the like may make sense—but only then. The enlightened competitor seems less utopian when one looks at the level of city league play, local tennis and running clubs, and so forth. Persons approaching the enlightened competitor exist in large numbers at this level, where personal monetary gain is not a factor. Their competition is to them a source of pride, without the slightest desire to cheat or hold opponents in contempt.

Competition is a mixed good; it does have its risks. Competition makes 21
some persons anything but enlightened competitors. But critics such as Kohn have painted a far too bleak picture of it. The suspicious, contemptuous, deceitful, and insecure competitor—too often portrayed as typical—is far more the exception than the rule at the level of sport where persons still rival simply for the sake of the rivalry.

QUESTIONS FOR MEANING

1. According to Eggerman, what is the distinction between "rivalry" and "competition"? What is the difference between "losing" and "failing"?
2. Why does Eggerman restrict his essay to discussing the effects of competition on adults?
3. What does Eggerman mean by "anti-humanistic"?
4. In what sense is competition "artificial"? For what type of challenge is it a substitute?
5. Vocabulary: fabricate (4), insidious (5), anesthetized (5), impairment (7), deleterious (11), hedonist (11), intrinsic (15).

QUESTIONS ABOUT STRATEGY

1. In responding to Alfie Kohn's essay, Eggerman uses both quotation and paraphrase. Do these references convey a fair sense of Kohn's argument as a whole?

2. Why does Eggerman discuss the negative effects of competition before discussing beneficial effects? How does this strategy reflect his point of view?

3. How convincing are the "psychological studies" that are cited in paragraphs 11 and 14?

4. Where does Eggerman summarize the way in which competition should be approached?

JENNIFER RING

Perfection on the Wing

Jennifer Ring received her doctorate from the University of California at Berkeley in 1979 and now teaches political theory at Stanford and the University of California, Davis. The following selection is adapted from a longer essay on women and competitive sports which Ring contributed to an anthology published in **1987,** Competition: A Feminist Taboo?

I don't compete in athletics. I have never entered a running race or a   1
bicycle race. I have participated in sailboat races, but always as crew, never as skipper, and not even the sailboard I bought has tempted me to try my skills against another sailor. This is not very odd. My life's work is scholarly, not athletic. I don't seem to have much trouble competing in academic life, although I haven't had occasion to analyze that corner of my soul. But my athletic life is a puzzle to me. There would be no reason for my concern and curiosity were it not for the fact that in my own eyes—and I am sure that any random sampling of friends and acquaintances would agree—I am one of the most competitive people I know, and have one of the most obsessive athletic spirits as well. The two simply do not seem to come together at the same time for me.

My interest in sports was a source of joy and embarrassment to me when   2
I was growing up. The sexual conventions of the 1950s and 1960s were enough to crush the exuberance of any athletic girl, to saddle her with the patronizing title of tomboy, and to make her apologetic rather than proud of strength, speed, and aggressiveness. I was as obsessed as any boy with baseball, but I had to cultivate elaborate fantasies of a girls' Little League being organized by the time I would turn nine and be old enough to play in it. I was pretty good in pick-up street games: a slugger who could also pitch. But by the time I entered junior high school it was difficult to find other girls interested in playing baseball, and nobody thought my continued interest in the sport was a good thing.

The next time the athlete in me emerged, I found myself swimming laps   3
for short distances while an undergraduate at UCLA. Early in my graduate
career at Berkeley my daily swim had lengthened to a mile or more, and I
was feeling waterlogged, began running at the track to dry out, and the distance grew each year. By the time I started work on my doctoral dissertation,
I was running the toughest trails in the Berkeley hills. The sweeping pano-
rama of San Francisco Bay took my mind off my lungs and legs, although on
my favorite run there was no avoiding "the connector," a stretch straight up
the side of a hill connecting the steepest segments of the trail. As my dissertation progressed, my distances grew. During the last year of work I ran the
entire trail several times a week, with shorter runs on my "easy" days. During
the last few months, I couldn't live with myself whenever I had to walk up
part of the connector.

My compulsion for distance has abated somewhat since then. But still, if a   4
day passes without a workout that has left me drenched in sweat and groping
for energy for an hour or so afterward, I spend the evening distracted by
nervous energy and a hair-trigger temper. I have expanded the activities that
fulfill my need for a daily dose of pain and exhaustion to include weight
lifting, and reintroduced an occasional swim. I became interested in wind-
surfing because it looked like it might provide me with a *relaxing* occasional
substitute for the usual daily exercise grind. But it turned out to be more
"my" type of sport than I had imagined. The winds increase with each month
of summer in the San Francisco Bay, and the challenge is now to stay with
the 20- to 25-knot blows of August as they threaten to wrench the sail out
of my hands and launch me into the chilly water. I come home aching, exhausted and exhilarated (and wet), and spend the following morning working
out with weights to strengthen my upper body, determined to last longer the
next time out. Addiction to tests of physical endurance has become a way of
life, and still I don't compete. I can't say that my competitive spirit has actually broken somewhere along the line, but, as often happens with thwarted
aggressive energy, it has turned inward.

I am tempted to think of this as a woman's problem. But it also reflects an   5
aspect of life in the United States that, while perhaps more characteristic of
the way women must live, is not confined to feminine experience. There exists a group of men and women who are reluctant to acknowledge the role
played by competition in their lives. Those engaged in the genteel occupations of the middle class—academia, the arts, the professions—are likely to
downplay the mandate to compete and win. The tendency is to renounce the
crude desire to better one's opponents, to speak rather, of a community of
peers, of "colleagues" rather than "rivals," denying the embarrassing ambition
and competitiveness required to become a member of the "team" in the first
place. The needs of this elite class parallel those of the competitive woman
who has been taught that it is unbecoming to lust after overt victory and has
been discouraged from pitting her strength against rivals. Members of this
class strive for personal excellence, often regarding themselves as exceptional in one way or another. But they are reluctant to admit that their su-

periority comes at the price of victory over their peers. They experience the full force of the contradiction between the clashing U.S. ideals of liberty and equality. This is not an entirely new phenomenon,[1] but it has characterized a segment of life in the United States since the early 1970s. This happens to coincide with efforts during the late 1960s to understand "manhood" as not necessarily warlike. And of course it coincides with the emergence of the contemporary women's movement.

Endurance sports—long-distance running, marathons, triathlons[2]—which have so recently emerged seem to serve the needs of women and "new men" to compete athletically, but not in the traditional ways. Many women are competing in athletics for the first time through long-distance running and other endurance sports. Such competition is a solitary business. Even in a race, competitors provide as much comfort as challenge, lend as much energy as they take, serve as excuses to fire up the real competition, the one with oneself. The actual victories are subtle and momentary: seconds or minutes off previous personal records, which are soon accepted as complacently as if they had always been possible. Best times are rapidly converted into challenges for the future. Or—Spartan voluptuousness—pleasure is taken in each newly displayed definition of muscle, as the body hardens beyond what had previously been accepted as hard. As these achievements are absorbed into what endurance athletes come to expect of themselves, they need something more to bring the next rush of pride. Long-distance runners exemplify the restlessness of this competitive spirit. In their striving for elusive perfection, a humble two or three miles a day grow to five or six, to an obsession with eight, ten, and fifteen—and the rest of life becomes subordinated to the demands of so much daily energy expenditure. When the switch is made from running to racing, one would think that the concrete results of the race would satisfy the need for acknowledgment of excellence. But they don't necessarily, and the challenges continue: to finish well in shorter distances, to move on to marathons. Eventually, even several marathons a year can be taken in stride, and it is apparent once again that there is no victory against others that can finally satisfy, because there is no final victory over the self.   6

It is the educated middle class that seems to find these obsessive physical tests most compelling.[3] They often describe the pleasures of endurance sports in terms of getting "high" on the discipline of workouts, on oxygen, on scenery, and on solitude. But pushing one's physical limits to the point of thorough collapse, driving away all but pure physical sensation, the sweet opium of complete exhaustion, seems to fill a more profound need than the one created by boredom, or than the search for a new high. Addiction to oxygen depletion signifies a deeper yearning in the souls of those who crave it.   7

Could this be a new vision of competition in the United States, one that, precisely because it is private rather than openly aggressive, is more acceptable for women? Perhaps it's a new form of masochism, a tendency that has been regarded as peculiarly feminine, at least since the time Freud suggested it.[4] Or is it simply an avoidance of the overt competition from which women have been discouraged for so long? Team sports is one way boys in the United   8

States are taught about democratic participation. Perhaps girls also need experience on teams so that women will not be bereft of a certain sort of effectiveness in U.S. life. Excelling in individual sports may circumvent access to the social, economic, and political skills which call for teamwork. Do women have to learn to compete in the traditional ways before they can have the luxury of withdrawing?

There are aspects of endurance sports that harken back to early U.S. history, to the necessity for hardness and independence faced by the settlers of the North American continent. Feminist historians refer to the tests of physical bravery and endurance experienced by pioneer women. From an 1838 diary: "We had some frightful places to pass. . . . We passed along the steep sides of mountains where every step the loose earth slid from beneath our horses' feet. . . . My horse fell and tumbled me over his head. Did not hurt me. . . . Left the campground half past four in the morning after a sleepless night with a toothache."[5] It may be that this ideal of hardened independence has been lost in the United States, replaced by a corporate ideal for which team sports provides a better metaphor.[6] Perhaps the emergence of endurance sports evokes a nostalgia for the rugged individualism of frontier America, which is missed most poignantly by middle-class corporate men and by women who were discouraged from ruggedness as soon as men became urbanized. The attraction these sports hold for women gives the appearance of picking up their history where it left off, before the comforts of urban life could impose a feminine ideal that was soft and dependent. The "new men" attracted to endurance sports might also be striving for a lost ideal of toughness, a genuine strength that does not rely on a dependent woman for verification, or on the destruction of a rival or an enemy for a sense of self-worth.

The recent prominence of endurance sports may also tacitly acknowledge that the mandate to succeed in this country is impossible to fulfill. Success is the imperative, sure enough, but it is so ill-defined that no one can ever be confident that it is securely within his or her grasp. Whoever "succeeds" in the United States often makes more enemies than friends, and faces the prospect of continually fighting off the next comer and of deciding that that particular success was not sufficient protection against mediocrity anyway. The next comer emerges, after all, from within. And nothing disintegrates more quickly than satisfaction with one's own achievements.[7] Perhaps it is best to acknowledge that the only possible victory is private, psychological, a victory over the self. The hardest part of such an admission is relinquishing clear-cut victory for anybody. But the promise is a sense of community *within* the competition. Striving for excellence without having to destroy a field of competitors seems a worthy vision for athletes and citizens in the United States, an effort to embrace freedom and equality at one and the same time.

Notes

1. As early as the 1830s, visitors to the new American democracy observed its citizens driving themselves beyond anything Europeans had ever witnessed. Instead of the old European class

structure defining limits to what was possible in life, the United States was already manifesting symptoms of endurance addiction, signs of things to come. Alexis de Tocqueville, the French aristocrat who visited this country in 1831 and wrote a book describing "Democracy in America," noted: "In proportion as castes disappear and the classes of society approximate, . . . the image of ideal perfection, forever on the wing, presents itself to the human mind." Americans, he wrote, displayed a "strange unrest . . . as old as the world; the novelty is to see a whole people furnish an exemplification of it." Americans were "forever brooding over advantages they do not possess. It is strange to see with what feverish ardor the Americans pursue their own welfare; and to watch the vague dread that constantly torments them." *Democracy in America* (New York: Vintage, 1945), vol. 2, 144.

2. The triathlon is a race that combines long-distance swimming, 100-plus miles of bicycle riding, and a marathon in a single day. Best times for the entire event average about nine hours.

3. The average age of triathletes is thirty; 65 percent are college graduates; and their average annual income is $32,000, according to *Tri-Athlete* 1, no. 1 (May 1983).

4. See Sigmund Freud, "Femininity," in *New Introductory Lectures on Psychoanalysis,* ed. James Strachey (New York: Norton, 1964; originally published in 1933): "The suppression of women's aggressiveness which is prescribed for them constitutionally and imposed on them socially favors the development of powerful masochistic impulses, which succeed, as we know, in binding erotically the destructive trends which have been diverted inwards. Thus masochism, as people say, is truly feminine" (p. 102).

5. Diary of Mary Richardson Walker, June 10 to December 21, 1838, quoted in Eleanor Flexner, *Century of Struggle, The Women's Rights Movement in the United States* (Cambridge: Harvard Belknap, 1975), 159.

6. Barbara Ehrenreich, in *The Hearts of Men* (New York: Anchor Doubleday, 1983), discusses the pressure for men in the 1950s to conform to the standards of corporate capitalism, and the consequent rage that was directed onto a "safe" target—women. Not until the 1960s did men begin to question both the definition of aggressive, competitive manhood that had grown out of American history, and its contradiction as manifested in "gray flannel" conformity.

7. For a fuller commentary on this phenomenon as a theme of life in the United States, see Richard Sennett and Jonathan Cobb, *The Hidden Injuries of Class* (New York: Vintage, 1973). The relationship between celebrity and U.S. class structure—the American abhorrence of mediocrity represented by anonymity—was actually remarked upon by John Adams, as early as 1791, in his *Discourses on Davila.*

QUESTIONS FOR MEANING

1. Ring opens her essay by claiming that she doesn't compete in athletics. What does she mean by this? Is there another sense in which she does compete?

2. What does Ring mean when she writes of "the contradiction between the clashing U.S. ideals of liberty and equality"?

3. What does Ring mean by "new men" in paragraph 6?

4. In what sense can physical exhaustion be an "opium"?

5. What sociological factors might explain the popularity of endurance sports in recent years?

6. Vocabulary: patronizing (2), complacently (6), voluptuousness (6), masochism (8), bereft (8), verification (9), imperative (10).

QUESTIONS ABOUT STRATEGY

1. How does Ring's personal experience support the thesis of this essay? At what point does she move beyond the narration of this experience, and why was it useful to do so?
2. Where does Ring link competition to gender? What does this reveal about the audience for which this essay was originally written?
3. What is the quotation from a pioneer diary in paragraph 9 meant to illustrate?

VERA J. ELLESON
Is Competition a Cultural Imperative?

Although some writers believe that the urge to compete is inborn and instinctive, others believe that it is a learned type of behavior that is acquired through training and environment. As the title of her essay suggests, Vera J. Elleson is concerned with the extent to which American culture fosters competition. The following essay is a condensation by Education Digest *of a **1983** study Elleson published in* The Personnel and Guidance Journal *while she was completing her doctorate at the University of Missouri.*

There is a prevailing mode of competition in American culture—a general   1 tendency to view and judge self and others in terms of a hierarchical structure of bad to good and low value to high worth. The American way of life presupposes climbing the ladder to success, often, unfortunately, by pulling or pushing others down and trampling on the bodies or psyches of those one wishes to surpass.

Competitive strivings appear early in life as children vie to establish their   2 places within the family unit and to assure themselves of an adequate supply of parental love, space, and possessions. The evidence of an emphasis on competitiveness as the predominant mode of behavior in our society is overwhelming. Western industrialization set the stage, and urbanization provided the impetus for competition to spread throughout the land and also for it to permeate the disparate areas of education, social life, industry, athletics, and scientific research.

The field of education is of particular interest because it is where the   3 citizens of any nation are trained for the roles they will assume in adult life. Despite a general consensus that competition is the best way to get children to work, research indicates that competitive incentives lead to better performance only for boring tasks. (My personal experience as a school counselor and as a student confirms the view that many teachers are capable of minimizing the repetitive tasks and providing an atmosphere free of monotony.)

The detrimental effects of poorly managed competition are numerous and   4
serious. They range from school children who withdraw from learning, to athletes who cheat, to workers who neglect to develop their career skills fully and neglect to attend to their families. Human beings and institutions are separated by denominationalism, deception, and lack of trust. Mental and physical health suffer. Personal security and creativity diminish, and general sharing, caring, and friendliness are stifled.

The prevailing mode of competition in American culture thus continues   5
despite convincing evidence that it is damaging to physical, spiritual, emotional, and social health. And what is the reaction of members of the helping professions? Are they creative agents of cultural change or are they dispensers of bandages to the injured and facilitators of adjustment to "the way things are?"

Making a Difference

We can have an impact—on the setting in which we work, our friends,   6
family, co-workers, and profession. Each of us must begin with ourselves. Most of us have been acculturated to a competitive mode of behavior. We must recognize how we view and interact with others. It is time now to change what is not positive and growth-enhancing.

Each of us should pause and ask, "Do I put others down or fail to support   7
others in my attempt to get ahead? Do my competitive strivings interfere with my own emotional well-being, with the development of trust between me and others, and with my personal or professional effectiveness?" How often do educators motivate students by setting them against each other in a vicious struggle for a position at the top? Or do they work cooperatively with students, each learning from and teaching the other?

Work environments are influenced by the people who occupy them. One   8
can question the value of a competitive atmosphere. One can suggest, encourage, and model cooperation in committee work, organizational planning, and the performance of everyday activities and tasks. Cooperative support for peers is little seen but long remembered as we move slowly through our professional lives.

Clients are influenced by the values of their counselors. It is important to   9
help clients recognize the dangers of unhealthy management of competition. Some clients value a cooperative, educational work and family atmosphere but may not recognize this as the source of their discontent or realize that they can make choices in this regard. It is the function of counseling not to discourage or encourage particular choices but rather to facilitate a free and open process of decision making.

Competition, although perhaps a part of normal development, is dispro-   10
portionately reinforced in American culture. Members of the helping profes-

sions have a responsibility to create and protect environments in which the needs of people take precedence over the concern for things. Each person can have an impact. The efforts of single persons, like the ripples from a stone cast into a pond, can combine with the efforts of counselors and others across the land to create a wave of energy that will be a force for health and growth.

QUESTIONS FOR MEANING

1. When and why do competitive feelings first appear?
2. What harmful effects of competition are cited by Elleson?
3. What does Elleson mean by "the helping professions"? Is her advice relevant to other professions as well?
4. According to Elleson, what is the proper function of counseling?
5. Vocabulary: hierarchical (1), impetus (2), permeate (2), disparate (2), detrimental (4), denominationalism (4), acculturated (6), facilitate (9).

QUESTIONS ABOUT STRATEGY

1. Does Elleson make any unsupported generalizations?
2. This essay was originally written for a journal read by guidance counselors. Is competition an appropriate topic for this audience? What changes would Elleson need to make if she wanted to revise her essay for a general audience?
3. Why does Elleson conclude her essay by insisting that individuals can make a difference?

HARVEY L. RUBEN
Dealing with Success

*Failure is obviously one of the risks of competition, but winning can also cause problems. Successful competitors may find themselves cut off from former friends and associates; they may also become the target other competitors now aim for. The risk of becoming a "sore winner" is the topic of the following selection by Harvey L. Ruben, M.D. It is taken from his **1980** book,* Competing.

It's a recognized fact that celebrities have a higher rate of emotional problems (including suicidal tendencies) than the population at large. Celebrity status—which in our culture represents the pinnacle of success—seems to bring with it a host of traumas from which the rest of the population, moderately or not at all successful, does not suffer. 1

Why should this be so? Why should precisely those people who have reached the top of their professions be among the most prone to self-destructive involvement in drugs and alcohol? Why should they be among those who are most attracted to suicide as a way of dealing with their problems? 2

According to the Horatio Alger myth, if you work hard and have good luck along the way, you will triumph over early adversities, beat out your rivals for any position you want, and attain the position most valued in our society: that of the unqualified Success. In fact, attaining success, unqualified or otherwise, is seldom as straightforward as this. I have treated numerous patients, many of them enjoying the finest fruits of official success, who would attest to the fact that "making it" is anything but a free trip to Paradise. 3

Inherent in the very notion of success is the fact that you have beaten out others in the race—and that fact often proves to be the psychological undoing of many a highly successful competitor. Many a winner is burdened by considerable guilt for having won out over rivals; this feeling can diminish pleasure in one's own victory. 4

To put it another way, the person who has succeeded well in a competitive effort is bound to have elicited, at some step along the way, the envy and resentment of those in the race who have not succeeded as well. This seems an inevitable consequence of human interaction: those on high, whatever their purity of motives or the honesty of their competitive designs, are sure to be envied by those who have fallen by the wayside. 5

This has a deep and not altogether salutary effect on the psychologies of both the victors and the vanquished. The losers (or at least the sore losers) very often indulge in escapist rationalizations to explain why they have been beaten, and at the same time focus a great deal of their resentment on those they see as responsible for their defeat. The victors, on the other hand, have to contend with the fact that, although they have carried away the laurels, they have in the process lost the camaraderie, the pre-competition friend- 6 ships which they had hitherto enjoyed. They are no longer "one of the gang," striving for a common goal; they have become Number One, and have therefore become automatically isolated from the field in which, a short time ago, they found their most sympathetic allies.

Military people speak frequently about "the loneliness of command." The phrase is applicable as well to many nonmilitary situations, in which one person finds himself or herself suddenly raised above those who until then have been peers. A common result of being catapulted abruptly to a position of eminence is a feeling of isolation, a conviction that those who were recently your friends have somehow, overnight, become your opponents.   7

Highly successful competitors, for this reason, are seldom able to trust those with whom they have established long competitive contacts. Like the gunfighter in the Old West, the top dog in any competitive venture is always the standard against which the other competitors must measure their own efforts; this means that it is nearly impossible for them to relate to Number One in the same way they relate to those who have not achieved such eminence. The person on top, for his part, frequently is in the painful position of experiencing his old friends as jealous of his new power, as conspiring to unseat him, of biding their time until he makes a mistake that will give one of them a shot at the top post. His vision of his former friends as conspirators against him, moreover, is often not merely a paranoid delusion: the person at the top has good reason to suppose that he or she is the target of competitive attacks on his authority, since competition in human affairs never ceases.   8

The effect of this on the successful competitor's personal life is often severe. Such a person will often experience difficulty in forming close attachments; even when he does manage to do so, he may still feel wary of really opening up to his friends, for fear that underneath their affable exteriors they too are out to unseat him.   9

Simply because you might become successful and then be the target of envy for your peers does not mean you should refuse ever to compete. What you should do, though, is to assess sensibly what you want out of success, and what price you are willing to pay to get it. This goes back to what I said earlier about needing to weigh the costs and the benefits of competition; remembering this whenever you enter a competitive situation may help you avoid some of the more egregious hazards of getting to the top of the heap. Forgetting it may mean that you turn into someone who can never be satisfied with any single victory: someone who, like the gunfighter constantly looking over his shoulder, must be ever prepared to counter another attack, ever ready to doubt a friend, to withdraw into isolation in the mistaken belief that "Winning is All."   10

For the person who is as nervous about holding on to his victory as the sore loser is about disguising his defeat, winning can become a kind of millstone around the neck rather than the amulet he or she hoped it would be. Balance is needed, then, in winning and losing alike; it may be less socially acceptable to be a sore loser, but psychologically it's no less painful to be a "sore winner."   11

QUESTIONS FOR MEANING

1. What does Ruben mean by "the Horatio Alger myth"? Where does this myth come from?
2. How can successful competition eventually lead to isolation?
3. Does Reuben believe competition should be avoided?
4. According to this essay, how can we try to avoid the ill feelings that competition can produce?
5. Vocabulary: pinnacle (1), attest (3), elicited (5), salutary (6), camaraderie (6), eminence (7), paranoid (8), egregious (10), amulet (11).

QUESTIONS ABOUT STRATEGY

1. Ruben claims that it is "a recognized fact that celebrities have a higher rate of emotional problems (including suicidal tendencies) than the population at large." Was he right to assume that this claim could stand alone, or should he have provided evidence to support it?
2. Consider the analogy Ruben makes between successful competitors and "the gun fighter in the Old West." What does this comparison imply about the nature of competition? Does this implication support Ruben's thesis?
3. Paragraph 2 consists entirely of questions. Is this a useful way of beginning an essay? Does Ruben answer the questions he has raised?

ONE STUDENT'S ASSIGNMENT

Write an argument for or against competition that will draw primarily upon your own personal experience. You might focus your essay on the effects of either competitive sports or academic competition for high grades. If you include any material from sources besides your personal experience, use oen of the documentation styles favored by the Council of Biology Editors.

Competition: An Abused Privilege
Tim Paetsch

Competition is a privilege. Although it does not guarantee   1
triumph, it enables us to define personal goals and to pursue
them, which is better than simply living from day to day.
Even when we encounter failure, competition can be exciting
and enjoyable. Therefore, we must view the basic principles
of competition as beneficial. Unfortunately, this privilege
is often abused. When winning is an obsession rather than a
goal, competition becomes an event filled with anxiety in—
stead of pleasure. This can be seen often in high school

sports--more often than we would like to believe. Many parents and coaches are putting too much pressure on young athletes, leading them to put even more pressure on themselves
until they burn out.

Sports like wrestling are particularly vulnerable to the   2
burnout dilemma because participants have no teammates to
blend in with and help them accept defeat. When a wrestler
screws up, all of the criticism and ridicule is directed at
him alone.

I started to wrestle in fourth grade and enjoyed the sport   3
for several years, but I eventually witnessed many cases of
burnout. A wrestler in my home town had great success as a
youngster, but in high school the coaches expected too much
from him, causing him to quit the sport after his sophomore
year. As seniors, two top-notch wrestlers didn't join their
defending state champion team because "it's not worth it
anymore." And Mark Schwab, a two-time Junior National Champion, nearly became a full-time beach bum because he was sick
of wrestling.

Eventually, I also fell victim to burnout. Before entering   4
high school I won several state titles and two regional national titles. I competed almost anonymously, with little
coaching. When I became a high school wrestler, everything
seemed to change. I had full-time coaches and fans with high
expectations. I now had to perform in front of crowds of people who all knew me. If I lost, the day after the match,
classmates would ask me, "What happened? How did you lose?"
This led me to worry: "I can't screw up anymore, or else I'll
have to keep answering to everyone in school." Eventually I
began to avoid people whenever possible because I knew the
topic of wrestling would immediately pop up. After high
school I was so sick of the sport that I hung up my wrestling
shoes and vowed never to wrestle again.

It's sad when pressure causes young athletes to relinquish   5
all of the benefits of competition. What can be done to make
athletic competition the enjoyable experience that it
should be in high school?

First, coaches should make training seem less monotonous.   6
Training is a necessity in most sports, and it needs to be
vigorous, but the usually loathed conditioning exercises
are much more tolerable if coaches vary workouts. For example, rather than always sending the whole team out for a
five mile run, a coach could break the team into partners or

small groups and have continuous relay races with various
exercises and drills. To provide incentive for the whole
team, he could exempt them from some other exercises if
everybody finishes in a given amount of time.

Second, we must help competitors realize that an opponent   7
is not an enemy. One high school coach told me not to talk to
any of my opponents because it would keep them uncertain of
me and make them nervous. In other words, it would "psych
them out." In actuality, I became just as nervous as my opponent. I was as uncertain of him as he was of me, and he seemed
as inhuman as I. When I used to wrestle in kids tournaments, I
would find my opponent and talk to him before the match. Both
of us were less nervous, making it easier for us to wrestle up
to our ability. After the match we would go to the concession
stand, have a couple of sodas, and there were no hard feelings. I see no reason why high school athletes couldn't do
the same.

Third, we must limit the involvement of coaches at an ac-   8
tual competitive event. I realize that the coach is essential during the performance for some team sports, but in many
cases he becomes overinvolved. Coaches often bark out so
many instructions at an athlete that it only confuses and
frustrates him. If a young athlete has not learned something
in practice, he certainly cannot be expected to learn and execute it in a matter of seconds in the midst of competition.

Involvement of parents and friends also needs reform in   9
some cases. Parents often see their kids as extensions of
themselves competing, causing them to sometimes behave outrageously, belittling and embarrassing young competitors (1).
Parents need to back off and let athletes compete for their
own benefit. If you are a friend of an athlete, don't show over
concern when he or she loses or makes a mistake. The athlete
would rather learn from the mistake and move on than have a
sympathetic friend dwell upon a failure.

Finally, we must prevent competitors from putting too much   10
pressure on themselves. Having goals and striving for them
is beneficial, but when a person cannot fall asleep at night
or vomits because he is so nervous about how he will perform,
then there is a definite problem. Not only is the sport no
longer enjoyable, but performance is usually jeopardized.
As Ross Wetzsteon pointed out in "The Winner Instinct," the
actual pursuit of a goal is usually more exciting and rewarding than its realization (2). Why ruin the process by turning

athletes into nauseated insomniacs? Coaches, parents, and
competitors must work together to prevent pressure from
building up so that athletes can enjoy pursuing their goals
even if they don't always achieve them.

References*

(1) Martin, K. 1986. Is winning everything? Pages 328–331 in
     R. K. Miller, The informed argument. Harcourt Brace
     Jovanovich, San Diego.
(2) Wetzsteon, R. 1984. The winner instinct. Pages 325–327
     in R. K. Miller, The informed argument. Harcourt Brace
     Jovanovich, San Diego.

SUGGESTIONS FOR WRITING

1. Drawing upon your own experience as well as the essay by Katherine Martin, write an essay for or against encouraging children to compete in sports.
2. To what extent is competition useful in the classroom? Write an argument for or against encouraging academic competition among high school students.
3. Compare the essays by Kohn and Eggerman and determine which is stronger.
4. Write an argument on the positive and/or negative effects of competition among college students.
5. If you believe that competition can be good or bad depending on the situation, write an essay designed to establish the nature of healthy competition.
6. Do an informal survey among your friends and neighbors to determine how the people you know view competition. Try to speak to an equal number of men and women. Drawing upon your survey, write an essay that will support or challenge the claim that men are more competitive than women.

*This essay illustrates how numbered references can be used within an essay if they correspond correctly with the right source within the reference list at the end of the paper. Unlike numbered footnotes, in which the same number is never repeated within a single paper, numbered references allow for repeating the same number whenever the same source is cited. Thus, if Tim had wished to cite Martin's essay as support for another point he wanted to make, (1) would have appeared a second time within the text. The use of numbered references is limited mainly to scientific and technical writing, and their form can vary. Tim's reference list follows one of the forms recognized by the Council of Biology Editors in *CBE Style Manual: A Guide for Authors, Editors, and Publishers in the Biological Sciences.* You should note, however, that the *CBE Manual* emphasizes that documentation styles vary from one journal to another, and writers planning to publish within a specific journal should follow the form that is used by that journal. If you would like to examine an extended example of a numbered system used in a scientific article, consult any issue of *Science,* a highly respected journal found in most libraries [editor's note].

Higher Education: What's the Point?

LYNNE V. CHENEY

Students of Success

Lynne V. Cheney has a Ph.D. in English from the University of Wisconsin. The author of two novels, she has taught English at George Washington University and the University of Wyoming. More recently, she has served as Chairman of the National Endowment for the Humanities. Her belief in the importance of the humanities is apparent in the following essay, first published in Newsweek *in 1986.*

Not long ago, my college-age daughter read about a software genius who   1
became a multimillionaire before he was 30. "That does it," she said, "I'm
going into computers."

This daughter, who has never met a political science course she didn't like,   2
was only joking. But a study conducted by the Carnegie Foundation shows
that many young people do think seriously along these lines. Instead of choosing
college majors—and careers—according to their interests, they are channel-
ing themselves into fields that promise to be profitable: business, engineering,
computer science, allied health programs.

Given the high cost of a college education, this trend is not surprising. A   3
bachelor's degree now costs $40,000 at an average independent college. Can
we expect students to major in the liberal arts when their starting salaries
will be significantly lower than they are for business and professional majors?
Shouldn't they get the best possible return on their investment?

They should, but I would suggest that there are better ways to calculate   4
profit and loss than by looking at starting salaries. Consider, first of all, that
very few people stay in the same line of work over a lifetime. They switch
jobs, even change professions, and what is crucial for advancement is not
specialized training but the ability to think critically and judge wisely. Given
the difficulty of predicting which skills will be in demand even five years from
now, let alone over a lifetime, a student's best career preparation is one that

emphasizes general understanding and intellectual curiosity: a knowledge of how to learn and the desire to do it. Literature, history, philosophy and the social sciences—majors that students avoid today—are the ones traditionally believed to develop such habits of mind.

I recently conducted an informal survey of successful Americans, and while 5
several dozen phone calls aren't proof of the value of a liberal-arts major, the results are suggestive. The communications world, for example, is dominated by liberal-arts majors. Thomas H. Wyman, chairman of CBS, majored in English, as did Cathleen Black, publisher of USA Today. Washington Post columnist William Raspberry studied history; NBC News anchorman Tom Brokaw, political science.

In public life, too, leaders more often than not were students of the liberal 6
arts. They form a majority in the president's cabinet. Secretary of State George Shultz and Secretary of Energy John Herrington majored in economics. Interior Secretary Donald Hodel majored in government, and Transportation Secretary Elizabeth Dole, political science. Secretary of the Treasury James Baker read history with a minor in classics; Secretary of Education William Bennett studied philosophy.

The president himself majored in economics and sociology. His commu- 7
nications director, Pat Buchanan, majored in English and philosophy. White House chief of staff (and former treasury secretary) Donald Regan was an English major and before he came to government had a remarkably success- ful business career as the head of Merrill Lynch. Secretary of Commerce Malcolm Baldrige headed Scovill Manufacturing, and now the former English major is leading a campaign for clear writing in government.

Executives like Regan and Baldrige are not unusual. According to a recent 8
report in Fortune magazine, 38 percent of today's CEO's majored in the lib- eral arts, and a close reading of The New York Times shows that 9 of the top 13 executives at IBM are liberal-arts majors. At AT&T, a study showed social- science and humanities graduates moving into middle management faster than engineers and doing at least as well as their business and engineering coun- terparts in reaching top management levels.

For several years now, corporate executives have extolled the wide range 9
of knowledge and interests that a study of the liberal arts encourages. And now under Tom Wyman's direction, CBS has funded an organization that investigates exactly why it is that liberal-arts training is valuable to the Amer- ican corporation. "In an increasingly competitive, internationally oriented and technologically innovative society," Wyman recently wrote, "successful exec- utives will be those who can understand—and interpret—complex relation- ships and who are capable of continually reconsidering assumptions underlying old operating practices."

In the past, such top-level views did not always filter down to where entry- 10
level hiring is done. But reports from that front are encouraging. A study by Northwestern University shows that many major companies plan to increase their hiring of liberal-arts graduates by some 20 percent in 1986. Or as one

employer recently told "Today" show viewers, "Those that are involved in recruiting people to the company are looking for . . . broader skills . . . Then we will worry about teaching them terminology, specifics of the jobs."

I don't mean to argue that liberal arts is the only road to success. The average starting salary for engineers remains impressively high, almost $30,000 compared to $21,000 for a liberal-arts graduate. In fact, my informal survey also shows that engineers are doing well in a variety of fields. Chrysler chairman Lee Iacocca was an engineering major, as was former Delaware Gov. Pete du Pont. My point is that there are many paths to success and students shouldn't force themselves down any single one if their true interests lie elsewhere. College should be a time for intellectual enthusiasm, for trying to read one's way through the library, for heated debate with those who see the world differently. College should be a time for learning to enjoy the life of the mind rather than for learning to tolerate what one doesn't find interesting. 11

Students who follow their hearts in choosing majors will most likely end up laboring at what they love. They're the ones who will put in the long hours and intense effort that achievement requires. And they're the ones who will find the sense of purpose that underlies most human happiness. 12

QUESTIONS FOR MEANING

1. What explanation does Cheney provide for student interest in fields that are likely to be profitable?
2. According to Cheney, what is the best type of career preparation and why does she believe this is so?
3. What disadvantages might a student who has majored in one of the liberal arts encounter when seeking an entry-level position?
4. What is the thesis of this essay, and in what paragraph does it occur?
5. What does Cheney mean by "the life of the mind"? Can the mind have a life independent of the body? If so, how can this life be nourished?
6. Does Cheney believe that students should be compelled to study the liberal arts?
7. Vocabulary: software (1), suggestive (5), extolled (9), innovative (9), terminology (10).

QUESTIONS ABOUT STRATEGY

1. How effective are the examples Cheney cites as the result of her "informal survey"? Why was it important for Cheney to cite examples from business as well as government?

2. Why does Cheney begin her argument with an anecdote about her college-age daughter? Is this a good opening for the essay that follows?
3. Does Cheney make any concessions which show that she understands why students may choose majors in fields such as business and engineering? Is she unfair, in any way, to students who make such career choices?

NORMAN COUSINS

How to Make People Smaller Than They Are

For more than thirty years, Norman Cousins was one of the most influential editors in this country. After working as an editor for the New York Evening Post *and* Current History, *Cousins joined the* Saturday Review *in 1940. It is with this magazine that he is most readily identified. As executive editor of the* Review *from 1942 to 1971, and again from 1975 to 1978, Cousins was in a position to champion numerous liberal causes, including the importance of education. Almost paralyzed with a serious disease in the mid-1960s, Cousins was given only a few months to live, but he fought his way back to health through a remarkable effort of will, which he describes in one of his best known books,* Anatomy of an Illness as Perceived by the Patient: Reflections on Healing and Regeneration *(1979). In his long career, Cousins has been awarded nearly fifty honorary doctorates. He is now Professor of Medical Humanities at UCLA. Cousins has been a strong advocate of culture, as can be seen in the following* **1978** *essay, one of his last columns as editor of the* Saturday Review.

Three months ago in this space we wrote about the costly retreat from   1
the humanities on all the levels of American education. Since that time, we
have had occasion to visit a number of campuses and have been troubled to
find that the general situation is even more serious than we had thought. It
has become apparent to us that one of the biggest problems confronting
American education today is the increasing vocationalization of our colleges
and universities. Throughout the country, schools are under pressure to become job-training centers and employment agencies.

The pressure comes mainly from two sources. One is the growing deter-   2
mination of many citizens to reduce taxes—understandable and even commendable in itself, but irrational and irresponsible when connected to the
reduction or dismantling of vital public services. The second source of pressure comes from parents and students who tend to scorn courses of study
that do not teach people how to become attractive to employers in a rapidly
tightening job market.

It is absurd to believe that the development of skills does not also require   3
the systematic development of the human mind. Education is being measured more by the size of the benefits the individual can extract from society
than by the extent to which the individual can come into possession of his
or her full powers. The result is that the life-giving juices are in danger of
being drained out of education.

Emphasis on "practicalities" is being characterized by the subordination   4
of words to numbers. History is seen not as essential experience to be transmitted to new generations, but as abstractions that carry dank odors. Art is
regarded as something that calls for indulgence or patronage and that has no
place among the practical realities. Political science is viewed more as a specialized subject for people who want to go into politics than as an opportunity for citizens to develop a knowledgeable relationship with the systems by
which human societies are governed. Finally, literature and philosophy are
assigned the role of add-ons—intellectual adornments that have nothing to
do with "genuine" education.

Instead of trying to shrink the liberal arts, the American people ought to   5
be putting pressure on colleges and universities to increase the ratio of the
humanities to the sciences. Most serious studies of medical-school curricula
in recent years have called attention to the stark gaps in the liberal education
of medical students. The experts agree that the schools shouldn't leave it up
to students to close those gaps.

The irony of the emphasis being placed on careers is that nothing is more   6
valuable for anyone who has had a professional or vocational education than
to be able to deal with abstractions or complexities, or to feel comfortable
with subtleties of thought or language, or to think sequentially. The doctor
who knows only disease is at a disadvantage alongside the doctor who knows
at least as much about people as he does about pathological organisms. The
lawyer who argues in court from a narrow legal base is no match for the
lawyer who can connect legal precedents to historical experience and who
employs wide-ranging intellectual resources. The business executive whose
competence in general management is bolstered by an artistic ability to deal
with people is of prime value to his company. For the technologist, the engineering of consent can be just as important as the engineering of moving
parts. In all these respects, the liberal arts have much to offer. Just in terms
of career preparation, therefore, a student is shortchanging himself by short-
cutting the humanities.

But even if it could be demonstrated that the humanities contribute noth-   7
ing directly to a job, they would still be an essential part of the educational
equipment of any person who wants to come to terms with life. The humanities would be expendable only if human beings didn't have to make decisions
that affect their lives and the lives of others; if the human past never existed
or had nothing to tell us about the present; if thought processes were irrelevant to the achievement of purpose; if creativity was beyond the human
mind and had nothing to do with the joy of living; if human relationships

were random aspects of life; if human beings never had to cope with panic or pain, or if they never had to anticipate the connection between cause and effect; if all the mysteries of mind and nature were fully plumbed; and if no special demands arose from the accident of being born a human being instead of a hen or a hog.

Finally, there would be good reason to eliminate the humanities if a free   8
society were not absolutely dependent on a functioning citizenry. If the main purpose of a university is job training, then the underlying philosophy of our government has little meaning. The debates that went into the making of American society concerned not just institutions or governing principles but the capacity of humans to sustain those institutions. Whatever the disagreements were over other issues at the American Constitutional Convention, the fundamental question sensed by everyone, a question that lay over the entire assembly, was whether the people themselves would understand what it meant to hold the ultimate power of society, and whether they had enough of a sense of history and destiny to know where they had been and where they ought to be going.

Jefferson was prouder of having been the founder of the University of   9
Virginia than of having been President of the United States. He knew that the educated and developed mind was the best assurance that a political system could be made to work—a system based on the informed consent of the governed. If this idea fails, then all the saved tax dollars in the world will not be enough to prevent the nation from turning on itself.

QUESTIONS FOR MEANING

1. According to Cousins, what are the two main sources of pressure for changes in the nature of American higher education?
2. How should the quality of an education be measured? How do many people tend to measure it? Explain the distinction Cousins draws in paragraph 3, and ask yourself if Cousins would approve of the education you are receiving.
3. One of the unfortunate signs of modern education, as Cousins sees it, is "the subordination of words to numbers." He lists several disciplines that no longer enjoy the respect they once inspired. Are these disciplines responsible in any way for their own decline? What are the "numbers" courses that now seem more serious and practical?
4. Cousins argues that doctors, lawyers, and business executives have an advantage if they have been broadly educated and not just narrowly trained. Would you like to go to a doctor who had majored in English or history as an undergraduate? Would you feel more or less confidence in him or her?
5. What does Cousins mean by "an artistic ability to deal with people"? Define this ability and explain how it can be gained through a college education. Is this something that comes from studying the liberal arts, or are there other sources as well—sources outside of school?

QUESTIONS ABOUT STRATEGY

1. Consider the title of this essay. What does it tell you about Cousins's conception of human nature?
2. What premise underlies Cousins's argument? Where does he state it? Are you persuaded that a liberal education satisfies the principle the premise involves?
3. Why does Cousins use "we" in his opening sentence? What does this tell you about how he sees himself when writing for the magazine in which this essay was originally published?
4. In paragraphs 6–8, Cousins advances three arguments on behalf of the humanities. Why are they arranged in the order in which he has them?
5. Most of paragraph 7 is a long sentence linked together with semicolons. What stylistic device enables Cousins to write such a long sentence, and what do you think motivated him to do it?
6. How effective is this argument? Does Cousins respond to your own needs and concerns, or does he write over them—obsessed with an ideal that you do not share?

JOHN HENRY NEWMAN
Knowledge as Its Own End

One of the most influential religious thinkers of the nineteenth century, John Henry Newman (1801–1890) attended Trinity College, Oxford, before becoming a Fellow of Oriel College in 1822. In 1824 he became a minister in the Church of England, and four years later he became vicar of St. Mary's Church in Oxford where his sermons drew a large audience. During the second half of the 1830s, he was one of the principal figures of "The Oxford Movement," a movement which began as a protest against the right of the British government to regulate the Anglican Church and which became increasingly controversial as the decade progressed. Newman published the "Tracts for the Times," a series of arguments through which the movement sought to advance its views. The most controversial of these tracts was number 90 (1841) which argued that the doctrines of the Church of England were compatible with Roman Catholicism on almost all points. Newman gave his last sermon as an Anglican in 1843; two years later, he converted to Catholicism—a decision for which he was much criticized in England. In 1847 he became a Catholic priest. Upon the petition of Catholic laymen, he was made a Cardinal by Pope Leo XIII in 1879.

Newman's greatest influence has been through his writing. His most important works include Apologia pro Vita Sua *(1864),* An Essay in Aid of a Grammar of Assent *(1870), and* The Idea of a University *(**1873**), from which the following selection is taken. It originated in a series of lectures Newman gave in 1852 in Dublin, where he was instrumental in founding the Catholic University of Ireland.*

Things, which can bear to be cut off from everything else and yet persist   1
in living, must have life in themselves; pursuits, which issue in nothing, and still maintain their ground for ages, which are regarded as admirable, though they have not as yet proved themselves to be useful, must have their sufficient end in themselves, whatever it turn out to be. And we are brought to the same conclusion by considering the force of the epithet, by which the knowledge under consideration is popularly designated. It is common to speak of *"liberal* knowledge," of the *"liberal* arts and studies," and of a *"liberal* education," as the especial characteristic or property of a University and of a gentleman; what is really meant by the word? Now, first, in its grammatical sense it is opposed to *servile;* and by "servile work" is understood, as our catechisms inform us, bodily labour, mechanical employment, and the like, in which the mind has little or no part. Parallel to such servile works are those arts, if they deserve the name, of which the poet speaks, which owe their origin and their method to hazard, not to skill; as, for instance, the practice and operations of an empiric. As far as this contrast may be considered as a guide into the meaning of the word, liberal education and liberal pursuits are exercises of mind, of reason, of reflection.

But we want something more for its explanation, for there are bodily exercises which are liberal, and mental exercises which are not so. For instance, in ancient times the practitioners in medicine were commonly slaves; yet it was an art as intellectual in its nature, in spite of the pretence, fraud and quackery with which it might then, as now, be debased, as it was heavenly in its aim. And so in like manner, we contrast a liberal education with a commercial education or a professional; yet no one can deny that commerce and the professions afford scope for the highest and most diversified powers of mind. There is then a great variety of intellectual exercises, which are not technically called "liberal"; on the other hand, I say, there are exercises of the body which do receive that appellation. Such, for instance, was the palæstra, in ancient times; such the Olympic games, in which strength and dexterity of body as well as of mind gained the prize. In Xenophon we read of the young Persian nobility being taught to ride on horseback and to speak the truth; both being among the accomplishments of a gentleman. War, too, however rough a profession, has ever been accounted liberal, unless in cases when it becomes heroic, which would introduce us to another subject.

Now comparing these instances together, we shall have no difficulty in determining the principle of this apparent variation in the application of the term which I am examining. Manly games, or games of skill, or military prowess, though bodily, are, it seems, accounted liberal; on the other hand, what is merely professional, though highly intellectual, nay, though liberal in comparison of trade and manual labour, is not simply called liberal, and mercantile occupations are not liberal at all. Why this distinction? because that alone is liberal knowledge, which stands on its own pretensions, which is independent of sequel, expects no complement, refuses to be *informed* (as it is called) by any end, or absorbed into any art, in order duly to present itself to our contemplation. The most ordinary pursuits have this specific character, if they are self-sufficient and complete; the highest lose it, when they minister to something beyond them. It is absurd to balance, in point of worth and importance, a treatise on reducing fractures with a game of cricket or a fox-chase; yet of the two the bodily exercise has that quality which we call "liberal," and the intellectual has not. And so of the learned professions altogether, considered merely as professions; although one of them be the most popularly beneficial, and another the most politically important, and the third the most intimately divine of all human pursuits, yet the very greatness of their end, the health of the body, or of the commonwealth, or of the soul, diminishes, not increases, their claim to the appellation "liberal," and that still more, if they are cut down to the strict exigencies of that end. If, for instance, Theology instead of being cultivated as a contemplation, be limited to the purposes of the pulpit or be represented by the catechism, it loses—not its usefulness, not its divine character, not its meritoriousness, (rather it gains a claim upon these titles by such charitable condescension),—but it does lose the particular attribute which I am illustrating; just as a face worn by tears and fasting loses its beauty, or a labourer's hand loses its delicateness;—for

Theology thus exercised is not simple knowledge, but rather is an art or a business making use of Theology. And thus it appears that even what is supernatural need not be liberal, nor need a hero be a gentleman, for the plain reason that one idea is not another idea. And in like manner the Baconian Philosophy, by using its physical sciences in the service of man, does thereby transfer them from the order of Liberal Pursuits to, I do not say the inferior, but the distinct class of the Useful. And, to take a different instance, hence again, as is evident, whenever personal gain is the motive, still more distinctive an effect has it upon the character of a given pursuit; thus racing, which was a liberal exercise in Greece, forfeits its rank in times like these, so far as it is made the occasion of gambling.

All that I have been now saying is summed up in a few characteristic   4
words of the great Philosopher [Aristotle]. "Of possessions," he says, "those rather are useful, which bear fruit; those *liberal, which tend to enjoyment.* By fruitful, I mean, which yield revenue; by enjoyable, where *nothing accrues of consequence beyond the using."*

QUESTIONS FOR MEANING

1. How does Newman define the liberal arts? Why is it that the study of medicine, law, or engineering is not "liberal" in Newman's sense of the term?
2. Who was Xenophon? If you've never heard of him, what can you conclude about him from the context in which he is mentioned (paragraph 2)? How could you learn more about him?
3. Does Newman believe that liberal knowledge is superior to other forms of knowledge?
4. What does Newman mean by "Baconian Philosophy" in paragraph 3?
5. Vocabulary: epithet (1), servile (1), empiric (1), dexterity (2), treatise (3), exigencies (3), accrues (4).

QUESTIONS ABOUT STRATEGY

1. How would you describe Newman's sentence structure? Is his style appropriate for his topic?
2. Like many other nineteenth-century prose writers, Newman tended to write long paragraphs. Could any of the paragraphs in this selection be broken up?
3. Consider the analogy that Newman makes in paragraph 3 between a "business making use of Theology" and a face "worn by tears and fasting" that has lost its beauty or "a labourer's hand" that has lost its "delicateness." What do these lines reveal about Newman's values?

CARRIE TUHY
So Who Needs College?

The debate over the purpose of higher education took on new urgency in the 1980s, when unemployment began to rise after a decade of high inflation that had significantly increased the cost of a college education. Many college graduates in the early 1980s found it difficult to find jobs within their chosen fields. The number of majors in such subjects as English, history, and philosophy continued to decline as students turned to such majors as business and computer science that seemed more "practical." For many students, job training became more important than general education. Vocational schools began to attract an increasing number of students who might otherwise have gone to a college or university. The advantages of vocational training are considered in the following **1982** *essay by Carrie Tuhy, a staff writer for* Money *magazine.*

Career seekers, the want ads are trying to tell you something. Despite the 1 highest unemployment rate since 1941, Sunday papers across America are thick with job postings for specialized skills. Employers seem unable to find enough qualified people for such positions as bank teller, commercial artist, computer programmer, data processor, electronics technician, medical technologist, nurse, office manager, salesperson and secretary. Fewer and fewer classified ads stipulate college as a requirement.

The message is clear: even a severe recession hasn't caused a labor surplus in certain occupations. But the message goes deeper. In good times as well as bad, a bachelor's degree is becoming less valuable for some careers. As students head off to college this month, they and their parents may wonder whether the diploma is still worth its price in tuition, room, board and four years of forgone income.

The majority of openings, now and for the economic recovery that could 3 be getting under way, require types of skills more likely to be acquired in a technical or trade school or on the job than on an ivied campus. Technical school graduates are routinely landing jobs with higher starting pay than newly minted bachelors of arts can command. A computer programmer fresh from a six-month course can earn up to $14,000 a year while an English major is rewriting his résumé for the umpteenth time. Clearly, the $5,000 certificate of technical competence is gaining on the $50,000 sheepskin.

While graduates of four-year colleges still have a small financial edge, that 4 advantage is narrowing. In the 1960s, beginning salaries for college men started an average of 24% higher than for the work force as a whole. That differential is now down to 5%. Projections of the lifetime return on an investment in a college education are still more disillusioning. The foremost specialist in such estimates, Richard Freeman of the National Bureau of Economic Research, predicts that the class of '82 will realize only 6% or 7% a year on its education costs in the form of higher earnings compared with the 11% return projected for the class of '62. Concludes Finis Welch, an economist at UCLA: "A college degree today is not a ticket to a high-paying job or an insurance policy against unemployment." . . .

In fact, going to college may even be a hindrance for some people with   5
extraordinary talent or ambition. They often feel that college bottles up their drive. Still, you shouldn't overlook educational values that cannot be measured in dollars. Pursuing a bachelor's degree can stretch the mind, help a young person gain maturity and generally enrich anyone's life. Indisputably too, college remains essential in preparing for the professions and advantageous in getting interviews for some occupations. You may not need a B.A. to do the work of an advertising copywriter, broker or journalist—to cite some conspicuous examples—but a diploma still helps you to get in the door. Degreeless applicants may have to start lower or fight harder to enter such fields, and they may be passed over for promotions, particularly to management levels.

Conversely, doors stand wide open to rewarding careers, especially in   6
technical fields, for those with the right nonacademic training. Trade and technical schools are quickly outgrowing their matchbook-cover image—DRAW THIS DOG AND EARN BIG MONEY! Despite the continuing shabby practices of a few institutions, most of the nation's 7,000 private vocational schools for high school graduates competently provide training for all manner of careers from actor to X-ray technician.

The emphasis in vocational education is switching from training blue-   7
collar factory hands and brown-collar repairmen to preparing gray-collar technicians. Also, high-tech companies with a vested interest in a competent work force have taken it upon themselves to educate people in specialized skills. The list of those companies starts with AT&T, IBM and Xerox but goes on to include such somewhat smaller firms as Bell & Howell, Control Data and Wang. One of several courses sponsored by Bell & Howell's DeVry Institute of Technology in Chicago trains technicians to build product prototypes by following engineering drawings; the course takes 20 months and leads to jobs starting at $18,000 a year.

Profit-making trade schools are flourishing even as university enrollments   8
dwindle. One of the country's largest commercial schools, National Education Corp. (NEC), based in Newport Beach, Calif., has more than 100,000 students in 70 branches. Graduates repair jets (average starting salary: $15,000), manage radio stations ($30,000), write computer programs and design microprocessor chips (both $12,000).

Fees are often substantial at a high-tech school, but because the training   9
is condensed it costs far less than getting a university degree. A six-month course in computers at NEC's National Institute of Technology costs $5,000; a two-year program in electronics engineering is $7,900. Says Wayne Gilpin, president of the institute, with a touch of braggadocio: "Our students may not be able to quote Byron, but they are technically sharp. They can sit alongside four-year graduates from Purdue and MIT."

Trade school students should face the fact that they won't sit beside many   10
of those Purdue and MIT graduates. Electrical engineers, for example, can

get jobs researching and developing new technology at salaries ranging from $23,000 to $30,000, while technicians are more likely to work at repairing those creations at $18,000 to $22,000.

Even so, bright people can advance surprisingly far on trade school train- 11
ing. One example: Ronald Billodeaux, now 29, who completed an electronics course at Little Rock's United Electronics (now called Arkansas College of Technology) and got a job maintaining equipment for Geophysical Services Inc., a Texas Instruments subsidiary that provides exploration data for oil companies. Over the years, Billodeaux helped search for oil in Africa, South America and Australia. Last year the company wanted to move him to London to oversee Middle Eastern and African operations, but he balked at further travel. Almost immediately, Mobil hired him away as a supervisor to scout oil prospects in the Gulf of Mexico.

Two-year community colleges and private junior colleges offer vocational 12
training at a considerably lower cost than private technical schools do. Tuition averages $500 a year for such job-oriented studies as auto mechanics, data processing, police science and real estate sales. Says Roger Yarrington, until recently executive director of the American Association of Junior and Community Colleges: "The use of these schools has shifted from university preparation to job preparation." But community colleges, with their multitude of majors, may not have the resources to give as thorough and up-to-date training as you can get at single-subject technical schools. NEC, for example, is spending more than $1 million this year on new equipment.

What is most valuable in vocational education—whether at a community 13
college or a technical school—is hands-on training. In choosing a program, you should ask about not only the school's resources but also about the time devoted to learning by doing and the companies that hire the most students. Then query those companies' personnel managers on how they rate the school's courses.

Employers say the best preparation combines study with work alongside 14
people in the field. At the Fashion Institute of Design and Merchandising, a California junior college with branches in San Francisco and Los Angeles, Constance Bennett, 23, spent her second year working as an intern at Hang Ten, a sportswear manufacturer. The experience serves her well in her present job at Koret of North America, a San Francisco sportswear company. During a 21-month course at the Culinary Institute of America in Hyde Park, N.Y., the Harvard of *haute cuisine*, students get experience in some of the nation's best-known kitchens. John Doherty, 24, spent more than a quarter of his course at the Waldorf Astoria in New York City. After graduation in 1978, he was hired as a cook there; he has since risen to second in command of a kitchen with 170 cooks.

The best deal, of course, is getting paid to learn a skill. Competition for 15
apprenticeships is always stiff, and a slack economy has cut the number of openings. But as business revives, so will the need for trainees. Along with the standard apprenticeships for plumbers, pipefitters and carpenters, there are programs in hundreds of occupations including biomedical equipment technician, film and video editor, recording engineer, meteorologist and chef.

Frank Ruta, 24, learned to cook and run a kitchen in a three-year apprentice-ship arranged by the American Culinary Federation. Instead of forking out more than $13,000 to attend the Culinary Institute of America, he hired on at the Lemon Tree, a restaurant in his home town of McKeesport, Pa., at $3.25 an hour and got a 25¢ raise every six months. Ruta learned to cook well enough to satisfy a range of tastes, in politics as well as palates. As personal chef to the First Family, he has served the Carters and the Reagans.

The Labor Department's Bureau of Apprenticeship and Training super-   16
vises programs in some 500 trades. Thirty years ago, federal regulation was aimed against racism, favoritism and exploitation in handing out job assign-ments. Today the bureau mainly monitors wages: apprentices at first average about $6 an hour, 40% to 50% of skilled workers' pay. State agencies with information about apprenticeships are listed in phone directories; look under "state government" for the employment security administration.

However, some of the most respected employer-sponsored programs, such   17
as those run by Kodak, General Electric and Westinghouse, are not listed with government offices. You can find them by asking major employers in your chosen field. Apprenticeships are investments of time rather than money; it takes five years to qualify as a journeyman machinist—only a year less than it usually requires to earn a bachelor's degree and an M.B.A. Though appren-tices start with no job guarantee, a company that spends up to six years training a person is likely to keep him.

Even without training, high school graduates sometimes can land worth-   18
while jobs in marketing, retailing and a few other fields. Continental Illinois National Bank in Chicago occasionally hires promising teenagers as trainees at $10,000 a year. In five years, they can rise to loan service representative at $27,000—a position and a salary few people fresh from a liberal arts col-lege would qualify for in less than two or three years.

In some government-regulated sales fields—particularly real estate, secu-   19
rities and insurance—a mere office clerk can impress the boss by passing the licensing exam. Judith Briles, 36, started as a secretary in a brokerage house with just a high school diploma and a housewife's experience. She quickly learned the business and got a stockbroker's license. After 10 years in the field, she was earning $150,000 a year in commissions at E.F. Hutton in San Jose.

Only after opening her own investment advisory company in 1978 did she   20
go to college—to hone her management skills. At Pepperdine University in Malibu, Calif., she took an entrance exam to determine how much her life's experience should count toward her degree. It counted a lot. In two years of part-time study, she bypassed a bachelor's degree and won an M.B.A.

QUESTIONS FOR MEANING

1. What does Tuhy mean by "sheepskin" in paragraph 3?
2. According to this argument, what is the principal advantage of technical training over general education? What is the principal career risk in choos-ing an education of this sort?

3. Why does Tuhy prefer private technical schools to community colleges that offer technical training?
4. How can you go about evaluating a vocational education program? What is the most important aspect in such programs? How can you determine the likelihood of getting a job upon completing your studies at a school you are considering attending?
5. Vocabulary: stipulate (1), braggadocio (9), and hone (20).

QUESTIONS ABOUT STRATEGY

1. What sort of tone does Tuhy adopt toward the various people she describes in her essay? What does this reveal about her values? Why doesn't she describe anyone who has paid for a vocational education and then been unable to find work?
2. This article was originally written for *Money* magazine. Assuming that Tuhy had a good sense of the audience she was writing for, what sort of people read this magazine?
3. Where does Tuhy concede that vocational education has its limitations? Why does she have an obligation to remind her readers that this is so?
4. Tuhy concludes her argument with one final example. Is this a good way to bring an essay to a close? Is the example strong enough to justify concluding without further commentary?

CAROLINE BIRD
Where College Fails Us

After working as a researcher for Newsweek *and* Fortune *magazines in the mid-1940s, Caroline Bird went on to a successful career in public relations. Her many books reflect her interest in business and, in particular, the position of women in the business world. These books include* Born Female: The High Cost of Keeping Women Down *(1968),* Everything a Woman Needs to Know to Get Paid What She's Worth *(1973),* What Women Want *(1978), and* The Two Paycheck Marriage *(1979). The following essay, which has appeared in many anthologies since its first publication in* **1975,** *is probably Bird's best-known work. Drawing upon her knowledge of the economy and her skills as a researcher, Bird makes a well-supported attack upon the much cherished notion that going to college leads to a good paying job.*

1   The case *for* college has been accepted without question for more than a generation. All high school graduates ought to go, says Conventional Wisdom and statistical evidence, because college will help them earn more money, become "better" people, and learn to be more responsible citizens than those who don't go.

2   But college has never been able to work its magic for everyone. And now that close to half our high school graduates are attending, those who don't fit the pattern are becoming more numerous, and more obvious. College graduates are selling shoes and driving taxis; college students sabotage each other's experiments and forge letters of recommendation in the intense competition for admission to graduate school. Others find no stimulation in their studies, and drop out—often encouraged by college administrators.

3   Some observers say the fault is with the young people themselves—they are spoiled, stoned, overindulged, and expecting too much. But that's mass character assassination, and doesn't explain all campus unhappiness. Others blame the state of the world, and they are partly right. We've been told that young people have to go to college because our economy can't absorb an army of untrained eighteen-year-olds. But disillusioned graduates are learning that it can no longer absorb an army of trained twenty-two-year-olds, either.

4   Some adventuresome educators and campus watchers have openly begun to suggest that college may not be the best, the proper, the only place for every young person after the completion of high school. We may have been looking at all those surveys and statistics upside down, it seems, and through the rosy glow of our own remembered college experiences. Perhaps college doesn't make people intelligent, ambitious, happy, liberal, or quick to learn new things—maybe it's just the other way around, and intelligent, ambitious, happy, liberal, and quick-learning people are merely the ones who have been attracted to college in the first place. And perhaps all those successful col-

lege graduates would have been successful whether they had gone to college or not. This is heresy to those of us who have been brought up to believe that if a little schooling is good, more has to be much better. But contrary evidence is beginning to mount up.

The unhappiness and discontent of young people is nothing new, and   5 problems of adolescence are always painfully intense. But while traveling around the country, speaking at colleges, and interviewing students at all kinds of schools—large and small, public and private—I was overwhelmed by the prevailing sadness. It was as visible on campuses in California as in Nebraska and Massachusetts. Too many young people are in college reluctantly, because everyone told them they ought to go, and there didn't seem to be anything better to do. Their elders sell them college because it's good for them. Some never learn to like it, and talk about their time in school as if it were a sentence to be served.

Students tell us the same thing college counselors tell us—they go be-   6 cause of pressure from parents and teachers, and stay because it seems to be an alternative to a far worse fate. It's "better" than the Army or a dead-end job, and it has to be pretty bad before it's any worse than staying at home.

College graduates say that they don't want to work "just" for money: They   7 want work that matters. They want to help people and save the world. But the numbers are stacked against them. Not only are there not enough jobs in world-saving fields, but in the current slowdown it has become evident that there never were, and probably never will be, enough jobs requiring higher education to go around.

Students who tell their advisers they want to help people, for example,   8 are often directed to psychology. This year the Department of Labor estimates that there will be 4,300 new jobs for psychologists, while colleges will award 58,430 bachelor's degrees in psychology.

Sociology has become a favorite major on socially conscious campuses, but   9 graduates find that social reform is hardly a paying occupation. Male sociologists from the University of Wisconsin reported as gainfully employed a year after graduation included a legal assistant, sports editor, truck unloader, Peace Corps worker, publications director, and a stockboy—but no sociologist per se. The highest paid worked for the post office.

Publishing, writing, and journalism are presumably the vocational goal of   10 a large proportion of the 104,000 majors in Communications and Letters expected to graduate in 1975. The outlook for them is grim. All of the daily newspapers in the country combined are expected to hire a total of 2,600 reporters this year. Radio and television stations may hire a total of 500 announcers, most of them in local radio stations. Nonpublishing organizations will need 1,100 technical writers, and public-relations activities another 4,400. Even if new graduates could get all these jobs (they can't, of course), over 90,000 of them will have to find something less glamorous to do.

Other fields most popular with college graduates are also pathetically small.   11 Only 1,900 foresters a year will be needed during this decade, although schools of forestry are expected to continue graduating twice as many. Some will get sub-professional jobs as forestry aides. Schools of architecture are expected to turn out twice as many as will be needed, and while all sorts of people want to design things, the Department of Labor forecasts that there will be jobs for only 400 new industrial designers a year. As for anthropologists, only 400 will be needed every year in the 1970s to take care of all the college courses, public-health research, community surveys, museums, and all the archaeological digs on every continent. (For these jobs graduate work in anthropology is required.)

Many popular occupations may seem to be growing fast without necessarily offering employment to very many. "Recreation work" is always cited as an expanding field, but it will need relatively few workers who require more special training than life guards. "Urban planning" has exploded in the media, so the U.S. Department of Labor doubled its estimate of the number of jobs to be filled every year in the 1970s—to a big, fat 800. A mere 200 oceanographers a year will be able to do all the exploring of "inner space"—and all that exciting underwater diving you see demonstrated on television—for the entire decade of the 1970s.   12

Whatever college graduates *want* to do, most of them are going to wind up doing what *there is* to do. During the next few years, according to the Labor Department, the biggest demand will be for stenographers and secretaries, followed by retail-trade salesworkers, hospital attendants, bookkeepers, building custodians, registered nurses, foremen, kindergarten and elementary school teachers, receptionists, cooks, cosmetologists, private-household workers, manufacturing inspectors, and industrial machinery repairmen. These are the jobs which will eventually absorb the surplus archaeologists, urban planners, oceanographers, sociologists, editors, and college professors.   13

Vocationalism is the new look on campus because of the discouraging job market faced by the generalists. Students have been opting for medicine and law in droves. If all those who check "doctor" as their career goal succeed in getting their MDs, we'll immediately have ten times the target ratio of doctors for the population of the United States. Law schools are already graduating twice as many new lawyers every year as the Department of Labor thinks we will need, and the oversupply grows annually.   14

Specialists often find themselves at the mercy of shifts in demand, and the narrower the vocational training, the more risky the long-term prospects. Engineers are the classic example of the "Yo-Yo" effect in supply and demand. Today's shortage is apt to produce a big crop of engineering graduates after the need has crested, and teachers face the same squeeze.   15

Worse than that, when the specialists turn up for work, they often find that they have learned a lot of things in classrooms that they will never use, that they will have to learn a lot of things on the job that they were never taught, and that most of what they have learned is less likely to "come in handy later" than to fade from memory. One disillusioned architecture student, who had already designed and built houses, said, "It's the degree you need, not everything you learn getting it."   16

A diploma saves the employer the cost of screening candidates and gives   17
him a predictable product: He can assume that those who have survived the
four-year ordeal have learned how to manage themselves. They have learned
how to budget their time, meet deadlines, set priorities, cope with impersonal
authority, follow instructions, and stick with a task that may be tiresome
without direct supervision.

The employer is also betting that it will be cheaper and easier to train the   18
college graduate because he has demonstrated his ability to learn. But if the
diploma serves only to identify those who are talented in the art of school-
work, it becomes, in the words of Harvard's Christopher Jencks, "a hell of an
expensive aptitude test." It is unfair to the candidates because they themselves must bear the cost of the screening—the cost of college. Candidates
without the funds, the academic temperament, or the patience for the four-
year obstacle race are ruled out, no matter how well they may perform on
the job. But if "everyone" has a diploma, employers will have to find another
way to choose employees, and it will become an empty credential.

(Screening by diploma may in fact already be illegal. The 1971 ruling of   19
the Supreme Court in *Griggs* v. *Duke Power Co.* contended that an employer
cannot demand a qualification which systematically excludes an entire class
of applicants, unless that qualification reliably predicts success on the job.
The requiring of a high school diploma was outlawed in the *Griggs* case, and
this could extend to a college diploma.)

The bill for four years at an Ivy League college is currently climbing toward   20
$25,000; at a state university, a degree will cost the student and his family
about $10,000 (with taxpayers making up the difference).

Not many families can afford these sums, and when they look for financial   21
aid, they discover that someone else will decide how much they will actually
have to pay. The College Scholarship Service, which establishes a family's
degree of need for most colleges, is guided by noble principles: uniformity of
sacrifice, need rather than merit. But families vary in their willingness to
"sacrifice" as much as the bureaucracy of the CSS thinks they ought to. This
is particularly true of middle-income parents, whose children account for the
bulk of the country's college students. Some have begun to rebel against this
attempt to enforce the same values and priorities on all. "In some families, a
college education competes with a second car, a color television, or a trip to
Europe—and it's possible that college may lose," one financial-aid officer recently told me.

Quite so. College is worth more to some middle-income families than to   22
others. It is chilling to consider the undercurrent of resentment that families
who "give up everything" must feel toward their college-age children, or the
burden of guilt children must bear every time they goof off or receive less
than top grades in their courses.

The decline in return for a college degree within the last generation has   23
been substantial. In the 1950s, a Princeton student could pay his expenses
for the school year—eating club and all—on less than $3,000. When he grad-
uated, he entered a job market which provided a comfortable margin over
the earnings of his agemates who had not been to college. To be precise, a

freshman entering Princeton in 1956, the earliest year for which the Census has attempted to project lifetime earnings, could expect to realize a 12.5 percent return on his investment. A freshman entering in 1972, with the cost nearing $6,000 annually, could expect to realize only 9.3 percent, less than might be available in the money market. This calculation was made with the help of a banker and his computer, comparing college as an investment in future earnings with other investments available in the booming money market of 1974, and concluded that in strictly financial terms, college is not always the best investment a young person can make.

I postulated a young man (the figures are different with a young woman, but the principle is the same) whose rich uncle would give him, in cash, the total cost of four years at Princeton—$34,181. (The total includes what the young man would earn if he went to work instead of to college right after high school.) If he did not spend the money on Princeton, but put it in the savings bank at 7.5 percent interest compounded daily, he would have, at retirement age sixty-four, more than five times as much as the $199,000 extra he could expect to earn between twenty-two and sixty as a college man rather than a mere high school graduate. And with all that money accumulating in the bank, he could invest in something with a higher return than a diploma. At age twenty-eight, when his nest egg had reached $73,113, he could buy a liquor store, which would return him well over 20 percent on his investment, as long as he was willing to mind the store. He might get a bit fidgety sitting there, but he'd have to be dim-witted to lose money on a liquor store, and right now we're talking only about dollars. 24

If the young man went to a public college rather than Princeton, the investment would be lower, and the payoff higher, of course, because other people—the taxpayers—put up part of the capital for him. But the difference in return between an investment in public and private colleges is minimized because the biggest part of the investment in either case is the money a student might earn if he went to work, not to college—in economic terms, his "foregone income." That he bears himself. 25

Rates of return and dollar signs on education are a fascinating brain teaser, and, obviously, there is a certain unreality to the game. But the same unreality extends to the traditional calculations that have always been used to convince taxpayers that college is a worthwhile investment. 26

The ultimate defense of college has always been that while it may not teach you anything vocationally useful, it will somehow make you a better person, able to do anything better, and those who make it through the process are initiated into the "fellowship of educated men and women." In a study intended to probe what graduates seven years out of college thought their colleges should have done for them, the Carnegie Commission found that most alumni expected the "development of my abilities to think and express myself." But if such respected educational psychologists as Bruner and Piaget are right, specific learning skills have to be acquired very early in life, perhaps even before formal schooling begins. 27

So, when pressed, liberal-arts defenders speak instead about something more encompassing, and more elusive. "College changed me inside," one 28 graduate told us fervently. The authors of a Carnegie Commission report, who obviously struggled for a definition, concluded that one of the common threads in the perceptions of a liberal education is that it provides "an integrated view of the world which can serve as an inner guide." More simply, alumni say that college should have "helped me to formulate the values and goals of my life."

In theory, a student is taught to develop these values and goals himself,   29
but in practice, it doesn't work quite that way. All but the wayward and the saintly take their sense of the good, the true, and the beautiful from the people around them. When we speak of students acquiring "values" in college, we often mean that they will acquire the values—and sometimes that means only the tastes—of their professors. The values of professors may be "higher" than many students will encounter elsewhere, but they may not be relevant to situations in which students find themselves in college and later.

Of all the forms in which ideas are disseminated, the college professor   30
lecturing a class is the slowest and most expensive. You don't have to go to college to read the great books or learn about the great ideas of Western Man. Today you can find them everywhere—in paperbacks, in the public libraries, in museums, in public lectures, in adult-education courses, in abridged, summarized, or adapted form in magazines, films, and television. The problem is no longer one of access to broadening ideas; the problem is the other way around: how to choose among the many courses of action proposed to us, how to edit the stimulations that pour into our eyes and ears every waking hour. A college experience that piles option on option and stimulation on stimulation merely adds to the contemporary nightmare.

What students and graduates say that they did learn on campus comes   31
under the heading of personal, rather than intellectual, development. Again and again I was told that the real value of college is learning to get along with others, to practice social skills, to "sort out my head," and these have nothing to do with curriculum.

For whatever impact the academic experience used to have on college   32
students, the sheer size of many undergraduate classes in the 1970s dilutes faculty-student dialogue, and, more often than not, they are taught by teachers who were hired when colleges were faced with a shortage of qualified instructors, during their years of expansion and when the big rise in academic pay attracted the mediocre and the less than dedicated.

On the social side, colleges are withdrawing from responsibility for feed-   33
ing, housing, policing, and protecting students at a time when the environment of college may be the most important service it could render. College officials are reluctant to "intervene" in the personal lives of the students. They no longer expect to take over from parents, but often insist that students—who have, most often, never lived away from home before—take full adult responsibility for their plans, achievements, and behavior.

Most college students do not live in the plush, comfortable country-club-   34
like surroundings their parents envisage, or, in some cases, remember. Open dorms, particularly when they are coeducational, are noisy, usually over-

crowded, and often messy. Some students desert the institutional "zoos" (their own word for dorms) and move into run-down, overpriced apartments. Bulletin boards in student centers are littered with notices of apartments to share and the drift of conversation suggests that a lot of money is dissipated in scrounging for food and shelter.

Taxpayers now provide more than half of the astronomical sums that are 35 spent on higher education. But less than half of today's high school graduates go on, raising a new question of equity: Is it fair to make all the taxpayers pay for the minority who actually go to college? We decided long ago that it is fair for childless adults to pay school taxes because everyone, parents and nonparents alike, profits by a literate population. Does the same reasoning hold true for state-supported higher education? There is no conclusive evidence on either side.

Young people cannot be expected to go to college for the general good of 36 mankind. They may be more altruistic than their elders, but no great numbers are going to spend four years at hard intellectual labor, let alone tens of thousands of family dollars, for "the advancement of human capability in society at large," one of the many purposes invoked by the Carnegie Commission report. Nor do any considerable number of them want to go to college to beat the Russians to Jupiter, improve the national defense, increase the Gross National Product, lower the crime rate, improve automobile safety, or create a market for the arts—all of which have been suggested at one time or other as benefits taxpayers get for supporting higher education.

One sociologist said that you don't have to have a reason for going to 37 college because it's an institution. His definition of an institution is something everyone subscribed to without question. The burden of proof is not on why you should go to college, but why anyone thinks there might be a reason for not going. The implication—and some educators express it quite frankly—is that an eighteen-year-old high school graduate is still too young and confused to know what he wants to do, let alone what is good for him.

Mother knows best, in other words. 38

It had always been comfortable for students to believe that authorities, 39 like Mother, or outside specialists, like educators, could determine what was best for them. However, specialists and authorities no longer enjoy the credibility former generations accorded them. Patients talk back to doctors and are not struck suddenly dead. Clients question the lawyer's bills and sometimes get them reduced. It is no longer self-evident that all adolescents must study a fixed curriculum that was constructed at a time when all educated men could agree on precisely what it was that made them educated.

The same with college. If high school graduates don't want to continue 40 their education, or don't want to continue it right away, they may perceive more clearly than their elders that college is not for them.

College is an ideal place for those young adults who love learning for its 41 own sake, who would rather read then eat, and who like nothing better than writing research papers. But they are a minority, even at the prestigious colleges, which recruit and attract the intellectually oriented.

The rest of our high school graduates need to look at college more closely   42
and critically, to examine it as a consumer product, and decide if the cost in
dollars, in time, in continued dependency, and in future returns, is worth the
very large investment each student—and his family—must make.

QUESTIONS FOR MEANING

1. What does Bird see as the principal failure of college education? Why is
   college a "four year ordeal," and a "four year obstacle race"? Who should
   go to college, and who should not?
2. What risks does Bird concede to be in choosing a vocational education?
3. How do values differ from taste (paragraph 29)?
4. What does Bird mean when she demands that college should be examined
   as "a consumer product"?
5. How does Bird characterize the average college teacher? Is her appraisal
   justified by your own experience, or does it seem unfair?
6. Bird argues that college dorms are "noisy, usually overcrowded, and often
   messy," a far cry from the "country-clublike surroundings" many parents
   imagine. Is she right? What is your own dorm like? Are you getting good
   value for your money? Does Bird overlook any advantages to living in a
   dorm?
7. Have colleges changed in the years since this essay was written? What
   would Bird think of the school you attend?
8. Does Bird ever reveal what will happen to the thousands of high school
   graduates she would discourage from going to college? What do you think
   would happen if college attendance was suddenly reduced by half?
9. Vocabulary: pathetically (11), postulated (24), integrated (28), abridged
   (30), envisage (34), dissipated (34), altruistic (36), and credibility (39).

QUESTIONS ABOUT STRATEGY

1. In her opening paragraph, Bird introduces the three main arguments that
   people usually advance on behalf of going to college. If you study her
   essay, you will find that she responds to each of these arguments in the
   order in which she introduces them. This helps make her argument seem
   well-organized. But are there any arguments for college education that she
   overlooks?
2. Why does Bird put quotation marks around "better" in paragraph 1?
3. Was this essay originally intended for an audience of students or an audience of college graduates? Could someone understand Bird's argument
   before going to college, or is a college education necessary to understand
   what Bird is saying? If the latter is true, how does this affect the credibility
   of the argument? Define Bird's audience. Then explain what you think she
   was trying to accomplish with this essay.
4. Bird uses many statistics to strengthen her argument. Does she reveal
   where she got them? Are you impressed by the various numbers she cites

concerning job placement and the value of a college education as an investment? How vital are these numbers to the argument as a whole? Would you take Bird seriously without them?

5. What is the function of paragraphs 24–25? How useful is this example?

6. In paragraphs 38–40, Bird rejects the argument that many high school graduates are too young and confused to know what to do with their lives— and the implied argument that college gives them the time to "grow up." When you graduated from high school, how many of your friends had clear career goals? Now that you are in college, do your fellow students seem more mature? Do you agree with this aspect of Bird's argument?

ALLAN BLOOM
The Poverty of an Open Mind

Allan Bloom taught at Yale, Cornell, and the University of Toronto before returning to the University of Chicago where he had received his Ph.D. At Chicago, he is co-director of the John M. Olin Center for Inquiry into the Theory and Practice of Democracy. His books include Shakespeare's Politics, *translations of Plato's* Republic *and Rousseau's* Emile, *and* The Closing of the American Mind. *Subtitled "How Higher Education Has Failed Democracy and Impoverished the Souls of Today's Students,"* The Closing of the American Mind *was one of the most controversial books of **1987.** "The Poverty of an Open Mind" is an editor's title for the introduction to Bloom's book, from which the following selection was taken.*

There is one thing a professor can be absolutely certain of: almost every   1
student entering the university believes, or says he believes, that truth is relative. If this belief is put to the test, one can count on the students' reaction: they will be uncomprehending. That anyone should regard the proposition as not self-evident astonishes them, as though he were calling into question $2+2=4$. These are things you don't think about. The students' backgrounds are as various as America can provide. Some are religious, some atheists; some are to the Left, some to the Right; some intend to be scientists, some humanists or professionals or businessmen; some are poor, some rich. They are unified only in their relativism and in their allegiance to equality. And the two are related in a moral intention. The relativity of truth is not a theoretical insight but a moral postulate, the condition of a free society, or so they see it. They have all been equipped with this framework early on, and it is the modern replacement for the inalienable natural rights that used to be the traditional American grounds for a free society. That it is a moral issue for students is revealed by the character of their response when challenged—a

combination of disbelief and indignation: "Are you an absolutist?," the only alternative they know, uttered in the same tone as "Are you a monarchist?" or "Do you really believe in witches?" This latter leads into the indignation, for someone who believes in witches might well be a witchhunter or a Salem judge. The danger they have been taught to fear from absolutism is not error but intolerance. Relativism is necessary to openness; and this is the virtue, the only virtue, which all primary education for more than fifty years has dedicated itself to inculcating. Openness—and the relativism that makes it the only plausible stance in the face of various claims to truth and various ways of life and kinds of human beings—is the great insight of our times. The true believer is the real danger. The study of history and of culture teaches that all the world was mad in the past; men always thought they were right, and that led to wars, persecutions, slavery, xenophobia, racism, and chauvinism. The point is not to correct the mistakes and really be right; rather it is not to think you are right at all.

The students, of course, cannot defend their opinion. It is something with   2
which they have been indoctrinated. The best they can do is point out all the opinions and cultures there are and have been. What right, they ask, do I or anyone else have to say one is better than the others? If I pose the routine questions designed to confute them and make them think, such as, "If you had been a British administrator in India, would you have let the natives under your governance burn the widow at the funeral of a man who had died?," they either remain silent or reply that the British should never have been there in the first place. It is not that they know very much about other nations, or about their own. The purpose of their education is not to make them scholars but to provide them with a moral virtue—openness.

Every educational system has a moral goal that it tries to attain and that   3
informs its curriculum. It wants to produce a certain kind of human being. This intention is more or less explicit, more or less a result of reflection; but even the neutral subjects, like reading and writing and arithmetic, take their place in a vision of the educated person. In some nations the goal was the pious person, in others the warlike, in others the industrious. Always important is the political regime, which needs citizens who are in accord with its fundamental principle. Aristocracies want gentlemen, oligarchies men who respect and pursue money, and democracies lovers of equality. Democratic education, whether it admits it or not, wants and needs to produce men and women who have the tastes, knowledge, and character supportive of a democratic regime. Over the history of our republic, there have obviously been changes of opinion as to what kind of man is best for our regime. We began with the model of the rational and industrious man, who was honest, respected the laws, and was dedicated to the family (his own family—what has in its decay been dubbed the nuclear family). Above all he was to know the rights doctrine; the Constitution, which embodied it; and American history, which presented and celebrated the founding of a nation "conceived in liberty and dedicated to the proposition that all men are created equal." A powerful attachment to the letter and the spirit of the Declaration of Inde-

pendence gently conveyed, appealing to each man's reason, was the goal of the education of democratic man. This called for something very different from the kinds of attachment required for traditional communities where myth and passion as well as severe discipline, authority, and the extended family produced an instinctive, unqualified, even fanatic patriotism, unlike the reflected, rational, calm, even self-interested loyalty—not so much to the country but to the form of government and its rational principles—required in the United States. This was an entirely new experiment in politics, and with it came a new education. This education has evolved in the last half-century from the education of democratic man to the education of the democratic personality.

The palpable difference between these two can easily be found in the   4
changed understanding of what it means to be an American. The old view was that, by recognizing and accepting man's natural rights, men found a fundamental basis of unity and sameness. Class, race, religion, national origin or culture all disappear or become dim when bathed in the light of natural rights, which give men common interests and make them truly brothers. The immigrant had to put behind him the claims of the Old World in favor of a new and easily acquired education. This did not necessarily mean abandoning old daily habits or religions, but it did mean subordinating them to new principles. There was a tendency, if not a necessity, to homogenize nature itself.

The recent education of openness has rejected all that. It pays no atten-   5
tion to natural rights or the historical origins of our regime, which are now thought to have been essentially flawed and regressive. It is progressive and forward-looking. It does not demand fundamental agreement or the abandonment of old or new beliefs in favor of the natural ones. It is open to all kinds of men, all kinds of life-styles, all ideologies. There is no enemy other than the man who is not open to everything. But when there are no shared goals or vision of the public good, is the social contract any longer possible? . . .

The upshot of all this for the education of young Americans is that they   6
know much less about American history and those who were held to be its heroes. This was one of the few things that they used to come to college with that had something to do with their lives. Nothing has taken its place except a smattering of facts learned about other nations or cultures and a few social science formulas. None of this means much, partly because little attention has been paid to what is required in order truly to convey the spirit of other places and other times to young people, or for that matter to anyone, partly because the students see no relevance in any of it to the lives they are going to lead or to their prevailing passions. It is the rarest of occurrences to find a youngster who has been infused by this education with a longing to know all about China or the Romans or the Jews.

All to the contrary. There is an indifference to such things, for relativism   7
has extinguished the real motive of education, the search for a good life. Young Americans have less and less knowledge of and interest in foreign places. In the past there were many students who actually knew something about and loved England, France, Germany, or Italy, for they dreamed of

living there or thought their lives would be made more interesting by assimilating their languages and literatures. Such students have almost disappeared, replaced at most by students who are interested in the political problems of Third World countries and in helping them to modernize, with due respect to their old cultures, of course. This is not learning from others but condescension and a disguised form of a new imperialism. It is the Peace Corps mentality, which is not a spur to learning but to a secularized version of doing good works.

Actually openness results in American conformism—out there in the rest   8
of the world is a drab diversity that teaches only that values are relative, whereas here we can create all the life-styles we want. Our openness means we do not need others. Thus what is advertised as a great opening is a great closing. No longer is there a hope that there are great wise men in other places and times who can reveal the truth about life—except for the few remaining young people who look for a quick fix from a guru. Gone is the real historical sense of a Machiavelli who wrested a few hours from each busy day in which "to don regal and courtly garments, enter the courts of the ancients and speak with them."

None of this concerns those who promote the new curriculum. The point   9
is to propagandize acceptance of different ways, and indifference to their real content is as good a means as any. It was not necessarily the best of times in America when Catholics and Protestants were suspicious of and hated one another, but at least they were taking their beliefs seriously, and the more or less satisfactory accommodations they worked out were not simply the result of apathy about the state of their souls. Practically all that young Americans have today is an insubstantial awareness that there are many cultures, accompanied by a saccharine moral drawn from that awareness: We should all get along. Why fight? In 1980, during the crisis with Iran, the mother of one of the hostages expressed our current educational principles very well. She went to Iran to beg for her son's release, against the express wishes of the government of her country, the very week a rescue of the hostages was attempted. She justified her conduct by explaining that a mother has a right to try to save her son and also to learn a new culture. These are two basic rights, and her trip enabled her to kill two birds with one stone. . . .

One of the techniques of opening young people up is to require a college   10
course in a non-Western culture. Although many of the persons teaching such courses are real scholars and lovers of the areas they study, in every case I have seen this requirement—when there are so many other things that can and should be learned but are not required, when philosophy and religion are no longer required—has a demagogic intention. The point is to force students to recognize that there are other ways of thinking and that Western ways are not better. It is again not the content that counts but the lesson to be drawn. Such requirements are part of the effort to establish a world community and train its member—the person devoid of prejudice. But if the students were really to learn something of the minds of any of these non-Western cultures—which they do not—they would find that each and every

one of these cultures is ethnocentric. All of them think their way is the best way, and all others are inferior. Herodotus tells us that the Persians thought that they were the best, that those nations bordering on them were next best, that those nations bordering on the nations bordering on them were third best, and so on, their worth declining as the concentric circles were farther from the Persian center. This is the very definition of ethnocentrism. Something like this is as ubiquitous as the prohibition against incest between mother and son.

Only in the Western nations, i.e., those influenced by Greek philosophy, is   11 there some willingness to doubt the identification of the good with one's own way. One should conclude from the study of non-Western cultures that not only to prefer one's own way but to believe it best, superior to all others, is primary and even natural—exactly the opposite of what is intended by requiring students to study these cultures. What we are really doing is applying a Western prejudice—which we covertly take to indicate the superiority of our culture—and deforming the evidence of those other cultures to attest to its validity. The scientific study of other cultures is almost exclusively a Western phenomenon, and in its origin was obviously connected with the search for new and better ways, or at least for validation of the hope that our own culture really is the better way, a validation for which there is no felt need in other cultures. If we are to learn from those cultures, we must wonder whether such scientific study is a good idea. Consistency would seem to require professors of openness to respect the ethnocentrism or closedness they find everywhere else. However, in attacking ethnocentrism, what they actually do is assert unawares the superiority of their scientific understanding and the inferiority of the other cultures which do not recognize it at the same time that they reject all such claims to superiority. They both affirm and deny the goodness of their science. They face a problem akin to that faced by Pascal in the conflict between reason and revelation, without the intellectual intransigence that forced him to abandon science in favor of faith.

The reason for the non-Western closedness, or ethnocentrism, is clear.   12 Men must love and be loyal to their families and their peoples in order to preserve them. Only if they think their own things are good can they rest content with them. A father must prefer his child to other children, a citizen his country to others. That is why there are myths—to justify these attachments. And a man needs a place and opinions by which to orient himself. This is strongly asserted by those who talk about the importance of roots. The problem of getting along with outsiders is secondary to, and sometimes in conflict with, having an inside, a people, a culture, a way of life. A very great narrowness is not incompatible with the health of an individual or a people, whereas with great openness it is hard to avoid decomposition. The firm binding of the good with one's own, the refusal to see a distinction between the two, a vision of the cosmos that has a special place for one's people, seem to be conditions of culture. This is what really follows from the study of non-Western cultures proposed for undergraduates. It points them back to passionate attachment to their own and away from the science which liberates them from it. Science now appears as a threat to culture and a dangerous uprooting charm. In short, they are lost in a no-man's-land between the goodness of knowing and goodness of culture, where they have been placed by their teachers who no longer have the resources to guide them. Help must be sought elsewhere.

Greek philosophers were the first men we know to address the problems   13
of ethnocentrism. Distinctions between the good and one's own, between nature and convention, between the just and the legal are the signs of this movement of thought. They related the good to the fulfillment of the whole natural human potential and were aware that few, if any, of the nations of men had ways that allowed such fulfillment. They were open to the good. They had to use the good, which was not their own, to judge their own. This was a dangerous business because it tended to weaken wholehearted attachment to their own, hence weaken their peoples as well as to expose themselves to the anger of family, friends, and countrymen. Loyalty versus quest for the good introduced an unresolvable tension into life. But the awareness of the good as such and the desire to possess it are priceless humanizing acquisitions.

This is the sound motive contained, along with many other less sound   14
ones, in openness as we understand it. Men cannot remain content with what is given them by their culture if they are to be fully human. This is what Plato meant to show by the image of the cave in the *Republic* and by representing us as prisoners in it. A culture is a cave. He did not suggest going around to other cultures as a solution to the limitations of the cave. Nature should be the standard by which we judge our own lives and the lives of peoples. That is why philosophy, not history or anthropology, is the most important human science. Only dogmatic assurance that thought is culture-bound, that there is no nature, is what makes our educators so certain that the only way to escape the limitations of our time and place is to study other cultures. History and anthropology were understood by the Greeks to be useful only in discovering what the past and other peoples had to contribute to the discovery of nature. Historians and anthropologists were to put peoples and their conventions to the test, as Socrates did individuals, and go beyond them. These scientists were superior to their subjects because they saw a problem where others refused to see one, and they were engaged in the quest to solve it. They wanted to be able to evaluate themselves and others.

This point of view, particularly the need to know nature in order to have   15
a standard, is uncomfortably buried beneath our human sciences, whether they like it or not, and accounts for the ambiguities and contradictions I have been pointing out. They want to make us culture-beings with the instruments that were invented to liberate us from culture. Openness used to be the virtue that permitted us to seek the good by using reason. It now means accepting everything and denying reason's power. The unrestrained and thoughtless pursuit of openness, without recognizing the inherent political, social, or cultural problem of openness as the goal of nature, has rendered openness meaningless. Cultural relativism destroys both one's own and the

good. What is most characteristic of the West is science, particularly understood as the quest to know nature and the consequent denigration of convention—i.e., culture or the West understood as a culture—in favor of what is accessible to all men as men through their common and distinctive faculty, reason. Science's latest attempts to grasp the human situation—cultural relativism, historicism, the fact-value distinction—are the suicide of science. Culture, hence closedness, reigns supreme. Openness to closedness is what we teach.

Cultural relativism succeeds in destroying the West's universal or intellectually imperialistic claims, leaving it to be just another culture. So there is equality in the republic of cultures. Unfortunately the West if defined by its need for justification of its ways or values, by its need for discovery of nature, by its need for philosophy and science. This is its cultural imperative. Deprived of that, it will collapse. The United States is one of the highest and most extreme achievements of the rational quest for the good life according to nature. What makes its political structure possible is the use of the rational principles of natural right to found a people, thus uniting the good with one's own. Or, to put it otherwise, the regime established here promised untrammeled freedom to reason—not to everything indiscriminately, but to reason, the essential freedom that justifies the other freedoms, and on the basis of which, and for the sake of which, much deviance is also tolerated. An openness that denies the special claim of reason bursts the mainspring keeping the mechanism of this regime in motion. And this regime, contrary to all claims to the contrary, was founded to overcome ethnocentrism, which is in no sense a discovery of social science.   16

It is important to emphasize that the lesson the students are drawing from their studies is simply untrue. History and study of cultures do not teach or prove that values or cultures are relative. All to the contrary, that is a philosophical premise that we now bring to our study of them. This premise is unproven and dogmatically asserted for what are largely political reasons. History and culture are interpreted in the light of it, and then are said to prove the premise. Yet the fact that there have been different opinions about good and bad in different times and places in no way proves that none is true or superior to others. To say that it does so prove is as absurd as to say that the diversity of points of view expressed in a college bull session proves there is no truth. On the face of it, the difference of opinion would seem to raise the question as to which is true or right rather than to banish it. The natural reaction is to try to resolve the difference, to examine the claims and reasons for each opinion.   17

Only the unhistorical and inhuman belief that opinions are held for no reason would prevent the undertaking of such an exciting activity. Men and nations always think they have reasons, and it could be understood to be historians' and social scientists' most important responsibility to make explicit and test those reasons. It was always known that there were many and conflicting opinions about the good, and nations embodying each of them. Herodotus was at least as aware as we are of the rich diversity of cultures.   18

But he took that observation to be an invitation to investigate all of them to see what was good and bad about each and find out what he could learn about good and bad from them. Modern relativists take that same observation as proof that such investigation is impossible and that we must be respectful of them all. Thus students, and the rest of us, are deprived of the primary excitement derived from the discovery of diversity, the impulse of Odysseus, who, according to Dante, traveled the world to see the virtues and vices of men. History and anthropology cannot provide the answers, but they can provide the material on which judgment can work.

I know that men are likely to bring what are only their prejudices to the judgment of alien peoples. Avoiding that is one of the main purposes of education. But trying to prevent it by removing the authority of men's reason is to render ineffective the instrument that can correct their prejudices. True openness is the accompaniment of the desire to know, hence of the awareness of ignorance. To deny the possibility of knowing good and bad is to suppress true openness. A proper historical attitude would lead one to doubt the truth of historicism (the view that all thought is essentially related to and cannot transcend its own time) and treat it as a peculiarity of contemporary history. Historicism and cultural relativism actually are a means to avoid testing our own prejudices and asking, for example, whether men are really equal or whether that opinion is merely a democratic prejudice. . . .   19

Thus there are two kinds of openness, the openness of indifference—promoted with the twin purposes of humbling our intellectual pride and letting us be whatever we want to be, just as long as we don't want to be knowers—and the openness that invites us to the quest for knowledge and certitude, for which history and the various cultures provide a brilliant array of examples for examination. This second kind of openness encourages the desire that animates and makes interesting every serious student—"I want to know what is good for me, what will make me happy"—while the former stunts that desire.   20

Openness, as currently conceived, is a way of making surrender to whatever is most powerful, or worship of vulgar success, look principled. It is historicism's ruse to remove all resistance to history, which in our day means public opinion, a day when public opinion already rules. How often I have heard the abandonment of requirements to learn languages or philosophy or science lauded as a progress of openness. Here is where the two kinds of openness clash. To be open to knowing, there are certain kinds of things one must know which most people don't want to bother to learn and which appear boring and irrelevant. Even the life of reason is often unappealing; and useless knowledge, i.e., knowledge that is not obviously useful for a career, has no place in the student's vision of the curriculum. So the university that stands intransigently for humane learning must necessarily look closed and rigid. If openness means to "go with the flow," it is necessarily an accommodation to the present. That present is so closed to doubt about so many things impeding the progress of its principles that unqualified openness to it would mean forgetting the despised alternatives to it, knowledge of which   21 makes us aware of what is doubtful in it. True openness means closedness to all the charms that make us comfortable with the present.

When I was a young teacher at Cornell, I once had a debate about educa- 22 tion with a professor of psychology. He said that it was his function to get rid of prejudices in his students. He knocked them down like tenpins. I began to wonder what he replaced those prejudices with. He did not seem to have much of an idea of what the opposite of a prejudice might be. He reminded me of the little boy who gravely informed me when I was four that there is no Santa Claus, who wanted me to bathe in the brilliant light of truth. Did this professor know what those prejudices meant for the students and what effect being deprived of them would have? Did he believe that there are truths that could guide their lives as did their prejudices? Had he considered how to give students the love of the truth necessary to seek unprejudiced beliefs, or would he render them passive, disconsolate, indifferent, and subject to authorities like himself, or the best of contemporary thought? My informant about Santa Claus was just showing off, proving his superiority to me. He had not created the Santa Claus that had to be there in order to be refuted. Think of all we learn about the world from men's belief in Santa Clauses, and all that we learn about the soul from those who believe in them. By contrast, merely methodological excision from the soul of the imagination that projects Gods and heroes onto the wall of the cave does not promote knowledge of the soul; it only lobotomizes it, cripples its powers.

I found myself responding to the professor of psychology that I personally 23 tried to teach my students prejudices, since nowadays—with the general success of his method—they had learned to doubt beliefs even before they believed in anything. Without people like me, he would be out of business. Descartes had a whole wonderful world of old beliefs, of prescientific experience and articulations of the order of things, beliefs firmly and even fanatically held, before he even began his systematic and radical doubt. One has to have the experience of really believing before one can have the thrill of liberation. So I proposed a division of labor in which I would help to grow the flowers in the field and he could mow them down.

Prejudices, strong prejudices, are visions about the way things are. They 24 are divinations of the order of the whole of things, and hence the road to a knowledge of that whole is by the way of erroneous opinions about it. Error is indeed our enemy, but it alone points to the truth and therefore deserves our respectful treatment. The mind that has no prejudices at the outset is empty. It can only have been constituted by a method that is unaware of how difficult it is to recognize that a prejudice is a prejudice. Only Socrates knew, after a lifetime of unceasing labor, that he was ignorant. Now every high-school student knows that. How did it become so easy? What accounts for our amazing progress? Could it be that our experience has been so impoverished by our various methods, of which openness is only the latest, that there is nothing substantial enough left there to resist criticism, and we therefore have no world left of which to be really ignorant? Have we so simplified the soul that it is no longer difficult to explain? To an eye of dogmatic skepticism, nature herself, in all her lush profusion of expressions, might appear to be a prejudice. In her place we put a gray network of critical concepts, which were invented to interpret nature's phenomena but which strangled them and therewith destroyed their own *raison d'être*. Perhaps it is our first task to resuscitate those phenomena so that we may again have a world to which we can put our questions and be able to philosophize. This seems to me to be our educational challenge.

QUESTIONS FOR MEANING

1. According to Bloom, how has education changed in the way it prepares young men and women for life in a democracy?
2. What should be the real motive and purpose of education?
3. What does Bloom mean by "cultural relativism," "ethnocentrism," and "historicism"?
4. Why does Bloom object to undergraduate courses in non-Western culture? Is he opposed to the study of other cultures?
5. What are the two kinds of openness identified by Bloom?
6. Vocabulary: postulate (1), xenophobia (1), chauvinism (1), palpable (4), regressive (5), secularized (7), apathy (9), demagogic (10), denigration (15), dogmatically (17), ruse (21), lauded (21), lobotomizes (22).

QUESTIONS ABOUT STRATEGY

1. Where does Bloom summarize the views he rejects? Does he distinguish clearly between these views and his own?
2. What point is Bloom making by mentioning the American woman who went to Iran to try to get her son released from captivity? How does this example relate to the rest of his argument?
3. Does Bloom overgeneralize at any point?
4. Judging from your reading of this argument, for what sort of audience was Bloom originally writing?
5. How fair is Bloom's characterization of the average college student?

DAVID G. WINTER, ABIGAIL J. STEWART, AND DAVID C. McCLELLAND

Grading the Effects of a Liberal Arts Education

It is easy to generalize about education but hard to prove that some forms of education are more valuable than others. Advocates of the liberal arts have traditionally argued that the study of history, literature, and philosophy, together with the study of science, mathematics, and at least one foreign language, is of greater value than an education devoted exclusively to job training. Assumptions of this sort can be found in the essays by Hesburgh, Solomon, Cousins, and Thomas. In **1978,** *a team of psychologists put these assumptions to the test by conducting a study designed to determine if a liberal arts education yields specific skills that can be measured and compared to the abilities of students who have undergone other types of education.*

David G. Winter is a former Rhodes Scholar with a Ph.D. in psychology from Harvard. A contributor to numerous journals, he is the author of The Power Motive *(1973) and* The Don Juan Legend *(1975). He is married to Abigail J. Stewart, who teaches psychology at Boston University. Her principal research interests include personality and adaptation to stress. A graduate of Wesleyan University, Stewart has a M.Sc. from the London School of Economics and a Ph.D. from Harvard—where David C. McClelland has taught since 1956. His books include* The Roots of Consciousness *(1964),* The Drinking Man *(1971),* Power: The Inner Experience *(1975), and* The Achieving Society *(1976). For his research in psychology, McClelland has been awarded fellowships and grants from the Guggenheim, Carnegie, and Ford Foundations, the National Institute of Mental Health, and the U.S. State Department.*

For more than 2,000 years, a liberal education has been the ideal of the West—for the brightest, if not for all, students. The tradition goes back to Plato, who argued in *The Republic* that leadership should be entrusted to the philosopher—"a lover not of a part of wisdom only, but of the whole . . . able to distinguish the idea from the objects which participate in the idea." More recently, in a World War II-era treatise, a Harvard University committee concluded that a liberal education best prepared an individual to become "an expert in the general art of the free man and the citizen." The report, which led to the introduction of Harvard's general education curriculum, concluded, "The fruit of education is intelligence in action. The aim is mastery of life." 1

In recent years, the fruit has spoiled and such high-sounding rhetoric has been increasingly challenged. Critics have charged that liberal arts education is elitist education, based on undefined and empty shibboleths. Caroline Bird, social critic and author, argues in *The Case Against College* that the liberal arts are a religion, "the established religion of the ruling class." Bird writes, "The exalted language, the universalistic setting, the ultimate value, the in- 2 ability to define, the appeal to personal witness . . . these are all the familiar modes of religious discourse."

Students in the 1960s charged that such traditional liberal arts courses as 3 "Western Thought and Institutions" and "Contemporary Civilization" were ethnocentric and imperialistic. Other students found little stimulation in a curriculum that emphasized learning to both formulate ideas and engage in rational discourse. They preferred, instead, to express themselves in experience and action; they favored feeling over thought, the nonverbal over the verbal, the concrete over the abstract. In the inflationary, job-scarce economy of the 1970s, many students argue that the liberal arts curriculum is "irrelevant" because it neither prepares them for careers nor teaches them marketable skills. In its present form, moreover, liberal arts education is expensive education.

Partly in response to these charges and, more immediately to faculty dis- 4 content, Harvard recently approved a redesigning of the liberal arts program. Faculty had complained that the growing numbers and varieties of courses had "eroded the purpose of the existing general education program." Students, they felt, could use any number of courses to satisfy the university's minimal requirements, making those requirements meaningless. The new core curriculum will require students to take eight courses carefully distributed among five basic areas of knowledge.* The Harvard plan proposed to give students "a critical appreciation of the ways in which we gain knowledge and understanding of ourselves." Plausible as this credo may be, it rests on rhetoric and not solid research evidence—like curriculum innovations of the 1960s.

In an era of educational accounting and educational accountability, it would 5 be helpful to have a way of determining what the essential and most valuable "core" of a university education is and what is peripheral and mere tradition. What are the actual effects of a liberal education, this most persistent of Western ideals? It is sobering to realize that we have little firm evidence.

Against this background, we recently designed and carried out a new study 6 to get some of the evidence. Our findings suggest that liberal arts education does, in fact, change students more or less as Plato envisioned, so that the durability of this educational ideal in Western civilization may not be undeserved. In our research, liberal education appears to promote increases in conceptual and social-emotional sophistication. Thus, according to a number of new tests we developed, students trained in the liberal arts are better able to formulate valid concepts, analyze arguments, define themselves, and orient themselves maturely to their world. The liberal arts education in at least one college also seems to increase the leadership motivation pattern—a desire for power, tempered by self-control.

The precise concept of a liberal education remains unclear. Is it the study 7 of certain "core" disciplines or bodies of knowledge—courses in Western civilization or modern literature, or a particular set of "Great Books"? Does it

---

*These are (1) letters and arts; (2) history; (3) social and philosophical analysis; (4) science and mathematics; (5) foreign languages and cultures.

require a multidisciplinary approach, as, for example, in courses entitled "Science and Responsibility" or "Freedom and Authority in the Modern Novel"? Many professors argue that the essence is not *what* is learned, but *how* it is taught—with an emphasis on concepts rather than facts, on independent inquiry rather than learning by rote. Some educators, perhaps half-facetiously, contend that liberal arts include everything that is not of obvious practical or vocational use!

The Harvard committee during World War II theorized that general education fostered four traits of mind: thinking effectively, communicating thought, making relevant judgments, and discriminating among values. Some 33 years later, the committee headed by present dean Henry Rosovsky characterized the goals of the liberally educated person in similarly luxuriant language: to "think and write clearly and effectively"; to have "some understanding of, and experience in thinking about, moral and ethical problems"; and to use experiences in the context of "other cultures and other times." 8

Still, these traits and skills remain largely unmeasured and ignored by psychologists who, even when they study "thinking," focus on much more elemental and simple processes. Most of the abundant research on the effects of higher education have focused on changes in personality, values, and beliefs. Even here, the conclusions are largely equivocal: many college "effects" are due to the process by which the students were chosen in the first place and not to the changes that occur during college. Studies have shown, for instance, that attitudes are stabilized as much as they are altered during college. 9

We started our study from two fundamental premises: first, that the evidence to date was probably more a reflection of the testing procedures used than of the efficacy of higher education; and, second, that new tests should be modeled on what university students actually do rather than on what researchers can easily score. If liberal education teaches articulate formation of complex concepts, then student research subjects should be asked to form concepts from complex material and then scored on how well they articulate them, rather than being asked to choose the "best" of five concepts by putting a check mark in one of the boxes. In more formal terms, tests of the effects of education should be *operant* tests that require operating on material and making up answers, rather than *respondent* tests that merely ask for choices from among precoded alternatives. 10

Any study of the effects of higher education has the difficult task of distinguishing educational effects from simple maturational effects. In order to have some control over the effects of maturation, therefore, we tested students who were receiving three different *kinds* of higher education: 11

  1. A traditional four-year liberal arts education at a prestigious Eastern U.S. institution. By any definition, students attending this school enjoy a curriculum that is considered liberal arts. It is a well-endowed, private college with a tradition of scholarly excellence, an eminent faculty, and great prestige. Its students, drawn from this country and 12

abroad, must satisfy very competitive admissions standards. The college accepts 20 percent of all applicants. Approximately two-thirds of its students are men and one-third women. The curriculum emphasizes broad, interdisciplinary survey courses in the sciences, humanities, and social sciences, and individualized scholarship at all stages of the college career.

2. A four-year undergraduate program for training teachers and other   13
professionals. The offerings at this state-controlled institution have been expanded in recent years to include such general and career programs as law enforcement and health education. The college's students, drawn from a large metropolitan area, must pass moderately competitive admissions standards; about one-half of those who apply are accepted. The student body is about evenly divided between men and women.

3. A two-year community college that offers career programs in data   14
processing, electronics, nursing, secretarial skills, and business administration. A publicly controlled institution, our community college is situated in a city and draws most of its students from nearby suburbs. It has a relatively nonselective admissions policy, accepting about 70 percent of those who apply. The student body is 60 percent male.

We administered three kinds of tests to a total of 414 students, half men   15
and half women, drawn from the first-year and last-year classes of the three colleges. We controlled statistically for intelligence and social class, to eliminate differences in performance based on these two characteristics. By comparing the test scores of first- and last-year students at each school, we hoped to determine the degree and nature of any changes brought about by the educational programs. By evaluating all three schools together, we hoped to find out whether the liberal arts school has a unique impact on its students.

With our new Test of Thematic Analysis, we examined the students' abil-   16
ities to create and express sophisticated concepts (see box, pages 392–93). We asked them to read two groups of brief, imaginative stories and then to describe the differences between the two in any way they liked. We awarded positive values to their work when they perceived characteristics of both story groups that could sensibly be compared and contrasted, used examples and qualifications to strengthen their arguments, legitimately redefined aspects of stories to support their theses, and found general categories to group apparently unrelated elements. When they compared unlike things or used affective and subjective phrasing such as "It makes the reader nervous" or "It left me satisfied," we awarded negative values.

At all three institutions, last-year students scored higher than first-year   17
students, but seniors at the liberal arts college far outdistanced their counterparts at the teachers' and community colleges.

Thus, a typical freshman at any of the schools might describe the differ-   18
ences between the two groups of stories in rather wandering terms: "Group B stories are more exciting than Group A stories. They were about nasty

TESTING ONE, TWO, THREE SETS OF STUDENTS

In the Test of Thematic Analysis—a measure of complex concept formation—students were asked to compare and contrast two groups of brief stories, labeled A and B. Below are sample stories taken from each group, followed
by typical responses written by a final-year student at each of the three
colleges in our study.

Researchers scored answers in terms of the sophistication shown in the
analysis and in the writing. Subjective opinions, based on emotional reactions to stories, and comparisons between totally dissimilar events or ideas
were scored negatively. Statements supported by specific examples and parallel comparisons were considered evidence of complex reasoning and were
scored positively. The liberal arts students—especially seniors—scored significantly higher on this test than did their counterparts at the other
two schools.

Group A Story

It is a trial and the people are lawyers.

They are all involved in various machinations against the others in the
trial which is to reveal graft.

All the trust that each put in someone else has been shattered by the
letter which reveals the various plots and subplots taking place during
the trial.

They will all be thrown in jail.

Group B Story

They are all politicians at a debate. One of them just got a special-delivery
letter from a colleague not able to attend.

The man who wrote the letter is held in high esteem by the others.

They are all depending on the person who wrote the letter and now he
has disappointed them.

They will seek a new "leader," someone to respect more than the others
and to look to him for guidance.

Senior at the Liberal Arts College

"In each of the stories there are two major relationships: that among the
figures described and (usually implicitly [*qualification*, scored +1]) that

leaders and I don't like that. Group B stories show people as not trusting
each other." A typical final-year student at our liberal arts college might put
what is essentially the same contrast in these terms: "Both groups of stories
involve relations to authority. In Group A, authority is either accepted or
actively rejected; while Group B stories involve moderate suspicion of au-

between the group in the picture and the writer of the story [*overarching issue,* followed by a *parallel comparison* between the two groups, both scored +1]. In Group A, each writer feels that self-interest divides the figures from one another and that what they are doing is either criminal—hence to his own disadvantage—or at least not helpful to him. In Group B, each writer conceives of a cooperative relationship among the figures in the picture and thinks of them as performing a service which may benefit him (*e.g.,* medical progress, newscasting [*examples,* scored +1]) or is at least in itself worthwhile [*subsuming alternatives,* scored +1]—thoughtful speaking on controversial issues, leadership for those who feel they need it."

Senior at the Teachers' College

"Whoever wrote Group A does not have a very positive image of man. In all four stories, man is dishonest, out for himself, arrogant, materialistic and all the uncomplimentary character defects I can think of. But I must admit they make for more interesting reading [*subjective reaction,* scored −1]. Everyone is manipulating everyone else for his own benefit. . . .

"Group B is very factual but rather cut and dry—no human emotions involved whatsoever ["apples and oranges," *nonparallel comparison* with Group A, scored −1]. I personally enjoy reading stories which include people's feelings, reactions and emotions; showing both their human weaknesses and their great strengths."

Sophomore (final year) at the Community College

"It seems to be that in the stories in Group A, in every case, each story makes the reader have a bad feeling [*affective reaction,* scored −1]. The people in the higher positions such as lawyers or politicians are generally men who should be respected. In the stories, however, they come across as cheaters, liars, men out to better themselves and cheat the people. The people who trust them and are more or less considered 'good people,' who come out of the stories in a disillusioned way but also appear as the ones who the reader should 'root' for to win in the end.

"In Group B stories, there is an element of togetherness and cooperation of the people in the stories ["apples and oranges," *nonparallel comparison* with Group A, scored −1]. I as the reader came out of these stories with an easier feeling and with more respect for the people involved [*subjective reaction,* scored −1]."

thority. While story A-4, an animal fable, might seem an exception to the rule, it does, in fact, fit if one considers the phrase 'king of the beasts' as representing symbolic authority."

Liberal education, then, seems to affect the way in which people marshal, 19 organize, and "operate" on facts. These processes are spontaneous, self-initiated, and active, and are the same ones called for by an essay assignment to "compare and contrast the Renaissance and the Reformation," or an examination question asking, "What are the essential differences between normal and malignant cells?" We believe these processes are more central to a liberal education than learning simple concepts and memorizing detailed facts. Indeed, we gave the students an adaptation of a standard reading-comprehension test and found that none of the three schools significantly affected the ability to learn and remember isolated facts.

As another means of probing the conceptual processes and reasoning abil-   20
ities of the three groups of students, Abigail Stewart devised an Analysis of Argument test. The test first quotes an extreme, unpopular, and rather badly argued position on a controversial issue. Students must attack this position and support their own stance with reasoned argument. Again, the quality of the attacks improved from first to final year at all three schools, but more so at our liberal arts institution. Thus, a typical first-year student would dispute a series of facts: "X is wrong when he says that . . ." A final-year attack focused on a more abstract, general principle, such as faulty logic: "X's arguments all derive from a confusion of association with causation."

In the second step of Stewart's test, students switched sides and had to   21
defend the position they had formerly attacked. Most floundered and simply substituted a blank endorsement for a blanket attack. Only our final-year liberal arts students were able to craft a limited, qualified endorsement of a position they had opposed. They could respond: "While there are flaws in X's whole line of reasoning, it must be admitted that some of his particular claims and examples are true." In other words, the liberally educated students were better able to argue both sides of a question, but with integrity and intelligence rather than by simply espousing the other point of view uncritically.

The other changes in student ability unique to, or more pronounced at,   22
the liberal arts college involved measures in the Thematic Apperception Test (TAT), a "projective" test that clinicians have used for over 40 years to assess personality. Subjects see a series of vague and ambiguous pictures—a man wearing the uniform of a ship's captain talking with a man in a business suit, for example, or two women in lab coats using equipment such as a test tube—and must tell or write stories about the pictures. Researchers may use any number of scoring systems to analyze the results, depending on the personality characteristics that interest them. We were looking for three elements in the responses: self-definition, maturity of adaptation to the environment, and the leadership motivation pattern.

A story that scores high in self-definition uses causal words such as "be-   23
cause" and "in order to," and portrays characters who take actions for reasons, for example: "After being miserable for a while, the woman in the picture will realize that her love affair won't work and will leave." Low-scoring stories portray ineffective actions, events with no apparent causes, and characters who experience intense feelings in response to others' actions, but who are unable to act themselves: "The man and woman pictured will try desperately to establish a love relationship, but will end up feeling only more alone." In a

number of studies, people who score high in self-definition act instrumentally (that is, effectively and constructively), often in ways that go beyond ascribed roles. Self-defining women, for example, tend to seek careers as well as marriage, and in many different ways are not limited by traditional sex roles. Thus, self-definition is associated with an instrumental, effective style of translating thought into action. When compared with the teachers' and community colleges, the liberal arts college produced unique and significant gains in student self-definition.

Maturity of adaptation to the environment refers to success in developing 24 characteristics that personality theorists have identified as representing the highest level of personality growth or maturity. Drawing on the ideas of Freud and Erik Erickson, who described the "stages" of development, Stewart recently worked out a TAT measure of this adaptation. As we expected, students at all three institutions showed higher stages of adaptation over time, but those at the liberal arts college showed larger, more significant gains. In terms of particular scoring categories from the Stewart measure, this means that students, our liberal arts students in particular: (1) see authority in complex, versus simplistic, pro and con terms; (2) view other people as differentiated beings in their own right, rather than as simple means of gratifying their (the students') desires; (3) integrate both joy and sorrow into their moods; (4) are able to work without falling victim to passivity, self-doubt, or anxiety about failure.

Seniors at the teachers' and community colleges scored higher than fresh- 25 men in both maturity of adaptation and self-definition, suggesting that almost any kind of higher education, or even just physical and social maturation, has some influence on these variables. But for all measures, the gains at the liberal arts college were significantly greater.

It appears that the liberal arts college also fosters a unique pattern of 26 motivation in its students: strong concern for power and weak concern for affiliation, combined with high self-control or ability to inhibit activity. Thus, the final-year liberal arts students wrote more TAT stories with the following combination of characteristics: (1) one character has an impact (or tries to) on another; (2) activity is restrained or inhibited—as indicated by the use of such words as "not" or "cannot"; and (3) characters do not show concern with establishing and maintaining warm, friendly relations with others.

David McClelland, of Harvard, has called this set of characteristics the 27 leadership or "imperial" motive pattern. In a series of experiments, McClelland has demonstrated that it is usually found in individuals who are considered effective leaders—managers who have a talent for creating in their subordinates such qualities as high morale, a sense of responsibility, organizational clarity, and "team spirit." For, while the qualities of an imperial motive suggest that a person is not compassionate, they generally dictate that he will be fair, treating others in an impartial manner that subordinates seem to appreciate.

The present study of only three colleges limits inference and further spec- 28 ulation. We must study other liberal arts schools to discover whether they have the same impact on the students as the liberal arts college discussed here. The issue will likely be complex. Indeed, data we recently collected from another college similar to the liberal arts school we examined suggest that liberal education there increases self-definition, but decreases maturity and has little or no effect on the imperial pattern.

When we know more about what causes the kinds of changes in students 29 detailed here, then our research can contribute to shaping educational policy. But who can say, from the evidence now at hand, that the effects of liberal education at our liberal arts college, or anywhere else, are caused by course requirements at all? It may be that the worth of an education at any school is determined more by faculty quality, library facilities, the size of the endowment, or even by the self-fulfilling anticipations and beliefs of faculty and students. We are currently seeking answers to these questions, taking our new test procedures to students at more than 15 different post-secondary-school institutions. During the next year or two, we hope to point to specific qualities of liberal arts colleges that leave their particular imprints on the students.

Still, the changes unique to, or enhanced by, attendance at our liberal arts 30 college do establish at least a prima-facie for education in the liberal arts. The pious goals and extravagant language of liberal arts educators must yet be analyzed, broken down into specific skills. With tests to measure student abilities in these skills, we can determine whether liberal arts education is doing what its proponents claim and how its performance can be improved.

QUESTIONS FOR MEANING

1. In what paragraphs do the authors state the thesis of their argument by summarizing the results of their research?
2. What specific abilities did liberal arts students prove to master, excelling students in the other two schools involved in this study?
3. What types of courses constitute the "liberal arts," and how are such courses usually best taught? What is the advantage of this type of teaching? Have you ever taken a course that was taught this way? What did you like or dislike about it?
4. What two premises determined the way in which the authors of this study went about conducting their research?
5. Explain the differences between operant and respondent testing. Can you give examples of these tests from your own experience in school?
6. What variables did the authors need to consider in analyzing their data? What steps did they take to make sure they were making fair comparisons?
7. In evaluating student responses to their Test of Thematic Analysis, what strengths and weaknesses were the researchers looking for? Explain in your own words why points were awarded and subtracted.
8. In the Analysis of Argument test, why were the essays of liberal arts students considered the strongest and most sophisticated?

9. What do the authors mean by "self-definition" in paragraphs 22 and 23?
10. Vocabulary: shibboleths (2), imperialistic (3), plausible (4), credo (4), innovations (4), peripheral (5), rote (7), facetiously (7), equivocal (9), eminent (12), floundered (21), affiliation (26), and prima-facie (30).

QUESTIONS ABOUT STRATEGY

1. In paragraphs 2 and 3, the authors summarize the main objections to liberal arts education. What advantage is there to doing this so early in their essay?
2. Do the authors explain their tests clearly? Do they tell you enough about them so that you can understand what the tests were designed to reveal? Similarly, how clearly do they report the results of their tests?
3. Where do the authors caution their readers, pointing out that their conclusions are only tentative an subject to further research? Do they provide any evidence to suggest that their initial results may be disputable?
4. Although their research supported the value of a liberal arts education, do the authors have any reservations about the liberal arts—or liberal arts educators? Consider the tone they adopt when discussing faculty and students at liberal arts schools.
5. Judging from this essay, what type of education do you think the authors had? Do you think they had any biases that may have affected their research? Can you point to anything in the essay that suggest that this may have been the case?

ONE STUDENT'S ASSIGNMENT

What should students expect from college? Draw upon your own expectations, material in The Informed Argument, *and at least two sources that you have found on your own through library research. At least one of these additional sources should be an article in a scholarly journal. Choose a documentation style suitable for your major.*

The Career Rut
Janet Jurgella

If one more person asks me why I'm going to college, I think   1
I'll scream. The fact that I am a married, non-working mother
of four young children causes some people to question my desire for a college degree. "Do you want to teach?" they ask.
Or "Are you going back to work when the kids are in school?"

Many people just assume that all college students are looking for their niche in the work force. I, for one, have no
desire to work outside my home, although I don't usually admit it.

But I will admit that Caroline Bird is telling me nothing   2
new when she speaks of "where college fails us." She says
that today's student will not get out of college what he or
she puts into it—monetarily or emotionally. And she feels a
college diploma is no assurance to an employer that the graduate has the right credentials for the job (372–75). Both
points are obvious and accepted in many other situations,
too. A worker who puts years into an apprenticeship may not
be accepted into the profession; or an heir to a business
might work tirelessly as a junior executive only to find that
Dear Old Dad squandered away the family fortune during his
last trip to Vegas. And, in reference to the second point,
are there <u>any</u> guarantees that an applicant is perfect for the
job? Don't you think that maybe sometimes the personnel director simply closes his eyes and points?

So those people, like myself, who invest in a college edu-   3
cation knowing the degree may not help them get a job must
have other reasons for doing so. What might they be?

Joseph Cangemi of Western Kentucky University asked col-   4
lege students, professors, and administrators what they
thought was the major purpose of higher education. His survey included twelve items which the respondents scaled from
"unimportant" to "more than important." "Unimportant" meant
the respondent did not expect a college to provide such, and
"more than important" indicated such a provision was imperative (Cangemi 152). Cangemi found essential agreement that
higher education has a real purpose of contributing toward a
student's psychological health, self-development, and realization of potential (151). Surprisingly, those areas
which would usually be considered career related did not receive high importance ratings.

Of course, we all realize that most students need to learn   5
practical skills which will improve their chance of decent
employment after graduation. But there are other important
skills a university can teach that seemingly have nothing to
do with a career. Norman Cousins, in his essay "How to Make
People Smaller Than They Are," argues that the increasing
vocationalization of higher education is narrowing the hu-

man mind. He believes that the most valuable asset a businessman can have is the ability "to deal with abstractions or
complexities, or to feel comfortable with subtleties of
thought or language, or to think sequentially" (359). And
it's the humanities courses, like English and philosophy,
which can teach this ability. In fact, Cousins thinks such
courses should be left out of the curriculum only if we believe the student will never need to make an important decision, the past won't influence his life, his creativity
won't bring happiness, he'll never have an intimate relationship, or will never face pain and unhappiness (359–60).
In other words, he believes that knowledge about life is more
important than knowledge about business. In my opinion,
life's challenges will be handled more effectively if they
are dealt with on this broad problem–solving level. A minor
glitch during a business day needn't become a crisis if it is
handled with the sort of calm, creative attitude of one who
has been there before, whether in theory or practice.

    Since I don't plan on being a future job seeker, you may
think I am in no position to put down Caroline Bird's data.
But I can still sympathize with career–minded students who
wonder if their four or more years in college will be worth
it. James Pickering and Nicholas Vacc of the University of
North Carolina believe that colleges should offer better career guidance for their students. They think there is a need
for "closer scrutiny of career intervention goals, processes, and outcomes" (Pickering and Vacc 149). If better
individual counseling were provided, fewer young people
would be surprised at the lack of jobs available upon graduation, say Pickering and Vacc. Communication would be more
open and students would be more aware, opting to change majors, go right into the job market, or tough it out in their
chosen field of study.

    But students should realize that uncertainty is part of
every phase of life and that they may regret bypassing a college degree. In any event, the decision is individual and
personal. I find it difficult to accept generalizations
about the value or failings of a college education when there
are so many factors which can influence a student. Whether
higher education helps the student with career goals or simply helps him grow is something that he alone can decide. My
own late arrival at higher education was prompted by an in-

6

7

terest in literature and writing. For me, the importance of
obtaining a college degree is secondary to the stimulation,
the insight, and the challenges that I know I will meet during the course of my studies.

Works Cited

Bird, Caroline. "Where College Fails Us." <u>The Informed Ar-</u>
<u>gument</u>. Ed. Robert K. Miller. San Diego: Harcourt, 1989.
370–77.

Cangemi, Joseph P. "The Real Purpose of Higher Education: Developing Self–Actualizing Personalities." <u>Education</u> 105
(Winter 1984): 151–4.

Cousins, Norman. "How to Make People Smaller Than They Are."
<u>The Informed Argument</u>. Ed. Robert K. Miller. San Diego:
Harcourt, 1989. 358–60.

Pickering, James W. and Nicholas A. Vacc. "Effectiveness of
Career Development Interventions for College Students:
A Review of Published Research." <u>The Vocational Guid-</u>
<u>ance Quarterly</u> 32 (March 1984): 149–59.

SUGGESTIONS FOR WRITING

1. Both Caroline Bird and Carrie Tuhy question the value of a college education as a means of securing a good job. How do you think your education will affect your own career? If you believe that a college education
is essential for employment in your chosen field, write an essay designed
to prove that this is so.

2. Write a defense for one course that you believe all students should take,
regardless of their major.

3. Evaluate the basic degree requirements at your school. Will they give you
the sort of knowledge that Newman and Cousins recommend? Are there
too many requirements? Can requirements be satisfied with courses that
offer little substance? If you believe that the degree requirements should
be changed in some way, write an essay explaining and supporting your
view.

4. Write an essay arguing on behalf of learning a foreign language.

5. Did your high school give you an adequate preparation for college? If you
are finding college more difficult than it should be, and believe that this
is because your high school education was weak, write an essay describing what was wrong at your school. Argue on behalf of a necessary
reform.

6. Writing more than ten years ago, Caroline Bird commented on the large number of students graduating from American colleges and argued that the economy could not absorb so many graduates. Every year since then, our colleges and universities have continued to produce hundreds of thousands of new graduates. Write an essay that will argue one of the following propositions: (1) College entrance requirements should be made more rigorous and selective so that degrees will carry more prestige; or (2) the government has a responsibility to ensure that everyone in the country, regardless of background, has access to higher education.

7. Do you learn anything important in college outside of the classroom that could not be leaned elsewhere? Is so, write an essay identifying this knowledge and arguing on behalf of its importance.

8. Consider the length of a college education. Are four years too little or too much?

9. How does the reading you do as a class assignment differ from the reading you do on your own? Write an essay in defense of reading that will explain why it is important to discuss what one has read.

10. What is the relationship between higher education and freedom? Write an essay explaining how knowledge can make one free.

11. If you are planning to drop out of college, or to take at least a semester off, write an argument that will justify your decision. Assume that you are writing for an audience that believes that you should remain in school.

Section 8
Literary Criticism: What Does a Poem Mean?

Stopping by Woods on a Snowy Evening

Whose woods these are I think I know.
His house is in the village though;
He will not see me stopping here
To watch his woods fill up with snow.

5   My little horse must think it queer
To stop without a farmhouse near
Between the woods and frozen lake
The darkest evening of the year.

He gives his harness bells a shake
10   To ask if there is some mistake.
The only other sound's the sweep
Of easy wind and downy flake.

The woods are lovely, dark and deep.
But I have promises to keep,
15   And miles to go before I sleep
And miles to go before I sleep.

Robert Frost

The steaming horses think it queer

Bo

little how   must
The troul   tejous   th think it queer

To
We stop with not a farm house near

the woods   an afrozen
Between a forest and a lake

The darkest evening of the year

She   her
He gives harness bells a shake

To ask if there is some mistake

The only other sounds the sweep

clowny
Of easy wind and faily flake.

The woods are lovely dark and deep

But I have promises to keep

That bid me

And miles to go before I sleep

And miles to go before I sleep

Facsimile of Robert Frost's handwritten draft of the last three stanzas of "Stopping by Woods on a Snowy Evening."

JOHN HOLMES

On Frost's "Stopping by Woods on a Snowy Evening"

Poet and educator John Holmes (1904–1962) graduated from Tufts College in 1929. He taught briefly at Lafayette College in Pennsylvania before returning to Tufts in 1934, where he taught poetry until his death twenty-eight years later. He was poetry critic for the Boston Evening Transcript, *and a reviewer for the* New York Times *and the* Atlantic Monthly. *His many books include* Address to the Living *(1937)*, The Poet's Work *(1939)*, Fair Warning *(1939)*, Map of My Country *(1943)*, The Symbols *(1955)*, Writing Poetry *(1960), and* The Fortune Teller *(1961). His explication of "Stopping By Woods on a Snowy Evening" was origi-nally published in* **1943.** *It demonstrates what an intelligent reader can learn from studying a poet's revisions.*

This facsimile [on the previous page] is a reproduction of the last three stanzas of "Stopping by Woods on a Snowy Evening" as Robert Frost worked it out. We know from the poet that he had just written the long poem, "New Hampshire," in one all-night unbroken stretch of composition, and that he then turned a page of his workbook and wrote this short poem without stop-ping. This fact has interesting implications. "New Hampshire" is a discourse in the idiomatic blank verse that is so peculiarly Frost's own style—the rhythms of natural speech matched to the strict but inconspicuous iambic pentame-ter, the beat always discernible but never formal. It is reasonable to suppose that after the hours spent in writing the long poem, in its loosened but never loose manner, he was ready, unconsciously, for a poem in strict pattern. He had also obviously had in his head for some time the incident on which the short poem was to be based, as well as the use he wished to make of it. He committed himself, as he has said, to the four-stress iambic line and to the *aaba* rime-scheme, in the first stanza, which he wrote rapidly and did not revise. He knew what he had seen, and he knew how he wanted to write it.

> Whose woods these are I think I know.
> His house is in the village though;
> He will not see me stopping here
> To watch his woods fill up with snow.

"That went off so easily I was tempted into the added difficulty of picking up my 3 for my 1-2-4 to go on with in the second stanza. I was amused and scared at what that got me into," Frost says. The facsimile shows what it got him into, how he got out of it, and how he achieved the poem as it meant itself to be written.

It began with what was the actual experience of stopping at night by some dark woods in winter, and the fact that there were two horses. He remembered what he saw then. "The steaming horses think it queer." But the poem needs truth more than fact, and he cancels the line, and begins again, "The horse begins to think it queer," but doesn't like the word "begins," needing in the allowed space a word that will particularize the horse, so writes "The little horse must think it queer." Now he runs into a grammatical difficulty, which must somehow be solved before he gets on into the poem he already feels sure of. "I launched into the construction 'My little horse must think it queer that we should stop.' I didn't like omitting the 'that' and I had no room for 'should.' I had the luck to get out of it with the infinitive." This groping and warming-up has a kind of impatience, an urgency to get on with the poem, but not until all the parts are right. At this point the poet knew and did not know how the poem would end. He knew the feel, and the sense, and almost everything about the form—certainly enough to know when he got off the track.

Whether he revised the third line here or later we cannot know. But we   4
can see in several places in this poem his changes toward particularization. The line "Between a forest and a lake" is a notation, and "Between the woods and frozen lake" is a finished line of poetry. "A forest" is too big, too vague, but "the woods" is definite, and bounded; you get lost in a forest, but you can walk through and out of the woods, and probably you know who owns it—Vermonters do, as he has said in the first stanza. "A lake" has not the specific condition or picture of "frozen lake." This sort of revision, or what Frost calls, "touching up," is what makes a poem—this, plus the first inspiration. Either one, without the other, is unlikely to make a good poem.

The next stanza comes easier, because the rime-scheme has been deter-   5
mined, and one unexpected obstacle has been overcome. But once more there is a delay, as the poet makes a decision as to the "he" or "she"—and the more important and more interesting one about the falling snow. In writing "downy flake" for "fall of flake" the gain is great not only for accuracy of feeling and fact, but also for the music of the lines. The simple alliteration in "fall of flake" is canceled in favor of the word, one word, "downy," which blends with the vowel-chords a poet half-consciously makes and modulates as he goes. In this instance, it half-chimes with "sounds" and adds a rounder, fuller, and yet quieter tone.

Now the carry-over rime is "sweep," a fortunate one, really, and important   6
to the final solution of the rime-scheme. It is not too much to assume, knowing all we know about the circumstances of the writing of this poem—the all-night composition of "New Hampshire," and the sudden urge to catch and shape still another saved idea—that the darker, more confident, more rapid strokes of the pen show the poet's growing excitement. The end is in sight. The thing he believed could happen will happen, surely now, and he must hurry to get it onto the page. This is the real moment of power, and any poet's greatest satisfaction.

"The woods are lovely dark and deep / But I have promises to keep." The   7
first two lines of the last stanza come fast, and flow beautifully, the crest of the poem's emotion and its music. We cannot know whether he had held

them in his head, or had swept up to and into them as he felt the destined pattern fulfilling itself.

Then, with success in sight, there comes an awkward and unexpected stumble. He writes, "That bid me give the reins a shake," which may have been the fact and the action. But the rime is wrong. Not only has the rime been used in the previous stanza, but so has the image of the horse shaking his head and reins. Things are moving fast now, no doubt impatiently, but certainly with determination, shown in the heavy black lines of abrupt cancellation. He strikes out "me give the reins a shake," and writes above it, so the line will read, "That bid me on, and there are miles," and then the whole thing comes through! Of course! "Miles to go . . ." 8

That's what it was supposed to be—the feeling of silence and dark, almost overpowering the man, but the necessity of going on. "And miles to go before I sleep." Then the triumph in the whole thing, the only right and perfect last line, solving the problem of the carried-over rime, keeping the half-tranced state, and the dark, and the solitude, and man's great effort to be responsible man . . . the repetition of that line. 9

"Stopping by Woods on a Snowy Evening" can be studied as perfected structure, with the photostat manuscript to show that art is not, though it must always appear to be, effortless. It can be thought of as a picture: the whites, grays, and blacks of the masses and areas of lake, field, and woods, with the tiny figure of the man in the sleigh, and the horse. And it can be thought of as a statement of man's everlasting responsibility to man; though the dark and nothingness tempt him to surrender, he will not give in. 10

QUESTIONS FOR MEANING

1. What is the connection between "Stopping by Woods on a Snowy Evening" and the long poem "New Hampshire"?
2. Do you understand what Holmes means by "blank verse," "iambic pentameter," and "rime-scheme"? Identify any other vocabulary that seems peculiar to the analysis of poetry. If you have never studied poetry before, how can you find out what these terms mean?
3. Explain what Holmes means in paragraph 3 when he writes, "the poem needs truth more than fact."
4. According to Holmes, what are the two essential steps in the process of writing poetry?
5. What theme or themes does Holmes find in this poem?
6. Vocabulary: facsimile (1), idiomatic (1), inconspicuous (1), discernible (1), and modulates (5).

QUESTIONS ABOUT STRATEGY

1. Why was it useful for Holmes to reproduce a partial facsimile of the original manuscript of "Stopping by Woods on a Snowy Evening"? If he had been unable to do so, what sort of changes would he have had to make in his essay?

2. How can studying the manuscript version of a poem help us to better understand the finished version? Explain why Frost deleted "steaming" and why two horses were turned into one "little" horse. Explain also why Frost changed "a forest" to "the woods" and "a lake" to "frozen lake." Do you agree with Holmes's interpretation of these changes? Could the changes mean anything else?

3. What does this essay reveal about the nature of literary criticism? How does reading critically differ from other types of reading?

EARL DANIELS
Misreading Poetry

Earl Daniels (1893–1970) was a teacher, critic, and poet. He graduated from Clark University in 1914 and served in the Army during World War I. After the war, he returned to school—receiving his A.M. from the University of Chicago in 1922 and his Ph.D. from Harvard in 1926. His poetry was published in Harper's, America, *and* New Masses. *But Daniels is remembered principally for his long association with Colgate University, where he taught from 1930 to 1961. After his retirement, he gave to Colgate a library of over four thousand books, including manuscripts and first editions. "Misreading Poetry" is an editor's title for an excerpt from the introductory chapter of* The Art of Reading Poetry, *a college textbook first published in* **1941**.

If you are one of those taught to approach the presence of the poem in quest of vital lesson, of profound comment on man and the universe, the answer is, *Don't*. Here should be no halfway measures, no reducing the urge to philosophy by half, no gradual tapering-off. You may, after all, rest comfortable in the assurance that if philosophy and morals are present in any vital way, they will make themselves felt without your conscious searching for them, insistent on their share in your awareness of the complete poem.   1

The way of a group of college freshmen with . . . ["Stopping by Woods on a Snowy Evening"] illustrates how deadly this concern about morals may be. . . .   2

Here are some interpretations by freshmen who were supposed to be better-than-average students.   3

> a) In this poem the underlying thought seems to be that of suicide. . . . The last four lines of the poem indicate that the person decides he has more work to do on earth before he dies in order to fulfill a promise of some kind.

> b) A man who has promised to leave town after committing some crime, and has been told "to get going and don't stop." The line, "The darkest evening

of the year," might mean the disgrace he has brought on himself; and, "I have promises to keep," may mean he has promised to get out of the country.

c) If he didn't mention that the owner of the woods lived in the village, I would say he was talking about the life he has yet to live before he meets his Maker.

d) It deals with the thought of eternal rest. . . . But then the subject is brought back to reality with the thought of the things he has yet to do, and the rest of his life he has yet to spend.

e) It may represent one who is tired of life's hardships, and is tempted to drop by the wayside in some secluded retreat, but who must press on since he has many years of work ahead and many obligations to fulfill before such rest may be his.

f) Almost every day we find ourselves faced with the lures of temptation. We realize that we ought to keep on our way, yet the temptation to stay where all is peaceful and quiet is often too great for us to resist. While we are here in college we are often tempted to do the easiest thing. That is, to neglect our studies and to run around and have a good time. However we know that there are promises to be kept and obligations to be filled. We have been sent here by our parents for the purpose of receiving an education, and there is no doubt that our duty is to do all in our power to take advantage of this opportunity.

g) I am a college man. I am taking a pre-med course. I am away from home. I am open to temptations that college may offer me. Am I to take advantage of their owner's absence to sit and gaze in his woods—to take advantage of being away from my parents to stop by the wayside and admire the beautiful sirens? Or, am I to be a second Ulysses and have sufficient will power to overcome these temptations? Am I to stop where there is "easy wind and downy flake"— to sit back in my chair, just to dream and forget all hardships? Or am I to heed the impatience of the horse and the warning of the harness bell—to awaken to my willing call for me to go on? True, it is dark now, and I cannot see well, but do I not remember the vows that I have made—to go through at all costs? Yes, I must go through those long miles of roads rougher than *I* can imagine, before *I* call for time out.

Comments *f* and *g* are especially nauseous misunderstandings, and they represent the cardinal sin of personal application. To make a poem mean privately, to ourselves alone, to look first for directions about *our* life and *our* problems—no going wrong can be more abysmally bad. Like the old hocus-pocus magic-formula way in which the Bible used to be consulted, you put your question, open the book at random, drop an equally random finger on the page, and there you are—provided you are ingenious enough in twisting words to meet special situations and personal needs. The method is equally unintelligent with the Bible and with poetry, and to resort to it is to proclaim oneself part of an intellectual underworld of superstition and ignorance. The poet's message, so far as he has a message for the individual, is a message to the individual not in his private and peculiar selfhood, but in his representative capacity as a normal human being, as a man; it is part of the universality of the poet's speaking.

If facile talk about appreciation, concern with peripheral things, and preoccupation with morals and the meaning of life are heresies, what is sound doctrine in the reading of poetry? What is orthodox? What is a right approach to Frost's poem, or to any poem? The simple, natural approach, the easiest way. What is obvious in "Stopping by Woods on a Snowy Evening" is that the poet has had a perfectly everyday experience. On a snow-filled winter's afternoon, he has come to a patch of woodland; for no reason, save that he simply and unashamedly likes to, he has stopped, just to watch the woods fill up with snow. That is the experience, the start of the poem, which, from such an unassuming start, got itself written because *the poet enjoyed the experience,* remembered it, and something made him want to try to put it in words, *just for fun: the poem is a record of experience to be shared with a reader,* who must take it at this simple face value if he is to read the poem as it should be read. Most poems probably begin much like this. And if someone says, "It may never have happened to Frost; he may have imagined it all," the answer is that in literature and the arts there is no essential difference between experience in actuality and experience in imagination; both are the stuff of poems, in the broadest sense of the term, *experience.* It is really very little a reader's business whether a writer is using memory or imagination, so long as the reality of the result is not affected. Frost may, indeed, have imagined it all, so far as we have a right to know, or care.

But why should a poet want to share experience, if he has nothing "important" to say, no "lesson" to teach, if he is not intent on "improving society," and "bettering the conditions of the human race"? Like so many facts, this is a mystery, hid in elemental human nature. Men do act this way: human nature prompts them to want to tell others what has happened to them. All conversation is built on that ancient formula, "Have you heard this one?" The questioner hopes "this one" has not been heard, so that he can go on and tell his story, enjoy sharing his experience. 6

The woman in the [following] parable is a case in point. She had lost her money. It is not significant that she went on an orgy of spring cleaning, turning the house upside down, or that she found her money. But when she found it, and this is the important thing, her next move was to give a party, inviting friends and neighbors for miles around, just that they might rejoice with her because she had found what had been lost: in other words, that they might share her experience. So the poet, though tangibilities like money may not be involved. Something emotionally stirring has happened, and he makes a poem, which is his invitation to his friends and neighbors to rejoice with him. How ungracious of the friends and neighbors of the woman, if they had hunted for lessons in the experience, emphasized, perhaps, the moral that in the future she must be more careful about her money, suggested it was all an illustration of the guidance of a good providence, enabling her to recover her fortune—or any other testimony a dyed-in-the-wool moralist might strain to discover. They had been invited to a party; the woman didn't want lessons; she wanted them to have a good time with her. No less ungracious is the reader who would deduce moral teaching from "Stopping by Woods on a Snowy Evening," and from many other poems, when what the poet wants is that we should have a good time at his party, along with him, because he, in the first place, had a good time with his experience. Such sharing is the 7 request every good poet makes of his readers, and it leads straight to an idea at the heart of all poetry, the irrefragable cornerstone on which poetry rests. That idea . . . is that *poetry, reduced to its simplest, is only experience.* Experience moved the poet; he enjoyed it, and wanted to put it down on paper, as experience and nothing else, partly because writing is a self-contained action which is fun for the writer, partly because he wanted the reader to enjoy the experience with him. If we are to learn to read, we must begin with elemental, irreducible facts like this.

QUESTIONS FOR MEANING

1. Consider the student interpretations of "Stopping by Woods on a Snowy Evening" that Daniels reports. Of interpretations *a* through *e,* which is the most and least intelligent? Explain why Daniels objects to *f* and *g.* What does he mean when he protests against "twisting words to meet special situations and personal needs"?
2. According to Daniels, how *should* we read poetry?
3. How does Daniels define "experience"?
4. Does Daniels imply that poetry is without moral content, and that writing poetry is always fun? How do you know if a poem is profound—and that the poet has asked us to do more than have "a good time at his party"?
5. Vocabulary: abysmally (4), ingenious (4), facile (5), heresies (5), orthodox (5), tangibilities (7), irrefragable (7), and irreducible (7).

QUESTIONS ABOUT STRATEGY

1. Is Daniels fair to students? Are the student interpretations that he reports reasonably representative of how "better-than-average" college freshmen respond to "Stopping by Woods on a Snowy Evening"?
2. Why does Daniels emphasize that reading poetry should be fun? What has he assumed about his audience?
3. Explain the parable in paragraph 7 and the point it is meant to illustrate.

JOHN CIARDI

Robert Frost: The Way to the Poem

The son of Italian immigrants, John Ciardi (1916–1986) taught English at Harvard from 1946 to 1953 and at Rutgers from 1953 to 1961, when he gave up teaching in order to be a full-time writer and poet. His many volumes of poetry include Homeward to America *(1940),* Other Skies *(1947),* Live Another Day *(1949),* If I Marry You: A Sheaf of Love Poems *(1958), and* In the Stoneworks *(1961). He is also the author of* How Does a Poem Mean?—*a highly respected book of criticism on the nature of poetry—and a fine translation of Dante's* Divine Comedy. *A fellow of the American Academy of Arts and Letters, Ciardi won many awards, most notably the Prix de Rome (1956–1957). As poetry editor for the* Saturday Review *from 1956 to 1972, he was in a position not only to encourage new poets but also to challenge conventional ideas about well-known poems. His columns were frequently controversial, as can be seen from the letters inspired by the following* **1958** *essay on Frost. At a time when many readers liked to see Frost as a grandfatherly nature poet, a sort of literary Norman Rockwell, Ciardi was one of the first critics to emphasize the element of despair that can be found in much of Frost's work.*

1   The School System has much to say these days of the virtue of reading widely, and not enough about the virtues of reading less but in depth. There are any number of reading lists for poetry, but there is not enough talk about individual poems. Poetry, finally, is one poem at a time. To read any one poem carefully is the ideal preparation for reading another. Only a poem can illustrate how poetry works.

2   Above, therefore, is a poem ["Stopping by Woods on a Snowy Evening"]—one of the master lyrics of the English language, and almost certainly the best-known poem by an American poet. What happens in it?—which is to say, not *what* does it mean, but *how* does it mean? How does it go about being a human reenactment of human experience? The author—perhaps the thousandth reader would need to be told—is Robert Frost.

3   Even the TV audience can see that this poem begins as a seemingly-simple narration of a seemingly-simple incident but ends by suggesting meanings far beyond anything specifically referred to in the narrative. And even readers with only the most casual interest in poetry might be made to note the additional fact that, though the poem suggests those larger meanings, it is very careful never to abandon its pretense to being simple narration. There is duplicity at work. The poet pretends to be talking about one thing, and all the while he is talking about many others.

4   Many readers are forever unable to accept the poet's essential duplicity. It is almost safe to say that a poem is never about what it seems to be about. As much could be said of the proverb. The bird in the hand, the rolling stone, the stitch in time never (except by an artful double-deception) intend any sort of statement about birds, stones, or sewing. The incident of this poem, one must conclude, is at root a metaphor.

Duplicity aside, this poem's movement from the specific to the general   5
illustrates one of the basic formulas of all poetry. Such a grand poem as
Arnold's "Dover Beach" and such lesser, though unfortunately better known,
poems as Longfellow's "The Village Blacksmith" and Holmes's "The Cham-
bered Nautilus" are built on the same progression. In these three poems,
however, the generalization is markedly set apart from the specific narration,
and even seems additional to the telling rather than intrinsic to it. It is this
sense of division one has in mind in speaking of "a tacked-on moral."

There is nothing wrong-in-itself with a tacked-on moral. Frost, in fact, makes   6
excellent use of the device at times. In this poem, however, Frost is careful
to let the whatever-the-moral-is grow out of the poem itself. When the action
ends the poem ends. There is no epilogue and no explanation. Everything
pretends to be about the narrated incident. And that pretense sets the basic
tone of the poem's performance of itself.

The dramatic force of that performance is best observable, I believe, as a   7
progression in three scenes.

In scene one, which coincides with stanza one, a man—a New England   8
man—is driving his sleigh somewhere at night. It is snowing, and as the man
passes a dark patch of woods he stops to watch the snow descend into the
darkness. We know, moreover, that the man is familiar with these parts (he
knows who owns the woods and where the owner lives), and we know that
no one has seen him stop. As scene one forms itself in the theatre of the
mind's-eye, therefore, it serves to establish some as yet unspecified relation
between the man and the woods.

It is necessary, however, to stop here for a long parenthesis: Even so sim-   9
ple an opening statement raises any number of questions. It is impossible to
address all the questions that rise from the poem stanza by stanza, but two
that arise from stanza one illustrate the sort of thing one might well ask of
the poem detail by detail.

Why, for example, does the man not say what errand he is on? What is   10
the force of leaving the errand generalized? He might just as well have told
us that he was going to the general store, or returning from it with a jug of
molasses he had promised to bring Aunt Harriet and two suits of long under-
wear he had promised to bring the hired man. Frost, moreover, can handle
homely detail to great effect. He preferred to leave his motive generalized. Why?

And why, on the other hand, does he say so much about knowing the   11
absent owner of the woods and where he lives? Is it simply that one set of
details happened-in whereas another did not? To speak of things "happening-
in" is to assault the integrity of a poem. Poetry cannot be discussed meaningfully unless one can assume that everything in the poem—every last comma
and variant spelling—is in it by the poet's specific act of choice. Only bad
poets allow into their poems what is haphazard or cheaply chosen.

The errand, I will venture a bit brashly for lack of space, is left generalized   12
in order the more aptly to suggest *any* errand in life and, therefore, life itself.
The owner is there because he is one of the forces of the poem. Let it do to

say that the force he represents is the village of mankind (that village at the edge of winter) from which the poet finds himself separated (has separated himself?) in his moment by the woods (and to which, he recalls finally, he has promises to keep). The owner is he-who-lives-in-his-village-house, thereby locked away from the poet's awareness of the-time-the-snow-tells as it engulfs and obliterates the world the village man allows himself to believe he "owns." Thus, the owner is a representative of an order of reality from which the poet has divided himself for the moment, though to a certain extent he ends by reuniting with it. Scene one, therefore, establishes not only a relation between the man and the woods, but the fact that the man's relation begins with his separation (though momentarily) from mankind.

End parenthesis one, begin parenthesis two.   13

Still considering the first scene as a kind of dramatic performance of forces,   14
one must note that the poet has meticulously matched the simplicity of his language to the pretended simplicity of the narrative. Clearly, the man stopped because the beauty of the scene moved him, but he neither tells us that the scene is beautiful nor that he is moved. A bad writer, always ready to overdo, might have written: "The vastness gripped me, filling my spirit with the slow steady sinking of the snow's crystalline perfection into the glimmerless profundities of the hushed primeval wood." Frost's avoidance of such a spate illustrates two principles of good writing. The first, he has stated himself in "The Mowing": "Anything *more* than the truth would have seemed too weak" (italics mine). Understatement is one of the basic sources of power in English poetry. The second principle is to let the action speak for itself. A good novelist does not tell us that a given character is good or bad (at least not since the passing of the Dickens tradition): he shows us the character in action and then, watching him, we know. Poetry, too, has fictional obligations: even when the characters are ideas and metaphors rather than people, they must be *characterized in action*. A poem does not *talk about* ideas; it *enacts* them. The force of the poem's performance, in fact, is precisely to act out (and thereby to make us act out empathetically, that is, to *feel out*, that is, *to identify with*) the speaker and why he stopped. The man is the principal actor in this little "drama of why" and in scene one he is the only character, though as noted, he is somehow related to the absent owner.

End second parenthesis.   15

In scene two (stanzas two and three) a *foil* is introduced. In fiction and   16
drama, a foil is a character who "plays against" a more important character. By presenting a different point of view or an opposed set of motives, the foil moves the more important character to react in ways that might not have found expression without such opposition. The more important character is thus more fully revealed—to the reader and to himself. The foil here is the horse.

The horse forces the question. Why did the man stop? Until it occurs to   17
him that his "little horse must think it queer" he had not asked himself for reasons. He had simply stopped. But the man finds himself faced with the question he imagines the horse to be asking: what *is* there to stop for out

there in the cold, away from bin and stall (house and village and mankind?) and all that any self-respecting beast could value on such a night? In sensing that other view, the man is forced to examine his own more deeply.

In stanza two the question arises only as a feeling within the man. In stanza three, however (still scene two), the horse acts. He gives his harness bells a shake. "What's wrong?" he seems to say. "What are we waiting for?"   18

By now, obviously, the horse—without losing its identity as horse—has also become a symbol. A symbol is something that stands for something else. Whatever that something else may be, it certainly begins as that order of life that does not understand why a man stops in the wintry middle of nowhere to watch the snow come down. (Can one fail to sense by now that the dark and the snowfall symbolize a death-wish, however momentary, *i.e.*, that hunger for final rest and surrender that a man may feel, but not a beast?)   19

So by the end of scene two the performance has given dramatic force to three elements that work upon the man. There is his relation to the world of the owner. There is his relation to the brute world of the horse. And there is that third presence of the unownable world, the movement of the all-engulfing snow across all the orders of life, the man's, the owner's, and the horse's—with the difference that the man knows of that second dark-within-the-dark of which the horse cannot, and the owner will not, know.   20

The man ends scene two with all these forces working upon him simultaneously. He feels himself moved to a decision. And he feels a last call from the darkness: "the sweep / Of easy wind and downy flake." It would be so easy and so downy to go into the woods and let himself be covered over.   21

But scene three (stanza four) produces a fourth force. This fourth force can be given many names. It is certainly better, in fact, to give it many names than to attempt to limit it to one. It is social obligation, or personal commitment, or duty, or just the realization that a man cannot indulge a mood forever. All of these and more. But, finally, he has a simple decision to make. He may go into the woods and let the darkness and the snow swallow him from the world of beast and man. Or he must move on. And unless he is going to stop here forever, it is time to remember that he has a long way to go and that he had best be getting there. (So there is something to be said for the horse, too.)   22

Then and only then, his question driven more and more deeply into himself by these cross-forces, does the man venture a comment on what attracted him "The woods are lovely, dark and deep." His mood lingers over the thought of that lovely dark-and-deep (as do the very syllables in which he phrases the thought), but the final decision is to put off the mood and move on. He has his man's way to go and his man's obligations to tend to before he can yield. He has miles to go before his sleep. He repeats that thought and the performance ends.   23

But why the repetition? The first time Frost says "And miles to go before I sleep," there can be little doubt that the primary meaning is: "I have a long way to go before I get to bed tonight." The second time he says it, however, "miles to go" and "sleep" are suddenly transformed into symbols. What are   24 those "something-elses" the symbols stand for? Hundreds of people have tried to ask Mr. Frost that question and he has always turned it away. He has turned it away *because he cannot answer it.* He could answer some part of it. But some part is not enough.

For a symbol is like a rock dropped into a pool: it sends out ripples in all directions, and the ripples are in motion. Who can say where the last ripple disappears? One may have a sense that he knows the approximate center point of the ripples, the point at which the stone struck the water. Yet even then he has trouble marking it surely. How does one make a mark on water? Oh very well—the center point of that second "miles to go" is probably approximately in the neighborhood of being close to meaning, perhaps, "the road of life"; and the second "before I sleep" is maybe that close to meaning "before I take my final rest," the rest in darkness that seemed so temptingly dark-and-deep for the moment of the mood. But the ripples continue to move and the light to change on the water, and the longer one watches the more changes he sees. Such shifting-and-being-at-the-same-instant is of the very sparkle and life of poetry. One experiences it as one experiences life, for every time he looks at an experience he sees something new, and he sees it change as he watches it. And that sense of continuity in fluidity is one of the primary kinds of knowledge, one of man's basic ways of knowing, and one that only the arts can teach, poetry foremost among them.

Frost himself certainly did not ask what that repeated last line meant. It came to him and he received it. He "felt right" about it. And what he "felt right" about was in no sense a "meaning" that, say, an essay could apprehend, but an act of experience that could be fully presented only by the dramatic enactment of forces which is the performance of the poem.

Now look at the poem in another way. Did Frost know what he was going to do when he began? Considering the poem simply as an act of skill, as a piece of juggling, one cannot fail to respond to the magnificent turn at the end where, with one flip, seven of the simplest words in the language suddenly dazzle full of never-ending waves of thought and feeling. Or, more precisely, of felt-thought. Certainly an equivalent stunt by a juggler—could there be an equivalent—would bring the house down. Was it to cap his performance with that grand stunt that Frost wrote the poem?

Far from it. The obvious fact is that *Frost could not have known he was going to write those lines until he wrote them.* Then a second fact must be registered: *he wrote them because, for the fun of it, he had got himself into trouble.*

Frost, like every good poet, began by playing a game with himself. The most usual way of writing a four line stanza with four feet to the line is to rhyme the third line with the first, and the fourth line with the second. Even that much rhyme is so difficult in English that many poets and almost all of the anonymous ballad makers do not bother to rhyme the first and third lines at all, settling for two rhymes in four lines as good enough. For English is a rhyme-poor language. In Italian and in French, for example, so many words end with the same sounds that rhyming is relatively easy—so easy that many

25

26

27

28

29

modern French and Italian poets do not bother to rhyme at all. English, being a more agglomerate language, has far more final sounds, hence fewer of them rhyme. When an Italian poet writes a line ending with "vita" (life) he has literally hundreds of rhyme choices available. When an English poet writes "life" at the end of a line he can summon "strife, wife, knife, fife, rife," and then he is in trouble. Now "life-strife" and "life-rife" and "life-wife" seem to offer a combination of possible ideas that can be related by more than just the rhyme. Inevitably, therefore, the poets have had to work and rework these combinations until the sparkle has gone out of them. The reader is normally tired of such rhyme-led associations. When he encounters "life-strife" he is certainly entitled to suspect that the poet did not really want to say "strife"— that had there been in English such a word as, say, "hife," meaning "infinite peace and harmony," the poet would as gladly have used that word instead of "strife." Thus, the reader feels that the writing is haphazard, that the rhyme is making the poet say things he does not really feel, and which, therefore, the reader does not feel except as boredom. One likes to see the rhymes fall into place, but he must end with the belief that it is the poet who is deciding what is said and not the rhyme scheme that is forcing the saying.

So rhyme is a kind of game, and an especially difficult one in English. As in every game, the fun of the rhyme is to set one's difficulties high and then to meet them skillfully. As Frost himself once defined freedom, it consists of "moving easy in harness." 30

In "Stopping by Woods on a Snowy Evening" Frost took a long chance. He decided to rhyme not two lines in each stanza, but three. Not even Frost could have sustained that much rhyme in a long poem (as Dante, for example, with the advantage of writing in Italian, sustained triple rhyme for thousands of lines in "The Divine Comedy"). Frost would have known instantly, therefore, when he took the original chance, that he was going to write a short poem. He would have had that much foretaste of it. 31

So the first stanza emerged rhymed a-a-b-a. And with the sure sense that this was to be a short poem, Frost decided to take an additional chance and to redouble: in English three rhymes in four lines is more than enough; there is no need to rhyme the fourth line. For the fun of it, however, Frost set himself to pick up that loose rhyme and to weave it into the pattern, thereby accepting the all but impossible burden of quadruple rhyme. 32

The miracle is that it worked. Despite the enormous freight of rhyme, the poem not only came out as a neat pattern, but managed to do so with no sense of strain. Every word and every rhyme falls into place as naturally and as inevitably as if there were no rhyme restricting the poet's choices. 33

That ease-in-difficulty is certainly inseparable from the success of the poem's performance. One watches the skill-man juggle three balls, then four, then five, and every addition makes the trick more wonderful. But unless he makes the hard trick seem as easy as an easy trick, then all is lost. 34

The real point, however, is not only that Frost took on a hard rhyme-trick and made it seem easy. It is rather as if the juggler, carried away, had tossed up one more ball than he could really handle, and then amazed himself by 35 actually handling it. So with the real triumph of his poem. Frost could not have known what a stunning effect his repetition of the last line was going to produce. He could not even know he was going to repeat the line. He simply found himself up against a difficulty he almost certainly had not foreseen and he had to improvise to meet it. For in picking up the rhyme from the third line of stanza one and carrying it over into stanza two, he had created an endless chain-link form within which each stanza left a hook sticking out for the next stanza to hang on. So by stanza four, feeling the poem rounding to its end, Frost had to do something about that extra rhyme.

He might have tucked it back into a third line rhyming with the *know-* 36 *though-snow* of stanza one. He could thus have rounded the poem out to the mathematical symmetry of using each rhyme four times. But though such a device might be defensible in theory, a rhyme repeated after eleven lines is so far from its original rhyme sound that its feeling as rhyme must certainly be lost. And what good is theory if the reader is not moved by the writing?

It must have been in some such quandary that the final repetition sug- 37 gested itself—a suggestion born of the very difficulties the poet had let himself in for. So there is that point beyond mere ease in handling a hard thing, the point at which the very difficulty offers the poet the opportunity to do better than he knew he could. What, aside from having that happen to oneself, could be more self-delighting than to participate in its happening by one's reader-identification with the poem?

And by now a further point will have suggested itself: that the human- 38 insight of the poem and the technicalities of its poetic artifice are inseparable. Each feeds the other. That interplay is the poem's meaning, a matter not of WHAT DOES IT MEAN, for no one can ever say entirely what a good poem means, but of HOW DOES IT MEAN, a process one can come much closer to discussing.

There is a necessary epilogue. Mr. Frost has often discussed this poem on 39 the platform, or more usually in the course of a long-evening-after a talk. Time and again I have heard him say that he just wrote it off, that it just came to him, and that he set it down as it came.

Once at Bread Loaf, however, I heard him add one very essential piece to 40 the discussion of how it "just came." One night, he said, he had sat down after supper to work at a long piece of blank verse. The piece never worked out, but Mr. Frost found himself so absorbed in it that, when next he looked up, dawn was at his window. He rose, crossed to the window, stood looking out for a few minutes, and *then* it was that "Stopping by Woods" suddenly "just came," so that all he had to do was cross the room and write it down.

Robert Frost is the sort of artist who hides his traces. I know of no Frost 41 worksheets anywhere. If someone has raided his wastebasket in secret, it is possible that such worksheets exist somewhere, but Frost would not willingly allow anything but the finished product to leave him. Almost certainly, therefore, no one will ever know what was in that piece of unsuccessful blank verse he had been working at with such concentration, but I for one would stake my life that could that worksheet be uncovered, it would be found to contain the germinal stuff of "Stopping by Woods"; that what was a-simmer in him all night without finding its proper form, suddenly, when he let his still-occupied mind look away, came at him from a different direction, offered itself in a different form, and that finding that form exactly right the impulse proceeded to marry itself to the new shape in one of the most miraculous performances of English lyricism.

And that, too—whether or not one can accept so hypothetical a discussion—is part of HOW the poem means. It means that marriage to the perfect form, the poem's shapen declaration of itself, its moment's monument fixed beyond all possibility of change. And thus, finally, in every truly good poem, "How does it mean?" must always be answered "Triumphantly." Whatever the poem "is about," *how* it means is always how Genesis means: the word become a form, and the form become a thing, and—when the becoming is true—the thing become a part of the knowledge and experience of the race forever.

42

Letters to the Editor of the *Saturday Review*

Finding Each Other

The article "Robert Frost: The Way to the Poem," by John Ciardi (*SR* Apr. 12), is one of the most excellent pieces of explication I have had an opportunity to read. It is simple, thorough, and clear, and at the same time provocative response to the deepest and most far-reaching values in poetry. The essay, just as it is, would be a boon to many students and teachers who together are seeking to find each other as they attend to a poem.

Joseph H. Jenkins

Petersburg, Va.

Poking and Picking

Robert Frost's miracle, "Stopping by Woods on a Snowy Evening," comprises four stanzas, sixteen lines, 108 words. John Ciardi's analysis of it runs to ten full columns. This flushes an old question: Does such probing, poking, and picking really lead "The Way to the Poem"?

William L. Hassett

Des Moines, Ia.

Critical Absurdity

I have just discovered, by way of John Ciardi's analysis of Robert Frost's poem, "Stopping by Woods on a Snowy Evening," that this charmingly simple, eloquent, lyrical little poem, long one of my favorites, is supposedly fraught with duplicity of meaning and symbolism, including a disguised death-wish, and that it is not at all about what it seems to be about.

This is really a new high in critical absurdity. If the presentation of this leading, cover-featured article were not so obviously straight-faced, I would have considered this a nice parody of much present-day "criticism." Who is Mr. Ciardi trying to kid? Or is he himself merely kidded? I am sure Mr. Frost must be highly amused or shaking his head in amazement at the awesome proportions his innocent poetic images have assumed ("By now, obviously, the horse has also become a symbol").

Mrs. Beverly Travers

New Orleans, La.

Enhance a Rainbow

It seems to us that when a poet uses the skill Frost employs in creating a mood, sharing an experience, one should accept it as given, without further analysis. One does not enhance a rainbow by subjecting it to a spectrometric analysis.

John G. Gosselink

Hartford City, Ind.

No Death-Wish

I was a little shocked when I read Ciardi's interpretation of the dark and snowfall in Frost's "Stopping by Woods on a Snowy Evening" as a death-wish. I suppose every person must interpret poems like this in terms of his own experience. To me, it seems to say that there is a certain deep satisfaction in stopping to lose oneself in the contemplation of beauty. The experience itself is significant in that it brings the individual into a sense of relationship to basic reality. But one cannot escape too long into these subjective experiences. There is work to do; obligations must be met; one cannot spend his whole life escaping from these practical realities.

J. Josephine Leamer

Gardiner, Mont.

Superfluous Info

I am used to most magazines pointing out the obvious, but when *SR* tells me that a symbol stands for something else (John Ciardi's article on Robert Frost), I am really hurt. Chances are, if I thought a symbol was something other than something else, I wouldn't be reading *SR* or any other magazine.

Marjorie Duryic

Everett, Wash.

Simple Narrative

Why Mr. Ciardi had to pick such, as he himself states, "a simple narrative" to expound upon I'll never know. If one thought of poetry as Mr. C does, the joy of just reading beautiful poetry would be gone completely. One would begin to spend all his time searching for symbols and such.

H. Clay Barnard

Sausalito, Calif.

Penetrating Analysis

I have just finished reading John Ciardi's penetrating analysis of Robert Frost's familiar lyric. This is distinguished service in the cause of criticism. More articles like this and we *will* develop a poetry-reading America.

Sister Mary Denise, RSM

Dallas, Pa.

Its Essence

Through the years I've read "Stopping by Woods on a Snowy Evening" many times and felt that with each reading I had extracted its meaning to the point where I felt certain that there was no more it could tell me. John Ciardi has exposed new and deeper meanings to me and, as an excellent teacher, has dissected and made clear its very essence.

Lloyd Rodnick

Detroit, Mich.

Heavy Limbs

Ciardi has some very interesting ideas. But wouldn't it be better to develop them in a separate essay? It seems to me that the literary woods is too full of heavy limbs falling upon little delicate branches.

Gary Thornburg

Losantville, Ind.

No Discords

Ciardi's calm, cleanly developed, and illuminating article on Frost's poem surely is a savory example of what his readers have clamored for all these months. In this essay one finds all of Mr. Ciardi's inspiring adherence to principles and none of those bubonic symptoms which many of his readers have denounced. Personally, I am pleased to find also fewer coinings of discordant and sometimes hideous compounds, an indulgence that often spoils the point of what Mr. Ciardi has to say.

Earl Clendenon

Chicago, Ill.

Frost's Analyst?

The business of equating this poem with all the current philosophical symbols that are in Ciardi's mind is, of course, Ciardi's privilege. But why should he speak as Frost's analyst?

Harvey Parker

Vista, Calif.

Pedantic Reparation

Ciardi very pedantically makes complete reparation for last year's storm-provoking criticism of Anne Morrow Lindbergh's delicate and deep poetry. Many college and high-school teachers will be able to use such an exhaustive analysis in the classroom.

Joseph A. McNulty

Philadelphia, Pa.

Self-Anointed Thor

After reading Ciardi's uncomprehending, clinical, anti-poetical "appreciation" of my friend Robert Frost's great lyric, I was so moved, in sundry unprintable ways, that I thought to write Robert: the essay reminded me throughout of a humorless pathologist slicing away with his microtome at a biopsy.

However, what I wanted to say "just came to me" and I simply "wrote it down"—on a Remington Noiseless which I use for all composition, including poetry. It took twenty minutes, from gag to madrigal—some twenty more to add an effort to refute Mr. Ciardi's contention that English is a knobby tongue to rhyme—and I forward the result to you, in the hope that you might print it as one (largely commercial) writer's testament that, to some of us, things do come, we do just write them down, and we know enough English to find little trouble in double-rhyming a ballad, even in what Mr. Ciardi regards as the difficult scheme of Frost's poem. I also felt J.C. should learn that "know," "here," "lake," and "sweep" hardly baffle an idle versifier—and Robert's variation of the ballad form is not beyond the reach even of typewriter poets like me.

Mr. Ciardi, neo-master of critique, finds it easy to demolish the avowedly amateur verses of Anne Lindbergh with his little mechanic's hammer; but he did not realize that when he undertook to acclaim a true poet his implement might bounce from the granite with predictable damage to the self-anointed Thor. Ciardi must be all Ph.D., and of the new academic sub-species.

Philip Wylie

Miami, Fla.

Stopping to Write a Friend on a Thick Night

> In this week's *Saturday Review*
> The first bit, Robert, deals with you.
> At least, its author, John Ciardi
> Tears a poem of yours in two
>
> And shreds the halves. His toy lombard, he
> Loads with treacle praise, and lardy,
> Salutes your metaphor and tmesis
> And fires again to call you hardy.
>
> Art, to him, is just its pieces,
> The obvious, his noblest thesis—
> Who even calls down holocaust
> On his own tongue—the mangling Jesus!
>
> Your blanket snow's thus double-crossed
> By one who should be blanket-tossed
> And he has miles to go to Frost
> And years to learn it's Frost he lost.

JOHN CIARDI
Letter to the Letter Writers

I have never known a magazine with *SR*'s knack for calling forth Letters   43
to the Editor. No one writing for *SR* need suffer from a sense that his ideas
have disappeared into the void: he will hear from the readers. I have been
hearing of late, and the charge this time, made by some readers, is that I
have despoiled a great poem in my analysis of Robert Frost's "Stopping by
Woods on a Snowy Evening" (*SR* Apr. 12).

The Frost article was self-declaredly an effort at close analysis. I believe   44
the poem to be much deeper than its surfaces, and I set out to ask what sort
of human behavior it is that presents a surface of such simplicity while stirring such depths of multiple responses. It may be that I analyzed badly, but
the more general charge seems to be that all analysis is inimical to poetry,
and that general charge is certainly worth a closer look.

A number of readers seem to have been offended by the fact that the   45
analysis was longer than the poem, which, as one reader put it, "comprises
four stanzas, sixteen lines, 108 words" (rather technical analysis, that sort of
word-counting), whereas my article ran to "ten full columns."

A first clear assumption in this reader's mind is the assertion that an analysis   46
must not be longer than what it analyzes. I can see no way of defending that
assumption. If there is to be any analysis at all, it is in the nature of things
that the analysis be longer than the poem or the passages it analyzes. One
hundred and eight words will hardly do simply to describe the stanzaic form
and rhyme scheme of the poem, without any consideration of the nature of
the rhyme problem. Analysis and the poem are simply enough tortoise and
hare. The difference from the fable is that the poetic hare does not lie down
and sleep. The unfabled tortoise, however, may still hope to crawl after and,
in some sense, to mark the way the hare went.

The second assumption is that analysis obscures ("does not lead the way   47
to") a poem, and amounts in fact to mere "probing, poking, and picking." The
charge as made is not specifically against my article but against all analysis.
The question may, therefore, be simply located: should poetry be talked about
at all?

A number of readers clearly take the position that it must not be. "One   48
should accept it (the experience of the poem) as given, without further
analysis," asserts one reader. "One does not enhance a rainbow by subjecting
it to spectrometric analysis." An unwavering position and an interesting figure of speech. I am drawn to that rainbow and fascinated by this use of the
word "enhance." By "spectrometric analysis" I take the gentleman to mean
"investigating the physical nature of" but said, of course, with an overtone of
disdain at the idea of seeing "beauty" meaningfully through any "instrument."
That disdain aside, however, one may certainly ask why detailed knowledge
of the physical phenomena that produce a rainbow should "unenhance" the
rainbow's emotional value. Is speculation into the nature of things to be taken
as a destruction of nature?

Two years ago, looking down on Rome from the Gianiculum, I saw two   49
complete rainbows in the sky at once, not just pieces of rainbows but complete arcs with both ends of each arc visible at once in a great bridge above
the city. And in what way did it hurt me as part of my instant delight to
register some sense of the angle at which the sun had to hit the atmosphere
in order to produce such a prodigy? I must insist on remaining among those
who are willing to learn about rainbows.

Such disdain seems to be shared by many of our readers. Mr. Philip Wylie,   50
a man described to me as an author, filed the strongest, or at least the longest, of the recent objections. My "implement," as he sees it, bounces "from
the granite (of the poem) with predictable damage to the self-anointed Thor.
Ciardi must be all Ph.D., and of the new academic sub-species."

Not exactly factual, since I do not own a Ph.D., but fair enough: giving   51
lumps is a time-honored literary game and anyone with a typewriter may
play. Mr. Wylie's indignation is largely against my way of dealing with Mr.

Frost's poem, and that is a charge I must waive—he may be right, he may be wrong; no score. One part of his charge, however, is a more general anger at the idea that anyone should go into a detailed analysis of the rhyme scheme of a poem that "just came" to the poet. Once again the basic charge is that poetry is damaged by analysis. One should "just let it come."

Many others have joined Mr. Wylie in his defense of the untouchable-   52
spontaneous. "Get your big clumsy feet off that miracle," says one reader I find myself especially drawn to. "What good do you think you do," writes another, "when you tear apart a thing as lovely as Mr. Frost's poem?" Another: "A dissecting kit belongs in the laboratory, not the library." And still another: "If one thought of poetry as Mr. C does, the joy of just reading beautiful poetry would be gone completely. One would begin to spend all his time dealing with symbols and such."

I must, parenthetically, reject some of the terms of that last letter. "Begin   53
to spend *all* his time," is the writer's idea: that "all" is no part of mine. I shall pass the sneer contained in the phrase "symbols and such." But I cannot accept the responsibility for defending myself when misquoted. One reader, for example, accuses me of stating that a poem "is not at all about what it seems to be about." I can only reply that those are his terms, not mine, and that I have no thought of defending them.

It is that "all" in the first quotation, however, that locates the central mis-   54
understanding. "Once one begins to analyze," the assumption runs, "he begins to spend all of his time 'merely analyzing' and the analysis not only takes the place of the poem but leads to the poem's destruction."

Were there no misconception involved, this reader's anger would certainly   55
be justified. What is misconceived is the idea that the analysis is intended to take the place of the poem. Far from it. One takes a poem apart only in order to put it back together again with greater understanding. The poem itself is the thing. A good poem is a hanging gull on a day of perfect winds. We sit below and watch it own the air it rides: a miracle from nature. There it hangs on infallible wings. But suppose one is interested in the theory of flight (as the gull itself, to be sure, need not be) and suppose one notices that the gull's wings can perform miracles in the air because they have a particular curvature and a particular sort of leading and trailing edge. And suppose he further notices that the gull's tail feathers have a great deal to do with that seemingly effortless mastery. Does that man cease to see the gull? Does he see nothing but diagrams of airflow and lift to the total damnation of all gulls? Or does he see the gull not only as the miracle of a perfect thing, but as the perfect thing in the enmarveling system of what encloses it?

The point involves the whole nature of perception. Do we "see" with our   56
eyes? I must believe that it is the mind that sees, and that the eyes are only the windows we see through. We see with the patterns of what we know. Let any layman look into a tide-pool and list what he sees there. Then let him call an imaginative biologist and ask the biologist what he sees. The layman will have seen things, but the biologist will see systems, and the things in place in those systems.

He will also see many things simultaneously. A basic necessity to all poetic   57
communication is what I have called *fluency* in an earlier article in these
pages. Fluency is the ability to receive more than one meaning, impression,
stimulus—call it what you please—at the same time. Analysis must always
fumble and be long-winded because it must consider those multiple impressions doggedly and one by one. If such itemized dealing accurately locates
true elements of the poem, the itemization will have served its purpose, and
that purpose must certainly be defended as one that has summoned some of
the best minds of all ages. What analysis does, though laboriously, is to establish patterns one may see with.

But there then remains the reader's work. It is up to him, guided by the   58
analysis, to read the poem with the fluency it requires, and which analysis
does not hope to achieve. Certainly, whatever is said here, poetry will be
talked about and must be talked about. The one point of such talk, however,
is to lead the reader more richly to the threshold of the poem. Over that
threshold he must take himself. And I, for one, must suspect that if he refuses to carry anything as cumbersome as detail across that threshold, he
will never furnish the house of his own mind.

QUESTIONS FOR MEANING

1. Explain the distinction that Ciardi makes between *how* a poem means
   and *what* a poem means. Paraphrase paragraphs 2, 38, and 42.
2. In paragraphs 3, 4, and 5, what does Ciardi mean by "duplicity"?
3. What is the topic statement of paragraph 11? Is this the premise that
   underlines Ciardi's approach to poetry?
4. According to Ciardi, what two principles are essential to writing good
   poetry?
5. Explain what Ciardi means by "foil" in paragraph 16.
6. Why does Ciardi believe that the horse in the poem is a symbol? Where
   does he define what he means by "symbol"?
7. What are the four dramatic forces that Ciardi identifies in "Stopping by
   Woods on a Snowy Evening"?
8. How does Ciardi explain Frost's decision to end his poem by repeating,
   "And miles to go before I sleep"? What technical problems did this decision solve for Frost, and why does Ciardi consider it a brilliant solution?
   What is the significance of the repetition?
9. Summarize the objections to Ciardi's essay that appear in the letters it
   inspired. What bothered people the most? Which is the best letter and
   which the silliest?
10. In responding to his critics, what did Ciardi identify as the major issue in
    the controversy over his interpretation of the poem? What is his re-
    sponse to this question? Had he anticipated it at any point in his original
    essay?
11. Explain what Ciardi means by "fluency" in the last two paragraphs of his
    "Letter to Letter Writers."

12. Vocabulary: epilogue (6), integrity (11), brashly (12), obliterates (12), spate (14), emphatically (14), haphazard (29), quandary (37), artifice (38), germinal (41), lyricism (41), despoiled (43), inimical (44), disdain (48), prodigy (49), indignation (51), and waive (51).

QUESTIONS ABOUT STRATEGY

1. What is the function of paragraph 1? How does it serve to prepare readers for the essay that follows?
2. Why are paragraphs 9 through 15 parenthetical to the primary purpose of Ciardi's essay?
3. Does Ciardi make any claims that he fails to support?
4. How useful is the analogy in paragraph 25? Did it help you to understand the nature of poetry?
5. Several of his critics complained that Ciardi's essay is too long. Do you agree? If so, what would you cut? How does Ciardi himself respond to this charge?
6. Which of Ciardi's critics makes an ad hominem argument? In responding to criticism, does Ciardi ever resort to sarcasm?
7. How effectively has Ciardi answered his critics? If you were amused by any of the letters to the editor, was Ciardi's rebuttal strong enough to win back your confidence in him?

HERBERT R. COURSEN, JR.

The Ghost of Christmas Past: "Stopping by Woods on a Snowy Evening"

Herbert R. Coursen, Jr., graduated from Amherst College in 1954 and received his Ph.D. from the University of Connecticut in 1965. Since 1964 he has taught English at Bowdoin College, where he is now Professor of Creative Writing and Shakespeare. A former fighter pilot in the U.S. Air Force, Coursen has published in periodicals as diverse as Studies in Philology *and* Sports Illustrated. *He is the author of several works of criticism, including* The Rarer Action: Hamlet's Mousetrap *(1969),* Shaping the Self: Style and Technique in the Narrative *(1975), and* Christian Ritual and the World of Shakespeare *(1976). He has also written a novel,* After the War *(1980), and many volumes of poetry, including* Storm in April *(1973),* Fears in the Night *(1976), and* Walking Away *(1977). The following essay on Frost was first published in December* **1962.** *As you read it, you should be prepared to smile.*

Much ink has spilled on many pages in exegesis of this little poem. Actually, critical jottings have only obscured what has lain beneath critical noses all these years. To say that the poem means merely that a man stops one night to observe a snowfall, or that the poem contrasts the mundane desire for creature comfort with the sweep of aesthetic appreciation, or that it renders worldly responsibilities paramount, or that it reveals the speaker's latent death-wish is to miss the point rather badly. Lacking has been that mind simple enough to see what is *really* there.   1

The first line ("Whose woods these are I think I know") shows that the speaker has paused aside a woods of whose ownership he is fairly sure. So much for paraphrase. Uncertainty vanishes with the next two lines ("His house is in the village though; / He will not see me stopping here"). The speaker knows (a) where the owner's home is located, and (b) that the owner won't be out at the woods tonight. Two questions arise immediately: (a) how does the speaker know? and (b) how does the speaker know? As will be made manifest, only one answer exists to each question.   2

The subsequent two quatrains force more questions to pop up. On auditing the first two lines of the second quatrain ("My little horse must think it queer / To stop without a farmhouse near"), we must ask, "Why does the little 'horse' think oddly of the proceedings?" We must ask also if this *is*, as the speaker claims, the "darkest evening of the year." The calendar date of this occurrence (or lack of occurrence) by an unspecified patch of trees is essential to an apprehension of the poem's true meaning. In the third quatrain, we hear "harness bells" shook. Is the auditory image really an allusion? Then there is the question of the "horse's" identity. Is this really Equus Caballus? This question links itself to that of the *driver's* identity and reiterates   3 the problem of the animal's untoward attitude toward this evidently unscheduled stop.

The questions have piled up unanswered as we reach the final quatrain   4
and approach the ultimate series of poetic mysteries to be resolved. Clearly, all of the questions asked thus far (save possibly the one about the "horse's" identity) are ones which any normal reader, granted the training in close analysis provided by a survey course in English Literature during his sophomore year in college, might ask. After some extraneous imagery ("The woods are lovely, dark and deep" has either been established or is easily adduced from the dramatic situation), the final three lines hold out the key with which the poem's essence may be released. What, to ask two more questions, are the "promises" which the speaker must "keep," and why are the last two lines so redundant about the distance he must cover before he tumbles into bed? Obviously, the obligations are important, the distance great.

Now, if we swing back to one of the previous questions, the poem will   5
begin to unravel. The "darkest evening of the year" in New England is December 21st, a date near that on which the western world celebrates Christmas. It may be that December 21st *is* the date of the poem, or (and with poets this seems more likely) that this is the closest the poet can come to Christmas without giving it all away. Who has "promises to keep" at or near this date, and who must traverse much territory to fulfill these promises? Yes, and who but St. Nick would know the location of *each* home? Only he would know who had "just settled down for a long winter's nap" (the poem's third line—"He will not see me stopping here"—is clearly a veiled allusion) and would not be out inspecting his acreage this night. The unusual phrase "fill up with snow," in the poem's fourth line, is a transfer of Santa's occupational preoccupation to the countryside; he is mulling the filling of countless stockings hung above countless fireplaces by countless careful children. "Harness bells," of course, allude to "Sleighing Song," a popular Christmas tune of the time the poem was written in which the refrain "Jingle Bells! Jingle Bells!" appears; thus again we are put on the Christmas track. The "little horse," like the date, is another attempt at poetic obfuscation. Although the "rein-reindeer" ambiguity has been eliminated from the poem's final version, probably because too obvious, we may speculate that the animal is really a reindeer disguised as a horse by the poet's desire for obscurity, a desire which we must concede has been fulfilled up to now.

The animal is clearly concerned, like the faithful Rudolph—another possi-   6
ble allusion (post facto, hence unconscious)—lest his master fail to complete his mission. Seeing no farmhouse in the second quatrain, but pulling a load of presents, no wonder the little beast wonders! It takes him a full two quatrains to rouse his driver to remember all the empty stockings which hang ahead. And Santa does so reluctantly at that, poor soul, as he ponders the myriad farmhouses and villages which spread between him and his own "winter's nap." The modern St. Nick, lonely and overworked, tosses no "Happy Christmas to all and to all a good night!" into the precipitation. He merely shrugs his shoulders and resignedly plods away.

QUESTIONS FOR MEANING

1. What interpretations of the poem does Coursen reject?
2. On what "evidence" does Coursen base his claim that "Stopping by Woods on a Snowy Evening" is about an overworked Santa Claus? Could anyone take this argument seriously?
3. Identify the allusion in the essay's title. What famous writer wrote about "the Ghost of Christmas Past"?
4. Vocabulary: exegesis (1), mundane (1), aesthetic (1), paramount (1), latent (1), quatrains (3), auditing (3), apprehension (3), auditory (3), reiterates (3), extraneous (4), adduced (4), traverse (5), obfuscation (5), and myriad (6).

QUESTIONS ABOUT STRATEGY

1. At what point in this essay did you first become aware that you were reading a parody? Rereading the essay, can you find any clues that you originally overlooked?
2. How does Coursen's diction contribute to the essay's humor? Can you identify any comic shifts in style?
3. How does Coursen account for discrepancies between his thesis and the language of the poem itself?
4. What is the point of this essay? Is Coursen ridiculing the nature of literary criticism, or is he simply making a good-humored joke? How would you describe his tone?

WILLIAM H. SHURR

Once More to the "Woods": A New Point of Entry into Frost's Most Famous Poem

Born in Evanston, Illinois, William H. Shurr attended Loyola University in Chicago, where he graduated in 1955, but remained to continue his study of philosophy and theology. He received his Ph.D. from the University of North Carolina at Chapel Hill in 1968, and has taught English at Washington State University and the University of Tennessee. His books include Prose and Poetry of England *(1965) and* The Mystery of Iniquity: Melville as Poet 1857–91 *(1972). His essay on Frost was first published in the* New England Quarterly *in **1974**. As you read it, you should be careful to note the way in which Shurr draws upon earlier critics and incorporates their views into his essay while still advancing a thesis of his own.*

"Stopping by Woods on a Snowy Evening" may be the best-known poem   1
ever written by an American. It is surely one of the most commented upon—
so much so that readers, critics, and the author himself frequently pleaded
for a moratorium to criticism. Only the promise of a truly new "point of
entry" can justify still another expenditure of effort, readers' and writer's, on
the subject. The argument that follows presents a new interpretation of the
poem based on a study of Frost's specific diction and its provenance. The
interpretation thus established generates two insights: that Frost, in this poem,
is responding negatively to one of the most profound and typical elements in
the American experience; and that several other early poems, which Frost
was always careful to popularize, can now be linked to a coherent series of
statements. This cluster of poems documents a significant moment of change
in the evolution of Frost's consciousness and of American consciousness
generally.

Commentary of Robert Frost's "Stopping by Woods on a Snowy Evening"   2
is already extensive enough for us to determine something like a *stemma* of
critical traditions. The most common interpretation, thematically, has been
that the poem is an ethical statement concerning social commitments and
obligations to which a man must listen. This obvious view responds to the
attention-soliciting repetition with which the poem ends. Louis Untermeyer
was one of the earliest to put this interpretation into writing. Reginald Cook,
Robert Doyle, D. J. Lepore, and Stanley Poss have continued to accept this
reading as adequate.[1]

---

[1] See Louis Untermeyer's *Come In* (New York, 1943), later amplified and published as *The Pocket Book of Robert Frost's Poems* (New York, 1956), 192. Reginald L. Cook, *The Dimensions of Robert Frost* (New York, 1958). John Robert Doyle, *The Poetry of Robert Frost: An Analysis* (Johannesburg, Witwatersrand, and New York, 1965), 195. D. J. Lepore, "Setting and/or Statement," *English Journal*, LV, 624–626. Stanley Poss, "Low Skies, Some Clearing, Local Frost," *New England Quarterly*, XLI, 438–442.

The second major tradition of interpretation was strikingly stated by John   3
Ciardi in his 1958 article in *The Saturday Review:* "Can one fail to sense by
now that the dark and snowfall symbolize a deathwish, however momentary,
i.e., that hunger for final rest and surrender that a man may feel, but not a
beast?" The insight had been anticipated a decade earlier by Wellek and
Warren in *Theory of Literature,* where *sleep* was seen as a "natural symbol"
for *death.* It continues as a tradition in Leonard Unger and William Van
O'Connor, in John Lynen, Lawrance Thompson, and James Armstrong. Lloyd
Dendinger, more recently, has seen the lure of death operating thematically
in the poem, but proposes the "lure of wilderness" typical in American letters
as even more basic to the poem.[2] One must note however that Frost objected
strongly to Ciardi's thesis: "That's all right, but it's hardly a death poem."[3]

These two interpretations can stand together. Ciardi conflated them in his   4
Saturday Review article by saying that the speaker in the poem is finally
recalled from the attractive power of the death wish by his sense of belong-
ing to the world of man; the social side of his nature prevails over the psychic
lure of the depths.

A third tradition of interpretation can be discerned in which the "dark   5
woods" stand out as the central symbol to be explicated. Robert Langbaum
used the terminology of theological existentialism when he analyzed the poem
as a "momentary insight into the nonhuman otherness of nature." John Ogilvie rightly discerned that imagery of the dark woods is pervasive in Frost's
early poetry; for him the woods symbol implied the poet's desire for isolation
and his need to explore the inner self. George Nitchie, surveying the whole
range of Frost's poetry, read this poem as a "yearning back to Eden . . . an
imagined withdrawal from the complicated world we all know into a mysterious loveliness symbolized by woods or darkness."[4] One finds a vagueness
in all of these readings, as if they were not based on sufficient evidence to
make the readings definite or persuasive.

Finally, one may mention a fourth tradition of interpreting the poem. This   6
is a blatant allegorization, particularly of the first stanza. I know whose woods
these are; He made them; His house is in the village; the village church. This
makes the poem a religious allegory of fairly simpleminded type. If done with
some irony it could take its place beside the successful spoof of symbol hunting generally, Herbert Coursen's "proof" that the speaker is really Santa Claus

[2]John Ciardi, "Robert Frost: The Way to the Poem," *Saturday Review,* 40 (April 12, 1958), 15ff. Rene Wellek and Austin Warren, *Theory of Literature* (New York, 1949, 1955); the passage relevant to Frost can be found on 194–195 of the first edition and 179 of the second edition. Leonard Unger and William Van O'Connor, *Poems for Study* (New York, 1953), 600. John F. Lynen, *The Pastoral Art of Robert Frost* (New Haven: Yale Univ. Press, 1960). Lawrance Thompson, *Fire and Ice: The Art and Thought of Robert Frost* (New York, 1961), 27. James Armstrong, "The 'Death Wish' in 'Stopping by Woods,'" *College English,* XXV, 440–445. Lloyd N. Dendinger, "The Irrational Appeal of Frost's Dark Deep Woods," *Southern Review,* II, 822–829.

[3]Quoted in Louis Mertins, *Robert Frost: Life and Talks—Walking* (Norman, 1965), 371.

[4]Robert Langbaum, "The New Nature Poetry," *American Scholar,* XXVIII, 323–340. John T. Ogilvie, "From Woods to Stars: A Pattern of Imagery in Robert Frost's Poetry," *South Atlantic Quarterly,* LVIII, 64–76. George W. Nitchie, *Human Values in the Poetry of Robert Frost* (Durham, 1960).

and that he must get on with the distribution of toys he has promised to all good children.[5] But the allegory is presented seriously. Although I have not seen this tradition in print, each year students have assured me that it was the quasi-official interpretation whenever they came 'round, dutifully, almost ritually, to "doing" the poem again in secondary school English classes. The curious thing about this interpretation is that it bears some similarity to the one which I am about to propose. Allegory is too blunt an instrument to use for analysis here, but there is convincing evidence that the poem is the record of a religious experience; or, since it is more precise to be more general here, say rather that the poem is a record of the mind's encounter with transcendence. Emerson achieved it, and on very nearly the same New England ground. His experience is joyfully recorded in the first chapter of *Nature*. In the first two paragraphs he lays down two conditions for this experience, "solitude" and "reverence"—conditions which are also prominent in the poem by Frost. The experience itself is recorded thus:

> In the woods, is perpetual youth. . . . In the woods, we return to reason and faith. There I feel that nothing can befall me in life—no disgrace, no calamity (leaving me my eyes), which nature cannot repair. Standing on the bare ground,— my head bathed by the blithe air, and uplifted into infinite space,—all mean egotism vanishes. I become a transparent eye-ball. I am nothing. I see all. The currents of the Universal Being circulate through me; I am part or particle of God.

The notion of "transparence" is repeated frequently in the essay, for example in Chapter 6: "If the Reason be stimulated to more earnest vision, outlines and surfaces become transparent, and are no longer seen; causes and spirits are seen through them."[6] In similar woodland circumstances Frost's mind also threatens to become transparent, but his reaction is different. As he later told a questioner, "I thought it was about time I was getting the hell out of there."[7]   7

An analysis of the structure of Frost's poem shows that line 13, "The woods are lovely, dark and deep," is central. From the first line, irrelevancies tug at his attention: the curious question of the *ownership* of these woods (Emerson would have dismissed the question by asserting that nobody owns the landscape), the sudden attention to the trivial subject of the horse's response to a pause in their journey, and finally the abrupt shift to auditory sensation in the analysis of the sound of snow falling. In other words, there is only one assertion in the poem about the subject most under consideration: "The woods are lovely, dark and deep." All of Frost's attention to the actual woods is concentrated here; it is here that the subject itself is finally able to gain   8

[5] "The Ghost of Christmas Past: 'Stopping by Woods on a Snowy Evening.'" *College English*, XXII, 236ff.

[6] I quote from the splendid edition of *Nature* by Merton M. Sealts, Jr., and Alfred R. Ferguson (New York, 1969), 8, 24.

[7] Quoted in Mertins, 304.

ascendancy over the side issues which attempt to snag the mind on its route towards this center. A major effect with which criticism of the poem must concern itself is the tension created by the actual subject of the poem and the speaker's resistance to it for three-fourths of the poem. When the assertion is finally made, its diction assumes supreme importance.

The speculation that this resistance is primarily to the lure of death is finally inadequate. Whatever associations with death the words "sleep" and "dark" may have, they also are appropriate to another area of experience to be set forth in a moment. A more problematical aspect of the death-wish interpretation is the existence in the poem of a concrete symbol of death, a symbol which is not at the center of focus. If death appears in the poem, it is represented by the "frozen lake" mentioned almost casually in line 7. This symbol takes its meaning from well-documented facts in Frost's life. Frost's early obsession with suicide usually took the form of death by drowning, and according to his family the lake of this poem was between the Frost farm and the nearest town of West Derry, a drive which the poet often had to take.[8] This information underlines the statement of the poem that while the speaker may feel caught between the lure of death and *something else* ("Between the woods and frozen lake"), it is the something else represented by the woods that mainly occupies his attention. If *lake* is associated in his mind with *death,* what then, does the more central assertion about the *woods* mean?

The "new point of entry" mentioned in my title, and which brings many of these materials together, involves a climactic phrase from a poem by Henry Vaughan, "The Night." The phrase reads "A deep but dazzling darkness." It will be seen to have immediate correspondences with line 13 of Frost's poem, "The woods are lovely, *dark* and *deep,*" prepared for earlier by "The *darkest* evening of the year" in line 8. Vaughan's poem works in the tradition of mystical theology which conceives of the soul's ascent to God as a passage through various well-defined stages of illumination until the final stage is reached in which the brightness is so intense that the seeker's senses and mind are blanked out, as it were by overstimulation. When the soul is wrapped in this dark night or cloud of unknowing, it knows, paradoxically, that it has arrived at the right place, at its spiritual center. The night becomes luminous, a deep but dazzling darkness which is God. One of the traditional sources for this notion of Divine Darkness is Dionysius the Areopagite, in his *De Mystica Theologia* (I, i):

> As for thee, dear Timothy, I counsel that in the earnest exercise of mystical contemplation thou leave the senses and the operations of the intellect and all things that the senses or the intellect can perceive, and all things in this world of nothingness or that world of being: and that, thine understanding being laid to rest, thou ascend (so far as thou mayest) towards union with Him whom neither being nor understanding can contain. For by the unceasing and absolute

9

10

---

[8] See Lawrance Thompson, *Robert Frost: The Early Years, 1874–1915* (New York, 1966), 548.

renunciation of thyself and all things, thou shalt in pureness cast all things aside, and be released from all, and so shalt be led upwards to the Ray of that Divine Darkness which exceedeth all existence.

Throughout his poem, Vaughan works with these same paradoxes of darkness and vision and the finding of oneself in the total abandonment of the self. His final stanza reads:

> There is in God (some say)
> A deep, but dazzling darkness; As men here
> Say it is late and dusky, because they
>   See not all clear;
>   O for that night! where I in him
> Might live invisible and dim.

The stanza sketches two alternative responses possible for one who approaches this kind of night. The practical New Englander (Frost) may say, equivalently, "it is late and dusky," and escape back to the brightly lit interior of home and family. The Anglican mystic (Vaughan) stays with the experience and relishes the slow and dangerous knowledge it provides.

    The question of biography must remain subsidiary to literary analysis, but [11] there is much in Frost's early life to explain his resistance to this kind of experience. His mother, always something of a religious fanatic, was a devoted Swedenborgian during Frost's early boyhood. Among the stories she told the children were those of the Biblical Samuel, Joan of Arc, and Swedenborg himself, all of whom were granted direct auditory communication from the supernatural world. His mother encouraged the sensitive young boy to develop his own gifts of second sight and second hearing. When he actually began hearing the sound of voices from another world, "he almost scared himself out of his wits,"[9] a phrase that corresponds with Frost's own later statement of his desire to get "the hell out of there" when something similar seemed about to occur.

    The question remains, of course, whether Frost knew this passage from [12] Vaughan. The answer can be a confident "yes," merely on the basis of Frost's well-known competence in the documents of his trade. But we can come closer. No fewer than three writers must have thrust Vaughan's lines upon his attention with new freshness, shortly before Frost came to write his own poem. The year before, Herbert J. C. Grierson published his famous anthology *Metaphysical Lyrics and Poems of the Seventeenth Century*.[10] The volume, which included Vaughan's "The Night," was to start a renascence of interest in the Metaphysical Poets. T. S. Eliot, that same year, wrote his essay on the Metaphysical Poets as a review of this book, and published it the first

---

[9]Thompson, *Robert Frost*, 36.

[10]The book was published by Oxford University Press in 1921. It is from this edition that I have cited Vaughan's "The Night" above.

of many times in the London *Times* Literary Supplement (October 20, 1921). Frost was very much aware of what Eliot was doing, as he would be for several years to come. He could hardly have ignored a book of poems that was promising to revise the official history of English letters. But a second book was also available which put Vaughan's poem explicitly in the mystical tradition and in the context of "Divine Darkness" literature. This was Evelyn Underhill's *Mysticism,* a sensitively written book full of marvelous quotations, so popular that it went through twelve editions between 1911 and 1930. Miss Underhill's emphasis was on the Anglican mystical tradition, in which Eliot (again) was becoming so totally interested. Miss Underhill cites the final stanza of Vaughan's "The Night" on the same page that she quotes the passage from Dionysius the Areopagite introduced above.

In the absence of actual records, it always seems tendentious to propose "probable" sources for a particular literary work. But the question of sources is not crucial in this instance. A more fertile source of investigation (as in the case of the Freudian criticism which posits a death wish here) is the more general question of *provenance:* analogous areas of human experience where similar diction is employed. The three authors mentioned above provide, then, a possible source for Frost's diction, and a certain analogue to both experience and diction. Frost, in the central statement of this poem, employs the vocabulary characteristic of this same kind of mysticism.

A well-known source of Frost's early thought provides a still richer trove of analogues. This is William James. Frost already knew the writings of the noted psychologist when he sought admission to Harvard as a special student in 1897. James was on leave of absence when Frost was there, but one of his professors used James's shorter *Psychology* as his text. Frost used this text, as well as James's *Talks to Teachers on Psychology,* when he was a teacher at the Plymouth Normal School in 1911–1912.[11] Frost himself said in 1932, "The most valuable teacher I had at Harvard I never had. . . . He was William James. His books meant a great deal to me."[12]

In James's *The Varieties of Religious Experience* (1902), Frost would have found the same vocabulary of mysticism used by Vaughan, though not the citation from the poet himself. In Lectures XVI and XVII, for example, James quotes from Henry Suso, German mystic of the fourteenth century, on the state of the soul in mystical rapture, "lost in the stillness of the glorious *dazzling obscurity* and of the naked simple unity. It is in this modeless *where* that the highest bliss is to be found." A night-time experience, close to Frost's in "Stopping by Woods," is also quoted: "The perfect stillness of the night was thrilled by a more solemn silence. The darkness held a presence that was all the more felt because it was not seen. I could not any more have doubted that *He* was there than that I was. Indeed, I felt myself to be, if possible, the less real of the two." To select a final citation, among many that relate to the vocabulary of Frost's poem, James quotes St. Teresa of

[11] Thompson, *Robert Frost: The Early Years;* see 231–232, 239–241, 372.

[12] Lawrance Thompson, *Robert Frost: The Years of Triumph, 1915–1938* (New York: 1970), 643.

Avila on the mystic's sense of nothingness, the threat of abandonment of one's being. The metaphors of wakefulness and sleep are especially pertinent: "In the orison of union, the soul is fully awake as regards God, but wholly asleep as regards things of this world and in respect of herself. During the short time the union lasts, she is as it were deprived of every feeling, and even if she would, she could not think of any single thing."[13] The provenance of Frost's imagery is, now, quite clear. The words and images do not characterize Freud's descriptions of the death-wish; they are found, however, throughout a large range of literature which attempts to describe a particular kind of mystical experience, an encounter with the Absolute in which man's own sense of selfhood is threatened with annihilation.

This kind of imagery, for this kind of terrifying experience of transcendent being, is deeply rooted in the human mind. In Greek mythology, high in the genealogy of the pre-divine entities, Sleep is the child of Night. One step further back, according to Hesiod's *Theogony*, is the father of Night, Chaos, the formlessness from which everything originates. Both Sleep and Night are mentioned in Frost's poem, as is also, by the implications of my argument, the Father of them all. One must point out, for those who espouse the death-wish interpretation, that Erebus is *another* child of Chaos, the sister of Sleep, and represents in mythological thought a distinctly different approach to the origin of all being. If we can reduce the statements of Frost's speaker here to mythological thought-patterns, they fall clearly into line with what I have been proposing. Frost's repeated line at the end of the poem, "And miles to go before I sleep," emphasizes his preference for other things, other "promises" he has made to himself, before he is ready to face this Night which exposes the sleeper to the infinite abandonment of forms, Chaos. 16

What all of these considerations lead to is the conclusion that "Stopping by Woods" is a decisive poem in the mental development of Robert Frost. It clearly describes the goal of a road not taken. This is the road of the holy man, whose goal is absorption in transcendent being. In determining the parameters of his genius Frost came upon this area, as is clearly shown by the vocabulary of this poem. Where the earlier Transcendentalists found in this experience the goal of their desires, Frost's later American draws the line and retreats. The poem is a statement of resistance to a particular kind of experience which the speaker finds radically uncongenial. Frost is on territory too personally threatening to cultivate as his own field of creative endeavor.[14] 17

Frost has several poems which verge upon the edge of this same emblematical night, where one knows that one will lose himself, and where the mystic trusts he will finally find himself and a total transforming wisdom as well. This cluster of poems has its own dramatic structure. We may sketch it lightly, 18

[13]*The Varieties of Religious Experience* was published in New York by Longmans, Green and Co., 1902; I quote from the edition published in New York by the New American Library of World Literature, 1958, 322, 67, 313.

[14]Eban Bass has recently discerned a grouping of Frost's poems which he calls the "poetry of fear." He finds, though, that the fear remains enigmatic. See *American Literature*, XLIII, 603–615.

with some well-known poems, to show the general curve; many more poems could be plotted along the points on this graph. The poems chosen are the ones Frost came back to again and again in his public readings. Several years earlier, in "An Old Man's Winter Night," the subject of the poem is vaguely troubled by a sense of presences in the night. But because of aloneness and feeble old age he is unable to confront them directly: "One aged man—one man—can't keep a house, / A farm, a countryside. . . ." Here is the beginning of the fear that will develop of the formlessness that lies outside of artificially established human boundaries. Another poem from the same volume (*Mountain Interlude*, 1916) confirms Frost's own preferences for the earthly and the particular. The famous "Birches" expresses a conscious choice of one direction over another as proper for human cultivation: "Earth's the right place for love:"[15]

> I'd like to go by climbing a birch-tree,
> And climb black branches up a snow-white trunk
> *Toward* heaven, till the tree could bear no more,
> But dipped its top and set me down again.

In other words, there is an unwillingness to cope with the experience of transcendence expressed several years before the moment in July, 1922, when "Stopping by Woods on a Snowy Evening" was written. A few years later, in *West-Running Brook* (1928), Frost printed "Acquainted with the Night." The speaker is again alone, again it is night. He feels totally isolated in a lifeless city and a loveless universe. A sign of the powerful feeling locked in this poem is the fact that it is held together by a tight terza rima, a form unusual in Frost. Panic, caused by a perception of limitlessness, is very close to the surface. Again, in "Desert Places" (1936), in a setting similar to that of "Stopping by Woods," the speaker has a sense of a universe that is no longer inhabited, whether these be the vast interstellar spaces or his own spaces "so much nearer home." In these poems the reason for his earlier rejection of the transcendent experience is developed: it is as if acceptance would have set him loose to wander in total isolation in the infinite formlessness of the universe. A final note to the explanation of Frost's resistance to the transcendent experience, as he recorded it in "Stopping by Woods," is stated in "Design" (from *A Further Range*, 1936). This is another closely knit poem, a well-designed sonnet more tightly unified by the use of only three rhymes. The "design" or providence which brings the moth and the dimpled spider together on the diseased flower is probably the "design of *darkness* to appall." The negative vastness that tenants the universe probably shapes things malevolently. One who perceived transcendence in this way could hardly be expected to cry, with Henry Vaughan, "O for the night. . . ."[16]

---

[15] A similar reading of "Birches" is offered by Anna K. Juhnke, "Religion in Robert Frost's Poetry: The Play for Self-Possessions," *American Literature*, XXXVI, 153–164.

[16] Some other poems of Frost that might be considered as part of this same cluster are "A Passing Glimpse," "Beeches," and "For Once, Then, Something,"—all of which state a choice of a circumscribed area of poetic inquiry in place of a limitless one. "Come In" is also interesting as a definite refusal to enter the dark woods.

QUESTIONS FOR MEANING

1. How does Shurr justify writing this essay? What are the two new insights into the poem that he claims to offer?
2. What are the four traditional approaches to "Stopping by Woods on a Snowy Evening" that Shurr rejects? Why does he find these interpretations to be inadequate?
3. What does Shurr mean in paragraph 6 when he states that "Stopping by Woods on a Snowy Evening" is "a record of the mind's encounter with transcendence"?
4. Who was Ralph Waldo Emerson, and what was his experience in "the woods"?
5. What support does Shurr offer for his claim that Frost must have been familiar with "The Night" by Henry Vaughan?
6. Explain the concept of "Divine Darkness" discussed in paragraphs 10 and 15.
7. Who were the Transcendentalists, alluded to in paragraph 17?
8. In what sense is "Stopping by Woods on a Snowy Evening" a religious poem? According to Shurr, what is it that Frost rejects in this poem? Has he rejected God?
9. Vocabulary: moratorium (1), expenditure (1), provenance (1), *stemma* (2), conflated (4), psychic (4), theological (5), existentialism (5), ascendancy (8), paradoxically (10), subsidiary (11), tendentious (13), analogues (14), pertinent (15), orison (15), espouse (16), uncongenial (17), emblematical (18), terza rima (18), and malevolently (18).

QUESTIONS ABOUT STRATEGY

1. Why does Shurr begin his essay by summarizing earlier interpretations of the poem?
2. How good is Shurr's research? Does he convince you that he has made a thorough study of the poem and the criticism it has inspired?
3. Why is it important for Shurr to link Frost to Emerson and James—and not just to Henry Vaughan?
4. Why does Shurr conclude his argument by comparing "Stopping by Woods on a Snowy Evening" with several other poems by Frost?

N. ARTHUR BLEAU
Robert Frost's Favorite Poem

*As the essays in this section have revealed, literary criticism is often argumentative. Critics often disagree about the meaning of literature, and the greatest controversy is frequently provoked by the most familiar poems and stories. Many critics would argue that a work of art has a life of its own that is independent of the author's intentions. But to know something of the circumstances under which a work is composed can sometimes help us to understand it. In forming your own judgment of "Stopping by Woods on a Snowy Evening," you may want to consider the following postscript: a **1978** narrative account of a conversation between Frost and one of his admirers which had occurred many years earlier.*

Robert Frost revealed his favorite poem to me. Furthermore, he gave me   1
a glimpse into his personal life that exposed the mettle of the man. I cherish
the memory of that conversation, and vividly recall his description of the
circumstances leading to the composition of his favorite work.

We were in my hometown—Brunswick, Maine. It was the fall of 1947, and   2
Bowdoin College was presenting its annual literary institute for students and
the public. Mr. Frost had lectured there the previous season; and being well
received, he was invited for a return engagement.

I attended the great poet's prior lecture and wasn't about to miss his en-   3
core—even though I was quartered 110 miles north at the University of Maine.
At the appointed time, I was seated and eagerly awaiting his entrance—armed
with a book of his poems and unaware of what was about to occur.

He came on strong with a simple eloquence that blended with his stature,   4
bushy white hair, matching eyebrows, and well-seasoned features. His topics
ranged from meter to the meticulous selection of a word and its varying
interpretations. He then read a few of his poems to accentuate his message.

At the conclusion of the presentation, Mr. Frost asked if anyone had ques-   5
tions. I promptly raised my hand. There were three other questioners, and
their inquiries were answered before he acknowledged me. I asked, "Mr. Frost,
what is your favorite poem?" He quickly replied, "They're all my favorites.
It's difficult to single out one over another!"

"But, Mr. Frost," I persisted, "surely there must be one or two of your   6
poems which have a special meaning to you—that recall some incident perhaps." He then astonished me by declaring the session concluded; where-
upon, he turned to me and said, "Young man, you may come up to the podium
if you like." I was there in an instant.

We were alone except for one man who was serving as Mr. Frost's host.   7
He remained in the background shadows of the stage. The poet leaned casually against the lectern—beckoning me to come closer. We were side by
side leaning on the lectern as he leafed the pages of the book.

"You know—in answer to your question—there is one poem which comes   8
readily to mind; and I guess I'd have to call it my favorite," he droned in a
pensive manner. "I'd have to say 'Stopping by Woods on a Snowy Evening' is
that poem. Do you recall in the lecture I pointed out the importance of the
line 'The darkest evening of the year'?" I acknowledged that I did, and he
continued his thoughtful recollection of a time many years before. "Well—
the darkest evening of the year is on December twenty-second—which is the
shortest day of the year—just before Christmas."

I wish I could have recorded the words as he reflectively meted out his   9
story, but this is essentially what he said.

The family was living on a farm. It was a bleak time both weatherwise and   10
financially. Times were hard, and Christmas was coming. It wasn't going to
be a very good Christmas unless he did something. So—he hitched up the
wagon filled with produce from the farm and started the long trek into town.

When he finally arrived, there was no market for his goods. Times were   11
hard for everybody. After exhausting every possibility, he finally accepted the
fact that there would be no sale. There would be no exchange for him to get
a few simple presents for his children's Christmas.

As he headed home, evening descended. It had started to snow, and his   12
heart grew heavier with each step of the horse in the gradually increasing
accumulation. He had dropped the reins and given the horse its head. It knew
the way. The horse was going more slowly as they approached home. It was
sensing his despair. There is an unspoken communication between a man
and his horse, you know.

Around the next bend in the road, near the woods, they would come into   13
view of the house. He knew the family was anxiously awaiting him. How could
he face them? What could he possibly say or do to spare them the disappointment he felt?

They entered the sweep of the bend. The horse slowed down and then   14
stopped. It knew what he had to do. He had to cry, and he did. I recall the
very words he spoke. "I just sat there and bawled like a baby"—until there
were no more tears.

The horse shook its harness. The bells jingled. They sounded cheerier. He   15
was ready to face his family. It would be a poor Christmas, but Christmas is
a time of love. They had an abundance of love, and it would see them through
that Christmas and the rest of those hard times. Not a word was spoken, but
the horse knew he was ready and resumed the journey homeward.

The poem was composed some time later, he related. How much later I do   16
not know, but he confided that these were the circumstances which eventually inspired what he acknowledged to be his favorite poem.

I was completely enthralled and, with youthful audacity, asked him to tell   17
me about his next favorite poem. He smiled relaxedly and readily replied,
"That would have to be 'Mending Wall.' Good fences do make good neighbors,
you know! We always looked forward to getting together and walking the
lines—each on his own side replacing the stones the winter frost had tum-

bled. As we moved along, we'd discuss the things each had experienced during the winter—and also what was ahead of us. It was a sign of spring!"

The enchantment was broken at that moment by Mr. Frost's host, who 18 had materialized behind us to remind him of his schedule. He nodded agreement that it was time to depart, turned to me and with a smile extended his hand. I grasped it, and returned his firm grip as I expressed my gratitude. He then strode off to join his host, who had already reached the door at the back of the stage. I stood there watching him disappear from sight.

I've often wondered why he suddenly changed his mind and decided to 19 answer my initial question by confiding his memoir in such detail. Perhaps no one had ever asked him; or perhaps I happened to pose it at the opportune time. Then again—perhaps the story was meant to be related, remembered and revealed sometime in the future. I don't know, but I'm glad he did—so that I can share it with you.

A Note by Lesley Frost

For many years I have assumed that my father's explanation to me, given 20 sometime in the forties, I think, of the circumstances round and about his writing "Stopping by Woods" was the only one he gave (of course, excepting to my mother), and since he expressed the hope that it need not be repeated fearing pity (pity, he said, was the *last* thing he wanted or needed), I have left it at that. Now, in 1977, I find there was at least one other to whom he vouchsafed the honor of hearing the truth of how it all was that Xmas eve when "the little horse" (Eunice) slows the sleigh at a point between woods, a hundred yards or so north of our farm on the Wyndham Road. And since Arthur Bleau's moving account is so closely, word for word, as I heard it, it would give me particular reason to hope it might be published. I would like to add my own remembrance of words used in the telling to me: "A man has as much right as a woman to a good cry now and again. The snow gave me its shelter; the horse understood and gave me the time." (Incidentally, my father had a liking for certain Old English words. *Bawl* was one of them. Instead of "Stop crying," it was "Oh, come now, quit bawling." Mr. Bleau is right to say my father bawled like a baby.)

QUESTIONS FOR MEANING

1. Summarize the experience that led Frost to write "Stopping by Woods on a Snowy Evening."
2. Of the various critics included in this section, who would be the most likely to use Bleau's testimony to reinforce his own interpretation of the poem?
3. Does the biographical information reported in this essay change your own perception of the poem?

4. What does this essay reveal about N. Arthur Bleau? What was he like in 1947? What was he like thirty years later?
5. Vocabulary: mettle (1), accentuate (4), droned (8), pensive (8), meted (9), enthralled (17), audacity (17), and opportune (19).

QUESTIONS ABOUT STRATEGY

1. How important is the note by Leslie Frost supporting the substance of Bleau's report? Would you take Bleau seriously without this reinforcement? If so, why? If not, why not?
2. Leslie Frost describes Bleau's essay as "moving." Do you agree? How would you describe the style and pace of this essay? How good is Bleau's writing?
3. What is the function of paragraph 9? Why does it come at this point, after Bleau has already quoted Frost in paragraphs 6 and 8?

One Student's Assignment

Study "Stopping by Woods on a Snowy Evening" and read at least one essay about the poem in The Informed Argument. *Demonstrate that this essay does not entirely explain the poem by offering an interpretation of your own. When writing about the poem, be careful to support whatever you claim with evidence from the poem itself. Use MLA style documentation.*

A View of the Woods
Kim Bassuener

Like any great poem, "Stopping by Woods on a Snowy Evening"   1
by Robert Frost has a number of possible meanings. According
to one famous interpretation, this poem is about death and
despair (Ciardi 414). This is a valid interpretation, but I
think that it is too narrow. Part of the delight of reading
poetry is discovering the variety of meanings which can be
derived from any one poem. Another way of reading "Stopping
by Woods on a Snowy Evening" is to see it as a poem about how
far man has come from nature.

In the very first line, the narrator reflects, "Whose   2
woods these are I think I know." His uncertainty about who
owns the woods suggests that whoever owns them does not visit
them often or does not take enough pride in them to let other

people know that he owns them. Frost continues to convey the
distance between owner and woods in the second line: "His
house is in the village though." It is clear that the owner
prefers civilization and people to nature. The third line
also supports this idea: "He will not see me stopping here"
emphasizes that the owner of the woods is removed from them.
It is almost as if the poem is saying that the owner does not
really own these woods which he cannot even see. The last
line of the first stanza, "To watch his woods fill up with
snow," uses "his" ironically. After the way the first
three lines imply a sense of casual and remote ownership, the
"his" in line 4 cannot be taken seriously. Nature is filling
up the woods with snow, and we can only watch what ultimately
seems to belong to nature, not man.

The second stanza further states how far away man has come   3
from nature with "My little horse must think it queer" (5).
The reader should ask why a horse would think it strange to
stop by some woods. One of nature's creatures, a horse should
love to be out in nature. Instead, it thinks it odd "To stop
without a farmhouse near" (6). This shows that man has taken
this animal from nature and made it dependent upon civilization. The horse would feel comfortable only if a farmhouse
was nearby, and perhaps this is why it is "little."

Frost reminds us about the animal's confusion in the third   4
stanza: "He gives his harness bells a shake / To ask if there
is some mistake" (9—10). Thoroughly domesticated, the horse
cannot understand why its master would want to stop by woods.
The next two lines in this stanza contrast with the last two
lines of the second stanza. Although we have already been
told that the lake is "frozen" (7) and that this is "The darkest evening of the year" (8), the narrator now seems to forget that nature is potentially dangerous. "The only other
sound's the sweep / Of easy wind and downy flake" (11—12)
makes nature seem harmless and even comforting. The narrator
seems to feel detached from the scene, like something watching a snow storm on television. Any forest animal would know
that this is no night to play with. A cold, dark, snowy night
is no time to get sentimental about nature. But the poor human being cannot comprehend the true power of what he is only
visiting.

The last stanza continues to portray the traveler as a de-   5
tached observer. When the narrator observes, "The woods are

lovely, dark, and deep" (13), he seems to see nature as something scenic—-like a picture on a wall. He would like to look longer, but other values are more important to him: "But I have promises to keep / And miles to go before I sleep / And miles to go before I sleep" (14—16). His life is someplace else. He is not a part of the scene that has briefly caught his attention.

When everything in the poem is taken into consideration, 6 it seems safe to believe that Frost could have written this poem to show a conflict between man and nature. Although the man in the poem seems able to find pleasure in looking at nature, he is too far removed from it to be able to understand what he is looking at.

Works Cited*

Ciardi, John. "Robert Frost: The Way to the Poem." <u>The Informed Argument</u>. Ed. Robert K. Miller. San Diego: Harcourt, 1989. 411—18.

---

*This citation follows the MLA form for a work in an anthology as given on p. 55. An alternative form recommended by the MLA is to give the complete data of the article's original publication as well as the complete data for the source in which it has been read. Here is how the Ciardi citation would look in this alternative form:

Ciardi, John. "Robert Frost: The Way to the Poem." <u>Saturday Review</u> 40 (12 Apr. 1958): 15+. Rpt. in <u>The Informed Argument</u>. Ed. Robert K. Miller. San Diego: Harcourt, 1989. 411–18.

Ciardi's essay began on page 15 and ended on page 65 in the magazine in which it first appeared, but it was not a 50-page-long article so it would be a mistake to write 15–65. As often happens in general circulation magazines, the article was broken up and "continued" on a number of different pages. In a case like this in which the pages are not continuous, use the plus sign (+) immediately after the page on which the material begins. Note that the abbreviation "Rpt." is used for "reprinted."

Of the two ways of citing material in an anthology, this alternative form is the more scholarly. Check with your instructor to find if he or she requires the additional information that is included within this form [editor's note].

SUGGESTIONS FOR WRITING

1. Write an explication of "Stopping by Woods on a Snowy Evening," drawing upon at least three of the essays in this unit.
2. Explicate one of the following poems. Do research if you wish, but make sure your interpretation explains the language of the poem you have chosen and not just the feelings it has inspired within you.

A Valediction: Forbidding Mourning

As virtuous men pass mildly away,
    And whisper to their souls to go,
While some of their sad friends do say,
    The breath goes now, and some say, no:

5   So let us melt, and make no noise,
    No tear-floods, nor sigh-tempests move;
'Twere profanation of our joys
    To tell the laity our love.

Moving of th' earth brings harms and fears,
10   Men reckon what it did and meant,
But trepidation of the spheres,
    Though greater far, is innocent.

Dull sublunary lovers' love
    (Whose soul is sense) cannot admit
15   Absence, because it doth remove
    Those things which elemented it.

But we by a love so much refined,
    That ourselves know not what it is,
Inter-assurèd of the mind,
20   Care less, eyes, lips, and hands to miss.

Our two souls therefore, which are one,
    Though I must go, endure not yet
A breach, but an expansion,
    Like gold to airy thinness beat.

25   If they be two, they are two so
    As stiff twin compasses are two;
Thy soul the fixed foot, makes no show
    To move, but doth, if th' other do.

And though it in the center sit,
30   Yet when the other far doth roam,
It leans, and hearkens after it,
    And grows erect, as that comes home.

Such wilt thou be to me, who must
    Like th' other foot, obliquely run;
35   Thy firmness makes my circle just,
    And makes me end, where I begun.

John Donne
1572–1631

The Night

Through that pure virgin shrine,
That sacred veil drawn o'er Thy glorious noon,
That men might look and live, as glowworms shine,
    And face the moon,
5   Wise Nicodemus saw such light
As made him know his God by night.

Most blest believer he!
Who in that land of darkness and blind eyes
Thy long-expected healing wings could see,
10   When Thou didst rise!
And, what can never more be done,
Did at midnight speak with the Sun!

O who will tell me where
He found Thee at that dead and silent hour?
15   What hallowed solitary ground did bear
    So rare a flower,
Within whose sacred leaves did lie
The fulness of the Deity?

No mercy-seat of gold,
20   No dead and dusty cherub, nor carved stone,
But His own living works did my Lord hold
    And lodge alone;
Where trees and herbs did watch and peep
And wonder, while the Jews did sleep.

25   Dear night! this world's defeat;
The stop to busy fools; care's check and curb;
The day of spirits; my soul's calm retreat
    Which none disturb!

Christ's progress, and His prayer time;
30   The hours to which high heaven doth chime;

God's silent, searching flight;
When my Lord's head is filled with dew, and all
His locks are wet with the clear drops of night;
His still, soft call;
35   His knocking time; the soul's dumb watch,
When spirits their fair kindred catch.

Were all my loud, evil days
Calm and unhaunted as is thy dark tent,
Whose peace but by some angel's wing or voice
40   Is seldom rent,
Then I in heaven all the long year
Would keep, and never wander here.

But living where the sun
Doth all things wake, and where all mix and tire
45   Themselves and others, I consent and run
To every mire,
And by this world's ill-guiding light,
Err more than I can do by night.

There is in God, some say,
50   A deep but dazzling darkness, as men here
Say it is late and dusky; because they
See not all clear.
O for that night! where I in Him
Might live invisible and dim!

Henry Vaughan
1622–1695

The Sick Rose

O Rose, thou art sick.
The invisible worm
That flies in the night
In the howling storm

5   Has found out thy bed
Of crimson joy,
And his dark secret love
Does thy life destroy.

William Blake
1757–1827

Ode on a Grecian Urn

Thou still unravished bride of quietness,
    Thou foster-child of silence and slow time,
Sylvan historian, who canst thus express
    A flowery tale more sweetly than our rhyme:
5   What leaf-fringed legend haunts about thy shape
        Of deities or mortals, or of both,
            In Tempe or the dales of Arcady?
    What men or gods are these? What maidens loth?
What mad pursuit? What struggle to escape?
10   What pipes and timbrels? What wild ecstacy?

Heard melodies are sweet, but those unheard
    Are sweeter; therefore, ye soft pipes, play on;
Not to the sensual ear, but, more endeared,
    Pipe to the spirit ditties of no tone:
15   Fair youth, beneath the trees, thou canst not leave
        Thy song, nor ever can those trees be bare;
            Bold lover, never, never canst thou kiss,
    Though winning near the goal—yet, do not grieve;
        She cannot fade, though thou hast not thy bliss,
20   For ever wilt thou love, and she be fair!

Ah, happy, happy boughs! that cannot shed
    Your leaves, nor ever bid the spring adieu;
And, happy melodist, unwearièd,
    For ever piping songs for ever new;
25   More happy love! more happy, happy love!
        For ever warm and still to be enjoyed,
            For ever panting and for ever young;
All breathing human passion far above,
    That leaves a heart high-sorrowful and cloyed,
30   A burning forehead, and a parching tongue.

Who are these coming to the sacrifice?
    To what green altar, O mysterious priest,
Lead'st thou that heifer lowing at the skies,
    And all her silken flanks with garlands drest?
35   What little town by river or sea shore,
        Or mountain-built with peaceful citadel,
            Is emptied of its folk, this pious morn?
And, little town, thy streets for evermore
    Will silent be; and not a soul to tell
40   Why thou art desolate, can e'er return.

O Attic shape! Fair attitude! with brede
    Of marble men and maidens overwrought,
With forest branches and the trodden weed;
    Thou, silent form, dost tease us out of thought
45   As doth eternity: Cold Pastoral!

When old age shall this generation waste,
　　Thou shalt remain, in midst of other woe
　Than ours, a friend to man, to whom thou say'st,
Beauty is truth, truth beauty,—that is all
50　　　Ye know on earth, and all ye need to know.

John Keats
1795–1821

Brahma

　If the red slayer thinks he slays,
　　Or if the slain think he is slain,
　They know not well the subtle ways
　　I keep, and pass, and turn again,

5　Far or forgot to me is near;
　　Shadow and sunlight are the same;
　The vanished gods to me appear;
　　And one to me are shame and fame.

　They reckon ill who leave me out;
10　　When me they fly, I am the wings;
　I am the doubter and the doubt,
　　And I the hymn the Brahmin sings.

　The strong gods pine for my abode,
　　And pine in vain the sacred Seven;
15　But thou, meek lover of the good!
　　Find me, and turn thy back on heaven.

Ralph Waldo Emerson
1803–1882

I Saw in Louisiana a Live-Oak Growing

I saw in Louisiana a live-oak growing,
All alone stood it and the moss hung down from the branches,
Without any companion it grew there uttering joyous leaves of dark
　green,
And its look, rude, unbending, lusty, made me think of myself,
5　But I wonder'd how it could utter joyous leaves standing alone there
　　without its friend near, for I knew I could not,
And I broke off a twig with a certain number of leaves upon it, and
　twined around it a little moss,
And brought it away, and I have placed it in sight in my room,
It is not needed to remind me as of my own dear friends,

(For I believe lately I think of little else than of them,)
10   Yet it remains to me a curious token, it makes me think of manly
           love;
       For all that, and though the live-oak glistens there in Louisiana
           solitary in a wide flat space,
       Uttering joyous leaves all its life without a friend a lover near,
       I know very well I could not.

                                                    Walt Whitman
                                                    1819–1892

Dover Beach

       The sea is calm tonight.
       The tide is full, the moon lies fair
       Upon the straits; on the French coast the light
       Gleams and is gone; the cliffs of England stand,
5   Glimmering and vast, out in the tranquil bay.
       Come to the window, sweet is the night-air!
       Only, from the long line of spray
       Where the sea meets the moon-blanched land.
       Listen! you hear the grating roar
10   Of pebbles which the waves draw back, and fling,
       At their return, up the high strand,
       Begin, and cease, and then again begin,
       With tremulous cadence slow, and bring
       The eternal note of sadness in.

15   Sophocles long ago
       Heard it on the Aegean, and it brought
       Into his mind the turbid ebb and flow
       Of human misery; we
       Find also in the sound a thought,
20   Hearing it by this distant northern sea.

       The Sea of Faith
       Was once, too, at the full, and round earth's shore
       Lay like the folds of a bright girdle furled.
       But now I only hear
25   Its melancholy, long, withdrawing roar,
       Retreating, to the breath
       Of the night-wind, down the vast edges drear
       And naked shingles of the world.

       Ah, love, let us be true
30   To one another! for the world, which seems
       To lie before us like a land of dreams,
       So various, so beautiful, so new,

Hath really neither joy, nor love, nor light,
Nor certitude, nor peace, nor help for pain;
35   And we are here as on a darkling plain
Swept with confused alarms of struggle and flight,
Where ignorant armies clash by night.

Matthew Arnold
1822–1888

A Bird Came Down the Walk

A Bird came down the Walk—
He did not know I saw—
He bit an Angleworm in halves
And ate the fellow, raw,

5   And then he drank a Dew
From a convenient Grass—
And then hopped sidewise to the Wall
To let a Beetle pass—

He glanced with rapid eyes
10   That hurried all around—
They looked like frightened Beads, I thought—
He stirred his Velvet Head

Like one in danger, Cautious,
I offered him a Crumb
15   And he unrolled his feathers
And rowed him softer home—

Than Oars divide the Ocean,
Too silver for a seam—
Or Butterflies, off Banks of Noon
20   Leap, plashless as they swim.

Emily Dickinson
1830–1886

Section 9
Some Classic Arguments

PLATO
The Allegory of the Cave

One of the most important thinkers in the history of Western civilization, Plato (c. 428–348 B.C.) grew up in Athens during the difficult years of the Peloponnesian War. He was the student of Socrates, and it is through Plato that Socratic thought has been passed down to us. Socrates is the principal figure in Plato's early dialogues—discussing with the young such questions as "What should men live for?" and "What is the nature of virtue?" Plato devoted his life to answering questions of this sort and teaching others to understand them. In 387 B.C., he founded his Academy, the world's first university, where he taught the future rulers of numerous Greek states. The Academy survived for almost a thousand years, before closing in A.D. 529.

Plato's major works include the Gorgias, Meno, Phaedo, Symposium, The Republic, *and* Phaedrus. *In each of these works, Plato insists upon two ideas that are fundamental to his philosophy. He believed that man has an immortal soul existing separately from the body both before birth and after death. Also, he believed that the physical world consists only of appearances; truth consists of ideas that can be discovered and understood only through systematic thought.*

"The Allegory of the Cave" is taken from The Republic, *which is Plato's greatest work. It is written in the form of a dialogue. The speaker is Socrates, and his "audience" is Glaucon, Plato's brother. But the dialogue should be regarded as a literary device, rather than an actual conversation. Its ultimate audience consists of everyone who wants to think seriously about the nature of truth, justice, and wisdom.*

Next, said I, here is a parable to illustrate the degrees in which our nature   1
may be enlightened or unenlightened. Imagine the condition of men living in a sort of cavernous chamber underground, with an entrance open to the light and a long passage all down the cave. Here they have been from childhood, chained by the leg and also by the neck, so that they cannot move and can see only what is in front of them, because the chains will not let them turn their heads. At some distance higher up is the light of a fire burning behind them; and between the prisoners and the fire is a track with a parapet built along it, like the screen at a puppet-show, which hides the performers while they show their puppets over the top.

I see, said he.   2

Now behind this parapet imagine persons carrying along various artificial   3
objects, including figures of men and animals in wood or stone or other materials, which project above the parapet. Naturally, some of these persons will
be talking, others silent.

It is a strange picture, he said, and a strange sort of prisoners.   4

Like ourselves, I replied; for in the first place prisoners so confined would   5
have seen nothing of themselves or of one another, except the shadows thrown
by the fire-light on the wall of the Cave facing them, would they?

Not if all their lives they have been prevented from moving their heads.   6

And they would have seen as little of the objects carried past.   7

Of course.   8

Now, if they could talk to one another, would they not suppose that their   9
words referred only to those passing shadows which they saw?

Necessarily.   10

And suppose their prison had an echo from the wall facing them? When   11
one of the people crossing behind them spoke, they could only suppose that
the sound came from the shadow passing before their eyes.

No doubt.   12

In every way, then, such prisoners would recognize as reality nothing but   13
the shadows of those artificial objects.

Inevitably.   14

Now consider what would happen if their release from the chains and the   15
healing of their unwisdom should come about in this way. Suppose one of
them set free and forced suddenly to stand up, turn his head, and walk with
eyes lifted to the light; all these movements would be painful, and he would
be too dazzled to make out the objects whose shadows he had been used to
see. What do you think he would say, if someone told him that what he had
formerly seen was meaningless illusion, but now, being somewhat nearer to
reality and turned towards more real objects, he was getting a truer view?
Suppose further that he were shown the various objects being carried by and
were made to say, in reply to questions, what each of them was. Would he
not be perplexed and believe the objects now shown him to be not so real
as what he formerly saw?

Yes, not nearly so real.   16

And if he were forced to look at the fire-light itself, would not his eyes   17
ache, so that he would try to escape and turn back to the things which he
could see distinctly, convinced that they really were clearer than these other
objects now being shown to him?

Yes.   18

And suppose someone were to drag him away forcibly up the steep and   19
rugged ascent and not let him go until he had hauled him out into the sunlight, would he not suffer pain and vexation at such treatment, and, when he
had come out into the light, find his eyes so full of its radiance that he could
not see a single one of the things that he was now told were real?

Certainly he would not see them all at once.   20

He would need, then, to grow accustomed before he could see things in that upper world. At first it would be easiest to make out shadows, and then the images of men and things reflected in water, and later on the things themselves. After that, it would be easier to watch the heavenly bodies and the sky itself by night, looking at the light of the moon and stars rather than the Sun and the Sun's light in the day-time.   21

Yes, surely.   22

Last of all, he would be able to look at the Sun and contemplate its nature, not as it appears when reflected in water or any alien medium, but as it is in itself in its own domain.   23

No doubt.   24

And now he would begin to draw the conclusion that it is the Sun that produces the seasons and the course of the year and controls everything in the visible world, and moreover is in a way the cause of all that he and his companions used to see.   25

Clearly he would come at last to that conclusion.   26

Then if he called to mind his fellow prisoners and what passed for wisdom in his former dwelling-place, he would surely think himself happy in the change and be sorry for them. They may have had a practice of honouring and commending one another, with prizes for the man who had the keenest eye for the passing shadows and the best memory for the order in which they followed or accompanied one another, so that he could make a good guess as to which was going to come next. Would our released prisoner be likely to covet those prizes or to envy the men exalted to honour and power in the Cave? Would he not feel like Homer's Achilles, that he would far sooner 'be on earth as a hired servant in the house of a landless man' or endure anything rather than go back to his old beliefs and live in the old way?   27

Yes, he would prefer any fate to such a life.   28

Now imagine what would happen if he went down again to take his former seat in the Cave. Coming suddenly out of the sunlight, his eyes would be filled with darkness. He might be required once more to deliver his opinion on those shadows, in competition with the prisoners who had never been released, while his eyesight was still dim and unsteady; and it might take some time to become used to the darkness. They would laugh at him and say that he had gone up only to come back with his sight ruined; it was worth no one's while even to attempt the ascent. If they could lay hands on the man who was trying to set them free and lead them up, they would kill him.   29

Yes, they would.   30

Every feature in this parable, my dear Glaucon, is meant to fit our earlier analysis. The prison dwelling corresponds to the region revealed to us through the sense of sight, and the fire-light within it to the power of the Sun. The ascent to see the things in the upper world you may take as standing for the upward journey of the soul into the region of the intelligible; then you will be in possession of what I surmise, since that is what you wish to be told. Heaven knows whether it is true; but this, at any rate, is how it appears to me. In the world of knowledge, the last thing to be perceived and only with   31 great difficulty is the essential Form of Goodness. Once it is perceived, the conclusion must follow that, for all things, this is the cause of whatever is right and good; in the visible world it gives birth to light and to the lord of light, while it is itself sovereign in the intelligible world and the parent of intelligence and truth. Without having had a vision of this Form no one can act with wisdom, either in his own life or in matters of state.

So far as I can understand, I share your belief.   32

Then you may also agree that it is no wonder if those who have reached   33
this height are reluctant to manage the affairs of men. Their souls long to spend all their time in that upper world—naturally enough, if here once more our parable holds true. Nor, again, is it at all strange that one who comes from the contemplation of divine things to the miseries of human life should appear awkward and ridiculous when, with eyes still dazed and not yet accustomed to the darkness, he is compelled, in a law-court or elsewhere, to dispute about the shadows of justice or the images that cast those shadows, and to wrangle over the notions of what is right in the minds of men who have never beheld Justice itself.

It is not at all strange.   34

No; a sensible man will remember that the eyes may be confused in two   35
ways—by a change from light to darkness or from darkness to light; and he will recognize that the same thing happens to the soul. When he sees it troubled and unable to discern anything clearly, instead of laughing thoughtlessly, he will ask whether, coming from a brighter existence, its unaccustomed vision is obscured by the darkness, in which case he will think its condition enviable and its life a happy one; or whether, emerging from the depths of ignorance, it is dazzled by excess of light. If so, he will rather feel sorry for it; or, if he were inclined to laugh, that would be less ridiculous than to laugh at the soul which has come down from the light.

That is a fair statement.   36

If this is true, then, we must conclude that education is not what it is said   37
to be by some, who profess to put knowledge into a soul which does not possess it, as if they could put sight into blind eyes. On the contrary, our own account signifies that the soul of every man does possess the power of learning the truth and the organ to see it with; and that, just as one might have to turn the whole body round in order that the eye should see light instead of darkness, so the entire soul must be turned away from this changing world, until its eye can bear to contemplate reality and that supreme splendour which we have called the Good. Hence there may well be an art whose aim would be to effect this very thing, the conversion of the soul, in the readiest way; not to put the power of sight into the soul's eye, which already has it, but to ensure that, instead of looking in the wrong direction, it is turned the way it ought to be.

Yes, it may well be so.   38

It looks, then, as though wisdom were different from those ordinary vir-   39
tues, as they are called, which are not far removed from bodily qualities, in that they can be produced by habituation and exercise in a soul which has

not possessed them from the first. Wisdom, it seems, is certainly the virtue of some diviner faculty, which never loses its power, though its use for good or harm depends on the direction towards which it is turned. You must have noticed in dishonest men with a reputation for sagacity the shrewd glance of a narrow intelligence piercing the objects to which it is directed. There is nothing wrong with their power of vision, but it has been forced into the service of evil, so that the keener its sight, the more harm it works.

Quite true.   40

And yet if the growth of a nature like this had been pruned from earliest   41
childhood, cleared of those clinging overgrowths which come of gluttony and all luxurious pleasure and, like leaden weights charged with affinity to this mortal world, hang upon the soul, bending its vision downwards; if, freed from these, the soul were turned round towards true reality, then this same power in these very men would see the truth as keenly as the objects it is turned to now.

Yes, very likely.   42

Is it not also likely, or indeed certain after what has been said, that a state   43
can never be properly governed either by the uneducated who know nothing of truth or by men who are allowed to spend all their days in the pursuit of culture? The ignorant have no single mark before their eyes at which they must aim in all the conduct of their own lives and of affairs of state; and the others will not engage in action if they can help it, dreaming that, while still alive, they have been translated to the Islands of the Blest.

Quite true.   44

It is for us, then, as founders of a commonwealth, to bring compulsion to   45
bear on the noblest natures. They must be made to climb the ascent to the vision of Goodness, which we called the highest object of knowledge; and, when they have looked upon it long enough, they must not be allowed, as they now are, to remain on the heights, refusing to come down again to the prisoners or to take any part in their labours and rewards, however much or little these may be worth.

Shall we not be doing them an injustice, if we force on them a worse life   46
than they might have?

You have forgotten again, my friend, that the law is not concerned to make   47
any one class specially happy, but to ensure the welfare of the common-wealth as a whole. By persuasion or constraint it will unite the citizens in harmony, making them share whatever benefits each class can contribute to the common good; and its purpose in forming men of that spirit was not that each should be left to go his own way, but that they should be instrumental in binding the community into one.

True, I had forgotten.   48

You will see, then, Glaucon, that there will be no real injustice in compel-   49
ling our philosophers to watch over and care for the other citizens. We can fairly tell them that their compeers in other states may quite reasonably re-fuse to collaborate: there they have sprung up, like a self-sown plant, in de-

spite of their country's institutions; no one has fostered their growth, and they cannot be expected to show gratitude for a care they have never received. 'But,' we shall say, 'it is not so with you. We have brought you into existence for your country's sake as well as for your own, to be like leaders and king-bees in a hive; you have been better and more thoroughly educated than those others and hence you are more capable of playing your part both as men of thought and as men of action. You must go down, then, each in his turn, to live with the rest and let your eyes grow accustomed to the darkness. You will then see a thousand times better than those who live there always; you will recognize every image for what it is and know what it represents, because you have seen justice, beauty, and goodness in their reality; and so you and we shall find life in our commonwealth no mere dream, as it is in most existing states, where men live fighting one another about shadows and quarreling for power, as if that were a great prize; whereas in truth government can be at its best and free from dissension only where the destined rulers are least desirous of holding office.'

Quite true.   50

Then will our pupils refuse to listen and to take their turns at sharing in   51
the work of the community, though they may live together for most of their time in a purer air?

No; it is a fair demand, and they are fair-minded men. No doubt, unlike   52
any ruler of the present day, they will think of holding power as an unavoidable necessity.

Yes, my friend; for the truth is that you can have a well-governed society   53
only if you can discover for your future rulers a better way of life than being in office; then only will power be in the hands of men who are rich, not in gold, but in the wealth that brings happiness, a good and wise life. All goes wrong when, starved for lack of anything good in their own lives, men turn to public affairs hoping to snatch from thence the happiness they hunger for. They set about fighting for power, and this internecine conflict ruins them and their country. The life of true philosophy is the only one that looks down upon offices of state; and access to power must be confined to men who are not in love with it; otherwise rivals will start fighting. So whom else can you compel to undertake the guardianship of the commonwealth, if not those who, besides understanding best the principles of government, enjoy a nobler life than the politician's and look for rewards of a different kind?

There is indeed no other choice.   54

QUESTIONS FOR MEANING

1. Describe the cave and the situation of the men who live within it. What must be done before anyone can leave the cave?
2. According to Plato, the men in the cave see only the moving shadows of artificial objects that are paraded before them. What activities do people pursue today that involve watching artificial images move across a screen?

If you spent a lifetime watching such images, would you mistake the artificial for the real?

3. Having escaped from the cave, why would anyone want to return to it?

4. In paragraph 29, Plato claims that the men in the cave would kill someone who returned from the upper world to teach them the truth. What reason did Plato have for making this claim?

5. What does "The Allegory of the Cave" reveal about the importance of education? Why is education necessary before one can leave the cave? How does Plato perceive the nature of education?

6. What types of people should be excluded from government in an ideal republic? Why would it be necessary to force philosophers to rule, and why does Plato believe that making such men rule against their will is ethically defensible?

7. If philosophers are attuned to a higher "reality" than the men and women they govern, how can they understand the problems of the people they rule?

8. What would Plato think of American politics?

9. Vocabulary: parapet (1), perplexed (15), vexation (19), surmise (31), affinity (41), and collaborate (49).

QUESTIONS ABOUT STRATEGY

1. What assumptions about human nature underlie Plato's allegory? What assumptions does he make about the nature of government? If you were to summarize Plato's argument and put it into deductive form, what would be your premise?

2. How effective is the use of dialogue as a method for developing an argument? Is it hard to follow?

3. What role does Glaucon serve? Why does he usually agree rather than ask difficult questions?

4. What is the function of paragraph 31?

NICCOLÒ MACHIAVELLI
Should Princes Tell the Truth?

Historian, playwright, poet, and political philosopher, Niccolò Machiavelli (1469–1527) lived in Florence during the turbulence of the Italian Renaissance. From 1498 to 1512, he served in the Chancellery of the Florentine Republic and held the position of secretary for the committee in charge of diplomatic relations and military operations. In fulfilling his responsibilities, Machiavelli traveled to France, Germany, and elsewhere in Italy—giving him the opportunity to observe numerous rulers and the strategies they used to maintain and extend their power. When the Florentine Republic collapsed in 1512 and the Medici returned to power, Machiavelli was dismissed from office, tortured, and temporarily exiled. He retired to an estate not far from Florence and devoted himself to writing the books for which he is now remembered: The Prince *(**1513**)*, The Discourses *(1519)*, The Art of War *(1519–1520), and the* Florentine History *(1525). Of these works the most famous is* The Prince.*

In writing The Prince, *Machiavelli set out to define the rules of politics as he understood them. His work became a handbook on how to acquire and maintain power. Machiavelli's experience taught him that successful rulers are not troubled by questions of ethics. He observed that it is better to be feared than to be loved. As the following excerpt reveals, he believed that virtues such as honesty are irrelevant to the successful pursuit of power. The amorality of Machiavelli's book continues to disturb many readers, and its shrewd observations on the nature of politics have made the author's name synonymous with craftiness and intrigue.*

How laudable it is for a prince to keep good faith and live with integrity, and not with astuteness, every one knows. Still the experience of our times shows those princes to have done great things who have had little regard for good faith, and have been able by astuteness to confuse men's brains, and who have ultimately overcome those who have made loyalty their foundation.   1

You must know, then, that there are two methods of fighting, the one by law, the other by force: the first method is that of men, the second of beasts; but as the first method is often insufficient, one must have recourse to the second. It is therefore necessary for a prince to know well how to use both the beast and the man. This was covertly taught to rulers by ancient writers, who relate how Achilles and many others of those ancient princes were given to Chiron the centaur to be brought up and educated under his discipline. The parable of this semi-animal, semi-human teacher is meant to indicate that a prince must know how to use both natures, and that the one without the other is not durable.   2

A prince being thus obliged to know well how to act as a beast must imitate the fox and the lion, for the lion cannot protect himself from traps, and the fox cannot defend himself from wolves. One must therefore be a fox to recognise traps, and a lion to frighten wolves. Those that wish to be only   3 lions do not understand this. Therefore, a prudent ruler ought not to keep faith when by so doing it would be against his interest, and when the reasons which made him bind himself no longer exist. If men were all good, this precept would not be a good one; but as they are bad, and would not observe their faith with you, so you are not bound to keep faith with them. Nor have legitimate grounds ever failed a prince who wished to show colourable excuse for the non-fulfilment of his promise. Of this one could furnish an infinite number of modern examples, and show how many times peace has been broken, and how many promises rendered worthless by the faithlessness of princes, and those that have been best able to imitate the fox have succeeded best. But it is necessary to be able to disguise this character well, and to be a great feigner and dissembler; and men are so simple and so ready to obey present necessities, that one who deceives will always find those who allow themselves to be deceived.

I will only mention one modern instance. Alexander VI did nothing else   4
but deceive men, he thought of nothing else, and found the occasion for it; no man was ever more able to give assurances, or affirmed things with stronger oaths, and no man observed them less; however, he always succeeded in his deceptions, as he well knew this aspect of things.

It is not, therefore, necessary for a prince to have all the above-named   5
qualities, but it is very necessary to seem to have them. I would even be bold to say that to possess them and always to observe them is dangerous, but to appear to possess them is useful. Thus it is well to seem merciful, faithful, humane, sincere, religious, and also to be so; but you must have the mind so disposed that when it is needful to be otherwise you may be able to change to the opposite qualities. And it must be understood that a prince, and especially a new prince, cannot observe all those things which are considered good in men, being often obliged, in order to maintain the state, to act against faith, against charity, against humanity, and against religion. And, therefore, he must have a mind disposed to adapt itself according to the wind, and as the variations of fortune dictate, and, as I said before, not deviate from what is good, if possible, but be able to do evil if constrained.

A prince must take great care that nothing goes out of his mouth which   6
is not full of the above-named five qualities, and, to see and hear him, he should seem to be all mercy, faith, integrity, humanity, and religion. And nothing is more necessary than to seem to have this last quality, for men in general judge more by the eyes than by the hands, for every one can see, but very few have to feel. Everybody sees what you appear to be, few feel what you are, and those few will not dare to oppose themselves to the many, who have the majesty of the state to defend them; and in the actions of men, and especially of princes, from which there is no appeal, the end justifies the means. Let a prince therefore aim at conquering and maintaining the state, and the means will always be judged honourable and praised by every one, for the vulgar is always taken by appearances and the issue of the event; and the world consists only of the vulgar, and the few who are not vulgar are isolated when the many have a rallying point in the prince. A certain prince

of the present time, whom it is well not to name, never does anything but preach peace and good faith, but he is really a great enemy to both, and either of them, had he observed them, would have lost him state or reputation on many occasions.

QUESTIONS FOR MEANING

1. What are the two methods of fighting cited by Machiavelli. Why is it important for princes to master both?
2. Machiavelli insists that princes must be both "lions" and "foxes." Explain what he means by this.
3. Under what circumstances should princes break their word?
4. Why is it useful for princes "to seem merciful, faithful, humane, sincere, religious, and also to be so"?
5. In paragraph 6, Machiavelli observes, "men in general judge more by the eyes than by the hands, for every one can see, but very few have to feel." What does this mean? Describe Machiavelli's opinion of the average man.

QUESTIONS ABOUT STRATEGY

1. What premise underlies Machiavelli's argument, and where does he first state it?
2. Consider the tone of this essay. What sort of assumptions has Machiavelli made about his audience?
3. Machiavelli mentions Alexander VI by name in paragraph 4, but refuses to identify the prince he alludes to in paragraph 6. What does this reveal?
4. How would you characterize Machiavelli's point of view? Is it cynical or realistic?

ANDREW MARVELL
To His Coy Mistress

Andrew Marvell (1621–1678) was a Puritan patriot and political writer who is now remembered for writing a book of poetry that was published after his death. He graduated from Trinity College, Cambridge, in 1639, and after the death of his father in 1641, he spent several years traveling in Europe, presumably as a tutor. Upon his return to England, he became tutor to a ward of Oliver Cromwell, the man who ruled England during the period between the execution of Charles I in 1649 and the restoration of the monarchy in 1660. Through his connection with Cromwell, Marvell became assistant Latin Secretary for the Council of State, but he was not seriously involved in government until 1658, when he was elected to Parliament. He served in Parliament for the next twenty years, and his political experience led him to write a number of prose satires on government and religion. Claiming that Marvell owed her money at the time of his death in 1678, his housekeeper went through his private papers, gathered together the miscellaneous poems that Marvell had written for his own pleasure, and arranged for their publication in **1681.**

The seventeenth century was a great age for English poetry, and Marvell cannot be said to rank with Shakespeare, Milton, or Donne. However, a few of his poems are so very fine that they have won for him an honored place in the history of literature. Of these poems the most famous is "To His Coy Mistress," an argument in the form of a poem.

To His Coy Mistress

Had we but world enough, and time,
This coyness, lady, were no crime.
We would sit down, and think which way
To walk, and pass our long love's day.
5   Thou by the Indian Ganges' side
Should'st rubies find: I by the tide
Of Humber would complain. I would
Love you ten years before the Flood,
And you should, if you please, refuse
10   Till the conversion of the Jews.
My vegetable love should grow
Vaster than empires, and more slow.
An hundred years should go to praise
Thine eyes, and on thy forehead gaze:
15   Two hundred to adore each breast:
But thirty thousand to the rest.
An age at least to every part,
And the last age should show your heart.
For, lady, you deserve this state,
20   Nor would I love at lower rate.
        But at my back I always hear
Time's winged chariot hurrying near;

And yonder all before us lie
Deserts of vast eternity.
25   Thy beauty shall no more be found,
Nor in thy marble vault shall sound
My echoing song; then worms shall try
That long preserved virginity,
And your quaint honor turn to dust,
30   And into ashes all my lust.
The grave's a fine and private place,
But none, I think, do there embrace.
       Now therefore, while the youthful hue
Sits on thy skin like morning dew,
35   And while thy willing soul transpires
At every pore with instant fires,
Now let us sport us while we may;
And now, like am'rous birds of prey,
Rather at once our time devour,
40   Than languish in his slow-chapt power,
Let us roll all our strength, and all
Our sweetness, up into one ball;
And tear our pleasures with rough strife
Thorough the iron gates of life.
45   Thus, though we cannot make our sun
Stand still, yet we will make him run.

                       Andrew Marvell

QUESTIONS FOR MEANING

1. What do we learn from the title of this poem? In the seventeenth century, "mistress" was a synonym for "sweetheart." But what does Marvell mean by "coy"?
2. What kind of woman inspired this poem? Identify the lines that reveal her character.
3. How does the poet feel about this woman? Does he love her? Is this a love poem?
4. What is the poet urging this woman to do? Under what circumstances would he be willing to spend more time pleading with her? Why is this not possible?
5. Why does the poet describe his feelings as a "vegetable love"? What are the implications of this phrase?
6. What is the "marble vault" referred to in line 26?
7. Identify the references to "Ganges" (line 5), "Humber" (line 7), and "the Flood" (line 8). What does Marvell mean by "Time's winged chariot" (line 22) and "the iron gates of life" (line 44)?
8. Explain the last two lines of the poem. Is the sun a figure of speech? How is it possible to make it "run" when we lack the power to make it stand still?

QUESTIONS ABOUT STRATEGY

1. This poem is divided into three sections. Consider separately the tone of each. How do they differ?
2. Summarize the argument of this poem in three sentences, one for each section. Is the conclusion valid, or does it rest upon a questionable premise?
3. What role does humor play in the poem? What serious emotions does the poet invoke in order to make his argument more persuasive?
4. How does Marvell use rhyme as a device for advancing his argument?

JONATHAN SWIFT

A Modest Proposal

For Preventing the Children of Poor People in Ireland from Being a Burden to Their Parents or Country, and for Making Them Beneficial to the Public

Jonathan Swift (1667–1745) was a clergyman, poet, wit, and satirist. Born in Ireland as a member of the Protestant ruling class, Swift attended Trinity College in Dublin before settling in England in 1689. For the next ten years, he was a member of the household of Sir William Temple at Moor Park, Surrey. It was there that Swift met Esther Johnson, the "Stella" to whom he later wrote a famous series of letters known as Journal to Stella *(1710–1713). Although he was ordained a priest in the Church of Ireland in 1695, and made frequent trips to Ireland, Swift's ambition always brought him back to England. His reputation as a writer grew rapidly after the publication of his first major work,* A Tale of a Tub, *in 1704. He became a writer on behalf of the ruling Tory party, and was appointed Dean of St. Patrick's Cathedral in Dublin as a reward for his services. When the Tories fell from power in 1714, Swift retired to Ireland, where he remained for the rest of his life, except for brief visits to England in 1726 and 1727. It was in Ireland that he wrote* Gulliver's Travels *(1726), which is widely recognized as one of the masterpieces of English literature, and "A Modest Proposal" (**1729**), one of the greatest of all essays.*

Ruled as an English colony and subject to numerous repressive laws, Ireland in Swift's time was a desperately poor country. Swift wrote "A Modest Proposal" in order to expose the plight of Ireland and the unfair policies under which it suffered. As you read it, you will find that Swift's proposal for solving the problem of poverty is anything but "modest." Even when we know that we are reading satire, this brilliant and bitter essay retains the power to shock all but the most careless of readers.

1   It is a melancholy object to those who walk through this great town or travel in the country, when they see the streets, the roads, and cabin doors, crowded with beggars of the female sex, followed by three, four, or six children, all in rags and importuning every passenger for an alms. These mothers, instead of being able to work for their honest livelihood, are forced to employ all their time in strolling to beg sustenance for their helpless infants, who, as they grow up, either turn thieves for want of work, or leave their dear native country to fight for the Pretender in Spain, or sell themselves to the Barbados.

2   I think it is agreed by all parties that this prodigious number of children in the arms, or on the backs, or at the heels of their mothers, and frequently of their fathers, is in the present deplorable state of the kingdom a very great additional grievance; and therefore whoever could find out a fair, cheap, and easy method of making these children sound, useful members of the com-

monwealth would deserve so well of the public as to have his statue set up for a preserver of the nation.

But my intention is very far from being confined to provide only for the   3
children of professed beggars; it is of a much greater extent, and shall take in the whole number of infants at a certain age who are born of parents in effect as little able to support them as those who demand our charity in the streets.

As to my own part, having turned my thoughts for many years upon this   4
important subject, and maturely weighed the several schemes of other projectors, I have always found them grossly mistaken in their computation. It is true, a child just dropped from its dam may be supported by her milk for a solar year, with little other nourishment; at most not above the value of two shillings, which the mother may certainly get, or the value in scraps, by her lawful occupation of begging; and it is exactly at one year that I propose to provide for them in such a manner as instead of being a charge upon their parents or the parish, or wanting food and raiment for the rest of their lives, they shall on the contrary contribute to the feeding, and partly to the clothing, of many thousands.

There is likewise another great advantage in my scheme, that it will pre-   5
vent those voluntary abortions, and that horrid practice of women murdering their bastard children, alas, too frequent among us, sacrificing the poor innocent babes, I doubt, more to avoid the expense than the shame, which would move tears and pity in the most savage and inhuman breast.

The number of souls in this kingdom being usually reckoned one million   6
and a half, of these I calculate there may be about two hundred thousand couples whose wives are breeders; from which number I subtract thirty thousand couples who are able to maintain their own children, although I apprehend there cannot be so many under the present distress of the kingdom; but this being granted, there will remain an hundred and seventy thousand breeders. I again subtract fifty thousand for those women who miscarry, or whose children die by accident or disease within the year. There only remain an hundred and twenty thousand children of poor parents annually born. The question therefore is, how this number shall be reared and provided for, which, as I have already said, under the present situation of affairs, is utterly impossible by all the methods hitherto proposed. For we can neither employ them in handicraft or agriculture; we neither build houses (I mean in the country) nor cultivate land. They can very seldom pick up a livelihood by stealing till they arrive at six years old, except where they are of towardly parts; although I confess they learn the rudiments much earlier, during which time they can however be looked upon only as probationers, as I have been informed by a principal gentleman in the country of Cavan, who protested to me that he never knew above one or two instances under the age of six, even in a part of the kingdom so renowned for the quickest proficiency in that art.

I am assured by our merchants that a boy or a girl before twelve years old   7
is no salable commodity; and even when they come to this age they will not yield above three pounds, or three pounds and half a crown at most on the

Exchange; which cannot turn to account either to the parents or the kingdom, the charge of nutriment and rags having been at least four times that value.

I shall now therefore humbly propose my own thoughts, which I hope will   8
not be liable to the least objection.

I have been assured by a very knowing American of my acquaintance in   9
London, that a young healthy child well nursed is at a year old a most delicious, nourishing, and wholesome food, whether stewed, roasted, baked, or boiled; and I make no doubt that it will equally serve in a fricassee or a ragout.

I do therefore humbly offer it to public consideration that of the hundred   10
and twenty thousand children, already computed, twenty thousand may be reserved for breed, whereof only one fourth part to be males, which is more than we allow to sheep, black cattle, or swine; and my reason is that these children are seldom the fruits of marriage, a circumstance not much regarded by our savages, therefore one male will be sufficient to serve four females. That the remaining hundred thousand may at a year old be offered in sale to the persons of quality and fortune through the kingdom, always advising the mother to let them suck plentifully in the last month, so as to render them plump and fat for a good table. A child will make two dishes at an entertainment for friends; and when the family dines alone, the fore or hind quarter will make a reasonable dish, and seasoned with a little pepper or salt will be very good boiled on the fourth day, especially in winter.

I have reckoned upon a medium that a child just born will weigh twelve   11
pounds, and in a solar year if tolerably nursed increaseth to twenty-eight pounds.

I grant this food will be somewhat dear, and therefore very proper for   12
landlords, who, as they have already devoured most of the parents, seem to have the best title to the children.

Infant's flesh will be in season throughout the year, but more plentiful in   13
March, and a little before and after. For we are told by a grave author, an eminent French physician, that fish being a prolific diet, there are more children born in Roman Catholic countries about nine months after Lent than at any other season; therefore, reckoning a year after Lent, the markets will be more glutted than usual, because the number of popish infants is at least three to one in this kingdom; and therefore it will have one other collateral advantage, by lessening the number of Papists among us.

I have already computed the charge of nursing a beggar's child (in which   14
list I reckon all cottagers, laborers, and four-fifths of the farmers) to be about two shillings per annum, rags included; and I believe no gentleman would repine to give ten shillings for the carcass of a good fat child, which, as I have said, will make four dishes of excellent nutritive meat, when he hath only some particular friend or his own family to dine with him. Thus the squire will learn to be a good landlord, and grow popular among the tenants; the mother will have eight shillings net profit, and be fit for work till she produces another child.

Those who are more thrifty (as I must confess the times require) may flay   15
the carcass; the skin of which artificially dressed will make admirable gloves
for ladies, and summer boots for fine gentlemen.

As to our city of Dublin, shambles may be appointed for this purpose in   16
the most convenient parts of it, and butchers we may be assured will not be
wanting; although I rather recommend buying the children alive, and dressing
them hot from the knife as we do roasting pigs.

A very worthy person, a true lover of his country, and whose virtues I   17
highly esteem, was lately pleased in discoursing on this matter to offer a
refinement upon my scheme. He said that many gentlemen of his kingdom,
having of late destroyed their deer, he conceived that the want of venison
might be well supplied by the bodies of young lads and maidens, not exceeding fourteen years of age nor under twelve, so great a number of both sexes
in every county being now ready to starve for want of work and service; and
these to be disposed of by their parents, if alive, or otherwise by their nearest
relations. But with due deference to so excellent a friend and so deserving a
patriot, I cannot be altogether in his sentiments; for as to the males, my
American acquaintance assured me from frequent experience that their flesh
was generally tough and lean, like that of our schoolboys, by continual exercise, and their taste disagreeable; and to fatten them would not answer the
charge. Then as to the females, it would, I think with humble submission, be
a loss to the public, because they soon would become breeders themselves;
and besides, it is not improbable that some scrupulous people might be apt
to censure such a practice (although indeed very unjustly) as a little bordering upon cruelty; which, I confess, hath always been with me the strongest
objection against any project, how well soever intended.

But in order to justify my friend, he confessed that this expedient was put   18
into his head by the famous Psalmanazar, a native of the island Formosa,
who came from thence to London about twenty years ago, and in conversation told my friend that in his country when any young person happened to
be put to death, the executioner sold the carcass to persons of quality as a
prime dainty; and that in his time the body of a plump girl of fifteen, who
was crucified for an attempt to poison the emperor, was sold to his Imperial
Majesty's prime minister of state, and other great mandarins of the court, in
joints from the gibbet, at four hundred crowns. Neither indeed can I deny
that if the same use were made of several plump young girls in this town,
who without one single groat to their fortunes cannot stir abroad without a
chair, and appear at the playhouse and assemblies in foreign fineries which
they never will pay for, the kingdom would not be the worse.

Some persons of a desponding spirit are in great concern about that vast   19
number of poor people who are aged, diseased, or maimed, and I have been
desired to employ my thoughts what course may be taken to ease the nation
of so grievous an encumbrance. But I am not in the least pain upon that
matter, because it is very well known that they are every day dying and
rotting by cold and famine, and filth and vermin, as fast as can be reasonably
expected. And as to the younger laborers, they are now in almost as hopeful

a condition. They cannot get work, and consequently pine away for want of nourishment to a degree that if any time they are accidentally hired to common labor, they have not strength to perform it; and thus the country and themselves are happily delivered from the evils to come.

I have too long digressed, and therefore shall return to my subject. I think 20 the advantages by the proposal which I have made are obvious and many, as well as of the highest importance.

For first, as I have already observed, it would greatly lessen the number 21 of Papists, with whom we are yearly overrun, being the principal breeders of the nation as well as our most dangerous enemies; and who stay at home on purpose to deliver the kingdom to the Pretender, hoping to take their advantage by the absence of so many good Protestants, who have chosen rather to leave their country than to stay at home and pay tithes against their conscience to an Episcopal curate.

Secondly, the poorer tenants will have something valuable of their own, 22 which by law may be made liable to distress, and help to pay their landlord's rent, their corn and cattle being already seized and money a thing unknown.

Thirdly, whereas the maintenance of an hundred thousand children, from 23 two years old and upwards, cannot be computed at less than ten shillings a piece per annum, the nation's stock will be thereby increased fifty thousand pounds per annum, besides the profit of a new dish introduced to the tables of all gentlemen of fortune in the kingdom who have any refinement in taste. And the money will circulate among ourselves, the goods being entirely of our own growth and manufacture.

Fourthly, the constant breeders, besides the gain of eight shillings sterling 24 per annum by the sale of their children, will be rid of the charge of maintaining them after the first year.

Fifthly, this food would likewise bring great custom to taverns, where the 25 vintners will certainly be so prudent as to procure the best receipts for dressing it to perfection, and consequently have their houses frequented by all the fine gentlemen, who justly value themselves upon their knowledge in good eating; and a skillful cook, who understands how to oblige his guests, will contrive to make it as expensive as they please.

Sixthly, this would be a great inducement to marriage, which all wise na- 26 tions have either encouraged by rewards or enforced by laws and penalties. It would increase the care and tenderness of mothers toward their children, when they were sure of a settlement for life to the poor babes, provided in some sort by the public, to their annual profit instead of expense. We should see an honest emulation among the married women, which of them could bring the fattest child to the market. Men would become as fond of their wives during the time of their pregnancy as they are now of their mares in foal, their cows in calf, or sows when they are ready to farrow; nor offer to beat or kick them (as is too frequent a practice) for fear of a miscarriage.

Many other advantages might be enumerated. For instance, the addition 27 of some thousand carcasses in our exportation of barreled beef, the propagation of swine's flesh, and improvements in the art of making good bacon, so much wanted among us by the great destruction of pigs, too frequent at our tables, which are no way comparable in taste or magnificence to a well-grown, fat, yearling child, which roasted whole will make a considerable figure at a lord mayor's feast or any other public entertainment. But this and many others I omit, being studious of brevity.

Supposing that one thousand families in this city would be constant   28
customers for infants' flesh, besides others who might have it at merry meetings, particularly weddings and christenings, I compute that Dublin would take off annually about twenty thousand carcasses, and the rest of the kingdom (where probably they will be sold somewhat cheaper) the remaining eighty thousand.

I can think of no one objection that will possibly be raised against this   29
proposal, unless it should be urged that the number of people will be thereby much lessened in the kingdom. This I freely own, and it was indeed one principal design in offering it to the world. I desire the reader will observe, that I calculate my remedy for this one individual kingdom of Ireland and for no other that ever was, is, or I think ever can be upon earth. Therefore let no man talk to me of other expedients: of taxing our absentees at five shillings a pound: of using neither clothes nor household furniture except what is of our own growth and manufacture: of utterly rejecting the materials and instruments that promote foreign luxury: of curing the expensiveness of pride, vanity, idleness, and gaming in our women: of introducing a vein of parsimony, prudence, and temperance: of learning to love our country, in the want of which we differ even from Laplanders and the inhabitants of Topinamboo: of quitting our animosities and factions, nor acting any longer like the Jews, who were murdering one another at the very moment their city was taken: of being a little cautious not to sell our country and conscience for nothing: of teaching landlords to have at least one degree of mercy toward their tenants: lastly, of putting a spirit of honesty, industry, and skill into our shopkeepers; who, if a resolution could now be taken to buy only our native goods, would immediately unite to cheat and exact upon us in the price, the measure, and the goodness, nor could ever yet be brought to make one fair proposal of just dealing, though often and earnestly invited to it.

Therefore I repeat, let no man talk to me of these and the like expedients,   30
till he hath at least some glimpse of hope that there will ever be some hearty and sincere attempt to put them in practice.

But as to myself, having been wearied out for many years with offering   31
vain, idle, visionary thoughts, and at length utterly despairing of success, I fortunately fell upon this proposal, which, as it is wholly new, so it hath something solid and real, of no expense and little trouble, full in our own power, and whereby we can incur no danger in disobliging England. For this kind of commodity will not bear exportation, the flesh being of too tender a consistence to admit a long continuance in salt, although perhaps I could name a country which would be glad to eat up our whole nation without it.

After all, I am not so violently bent upon my own opinion as to reject any   32
offer proposed by wise men, which shall be found equally innocent, cheap,

easy, and effectual. But before something of that kind shall be advanced in contradiction to my scheme, and offering a better, I desire the author or authors will be pleased maturely to consider two points. First, as things now stand, how they will be able to find food and raiment for an hundred thousand useless mouths and backs. And secondly, there being a round million of creatures in human figure throughout this kingdom, whose sole subsistence put into a common stock would leave them in debt two millions of pounds sterling, adding those who are beggars by profession to the bulk of farmers, cottagers, and laborers, with their wives and children who are beggars in effect; I desire those politicians who dislike my overture, and may perhaps be so bold to attempt an answer, that they will first ask the parents of these mortals whether they would not at this day think it a great happiness to have been sold for food at a year old in this manner I prescribe, and thereby have avoided such a perpetual scene of misfortunes as they have since gone through by the oppression of landlords, the impossibility of paying rent without money or trade, the want of common sustenance, with neither house nor clothes to cover them from the inclemencies of the weather, and the most inevitable prospect of entailing the like or greater miseries upon their breed forever.

I profess, in the sincerity of my heart, that I have not the least personal interest in endeavoring to promote this necessary work, having no other motive than the public good of my country, by advancing our trade, providing for infants, relieving the poor, and giving some pleasure to the rich. I have no children by which I can propose to get a single penny; the youngest being nine years old, and my wife past childbearing.   33

QUESTIONS FOR MEANING

1. What do we learn in this essay about the condition of Ireland in Swift's time, and how Ireland was viewed by England? Does Swift provide any clue about what has caused the poverty he describes?
2. What specific "advantages" does Swift cite on behalf of his proposal?
3. Why does Swift limit his proposal to infants? On what grounds does he exclude older children from consideration as marketable commodities? Why does he claim that we need not worry about the elderly?
4. What does this essay reveal about the relations between Catholics and Protestants in the eighteenth century?
5. Where in the essay does Swift tell us what he really wants? What serious reforms does he propose to improve conditions in Ireland?
6. Vocabulary: importuning (1), sustenance (1), prodigious (2), rudiments (6), ragout (9), collateral (13), desponding (19), inducement (26), emulation (26), propagation (27), parsimony (29) and incur (31).

QUESTIONS ABOUT STRATEGY

1. How does Swift present himself in this essay? Many readers have taken this essay seriously and come away convinced that Swift was heartless and cruel. Why is it possible for some readers to be deceived in this way?

What devices does Swift employ to create the illusion that he is serious? How does this strategy benefit the essay?

2. Does the language of the first few paragraphs contain any hint of irony? At what point in the essay did it first become clear to you that Swift is writing tongue in cheek?

3. Where in the essay does Swift pretend to anticipate objections that might be raised against his proposal? How does he dispose of these objections?

4. How does the style of this essay contrast with its subject matter? How does this contrast contribute to the force of the essay as a whole?

5. What is the function of the concluding paragraph?

6. What is the premise of this essay if we take its argument at face value? When we realize that Swift is writing ironically, what underlying premise begins to emerge?

7. What advantage is there in writing ironically? Why do you think Swift chose to treat his subject in this manner?

THOMAS JEFFERSON
The Declaration of Independence

Thomas Jefferson (1743–1826) was the third president of the United States and one of the most talented men ever to hold that office. A farmer, architect, writer, and scientist, Jefferson entered politics in 1769 as a member of the Virginia House of Burgesses. In 1775, he was a member of Virginia's delegation to the Second Continental Congress. He was governor of Virginia from 1779 to 1781, represented the United States in Europe from 1784 to 1789, and was elected to the first of two terms as president in 1801. Of all his many accomplishments, Jefferson himself was most proud of having founded the University of Virginia in 1819.

*Although the Continental Congress had delegated the responsibility for writing a declaration of independence to a committee that included Benjamin Franklin and John Adams as well as Jefferson, it was Jefferson who undertook the actual composition. His colleagues respected him as the best writer among them. Jefferson wrote at least two, and possibly three, drafts during the seventeen days allowed for the assignment. His work was reviewed by the other members of the committee, but they made only minor revisions—mainly in the first two paragraphs. When it came to adopting the declaration, Congress was harder to please. After lengthy and spirited debate, Congress made twenty-four changes and deleted over three hundred words. Nevertheless, "The Declaration of Independence," as approved by Congress on July 4, **1776,** is almost entirely the work of Jefferson. In addition to being an eloquent example of eighteenth-century prose, it is a clear example of deductive reasoning.*

When in the Course of human events, it becomes necessary for one people 1 to dissolve the political bands which have connected them with another, and to assume among the powers of the earth, the separate and equal station to which the Laws of Nature and of Nature's God entitle them, a decent respect to the opinions of mankind requires that they should declare the causes which impel them to the separation.

We hold these truths to be self-evident, that all men are created equal, 2 that they are endowed by their Creator with certain unalienable Rights, that among these are Life, Liberty and the pursuit of Happiness. That to secure these rights, Governments are instituted among Men, deriving their just powers from the consent of the governed. That whenever any Form of Government becomes destructive of these ends it is the Right of the People to alter or to abolish it, and to institute new Government, laying its foundation on such principles and organizing its powers in such form, as to them shall seem most likely to effect their Safety and Happiness. Prudence, indeed, will dictate that Governments long established should not be changed for light and transient causes; and accordingly all experience has shewn, that mankind are more disposed to suffer, while evils are sufferable, than to right themselves by abolishing the forms to which they are accustomed. But when a long train of abuses and usurpations, pursuing invariably the same Object evinces a design to reduce them under absolute Despotism, it is their right, it is their duty, to throw off such Government, and to provide new Guards for their future security. Such has been the patient sufferance of these Colonies; and such is now the necessity which constrains them to alter their former Systems of Government. The history of the present King of Great Britain is a history of repeated injuries and usurpations, all having in direct object the establishment of an absolute Tyranny over these States. To prove this, let Facts be submitted to a candid world.

He has refused his Assent to Laws, the most wholesome and necessary for   3
the public good.

He has forbidden his Governors to pass Laws of immediate and pressing   4
importance, unless suspended in their operation till his Assent should be obtained; and when so suspended, he has utterly neglected to attend to them. He has refused to pass other Laws for the accommodation of large districts of people, unless those people would relinquish the right of Representation in the Legislature, a right inestimable to them and formidable to tyrants only.

He has called together legislative bodies at places unusual, uncomfortable,   5
and distant from the depository of their public Records, for the sole purpose of fatiguing them into compliance with his measures.

He has dissolved Representative Houses repeatedly, for opposing with manly   6
firmness his invasions on the rights of the people.

He has refused for a long time, after such dissolutions, to cause others to   7
be elected; whereby the Legislative powers, incapable of Annihilation, have returned to the People at large for their exercise; the State remaining in the mean time exposed to all the dangers of invasion from without, and convulsions within.

He has endeavoured to prevent the population of these States; for that   8
purpose obstructing the Laws for Naturalization of Foreigners; refusing to pass others to encourage their migrations hither, and raising the conditions of new Appropriations of Lands.

He has obstructed the Administration of Justice, by refusing his Assent to   9
Laws for establishing Judiciary powers.

He has made Judges dependent on his Will alone, for the tenure of their   10
offices, and the amount and payment of their salaries.

He has erected a multitude of New Offices, and sent hither swarms of   11
Officers to harass our People, and eat out their substance.

He has kept among us, in times of peace, standing Armies without the   12
Consent of our legislatures.

He has affected to render the Military independent of and superior to the   13
Civil power.

He has combined with others to subject us to a jurisdiction foreign to our   14
constitution, and unacknowledged by our laws; giving his Assent to their Acts of pretended Legislation:

For Quartering large bodies of armed troops among us: 15

For protecting them, by a mock Trial, from punishment for any Murders   16
which they should commit on the Inhabitants of these States:

For cutting off our Trade with all parts of the world: 17

For imposing Taxes on us without our Consent: 18

For depriving us in many cases of the benefits of Trial by Jury: 19

For transporting us beyond Seas to be tried for pretended offences: 20

For abolishing the free System of English Laws in a neighbouring Prov-   21
ince, establishing therein an Arbitrary government, and enlarging its Boundaries so as to render it at once an example and fit instrument for introducing
the same absolute rule into these Colonies:

For taking away our Charters, abolishing our most valuable Laws, and al-   22
tering fundamentally the Forms of our Governments:

For suspending our own Legislatures, and declaring themselves invested   23
with power to legislate for us in all cases whatsoever.

He has abdicated Government here, by declaring us out of his Protection   24
and waging War against us.

He has plundered our seas, ravaged our Coasts, burnt our towns, and de-   25
stroyed the Lives of our people.

He is at this time transporting large Armies of foreign Mercenaries to com-   26
pleat the works of death, desolation and tyranny, already begun with circumstances of Cruelty & perfidy scarcely paralleled in the most barbarous ages,
and totally unworthy the Head of a civilized nation.

He has constrained our fellow Citizens taken Captive on the high Seas to   27
bear Arms against their Country, to become the executioners of their friends
and Brethren, or to fall themselves by their Hands.

He has excited domestic insurrections amongst us, and has endeavoured   28
to bring on the inhabitants of our frontiers, the merciless Indian Savages,
whose known rule of warfare, is an undistinguished destruction of all ages,
sexes and conditions.

In every stage of these Oppressions We have Petitioned for Redress in the   29
most humble terms: Our repeated Petitions have been answered only be repeated injury. A Prince, whose character is thus marked by every act which
may define a Tyrant, is unfit to be the ruler of a free people.

Nor have We been waiting in attentions to our Brittish brethren. We have   30
warned them from time to time of attempts by their legislature to extend an
unwarrantable jurisdiction over us. We have reminded them of the circumstances of our emigration and settlement here. We have appealed to their
native justice and magnanimity, and we have conjured them by the ties of
our common kindred to disavow these usurpations, which, would inevitably
interrupt our connections and correspondence. They too have been deaf to
the voice of Justice and of consanguinity. We must, therefore, acquiesce in
the necessity, which denounces our Separation, and hold them, as we hold
the rest of mankind, Enemies in War, in Peace Friends.

We, therefore, the Representatives of the united States of America, in Gen-   31
eral Congress, Assembled, appealing to the Supreme Judge of the world for
the rectitude of our intentions, do, in the Name, and by Authority of the good
People of these Colonies, solemnly publish and declare, That these United
Colonies are, and of Right ought to be Free and Independent States; that
they are Absolved from all Allegiance to the British Crown, and that all polit-

ical connection between them and the State of Great Britain, is and ought to be totally dissolved; and that as Free and Independent States, they have full Power to levy War, conclude Peace, contract Alliances, establish Commerce, and to do all other Acts and Things which Independent States may of right do. And for the support of this Declaration, with a firm reliance on the protection of divine Providence, we mutually pledge to each other our Lives, our Fortunes and our sacred Honor.

John Hancock	Geo. Taylor
Button Gwinnett	James Wilson
Lyman Hall	Geo. Ross
Geo Walton.	Caesar Rodney
Wm. Hooper	Geo Read
Joseph Hewes,	Tho M:Kean
John Penn	Wm. Floyd
Edward Rutledge.	Phil. Livingston
Thos. Heyward Junr.	Frans. Lewis
Thomas Lynch Junr.	Lewis Morris
Arthur Middleton	Richd. Stockton
Samuel Chase	Jno Witherspoon
Wm. Paca	Fras. Hopkinson
Thos. Stone	John Hart
Charles Carroll of Carrollton	Abra Clark
George Wythe	Josiah Bartlett
Richard Henry Lee	Wm: Whipple
Th: Jefferson	Saml. Adams
Benja. Harrison	John Adams
Thos. Nelson jr.	Robt. Treat Paine
Francis Lightfoot Lee	Elbridge Gerry
Carter Braxton	Step. Hopkins
Robt. Morris	William Ellery
Benjamin Rush	Roger Sherman
Benja. Franklin	Saml. Huntington
John Morton	Wm. Williams
Geo Clymer	Oliver Wolcott
Jas. Smith	Matthew Thornton

QUESTIONS FOR MEANING

1. What was the purpose of "The Declaration of Independence"? What reason does Jefferson himself give for writing it?
2. In paragraph 1, what does Jefferson mean by "the Laws of Nature and of Nature's God"?
3. Paragraphs 3–28 are devoted to enumerating a list of grievances against King George III. Which of these are the most important? Are any of them relatively trivial? Taken together do they justify Jefferson's description of

George III as "A Prince, whose character is thus marked by every act which may define a Tyrant"?

4. How would you summarize Jefferson's conception of the relationship between people and government?

5. How does Jefferson characterize his fellow Americans? At what points does he put the colonists in a favorable light?

6. What does Jefferson mean by "the Supreme Judge of the world"? Why does he express "a firm reliance on the protection of a divine Providence"?

7. Vocabulary: transient (2), evinces (2), usurpations (2), candid (2), annihilation (7), render (13), perfidy (26), unwarrantable (30), consanguinity (30), acquiesce (30), and rectitude (31).

QUESTIONS ABOUT STRATEGY

1. In paragraph 2, why does Jefferson declare certain truths to be "self-evident"? Paraphrase this paragraph and explain the purpose it serves in Jefferson's argument.

2. In evaluating "The Declaration of Independence" as an argument, what is more important: the general "truths" outlined in the second paragraph, or the specific accusations listed in the paragraphs that follow? If you were to write a counterargument to "The Declaration of Independence," on what points would you concentrate? Where is it most vulnerable?

3. Jefferson is often cited as a man of great culture and liberal values. Are there any points of "The Declaration of Independence" that now seem illiberal?

4. Does Jefferson use any loaded terms? He was forced to delete exaggerated language from his first two drafts of "The Declaration." Do you see any exaggerations that Congress failed to catch?

5. For what sort of audience did Jefferson write "The Declaration of Independence"? Is it directed primarily to the American people, the British government, or the world in general?

MARY WOLLSTONECRAFT
The Playthings of Tyrants

*An English writer of Irish extraction, Mary Wollstonecraft (1759–1797) was an
early advocate of women's rights. After working as a governess and a publisher's assistant, she went to France in 1792 in order to witness the French Revolution. She lived there with an American, Captain Gilbert Imlay, and had a
child by him in 1794. Her relationship with Imlay broke down soon afterwards,
and, in 1795, Wollstonecraft tried to commit suicide by drowning herself. She
was rescued, however, and returned to London, where she became a member of
a group of radical writers that included Thomas Paine, William Blake, and William Godwin. Wollstonecraft became pregnant by Godwin in 1796, and they
were married the following year. Their child, Mary (1797–1851), would eventually win fame as the author of* Frankenstein. *Wollstonecraft died only eleven
days after Mary's birth.*

Wollstonecraft's fame rests upon one work, A Vindication of the Rights of
Women *(**1792**). Although she had written about the need for educated women
several years earlier in* Thoughts on the Education of Daughters *(1787), she
makes a stronger and better-reasoned argument in her* Vindication. *"The Play-
things of Tyrants" is an editor's' title for an excerpt from the second chapter,
"The Prevailing Opinion of a Sexual Character Discussed." As the excerpt suggests, Wollstonecraft was not especially interested in securing political rights
for women. Her object was to emancipate women from the roles imposed upon
them by men and to urge women to think for themselves.*

To account for, and excuse the tyranny of man, many ingenious arguments   1
have been brought forward to prove, that the two sexes, in the acquirement
of virtue, ought to aim at attaining a very different character: or, to speak
explicitly, women are not allowed to have sufficient strength of mind to acquire what really deserves the name of virtue. Yet it should seem, allowing
them to have souls, that there is but one way appointed by Providence to
lead *mankind* to either virtue or happiness.

If then women are not a swarm of ephemeron triflers, why should they be   2
kept in ignorance under the specious name of innocence? Men complain, and
with reason, of the follies and caprices of our sex, when they do not keenly
satirize our headstrong passions and groveling vices.—Behold, I should answer, the natural effect of ignorance! The mind will ever be unstable that has
only prejudices to rest on, and the current will run with destructive fury
when there are no barriers to break its force. Women are told from their
infancy, and taught by the example of their mothers, that a little knowledge
of human weakness, justly termed cunning, softness of temper, *outward* obedience, and a scrupulous attention to a puerile kind of propriety, will obtain
for them the protection of man; and should they be beautiful, every thing
else is needless, for, at least, twenty years of their lives.

Thus Milton describes our first frail mother; though when he tells us that   3
women are formed for softness and sweet attractive grace, I cannot comprehend his meaning, unless, in the true Mahometan strain, he meant to deprive
us of souls, and insinuate that we were beings only designed by sweet attractive grace, and docile blind obedience, to gratify the senses of man when he
can no longer soar on the wing of contemplation.

How grossly do they insult us who thus advise us only to render ourselves   4
gentle, domestic brutes! For instance, the winning softness so warmly, and
frequently, recommended, that governs by obeying. What childish expressions, and how insignificant is the being—can it be an immortal one? who
will condescend to govern by such sinister methods! 'Certainly,' says Lord
Bacon, 'man is of kin to the beasts by his body; and if he be not of kin to
God by his spirit, he is a base and ignoble creature!' Men, indeed, appear to
me to act in a very unphilosophical manner when they try to secure the good
conduct of women by attempting to keep them always in a state of childhood.
Rousseau was more consistent when he wished to stop the progress of reason in both sexes, for if men eat of the tree of knowledge, women will come
in for a taste; but, from the imperfect cultivation which their understandings
now receive, they only attain a knowledge of evil.

Children, I grant, should be innocent; but when the epithet is applied to   5
men, or women, it is but a civil term for weakness. For if it be allowed that
women were destined by Providence to acquire human virtues, and by the
exercise of their understandings, that stability of character which is the firm-
est ground to rest our future hopes upon, they must be permitted to turn to
the fountain of light, and not forced to shape their course by the twinkling
of a mere satellite. Milton, I grant, was of a very different opinion; for he only
bends to the indefeasible right of beauty, though it would be difficult to render two passages which I now mean to contrast, consistent. But into similar
inconsistencies are great men often led by their senses.

> 'To whom thus Eve with *perfect beauty* adorn'd.
> 'My Author and Disposer, what thou bidst
> '*Unargued* I obey; So God ordains;
> 'God is *thy law; thou mine:* to know no more
> 'Is Woman's *happiest* knowledge and her *praise.*'

These are exactly the arguments that I have used to children; but I have   6
added, your reason is now gaining strength, and, till it arrives at some degree
of maturity, you must look up to me for advice—then you ought to *think,*
and only rely on God.

Yet in the following lines Milton seems to coincide with me; when he makes   7
Adam thus expostulate with his Maker.

> 'Hast thou not made me here thy substitute,
> 'And these inferior far beneath me set?
> 'Among *unequals* what society

'Can sort, what harmony or true delight?
'Which must be mutual, in proportion due
'Giv'n and receiv'd; but in *disparity*
'The one intense, the other still remiss
'Cannot well suit with either, but soon prove
'Tedious alike: of *fellowship* I speak
'Such as I seek, fit to participate
'All rational delight—'

In treating, therefore, of the manners of women, let us, disregarding sen-   8
sual arguments, trace what we should endeavour to make them in order to
cooperate, if the expression be not too bold, with the supreme Being.

By individual education, I mean, for the sense of the word is not precisely   9
defined, such an attention to a child as will slowly sharpen the senses, form
the temper, regulate the passions as they begin to ferment, and set the understanding to work before the body arrives at maturity; so that the man
may only have to proceed, not to begin, the important task of learning to
think and reason.

To prevent any misconstruction, I must add, that I do not believe that a   10
private education can work the wonders which some sanguine writers have
attributed to it. Men and women must be educated, in a great degree, by the
opinions and manners of the society they live in. In every age there has been
a stream of popular opinion that has carried all before it, and given a family
character, as it were, to the century. It may then fairly be inferred, that, till
society be differently constituted, much cannot be expected from education.
It is, however, sufficient for my present purpose to assert, that, whatever
effect circumstances have on the abilities, every being may become virtuous
by the exercise of its own reason; for if but one being was created with
vicious inclinations, that is positively bad, what can save us from atheism? or
if we worship a God, is not that God a devil?

Consequently, the most perfect education, in my opinion, is such an ex-   11
ercise of the understanding as is best calculated to strengthen the body and
form the heart. Or, in other words, to enable the individual to attain such
habits of virtue as will render it independent. In fact, it is a farce to call any
being virtuous whose virtues do not result from the exercise of its own reason. This was Rousseau's opinion respecting men: I extend it to women, and
confidently assert that they have been drawn out of their sphere by false
refinement, and not by an endeavour to acquire masculine qualities. Still the
regal homage which they receive is so intoxicating, that till the manners of
the times are changed, and formed on more reasonable principles, it may be
impossible to convince them that the illegitimate power, which they obtain,
by degrading themselves, is a curse, and that they must return to nature and
equality, if they wish to secure the placid satisfaction that unsophisticated
affections impart. But for this epoch we must wait—wait, perhaps, till kings
and nobles, enlightened by reason, and, preferring the real dignity of man to
childish state, throw off their gaudy hereditary trappings: and if then women

do not resign the arbitrary power of beauty—they will prove that they have *less* mind than man. . . .

Many are the causes that, in the present corrupt state of society, contrib-   12
ute to enslave women by cramping their understandings and sharpening their senses. One, perhaps, that silently does more mischief than all the rest, is their disregard of order.

To do every thing in an orderly manner, is a most important precept, which   13
women, who, generally speaking, receive only a disorderly kind of education, seldom attend to with that degree of exactness that men, who from their infancy are broken into method, observe. This negligent kind of guess-work, for what other epithet can be used to point out the random exertions of a sort of instinctive common sense, never brought to the test of reason? prevents their generalizing matters of fact—so they do to-day, what they did yesterday, merely because they did it yesterday.

This contempt of the understanding in early life has more baneful conse-   14
quences than is commonly supposed; for the little knowledge which women of strong minds attain, is, from various circumstances, of a more desultory kind than the knowledge of men, and it is acquired more by sheer observations on real life, than from comparing what has been individually observed with the results of experience generalized by speculation. Led by their dependent situation and domestic employments more into society, what they learn is rather by snatches; and as learning is with them, in general, only a secondary thing, they do not pursue any one branch with that persevering ardour necessary to give vigour to the faculties, and clearness to the judgment. In the present state of society, a little learning is required to support the character of a gentleman; and boys are obliged to submit to a few years of discipline. But in the education of women, the cultivation of the understanding is always subordinate to the acquirement of some corporeal accomplishment; even while enervated by confinement and false notions of modesty, the body is prevented from attaining that grace and beauty which relaxed half-formed limbs never exhibit. Besides, in youth their faculties are not brought forward by emulation; and having no serious scientific study, if they have natural sagacity it is turned too soon on life and manners. They dwell on effects, and modifications, without tracing them back to causes; and complicated rules to adjust behaviour are a weak substitute for simple principles.

As a proof that education gives this appearance of weakness to females,   15
we may instance the example of military men, who are, like them, sent into the world before their minds have been stored with knowledge or fortified by principles. The consequences are similar; soldiers acquire a little superficial knowledge, snatched from the muddy current of conversation, and, from continually mixing with society, they gain, what is termed a knowledge of the world; and this acquaintance with manners and customs has frequently been confounded with a knowledge of the human heart. But can the crude fruit of casual observation, never brought to the test of judgment, formed by comparing speculation and experience, deserve such a distinction? Soldiers, as well as women, practice the minor virtues with punctilious politeness. Where

is then the sexual difference, when the education has been the same? All the difference that I can discern, arises from the superior advantage of liberty, which enables the former to see more of life.

It is wandering from my present subject, perhaps, to make a political re-   16
mark; but, as it was produced naturally by the train of my reflections, I shall not pass it silently over.

Standing armies can never consist of resolute, robust men; they may be   17
well disciplined machines, but they will seldom contain men under the influence of strong passions, or with very vigorous faculties. And as for any depth of understanding, I will venture to affirm, that it is as rarely to be found in the army as amongst women; and the cause, I maintain, is the same. It may be further observed, that officers are also particularly attentive to their persons, fond of dancing, crowded rooms, adventures, and ridicule. Like the *fair* sex, the business of their lives is gallantry.—They were taught to please, and they only live to please. Yet they do not lose their rank in the distinction of sexes, for they are still reckoned superior to women, though in what their superiority consists, beyond what I have just mentioned, it is difficult to discover.

The great misfortune is this, that they both acquire manners before mor-   18
als, and a knowledge of life before they have, from reflections, any acquaintance with the grand ideal outline of human nature. The consequence is natural; satisfied with common nature, they become a prey to prejudices, and taking all their opinions on credit, they blindly submit to authority. So that, if they have any sense, it is a kind of instinctive glance, that catches proportions, and decides with respect to manners; but fails when arguments are to be pursued below the surface, or opinions analyzed.

May not the same remark be applied to women? Nay, the argument may   19
be carried still further, for they are both thrown out of a useful station by the unnatural distinctions established in civilized life. Riches and hereditary honours have made cyphers of women to give consequence to the numerical figure; and idleness has produced a mixture of gallantry and despotism into society, which leads the very men who are the slaves of their mistresses to tyrannize over their sisters, wives, and daughters. This is only keeping them in rank and file, it is true. Strengthen the female mind by enlarging it, and there will be an end to blind obedience; but, as blind obedience is ever sought for by power, tyrants and sensualists are in the right when they endeavor to keep women in the dark, because the former only want slaves, and the latter a play-thing. The sensualist, indeed, has been the most dangerous of tyrants, and women have been duped by their lovers, as princes by their ministers, whilst dreaming that they reigned over them.

QUESTIONS FOR MEANING

1. What's wrong with treating women as children and expecting "blind obedience"?
2. What causes does Wollstonecraft cite for the degradation of women? On what grounds does she defend their "follies" and "vices"?

3. What does Wollstonecraft mean by "false refinement" in paragraph 11? Explain why she believes it is dangerous to acquire "manners before morals."
4. Where in her essay does Wollstonecraft define the sort of education she believes women should receive? Why does she object to educating women privately in their homes?
5. Wollstonecraft was perceived as a radical by her contemporaries, and relatively few people took her ideas seriously. Looking back upon her work after almost two hundred years, can you find any traditional values that Wollstonecraft accepted without question? Could you argue that she was conservative in some ways?
6. Explain why "the sensualist" has been "the most dangerous of tyrants."
7. Vocabulary: ephemeron (2), specious (2), caprices (2), puerile (2), propriety (2), insinuate (3), docile (3), sanguine (10), desultory (14), corporeal (14), enervated (14), sagacity (14), punctilious (15) and cyphers (19).

QUESTIONS ABOUT STRATEGY

1. What is the premise of this argument? Where does Wollstonecraft first state it, and where is it restated?
2. What is the function of the last sentence in the second paragraph?
3. Why does Wollstonecraft quote John Milton and Francis Bacon? What do these quotations contribute to her argument?
4. Comment on the analogy Wollstonecraft makes between women and soldiers. What type of soldiers did she have in mind? Is her analogy valid?
5. Do you think Wollstonecraft wrote this argument primarily for men or for women? What kind of an audience could she have expected in the eighteenth century?

KARL MARX AND FRIEDRICH ENGELS
The Communist Manifesto

Karl Marx (1818–1883) was a German social scientist and political philosopher who believed that history is determined by economics. Originally intending to teach, Marx studied at the University of Berlin, receiving his Ph.D. in 1841. But, in 1842, he abandoned academics to become editor of the Rheinische Zeitung, *an influential newspaper published in Cologne. His editorials led the government to close the paper within a year, and Marx went into exile—first in France and Belgium, and eventually in England, where he spent the last thirty-three years of his life.*

It was in 1843 that Marx met Friedrich Engels (1820–1895), the son of a wealthy German industrialist with business interests in England. The two men discovered that they shared the same political beliefs, and they worked together closely for the next forty years. It was not until 1867 that Marx was able to publish the first volume of Das Kapital, *his most important work. The second and third volumes were published after his death, completed by Engels, who worked from the extensive notes that Marx left behind him.* Das Kapital, *or* Capital, *provided the theoretical basis for what is variously known as "Marxism" or "Communism." It is an indictment of nineteenth-century capitalism that predicts a proletarian revolution in which the workers would take over the means of production and distribute goods according to needs, creating an ideal society in which the state would wither away.*

But Marx and Engels had outlined their views long before the publication of Das Kapital. *In* **1848, *they published a pamphlet called* The Communist Manifesto. *It was written during a period of great political unrest. Within months of its publication, revolutions broke out in several European countries. Most of the revolutions of 1848 were quickly aborted, but "the specter of Communism" has continued to haunt the world. Here are the first few pages of this classic argument.*

A specter is haunting Europe—the specter of Communism. All the Powers   1
of old Europe have entered into a holy alliance to exorcise this specter; Pope and Czar, Metternich and Guizot, French Radicals and German police-spies.

Where is the party in opposition that has not been decried as communistic   2
by its opponents in power? Where the Opposition that has not hurled back the branding reproach of Communism against the more advanced opposition parties, as well as against its reactionary adversaries?

Two things result from this fact.   3

   I. Communism is already acknowledged by all European Powers to be   4
     itself a Power.

  II. It is high time that Communists should openly, in the face of the   5
     whole world, publish their views, their aims, their tendencies, and meet this nursery tale of the specter of Communism with a Manifesto of the party itself.

To this end, Communists of various nationalities have assembled in Lon-   6
don and sketched the following Manifesto, to be published in the English,
French, German, Italian, Flemish and Danish languages.

Bourgeois and Proletarians *

The history of all hitherto existing society is the history of class struggles.   7

Freeman and slave, patrician and plebeian, lord and serf, guild-master and   8
journeyman, in a word, oppressor and oppressed, stood in constant opposition to one another, carried on uninterrupted, now hidden, now open fight, a
fight that each time ended, either in a revolutionary re-constitution of society
at large, or in the common ruin of the contending classes.

In the earlier epochs of history we find almost everywhere a complicated   9
arrangement of society into various orders, a manifold gradation of social
rank. In ancient Rome we have patricians, knights, plebians, slaves; in the
Middle Ages, feudal lords, vassals, guild-masters, journeymen, apprentices, serfs;
in almost all of these classes, again, subordinate gradations.

The modern bourgeois society that has sprouted from the ruins of feudal   10
society, has not done away with class antagonisms. It has but established new
classes, new conditions of oppression, new forms of struggle in place of the
old ones.

Our epoch, the epoch of the bourgeoisie, possesses, however, this distinc-   11
tive feature; it has simplified the class antagonisms. Society as a whole is
more and more splitting up into two great hostile camps, into two great classes
directly facing each other: Bourgeoisie and Proletariat.

From the serfs of the Middle Ages sprang the chartered burghers of the   12
earliest towns. From these burgesses the first elements of the bourgeoisie
were developed.

The discovery of America, the rounding of the Cape, opened up fresh ground   13
for the rising bourgeoisie. The East Indian and Chinese markets, the coloni-
zation of America, trade with the colonies, the increase in the means of exchange and in commodities generally, gave to commerce, to navigation, to
industry, an impulse never before known, and thereby, to the revolutionary
element in the tottering feudal society, a rapid development.

The feudal system of industry, under which industrial production was mo-   14
nopolized by closed guilds, now no longer sufficed for the growing wants of
the new market. The manufacturing system took its place. The guild-masters
were pushed on one side by the manufacturing middle-class: division of labor
between the different corporate guilds vanished in the face of division of
labor in each single workshop.

Meantime the markets kept ever growing, the demand ever rising. Even   15
manufacture no longer sufficed. Thereupon, steam and machinery revolution-

*By bourgeoisie is meant the class of modern Capitalists, owners of the means of social production and
employers of wage labor. By proletariat, the class of modern wage laborers who, having no means of production of their own, are reduced to selling their labor-power in order to live. [Marx's note]

ized industrial production. The place of manufacture was taken by the giant, Modern Industry, the place of the industrial middle-class, by industrial millionaires, the leaders of whole industrial armies, the modern bourgeois.

Modern industry has established the world market, for which the discovery of America paved the way. This market has given an immense development to commerce, to navigation, to communication by land. This development has, in its turn, reacted on the extension of industry; and in proportion as industry, commerce, navigation, railways extended, in the same proportion the bourgeoisie developed, increased its capital, and pushed into the background every class handed down from the Middle Ages.   16

We see, therefore, how the modern bourgeoisie is itself the product of a long course of development, a series of revolutions in the modes of production and of exchange.   17

Each step in the development of the bourgeoisie was accompanied by a corresponding political advance of that class. An oppressed class under the sway of the feudal nobility, an armed and self-governing association in the medieval commune, here independent urban republic (as in Italy and Germany), there taxable "third estate" of the monarchy (as in France), afterwards, in the period of manufacture proper, serving either the semi-feudal or the absolute monarchy as a counterpoise against nobility, and, in fact, corner stone of the great monarchies in general, the bourgeoisie has at last, since the establishment of Modern Industry and of the world-market, conquered for itself, in the modern representative State, exclusive political sway. The executive of the modern State is but a committee for managing the common affairs of the whole bourgeoisie.   18

The bourgeoisie, historically, has played a most revolutionary part.   19

The bourgeoisie, wherever it has got the upper hand, has put an end to all feudal, patriarchal, idyllic relations. It has pitilessly torn asunder the motley feudal ties that bound man to his "natural superiors," and has left no other nexus between man and man than naked self-interest, than callous "cash payment." It has drowned the most heavenly ecstasies of religious fervor, of chivalrous enthusiasm, of Philistine sentimentalism, in the icy water of egotistical calculation. It has resolved personal worth into exchange value, and in place of the numberless indefeasible chartered freedoms, has set up that single, unconscionable freedom—Free Trade. In one word, for exploitation, veiled by religious and political illusions, it has substituted naked, shameless, direct, brutal exploitation.   20

The bourgeoisie has stripped of its halo every occupation hitherto honored and looked up to with reverent awe. It has converted the physician, the lawyer, the priest, the poet, the man of science, into its paid wage laborers.   21

The bourgeoisie has torn away from the family its sentimental veil, and has reduced the family relation to a mere money relation.   22

The bourgeoisie has disclosed how it came to pass that the brutal display of vigor in the Middle Ages, which reactionists so much admire, found its fitting complement in the most slothful indolence. It has been the first to show what man's activity can bring about. It has accomplished wonders far   23 surpassing Egyptian pyramids, Roman aqueducts and Gothic cathedrals; it has conducted expeditions that put in the shade all former Exoduses of nations and crusades.

The bourgeoisie cannot exist without constantly revolutionizing the instru-   24
ments of production, and thereby the relations of production, and with them the whole relations of society. Conservation of the old modes of production in unaltered form was, on the contrary, the first condition of existence for all earlier industrial classes. Constant revolutionizing of production, uninterrupted disturbance of all social conditions, everlasting uncertainty and agitation distinguish the bourgeois epoch from all earlier ones. All fixed, fast frozen relations, with their train of ancient and venerable prejudices and opinions, are swept away, all new formed ones become antiquated before they can ossify. All that is solid melts into the air, all that is holy is profaned, and man is at last compelled to face with sober senses, his real conditions of life, and his relations with his kind.

The need of a constantly expanding market for its products chases the   25
bourgeoisie over the whole surface of the globe. It must nestle everywhere, settle everywhere, establish connections everywhere.

The bourgeoisie has through its exploitation of the world-market given a   26
cosmopolitan character to production and consumption in every country. To the great chagrin of reactionists, it has drawn from under the feet of industry the national ground on which it stood. All old-established national industries have been destroyed or are daily being destroyed. They are dislodged by new industries, whose introduction becomes a life and death question for all civilized nations, by industries that no longer work up indigenous raw material, but raw material drawn from the remotest zones; industries whose products are consumed, not only at home, but in every quarter of the globe. In place of the old wants, satisfied by the productions of the country, we find new wants, requiring for their satisfaction the products of distant lands and climes. In place of the old local and national seclusion and self-sufficiency, we have intercourse in every direction, universal interdependence of nations. And as in material, so also in intellectual production. The intellectual creations of individual nations become common property. National onesidedness and narrowmindedness become more and more impossible, and from the numerous national and local literatures there arises a world-literature.

The bourgeoisie, by the rapid improvement of all instruments of produc-   27
tion, by the immensely facilitated means of communication, draws all, even the most barbarian nations into civilization. The cheap prices of its commodities are the heavy artillery with which it batters down all Chinese walls, with which it forces the barbarians' intensely obstinate hatred of foreigners to capitulate. It compels all nations, on pain of extinction, to adopt the bourgeois mode of production; it compels them to introduce what it calls civilization into their midst, i.e., to become bourgeois themselves. In a word, it creates a world after its own image.

The bourgeoisie has subjected the country to the rule of the towns. It has   28
created enormous cities, has greatly increased the urban population as com-

pared with the rural and has thus rescued a considerable part of the population from the idiocy of rural life. Just as it has made the country dependent on the towns, so it has made barbarian and semi-barbarian countries dependent on civilized ones, nations of peasants on nations of bourgeois, the East on the West.

The bourgeoisie keeps more and more doing away with the scattered state   29
of the population, of the means of production, and of property. It has agglomerated population, centralized means of production, and has concentrated property in a few hands. The necessary consequence of this was political centralization. Independent, or but loosely connected provinces, with separate interests, laws, governments, and systems of taxation, become lumped together in one nation, with one government, one code of laws, one national class interest, one frontier and one customs tariff.

The bourgeoisie, during its rule of scarce one hundred years, has created   30
more massive and more colossal productive forces than have all preceding generations together. Subjection of Nature's forces to man, machinery, application of chemistry to industry and agriculture, steam-navigation, railways, electric telegraphs, clearing of whole continents for cultivation, canalization of rivers, whole populations conjured out of the ground—what earlier century had even a presentiment that such productive forces slumbered in the lap of social labor?

We see then: the means of production and of exchange on whose founda-   31
tion the bourgeoisie built itself up, were generated in feudal society. At a certain stage in the development of these means of production and of exchange, the conditions under which feudal society produced and exchanged, the feudal organization of agriculture and manufacturing industry, in one word, the feudal relations of property became no longer compatible with the already developed productive forces; they became so many fetters. They had to burst asunder; they were burst asunder.

Into their places stepped free competition, accompanied by social and po-   32
litical constitution adapted to it, and by economical and political sway of the bourgeois class.

A similar movement is going on before our own eyes. Modern bourgeois   33
society with its relations of production, of exchange and of property, a society that has conjured up such gigantic means of production and of exchange, is like the sorcerer, who is no longer able to control the powers of the nether world whom he has called up by his spells. For many a decade past, the history of industry and commerce is but the history of the revolt of modern productive forces against modern conditions of production, against the property relations that are the conditions for the existence of the bourgeoisie and of its rule. It is enough to mention the commercial crises that by their periodical return put on its trial, each time more threateningly, the existence of the entire bourgeois society. In these crises a great part not only of the existing products, but also of the previously created productive forces, are periodically destroyed. In these crises there breaks out an epidemic that, in all earlier epochs, would have seemed an absurdity—the epidemic of overpro-

duction. Society suddenly finds itself put back into a state of momentary barbarism; it appears as if a famine, a universal war of devastation, had cut off the supply of every means of subsistence; industry and commerce seem to be destroyed; and why? Because there is too much civilization, too much means of subsistence, too much industry, too much commerce. The productive forces at the disposal of society no longer tend to further the development of the conditions of the bourgeois property; on the contrary, they have become too powerful for these conditions by which they are fettered, and as soon as they overcome these fetters they bring disorder into the whole of bourgeois society, endanger the existence of bourgeois property. The conditions of bourgeois society are too narrow to comprise the wealth created by them. And how does the bourgeoisie get over these crises? On the one hand by enforced destruction of a mass of productive forces; on the other, by the conquest of new markets, and by the more thorough exploitation of the old ones. That is to say, by paving the way for more extensive and more destructive crises, and by diminishing the means whereby crises are prevented.

The weapons with which the bourgeoisie felled feudalism to the ground are now turned against the bourgeoisie itself.   34

But not only has the bourgeoisie forged the weapons that bring death to itself; it has also called into existence the men who are to wield those weapons—the modern working class—the proletarians.   35

In proportion as the bourgeoisie, i.e., capital, is developed, in the same proportion is the proletariat, the modern working class, developed, a class of laborers who live only so long as they find work, and who find work only so long as their labor increases capital. These laborers, who must sell themselves piecemeal, are a commodity, like every other article of commerce, and are consequently exposed to all the vicissitudes of competition, to all the fluctuations of the market.   36

Owing to the extensive use of machinery and to division of labor, the work of the proletarians has lost all individual character, and, consequently, all charm for the workman. He becomes an appendage of the machine, and it is only the most simple, most monotonous and most easily acquired knack that is required of him. Hence, the cost of production of a workman is restricted almost entirely to the means of subsistence that he requires for his maintenance, and for the propagation of his race. But the price of a commodity, and also of labor, is equal to its cost of production. In proportion, therefore, as the repulsiveness of the work increases the wage decreases. Nay more, in proportion as the use of machinery and division of labor increases, in the same proportion the burden of toil increases, whether by prolongation of the working hours, by increase of the work enacted in a given time, or by increased speed of the machinery, etc.   37

Modern industry has converted the little workshop of the patriarchal master into the great factory of the industrial capitalist. Masses of laborers, crowded into factories, are organized like soldiers. As privates of the industrial army they are placed under the command of a perfect hierarchy of officers and sergeants. Not only are they the slaves of the bourgeois class and of the   38 bourgeois state, they are daily and hourly enslaved by the machine, by the overlooker, and, above all, by the individual bourgeois manufacturer himself. The more openly this despotism proclaims gain to be its end and aim, the more petty, the more hateful and the more embittering it is.

The less the skill and exertion or strength implied in manual labor, in other words, the more modern industry becomes developed, the more is the labor of men superseded by that of women. Differences of age and sex have no longer any distinctive social validity for the working class. All are instruments of labor, more or less expensive to use, according to their age and sex. 39

No sooner is the exploitation of the laborer by the manufacturer, so far at an end, that he receives his wages in cash, than he is set upon by the other portions of the bourgeoisie, the landlord, the shopkeeper, the pawnbroker, etc. 40

The lower strata of the middle class—the small trades-people, shopkeepers and retired tradesmen generally, the handicraftsmen and peasants— all these sink gradually into the proletariat, partly because their diminutive capital does not suffice for the scale on which Modern Industry is carried on, and is swamped in the competition with the large capitalists, partly because their specialized skill is rendered worthless by new methods of production. Thus the proletariat is recruited from all classes of the population. 41

The proletariat goes through various stages of development. With its birth begins its struggle with the bourgeoisie. At first the contest is carried on by individual laborers, then by the workpeople of a factory, then by the operatives of one trade, in one locality, against the individual bourgeois who directly exploits them. They direct their attacks not against the bourgeois conditions of production, but against the instruments of production themselves; they destroy imported wares that compete with their labor, they smash to pieces machinery, they set factories ablaze, they seek to restore by force the vanished status of the workman of the Middle Ages. 42

At this stage the laborers still form an incoherent mass scattered over the whole country, and broken up by their mutual competition. If anywhere they unite to form more compact bodies, this is not yet the consequence of their own active union, but of the union of the bourgeoisie, which class, in order to attain its own political ends, is compelled to set the whole proletariat in motion, and is moreover yet, for a time, able to do so. At this stage, therefore, the proletarians do not fight their enemies, but the enemies of their enemies, the remnants of absolute monarchy, the landowners, the non-industrial bourgeois, the petty bourgeoisie. Thus the whole historical movement is concentrated in the hands of the bourgeoisie, every victory so obtained is a victory for the bourgeoisie. 43

But with the development of industry the proletariat not only increases in number; it becomes concentrated in greater masses, its strength grows and it feels that strength more. The various interests and conditions of life within the ranks of the proletariat are more and more equalized, in proportion as machinery obliterates all distinctions of labor, and nearly everywhere reduces wages to the same low level. The growing competition among the bourgeois, 44 and the resulting commercial crisis, makes the wages of the workers even more fluctuating. The unceasing improvement of machinery, ever more rapidly developing, makes their livelihood more and more precarious; the collisions between individual workmen and individual bourgeois take more and more the character of collisions between two classes. Thereupon the workers begin to form combinations (Trades' Unions) against the bourgeois; they club together in order to keep up the rate of wages; they found permanent associations in order to make provision beforehand for these occasional revolts. Here and there the contest breaks out into riots.

Now and then the workers are victorious, but only for a time. The real 45 fruit of their battle lies not in the immediate result but in the ever-expanding union of workers. This union is helped on by the improved means of communication that are created by modern industry, and that places the workers of different localities in contact with one another. It was just this contact that was needed to centralize the numerous local struggles, all of the same character, into one national struggle between classes. But every class struggle is a political struggle. And that union, to attain which the burghers of the Middle Ages with their miserable highways, required centuries, the modern proletarians, thanks to railways, achieve in a few years.

This organization of the proletarians into a class, and consequently into a 46 political party, is continually being upset again by the competition between the workers themselves. But it ever rises up again, stronger, firmer, mightier. It compels legislative recognition of particular interests of the workers by taking advantage of the divisions among the bourgeoisie itself. Thus the ten hours' bill in England was carried.

Altogether collisions between the classes of the old society further, in many 47 ways, the course of development of the proletariat. The bourgeoisie finds itself involved in a constant battle. At first with the aristocracy; later on, with those portions of the bourgeoisie itself whose interests have become antagonistic to the progress of industry; at all times, with the bourgeoisie of foreign countries. In all these battles it sees itself compelled to appeal to the proletariat, to ask for its help, and thus, to drag it into the political arena. The bourgeoisie itself, therefore, supplies the proletariat with its own elements of political and general education; in other words, it furnishes the proletariat with weapons for fighting the bourgeoisie.

Further, as we have already seen, entire sections of the ruling classes are, 48 by the advance of industry, precipitated into the proletariat, or are at least threatened in their conditions of existence. These also supply the proletariat with fresh elements of enlightenment and progress.

Finally, in times when the class-struggle nears the decisive hour, the pro- 49 cess of dissolution going on within the ruling class—in fact, within the whole range of an old society—assumes such a violent, glaring character that a small section of the ruling class cuts itself adrift and joins the revolutionary class, the class that holds the future in its hands. Just as, therefore, at an earlier period, a section of the nobility went over to the bourgeoisie, so now a portion of the bourgeoisie goes over to the proletariat, and in particular, a portion of the bourgeois ideologists, who have raised themselves to the level of comprehending theoretically the historical movements as a whole.

Of all the classes that stand face to face with the bourgeoisie today the proletariat alone is a really revolutionary class. The other classes decay and finally disappear in the face of modern industry; the proletariat is its special and essential product.   50

The lower middle class, the small manufacturer, the shopkeeper, the artisan, the peasant, all these fight against the bourgeoisie, to save from extinction their existence as fractions of the middle class. They are therefore not revolutionary, but conservative. Nay, more; they are reactionary, for they try to roll back the wheel of history. If by chance they are revolutionary, they are so only in view of their impending transfer into the proletariat; they thus defend not their present, but their future interests; they desert their own standpoint to place themselves at that of the proletariat.   51

The "dangerous class," the social scum, that passively rotting mass thrown off by the lowest layers of old society, may, here and there, be swept into the movement by a proletarian revolution; its conditions of life, however, prepare it far more for the part of a bribed tool of reactionary intrigue.   52

In the conditions of the proletariat, those of the old society at large are already virtually swamped. The proletarian is without property; his relation to his wife and children has no longer anything in common with the bourgeois family relations; modern industrial labor, modern subjection to capital, the same in England as in France, in America as in Germany, has stripped him of every trace of national character. Law, morality, religion, are to him so many bourgeois prejudices, behind which lurk in ambush just as many bourgeois interests.   53

All the preceding classes that got the upper hand sought to fortify their already acquired status by subjecting society at large to their conditions of appropriation. The proletarians cannot become masters of the productive forces of society, except by abolishing their own previous mode of appropriation, and thereby also every other previous mode of appropriation. They have nothing of their own to secure and to fortify; their mission is to destroy all previous securities for and insurances of individual property.   54

All previous historical movements were movements of minorities, or in the interest of minorities. The proletarian movement is the self-conscious, independent movement of the immense majority. The proletariat, the lowest stratum of our present society, cannot stir, cannot raise itself up without the whole superincumbent strata of official society being sprung into the air.   55

Though not in substance, yet in form, the struggle of the proletariat with the bourgeoisie is at first a national struggle. The proletariat of each country must, of course, first of all settle matters with its own bourgeoisie.   56

In depicting the most general phases of the development of the proletariat, we traced the more or less veiled civil war, raging within existing society, up to the point where that war breaks out into open revolution, and where the violent overthrow of the bourgeoisie, lays the foundations for the sway of the proletariat.   57

Hitherto every form of society has been based, as we have already seen,   58
on the antagonism of oppressing and oppressed classes. But in order to op-
press a class, certain conditions must be assured to it under which it can, at
least, continue its slavish existence. The serf, in the period of serfdom, raised
himself to membership in the commune, just as the petty bourgeois, under
the yoke of feudal absolutism managed to develop into a bourgeois. The modern laborer, on the contrary, instead of rising with the progress of industry,
sinks deeper and deeper below the conditions of existence of his own class.
He becomes a pauper, and pauperism develops more rapidly than population
and wealth. And here it becomes evident that the bourgeoisie is unfit any
longer to be the ruling class in society, and to impose its conditions of existence upon society as an over-riding law. It is unfit to rule, because it is
incompetent to assure an existence to its slave within his slavery, because it
cannot help letting him sink into such a state that it has to feed him, instead
of being fed by him. Society can no longer live under this bourgeoisie; in
other words, its existence is no longer compatible with society.

The essential condition for the existence, and for the sway of the bour-   59
geois class, is the formation and augmentation of capital; the condition for
capital is wage labor. Wage labor rests exclusively on competition between
the laborers. The advance of industry, whose involuntary promoter is the
bourgeoisie, replaces the isolation of the laborers, due to competition, by
their involuntary combination, due to association. The development of Modern Industry, therefore, cuts from under its feet the very foundation on which
the bourgeoisie produces and appropriates products. What the bourgeoisie
therefore produces, above all, are its own grave diggers. Its fall and the victory of the proletariat are equally inevitable.

QUESTIONS FOR MEANING

1. Comment on the authors' claim in paragraph 7 that the "history of all
   hitherto existing society is the history of class struggles." What does this
   mean?
2. In paragraph 11, the authors write: "Society as a whole is more and more
   splitting up into two great hostile camps, into two great classes directly
   facing each other: Bourgeoisie and Proletariat." Has history proven them
   right? How would you describe class relations within the United States?
   Can American history be seen in Marxist terms?
3. Explain the distinction in paragraph 14 between the feudal and manufacturing systems of industry.
4. Do Marx and Engels concede that modern industry has accomplished anything admirable? Do they credit the bourgeoisie with any virtues?
5. Why do Marx and Engels believe that the bourgeoisie is unfit to rule? Why
   do they believe that the rise of the proletariat is inevitable?
6. What do Marx and Engels mean when they claim "there is too much civilization, too much means of subsistence, too much industry, too much
   commerce"? Paraphrase paragraph 33.

7. What is "the social scum" that Marx and Engels dismiss in paragraph 52? Why do they believe this class is dangerous?
8. Vocabulary: exorcise (1), patrician (8), plebeian (8), vassals (9), patriarchal (20), nexus (20), slothful (23), indigenous (26), agglomerated (29), presentiment (30), vicissitudes (36), diminutive (41), obliterates (44), precarious (44), and augmentation (59).

QUESTIONS ABOUT STRATEGY

1. Why do Marx and Engels open their manifesto by describing Communism as "a specter"? Explain what they mean by this and how it serves as an introduction to the political analysis that follows.
2. In interpreting history entirely in economic terms, are there any major conflicts that Marx and Engels overlook?
3. What is the function of paragraphs 31 and 32?
4. Can you point to anything in this work that reveals that Marx and Engels were writing for an international audience?
5. What parts of this essay are the strongest? Where do Marx and Engels make the most sense?
6. Can you identify any exaggerations in *The Communist Manifesto*? If you were to write a rebuttal, are there any claims that you could prove to be oversimplified?
7. Is this "manifesto" an argument or an exhortation? Is it designed to convince readers who have no political opinions, or to rally the men and women who are already committed to revolution? What is its purpose?

HENRY DAVID THOREAU
Resistance to Civil Government

Henry David Thoreau (1817–1862) was one of the most important American writers of the nineteenth century. A graduate of Harvard, Thoreau chose to live alone in a hut of his own making from 1845 to 1847 near Walden Pond outside of Concord, Massachusetts. He devoted himself there to living simply and striving to be self-sufficient—spending much of his time reading, thinking, and studying nature. The record of this experience can be found in Walden *(1854), Thoreau's most influential and widely read book. His other books include* A Week on the Concord and Merrimack River *(1849),* The Main Woods *(1864), and* Cape Cod *(1865). He was also the author of several important essays, foremost among which is the following selection—popularly known as "Civil Disobedience." It was first published in **1849,** during the Mexican War.*

I heartily accept the motto,—"That government is best which governs least;" and I should like to see it acted up to more rapidly and systematically. Carried out, it finally amounts to this, which also I believe,—"That government is best which governs not at all;" and when men are prepared for it, that will be the kind of government which they will have. Government is at best but an expedient; but most governments are usually, and all governments are sometimes, inexpedient. The objections which have been brought against a standing army, and they are many and weighty, and deserve to prevail, may also at last be brought against a standing government. The standing army is only an arm of the standing government. The government itself, which is only the mode which the people have chosen to execute their will, is equally liable to be abused and perverted before the people can act through it. Witness the present Mexican war, the work of comparatively a few individuals using the standing government as their tool; for, in the outset, the people would not have consented to this measure. 1

This American government,—what is it but a tradition, though a recent one, endeavoring to transmit itself unimpaired to posterity, but each instant losing some of its integrity? It has not the vitality and force of a single living man; for a single man can bend it to his will. It is a sort of wooden gun to the people themselves; and, if ever they should use it in earnest as a real one against each other, it will surely split. But it is not the less necessary for this; for the people must have some complicated machinery or other, and hear its din, to satisfy that idea of government which they have. Governments show thus how successfully men can be imposed on, even impose on themselves, for their own advantage. It is excellent, we must all allow; yet this government never of itself furthered any enterprise, but by the alacrity with which it got out of its way. *It* does not keep the country free. *It* does not settle the West. *It* does not educate. The character inherent in the American people has done all that has been accomplished; and it would have done somewhat 2 more, if the government had not sometimes got in its way. For government is an expedient by which men would fain succeed in letting one another alone; and, as has been said, when it is most expedient, the governed are most let alone by it. Trade and commerce, if they were not made of India rubber, would never manage to bounce over the obstacles which legislators are continually putting in their way; and, if one were to judge these men wholly by the effects of their actions, and not partly by their intentions, they would deserve to be classed and punished with those mischievous persons who put obstructions on the railroads.

But, to speak practically and as a citizen, unlike those who call themselves no-government men, I ask for, not at once no government, but at *once* a better government. Let every man make known what kind of government would command his respect, and that will be one step toward obtaining it.   3

After all, the practical reason why, when the power is once in the hands of the people, a majority are permitted, and for a long period continue, to rule, is not because they are most likely to be in the right, nor because this seems fairest to the minority, but because they are physically the strongest. But a government in which the majority rule in all cases cannot be based on justice, even as far as men understand it. Can there not be a government in which majorities do not virtually decide right and wrong, but conscience?— in which majorities decide only those questions to which the rule of expediency is applicable? Must the citizen ever for a moment, or in the least degree, resign his conscience to the legislator? Why has every man a conscience, then? I think that we should be men first, and subjects afterward. It is not desirable to cultivate a respect for the law, so much as for the right. The only obligation which I have a right to assume, is to do at any time what I think right. It is truly enough said, that a corporation has no conscience; but a corporation of conscientious men is a corporation *with* a conscience. Law never made men a whit more just; and, by means of their respect for it, even the well-disposed are daily made the agents of injustice. A common and natural result of an undue respect for law is, that you may see a file of soldiers, colonel, captain, corporal, privates, powder-monkeys and all, marching in admirable order over hill and dale to the wars, against their wills, aye, against their common sense and consciences, which makes it very steep marching indeed, and produces a palpitation of the heart. They have no doubt that it is a damnable business in which they are concerned; they are all peaceably inclined. Now, what are they? Men at all? or small moveable forts and magazines, at the service of some unscrupulous man in power? Visit the Navy Yard, and behold a marine, such a man as an American government can make, or such as it can make a man with its black arts, a mere shadow and reminiscence of humanity, a man laid out alive and standing, and already, as one may say, buried under arms with funeral accompaniments, though it may be   4

> "Not a drum was heard, not a funeral note,
>   As his corse to the rampart we hurried;

Not a soldier discharged his farewell shot
O'er the grave where our hero we buried."

The mass of men serve the State thus, not as men mainly, but as machines, 5
with their bodies. They are the standing army, and the militia, jailers, constables, *posse comitatus*, &c. In most cases there is no free exercise whatever
of the judgment or of the moral sense; but they put themselves on a level
with wood and earth and stones, and wooden men can perhaps be manufactured that will serve the purpose as well. Such command no more respect
than men of straw, or a lump of dirt. They have the same sort of worth only
as horses and dogs. Yet such as these even are commonly esteemed good
citizens. Others, as most legislators, politicians, lawyers, ministers, and officeholders, serve the State chiefly with their heads; and, as they rarely make
any moral distinctions, they are as likely to serve the devil, without intending
it, as God. A very few, as heroes, patriots, martyrs, reformers in the great
sense, and *men*, serve the State with their consciences also, and so necessarily resist it for the most part; and they are commonly treated by it as
enemies. A wise man will only be useful as a man, and will not submit to be
"clay," and "stop a hole to keep the wind away," but leave that office to his
dust at least:—

"I am too high-born to be propertied,
To be a secondary at control,
Or useful serving-man and instrument
To any sovereign state throughout the world."

He who gives himself entirely to his fellow-men appears to them useless 6
and selfish; but he who gives himself partially to them is pronounced a benefactor and philanthropist.

How does it become a man to behave toward this American government 7
to-day? I answer that he cannot without disgrace be associated with it. I
cannot for an instant recognize that political organization as *my* government
which is the *slave's* government also.

All men recognize the right of revolution; that is, the right to refuse allegiance to and to resist the government, when its tyranny or its inefficiency 8
are great and unendurable. But almost all say that such is not the case now.
But such was the case, they think, in the Revolution of '75. If one were to
tell me that this was a bad government because it taxed certain foreign commodities brought to its ports, it is most probable that I should not make an
ado about it, for I can do without them: all machines have their friction; and
possibly this does enough good to counterbalance the evil. At any rate, it is
a great evil to make a stir about it. But when the friction comes to have its
machine, and oppression and robbery are organized, I say, let us not have
such a machine any longer. In other words, when a sixth of the population of
a nation which has undertaken to be the refuge of liberty are slaves, and a

whole country is unjustly overrun and conquered by a foreign army, and subjected to military law, I think that it is not too soon for honest men to rebel and revolutionize. What makes this duty the more urgent is the fact, that the country so overrun is not our own, but ours is the invading army.

Paley, a common authority with many on moral questions, in his chapter   9
on the "Duty of Submission to Civil Government," resolves all civil obligation into expediency; and he proceeds to say, "that so long as the interest of the whole society requires it, that is, so long as the established government cannot be resisted or changed without public inconveniency, it is the will of God that the established government be obeyed, and no longer." . . . "This principle being admitted, the justice of every particular case of resistance is reduced to a computation of the quantity of the danger and grievance on the one side, and of the probability and expense of redressing it on the other." Of this, he says, every man shall judge for himself. But Paley appears never to have contemplated those cases to which the rule of expediency does not apply, in which a people, as well as an individual, must do justice, cost what it may. If I have unjustly wrested a plank from a drowning man, I must restore it to him though I drown myself. This, according to Paley, would be inconvenient. But he that would save his life, in such a case, shall lose it. This people must cease to hold slaves, and to make war on Mexico, though it cost them their existence as a people.

In their practice, nations agree with Paley; but does any one think that   10
Massachusetts does exactly what is right at the present crisis?

> "A drab of state, a cloth-o'-silver slut,
> To have her train borne up, and her soul trail in the dirt."

Practically speaking, the opponents to a reform in Massachusetts are not   11
a hundred thousand politicians at the South, but a hundred thousand merchants and farmers here, who are more interested in commerce and agriculture than they are in humanity, and are not prepared to do justice to the slave and to Mexico, *cost what it may.* I quarrel not with far-off foes, but with those who, near at home, co-operate with, and do the bidding of those far away, and without whom the latter would be harmless. We are accustomed to say, that the mass of men are unprepared; but improvement is slow, because the few are not materially wiser or better than the many. It is not so important that many should be as good as you, as that there be some absolute goodness somewhere; for that will leaven the whole lump. There are thousands who are *in opinion* opposed to slavery and to the war, who yet in effect do nothing to put an end to them; who, esteeming themselves children of Washington and Franklin, sit down with their hands in their pockets, and say that they know not what to do, and do nothing; who even postpone the question of freedom to the question of free-trade, and quietly read the prices-current along with the latest advices from Mexico, after dinner, and, it may be, fall asleep over them both. What is the price-current of an honest man and patriot to-day? They hesitate, and they regret, and sometimes they petition; but they do nothing in earnest and with effect. They will wait, well-

disposed, for others to remedy the evil, that they may no longer have it to regret. At most, they give only a cheap vote, and a feeble countenance and God-speed, to the right, as it goes by them. There are nine hundred and ninety-nine patrons of virtue to one virtuous man; but it is easier to deal with the real possessor of a thing than with the temporary guardian of it.

All voting is a sort of gaming, like chequers or backgammon, with a slight moral tinge to it, a playing with right and wrong, with moral questions; and betting naturally accompanies it. The character of the voters is not staked. I cast my vote, perchance, as I think right; but I am not vitally concerned that that right should prevail. I am willing to leave it to the majority. Its obligation, therefore, never exceeds that of expediency. Even voting *for the right* is *doing* nothing for it. It is only expressing to men feebly your desire that it should prevail. A wise man will not leave the right to the mercy of chance, nor wish it to prevail through the power of the majority. There is but little virtue in the action of masses of men. When the majority shall at length vote for the abolition of slavery, it will be because they are indifferent to slavery, or because there is but little slavery left to be abolished by their vote. *They* will then be the only slaves. Only *his* vote can hasten the abolition of slavery who asserts his own freedom by his vote.

I hear of a convention to be held at Baltimore, or elsewhere, for the selection of a candidate for the Presidency, made up chiefly of editors, and men who are politicians by profession; but I think, what is it to any independent, intelligent, and respectable man what decision they may come to, shall we not have the advantage of his wisdom and honesty, nevertheless? Can we not count upon some independent votes? Are there not many individuals in the country who do not attend conventions? But no: I find that the respectable man, so called, has immediately drifted from his position, and despairs of his country, when his country has more reason to despair of him. He forthwith adopts one of the candidates thus selected as the only *available* one, thus proving that he is himself *available* for any purposes of the demagogue. His vote is of no more worth than that of any unprincipled foreigner or hireling native, who may have been bought. Oh for a man who is a *man*, and, as my neighbor says, has a bone in his back which you cannot pass your hand through! Our statistics are at fault: the population has been returned too large. How many *men* are there to a square thousand miles in this country? Hardly one. Does not America offer any inducement for men to settle here? The American has dwindled into an Odd Fellow,—one who may be known by the development of his organ of gregariousness, and a manifest lack of intellect and cheerful self-reliance; whose first and chief concern, on coming into the world, is to see that the alms-houses are in good repair; and, before yet he lawfully donned the virile garb, to collect a fund for the support of the widows and orphans that may be; who, in short, ventures to live only by the aid of the mutual insurance company, which has promised to bury him decently.

It is not a man's duty, as a matter of course, to devote himself to the eradication of any, even the most enormous wrong; he may still properly have other concerns to engage him; but it is his duty, at least, to wash his hands of it, and, if he gives it no thought longer, not to give it practically his support. If I devote myself to other pursuits and contemplations, I must first see, at least, that I do not pursue them sitting upon another man's shoulders. I must get off him first, that he may pursue his contemplations too. See what gross inconsistency is tolerated. I have heard some of my townsmen say, "I should like to have them order me out to help put down an insurrection of the slaves, or to march to Mexico,—see if I would go;" and yet these very men have each, directly by their allegiance, and so indirectly, at least, by their money, furnished a substitute. The soldier is applauded who refuses to serve in an unjust war by those who do not refuse to sustain the unjust government which makes the war; is applauded by those whose own act and authority he disregards and sees at nought; as if the State were penitent to that degree that it hired one to scourge it while it sinned, but not to that degree that it left off sinning for a moment. Thus, under the name of order and civil government, we are all made at least to pay homage to and support our own meanness. After the first blush of sin, comes its indifference and from immoral it becomes, as it were, *un*moral, and not quite unnecessary to that life which we have made.

The broadest and most prevalent error requires the most disinterested   15
virtue to sustain it. The slight reproach to which the virtue of patriotism is commonly liable, the noble are most likely to incur. Those who, while they disapprove of the character and measures of a government, yield to it their allegiance and support, are undoubtedly its most conscientious supporters, and so frequently the most serious obstacles to reform. Some are petitioning the State to dissolve the Union, to disregard the requisitions of the President. Why do they not dissolve it themselves,—the union between themselves and the State,—and refuse to pay their quota into its treasury? Do not they stand in the same relation to the State, that the State does to the Union? And have not the same reasons prevented the State from resisting the Union, which have prevented them from resisting the State?

How can a man be satisfied to entertain an opinion merely, and enjoy *it?*   16
Is there any enjoyment in it, if his opinion is that he is aggrieved? If you are cheated out of a single dollar by your neighbor, you do not rest satisfied with knowing that you are cheated, or with saying that you are cheated, or even with petitioning him to pay you your due; but you take effectual steps at once to obtain the full amount, and see that you are never cheated again. Action from principle,—the perception and the performance of right,—changes things and relations; it is essentially revolutionary, and does not consist wholly with any thing which was. It not only divides states and churches, it divides families; aye, it divides the *individual,* separating the diabolical in him from the divine.

Unjust laws exist: shall we be content to obey them, or shall we endeavor   17
to amend them, and obey them until we have succeeded, or shall we transgress them at once? Men generally, under such a government as this, think that they ought to wait until they have persuaded the majority to alter them. They think that, if they should resist, the remedy would be worse than the evil. But it is the fault of the government itself that the remedy *is* worse than

the evil. *It* makes it worse. Why is it not more apt to anticipate and provide for reform? Why does it not cherish its wise minority? Why does it cry and resist before it is hurt? Why does it not encourage its citizens to be on the alert to point out its faults, and *do* better than it would have them? Why does it always crucify Christ, and excommunicate Copernicus and Luther, and pronounce Washington and Franklin rebels?

One would think, that a deliberate and practical denial of its authority was   18
the only offence never contemplated by government; else, why has it not assigned its definite, its suitable and proportionate penalty? If a man who has no property refuses but once to earn nine shillings for the State, he is put in prison for a period unlimited by any law that I know, and determined only by the discretion of those who placed him there; but if he should steal ninety times nine shillings from the State, he is soon permitted to go at large again.

If the injustice is part of the necessary friction of the machine of govern-   19
ment, let it go, let it go: perchance it will wear smooth,—certainly the machine will wear out. If the injustice has a spring, or a pulley, or a rope, or a crank, exclusively for itself, then perhaps you may consider whether the remedy will not be worse than the evil; but if it is of such a nature that it requires you to be the agent of injustice to another, then, I say, break the law. Let your life be a counter friction to stop the machine. What I have to do is to see, at any rate, that I do not lend myself to the wrong which I condemn.

As for adopting the ways which the State has provided for remedying the   20
evil, I know not of such ways. They take too much time, and a man's life will be gone. I have other affairs to attend to. I came into this world, not chiefly to make this a good place to live in, but to live in it, be it good or bad. A man has not every thing to do, but something; and because he cannot do *every thing*, it is not necessary that he should do *something* wrong. It is not my business to be petitioning the governor or the legislature any more than it is theirs to petition me; and, if they should not hear my petition, what should I do then? But in this case the State has provided no way: its very Constitution is the evil. This may seem to be harsh and stubborn and unconciliatory; but it is to treat with the utmost kindness and consideration the only spirit that can appreciate or deserves it. So is all change for the better, like birth and death which convulse the body.

I do not hesitate to say, that those who call themselves abolitionists should   21
at once effectually withdraw their support, both in person and property, from the government of Massachusetts, and not wait till they constitute a majority of one, before they suffer the right to prevail through them. I think that it is enough if they have God on their side, without waiting for that other one. Moreover, any man more right than his neighbors, constitutes a majority of one already.

I meet this American government, or its representative the State govern-   22
ment, directly, and face to face, once a year, no more, in the person of its tax-gatherer; this is the only mode in which a man situated as I am necessarily meets it; and it then says distinctly, Recognize me; and the simplest, the most effectual, and, in the present posture of affairs, the indispensablest mode

of treating with it on this head, of expressing your little satisfaction with and love for it, is to deny it then. My civil neighbor, the tax-gatherer, is the very man I have to deal with,—for it is, after all, with men and not with parchment that I quarrel,—and he has voluntarily chosen to be an agent of the government. How shall he ever know well what he is and does as an officer of the government, or as a man, until he is obliged to consider whether he shall treat me, his neighbor, for whom he has respect, as a neighbor and well-disposed man, or as a maniac and disturber of the peace, and see if he can get over this obstruction to his neighborliness without a ruder and more impetuous thought or speech corresponding with his action? I know this well, that if one thousand, if one hundred, if ten men whom I could name,—if ten *honest* men only,—aye, if *one* HONEST man, in the State of Massachusetts, *ceasing to hold slaves,* were actually to withdraw from this copartnership, and be locked up in the county jail therefor, it would be the abolition of slavery in America. For it matters not how small the beginning may seem to be: what is once well done is done for ever. But we love better to talk about it: that we say is our mission. Reform keeps many scores of newspapers in its service, but not one man. If my esteemed neighbor, the State's ambassador, who will devote his days to the settlement of the question of human rights in the Council Chamber, instead of being threatened with the prisons of Carolina, were to sit down the prisoner of Massachusetts, that State which is so anxious to foist the sin of slavery upon her sister,—though at present she can discover only an act of inhospitality to be the ground of a quarrel with her,—the Legislature would not wholly waive the subject the following winter.

Under a government which imprisons any unjustly, the true place for a just man is also a prison. The proper place to-day, the only place which Massachusetts has provided for her freer and less desponding spirits, is in her prisons, to be put out and locked out of the State by her own act, as they have already put themselves out by their principles. It is there that the fugitive slave, and the Mexican prisoner on parole, and the Indian come to plead the wrongs of his race, should find them; on that separate, but more free and honorable ground, where the State places those who are not *with* her but *against* her,—the only house in a slave-state in which a free man can abide with honor. If any think that their influence would be lost there, and their voices no longer afflict the ear of the State, that they would not be as an enemy within its walls, they do not know by how much truth is stronger than error, nor how much more eloquently and effectively he can combat injustice who has experienced a little in his own person. Cast your whole vote, not a strip of paper merely, but your whole influence. A minority is powerless while it conforms to the majority; it is not even a minority then; but it is irresistible when it clogs by its whole weight. If the alternative is to keep all just men in prison, or give up war and slavery, the State will not hesitate which to choose. If a thousand men were not to pay their tax-bills this year, that would not be a violent and bloody measure, as it would be to pay them, and enable the State to commit violence and shed innocent blood. This is, in fact, the definition of a peaceable revolution, if any such is possible. If the tax-gatherer, or any other public officer, asks me, as one has done, "But what shall I do?" my answer is, "If you really wish to do any thing, resign your office." When the subject has refused allegiance, and the officer has resigned his office, then the revolution is accomplished. But even suppose blood should flow. Is there not a sort of blood shed when the conscience is wounded? Through this wound a man's real manhood and immortality flow out, and he bleeds to an everlasting death. I see this blood flowing now.

I have contemplated the imprisonment of the offender, rather than the   24
seizure of his goods,—though both will serve the same purpose,—because they who assert the purest right, and consequently are most dangerous to a corrupt State, commonly have not spent much time in accumulating property. To such the State renders comparatively small service, and a slight tax is wont to appear exorbitant, particularly if they are obliged to earn it by special labor with their hands. If there were one who lived wholly without the use of money, the State itself would hesitate to demand it of him. But the rich man—not to make any invidious comparison—is always sold to the institution which makes him rich. Absolutely speaking, the more money, the less virtue; for money comes between a man and his objects, and obtains them for him; and it was certainly no great virtue to obtain it. It puts to rest many questions which he would otherwise be taxed to answer; while the only new question which it puts is the hard but superfluous one, how to spend it. Thus his moral ground is taken from under his feet. The opportunities of living are diminished in proportion as what are called the "means" are increased. The best thing a man can do for his culture when he is rich is to endeavour to carry out those schemes which he entertained when he was poor. Christ answered the Herodians according to their condition. "Show me the tribute-money," said he;—and one took a penny out of his pocket;—If you use money which has the image of Cæsar on it, and which he has made current and valuable, that is, *if you are men of the State,* and gladly enjoy the advantages of Cæsar's government, then pay him back some of his own when he demands it; "Render therefore to Cæsar that which is Cæsar's, and to God those things which are God's,"—leaving them no wiser than before as to which was which; for they did not wish to know.

When I converse with the freest of my neighbors, I perceive that, whatever   25
they may say about the magnitude and seriousness of the question, and their regard for the public tranquillity, the long and short of the matter is, that they cannot spare the protection of the existing government, and they dread the consequences of disobedience to it to their property and families. For my own part, I should not like to think that I ever rely on the protection of the State. But, if I deny the authority of the State when it presents its tax-bill, it will soon take and waste all my property, and so harass me and my children without end. This is hard. This makes it impossible for a man to live honestly and at the same time comfortably in outward respects. It will not be worth the while to accumulate property; that would be sure to go again. You must hire or squat somewhere, and raise but a small crop, and eat that soon. You

must live within yourself, and depend upon yourself, always tucked up and ready for a start, and not have many affairs. A man may grow rich in Turkey even, if he will be in all respects a good subject of the Turkish government. Confucius said,—"If a State is governed by the principles of reason, poverty and misery are subjects of shame; if a State is not governed by the principles of reason, riches and honors are the subjects of shame." No: until I want the protection of Massachusetts to be extended to me in some distant southern port, where my liberty is endangered, or until I am bent solely on building up an estate at home by peaceful enterprise, I can afford to refuse allegiance to Massachusetts, and her right to my property and life. It costs me less in every sense to incur the penalty of disobedience to the State, than it would to obey. I should feel as if I were worth less in that case.

Some years ago, the State met me in behalf of the church, and com- 26 manded me to pay a certain sum toward the support of a clergyman whose preaching my father attended, but never I myself. "Pay it," it said, "or be locked up in the jail." I declined to pay. But, unfortunately, another man saw fit to pay it. I did not see why the schoolmaster should be taxed to support the priest, and not the priest the schoolmaster; for I was not the State's schoolmaster, but I supported myself by voluntary subscription. I did not see why the lyceum should not present its tax-bill, and have the State to back its demand, as well as the church. However, at the request of the selectmen, I condescended to make some such statement as this in writing:—"Know all men by these presents, that I, Henry Thoreau, do not wish to be regarded as a member of any incorporated society which I have not joined." This I gave to the town-clerk; and he has it. The State, having thus learned that I did not wish to be regarded as a member of that church, has never made a like demand on me since; though it said that it must adhere to its original presumption that time. If I had known how to name them, I should then have signed off in detail from all the societies which I never signed on to; but I did not know where to find a complete list.

I have paid no poll-tax for six years. I was put into jail once on this ac- 27 count, for one night; and, as I stood considering the walls of solid stone, two or three feet thick, the door of wood and iron, a foot thick, and the iron grating which strained the light, I could not help being struck with the foolishness of that institution which treated me as if I were mere flesh and blood and bones, to be locked up. I wondered that it should have concluded at length that this was the best use it could put me to, and had never thought to avail itself of my services in some way. I saw that, if there was a wall of stone between me and my townsmen, there was a still more difficult one to climb or break through, before they could get to be as free as I was. I did not for a moment feel confined, and the walls seemed a great waste of stone and mortar. I felt as if I alone of all my townsmen had paid my tax. They plainly did not know how to treat me, but behaved like persons who are underbred. In every threat and in every compliment there was a blunder; for they thought that my chief desire was to stand the other side of that stone wall. I could not but smile to see how industriously they locked the door on my meditations, which followed them out again without let or hinderance, and *they* were really all that was dangerous. As they could not reach me, they had resolved to punish my body; just as boys, if they cannot come at some person against whom they have a spite, will abuse his dog. I saw that the State was half-witted, that it was timid as a lone woman with her silver spoons, and that it did not know its friends from its foes, and I lost all my remaining respect for it, and pitied it.

Thus the State never intentionally confronts a man's sense, intellectual or moral, but only his body, his senses. It is not armed with superior wit or honesty, but with superior physical strength. I was not born to be forced. I will breathe after my own fashion. Let us see who is the strongest. What force has a multitude? They only can force me who obey a higher law than I. They force me to become like themselves. I do not hear of *men* being *forced* to live this way or that by masses of men. What sort of life were that to live? When I meet a government which says to me, "Your money or your life," why should I be in haste to give it my money? It may be in a great strait, and not know what to do: I cannot help that. It must help itself; do as I do. It is not worth the while to snivel about it. I am not responsible for the successful working of the machinery of society. I am not the son of the engineer. I perceive that, when an acorn and a chestnut fall side by side, the one does not remain inert to make way for the other, but both obey their own laws, and spring and grow and flourish as best they can, till one, perchance, over-shadows and destroys the other. If a plant cannot live according to its nature, it dies; and so a man. 28

The night in prison was novel and interesting enough. The prisoners in their shirt-sleeves were enjoying a chat and the evening air in the door-way, when I entered. But the jailer said, "Come, boys, it is time to lock up;" and so they dispersed, and I heard the sound of their steps returning into the hollow apartments. My roommate was introduced to me by the jailer, as "a first-rate fellow and a clever man." When the door was locked, he showed me where to hang my hat, and how he managed matters there. The rooms were white-washed once a month; and this one, at least, was the whitest, most simply furnished, and probably the neatest apartment in the town. He naturally wanted to know where I came from, and what brought me there; and, when I had told him, I asked him in my turn how he came there, presuming him to be an honest man, of course; and, as the world goes, I believe he was. "Why," said he, "they accuse me of burning a barn; but I never did it." As near as I could discover, he had probably gone to bed in a barn when drunk, and smoked his pipe there; and so a barn was burnt. He had the reputation of being a clever man, had been there some three months waiting for his trial to come on, and would have to wait as much longer; but he was quite domesticated and contented, since he got his board for nothing, and thought that he was well treated. 29

He occupied one window, and I the other; and I saw, that, if one stayed there long, his principal business would be to look out the window. I had soon read all the tracts that were left there, and examined where former prisoners had broken out, and where a grate had been sawed off, and heard the history 30 of the various occupants of that room; for I found that even here there was a history and a gossip which never circulated beyond the walls of the jail. Probably this is the only house in the town where verses are composed, which are afterward printed in a circular form, but not published. I was shown quite a long list of verses which were composed by some young men who had been detected in a attempt to escape, who avenged themselves by singing them.

I pumped my fellow-prisoner as dry as I could, for fear I should never see   31
him again; but at length he showed me which was my bed, and left me to blow out the lamp.

It was like travelling into a far country, such as I had never expected to   32
behold, to lie there for one night. It seemed to me that I never had heard the town-clock strike before, nor the evening sounds of the village; for we slept with the windows open, which were inside the grating. It was to see my native village in the light of the middle ages, and our Concord was turned into a Rhine stream, and visions of knights and castles passed before me. They were the voices of old burghers that I heard in the streets. I was an involuntary spectator and auditor of whatever was done and said in the kitchen of the adjacent village-inn,—a wholly new and rare experience to me. It was a closer view of my native town. I was fairly inside of it. I never had seen its institutions before. This is one of its peculiar institutions; for it is a shire town. I began to comprehend what its inhabitants were about.

In the morning, our breakfasts were put through the hole in the door, in   33
small oblong-square tin pans, made to fit, and holding a pint of chocolate, with brown bread, and an iron spoon. When they called for the vessels again, I was green enough to return what bread I had left; but my comrade seized it, and said that I should lay that up for lunch or dinner. Soon after, he was let out to work at haying in a neighboring field, whither he went every day, and would not be back till noon; so he bade me good-day, saying that he doubted if he should see me again.

When I came out of prison,—for some one interfered, and paid the tax,—   34
I did not perceive that great changes had taken place on the common, such as he observed who went in a youth, and emerged a tottering and grayheaded man; and yet a change had to my eyes come over the scene,—the town, and State, and country,—greater than any that mere time could effect. I saw yet more distinctly the State in which I lived. I saw to what extent the people among whom I lived could be trusted as good neighbors and friends; that their friendship was for summer weather only; that they did not greatly purpose to do right; that they were a distinct race from me by their prejudices and superstitions, as the Chinamen and Malays are; that, in their sacrifices to humanity, they ran no risks, not even to their property; that, after all, they were not so noble but they treated the thief as he had treated them, and hoped, by a certain outward observance and a few prayers, and by walking in a particular straight though useless path from time to time, to save their souls. This may be to judge my neighbors harshly; for I believe that most of them are not aware that they have such an institution as the jail in their village.

It was formerly the custom in our village, when a poor debtor came out   35
of jail, for his acquaintances to salute him, looking through their fingers, which were crossed to represent the grating of a jail window, "How do ye do?" My neighbors did not thus salute me, but first looked at me, and then at one another, as if I had returned from a long journey. I was put into jail as I was going

to the shoemaker's to get a shoe which was mended. When I was let out the next morning, I proceeded to finish my errand, and having put on my mended shoe, joined a huckleberry party, who were impatient to put themselves under my conduct; and in half an hour,—for the horse was soon tackled,—was in the midst of a huckleberry field, on one of our highest hills, two miles off; and then the State was nowhere to be seen.

This is the whole history of "My Prisons."   36

I have never declined paying the highway tax, because I am as desirous of   37 being a good neighbor as I am of being a bad subject; and, as for supporting schools, I am doing my part to educate my fellow-countrymen now. It is for no particular item in the tax-bill that I refuse to pay it. I simply wish to refuse allegiance to the State, to withdraw and stand aloof from it effectually. I do not care to trace the course of my dollar, if I could, till it buys a man, or a musket to shoot one with,—the dollar is innocent,—but I am concerned to trace the effects of my allegiance. In fact, I quietly declare war with the State, after my fashion, though I will still make what use and get what advantage of her I can, as is usual in such cases.

If others pay the tax which is demanded of me, from a sympathy with the   38 State, they do but what they have already done in their own case, or rather they abet injustice to a greater extent than the State requires. If they pay the tax from a mistaken interest in the individual taxed, to save his property or prevent his going to jail, it is because they have not considered wisely how far they let their private feelings interfere with the public good.

This, then, is my position at present. But one cannot be too much on his   39 guard in such a case, lest his action be biassed by obstinacy, or an undue regard for the opinions of men. Let him see that he does only what belongs to himself and to the hour.

I think sometimes, Why, this people mean well; they are only ignorant;   40 they would do better if they knew how: why give your neighbors this pain to treat you as they are not inclined to? But I think, again, this is no reason why I should do as they do, or permit others to suffer much greater pain of a different kind. Again, I sometimes say to myself, When many millions of men, without heat, without ill-will, without personal feeling of any kind, demand of you a few shillings only, without the possibility, such is their constitution, of retracting or altering their present demand, and without the possibility, on your side, of appeal to any other millions, why expose yourself to this over-whelming brute force? You do not resist cold and hunger, the winds and the waves, thus obstinately; you quietly submit to a thousand similar necessities. You do not put your head into the fire. But just in proportion as I regard this as not wholly a brute force, but partly a human force, and consider that I have relations to those millions as to so many millions of men, and not of mere brute or inanimate things, I see that appeal is possible, first and instantaneously, from them to the Maker of them, and, secondly, from them to themselves. But, if I put my head deliberately into the fire, there is no appeal to fire or to the Maker of fire, and I have only myself to blame. If I could convince myself that I have any right to be satisfied with men as they are, and to treat them accordingly, and not according, in some respects, to my requisitions and expectations of what they and I ought to be, then, like a good Mussulman and fatalist, I should endeavor to be satisfied with things as they are, and say it is the will of God. And, above all, there is this difference between resisting this and a purely brute or natural force, that I can resist this with some effect, but I cannot expect, like Orpheus, to change the nature of the rocks and trees and beasts.

I do not wish to quarrel with any man or nation. I do not wish to split   41
hairs, to make fine distinctions, or set myself up as better than my neighbors. I seek rather, I may say, even an excuse for conforming to the laws of the land. I am but too ready to conform to them. Indeed I have reason to suspect myself on this head; and each year, as the tax-gatherer comes round, I find myself disposed to review the acts and position of the general and state governments, and the spirit of the people, to discover a pretext for conformity. I believe that the State will soon be able to take all my work of this sort out of my hands, and then I shall be no better a patriot than my fellow-countrymen. Seen from a lower point of view, the Constitution, with all its faults, is very good; the law and the courts are very respectable; even this State and this American government are, in many respects, very admirable and rare things, to be thankful for, such as a great many have described them; but seen from a point of view a little higher, they are what I have described them; seen from a higher still, and the highest, who shall say what they are, or that they are worth looking at or thinking of at all?

However, the government does not concern me much, and I shall bestow   42
the fewest possible thoughts on it. It is not many moments that I live under a government, even in this world. If a man is thought-free, fancy-free, imagination-free, that which is *not* never for a long time appearing *to be* to him, unwise rulers or reformers cannot fatally interrupt him.

I know that most men think differently from myself; but those whose lives   43
are by profession devoted to the study of these or kindred subjects, content me as little as any. Statesmen and legislators, standing so completely within the institution, never distinctly and nakedly behold it. They speak of moving society; but have no resting-place without it. They may be men of a certain experience and discrimination, and have no doubt invented ingenious and even useful systems, for which we sincerely thank them; but all their wit and usefulness lie within certain not very wide limits. They are wont to forget that the world is not governed by policy and expediency. Webster never goes behind government, and so cannot speak with authority about it. His words are wisdom to those legislators who contemplate no essential reform in the existing government; but for thinkers, and those who legislate for all time, he never once glances at the subject. I know of those whose serene and wise speculations on this theme would soon reveal the limits of his mind's range and hospitality. Yet, compared with the cheap professions of most reformers, and the still cheaper wisdom and eloquence of politicians in general, his are almost the only sensible and valuable words, and we thank Heaven for him.

Comparatively, he is always strong, original, and, above all, practical. Still his quality is not wisdom, but prudence. The lawyer's truth is not Truth, but consistency, or a consistent expediency. Truth is always in harmony with herself, and is not concerned chiefly to reveal the justice that may consist with wrong-doing. He well deserves to be called, as he has been called, the Defender of the Constitution. There are really no blows to be given by him but defensive ones. He is not a leader, but a follower. His leaders are the men of '87. "I have never made an effort," he says, "and never propose to make an effort; I have never countenanced an effort, and never mean to countenance an effort, to disturb the arrangement as originally made, by which the various States came into the Union." Still thinking of the sanction which the Constitution gives to slavery, he says, "Because it was a part of the original compact,—let it stand." Notwithstanding his special acuteness and ability, he is unable to take a fact out of its merely political relations, and behold it as it lies absolutely to be disposed of by the intellect,—what, for instance, it behoves a man to do here in America to-day with regard to slavery,—but ventures, or is driven, to make some such desperate answer as the following, while professing to speak absolutely, and as a private man,—from which what new and singular code of social duties might be inferred?—"The manner," says he, "in which the governments of those States where slavery exists are to regulate it, is for their own consideration, under their responsibility to their constituents, to the general laws of propriety, humanity, and justice, and to God. Associations formed elsewhere, springing from a feeling of humanity, or any other cause, have nothing whatever to do with it. They have never received any encouragement from me, and they never will."

They who know of no purer sources of truth, who have traced up its stream   44
no higher, stand, and wisely stand, by the Bible and the Constitution, and drink at it there with reverence and humility; but they who behold where it comes trickling into this lake or that pool, gird up their loins once more, and continue their pilgrimage toward its fountain-head.

No man with a genius for legislation has appeared in America. They are   45
rare in the history of the world. There are orators, politicians, and eloquent men, by the thousand; but the speaker has not yet opened his mouth to speak, who is capable of settling the much-vexed questions of the day. We love eloquence for its own sake, and not for any truth which it may utter, or any heroism it may inspire. Our legislators have not yet learned the comparative value of free-trade and of freedom, of union, and of rectitude, to a nation. They have no genius or talent for comparatively humble questions of taxation and finance, commerce and manufactures and agriculture. If we were left solely to the wordy wit of legislators in Congress for our guidance, uncorrected by the seasonable experience and the effectual complaints of the people, America would not long retain her rank among the nations. For eighteen hundred years, though perchance I have no right to say it, the New Testament has been written, yet where is the legislator who has wisdom and practical talent enough to avail himself of the light which it sheds on the science of legislation?

The authority of government, even such as I am willing to submit to,—for ⁴⁶ I will cheerfully obey those who know and can do better than I, and in many things even those who neither know nor can do so well,—is still an impure one: to be strictly just, it must have the sanction and consent of the governed. It can have no pure right over my person and property but what I concede to it. The progress from an absolute to a limited monarchy, from a limited monarchy to a democracy, is a progress toward a true respect for the individual. Is a democracy, such as we know it, the last improvement possible in government? Is it not possible to take a step further towards recognizing and organizing the rights of man? There will never be a really free and enlightened State, until the State comes to recognize the individual as a higher and independent power, from which all its own power and authority are derived, and treats him accordingly. I please myself with imagining a State at last which can afford to be just to all men, and to treat the individual with respect as a neighbor; which even would not think it inconsistent with its own repose, if a few were to live aloof from it, not meddling with it, nor embraced by it, who fulfilled all the duties of neighbors and fellow-men. A State which bore this kind of fruit, and suffered it to drop off as fast as it ripened, would prepare the way for a still more perfect and glorious State, which also I have imagined, but not yet anywhere seen.

QUESTIONS FOR MEANING

1. What is the only obligation that Thoreau recognizes?
2. What is Thoreau's opinion of the average man and woman?
3. Why is Thoreau unwilling to vote?
4. Under what circumstances did Thoreau believe that it was right to break the law? How can prison be "the true place for a just man"? Why was Thoreau imprisoned?
5. What does Thoreau mean when he declares, "the more money, the less virtue"? Why was he critical of the rich?
6. Would Thoreau approve of Social Security?
7. What type of government would please Thoreau?
8. Vocabulary: endeavoring (2), expediency (4), redressing (9), gregariousness (13), eradication (14), discretion (18), impetuous (22), exorbitant (24), snivel (28), fatalist (40), sanction (43).

QUESTIONS ABOUT STRATEGY

1. Consider the opening of paragraph 3. What advantage is there for Thoreau to declare that he intends to speak "practically and as a citizen"? Where else does he try to put himself in a favorable light? Does he ever put himself in a bad light?
2. Where does Thoreau first reveal his concern about slavery? Should he have said more about this issue?

3. Why do you think Thoreau chose to "quarrel not with far-off foes, but with those who, near at home, co-operate with, and do the bidding of those far away"?
4. Could Thoreau's argument be used for selfish purposes?
5. How does Thoreau respond to the argument that revolution often involves bloodshed? Where does he anticipate and respond to the argument that he enjoys the protection of the state he is unwilling to support?
6. What are the implications of the analogy Thoreau draws in paragraph 28 between the life of a man and the life of a plant?
7. What is the function of the eight-paragraph-long narration of Thoreau's one night in jail? What is it meant to illustrate? Does it reveal anything about Thoreau that he may not have intended to reveal?
8. This essay has been often reprinted as "Civil Disobedience." Which is the better title?

JOHN STUART MILL
Of the Liberty of Thought and Discussion

John Stuart Mill (1806–1873) was an economist, a philosopher, and a political reformer of remarkable intelligence. He began to study Greek when he was three years old, and Latin when he was seven. By the time he was twelve, he had mastered the best literature in both languages and moved on to study logic, mathematics, and political economy. Although Mill had one of the best minds in the nineteenth century, his rigorous education led to a nervous breakdown when he was twenty. He recovered his health only after he discovered the importance of poetry, music, and art—a process which he describes in his Auto- *biography (1873). His most important works include* A System of Logic *(1843),* The Principles of Political Economy *(1848),* Utilitarianism *(1863) and* On the Sub- *jection of Women (1869). The following essay is drawn from* On Liberty *(**1859**), a work that is widely recognized as one of the most carefully argued defenses of political and intellectual freedom ever written.*

The time, it is to be hoped, is gone by when any defense would be neces- 1
sary of the "liberty of the press" as one of the securities against corrupt or tyrannical government. No argument, we may suppose, can now be needed against permitting a legislature or an executive, not identified in interest with the people, to prescribe opinions to them and determine what doctrines or what arguments they shall be allowed to hear. This aspect of the question, besides, has been so often and so triumphantly enforced by preceding writers that it needs not be specially insisted on in this place. Though the law of England, on the subject of the press, is as servile to this day as it was in the

time of the Tudors, there is little danger of its being actually put in force against political discussion except during some temporary panic when fear of insurrection drives ministers and judges from their propriety,* and, speaking generally, it is not, in constitutional countries, to be apprehended that the government, whether completely responsible to the people or not, will often attempt to control the expression of opinion, except when in doing so it makes itself the organ of the general intolerance of the public. Let us suppose, therefore, that the government is entirely at one with the people, and never thinks of exerting any power of coercion unless in agreement with what it conceives to be their voice. But I deny the right of the people to exercise such coercion, either by themselves or by their government. The power itself is illegitimate. The best government has no more title to it than the worst. It is as noxious, or more noxious, when exerted in accordance with public opinion than when in opposition to it. If all mankind minus one were of one opinion, mankind would be no more justified in silencing that one person than he, if he had the power, would be justified in silencing mankind. Were an opinion a personal possession of no value except to the owner, if to be obstructed in the employment of it were simply a private injury, it would make some difference whether the injury was inflicted only on a few persons or on many. But the peculiar evil of silencing the expression of an opinion is that it is robbing the human race, posterity as well as the existing generation—those who dissent from the opinion, still more than those who hold it. If the opinion is right, they are deprived of the opportunity of exchanging error for truth; if wrong, they lose, what is almost as great a benefit, the clearer perception and livelier impression of truth produced by its collision with error.

It is necessary to consider separately these two hypotheses, each of which has a distinct branch of the argument corresponding to it. We can never be sure that the opinion we are endeavoring to stifle is a false opinion; and if we were sure, stifling it would be an evil still.

2

---

*These words had scarcely been written when, as if to give them an emphatic contradiction, occurred the Government Press Prosecutions of 1858. That ill-judged interference with the liberty of public discussion has not, however, induced me to alter a single word in the text, nor has it at all weakened my conviction that, moments of panic excepted, the era of pains and penalties for political discussion has, in our own country, passed away. For, in the first place, the prosecutions were not persisted in; and, in the second, they were never, properly speaking, political prosecutions. The offense charged was not that of criticizing institutions or the acts or persons of rulers, but of circulating what was deemed an immoral doctrine, the lawfulness of tyrannicide.

If the arguments of the present chapter are of any validity, there ought to exist the fullest liberty of professing and discussing, as a matter of ethical conviction, any doctrine, however immoral it may be considered. It would, therefore, be irrelevant and out of place to examine here whether the doctrine of tyrannicide deserves that title. I shall content myself with saying that the subject has been at all times one of the open questions of morals; that the act of a private citizen in striking down a criminal who, by raising himself above the law, has placed himself beyond the reach of legal punishment or control has been accounted by whole nations, and by some of the best and wisest of men, not a crime but an act of exalted virtue; and that, right or wrong, it is not of the nature of assassination, but of civil war. As such, I hold that the instigation to it, in a specific case, may be a proper subject of punishment, but only if an overt act has followed, and at least a probable connection can be established between the act and the instigation. Even then it is not a foreign government but the very government assailed which alone, in the exercise of self-defense, can legitimately punish attacks directed against its own existence. [Mill's note]

First, the opinion which it is attempted to suppress by authority may pos-   3
sibly be true. Those who desire to suppress it, of course, deny its truth; but
they are not infallible. They have no authority to decide the question for all
mankind and exclude every other person from the means of judging. To refuse a hearing to an opinion because they are sure that it is false is to assume
that *their* certainty is the same thing as *absolute* certainty. All silencing of
discussion is an assumption of infallibility. Its condemnation may be allowed
to rest on this common argument, not the worse for being common.

Unfortunately for the good sense of mankind, the fact of their fallibility is   4
far from carrying the weight in their practical judgment which is always allowed to it in theory; for while everyone well knows himself to be fallible,
few think it necessary to take any precautions against their own fallibility, or
admit the supposition that any opinion of which they feel very certain may
be one of the examples of the error to which they acknowledge themselves
to be liable. Absolute princes, or others who are accustomed to unlimited
deference, usually feel this complete confidence in their own opinions on
nearly all subjects. People more happily situated, who sometimes hear their
opinions disputed and are not wholly unused to be set right when they are
wrong, place the same unbounded reliance only on such of their opinions as
are shared by all who surround them, or to whom they habitually defer; for
in proportion to a man's want of confidence in his own solitary judgment
does he usually repose, with implicit trust, on the infallibility of "the world"
in general. And the world, to each individual, means the part of it with which
he comes in contact: his party, his sect, his church, his class of society; the
man may be called, by comparison, almost liberal and large-minded to whom
it means anything so comprehensive as his own country or his own age. Nor
is his faith in this collective authority at all shaken by his being aware that
other ages, countries, sects, churches, classes, and parties have thought, and
even now think, the exact reverse. He devolves upon his own world the responsibility of being in the right against the dissentient worlds of other people; and it never troubles him that mere accident has decided which of these
numerous worlds is the object of his reliance, and that the same causes which
make him a churchman in London would have made him a Buddhist or a
Confucian in Peking. Yet it is as evident in itself, as any amount of argument
can make it, that ages are no more infallible than individuals—every age having held many opinions which subsequent ages have deemed not only false
but absurd; and it is as certain that many opinions, now general, will be rejected by future ages, as it is that many, once general, are rejected by the
present.

The objection likely to be made to this argument would probably take   5
some such form as the following. There is no greater assumption of infallibility in forbidding the propagation of error than in any other thing which is
done by public authority on its own judgment and responsibility. Judgment
is given to men that they may use it. Because it may be used erroneously,
are men to be told that they ought not to use it at all? To prohibit what they
think pernicious is not claiming exemption from error, but fulfilling the duty

incumbent on them, although fallible, of acting on their conscientious conviction. If we were never to act on our opinions, because those opinions may be wrong, we should leave all our interests uncared for, and all our duties unperformed. An objection which applies to all conduct can be no valid objection to any conduct in particular. It is the duty of governments, and of individuals, to form the truest opinions they can; to form them carefully, and never impose them upon others unless they are quite sure of being right. But when they are sure (such reasoners may say), it is not conscientiousness but cowardice to shrink from acting on their opinions and allow doctrines which they honestly think dangerous to the welfare of mankind, either in this life or in another, to be scattered abroad without restraint, because other people, in less enlighted times, have persecuted opinions now believed to be true. Let us take care, it may be said, not to make the same mistake; but governments and nations have made mistakes in other things which are not denied to be fit subjects for the exercise of authority: they have laid on bad taxes, made unjust wars. Ought we therefore to lay on no taxes and, under whatever provocation, make no wars? Men and governments must act to the best of their ability. There is no such thing as absolute certainty, but there is assurance sufficient for the purposes of human life. We may, and must, assume our opinion to be true for the guidance of our own conduct; and it is assuming no more when we forbid bad men to pervert society by the propagation of opinions which we regard as false and pernicious.

I answer, that it is assuming very much more. There is the greatest difference between presuming an opinion to be true because, with every opportunity for contesting it, it has not been refuted, and assuming its truth for the purpose of not permitting its refutation. Complete liberty of contradicting and disproving our opinion is the very condition which justifies us in assuming its truth for purposes of action; and on no other terms can a being with human faculties have any rational assurance of being right. 6

When we consider either the history of opinion or the ordinary conduct of human life, to what is it to be ascribed that the one and the other are no worse than they are? Not certainly to the inherent force of the human understanding, for on any matter not self-evident there are ninety-nine persons totally incapable of judging of it for one who is capable; and the capacity of the hundredth person is only comparative, for the majority of the eminent men of every past generation held many opinions now known to be erroneous, and did or approved numerous things which no one will now justify. Why is it, then, that there is on the whole a preponderance among mankind of rational opinions and rational conduct? If there really is this preponderance—which there must be unless human affairs are, and have always been, in an almost desperate state—it is owing to a quality of the human mind, the source of everything respectable in man either as an intellectual or as a moral being, namely, that his errors are corrigible. He is capable of rectifying his mistakes by discussion and experience. Not by experience alone. There must be discussion to show how experience is to be interpreted. Wrong opinions and practices gradually yield to fact and argument; but facts and arguments, to produce any effect on the mind, must be brought before it. Very few facts 7 are able to tell their own story, without comments to bring out their meaning. The whole strength and value, then, of human judgment depending on the one property, that it can be set right when it is wrong, reliance can be placed on it only when the means of setting it right are kept constantly at hand. In the case of any person whose judgment is really deserving of confidence, how has it become so? Because he has kept his mind open to criticism of his opinions and conduct. Because it has been his practice to listen to all that could be said against him; to profit by as much of it as was just, and to expound to himself, and upon occasion to others, the fallacy of what was fallacious. Because he felt that the only way in which a human being can make some approach to knowing the whole of a subject is by hearing what can be said about it by persons of every variety of opinion, and studying all modes in which it can be looked at by every character of mind. No wise man ever acquired his wisdom in any mode but this; nor is it in the nature of human intellect to become wise in any other manner. The steady habit of correcting and completing his own opinion by collating it with those of others, so far from causing doubt and hesitation in carrying it into practice, is the only stable foundation for a just reliance on it; for, being cognizant of all that can, at least obviously, be said against him, and having taken up his position against all gainsayers—knowing that he has sought for objections and difficulties instead of avoiding them, and has shut out no light which can be thrown upon the subject from any quarter—he has a right to think his judgment better than that of any person, or any multitude, who have not gone through a similar process.

It is not too much to require that what the wisest of mankind, those who   8
are best entitled to trust their own judgment, find necessary to warrant their relying on it, should be submitted to by that miscellaneous collection of a few wise and many foolish individuals called the public. The most intolerant of churches, the Roman Catholic Church, even at the canonization of a saint admits, and listens patiently to, a "devil's advocate." The holiest of men, it appears, cannot be admitted to posthumous honors until all that the devil could say against him is known and weighed. If even the Newtonian philosophy were not permitted to be questioned, mankind could not feel as complete assurance of its truth as they now do. The beliefs which we have most warrant for have no safeguard to rest on but a standing invitation to the whole world to prove them unfounded. If the challenge is not accepted, or is accepted and the attempt fails, we are far enough from certainty still, but we have done the best that the existing state of human reason admits of: we have neglected nothing that could give the truth a chance of reaching us; if the lists are kept open, we may hope that, if there be a better truth, it will be found when the human mind is capable of receiving it; and in the meantime we may rely on having attained such approach to truth as is possible in our own day. This is the amount of certainty attainable by a fallible being, and this the sole way of attaining it.

Strange it is that men should admit the validity of the arguments for free   9
discussion, but object to their being "pushed to an extreme," not seeing that unless the reasons are good for an extreme case, they are not good for any

case. Strange that they should imagine that they are not assuming infallibility when they acknowledge that there should be free discussion on all subjects which can possibly be *doubtful,* but think that some particular principle or doctrine should be forbidden to be questioned because it is so *certain,* that is, because *they are certain* that it is certain. To call any proposition certain, while there is anyone who would deny its certainty if permitted, but who is not permitted, is to assume that we ourselves, and those who agree with us, are the judges of certainty, and judges without hearing the other side.

In the present age—which has been described as "destitute of faith, but   10
terrified at skepticism"—in which people feel sure, not so much that their opinions are true as that they should not know what to do without them— the claims of an opinion to be protected from public attack are rested not so much on its truth as on its importance to society. There are, it is alleged, certain beliefs so useful, not to say indispensable, to well-being that it is as much the duty of governments to uphold those beliefs as to protect any other of the interests of society. In a case of such necessity, and so directly in the line of their duty, something less than infallibility may, it is maintained, warrant, and even bind, governments to act on their own opinion confirmed by the general opinion of mankind. It is also often argued, and still oftener thought, that none but bad men would desire to weaken these salutary be- liefs; and there can be nothing wrong, it is thought, in restraining bad men and prohibiting what only such men would wish to practice. This mode of thinking makes the justification of restraints on discussion not a question of the truth of doctrines but of their usefulness, and flatters itself by that means to escape the responsibility of claiming to be an infallible judge of opinions. But those who thus satisfy themselves do not perceive that the assumption of infallibility is merely shifted from one point to another. The usefulness of an opinion is itself matter of opinion—as disputable, as open to discussion, and requiring discussion as much as the opinion itself. There is the same need of an infallible judge of opinions to decide an opinion to be noxious as to decide it to be false, unless the opinion condemned has full opportunity of defending itself. And it will not do to say that the heretic may be allowed to maintain the utility or harmlessness of his opinion, though forbidden to maintain its truth. The truth of an opinion is part of its utility. If we would know whether or not it is desirable that a proposition should be believed, is it possible to exclude the consideration of whether or not it is true? In the opinion, not of bad men, but of the best men, no belief which is contrary to truth can be really useful; and can you prevent such men from urging that plea when they are charged with culpability for denying some doctrine which they are told is useful, but which they believe to be false? Those who are on the side of received opinions never fail to take all possible advantage of this plea; you do not find *them* handling the question of ability as if it could be completely abstracted from that of truth; on the contrary, it is, above all, because their doctrine is "the truth" that the knowledge or the belief of it is held to be so indispensable. There can be no fair discussion of the question of usefulness when an argument so vital may be employed on one side, but

not on the other. And in point of fact, when law or public feeling do not permit the truth of an opinion to be disputed, they are just as little tolerant of a denial of its usefulness. The utmost they allow is an extenuation of its absolute necessity, or of the positive guilt of rejecting it.

In order more fully to illustrate the mischief of denying a hearing to opin- 11 ions because we, in our own judgment, have condemned them, it will be desirable to fix down the discussion to a concrete case; and I choose, by preference, the cases which are least favorable to me—in which the argument against freedom of opinion, both on the score of truth and on that of utility, is considered the strongest. Let the opinions impugned be the belief in a God and in a future state, or any of the commonly received doctrines of morality. To fight the battle on such ground gives a great advantage to an unfair antagonist, since he will be sure to say (and many who have no desire to be unfair will say it internally), Are these the doctrines which you do not deem sufficiently certain to be taken under the protection of law? Is the belief in a God one of the opinions to feel sure of which you hold to be assuming infallibility? But I must be permitted to observe that it is not the feeling sure of a doctrine (be it what it may) which I call an assumption of infallibility. It is the undertaking to decide that question *for others,* without allowing them to hear what can be said on the contrary side. And I denounce and reprobate this pretension not the less if put forth on the side of my most solemn convictions. However positive anyone's persuasion may be, not only of the falsity but of the pernicious consequences—not only of the pernicious consequences, but (to adopt expressions which I altogether condemn) the immorality and impiety of an opinion—yet if, in pursuance of that private judgment, though backed by the public judgment of his country or his contemporaries, he prevents the opinion from being heard in its defense, he assumes infallibility. And so far from the assumption being less objectionable or less dangerous because the opinion is called immoral or impious, this is the case of all others in which it is most fatal. These are exactly the occasions on which the men of one generation commit those dreadful mistakes which excite the astonishment and horror of posterity. It is among such that we find the instances memorable in history, when the arm of the law has been employed to root out the best men and the noblest doctrines; with deplorable success as to the men, though some of the doctrines have survived to be (as if in mockery) invoked in defense of similar conduct toward those who dissent from *them,* or from their received interpretation.

Mankind can hardly be too often reminded that there was once a man 12 called Socrates, between whom and the legal authorities and public opinion of his time there took place a memorable collision. Born in an age and country abounding in individual greatness, this man has been handed down to us by those who best knew both him and the age as the most virtuous man in it; while *we* know him as the head and prototype of all subsequent teachers of virtue, the source equally of the lofty inspiration of Plato and the judicious utilitarianism of Aristotle, *"i maestri di color che sanno,"* the two headsprings of ethical as of all other philosophy. This acknowledged master of all the eminent thinkers who have since lived—whose fame, still growing after more than two thousand years, all but outweighs the whole remainder of the names which make his native city illustrious—was put to death by his countrymen, after a judicial conviction, for impiety and immorality. Impiety, in denying the gods recognized by the State; indeed, his accuser asserted (see the *Apologia*) that he believed in no gods at all. Immorality, in being, by his doctrines and instructions, a "corruptor of youth." Of these charges the tribunal, there is every ground for believing, honestly found him guilty, and condemned the man who probably of all then born had deserved best of mankind to be put to death as a criminal.

To pass from this to the only other instance of judicial iniquity, the mention of which, after the condemnation of Socrates, would not be an anticlimax: the event which took place on Calvary rather more than eighteen hundred years ago. The man who left on the memory of those who witnessed his life and conversation such an impression of his moral grandeur that eighteen subsequent centuries have done homage to him as the Almighty in person, was ignominiously put to death, as what? As a blasphemer. Men did not merely mistake their benefactor, they mistook him for the exact contrary of what he was and treated him as that prodigy of impiety which they themselves are now held to be for their treatment of him. The feelings with which mankind now regard these lamentable transactions, especially the later of the two, render them extremely unjust in their judgment of the unhappy actors. These were, to all appearance, not bad men—not worse than men commonly are, but rather the contrary; men who possessed in a full, or somewhat more than a full measure, the religious, moral, and patriotic feelings of their time and people: the very kind of men who, in all times, our own included, have every chance of passing through life blameless and respected. The high priest who rent his garments when the words were pronounced, which, according to all the ideas of his country, constituted the blackest guilt, was in all probability quite as sincere in his horror and indignation as the generality of respectable and pious men now are in the religious and moral sentiments they profess; and most of those who now shudder at his conduct, if they had lived in his time, and been born Jews, would have acted precisely as he did. Orthodox Christians who are tempted to think that those who stoned to death the first martyrs must have been worse men than they themselves are ought to remember that one of those persecutors was Saint Paul. . . .

Let us now pass to the second division of the argument, and dismissing   14
the supposition that any of the received opinions may be false, let us assume them to be true and examine into the worth of the manner in which they are likely to be held when their truth is not freely and openly canvassed. However unwillingly a person who has a strong opinion may admit the possibility that his opinion may be false, he ought to be moved by the consideration that, however true it may be, if it is not fully, frequently, and fearlessly discussed, it will be held as a dead dogma, not a living truth. . . .

To what an extent doctrines intrinsically fitted to make the deepest   15
impression upon the mind may remain in it as dead beliefs, without being

ever realized in the imagination, the feelings, or the understanding, is exemplified by the manner in which the majority of believers hold the doctrines of Christianity. By Christianity, I here mean what is accounted such by all churches and sects—the maxims and precepts contained in the New Testament. These are considered sacred, and accepted as laws, by all professing Christians. Yet it is scarcely too much to say that not one Christian in a thousand guides or tests his individual conduct by reference to those laws. The standard to which he does refer it is the custom of his nation, his class, or his religious profession. He has thus, on the one hand, a collection of ethical maxims which he believes to have been vouchsafed to him by infallible wisdom as rules for his government; and, on the other, a set of everyday judgments and practices which go a certain length with some of those maxims, not so great a length with others, stand in direct opposition to some, and are, on the whole, a compromise between the Christian creed and the interests and suggestions of worldly life. To the first of these standards he gives his homage; to the other his real allegiance. All Christians believe that the blessed are the poor and humble, and those who are ill-used by the world; that it is easier for a camel to pass through the eye of a needle than for a rich man to enter the kingdom of heaven; that they should judge not, lest they be judged; that they should swear not at all; that they should love their neighbor as themselves; that if one take their cloak, they should give him their coat also; that they should take no thought for the morrow; that if they would be perfect they should sell all that they have and give it to the poor. They are not insincere when they say that they believe these things. They do believe them, as people believe what they have always heard lauded and never discussed. But in the sense of that living belief which regulates conduct, they believe these doctrines just up to the point to which it is usual to act upon them. The doctrines in their integrity are serviceable to pelt adversaries with; and it is understood that they are to be put forward (when possible) as the reasons for whatever people do that they think laudable. But anyone who reminded them that the maxims require an infinity of things which they never even think of doing would gain nothing but to be classed among those very unpopular characters who affect to be better than other people. The doctrines have no hold on ordinary believers—are not a power in their minds. They have an habitual respect for the sound of them, but no feeling which spreads from the words to the things signified and forces the mind to take *them* in and make them conform to the formula. Whenever conduct is concerned, they look round for Mr. A and B to direct them how far to go in obeying Christ.

Now we may be well assured that the case was not thus, but far otherwise, 16 with the early Christians. Had it been thus, Christianity never would have expanded from an obscure sect of the despised Hebrews into the religion of the Roman empire. When their enemies said, "See how these Christians love one another" (a remark not likely to be made by anybody now), they assuredly had a much livelier feeling of the meaning of their creed than they have ever had since. And to this cause, probably, it is chiefly owing that

Christianity now makes so little progress in extending its domain, and after eighteen centuries is still nearly confined to Europeans and the descendants of Europeans. Even with the strictly religious, who are much in earnest about their doctrines and attach a greater amount of meaning to many of them than people in general, it commonly happens that the part which is thus comparatively active in their minds is that which was made by Calvin, or Knox, or some such person much nearer in character to themselves. The sayings of Christ coexist passively in their minds, producing hardly any effect beyond what is caused by mere listening to words so amiable and bland. There are many reasons, doubtless, why doctrines which are the badge of a sect retain more of their vitality than those common to all recognized sects, and why more pains are taken by teachers to keep their meaning alive; but one reason certainly is that the peculiar doctrines are more questioned and have to be oftener defended against open gainsayers. Both teachers and learners go to sleep at their post as soon as there is no enemy in the field.

The same thing holds true, generally speaking, of all traditional doc-   17
trines—those of prudence and knowledge of life as well as of morals or religion. All languages and literatures are full of general observations on life, both as to what it is and how to conduct oneself in it—observations which everybody knows, which everybody repeats or hears with acquiescence, which are received as truisms, yet of which most people first truly learn the meaning when experience, generally of a painful kind, has made it a reality to them. How often, when smarting under some unforeseen misfortune or disappointment, does a person call to mind some proverb or common saying, familiar to him all his life, the meaning of which, if he had ever before felt it as he does now, would have saved him from the calamity. There are indeed reasons for this, other than the absence of discussion; there are many truths of which the full meaning *cannot* be realized until personal experience has brought it home. But much more of the meaning even of these would have been understood, and what was understood would have been far more deeply impressed on the mind, if the man had been accustomed to hear it argued *pro* and *con* by people who did understand it. The fatal tendency of mankind to leave off thinking about a thing when it is no longer doubtful is the cause of half their errors. A contemporary author has well spoken of "the deep slumber of a decided opinion."

But what! (it may be asked), Is the absence of unanimity an indispensable   18
condition of true knowledge? Is it necessary that some part of mankind should persist in error to enable any to realize the truth? Does a belief cease to be real and vital as soon as it is generally received—and is a proposition never thoroughly understood and felt unless some doubt of it remains? As soon as mankind have unanimously accepted a truth, does the truth persist within them? The highest aim and best result of improved intelligence, it has hitherto been thought, is to unite mankind more and more in the acknowledgment of all important truths; and does the intelligence only last as long as it has not achieved its object? Do the fruits of conquest perish by the very completeness of the victory?

I affirm no such thing. As mankind improve, the number of doctrines which   19
are no longer disputed or doubted will be constantly on the increase; and the
well-being of mankind may almost be measured by the number and gravity
of the truths which have reached the point of being uncontested. The cessation, on one question after another, of serious controversy is one of the
necessary incidents of the consolidation of opinion—a consolidation as salutary in the case of true opinions as it is dangerous and noxious when the
opinions are erroneous. But though this gradual narrowing of the bounds of
diversity of opinion is necessary in both senses of the term, being at once
inevitable and indispensable, we are not therefore obliged to conclude that
all its consequences must be beneficial. The loss of so important an aid to
the intelligent and living apprehension of a truth as is afforded by the necessity of explaining it to, or defending it against, opponents, though not sufficient to outweigh, is no trifling drawback from the benefit of its universal
recognition. Where this advantage can no longer be had, I confess I should
like to see the teachers of mankind endeavoring to provide a substitute for
it—some contrivance for making the difficulties of the question as present to
the learner's consciousness as if they were pressed upon him by a dissentient
champion, eager for his conversion.

But instead of seeking contrivances for this purpose, they have lost those   20
they formerly had. The Socratic dialectics, so magnificently exemplified in
the dialogues of Plato, were a contrivance of this description. They were
essentially a negative discussion of the great questions of philosophy and life,
directed with consummate skill to the purpose of convincing anyone who had
merely adopted the commonplaces of received opinion that he did not understand the subject—that he as yet attached no definite meaning to the
doctrines he professed; in order that, becoming aware of his ignorance, he
might be put in the way to obtain a stable belief, resting on a clear apprehension both of the meaning of doctrines and of their evidence. The school
disputations of the Middle Ages had a somewhat similar object. They were
intended to make sure that the pupil understood his own opinion, and (by
necessary correlation) the opinion opposed to it, and could enforce the grounds
of the one and confute those of the other. These last-mentioned contests had
indeed the incurable defect that the premises appealed to were taken from
authority, not from reason; and, as a discipline to the mind, they were in
every respect inferior to the powerful dialectics which formed the intellects
of the *"Socratici viri";* but the modern mind owes far more to both than it
is generally willing to admit, and the present modes of education contain
nothing which in the smallest degree supplies the place either of the one or
of the other. A person who derives all his instruction from teachers or books,
even if he escape the besetting temptation of contenting himself with cram,
is under no compulsion to hear both sides; accordingly it is far from a frequent accomplishment, even among thinkers, to know both sides; and the
weakest part of what everybody says in defense of his opinion is what he
intends as a reply to antagonists. It is the fashion of the present time to
disparage negative logic—that which points out weaknesses in theory or er-

rors in practice without establishing positive truths. Such negative criticism would indeed be poor enough as an ultimate result, but as a means to attaining any positive knowledge or conviction worthy the name it cannot be valued too highly; and until people are again systematically trained to it, there will be few great thinkers and a low general average of intellect in any but the mathematical and physical departments of speculation. On any other subject no one's opinions deserve the name of knowledge, except so far as he has either had forced upon him by others or gone through of himself the same mental process which would have been required of him in carrying on an active controversy with opponents. That, therefore, which, when absent, it is so indispensable, but so difficult, to create, how worse than absurd it is to forego when spontaneously offering itself! If there are any persons who contest a received opinion, or who will do so if law or opinion will let them, let us thank them for it, open our minds to listen to them, and rejoice that there is someone to do for us what we otherwise ought, if we have any regard for either the certainty or the vitality of our convictions, to do with much greater labor for ourselves.

It still remains to speak of one of the principal causes which make diversity of opinion advantageous, and will continue to do so until mankind shall have entered a stage of intellectual advancement which at present seems at an incalculable distance. We have hitherto considered only two possibilities: that the received opinion may be false, and some other opinion, consequently, true; or that, the received opinion being true, a conflict with the opposite error is essential to a clear apprehension and deep feeling of its truth. But there is a commoner case than either of these: when the conflicting doctrines, instead of being one true and the other false, share the truth between them, and the nonconforming opinion is needed to supply the remainder of the truth of which the received doctrine embodies only a part. Popular opinions, on subjects not palpable to sense, are often true, but seldom or never the whole truth. They are a part of the truth, sometimes a greater, sometimes a smaller part, but exaggerated, distorted, and disjointed from the truths by which they ought to be accompanied and limited. Heretical opinions, on the other hand, are generally some of these suppressed and neglected truths, bursting the bonds which kept them down, and either seeking reconciliation with the truth contained in the common opinion, or fronting it as enemies, and setting themselves up, with similar exclusiveness, as the whole truth. The latter case is hitherto the most frequent, as, in the human mind, one-sidedness has always been the rule, and many-sidedness the exception. Hence, even in revolutions of opinion, one part of the truth usually sets while another rises. Even progress, which ought to superadd, for the most part only substitutes one partial and incomplete truth for another; improvement consisting chiefly in this, that the new fragment of truth is more wanted, more adapted to the needs of the time than that which it displaces. Such being the partial character of prevailing opinions, even when resting on a true foundation, every opinion which embodies somewhat of the portion of truth which the common opinion omits ought to be considered precious, with whatever amount of error and confusion that truth may be blended. No sober judge of human affairs will feel bound to be indignant because those who force on our notice truths which we should otherwise have overlooked, overlook some of those which we see. Rather, he will think that so long as popular truth is one-sided, it is more desirable than otherwise that unpopular truth should have one-sided assertors, too, such being usually the most energetic and the most likely to compel reluctant attention to the fragment of wisdom which they proclaim as if it were the whole.

Thus, in the eighteenth century, when nearly all the instructed, and all 22 those of the uninstructed who were led by them, were lost in admiration of what is called civilization, and of the marvels of modern science, literature, and philosophy, and while greatly overrating the amount of unlikeness between the men of modern and those of ancient times, indulged the belief that the whole of the difference was in their own favor: with what a salutary shock did the paradoxes of Rousseau explode like bombshells in the midst, dislocating the compact mass of one-sided opinion and forcing its elements to recombine in a better form and with additional ingredients. Not that the current opinions were on the whole farther from the truth than Rousseau's were; on the contrary, they were nearer to it; they contained more of positive truth, and very much less of error. Nevertheless there lay in Rousseau's doctrine, and has floated down the stream of opinion along with it, a considerable amount of exactly those truths which the popular opinion wanted; and these are the deposit which was left behind them when the flood subsided. The superior worth of simplicity of life, the enervating and demoralizing effect of the trammels and hypocrisies of artificial society are ideas which have never been entirely absent from cultivated minds since Rousseau wrote; and they will in time produce their due effect, though at present needing to be asserted as much as ever, and to be asserted by deeds; for words, on this subject, have nearly exhausted their power.

In politics, again, it is almost a commonplace that a party of order or sta- 23 bility and a party of progress or reform are both necessary elements of a healthy state of political life, until the one or the other shall have so enlarged its mental grasp as to be a party equally of order and of progress, knowing and distinguishing what is fit to be preserved from what ought to be swept away. Each of these modes of thinking derives its utility from the deficiencies of the other; but it is in a great measure the opposition of the other that keeps each within the limits of reason and sanity. Unless opinions favorable to democracy and to aristocracy, to property and to equality, to cooperation and to competition, to luxury and to abstinence, to sociality and individuality, to liberty and discipline, and all the other standing antagonisms of practical life, are expressed with equal freedom and enforced and defended with equal talent and energy, there is no chance of both elements obtaining their due; one scale is sure to go up, and the other down. Truth, in the great practical concerns of life, is so much a question of the reconciling and combining of opposites that very few have minds sufficiently capacious and impartial to make the adjustment with an approach to correctness, and it has to be made by the tough process of a struggle between combatants fighting under hostile banners. On any of the great open questions just enumerated, if either of the two opinions has a better claim than the other, not merely to be tolerated, but to be encouraged and countenanced, it is the one which happens at the particular time and place to be in a minority. That is the opinion which, for the time being, represents the neglected interests, the side of human well-being which is in danger of obtaining less than its share. I am aware that there is not, in this country, any intolerance of differences of opinion on most of these topics. They are adduced to show, by admitted and multiplied examples, the universality of the fact that only through diversity of opinion is there, in the existing state of human intellect, a chance of fair play to all sides of the truth. When there are persons to be found who form an exception to the apparent unanimity of the world on any subject, even if the world is in the right, it is always probable that dissentients have something worth hearing to say for themselves, and that truth would lose something by their silence. . . .

I do not pretend that the most unlimited use of the freedom of enunciat- 24 ing all possible opinions would put an end to the evils of religious or philosophical sectarianism. Every truth which men of narrow capacity are in earnest about is sure to be asserted, inculcated, and in many ways even acted on, as if no other truth existed in the world, or at all events none that could limit or qualify the first. I acknowledge that the tendency of all opinions to become sectarian is not cured by the freest discussion, but is often heightened and exacerbated thereby; the truth which ought to have been, but was not, seen, being rejected all the more violently because proclaimed by persons regarded as opponents. But it is not on the impassioned partisan, it is on the calmer and more disinterested bystander, that this collision of opinions works its salutary effect. Not the violent conflict between parts of the truth, but the quiet suppression of half of it, is the formidable evil; there is always hope when people are forced to listen to both sides: it is when they attend only to one that errors harden into prejudices, and truth itself ceases to have the effect of truth by being exaggerated into falsehood. And since there are few mental attributes more rare than that judicial faculty which can sit in intelligent judgment between two sides of a question, of which only one is represented by an advocate before it, truth has no chance but in proportion as every side of it, every opinion which embodies any fraction of the truth, not only finds advocates, but is so advocated as to be listened to.

We have now recognized the necessity to the mental well-being of man- 25 kind (on which all their other well-being depends) of freedom of opinion, and freedom of the expression of opinion, on four distinct grounds, which we will now briefly recapitulate:

First, if any opinion is compelled to silence, that opinion may, for aught 26 we can certainly know, be true. To deny this is to assume our own infallibility.

Secondly, though the silenced opinion be an error, it may, and very com- 27 monly does, contain a portion of truth; and since the general or prevailing opinion on any subject is rarely or never the whole truth, it is only by the collision of adverse opinions that the remainder of the truth has any chance of being supplied.

Thirdly, even if the received opinion be not only true, but the whole truth; unless it is suffered to be, and actually is, vigorously and earnestly contested, it will, by most of those who receive it, be held in the manner of a prejudice, with little comprehension or feeling of its rational grounds. And not only this, but, fourthly, the meaning of the doctrine itself will be in danger of being lost or enfeebled, and deprived of its vital effect on the character and conduct: the dogma becoming a mere formal profession, inefficacious for good, but cumbering the ground and preventing the growth of any real and heartfelt conviction from reason or personal experience. 28

Before quitting the subject of freedom of opinion, it is fit to take some notice of those who say that the free expression of all opinions should be permitted on condition that the manner be temperate, and do not pass the bounds of fair discussion. Much might be said on the impossibility of fixing where these supposed bounds are to be placed; for if the test be offense to those whose opinions are attacked, I think experience testifies that this offense is given whenever the attack is telling and powerful, and that every opponent who pushes them hard, and whom they find it difficult to answer, appears to them, if he shows any strong feeling on the subject, an intemperate opponent. But this, though an important consideration in a practical point of view, merges in a more fundamental objection. Undoubtedly, the manner of asserting an opinion, even though it be a true one, may be very objectionable and may justly incur severe censure. But the principal offenses of the kind are such as it is mostly impossible, unless by accidental self-betrayal, to bring home to conviction. The gravest of them is, to argue sophistically, to suppress facts or arguments, to misstate the elements of the case, or misrepresent the opposite opinion. But all this, even to the most aggravated degree, is so continually done in perfect good faith by persons who are not considered, and in many other respects may not deserve to be considered, ignorant or incompetent, that it is rarely possible, on adequate grounds, conscientiously to stamp the misrepresentation as morally culpable, and still less could law presume to interfere with this kind of controversial misconduct. With regard to what is commonly meant by intemperate discussion, namely invective, sarcasm, personality, and the like, the denunciation of these weapons would deserve more sympathy if it were ever proposed to interdict them equally to both sides; but it is only desired to restrain the employment of them against the prevailing opinion; against the unprevailing they may not only be used without general disapproval, but will be likely to obtain for him who uses them the praise of honest zeal and righteous indignation. Yet whatever mischief arises from their use is greatest when they are employed against the comparatively defenseless; and whatever unfair advantage can be derived by any opinion from this mode of asserting it accrues almost exclusively to received opinions. The worst offense of this kind which can be committed by a polemic is to stigmatize those who hold the contrary opinion as bad and immoral men. To calumny of this sort, those who hold any unpopular opinion 29 are peculiarly exposed, because they are in general few and uninfluential, and nobody but themselves feels much interested in seeing justice done them; but this weapon is, from the nature of the case, denied to those who attack a prevailing opinion: they can neither use it with safety to themselves, nor, if they could, would it do anything but recoil on their own cause. In general, opinions contrary to those commonly received can only obtain a hearing by studied moderation of language and the most cautious avoidance of unnecessary offense, from which they hardly ever deviate even in a slight degree without losing ground, while unmeasured vituperation employed on the side of the prevailing opinion really does deter people from professing contrary opinions and from listening to those who profess them. For the interest, therefore, of truth and justice it is far more important to restrain this employment of vituperative language than the other; and, for example, if it were necessary to choose, there would be much more need to discourage offensive attacks on infidelity than on religion. It is, however, obvious that law and authority have no business with restraining either, while opinion ought, in every instance, to determine its verdict by the circumstances of the individual case—condemning everyone, on whichever side of the argument he places himself, in whose mode of advocacy either want of candor, or malignity, bigotry, or intolerance of feeling manifest themselves; but not inferring these vices from the side which a person takes, though it be the contrary side of the question to our own; and giving merited honor to everyone, whatever opinion he may hold, who has calmness to see and honesty to state what his opponents and their opinions really are, exaggerating nothing to their discredit, keeping nothing back which tells, or can be supposed to tell, in their favor. This is the real morality of public discussion; and if often violated, I am happy to think that there are many controversialists who to a great extent observe it, and a still greater number who conscientiously strive toward it.

QUESTIONS FOR MEANING

1. Why does Mill believe that controversy is important? Who is it that is most likely to benefit from public debate? Is anyone apt to be hurt?
2. How does Mill define "infallibility"? What help does he offer us in deciding whose judgment we can afford to trust?
3. Why does Mill describe the Catholic Church as the "most intolerant of Churches"? Do you know anything about English history that might help account for Mill's hostility to Catholicism?
4. How fair is Mill's appraisal of the average Christian? Does he himself believe in Christ? Why is he sympathetic to the people who were responsible for putting Christ to death?
5. What does Mill mean when he writes, "Both teachers and learners go to sleep at their post as soon as there is no enemy in the field"?
6. Do you know anything about the work of Rousseau cited in paragraph 22? If you've never heard of Rousseau, what could you infer about his work from Mill's references to it?

7. In addition to being a famous defense of freedom of thought and discussion, Mill's essay is also an argument about how men and women should argue. Define what he means by "the real morality of public discussion" in paragraph 29. According to Mill, what determines if an argument is "moral" or "immoral"?

8. How would John Stuart Mill feel about the classes you are taking this semester?

9. Would Mill tolerate the publication of pornography?

QUESTIONS ABOUT STRATEGY

1. Mill illustrates the danger of persecution by citing the examples of Socrates and Christ. Why does he discuss them in this order?

2. Mill tends to favor long ponderous paragraphs. What effect does his paragraphing have on your reading? Do you see any specific points at which a paragraph could be broken up?

3. What is the function of paragraph 5?

4. In paragraph 19 Mill writes, "The cessation, on one question after another, of serious controversy is one of the necessary incidents of the consolidation of opinion—a consolidation as salutary in the case of true opinions as it is dangerous and noxious when the opinions are erroneous." In making this concession, is Mill contradicting himself?

5. Why does Mill summarize his argument in paragraphs 25–28? And why does he alter the order in which he originally discussed his four basic points?

6. Judging from Mill's prose, what kind of man does he seem to have been? Specifically, to what extent does he sound like someone who tried to live according to the principles set forth in this argument?

MARK TWAIN
Fenimore Cooper's Literary Offenses

Mark Twain is the name Samuel Clemens (1835–1910) assumed in 1863 at the beginning of what would be a long, successful career as a writer. Once called "the Lincoln of our literature," he has remained one of the most widely read of major American writers—admired for his distinctive humor and also for the skill with which he used the written word to capture the varied forms of American dialect. His best known works include The Adventures of Tom Sawyer *(1876),* The Prince and the Pauper *(1877),* Life on the Mississippi *(1883),* A Connecticut Yankee in King Arthur's Court *(1889)—and* The Adventures of Huckleberry Finn *(1885), which is generally agreed to be his greatest work.*

In addition to his achievement as a writer of fiction, Twain is also valued for the penetrating social and literary criticism that can be found in his many essays. "Fenimore Cooper's Literary Offenses," written in **1895,** *is one of two essays Twain wrote to explain why he objected to James Fenimore Cooper (1789–1851)—an important American novelist whose reputation has never altogether recovered from Twain's charges. But you should try to read the following essay as an argument on how fiction should be written and not simply as an attack on Cooper.*

The Pathfinder *and* The Deerslayer *stand at the head of Cooper's novels as artistic creations. There are others of his works which contain parts as perfect as are to be found in these, and scenes even more thrilling. Not one can be compared with either of them as a finished whole.*

The defects in both of these tales are comparatively slight. They were pure works of art.—Prof. Lounsbury.

The five tales reveal an extraordinary fulness of invention.

. . . One of the very greatest characters in fiction, Natty Bumppo. . . .

The craft of the woodsman, the tricks of the trapper, all the delicate art of the forest, were familiar to Cooper from his youth up.—Prof. Brander Matthews.

Cooper is the greatest artist in the domain of romantic fiction yet produced by America.—Wilkie Collins.

It seems to me that it was far from right for the Professor of English   1
Literature in Yale, the Professor of English Literature in Columbia, and Wilkie Collins to deliver opinions on Cooper's literature without having read some of it. It would have been much more decorous to keep silent and let persons talk who have read Cooper.

Cooper's art has some defects. In one place in *Deerslayer,* and in the   2
restricted space of two-thirds of a page, Cooper has scored 114 offenses against literary art out of a possible 115. It breaks the record.

There are nineteen rules governing literary art in the domain of romantic   3
fiction—some say twenty-two. In *Deerslayer* Cooper violated eighteen of them. These eighteen require:

1. That a tale shall accomplish something and arrive somewhere. But the *Deerslayer* tale accomplishes nothing and arrives in the air.

2. They require that the episodes of a tale shall be necessary parts of the tale, and shall help to develop it. But as the *Deerslayer* tale is not a tale, and accomplishes nothing and arrives nowhere, the episodes have no rightful place in the work, since there was nothing for them to develop.

3. They require that the personages in a tale shall be alive, except in the cases of corpses, and that always the reader shall be able to tell the corpses from the others. But this detail has often been overlooked in the *Deerslayer* tale.

4. They require that the personages in a tale, both dead and alive, shall exhibit a sufficient excuse for being there. But this detail also has been overlooked in the *Deerslayer* tale.

5. They require that when the personages of a tale deal in conversation, the talk shall sound like human talk, and be talk such as human beings would be likely to talk in the given circumstances, and have a discoverable meaning, also a discoverable purpose, and a show of relevancy, and remain in the neighborhood of the subject in hand, and be interesting to the reader, and help out the tale, and stop when the people cannot think of anything more to say. But this requirement has been ignored from the beginning of the *Deerslayer* tale to the end of it.

6. They require that when the author describes the character of a personage in his tale, the conduct and conversation of that personage shall justify said description. But this law gets little or no attention in the *Deerslayer* tale, as Natty Bumppo's case will amply prove.

7. They require that when a personage talks like an illustrated, gilt-edged, tree-calf, hand-tooled, seven-dollar Friendship's Offering in the beginning of a paragraph, he shall not talk like a negro minstrel in the end of it. But this rule is flung down and danced upon in the *Deerslayer* tale.

8. They require that crass stupidities shall not be played upon the reader as "the craft of the woodsman, the delicate art of the forest," by either the author or the people in the tale. But this rule is persistently violated in the *Deerslayer* tale.

9. They require that the personages of a tale shall confine themselves to possibilities and let miracles alone; or, if they venture a miracle, the author must so plausibly set it forth as to make it look possible and reasonable. But these rules are not respected in the *Deerslayer* tale.

10. They require that the author shall make the reader feel a deep interest in the personages of his tale and in their fate; and that he shall make the reader love the good people in the tale and hate the bad ones. But the reader of the *Deerslayer* tale dislikes the good people in it, is indifferent to the others, and wishes they would all get drowned together.

11. They require that the characters in a tale shall be so clearly defined that the reader can tell beforehand what each will do in a given emergency. But in the *Deerslayer* tale this rule is vacated.

In addition to these large rules there are some little ones. These require that the author shall

12. *Say* what he is proposing to say, not merely come near it.
13. Use the right word, not its second cousin.
14. Eschew surplusage.
15. Not omit necessary details.
16. Avoid slovenliness of form.
17. Use good grammar.
18. Employ a simple and straightforward style.

Even these seven are coldly and persistently violated in the *Deerslayer* tale.

Cooper's gift in the way of invention was not a rich endowment; but such   4
as it was he liked to work it, he was pleased with the effects, and indeed he did some quite sweet things with it. In his little box of stage-properties he kept six or eight cunning devices, tricks, artifices for his savages and woodsmen to deceive and circumvent each other with, and he was never so happy as when he was working these innocent things and seeing them go. A favorite one was to make a moccasined person tread in the tracks of the moccasined enemy, and thus hide his own trail. Cooper wore out barrels and barrels of moccasins in working that trick. Another stage-property that he pulled out of his box pretty frequently was his broken twig. He prized his broken twig above all the rest of his effects, and worked it the hardest. It is a restful chapter in any book of his when somebody doesn't step on a dry twig and alarm all the reds and whites for two hundred yards around. Every time a Cooper person is in peril, and absolute silence is worth four dollars a minute, he is sure to step on a dry twig. There may be a hundred handier things to step on, but that wouldn't satisfy Cooper. Cooper requires him to turn out and find a dry twig; and if he can't do it, go and borrow one. In fact, the Leather Stocking Series ought to have been called the Broken Twig Series.

I am sorry there is not room to put in a few dozen instances of the delicate   5
art of the forest, as practiced by Natty Bumppo and some of the other Cooperian experts. Perhaps we may venture two or three samples. Cooper was a sailor—a naval officer; yet he gravely tells us how a vessel, driving toward a lee shore in a gale, is steered for a particular spot by her skipper because he knows of an *undertow* there which will hold her back against the gale and save her. For just pure woodcraft, or sailorcraft, or whatever it is, isn't that neat? For several years Cooper was daily in the society of artillery, and he ought to have noticed that when a cannon-ball strikes the ground it either buries itself or skips a hundred feet or so; skips again a hundred feet or so— and so on, till finally it gets tired and rolls. Now in one place he loses some "females"—as he always calls women—in the edge of a wood near a plain at night in a fog, on purpose to give Bumppo a chance to show off the delicate art of the forest before the reader. These mislaid people are hunting for a

fort. They hear a cannon-blast, and a cannon-ball presently comes rolling into the wood and stops at their feet. To the females this suggests nothing. The case is very different with the admirable Bumppo. I wish I may never know peace again if he doesn't strike out promptly and *follow the track* of that cannon-ball across the plain through the dense fog and find the fort. Isn't it a daisy? If Cooper had any real knowledge of Nature's ways of doing things, he had a most delicate art in concealing the fact. For instance: one of his acute Indian experts, Chingachgook (pronounced Chicago, I think), has lost the trail of a person he is tracking through the forest. Apparently that trail is hopelessly lost. Neither you nor I could ever have guessed out the way to find it. It was very different with Chicago. Chicago was not stumped for long. He turned a running stream out of its course, and there, in the slush in its old bed, were that person's moccasin-tracks. The current did not wash them away, as it would have done in all other cases—no, even the eternal laws of Nature have to vacate when Cooper wants to put up a delicate job of wood-craft on the reader.

We must be a little wary when Brander Matthews tells us that Cooper's   6
books "reveal an extraordinary fulness of invention." As a rule, I am quite willing to accept Brander Matthews's literary judgments and applaud his lucid and graceful phrasing of them; but that particular statement needs to be taken with a few tons of salt. Bless your heart, Cooper hadn't any more invention than a horse; and I don't mean a high-class horse, either; I mean a clothes-horse. It would be very difficult to find a really clever "situation" in Cooper's books, and still more difficult to find one of any kind which he has failed to render absurd by his handling of it. Look at the episodes of "the caves"; and at the celebrated scuffle between Maqua and those others on the table-land a few days later; and at Hurry Harry's queer water-transit from the castle to the ark; and at Deerslayer's half-hour with his first corpse; and at the quarrel between Hurry Harry and Deerslayer later; and at—but choose for yourself; you can't go amiss.

If Cooper had been an observer his inventive faculty would have worked   7
better; not more interestingly, but more rationally, more plausibly. Cooper's proudest creations in the way of "situations" suffer noticeably from the absence of the observer's protecting gift. Cooper's eye was splendidly inaccurate. Cooper seldom saw anything correctly. He saw nearly all things as through a glass eye, darkly. Of course a man who cannot see the commonest little every-day matters accurately is working at a disadvantage when he is constructing a "situation." In the *Deerslayer* tale Cooper has a stream which is fifty feet wide where it flows out of a lake; it presently narrows to twenty as it meanders along for no given reason, and yet when a stream acts like that it ought to be required to explain itself. Fourteen pages later the width of the brook's outlet from the lake has suddenly shrunk thirty feet, and become "the narrowest part of the stream." This shrinkage is not accounted for. The stream has bends in it, a sure indication that it has alluvial banks and cuts them; yet these bends are only thirty and fifty feet long. If Cooper had been a nice and punctilious observer he would have noticed that the bends were oftener nine hundred feet long than short of it.

Cooper made the exit of that stream fifty feet wide, in the first place, for   8
no particular reason; in the second place, he narrowed it to less than twenty
to accommodate some Indians. He bends a "sapling" to the form of an arch
over this narrow passage, and conceals six Indians in its foliage. They are
"laying" for a settler's scow or ark which is coming up the stream on its way
to the lake; it is being hauled against the stiff current by a rope whose sta-
tionary end is anchored in the lake; its rate of progress cannot be more than
a mile an hour. Cooper describes the ark, but pretty obscurely. In the matter
of dimensions "it was little more than a modern canal-boat." Let us guess,
then, that it was about one hundred and forty feet long. It was of "greater
breadth than common." Let us guess, then, that it was about sixteen feet
wide. This leviathan had been prowling down bends which were but a third
as long as itself, and scraping between banks where it had only two feet of
space to spare on each side. We cannot too much admire this miracle. A low-
roofed log dwelling occupies "two-thirds of the ark's length"—a dwelling ninety
feet long and sixteen feet wide, let us say—a kind of vestibule train. The
dwelling has two rooms—each forty-five feet long and sixteen feet wide, let
us guess. One of them is the bedroom of the Hutter girls, Judith and Hetty;
the other is the parlor in the daytime, at night it is papa's bedchamber. The
ark is arriving at the stream's exit now, whose width has been reduced to
less than twenty feet to accommodate the Indians—say to eighteen. There is
a foot to spare on each side of the boat. Did the Indians notice that there
was going to be a tight squeeze there? Did they notice that they could make
money by climbing down out of that arched sapling and just stepping aboard
when the ark scraped by? No, other Indians would have noticed these things,
but Cooper's Indians never notice anything. Cooper thinks they are marvelous creatures for noticing, but he was almost always in error about his Indians. There was seldom a sane one among them.

The ark is one hundred and forty feet long; the dwelling is ninety feet   9
long. The idea of the Indians is to drop softly and secretly from the arched
sapling to the dwelling as the ark creeps along under it at the rate of a mile
an hour, and butcher the family. It will take the ark a minute and a half to
pass under. It will take the ninety-foot dwelling a minute to pass under. Now,
then, what did the six Indians do? It would take you thirty years to guess,
and even then you would have to give it up, I believe. Therefore, I will tell
you what the Indians did. Their chief, a person of quite extraordinary intellect for a Cooper Indian, warily watched the canal-boat as it squeezed along
under him, and when he had got his calculations fined down to exactly the
right shade, as he judged, he let go and dropped. And *missed the house!*
That is actually what he did. He missed the house, and landed in the stern
of the scow. It was not much of a fall, yet it knocked him silly. He lay there
unconscious. If the house had been ninety-seven feet long he would have
made the trip. The fault was Cooper's, not his. The error lay in the construction of the house. Cooper was no architect.

There still remained in the roost five Indians. The boat has passed under   10
and is now out of their reach. Let me explain what the five did—you would

not be able to reason it out for yourself. No. 1 jumped for the boat, but fell in the water astern of it. Then No. 2 jumped for the boat, but fell in the water still farther astern of it. Then No. 3 jumped for the boat, and fell a good way astern of it. Then No. 4 jumped for the boat, and fell in the water *away* astern. Then even No. 5 made a jump for the boat—for he was a Cooper Indian. In the matter of intellect, the difference between a Cooper Indian and the Indian that stands in front of the cigarshop is not spacious. The scow episode is really a sublime burst of invention; but it does not thrill, because the inaccuracy of the detail throws a sort of air of fictitiousness and general improbability over it. This comes of Cooper's inadequacy as an observer.

The reader will find some examples of Cooper's high talent for inaccurate   11
observation in the account of the shooting-match in *The Pathfinder.*

> A common wrought nail was driven lightly into the target, its head having been first touched with paint.

The color of the paint is not stated—an important omission, but Cooper   12
deals freely in important omissions. No, after all, it was not an important omission; for this nailhead is *a hundred yards from* the marksmen, and could not be seen by them at that distance, no matter what its color might be. How far can the best eyes see a common house-fly? A hundred yards? It is quite impossible. Very well; eyes that cannot see a house-fly that is a hundred yards away cannot see an ordinary nail head at that distance, for the size of the two objects is the same. It takes a keen eye to see a fly or a nail-head at fifty yards—one hundred and fifty feet. Can the reader do it?

The nail was lightly driven, its head painted, and game called. Then the   13
Cooper miracles begin. The bullet of the first marksman chipped an edge of the nail-head; the next man's bullet drove the nail a little way into the target—and removed all the paint. Haven't the miracles gone far enough now? Not to suit Cooper; for the purpose of this whole scheme is to show off his prodigy,   Deerslayer-Hawkeye-Long-Rifle-Leather-Stocking-Pathfinder-Bumppo before the ladies.

> "Be all ready to clench it, boys!" cried out Pathfinder, stepping into his friend's tracks the instant they were vacant. "Never mind a new nail; I can see that, though the paint is gone, and what I can see I can hit at a hundred yards, though it were only a mosquito's eye. Be ready to clench!"
> The rifle cracked, the bullet sped its way, and the head of the nail was buried in the wood, covered by the piece of flattened lead.

There, you see, is a man who could hunt flies with a rifle, and command a   14
ducal salary in a Wild West show today if we had him back with us.

The recorded feat is certainly surprising just as it stands; but it is not   15
surprising enough for Cooper. Cooper adds a touch. He has made Pathfinder

do this miracle with another man's rifle; and not only that, but Pathfinder did not have even the advantage of loading it himself. He had everything against him, and yet he made that impossible shot; and not only made it, but did it with absolute confidence, saying, "Be ready to clench." Now a person like that would have undertaken that same feat with a brick-bat, and with Cooper to help he would have achieved it, too.

Pathfinder showed off handsomely that day before the ladies. His very first   16
feat was a thing which no Wild West show can touch. He was standing with the group of marksmen, observing—a hundred yards from the target, mind; one Jasper raised his rifle and drove the center off the bull's-eye. Then the Quartermaster fired. The target exhibited no result this time. There was a laugh. "It's a dead miss," said Major Lundie. Pathfinder waited an impressive moment or two; then said, in that calm, indifferent, know-it-all way of his, "No, Major, he has covered Jasper's bullet, as will be seen if anyone will take the trouble to examine the target."

Wasn't it remarkable! How *could* he see that little pellet fly through the   17
air and enter that distant bullet-hole? Yet that is what he did; for nothing is impossible to a Cooper person. Did any of those people have any deep-seated doubts about this thing? No; for that would imply sanity, and these were all Cooper people.

> The respect for Pathfinder's skill and for his *quickness and accuracy of sight* [the italics are mine] was so profound and general, that the instant he made this declaration the spectators began to distrust their own opinions, and a dozen rushed to the target in order to ascertain the fact. There, sure enough, it was found that the Quartermaster's bullet had gone through the hole made by Jasper's, and that, too, so accurately as to require a minute examination to be certain of the circumstance, which, however, was soon clearly established by discovering one bullet over the other in the stump against which the target was placed.

They made a "minute" examination; but never mind, how could they know   18
that there were two bullets in that hole without digging the latest one out? for neither probe nor eyesight could prove the presence of any more than one bullet. Did they dig? No; as we shall see. It is the Pathfinder's turn now; he steps out before the ladies, takes aim, and fires.

But, alas! here is a disappointment; an incredible, an unimaginable disap-   19
pointment—for the target's aspect is unchanged; there is nothing there but that same old bullet-hole!

> "If one dared to hint at such a thing," cried Major Duncan, "I should say that the Pathfinder has also missed the target!"

As nobody had missed it yet, the "also" was not necessary; but never mind   20
about that, for the Pathfinder is going to speak.

"No, no, Major," said he, confidently, "that *would* be a risky declaration. I didn't load the piece, and can't say what was in it; but if it was lead, you will find the bullet driving down those of the Quartermaster and Jasper, else is not my name Pathfinder."

A shout from the target announced the truth of this assertion.

Is the miracle sufficient as it stands? Not for Cooper. The Pathfinder speaks   21 again, as he "now slowly advances towards the stage occupied by the females":

"That's not all, boys, that's not all; if you find the target touched at all, I'll own to a miss. The Quartermaster cut the wood, but you'll find no wood cut by that last messenger."

The miracle is at last complete. He knew—doubtless *saw*—at the distance   22 of a hundred yards—that his bullet had passed into the hole *without fraying the edges.* There were now three bullets in that one hole—three bullets embedded processionally in the body of the stump back of the target. Everybody knew this—somehow or other—and yet nobody had dug any of them out to make sure. Cooper is not a close observer, but he is interesting. He is certainly always that, no matter what happens. And he is more interesting when he is not noticing what he is about than when he is. This is a considerable merit.

The conversations in the Cooper books have a curious sound in our mod-   23 ern ears. To believe that such talk really ever came out of people's mouths would be to believe that there was a time when time was of no value to a person who thought he had something to say; when it was the custom to spread a two-minute remark out to ten; when a man's mouth was a rolling-mill, and busied itself all day long in turning four-foot pigs of thought into thirty-foot bars of conversational railroad iron by attenuation; when subjects were seldom faithfully stuck to, but the talk wandered all around and arrived nowhere; when conversations consisted mainly of irrelevancies, with here and there a relevancy, a relevancy with an embarrassed look, as not being able to explain how it got there.

Cooper was certainly not a master in the construction of dialogue. Inac-   24 curate observation defeated him here as it defeated him in so many other enterprises of his. He even failed to notice that the man who talks corrupt English six days in the week must and will talk it on the seventh, and can't help himself. In the *Deerslayer* story he lets Deerslayer talk the showiest kind of book-talk sometimes, and at other times the basest of base dialects. For instance, when someone asks him if he has a sweetheart, and if so, where she abides, this is his majestic answer:

"She's in the forest—hanging from the boughs of the trees, in a soft rain— in the dew on the open grass—the clouds that float about in the blue heavens—

the birds that sing in the woods—the sweet springs where I slake my thirst—
and in all the other glorious gifts that come from God's Providence!"

And he preceded that, a little before, with this: 25

"It consarns me as all things that touches a fri'nd consarns a fri'nd."

And this is another of his remarks: 26

"If I was Injin born, now, I might tell of this, or carry in the scalp and boast
of the expl'ite afore the whole tribe; or if my inimy had only been a bear"

—and so on.

We cannot imagine such a thing as a veteran Scotch Commander-in-Chief   27
comporting himself in the field like a windy melodramatic actor, but Cooper
could. On one occasion Alice and Cora were being chased by the French
through a fog in the neighborhood of their father's fort:

> *"Point de quartier aux coquins!"* cried an eager pursuer, who seemed to
> direct the operations of the enemy.
> "Stand firm and be ready, my gallant 60ths!" suddenly exclaimed a voice
> above them; "wait to see the enemy; fire low, and sweep the glacis."
> "Father! father!" exclaimed a piercing cry from out the mist; "it is I! Alice!
> thy own Elsie! spare, O! save your daughters!"
> "Hold!" shouted the former speaker, in the awful tones of parental agony,
> the sound reaching even to the woods, and rolling back in solemn echo. " 'Tis
> she! God has restored me my children! Throw open the sally-port; to the field,
> 60ths, to the field! pull not a trigger, lest ye kill my lambs! Drive off these dogs
> of France with your steel!"

Cooper's word-sense was singularly dull. When a person has a poor ear for   28
music he will flat and sharp right along without knowing it. He keeps near
the tune, but it is *not* the tune. When a person has a poor ear for words, the
result is a literary flatting and sharping; you perceive what he is intending to
say, but you also perceive that he doesn't *say* it. This is Cooper. He was not
a word-musician. His ear was satisfied with the *approximate* word. I will
furnish some circumstantial evidence in support of this charge. My instances
are gathered from half a dozen pages of the tale called *Deerslayer*. He uses
"verbal," for "oral"; "precision," for "facility"; "phenomena," for "marvels";
"necessary," for "predetermined"; "unsophisticated," for "primitive"; "preparation," for "expectancy"; "rebuked," for "subdued"; "dependent on," for "resulting from"; "fact," for "condition"; "fact," for "conjecture"; "precaution," for
"caution"; "explain," for "determine"; "mortified," for "disappointed"; "mere-
tricious," for "factitious"; "materially," for "considerably"; "decreasing," for
"deepening"; "increasing," for "disappearing"; "embedded," for "enclosed";

"treacherous," for "hostile"; "stood," for "stooped"; "softened," for "replaced"; "rejoined," for "remarked"; "situation," for "condition"; "different," for "differing"; "insensible," for "unsentient"; "brevity," for "celerity"; "distrusted," for "suspicious"; "mental imbecility," for "imbecility"; "eyes," for "sight"; "counteracting," for "opposing"; "funeral obsequies," for "obsequies."

There have been daring people in the world who claimed that Cooper   29
could write English, but they are all dead now—all dead but Lounsbury. I don't remember that Lounsbury makes the claim in so many words, still he makes it, for he says that *Deerslayer* is a "pure work of art." Pure, in that connection, means faultless—faultless in all details—and language is a detail. If Mr. Lounsbury had only compared Cooper's English with the English which he writes himself—but it is plain that he didn't; and so it is likely that he imagines until this day that Cooper's is as clean and compact as his own. Now I feel sure, deep down in my heart, that Cooper wrote about the poorest English that exists in our language, and that the English of *Deerslayer* is the very worst that even Cooper ever wrote.

I may be mistaken, but it does seem to me that *Deerslayer* is not a work   30
of art in any sense; it does seem to me that it is destitute of every detail that goes to the making of a work of art; in truth, it seems to me that *Deerslayer* is just simply a literary *delirium tremens.*

A work of art? It has no invention; it has no order, system, sequence, or   31
result; it has no lifelikeness, no thrill, no stir, no seeming of reality; its characters are confusedly drawn, and by their acts and words they prove that they are not the sort of people the author claims that they are; its humor is pathetic; its pathos is funny; its conversations are—oh! indescribable; its love-scenes odious; its English a crime against the language.

Counting these out, what is left is Art. I think we must all admit that.   32

QUESTIONS FOR MEANING

1. What do Wilkie Collins and Twain mean by "romantic fiction"?
2. Demonstrate that you have understood Twain's first eleven rules for literature by paraphrasing them.
3. Why does Twain object to Cooper's use of the device of having a character cause alarm by stepping on a dry twig?
4. Why does Twain believe that Cooper was not observant?
5. What is wrong with Cooper's characterization of the Indians discussed in paragraph 10?
6. Why does Twain object to Cooper's dialogue?
7. Vocabulary: decorous (1), eschew (3), lucid (6), plausibly (7), leviathan (8), ducal (14), attenuation (23), obsequies (28).

QUESTIONS ABOUT STRATEGY

1. How important are the quotations that preface this essay?
2. Twain has been much praised for his humor. How does he use humor in this essay to make his point?

3. Did Twain persuade you that he has read Cooper carefully? If so, how? If not, why not?

4. Has Twain assumed that his audience is familiar with Cooper? Could someone who has not read Cooper understand this essay?

MARGARET SANGER
The Cause of War

A pioneering advocate of birth control, Margaret Sanger (1883–1966) was one of eleven children. She studied nursing and worked as an obstetrical nurse in the tenements of Manhattan's Lower East Side. She became convinced of the importance of birth control in 1912 when a young woman died in her arms after a self-induced abortion. Sanger went to Europe in 1913 to study contraception, and she is credited with having coined the phrase "birth control." Upon her return to the United States, she founded a magazine, Woman Rebel, *in which she could publish her views. In 1916, she was jailed for opening a birth control clinic in New York, the first of many times she would be imprisoned for her work. She founded the National Birth Control League in 1917, an organization that eventually became the Planned Parenthood Federation of America. By the time Sanger was elected the first president of the International Planned Parenthood Federation in 1952, her views had come to be widely accepted.*

A lecturer and a writer, Sanger published several books. The following essay is drawn from Woman and the New Race *(**1920**). Writing at a time when Europe had not yet recovered from the horrors of World War I, Sanger argued that the underlying cause of the war was excessive population growth. Although most historians would argue that the war had multiple causes, Sanger makes a strong case on behalf of her view.*

In every nation of militaristic tendencies we find the reactionaries de-   1
manding a higher and still higher birth rate. Their plea is, first, that great armies are needed to *defend* the country from its possible enemies; second, that a huge population is required to assure the country its proper place among the powers of the world. At bottom the two pleas are the same.

As soon as the country becomes overpopulated, these reactionaries pro-   2
claim loudly its moral right to expand. They point to the huge population, which in the name of patriotism they have previously demanded should be brought into being. Again pleading patriotism, they declare that it is the moral right of the nation to take by force such room as it needs. Then comes war—usually against some nation supposed to be less well prepared than the aggressor.

Diplomats make it their business to conceal the facts, and politicians vio-   3
lently denounce the politicians of other countries. There is a long beating of

tom-toms by the press and all other agencies for influencing public opinion. Facts are distorted and lies invented until the common people cannot get at the truth. Yet, when the war is over, if not before, we always find that "a place in the sun," "a path to the sea," "a route to India" or something of the sort is at the bottom of the trouble. These are merely other names for expansion.

The "need of expansion" is only another name for overpopulation. One   4
supreme example is sufficient to drive home this truth. That the Great War, from the horror of which we are just beginning to emerge, had its source in overpopulation is too evident to be denied by any serious student of current history.

For the past one hundred years most of the nations of Europe have been   5
piling up terrific debts to humanity by the encouragement of unlimited numbers. The rulers of these nations and their militarists have constantly called upon the people to breed, breed, breed! Large populations meant more people to produce wealth, more people to pay taxes, more trade for the merchants, more soldiers to protect the wealth. But more people also meant need of greater food supplies, an urgent and natural need for expansion.

As shown by C. V. Drysdale's famous "War Map of Europe," the great con-   6
flict began among the high birth rate countries—Germany, with its rate of 31.7, Austria-Hungary with 33.7 and 36.7, respectively, Russia with 45.4, Serbia with 38.6. Italy with her 38.7 came in, as the world is now well informed through the publication of secret treaties by the Soviet government of Russia, upon the promise of territory held by Austria. England, owing to her small home area, is cramped with her comparatively low birth rate of 26.3. France, among the belligerents, is conspicuous for her low birth rate of 19.9, but stood in the way of expansion of high birth rate Germany. Nearly all of the persistently neutral countries—Holland, Denmark, Norway, Sweden and Switzerland have low birth rates, the average being a little over 26.

Owing to the part Germany played in the war, a survey of her birth statis-   7
tics is decidedly illuminating. The increase in the German birth rate up to 1876 was great. Though it began to decline then, the decline was not sufficient to offset the tremendous increase of the previous years. There were more millions to produce children, so while the average number of births per thousand was somewhat smaller, the net increase in population was still huge. From 41,000,000 in 1871, the year the Empire was founded, the German population grew to approximately 67,000,000 in 1918. Meanwhile her food supply increased only a very small percent. In 1910, Russia had a birth rate even higher than Germany's had ever been—a little less than 48 per thousand. When czarist Russia wanted an outlet to the Mediterranean by way of Constantinople, she was thinking of her increasing population. Germany was thinking of her increasing population when she spoke as with one voice of a "place in the sun." . . .

The militaristic claim for Germany's right to new territory was simply a   8
claim to the right of life and food for the German babies—the same right that a chick claims to burst its shell. If there had not been other millions of people

claiming the same right, there would have been no war. But there *were* other millions.

The German rulers and leaders pointed out the fact that expansion meant   9
more business for German merchants, more work for German workmen at better wages, and more opportunities for Germans abroad. They also pointed out that lack of expansion meant crowding and crushing at home, hard times, heavy burdens, lack of opportunity for Germans, and what not. In this way, they gave the people of the Empire a startling and true picture of what would happen from overcrowding. Once they realized the facts, the majority of Germans naturally welcomed the so-called war of defense.

The argument was sound. Once the German mothers had submitted to the   10
plea for overbreeding, it was inevitable that imperialistic Germany should make war. Once the battalions of unwanted babies came into existence— babies whom the mothers did not want but which they bore as a "patriotic duty"—it was too late to avoid international conflict. The great crime of imperialistic Germany was its high birth rate.

It has always been so. Behind all war has been the pressure of population.   11
"Historians," says Huxley, "point to the greed and ambition of rulers, the reckless turbulence of the ruled, to the debasing effects of wealth and luxury, and to the devastating wars which have formed a great part of the occupation of mankind, as the causes of the decay of states and the foundering of old civilizations, and thereby point their story with a moral. But beneath all this superficial turmoil lay the deep-seated impulse given by unlimited multiplication."

Robert Thomas Malthus, formulator of the doctrine which bears his name,   12
pointed out, in the closing years of the eighteenth century, the relation of overpopulation to war. He showed that mankind tends to increase faster than the food supply. He demonstrated that were it not for the more common diseases, for plague, famine, floods and wars, human beings would crowd each other to such an extent that the misery would be even greater than it now is. These he described as "natural checks," pointing out that as long as no other checks are employed, such disasters are unavoidable. If we do not exercise sufficient judgment to regulate the birth rate, we encounter disease, starvation and war.

Both Darwin and John Stuart Mill recognized, by inference at least, the   13
fact that so-called "natural checks"—and among them war—will operate if some sort of limitation is not employed. In his *Origin of Species,* Darwin says: "There is no exception to the rule that every organic being naturally increases at so high a rate, if not destroyed, that the earth would soon be covered by the progeny of a single pair." Elsewhere he observes that we do not permit helpless human beings to die off, but we create philanthropies and charities, build asylums and hospitals and keep the medical profession busy preserving those who could not otherwise survive. John Stuart Mill, supporting the views of Malthus, speaks to exactly the same effect in regard to the multiplying power of organic beings, among them humanity. In other words,

let countries become overpopulated and war is inevitable. It follows as daylight follows the sunrise.

When Charles Bradlaugh and Mrs. Annie Besant were on trial in England   14
in 1877 for publishing information concerning contraceptives, Mrs. Besant put the case bluntly to the court and the jury:

"I have no doubt that if natural checks were allowed to operate right through   15
the human as they do in the animal world, a better result would follow. Among the brutes, the weaker are driven to the wall, the diseased fall out in the race of life. The old brutes, when feeble or sickly, are killed. If men insisted that those who were sickly should be allowed to die without help of medicine or science, if those who are weak were put upon one side and crushed, if those who were old and useless were killed, if those who were not capable of providing food for themselves were allowed to starve, if all this were done, the struggle for existence among men would be as real as it is among brutes and would doubtless result in the production of a higher race of men.

"But are you willing to do that or to allow it to be done?"   16

We are not willing to let it be done. Mother hearts cling to children, no   17
matter how diseased, misshapen and miserable. Sons and daughters hold fast to parents, no matter how helpless. We do not allow the weak to depart; neither do we cease to bring more weak and helpless beings into the world. Among the dire results is war, which kills off, not the weak and the helpless, but the strong and the fit.

What shall be done? We have our choice of one of three policies. We may   18
abandon our science and leave the weak and diseased to die, or kill them, as the brutes do. Or we may go on overpopulating the earth and have our famines and our wars while the earth exists. Or we can accept the third, sane, sensible, moral and practicable plan of birth control. We can refuse to bring the weak, the helpless and the unwanted children into the world. We can refuse to overcrowd families, nations and the earth. There are these ways to meet the situation, and only these three ways.

The world will never abandon its preventive and curative science; it may   19
be expected to elevate and extend it beyond our present imagination. The efforts to do away with famine and the opposition to war are growing by leaps and bounds. Upon these efforts are largely based our modern social revolutions.

There remains only the third expedient—birth control, the real cure for   20
war. This fact was called to the attention of the Peace Conference in Paris, in 1919, by the Malthusian League, which adopted the following resolution at its annual general meeting in London in June of that year:

"The Malthusian League desires to point out that the proposed scheme   21
for the League of Nations has neglected to take account of the important questions of *the pressure of population,* which *causes the great international economic competition* and rivalry, and of the *increase of population,* which is put forward as a justification for *claiming increase of territory.* It, therefore, wishes to put on record its belief that the League of Nations

will only be able to fulfill its aim *when it adds a clause* to the following effect:

" 'That each Nation desiring to enter into the League of Nations shall pledge   22
itself *so to restrict its birth rate* that its people shall be able to live in comfort *in their own dominions without need* for territorial expansion, and that it shall recognize that *increase of population shall not justify* a demand either for increase of territory or for the compulsion of other Nations to admit its emigrants; so that when all Nations in the League have shown their ability to live on their own resources without international rivalry, they will be in a position to fuse into an international federation, and territorial boundaries will then have little significance.' "

As a matter of course, the Peace Conference paid no attention to the   23
resolution, for, as pointed out by Frank A. Vanderlip, the American financier, that conference not only ignored the economic factors of the world situation, but seemed unaware that Europe had produced more people than its fields could feed. So the resolution amounted to so much propaganda and nothing more.

This remedy can be applied only by woman and she will apply it. She must   24
and will see past the call of pretended patriotism and of glory of empire and perceive what is true and what is false in these things. She will discover what base uses the militarist and the exploiter made of the idealism of peoples. Under the clamor of the press, permeating the ravings of the jingoes, she will hear the voice of Napoleon, the archtype of the militarists of all nations, calling for "fodder for cannon."

"Woman is given to us that she may bear children," said he. "Woman is   25
our property, we are not hers, because she produces children for us—we do not yield any to her. She is, therefore, our possession as the fruit tree is that of the gardener."

That is what the imperialist is *thinking* when he speaks of the glory of   26
the empire and the prestige of the nation. Every country has its appeal—its shibboleth—ready for the lips of the imperialist. German rulers pointed to the comfort of the workers, to old-age pensions, maternal benefits and minimum wage regulations, and other material benefits, when they wished to inspire soldiers for the Fatherland. England's strongest argument, perhaps, was a certain phase of liberty which she guarantees her subjects, and the protection afforded them wherever they may go. France and the United States, too, have their appeals to the idealism of democracy—appeals which the politicians of both countries know well how to use, though the peoples of both lands are beginning to awake to the fact that their countries have been living on the glories of their revolutions and traditions, rather than the substance of freedom. Behind the boast of old-age pensions, material benefits and wage regulations, behind the bombast concerning liberty in this country and tyranny in that, behind all the slogans and shibboleths coined out of the ideals of the peoples for the uses of imperialism, woman must and will see the iron hand of that same imperialism, condemning women to breed and men to die for the will of the rulers.

Upon woman the burden and the horrors of war are heaviest. Her heart is   27
the hardest wrung when the husband or the son comes home to be buried
or to live a shattered wreck. Upon her devolve the extra tasks of filling out
the ranks of workers in the war industries, in addition to caring for the children and replenishing the war-diminished population. Hers is the crushing
weight and the sickening of soul. And it is out of her womb that those things
proceed. When she sees what lies behind the glory and the horror, the boast-
ing and the burden, and gets the vision, the human perspective, she will end
war. She will kill war by the simple process of starving it to death. For she
will refuse longer to produce the human food upon which the monster feeds.

QUESTIONS FOR MEANING

1. According to Sanger, what motives have led governments to encourage
   population growth?
2. From an evolutionary point of view, why is war unacceptable as a "natural
   check" upon population growth?
3. What are the three policies that Sanger believes nations must inevitably
   choose among? Are there any alternatives that she overlooks?
4. The Second World War began less than twenty years after the publication
   of this essay. Do you know anything about the conditions under which
   that war began that could be used as evidence to support Sanger's thesis
   that "militarists" and "reactionaries" favor high birth rates?
5. Vocabulary: belligerents (6), conspicuous (6), turbulence (11), debasing
   (11), foundering (11), inference (13), progeny (13), base (24), jingoes
   (24), and bombast (26).

QUESTIONS ABOUT STRATEGY

1. Is Sanger ever guilty of oversimplification? Can you think of any causes of
   war that have nothing to do with population?
2. How useful are the statistics cited in paragraphs 6 and 7?
3. Of the various quotations that Sanger includes in her essay, which is the
   most effective?
4. How would you describe the tone of this essay? Is it suitable for the
   subject?
5. Do you detect any bias in this essay? Does Sanger ever seem to suggest
   that World War I was caused by one country in particular? Is such an
   implication historically valid?

GEORGE ORWELL
Politics and the English Language

George Orwell was the pseudonym adopted by Eric Arthur Blair (1903–1950)
upon the publication of his first book, Down and Out in Paris and London *(1933).*
Born the son of a British civil servant in India, he distinguished himself at an
early age by winning a King's scholarship to Eton, where he studied between
1917 and 1921. Deciding not to go on to a university, he joined the Indian Im-
perial Police, and served in Burma from 1922 to 1927—an experience upon
which he drew for his novel, Burmese Days *(1935), and essays like "Shooting an*
Elephant" and "A Hanging." During the 1930s Orwell published two more nov-
els, A Clergyman's Daughter *(1935) and* Keep the Aspidistra Flying *(1936), but*
most of his income came from writing book reviews and political journalism.
Throughout these years, Orwell thought of himself as a socialist, but he was ba-
sically a libertarian who could not reconcile himself to the regimentation of
party politics. With The Road to Wigan Pier *(1937) and* Homage to Catalonia
(1938), Orwell's work becomes increasingly political. His two most famous
books, Animal Farm *(1945) and* Nineteen Eighty-Four *(1949), reveal his convic-*
tion that social revolutions eventually lead to the subjugation of the individual
by an all-powerful and faceless state.

Orwell is a writer who makes readers think, but he is also one of the best
stylists in our century. His many essays are written with simplicity, clarity,
and grace. Orwell cared deeply about the importance of language, and in "Poli-
tics and the English Language" he offers a brilliant analysis of the many ways
in which language can be abused. This is an essay that every writer should
read. It was first published in **1946.**

Most people who bother with the matter at all would admit that the En-   1
glish language is in a bad way, but it is generally assumed that we cannot by
conscious action do anything about it. Our civilization is decadent and our
language—so the argument runs—must inevitably share in the general collapse. It follows that any struggle against the abuse of language is a sentimental archaism, like preferring candles to electric light or hansom cabs to
aeroplanes. Underneath this lies the half-conscious belief that language is a
natural growth and not an instrument which we shape for our own purposes.

Now, it is clear that the decline of a language must ultimately have politi-   2
cal and economic causes: it is not due simply to the bad influence of this or
that individual writer. But an effect can become a cause, reinforcing the original cause and producing the same effect in an intensified form, and so on
indefinitely. A man may take to drink because he feels himself to be a failure,
and then fail all the more completely because he drinks. It is rather the same
thing that is happening to the English language. It becomes ugly and inaccurate because our thoughts are foolish, but the slovenliness of our language
makes it easier for us to have foolish thoughts. The point is that the process
is reversible. Modern English, especially written English, is full of bad habits

which spread by imitation and which can be avoided if one is willing to take the necessary trouble. If one gets rid of these habits one can think more clearly, and to think clearly is a necessary first step towards political regeneration: so that the fight against bad English is not frivolous and is not the exclusive concern of professional writers. I will come back to this presently, and I hope that by that time the meaning of what I have said here will have become clearer. Meanwhile, here are five specimens of the English language as it is now habitually written.

These five passages have not been picked out because they are especially   3 bad—I could have quoted far worse if I had chosen—but because they illustrate various of the mental vices from which we now suffer. They are a little below the average, but are fairly representative samples. I number them so that I can refer back to them when necessary:

(1) I am not, indeed, sure whether it is not true to say that the Milton who once seemed not unlike a seventeenth-century Shelley had not become, out of an experience ever more bitter in each year, more alien[*sic*] to the founder of that Jesuit sect which nothing could induce him to tolerate.

> Professor Harold Laski (Essay in *Freedom of Expression*).

(2) Above all, we cannot play ducks and drakes with a native battery of idioms which prescribes such egregious collocations of vocables as the Basic *put up with* for *tolerate* or *put at a loss* for *bewilder.*

> Professor Lancelot Hogben (*Interglossa*).

(3) On the one side we have the free personality: by definition it is not neurotic, for it has neither conflict nor dream. It desires, such as they are, are transparent, for they are just what institutional approval keeps in the forefront of consciousness; another institutional pattern would alter their number and intensity; there is little in them that is natural, irreducible, or culturally dangerous. But *on the other side,* the social bond itself is nothing but the mutual reflection of these self-secure integrities. Recall the definition of love. Is not this the very picture of a small academic? Where is there a place in this hall of mirrors for either personality or fraternity?

> Essay on psychology in *Politics* (New York).

(4) All the "best people" from the gentlemen's clubs, and all the frantic fascist captains, united in common hatred of Socialism and bestial horror of the rising tide of the mass revolutionary movement, have turned to acts of provocation, to foul incendiarism, to medieval legends of poisoned wells, to legalize their own destruction of proletarian organizations, and rouse the agitated petty-bourgeoisie to chauvinistic fervor on behalf of the fight against the revolutionary way out of the crisis.

> Communist pamphlet

(5) If a new spirit *is* to be infused into this old country, there is one thorny and contentious reform which must be tackled, and that is the humanization and galvanization of the B.B.C. Timidity here will bespeak cancer and atrophy of the soul. The heart of Britain may be sound and of strong beat, for instance,

but the British lion's roar at present is like that of Bottom in Shakespeare's *Midsummer Night's Dream*—as gentle as any sucking dove. A virile new Britain cannot continue indefinitely to be traduced in the eyes or rather ears, of the world by the effete languors of Langham Place, brazenly masquerading as "standard English." When the Voice of Britain is heard at nine o'clock, better far and infinitely less ludicrous to hear aitches honestly dropped than the present priggish, inflated, inhibited, school-ma'amish arch braying of blameless bashful mewing maidens!

Letter in *Tribune.*

Each of these passages has faults of its own, but, quite apart from avoidable ugliness, two qualities are common to all of them. The first is staleness of imagery: the other is lack of precision. The writer either has a meaning and cannot express it, or he inadvertently says something else, or he is almost indifferent as to whether his words mean anything or not. The mixture of vagueness and sheer incompetence is the most marked characteristic of modern English prose, and especially of any kind of political writing. As soon as certain topics are raised, the concrete melts into the abstract and no one seems to think of turns of speech that are not hackneyed: prose consists less and less of *words* chosen for the sake of their meaning, and more and more of *phrases* tacked together like the sections of a prefabricated hen-house. I list below, with notes and examples, various of the tricks by means of which the work of prose-construction is habitually dodged: 4

Dying Metaphors

A newly invented metaphor assists thought by evoking a visual image, while on the other hand a metaphor which is technically "dead" (e.g., *iron resolution*) has in effect reverted to being an ordinary word and can generally be used without loss of vividness. But in between these two classes there is a huge dump of worn-out metaphors which have lost all evocative power and are merely used because they save people the trouble of inventing phrases for themselves. Examples are: *Ring the changes on, take up the cudgels for, toe the line, ride roughshod over, stand shoulder to shoulder with, play into the hands of, no axe to grind, grist to the mill, fishing in troubled waters, on the order of the day, Achilles' heel, swan song, hotbed.* Many of these are used without knowledge of their meaning (what is a "rift," for instance?), and incompatible metaphors are frequently mixed, a sure sign that the writer is not interested in what he is saying. Some metaphors now current have been twisted out of their original meaning without those who use them even being aware of the fact. For example, *toe the line* is sometimes written *tow the line.* Another example is *the hammer and the anvil,* now always used with the implication that the anvil gets the worst of it. In real life it is always the anvil that breaks the hammer, never the other way about: a writer who stopped to think what he was saying would be aware of this, and would avoid perverting the original phrase.   5

Operators or Verbal False Limbs

These save the trouble of picking out appropriate verbs and nouns, and at 6
the same time pad each sentence with extra syllables which give it an appearance of symmetry. Characteristic phrases are: *render inoperative, militate against, make contact with, be subjected to, give rise to, give grounds for, have the effect of, play a leading part (role) in, make itself felt, take effect, exhibit a tendency to, serve the purpose of, etc., etc.* The keynote is the elimination of simple verbs. Instead of being a single word, such as *break, stop, spoil, mend, kill,* a verb becomes a *phrase,* made up of a noun or adjective tacked on to some general-purpose verb such as *prone, serve, form, play, render.* In addition, the passive voice is wherever possible used in preference to the active, and noun constructions are used instead of gerunds (*by examination of* instead of *by examining*). The range of verbs is further cut down by means of the *-ize* and *de-* formation, and the banal statements are given an appearance of profundity by means of the *non un-* formation. Simple conjunctions and prepositions are replaced by such phrases as *with respect to, having regard to, the fact that, by dint of, in view of, in the interests of, on the hypothesis that;* and the ends of sentences are saved from anticlimax by such resounding commonplaces as *greatly to be desired, cannot be left out of account, a development to be expected in the near future, deserving of serious consideration, brought to a satisfactory conclusion,* and so on and so forth.

Pretentious Diction

Words like *phenomenon, element, individual* (as noun), *objective, cat-* 7
egorical, effective, virtual, basic, primary, promote, constitute, exhibit, exploit, utilize, eliminate, liquidate, are used to dress up simple statements and give an air of scientific impartiality to biased judgments. Adjectives like *epoch-making, epic, historic, unforgettable, triumphant, age-old, inevitable, inexorable, veritable,* are used to dignify the sordid processes of international politics, while writing that aims at glorifying war usually takes on an archaic color, its characteristic words being: *realm, throne, chariot, mailed fist, trident, sword, shield, buckler, banner, jackboot, clarion.* Foreign words and expressions such as *cul de sac, ancien régime, deus ex machina, mutatis mutandis, status quo, gleichshaltung, weltanschauung,* are used to give an air of culture and elegance. Except for the useful abbreviations *i.e., e.g.,* and *etc.,* there is no real need for any of the hundreds of foreign phrases now current in English. Bad writers, and especially scientific, political and sociological writers, are nearly always haunted by the notion that Latin or Greek words are grander than Saxon ones, and unnecessary words like *expedite, ameliorate, predict, extraneous, deracinated, clandestine, subaqueous* and hundreds of others constantly gain ground from their Anglo-

Saxon opposite numbers.[1] The jargon peculiar to Marxist writing (*hyena, hangman, cannibal, petty bourgeois, these gentry, lackey, flunkey, mad dog, White Guard,* etc.) consists largely of words and phrases translated from Russian, German or French; but the normal way of coining a new word is to use a Latin or Greek root with the appropriate affix and, where necessary, the *-ize* formation. It is often easier to make up words of this kind (*deregionalize, impermissible, extramarital, nonfragmentatory* and so forth) than to think up the English words that will cover one's meaning. The result, in general, is an increase in slovenliness and vagueness.

Meaningless Words

In certain kinds of writing, particularly in art criticism and literary criticism, it is normal to come across long passages which are almost completely lacking in meaning.[2] Words like *romantic, plastic, values, human, dead, sentimental, natural, vitality,* as used in art criticism, are strictly meaningless in the sense that they not only do not point to any discoverable object, but are hardly ever expected to do so by the reader. When one critic writes, "The outstanding feature of Mr. X's work is its living quality," while another writes, "The immediately striking thing about Mr. X's work is its peculiar deadness," the reader accepts this as a simple difference of opinion. If words like *black* and *white* were involved, instead of the jargon words *dead* and *living,* he would see at once that language was being used in an improper way. Many political words are similarly abused. The word *Fascism* has now no meaning except in so far as it signifies "something not desirable." The words *democracy, socialism, freedom, patriotic, realistic, justice,* have each of them several different meanings which cannot be reconciled with one another. In the case of a word like *democracy,* not only is there no agreed definition, but the attempt to make one is resisted from all sides. It is almost universally felt that when we call a country democratic we are praising it: consequently the defenders of every kind of regime claim that it is a democracy, and fear that they might have to stop using the word if it were tied down to any one meaning. Words of this kind are often used in a consciously dishonest way. That is, the person who uses them has his own private definition, but allows his hearer to think he means something quite different. Statements like *Marshal Pétain was a true patriot, The Soviet Press is the freest in the world, The Catholic Church is opposed to persecution,* are almost always made with intent to deceive. Other words used in variable

8

[1] An interesting illustration of this is the way in which the English flower names which were in use till very recently are being ousted by Greek ones, *snapdragon* becoming *antirrhinum, forget-me-not* becoming *myosotis,* etc. It is hard to see any practical reason for this change of fashion; it is probably due to an instinctive turning-away from the more homely word and a vague feeling that the Greek word is scientific.

[2] Example: "Comfort's catholicity of perception and image, strangely Whitmanesque in range, almost the exact opposite in aesthetic compulsion, continues to evoke that trembling atmospheric accumulative hinting at a cruel, an inexorably serene timelessness . . . Wrey Gardiner scores by aiming at simple bull's-eyes with precision. Only they are not so simple, and through this contented sadness runs more than the surface bittersweet of resignation." *(Poetry Quarterly.)*

meanings, in most cases more or less dishonestly, are: *class, totalitarian, science, progressive, reactionary, bourgeois, equality.*

Now that I have made this catalogue of swindles and perversions, let me   9
give another example of the kind of writing that they lead to. This time it must of its nature be an imaginary one. I am going to translate a passage of good English into modern English of the worst sort. Here is a well-known verse from *Ecclesiastes:*

> I returned and saw under the sun, that the race is not to the swift, nor the battle to the strong, neither yet bread to the wise, nor yet riches to men of understanding, nor yet favor to men of skill; but time and chance happeneth to them all.

Here it is in modern English:

> Objective consideration of contemporary phenomena compels the conclusion that success or failure in competitive activities exhibits no tendency to be commensurate with innate capacity, but that a considerable element of the unpredictable must invariably be taken into account.

This is a parody, but not a very gross one. Exhibit (3), above, for instance,   10
contains several patches of the same kind of English. It will be seen that I have not made a full translation. The beginning and ending of the sentence follow the original meaning fairly closely, but in the middle the concrete illustrations—race, battle, bread—dissolve into the vague phrase "success or failure in competitive activities." This had to be so, because no modern writer of the kind I am discussing—no one capable of using phrases like "objective consideration of contemporary phenomena"—would ever tabulate his thoughts in that precise and detailed way. The whole tendency of modern prose is away from concreteness. Now analyze these two sentences a little more closely. The first contains forty-nine words but only sixty syllables, and all its words are those of everyday life. The second contains thirty-eight words of ninety syllables: eighteen of its words are from Latin roots, and one from Greek. The first sentence contains six vivid images, and only one phrase ("time and chance") that could be called vague. The second contains not a single fresh, arresting phrase, and in spite of its ninety syllables it gives only a shortened version of the meaning contained in the first. Yet without a doubt it is the second kind of sentence that is gaining ground in modern English. I do not want to exaggerate. This kind of writing is not yet universal, and outcrops of simplicity will occur here and there in the worst-written page. Still, if you or I were told to write a few lines on the uncertainty of human fortunes, we should probably come much nearer to my imaginary sentence than to the one from *Ecclesiastes*.

As I have tried to show, modern writing at its worst does not consist in   11
picking out words for the sake of their meaning and inventing images in

order to make the meaning clearer. It consists in gumming together long strips of words which have already been set in order by someone else, and making the results presentable by sheer humbug. The attraction of this way of writing is that it is easy. It is easier—even quicker once you have the habit—to say *In my opinion it is a not unjustifiable assumption that* than to say I *think*. If you use ready-made phrases, you not only don't have to hunt about for words; you also don't have to bother with the rhythms of your sentences, since these phrases are generally so arranged as to be more or less euphonious. When you are composing in a hurry—when you are dictating to a stenographer, for instance, or making a public speech—it is natural to fall into a pretentious, Latinized style. Tags like *a consideration which we should do well to bear in mind* or *a conclusion to which all of us would readily assent* will save many a sentence from coming down with a bump. By using stale metaphors, similes and idioms, you save much mental effort, at the cost of leaving your meaning vague, not only for your reader but for yourself. This is the significance of mixed metaphors. The sole aim of a metaphor is to call up a visual image. When these images clash—as in *The Fascist octopus has sung its swan song, the jackboot is thrown into the melting pot*—it can be taken as certain that the writer is not seeing a mental image of the objects he is naming; in other words he is not really thinking. Look again at the examples I gave at the beginning of this essay. Professor Laski (1) uses five negatives in fifty-three words. One of these is superfluous, making nonsense of the whole passage, and in addition there is the slip *alien* for akin, making further nonsense, and several avoidable pieces of clumsiness which increase the general vagueness. Professor Hogben (2) plays ducks and drakes with a battery which is able to write prescriptions, and, while disapproving of the every-day phrase *put up with*, is unwilling to look *egregious* up in the dictionary and see what it means. (3), if one takes an uncharitable attitude towards it, is simply meaningless: probably one could work out its intended meaning by reading the whole of the article in which it occurs. In (4), the writer knows more or less what he wants to say, but an accumulation of stale phrases chokes him like tea leaves blocking a sink. In (5), words and meaning have almost parted company. People who write in this manner usually have a general emotional meaning—they dislike one thing and want to express solidarity with another—but they are not interested in the detail of what they are saying. A scrupulous writer, in every sentence that he writes, will ask himself at least four questions, thus: What am I trying to say? What words will express it? What image or idiom will make it clearer? Is this image fresh enough to have an effect? And he will probably ask himself two more: Could I put it more shortly? Have I said anything that is avoidably ugly? But you are not obliged to go to all this trouble. You can shirk it by simply throwing your mind open and letting the ready-made phrases come crowding in. They will construct your sentences for you—even think your thoughts for you, to a certain extent—and at need they will perform the important service of partially concealing your meaning even from yourself. It is at this point that the special connection between politics and the debasement of language becomes clear.

In our time it is broadly true that political writing is bad writing. Where it   12
is not true, it will generally be found that the writer is some kind of rebel,
expressing his private opinions and not a "party line." Orthodoxy, of whatever color, seems to demand a lifeless, imitative style. The political dialects
to be found in pamphlets, leading articles, manifestos, White Papers and the
speeches of under-secretaries do, of course, vary from party to party, but
they are all alike in that one almost never finds in them a fresh, vivid, homemade turn of speech. When one watches some tired hack on the platform
mechanically repeating the familiar phrases—*bestial atrocities, iron heel,
bloodstained tyranny, free peoples of the world, stand shoulder to shoulder*—one often has a curious feeling that one is not watching a live human
being but some kind of dummy; a feeling which suddenly becomes stronger
at moments when the light catches the speaker's spectacles and turns them
into blank discs which seem to have no eyes behind them. And this is not
altogether fanciful. A speaker who uses that kind of phraseology has gone
some distance towards turning himself into a machine. The appropriate noises
are coming out of his larynx, but his brain is not involved as it would be if
he were choosing his words for himself. If the speech he is making is one
that he is accustomed to make over and over again, he may be almost unconscious of what he is saying, as one is when one utters the responses in church.
And this reduced state of consciousness, if not indispensable, is at any rate
favorable to political conformity.

In our time, political speech and writing are largely the defense of the   13
indefensible. Things like the continuance of British rule in India, the Russian
purges and deportations, the dropping of the atom bombs on Japan, can indeed be defended, but only by arguments which are too brutal for most people to face, and which do not square with the professed aims of political
parties. Thus political language has to consist largely of euphemism, ques-
tion-begging and sheer cloudy vagueness. Defenseless villages are bombarded
from the air, the inhabitants driven out into the countryside, the cattle ma-
chine-gunned, the huts set on fire with incendiary bullets: this is called *pac-
ification.* Millions of peasants are robbed of their farms and sent trudging
along the roads with no more than they can carry: this is called *transfer of
population* or *rectification of frontiers.* People are imprisoned for years
without trial, or shot in the back of the neck or sent to die of scurvy in Arctic
lumber camps: this is called *elimination of unreliable elements.* Such
phraseology is needed if one wants to name things without calling up mental
pictures of them. Consider for instance some comfortable English professor
defending Russian totalitarianism. He cannot say outright, "I believe in killing
off your opponents when you can get good results by doing so." Probably,
therefore, he will say something like this:

"While freely conceding that the Soviet régime exhibits certain features   14
which the humanitarian may be inclined to deplore, we must, I think, agree
that a certain curtailment of the right to political opposition is an unavoidable
concomitant of transitional periods, and that the rigors which the Russian
people have been called upon to undergo have been amply justified in the
sphere of concrete achievement."

The inflated style is itself a kind of euphemism. A mass of Latin words fall   15
upon the facts like soft snow, blurring the outlines and covering up all the
details. The great enemy of clear language is insincerity. When there is a gap
between one's real and one's declared aims, one turns as it were instinctively
to long words and exhausted idioms, like a cuttlefish squirting out ink. In our
age there is no such thing as "keeping out of politics." All issues are political
issues, and politics itself is a mass of lies, evasions, folly, hatred and schizophrenia. When the general atmosphere is bad, language must suffer. I should
expect to find—this is a guess which I have not sufficient knowledge to verify—that the German, Russian and Italian languages have all deteriorated in
the last ten or fifteen years, as a result of dictatorship.

But if thought corrupts language, language can also corrupt thought. A   16
bad usage can spread by tradition and imitation, even among people who
should and do know better. The debased language that I have been discussing is in some ways very convenient. Phrases like *a not unjustifiable assumption, leaves much to be desired, would serve no good purpose, a
consideration which we should do well to bear in mind,* are a continuous
temptation, a packet of aspirins always at one's elbow. Look back through
this essay, and for certain you will find that I have again and again committed
the very faults I am protesting against. By this morning's post I have received
a pamphlet dealing with conditions in Germany. The author tells me that he
"felt impelled" to write it. I open it at random, and here is almost the first
sentence that I see: "(The Allies) have an opportunity not only of achieving
a radical transformation of Germany's social and political structure in such a
way as to avoid a nationalistic reaction in Germany itself, but at the same
time of laying the foundations of a co-operative and unified Europe." You see,
he "feels impelled" to write—feels, presumably, that he has something new
to say—and yet his words, like cavalry horses answer the bugle, group themselves automatically into the familiar dreary pattern. This invasion of one's
mind by read-made phrases (*lay the foundations, achieve a radical transformation*) can only be prevented if one is constantly on guard against them,
and every such phrase anaesthetizes a portion of one's brain.

I said earlier that the decadence of our language is probably curable. Those   17
who deny this would argue, if they produced an argument at all, that language merely reflects existing social conditions, and that we cannot influence
its development by any direct tinkering with words and constructions. So far
as the general tone or spirit of a language goes, this may be true, but it is
not true in detail. Silly words and expressions have often disappeared, not
through any evolutionary process but owing to the conscious action of a minority. Two recent examples were *explore every avenue* and *leave no stone
unturned,* which were killed by the jeers of a few journalists. There is a long
list of flyblown metaphors which could similarly be got rid of if enough people would interest themselves in the job; and it should also be possible to
laugh the *not un*-formation out of existence,[3] to reduce the amount of Latin

---

[3] One can cure oneself of the *not un*-formation by memorizing this sentence: *A not unblack dog was chasing
a not unsmall rabbit across a not ungreen field.*

and Greek in the average sentence, to drive out foreign phrases and strayed scientific words, and, in general, to make pretentiousness unfashionable. But all these are minor points. The defense of the English language implies more than this, and perhaps it is best to start by saying what it does *not* imply.

To begin with it has nothing to do with archaism, with the salvaging of   18 obsolete words and turns of speech, or with the setting up of a "standard English" which must never be departed from. On the contrary, it is especially concerned with the scrapping of every word or idiom which has outworn its usefulness. It has nothing to do with correct grammar and syntax, which are of no importance so long as one makes one's meaning clear, or with the avoidance of Americanisms, or with having what is called a "good prose style." On the other hand it is not concerned with fake simplicity and the attempt to make written English colloquial. Nor does it even imply in every case preferring the Saxon word to the Latin one, though it does imply using the fewest and shortest words that will cover one's meaning. What is above all needed is to let the meaning choose the word, and not the other way about. In prose, the worst thing one can do with words is to surrender to them. When you think of a concrete object, you think wordlessly, and then, if you want to describe the thing you have been visualizing you probably hunt about till you find the exact words that seem to fit. When you think of something abstract you are more inclined to use words from the start, and unless you make a conscious effort to prevent it, the existing dialect will come rushing in and do the job for you, at the expense of blurring or even changing your meaning. Probably it is better to put off using words as long as possible and get one's meaning as clear as one can through pictures or sensations. Afterwards one can choose—not simply *accept*—the phrases that will best cover the meaning, and then switch round and decide what impression one's words are likely to make on another person. This last effort of the mind cuts out all stale or mixed images, all prefabricated phrases, needless repetitions, and humbug and vagueness generally. But one can often be in doubt about the effect of a word or a phrase, and one needs rules that one can rely on when instinct fails. I think the following rules will cover most cases:

   (i) Never use a metaphor, simile or other figure of speech which you are used to seeing in print.

  (ii) Never use a long word where a short one will do.

 (iii) If it is possible to cut a word out, always cut it out.

 (iv) Never use the passive where you can use the active.

  (v) Never use a foreign phrase, a scientific word or a jargon word if you can think of an everyday English equivalent.

 (vi) Break any of these rules sooner than say anything outright barbarous.

These rules sound elementary, and so they are, but they demand a deep change in attitude in anyone who has grown used to writing in the style now fashionable. One could keep all of them and still write bad English, but one could not write the kind of stuff that I quoted in those five specimens at the beginning of this article.

I have not here been considering the literary use of language, but merely   19
language as an instrument for expressing and not for concealing or preventing thought. Stuart Chase and others have come near to claiming that all
abstract words are meaningless, and have used this as a pretext for advocating a kind of political quietism. Since you don't know what Fascism is, how
can you struggle against Fascism? One need not swallow such absurdities as
this, but one ought to recognize that the present political chaos is connected
with the decay of language, and that one can probably bring about some
improvement by starting at the verbal end. If you simplify your English, you
are freed from the worst follies of orthodoxy. You cannot speak any of the
necessary dialects, and when you make a stupid remark its stupidity will be
obvious, even to yourself. Political language—and with variations this is true
of all political parties, from Conservatives to Anarchists—is designed to make
lies sound truthful and murder respectable, and to give an appearance of
solidity to pure wind. One cannot change this all in a moment, but one can
at least change one's own habits, and from time to time one can even, if one
jeers loudly enough, send some wornout and useless phrase—some *jackboot,
Achilles' heel, hotbed, melting pot, acid test, veritable inferno* or other
lump of verbal refuse—into the dustbin where it belongs.

QUESTIONS FOR MEANING

1. Why should language concern everyone, and not just English teachers
   and professional writers? Explain what Orwell means by his claim that
   language can corrupt thought.
2. Many people believe that they sound "educated" by using big words and
   abstract phrases, and so "rain" becomes "precipitation" (or *shower activity*) and libraries become learning resource centers. Why does Orwell
   prefer simple, concrete language?
3. Why do people write badly? What causes does Orwell identify in his
   essay?
4. Explain in your own words what is wrong with each of the five writing
   samples that Orwell includes in paragraph 3.
5. What does Orwell mean by "verbal false limbs"?
6. Over forty years have passed since Orwell first published this essay, and
   some of the phrases he ridicules have fallen from general use. Demonstrate that you understand what Orwell is complaining about by citing
   contemporary examples of pretentious diction, meaningless words, and
   political double-talk.
7. What is the connection between politics and language?
8. Orwell's fourth rule for writing well is, "Never use the passive where you
   can use the active." Explain the difference between the passive and active voice, and give at least one example of each.
9. Why is Orwell's sixth rule important?

10. Vocabulary: archaism (1), slovenliness (2), regeneration (2), frivolous (2), egregious (3), metaphor (5), evocative (5), banal (6), euphonious (11), idioms (11), scrupulous (11), purges (13), euphemism (13), concomitant (14), and colloquial (18).

QUESTIONS ABOUT STRATEGY

1. What point is Orwell emphasizing in his first two paragraphs, and why is it important to establish this point early in the essay?
2. Comment on Orwell's use of analogy in paragraph 2. How does the comparison between drinking and writing help to clarify Orwell's point?
3. How would you describe Orwell's own style? Does he ever violate his own standards?
4. Orwell protested against the use of "dying metaphors." Can you find examples of figurative language in this essay that are fresh and original?
5. What is the function of paragraph 9? Orwell writes that it is "a parody, but not a very gross one." What does he mean by this, and what is he trying to accomplish by contrasting "modern English" with a verse from the King James version of the Bible?
6. Orwell writes, "Political language . . . is designed to make lies sound truthful and murder respectable, and give an appearance of solidity to pure wind." As writing, this sentence is admirably clear. But is it fair? Do you agree with Orwell about the language of politics, or do you think he weakens his case through overstatement?

MARTIN LUTHER KING, JR.
Letter from Birmingham Jail

Martin Luther King, Jr. (1929–1968) was the most important leader of the movement to secure civil rights for black Americans during the mid-twentieth century. Ordained a Baptist minister in his father's church in Atlanta, King went on to receive a Ph.D. from Boston University in 1955. Two years later, he became the founder and director of the Southern Christian Leadership Conference, an organization he continued to lead until his assassination in 1968. He first came to national attention by organizing a boycott of the buses in Montgomery, Alabama (1955–1956)—a campaign that he recounts in Stride Toward Freedom: The Montgomery Story *(1958). His other books include* The Measure of a Man *(1959),* Why We Can't Wait *(1963), and* Where Do We Go From Here: Chaos or Community? *(1967). An advocate of nonviolence, King was jailed fourteen times in the course of his work for civil rights. His efforts helped secure the passage of the Civil Rights Bill in 1963, and, during the last years of his life, he was the recipient of many awards, most notably the Nobel Peace Prize in 1964.*

"Letter from Birmingham Jail" was written in **1963,** *when King was jailed for eight days as the result of his campaign against segregation in Birmingham, Alabama. In it, King responds to white clergymen who had criticized his work and blamed him for breaking the law. But "Letter from Birmingham Jail" is much more than a rebuttal of criticism. It is a well-reasoned and carefully argued defense of civil disobedience as a means of securing civil liberties.*

April 16, 1963

My Dear Fellow Clergymen:

While confined here in the Birmingham city jail, I came across your recent   1
statement calling my present activities "unwise and untimely." Seldom do I pause to answer criticism of my work and ideas. If I sought to answer all the criticisms that cross my desk, my secretaries would have little time for anything other than such correspondence in the course of the day, and I would have no time for constructive work. But since I feel that you are men of genuine good will and that your criticisms are sincerely put forth, I want to try to answer your statement in what I hope will be patient and reasonable terms.

I think I should indicate why I am here in Birmingham, since you have   2
been influenced by the view which argues against "outsiders coming in." I have the honor of serving as president of the Southern Christian Leadership Conference, an organization operating in every southern state, with headquarters in Atlanta, Georgia. We have some eighty-five affiliated organizations across the South, and one of them is the Alabama Christian Movement for Human Rights. Frequently we share staff, educational, and financial resources with our affiliates. Several months ago the affiliate here in Birmingham asked us to be on call to engage in a nonviolent direct-action program if such were deemed necessary. We readily consented, and when the hour came we lived

up to our promise. So I, along with several members of my staff, am here because I was invited here. I am here because I have organizational ties here.

But more basically, I am in Birmingham because injustice is here. Just as the prophets of the eighth century B.C. left their villages and carried their "thus saith the Lord" far beyond the boundaries of their home towns, and just as the Apostle Paul left his village of Tarsus and carried the gospel of Jesus Christ to the far corners of the Greco-Roman world, so am I compelled to carry the gospel of freedom beyond my own home town. Like Paul, I must constantly respond to the Macedonian call for aid.   3

Moreover, I am cognizant of the interrelatedness of all communities and states. I cannot sit idly by in Atlanta and not be concerned about what happens in Birmingham. Injustice anywhere is a threat to justice everywhere. We are caught in an inescapable network of mutuality, tied in a single garment of destiny. Whatever affects one directly, affects all indirectly. Never again can we afford to live with the narrow, provincial, "outside agitator" idea. Anyone who lives inside the United States can never be considered an outsider anywhere within its bounds.   4

You deplore the demonstrations taking place in Birmingham. But your statement, I am sorry to say, fails to express a similar concern for the conditions that brought about the demonstrations. I am sure that none of you would want to rest content with the superficial kind of social analysis that deals merely with effects and does not grapple with underlying causes. It is unfortunate that demonstrations are taking place in Birmingham, but it is even more unfortunate that the city's white power structure left the Negro community with no alternative.   5

In any nonviolent campaign there are four basic steps: collection of the facts to determine whether injustices exist; negotiation; self-purification; and direct action. We have gone through all these steps in Birmingham. There can be no gainsaying the fact that racial injustice engulfs this community. Birmingham is probably the most thoroughly segregated city in the United States. Its ugly record of brutality is widely known. Negroes have experienced grossly unjust treatment in courts. There have been more unsolved bombings of Negro homes and churches in Birmingham than in any other city in the nation. These are the hard, brutal facts of the case. On the basis of these conditions, Negro leaders sought to negotiate with the city fathers. But the latter consistently refused to engage in good-faith negotiation.   6

Then, last September, came the opportunity to talk with leaders of Birmingham's economic community. In the course of the negotiations, certain promises were made by the merchants—for example, to remove the stores' humiliating racial signs. On the basis of these promises, the Reverend Fred Shuttlesworth and the leaders of the Alabama Christian Movement for Human Rights agreed to a moratorium on all demonstrations. As the weeks and months went by, we realized that we were the victims of a broken promise. A few signs, briefly removed, returned; the others remained.   7

As in so many past experiences, our hopes had been blasted, and the shadow of deep disappointment settled upon us. We had no alternative ex-   8 cept to prepare for direct action, whereby we would present our very bodies as means of laying our case before the conscience of the local and the national community. Mindful of the difficulties involved, we decided to undertake a process of self-purification. We began a series of workshops on nonviolence, and we repeatedly asked ourselves: "Are you able to accept blows without retaliating?" "Are you able to endure the ordeal of jail?" We decided to schedule our direct-action program for the Easter season, realizing that except for Christmas, this is the main shopping period of the year. Knowing that a strong economic-withdrawal program would be the by-product of direct action, we felt that this would be the best time to bring pressure to bear on the merchants for the needed change.

Then it occurred to us that Birmingham's mayoral election was coming up   9
in March, and we speedily decided to postpone action until after election day. When we discovered that the Commissioner of Public Safety, Eugene "Bull" Connor, had piled up enough votes to be in the run-off, we decided again to postpone action until the day after the run-off so that the demonstrations could not be used to cloud the issues. Like many others, we waited to see Mr. Connor defeated, and to this end we endured postponement after postponement. Having aided in this community need, we felt that our direct-action program could be delayed no longer.

You may well ask, "Why direct action? Why sit-ins, marches, and so forth?   10
Isn't negotiation a better path?" You are quite right in calling for negotiation. Indeed, this is the very purpose of direct action. Nonviolent direct action seeks to create such a crisis and foster such a tension that a community which has constantly refused to negotiate is forced to confront the issue. It seeks so to dramatize the issue that it can no longer be ignored. My citing the creation of tension as part of the work of the nonviolent-resister may sound rather shocking. But I must confess that I am not afraid of the word "tension." I have earnestly opposed violent tension, but there is a type of constructive, nonviolent tension which is necessary for growth. Just as Socrates felt that it was necessary to create a tension in the mind so that individuals could rise from the bondage of myths and half-truths to the unfettered realm of creative analysis and objective appraisal, so must we see the need for nonviolent gadflies to create the kind of tension in society that will help men rise from the dark depths of prejudice and racism to the majestic heights of understanding and brotherhood.

The purpose of our direct-action program is to create a situation so crisis-   11
packed that it will inevitably open the door to negotiation. I therefore concur with you in your call for negotiation. Too long has our beloved Southland been bogged down in a tragic effort to live in monologue rather than dialogue.

One of the basic points in your statement is that the action that I and my   12
associates have taken in Birmingham is untimely. Some have asked: "Why didn't you give the new city administration time to act?" The only answer that I can give to this query is that the new Birmingham administration must be prodded about as much as the outgoing one, before it will act. We are sadly mistaken if we feel that the election of Albert Boutwell as mayor will

bring the millennium to Birmingham. While Mr. Boutwell is a much more gentle person than Mr. Connor, they are both segregationists, dedicated to maintenance of the status quo. I have hoped that Mr. Boutwell will be reasonable enough to see the futility of massive resistance to desegregation. But he will not see this without pressure from devotees of civil rights. My friends, I must say to you that we have not made a single gain in civil rights without determined legal and nonviolent pressure. Lamentably, it is an historical fact that privileged groups seldom give up their privileges voluntarily. Individuals may see the moral light and voluntarily give up their unjust posture; but, as Reinhold Niebuhr has reminded us, groups tend to be more immoral than individuals.

We know through painful experience that freedom is never voluntarily   13
given by the oppressor; it must be demanded by the oppressed. Frankly, I have yet to engage in a direct-action campaign that was "well timed" in the view of those who have not suffered unduly from the disease of segregation. For years now I have heard the word "Wait!" It rings in the ear of every Negro with piercing familiarity. This "Wait" has almost always meant "Never." We must come to see, with one of our distinguished jurists, that "justice too long delayed is justice denied."

We have waited for more than 340 years for our constitutional and God-   14
given rights. The nations of Asia and Africa are moving with jetlike speed toward gaining political independence, but we still creep at horse-and-buggy pace toward gaining a cup of coffee at a lunch counter. Perhaps it is easy for those who have never felt the stinging darts of segregation to say, "Wait." But when you have seen vicious mobs lynch your mothers and fathers at will and drown your sisters and brothers at whim; when you have seen hate-filled policemen curse, kick, and even kill your black brothers and sisters; when you see the vast majority of your twenty million Negro brothers smothering in an airtight cage of poverty in the midst of an affluent society; when you suddenly find your tongue twisted and your speech stammering as you seek to explain to your six-year-old daughter why she can't go to the public amusement park that has just been advertised on television, and see tears welling up in her eyes when she is told that Funtown is closed to colored children, and see ominous clouds of inferiority beginning to form in her little mental sky, and see her beginning to distort her personality by developing an unconscious bitterness toward white people; when you have to concoct an answer for a five-year-old son who is asking, "Daddy, why do white people treat colored people so mean?"; when you take a cross-country drive and find it necessary to sleep night after night in the uncomfortable corners of your automobile because no motel will accept you; when you are humiliated day in and day out by nagging signs reading "white" and "colored"; when your first name becomes "nigger," your middle name becomes "boy" (however old you are) and your last name becomes "John," and your wife and mother are never given the respected title "Mrs."; when you are harried by day and haunted by night by the fact that you are a Negro, living constantly at tiptoe stance, never quite knowing what to expect next, and are plagued

with inner fears and outer resentments; when you are forever fighting a degenerating sense of "nobodiness"—then you will understand why we find it difficult to wait. There comes a time when the cup of endurance runs over, and men are no longer willing to be plunged into the abyss of despair. I hope, sirs, you can understand our legitimate and unavoidable impatience.

You express a great deal of anxiety over our willingness to break laws.   15
This is certainly a legitimate concern. Since we so diligently urge people to obey the Supreme Court's decision of 1954 outlawing segregation in the public schools, at first glance it may seem rather paradoxical for us consciously to break laws. One may well ask: "How can you advocate breaking some laws and obeying others?" The answer lies in the fact that there are two types of laws; just and unjust. I would be the first to advocate obeying just laws. One has not only a legal but a moral responsibility to obey just laws. Conversely, one has a moral responsibility to disobey unjust laws. I would agree with St. Augustine that "an unjust law is no law at all."

Now, what is the difference between the two? How does one determine   16
whether a law is just or unjust? A just law is a man-made code that squares with the moral law or the law of God. An unjust law is a code that is out of harmony with the moral law. To put it in the terms of St. Thomas Aquinas: An unjust law is a human law that is not rooted in eternal law and natural law. Any law that uplifts human personality is just. Any law that degrades human personality is unjust. All segregation statutes are unjust because segregation distorts the soul and damages the personality. It gives the segregator a false sense of superiority and the segregated a false sense of inferiority. Segregation, to use the terminology of the Jewish philosopher Martin Buber, substitutes an "I-it" relationship for an "I-thou" relationship and ends up relegating persons to the status of things. Hence segregation is not only politically, economically, and sociologically unsound, it is morally wrong and sinful. Paul Tillich has said that sin is separation. Is not segregation an existential expression of man's tragic separation, his awful estrangement, his terrible sinfulness? Thus it is that I can urge men to obey the 1954 decision of the Supreme Court, for it is morally right; and I can urge them to disobey segregation ordinances, for they are morally wrong.

Let us consider a more concrete example of just and unjust laws. An un-   17
just law is a code that a numerical or power majority group compels a minority group to obey but does not make binding on itself. This is *difference* made legal. By the same token, a just law is a code that a majority compels a minority to follow and that it is willing to follow itself. This is *sameness* made legal.

Let me give another explanation. A law is unjust if it is inflicted on a   18
minority that, as a result of being denied the right to vote, had no part in enacting or devising the law. Who can say that the legislature of Alabama which set up that state's segregation laws was democratically elected? Throughout Alabama all sorts of devious methods are used to prevent Negroes from becoming registered voters, and there are some counties in which,

even though Negroes constitute a majority of the population, not a single Negro is registered. Can any law enacted under such circumstances be considered democratically structured?

Sometimes a law is just on its face and unjust in its application. For instance, I have been arrested on a charge of parading without a permit. Now, there is nothing wrong in having an ordinance which requires a permit for a parade. But such an ordinance becomes unjust when it is used to maintain segregation and to deny citizens the First-Amendment privilege of peaceful assembly and protest.

I hope you are able to see the distinction I am trying to point out. In no sense do I advocate evading or defying the law, as would the rabid segregationist. That would lead to anarchy. One who breaks an unjust law must do so openly, lovingly, and with a willingness to accept the penalty. I submit that an individual who breaks a law that conscience tells him is unjust, and who willingly accepts the penalty of imprisonment in order to arouse the conscience of the community over its injustice, is in reality expressing the highest respect for law.

Of course, there is nothing new about this kind of civil disobedience. It was evidenced sublimely in the refusal of Shadrach, Meshach, and Abednego to obey the laws of Nebuchadnezzar, on the ground that a higher moral law was at stake. It was practiced superbly by the early Christians, who were willing to face hungry lions and the excruciating pain of chopping blocks rather than submit to certain unjust laws of the Roman Empire. To a degree, academic freedom is a reality today because Socrates practiced civil disobedience. In our own nation, the Boston Tea Party represented a massive act of civil disobedience.

We should never forget that everything Adolf Hitler did in Germany was "legal" and everything the Hungarian freedom fighters did in Hungary was "illegal." It was "illegal" to aid and comfort a Jew in Hitler's Germany. Even so, I am sure that, had I lived in Germany at the time, I would have aided and comforted my Jewish brothers. If today I lived in a Communist country where certain principles dear to the Christian faith are suppressed, I would openly advocate disobeying that country's anti-religious laws.

I must make two honest confessions to you, my Christian and Jewish brothers. First, I must confess that over the past few years I have been gravely disappointed with the white moderate. I have almost reached the regrettable conclusion that the Negro's great stumbling block in his stride toward freedom is not the White Citizen's Counciler or the Ku Klux Klanner, but the white moderate, who is more devoted to "order" than to justice; who prefers a negative peace which is the absence of tension to a positive peace which is the presence of justice; who constantly says, "I agree with you in the goal you seek, but I cannot agree with your methods of direct action"; who paternalistically believes he can set the timetable for another man's freedom; who lives by a mythical concept of time and who constantly advises the Negro to wait for a "more convenient season." Shallow understanding from people of good will is more frustrating than absolute misunderstanding from people of ill will. Lukewarm acceptance is much more bewildering than outright rejection.

I had hoped that the white moderate would understand that law and order exist for the purpose of establishing justice and that when they fail in this purpose they become the dangerously structured dams that block the flow of social progress. I had hoped that the white moderate would understand that the present tension in the South is a necessary phase of the transition from an obnoxious negative peace, in which the Negro passively accepted his unjust plight, to a substantive and positive peace, in which all men will respect the dignity and worth of human personality. Actually, we who engage in nonviolent direct action are not the creators of tension. We merely bring to the surface the hidden tension that is already alive. We bring it out in the open, where it can be seen and dealt with. Like a boil that can never be cured so long as it is covered up but must be opened with all its ugliness to the natural medicines of air and light, injustice must be exposed, with all the tension its exposure creates, to the light of human conscience and the air of national opinion, before it can be cured.   24

In your statement you assert that our actions, even though peaceful, must be condemned because they precipitate violence. But is this a logical assertion? Isn't this like condemning a robbed man because his possession of money precipitated the evil act of robbery? Isn't this like condemning Socrates because his unswerving commitment to truth and his philosophical inquiries precipitated the act by the misguided populace in which they made him drink hemlock? Isn't this like condemning Jesus because his unique God-consciousness and never-ceasing devotion to God's will precipitated the evil act of crucifixion? We must come to see that, as the federal courts have consistently affirmed, it is wrong to urge an individual to cease his efforts to gain his basic constitutional rights because the quest may precipitate violence. Society must protect the robbed and punish the robber.   25

I had also hoped that the white moderate would reject the myth concerning time in relation to the struggle for freedom. I have just received a letter from a white brother in Texas. He writes: "All Christians know that the colored people will receive equal rights eventually, but it is possible that you are in too great a religious hurry. It has taken Christianity almost two thousand years to accomplish what it has. The teachings of Christ take time to come to earth." Such an attitude stems from a tragic misconception of time, from the strangely irrational notion that there is something in the very flow of time that will inevitably cure all ills. Actually, time itself is neutral; it can be used either destructively or constructively. More and more I feel that the people of ill will have used time much more effectively than have the people of good will. We will have to repent in this generation not merely for the hateful words and actions of the bad people, but for the appalling silence of the good people. Human progress never rolls in on wheels of inevitability; it comes through the tireless efforts of men willing to be co-workers with God,   26 and without this hard work, time itself becomes an ally of the forces of social stagnation. We must use time creatively, in the knowledge that the time is always ripe to do right. Now is the time to make real the promise of democracy and transform our pending national elegy into a creative psalm of brotherhood. Now is the time to lift our national policy from the quicksand of racial injustice to the solid rock of human dignity.

You speak of our activity in Birmingham as extreme. At first I was rather   27
disappointed that fellow clergymen would see my nonviolent efforts as those of an extremist. I began thinking about the fact that I stand in the middle of two opposing forces in the Negro community. One is a force of complacency, made up in part of Negroes who, as a result of long years of oppression, are so drained of self-respect and a sense of "somebodiness" that they have adjusted to segregation; and in part of a few middle-class Negroes who, because of a degree of academic and economic security and because in some ways they profit by segregation, have become insensitive to the problems of the masses. The other force is one of bitterness and hatred, and it comes perilously close to advocating violence. It is expressed in the various black nationalist groups that are springing up across the nation, the largest and best-known being Elijah Muhammad's Muslim movement. Nourished by the Negro's frustration over the continued existence of racial discrimination, this movement is made up of people who have lost faith in America, who have absolutely repudiated Christianity, and who have concluded that the white man is an incorrigible "devil."

I have tried to stand between these two forces, saying that we need emu-   28
late neither the "do-nothingism" of the complacent nor the hatred and despair of the black nationalist. For there is the more excellent way of love and nonviolent protest. I am grateful to God that, through the influence of the Negro church, the way of nonviolence became an integral part of our struggle.

If this philosophy had not emerged, by now many streets of the South   29
would, I am convinced, be flowing with blood. And I am further convinced that if our white brothers dismiss as "rabble-rousers" and "outside agitators" those of us who employ nonviolent direct action, and if they refuse to support our nonviolent efforts, millions of Negroes will, out of frustration and despair, seek solace and security in black-nationalist ideologies—a development that would inevitably lead to a frightening racial nightmare.

Oppressed people cannot remain oppressed forever. The yearning for free-   30
dom eventually manifests itself, and that is what has happened to the American Negro. Something within has reminded him of his birthright of freedom, and something without has reminded him that it can be gained. Consciously or unconsciously, he has been caught up by the *Zeitgeist,* and with his black brothers of Africa and his brown and yellow brothers of Asia, South America, and the Caribbean, the United States Negro is moving with a sense of great urgency toward the promised land of racial justice. If one recognizes this vital urge that has engulfed the Negro community, one should readily understand

why public demonstrations are taking place. The Negro has many pent-up resentments and latent frustrations, and he must release them. So let him march; let him make prayer pilgrimages to the city hall; let him go on freedom rides—and try to understand why he must do so. If his repressed emotions are not released in nonviolent ways, they will seek expression through violence; this is not a threat but a fact of history. So I have not said to my people, "Get rid of your discontent." Rather, I have tried to say that this normal and healthy discontent can be channeled into the creative outlet of nonviolent direct action. And now this approach is being termed extremist.

But though I was initially disappointed at being categorized as an extre-   31
mist, as I continued to think about the matter I gradually gained a measure of satisfaction from the label. Was not Jesus an extremist for love: "Love your enemies, bless them that curse you, do good to them that hate you, and pray for them which despitefully use you, and persecute you." Was not Amos an extremist for justice: "Let justice roll down like waters and righteousness like an everflowing stream." Was not Paul an extremist for the Christian gospel: "I bear in my body the marks of the Lord Jesus." Was not Martin Luther an extremist: "Here I stand; I cannot do otherwise, so help me God." And John Bunyan: "I will stay in jail to the end of my days before I make a butchery of my conscience." And Abraham Lincoln: "This nation cannot survive half slave and half free." And Thomas Jefferson: "We hold these truths to be self-evident, that all men are created equal. . . ." So the question is not whether we will be extremists, but what kind of extremists we will be. Will we be extremists for hate or for love? Will we be extremists for the preservation of injustice or for the extension of justice? In that dramatic scene on Calvary's hill three men were crucified. We must never forget that all three were crucified for the same crime—the crime of extremism. Two were extremists for immorality, and thus fell below their environment. The other, Jesus Christ, was an extremist for love, truth, and goodness, and thereby rose above his environment. Perhaps the South, the nation, and the world are in dire need of creative extremists.

I had hoped that the white moderate would see this need. Perhaps I was   32
too optimistic; perhaps I expected too much. I suppose I should have realized that few members of the oppressor race can understand the deep groans and passionate yearnings of the oppressed race, and still fewer have the vision to see that injustice must be rooted out by strong, persistent, and determined action. I am thankful, however, that some of our white brothers in the South have grasped the meaning of this social revolution and committed themselves to it. They are still all too few in quantity, but they are big in quality. Some— such as Ralph McGill, Lillian Smith, Harry Golden, James McBride Dabbs, Ann Braden, and Sarah Patton Boyle—have written about our struggle in eloquent and prophetic terms. Others have marched with us down nameless streets of the South. They have languished in filthy, roach-infested jails, suffering the abuse and brutality of policemen who view them as "dirty nigger-lovers." Unlike so many of their moderate brothers and sisters, they have recognized

the urgency of the moment and sensed the need for powerful "action" antidotes to combat the disease of segregation.

Let me take note of my other major disappointment. I have been so greatly   33
disappointed with the white church and its leadership. Of course, there are
some notable exceptions. I am not unmindful of the fact that each of you has
taken some significant stands on this issue. I commend you, Reverend
Stallings, for your Christian stand on this past Sunday, in welcoming
Negroes to your worship service on a nonsegregated basis. I commend the
Catholic leaders of this state for integrating Spring Hill College several
years ago.

But despite these notable exceptions, I must honestly reiterate that I have   34
been disappointed with the church. I do not say this as one of those negative
critics who can always find something wrong with the church. I say this as a
minister of the gospel, who loves the church; who was nurtured in its bosom;
who has been sustained by its spiritual blessings and who will remain true to
it as long as the cord of life shall lengthen.

When I was suddenly catapulted into the leadership of the bus protest in   35
Montgomery, Alabama, a few years ago, I felt we would be supported by the
white church. I felt that the white ministers, priests, and rabbis of the South
would be among our strongest allies. Instead, some have been outright opponents, refusing to understand the freedom movement and misrepresenting
its leaders; all too many others have been more cautious than courageous
and have remained silent behind the anesthetizing security of stained-glass
windows.

In spite of my shattered dreams, I came to Birmingham with the hope that   36
the white religious leadership of this community would see the justice of our
cause and, with deep moral concern, would serve as the channel through
which our just grievances could reach the power structure. I had hoped that
each of you would understand. But again I have been disappointed.

There was a time when the church was very powerful—in the time when   37
the early Christians rejoiced at being deemed worthy to suffer for what they
believed. In those days the church was not merely a thermometer that recorded the ideas and principles of popular opinion; it was a thermostat that
transformed the mores of society. Whenever the early Christians entered a
town, the people in power became disturbed and immediately sought to convict the Christians for being "disturbers of the peace" and "outside agitators."
But the Christians pressed on, in the conviction that they were "a colony of
heaven," called to obey God rather than man. Small in number, they were big
in commitment. They were too God-intoxicated to be "astronomically intimidated." By their effort and example they brought an end to such ancient evils
as infanticide and gladiatorial contests.

Things are different now. So often the contemporary church is a weak,   38
ineffectual voice with an uncertain sound. So often it is an archdefender of
the status quo. Far from being disturbed by the presence of the church, the
power structure of the average community is consoled by the church's silent—and often even vocal—sanction of things as they are.

But the judgment of God is upon the church as never before. If today's   39
church does not recapture the sacrificial spirit of the early church, it will lose
its authenticity, forfeit the loyalty of millions, and be dismissed as an irrelevant social club with no meaning for the twentieth century. Every day I meet
young people whose disappointment with the church has turned into outright disgust.

Perhaps I have once again been too optimistic. Is organized religion too   40
inextricably bound to the status quo to save our nation and the world? Perhaps I must turn my faith to the inner spiritual church, the church within
the church, as the true *ekklesia* and the hope of the world. But again I am
thankful to God that some noble souls from the ranks of organized religion
have broken loose from the paralyzing chains of conformity and joined us as
active partners in the struggle for freedom. They have left their secure con-
gregations and walked the streets of Albany, Georgia, with us. They have
gone down the highways of the South on torturous rides for freedom. Yes,
they have gone to jail with us. Some have been dismissed from their churches,
have lost the support of their bishops and fellow ministers. But they have
acted in the faith that right defeated is stronger than evil triumphant. Their
witness has been the spiritual salt that has preserved the true meaning of
the gospel in these troubled times. They have carved a tunnel of hope through
the dark mountain of disappointment.

I hope the church as a whole will meet the challenge of this decisive hour.   41
But even if the church does not come to the aid of justice, I have no despair
about the future. I have no fear about the outcome of our struggle in Birmingham, even if our motives are at present misunderstood. We will reach
the goal of freedom in Birmingham and all over the nation, because the goal
of America is freedom. Abused and scorned though we may be, our destiny
is tied up with America's destiny. Before the pilgrims landed at Plymouth, we
were here. Before the pen of Jefferson etched the majestic words of the
Declaration of Independence across the pages of history, we were here. For
more than two centuries our forebears labored in this country without wages;
they made cotton king; they built the homes of their masters while suffering
gross injustice and shameful humiliation—and yet out of a bottomless vitality
they continued to thrive and develop. If the inexpressible cruelties of slavery
could not stop us, the opposition we now face will surely fail. We will win our
freedom because the sacred heritage of our nation and the eternal will of
God are embodied in our echoing demands.

Before closing I feel impelled to mention one other point in your state-   42
ment that has troubled me profoundly. You warmly commended the Birmingham police force for keeping "order" and "preventing violence." I doubt that
you would have so warmly commended the police force if you had seen its
dogs sinking their teeth into unarmed, nonviolent Negroes. I doubt that you
would so quickly commend the policemen if you were to observe their ugly
and inhumane treatment of Negroes here in the city jail; if you were to watch
them push and curse old Negro women and young Negro girls; if you were
to see them slap and kick old Negro men and young boys; if you were to
observe them, as they did on two occasions, refuse to give us food because

we wanted to sing our grace together. I cannot join you in your praise of the Birmingham police department.

It is true that the police have exercised a degree of discipline in handling the demonstrators. In this sense they have conducted themselves rather "nonviolently" in public. But for what purpose? To preserve the evil system of segregation. Over the past few years I have consistently preached that nonviolence demands that the means we use must be as pure as the ends we seek. I have tried to make clear that it is wrong to use immoral means to attain moral ends. But now I must affirm that it is just as wrong, or perhaps even more so, to use moral means to preserve immoral ends. Perhaps Mr. Connor and his policemen have been rather nonviolent in public, as was Chief Pritchett in Albany, Georgia, but they have used the moral means of nonviolence to maintain the immoral end of racial injustice. As T. S. Eliot has said, "The last temptation is the greatest treason: To do the right deed for the wrong reason." 43

I wish you had commended the Negro sit-inners and demonstrators of Birmingham for their sublime courage, their willingness to suffer, and their amazing discipline in the midst of great provocation. One day the South will recognize its real heroes. They will be the James Merediths, with the noble sense of purpose that enables them to face jeering and hostile mobs, and with the agonizing loneliness that characterizes the life of the pioneer. They will be old, oppressed, battered Negro women, symbolized in a seventy-two-year-old woman in Montgomery, Alabama, who rose up with a sense of dignity and with her people decided not to ride segregated buses, and who responded with ungrammatical profundity to one who inquired about her weariness: "My feets is tired, but my soul is at rest." They will be the young high school and college students, the young ministers of the gospel and a host of their elders, courageously and nonviolently sitting in at lunch counters and willingly going to jail for conscience' sake. One day the South will know that when these disinherited children of God sat down at lunch counters, they were in reality standing up for what is best in the American dream and for the most sacred values in our Judeo-Christian heritage, thereby bringing our nation back to those great wells of democracy which were dug deep by the founding fathers in their formulation of the Constitution and the Declaration of Independence. 44

Never before have I written so long a letter. I'm afraid it is much too long to take your precious time. I can assure you that it would have been much shorter if I had been writing from a comfortable desk, but what else can one do when he is alone in a narrow jail cell, other than write long letters, think long thoughts, and pray long prayers? 45

If I have said anything in this letter that overstates the truth and indicates an unreasonable impatience, I beg you to forgive me. If I have said anything that understates the truth and indicates my having a patience that allows me to settle for anything less than brotherhood, I beg God to forgive me. 46

I hope this letter finds you strong in the faith. I also hope that circumstances will soon make it possible for me to meet each of you, not as an integrationist or a civil-rights leader but as a fellow clergyman and a Chris- 47 tian brother. Let us all hope that the dark clouds of racial prejudice will soon pass away and the deep fog of misunderstanding will be lifted from our fear-drenched communities, and in some not too distant tomorrow the radiant stars of love and brotherhood will shine over our great nation with all their scintillating beauty.

Yours for the cause of Peace and Brotherhood,

Martin Luther King, Jr.

QUESTIONS FOR MEANING

1. What reason does King give for writing this letter? What justification does he provide for its length? How do these explanations work to his advantage?
2. One of the many charges brought against King at the time of his arrest was that he was an "outsider" who had no business in Birmingham. How does King defend himself? What three reasons does he cite to justify his presence in Birmingham?
3. King also responds to the criticism that his campaign for civil rights was "untimely." What is his defense against this charge?
4. What does King mean by nonviolent "direct-action"? What sort of activities did he lead people to pursue? Identify the four basic steps to a direct-action campaign and explain what such campaigns were meant to accomplish.
5. Why did King believe that a direct-action campaign was necessary in Birmingham? Why did the black community in Birmingham turn to King? What problems were they facing, and what methods had they already tried before deciding upon direct-action?
6. What was the 1954 Supreme Court decision that King refers to in paragraph 16? Why was King able to charge that the "rabid segregationist" breaks the law?
7. King's critics charged that he obeyed the law selectively. He answers by arguing there is a difference between just and unjust laws, and that moral law requires men and women to break unjust laws that are imposed upon them. How can you tell the difference between laws that you should honor and laws that you should break? What is King's definition of an unjust law, and what historical examples does he give to illustrate situations in which unjust laws have to be broken?
8. What does King mean when he complains of the "anesthetizing security of stained-glass windows"? How can churches make men and women feel falsely secure?

QUESTIONS ABOUT STRATEGY

1. Why did King address his letter to fellow clergymen? Why was he disappointed in them, and what did he expect his letter to accomplish?
2. Is there anything in the substance of this letter that reveals it was written for an audience familiar with the Bible and modern theology? Do you think

King intended this letter to be read only by clergymen? Can you point to anything that suggests King may have really written for a larger, more general audience?

3. How does King characterize himself in this letter? What sort of a man does he seem to be, and what role does his presentation of himself play in his argument? How does he establish that he is someone worth listening to—and that it is important to listen to what he has to say?

4. *Ekklesia* is Greek for assembly, congregation, or church. Why does King use this word in paragraph 40 instead of simply saying "the church"?

5. Martin Luther King had much experience as a preacher when he wrote this famous letter. Is there anything about its style that reminds you of oratory? How effective would this letter be if delivered as a speech?

BETTY FRIEDAN
The Importance of Work

Betty Friedan was one of the founders of the National Organization for Women, serving as NOW's first president between 1966 and 1970. Born in Peoria, Illinois, and educated at Smith College, the University of California, and the University of Iowa, Friedan has lectured at more than fifty universities and institutes. Her essays have appeared in numerous periodicals, including the Saturday Review, Harper's, McCall's, Redbook, Good Housekeeping, *and the* Ladies' Home Journal. *Her books include* It Changed My life *(1976) and* The Second Stage *(1981). The following essay is drawn from the book that made her famous,* The Feminine Mystique *(**1963***).*

A quarter of a century has now passed since Friedan published this book, and the leadership of the woman's movement has passed to a younger generation. But if the development of that movement could be traced back to the publication of a single work, it would have to be The Feminine Mystique. *Friedan believed that women needed to escape from the roles they had assumed as wives and mothers, and if her ideas no longer seem as bold as they once were, it is because she anticipated most of the concerns that would dominate the analysis of male/female relations during the 1970s and 1980s. "The Importance of Work" is an editor's title for the concluding pages of Friedan's book, an excerpt that reveals Friedan's conviction that women need to enter the mainstream of the American workforce—not simply as typists and file clerks, but as the full equals of men.*

The question of how a person can most fully realize his own capacities and thus achieve identity has become an important concern of the philosophers and the social and psychological thinkers of our time—and for good reason. Thinkers of other times put forth the idea that people were, to a great extent, defined by the work they did. The work that a man had to do to eat, to stay alive, to meet the physical necessities of his environment, dictated his identity. And in this sense, when work is seen merely as a means of survival, human identity was dictated by biology.

But today the problem of human identity has changed. For the work that defined man's place in society and his sense of himself has also changed man's world. Work, and the advance of knowledge, has lessened man's dependence on his environment; his biology and the work he must do for biological survival are no longer sufficient to define his identity. This can be most clearly seen in our own abundant society; men no longer need to work all day to eat. They have an unprecedented freedom to choose the kind of work they will do; they also have an unprecedented amount of time apart from the hours and days that must actually be spent in making a living. And suddenly one realizes the significance of today's identity crisis—for women, and increasingly, for men. One sees the human significance of work—not merely as the means of biological survival, but as the giver of self and the transcender of self, as the creator of human identity and human evolution.

For "self-realization" or "self-fulfillment" or "identity" does not come from   3
looking into a mirror in rapt contemplation of one's own image. Those who
have most fully realized themselves, in a sense that can be recognized by the
human mind even though it cannot be clearly defined, have done so in the
service of a human purpose larger than themselves. Men from varying disciplines have used different words for this mysterious process from which comes
the sense of self. The religious mystics, the philosophers, Marx, Freud—all
had different names for it: man finds himself by losing himself; man is defined
by his relation to the means of production; the ego, the self, grows through
understanding and mastering reality—through work and love.

The identity crisis, which has been noted by Erik Erikson and others in   4
recent years in the American man, seems to occur for lack of, and be cured
by finding, the work, or cause, or purpose that evokes his own creativity.
Some never find it, for it does not come from busy-work or punching a time
clock. It does not come from just making a living, working by formula, finding
a secure spot as an organization man. The very argument, by Riesman and
others, that man no longer finds identity in the work defined as a paycheck
job, assumes that identity for man comes through creative work of his own
that contributes to the human community: the core of the self becomes aware,
becomes real, and grows through work that carries forward human society.

Work, the shopworn staple of the economists, has become the new frontier   5
of psychology. Psychiatrists have long used "occupational therapy" with patients in mental hospitals; they have recently discovered that to be of real
psychological value, it must be not just "therapy," but real work, serving a
real purpose in the community. And work can now be seen as the key to the
problem that has no name. The identity crisis of American women began a
century ago, as more and more of the work important to the world, more and
more of the work that used their human abilities and through which they
were able to find self-realization, was taken from them.

Until, and even into, the last century, strong, capable women were needed   6
to pioneer our new land; with their husbands, they ran the farms and plan-
tations and Western homesteads. These women were respected and self-respecting members of a society whose pioneering purpose centered in the
home. Strength and independence, responsibility and self-confidence, self-
discipline and courage, freedom and equality were part of the American character for both men and women, in all the first generations. The women who
came by steerage from Ireland, Italy, Russia, and Poland worked beside their
husbands in the sweatshops and the laundries, learned the new language, and
saved to send their sons and daughters to college. Women were never quite
as "feminine," or held in as much contempt, in America as they were in Europe. American women seemed to European travelers, long before our time,
less passive, childlike, and feminine than their own wives in France or Germany or England. By an accident of history, American women shared in the
work of society longer, and grew with the men. Grade- and high-school education for boys and girls alike was almost always the rule; and in the West,
where women shared the pioneering work the longest, even the universities
were coeducational from the beginning.

The identity crisis for women did not begin in America until the fire and   7
strength and ability of the pioneer women were no longer needed, no longer
used, in the middle-class homes of the Eastern and Midwestern cities, when
the pioneering was done and men began to build the new society in industries and professions outside the home. But the daughters of the pioneer
women had grown too used to freedom and work to be content with leisure
and passive femininity.

It was not an American, but a South African woman, Mrs. Olive Schreiner,   8
who warned at the turn of the century that the quality and quantity of wom-
en's functions in the social universe were decreasing as fast as civilization
was advancing; that if women did not win back their right to a full share of
honored and useful work, woman's mind and muscle would weaken in a parasitic state; her offspring, male and female, would weaken progressively, and
civilization itself would deteriorate.

The feminists saw clearly that education and the right to participate in the   9
more advanced work of society were women's greatest needs. They fought
for and won the rights to new, fully human identity for women. But how very
few of their daughters and granddaughters have chosen to use their education and their abilities for any large creative purpose, for responsible work in
society? How many of them have been deceived, or have deceived themselves, into clinging to the outgrown, childlike femininity of "Occupation:
housewife"?

It was not a minor matter, their mistaken choice. We now know that the   10
same range of potential ability exists for women as for men. Women, as well
as men, can only find their identity in work that uses their full capacities. A
woman cannot find her identity through others—her husband, her children.
She cannot find it in the dull routine of housework. As thinkers of every age
have said, it is only when a human being faces squarely the fact that he can
forfeit his own life, that he becomes truly aware of himself, and begins to
take his existence seriously. Sometimes this awareness comes only at the
moment of death. Sometimes it comes from a more subtle facing of death:
the death of self in passive conformity, in meaningless work. The feminine
mystique prescribes just such a living death for women. Faced with the slow
death of self, the American woman must begin to take her life seriously.

"We measure ourselves by many standards," said the great American psy-   11
chologist William James, nearly a century ago. "Our strength and our intelligence, our wealth and even our good luck, are things which warm our heart
and make us feel ourselves a match for life. But deeper than all such things,
and able to suffice unto itself without them, is the sense of the amount of
effort which we can put forth."

If women do not put forth, finally, that effort to become all that they have   12
it in them to become, they will forfeit their own humanity. A woman today
who has no goal, no purpose, no ambition patterning her days into the future,
making her stretch and grow beyond that small score of years in which her
body can fill its biological function, is committing a kind of suicide. For that
future half a century after the child-bearing years are over is a fact that an

American woman cannot deny. Nor can she deny that as a housewife, the world is indeed rushing past her door while she just sits and watches. The terror she feels is real, if she has no place in that world.

The feminine mystique has succeeded in burying millions of American   13
women alive. There is no way for these women to break out of their comfortable concentration camps except by finally putting forth an effort—that human effort which reaches beyond biology, beyond the narrow walls of home, to help shape the future. Only by such a personal commitment to the future can American women break out of the housewife trap and truly find fulfillment as wives and mothers—by fulfilling their own unique possibilities as separate human beings.

QUESTIONS FOR MEANING

1. In her opening paragraph, Friedan writes, "when work is seen merely as a means of survival, human identity was dictated by biology." What does this mean?
2. Does Friedan believe that all types of work are equally satisfying? Where does she define the type of work that has "human significance"?
3. According to Friedan, what is the historical explanation for the identity crisis many American women suffered in recent decades?
4. What's wrong with "Occupation: housewife"? Why does Friedan believe that women cannot find fulfillment simply by being wives and mothers?
5. Explain Friedan's allusion to "feminists" in paragraph 9. Who were the early feminists, and what did they accomplish?
6. Although you have been given only the last few pages of Friedan's book, can you construct a definition for what she means by "the feminine mystique"?
7. Vocabulary: transcender (2), rapt (3), mystics (3), parasitic (8), deteriorate (8), and forfeit (10).

QUESTIONS ABOUT STRATEGY

1. What is the premise that underlies Friedan's argument on behalf of meaningful careers for women?
2. Why does Friedan discuss women within the context of psychological "identity"? Why is it important for her to link the needs of women with the needs of men?
3. Comment on Friedan's use of quotation. She refers, for support, to four men (Marx, Freud, Erik Erikson, and William James) and to only one woman, Olive Schreiner. Does her reliance upon male authorities help or hurt her argument?
4. When Friedan declares that housewives are "committing a kind of suicide" trapped within homes that are "comfortable concentration camps," is she drawing her work together with a forceful conclusion or weakening it through exaggeration?

SUGGESTIONS FOR WRITING

1. Defend or attack Plato's claim that "government can be at its best and free from dissension only where the destined rulers are least desirous of holding office."
2. Identify a modern politician who governs according to Machiavellian principles. Be careful not to make groundless accusations. Do research if necessary to write an argument that will include specific evidence.
3. Write a dialogue between Plato and Machiavelli on the question of how a republic should be ruled.
4. Respond to Marvell by writing an argument in defense of chastity.
5. Using "A Modest Proposal" as your model, write a satirical essay proposing a "solution" to a contemporary social problem other than poverty.
6. Write a counterargument to Jefferson, a "Declaration of Continued Dependence" from the point of view of George III.
7. Drawing upon the work of Mary Wollstonecraft, Margaret Sanger, and Betty Friedan, write a "Declaration of Independence for Women."
8. Marx and Engels predicted that communism would triumph in advanced industrialized nations with large proletariats. But Russia was primarily an agricultural country at the time of the Russian Revolution, and Marxism now seems to appeal principally to agricultural nations in Africa, Asia, and Central America. Defend or attack *The Communist Manifesto* in the light of twentieth century history.
9. Write a summary of John Stuart Mill's "Of the Liberty of Thought and Discussion."
10. Do a research paper on birth control in Mexico, India, or China.
11. Synthesize what Mark Twain and George Orwell taught about good writing style.
12. Analyze a speech by a contemporary politician, using the criteria of George Orwell.
13. Drawing upon "Resistance to Civil Government" and "Letter from Birmingham Jail," defend an illegal act that you would be willing to commit in order to fight for something in which you strongly believe.

PART 3

A Guide to Research

Writing may be hard work, but it's much easier when you have something to write about. If forced to write about an unfamiliar subject, even the best writers can find themselves drifting into wordiness, repetition, and vague generalizations. The great advantage of research is that it gives you the material for writing. You need to organize this material and determine its worth before you can write a good research paper. You also need to know how to handle the mechanics of a research paper, since this is the most formal type of writing that most students are expected to do. There are strict conventions that must be observed when you draw upon the work of others. But these conventions can be mastered easily by anyone willing to take the trouble. There is nothing especially difficult about writing a research paper if you approach it as a process that begins long before the assignment is due.

Your instructor may allow you to choose your own subject for research. Or you may be required to work on a subject that has been assigned to you. But in either case, there are two basic points that you need to remember when undertaking a research paper: (1) A graceful style cannot compensate for a failure to do thorough research. Even if you are an excellent writer, your paper will be superficial if your research has been superficial. (2) Although research is essential to the process of writing a research paper, there is more to the research paper than research alone. You can spend months investigating your subject, but your essay will be a failure if it consists of nothing more than one quotation after another. You should remember that you are a writer as well as an investigator, and your own thoughts and interpretations are ultimately as important as the research itself. You may occasionally have an assignment that requires nothing more than reporting on a technical question such as "How is gasoline refined?" or "How do eagles mate?" But most research papers require that the writer have a thesis and a point of view about the subject under consideration. Unless specifically instructed otherwise, you should think of the research paper as an extended form of argument—an argument which is supported by evidence you have discovered through research.

There are two types of research: primary and secondary. *Primary research* requires firsthand experimentation or analysis. This is the sort of research that is done in scientific laboratories and scholarly archives. Research of this sort is seldom expected of college students, although, if you interview someone, you are doing a type of primary research. An undergraduate research paper is usually confined to *secondary research,* which means the examination of what other people have already published on a given subject. In order to do this type of research efficiently, you must know where to look. And this means that you must be familiar with the resources that are available to you in your library and develop a strategy for using these resources effectively.

GETTING STARTED

Your primary goal in preliminary research is to get your subject in focus. This usually means narrowing your subject down to a specific topic. A clear focus is essential if your paper is to have depth and coherence. A ten-page paper on "The Question of Race in *Huckleberry Finn*" is likely to be much more thoughtful than one of that length on "Mark Twain: America's Favorite Writer." Moreover, the clearer your focus, the easier your research will be. When you know what you are looking for, you know what you need to read and what you can afford to pass over. This will keep you from feeling overwhelmed as your research progresses.

Different instructors make different assignments, and you should always be certain that you have understood what your instructor expects of you. But if you have been asked to write a fixed number of pages on a subject of your own choice, a good rule to follow is to narrow your subject as much as possible without narrowing yourself out of the library. Don't put yourself in the position of aimlessly reading dozens of books on an unnecessarily broad subject. On the other hand, don't make your subject so obscure that you will be unable to find enough material to write a paper of the length required.

If you know very little about your subject, you may want to begin your research by reading whatever can be found in a general encyclopedia, such as the *Encyclopedia Britannica* or the *Encyclopedia Americana.* Encyclopedias contain the basic background information that other works may assume you already possess. Within the reference rooms of most libraries, you can also find special encyclopedias and dictionaries for major fields such as art, biography, economics, education, history, law, literature, medicine, music, philosophy, and psychology. Do some preliminary reading in an encyclopedia if doing so will make you feel more comfortable with your subject, but do not spend a lot of time reading in the library at this early stage of your research. Although the reference room may be a good place to begin your work, it has a great disadvantage: The books in this room are seldom allowed to circulate. Your first day in the library should be devoted primarily to finding out what types of material are going to be available to you in the days ahead.

LOOKING FOR BOOKS

The first step in your search strategy should be to consult a standard (or computerized) card catalog. Never assume that your topic is so new, or so specialized, that the library will not have books on it. The card catalogs of most libraries include two or three cards for every book the library owns. This allows you to locate books in a variety of ways, depending upon how much you already know. You may be looking for books by a particular author, so libraries provide *author cards*. You may know the title of a book but not know who wrote it, so libraries also provide *title cards*. In many libraries, these two types of card are filed together in one catalog known as the *author/title catalog*. But when beginning a research paper, you may not know the names of any authors or titles of works within your subject. For this reason, books are also filed under subject headings.

The *subject catalog* is usually separate from the author/title catalog. Large subjects, like American history, are broken down into numerous subcategories. If you have chosen a large subject and are unsure about how to narrow it down, it is often useful to consult the subject catalog. Not only will you be able to see how professional indexers have divided the subject into manageable components, but you will also be able to see how many books are available within each subdivision.

When using the subject catalog, you should always begin your search under the most specific heading you can think of and then consult broader subjects only if it is necessary to do so. You can usually assume that the library has at least one book on the subject you are investigating. Your goal is to find it. Do not give up easily, and remember that you will often find it necessary to consider alternative headings under which the material you need may be catalogued. Books on the Civil War may be listed under "War Between the States," and books on nuclear energy may be listed under "Atomic Energy." Sometimes you will find a card that will direct you to the correct subject heading, just as the yellow pages in a telephone directory may tell you to "See Grocers-Retail" if you look up "Super Markets." But you may have to rely upon your own ingenuity. If you are sure that the library must have books on your subject and that you are simply unable to find the correct subject heading, ask a librarian for help.

Most American libraries use one of two systems for classifying the books in their collections: the Dewey Decimal system and the Library of Congress system. If you understand how these systems work, you can save valuable time in the library by knowing where to look for material when you are already working in the stacks.

The Dewey Decimal system classifies books numerically:

000–099	General Works
100–199	Philosophy
200–299	Religion

300–399	Social Sciences
400–499	Language
500–599	Natural Sciences
600–699	Technology
700–799	Fine Arts
800–899	Literature
900–999	History and Geography

These major divisions are subdivided by ten to identify specializations within each general field. For example, within the 800–899 category for literature, American literature is found between 810 and 819, English literature between 820 and 829, German literature between 830 and 839—and so forth. Specific numbers narrow these areas further, so that 811 represents American poetry, for example, and 812 American drama. Additional numbers after the decimal point enable catalogers to classify books more precisely: 812.54 would indicate an American play written since 1945. In order to distinguish individual books from others that are similar, an additional number is usually placed beneath the Dewey number. Most libraries that use the Dewey Decimal system combine it with one of three systems for providing what is called an "author mark." These systems (Cutter two-figure, Cutter three-figure, and Cutter-Sanborn) all work according to the same principle. Librarians consult a reference table which provides a numerical representation for the first four to six letters of every conceivable last name. The first letter of the author's last name is placed immediately before this number, and the first letter of the first significant word in the title is placed after the number. Here is a complete call number for *Cat on a Hot Tin Roof,* by the American playwright Tennessee Williams:

812.54
W675c

Although the Dewey Decimal system remains the most widely used system for the classification of books in American libraries, many university libraries prefer to use the Library of Congress system, which uses the alphabet to distinguish twenty-one major categories as opposed to Dewey's ten:

A	General Works
B	Philosophy, Psychology, and Religion
C	General History
D	Foreign History
E–F	American History (North and South)
G	Geography and Anthropology
H	Social Sciences

J	Political Science
K	Law
L	Education
M	Music
N	Fine Arts
P	Language and Literature
Q	Science
R	Medicine
S	Agriculture
T	Technology
U	Military Science
V	Naval Science
Z	Bibliography and Library Science

Each of these categories can be subdivided through additional letters and numbers. PR, for example, indicates English literature, and PS indicates American. The complete entry will usually involve three lines. Unless you are planning to become a librarian, you will not find it necessary to memorize the complete code. But whether you are using Dewey or the Library of Congress, *always be sure to copy down the complete call number for any book you wish to find.* If you leave out part of the number you may find yourself wandering in the stacks and unable to find the book you want.

The call number always appears in the upper left hand corner of the author, title, and subject cards. Figure 1 (p. 580) shows four sample cards for the same book, using the Library of Congress system. Each card has a different heading but otherwise contains the same information: the title of the book and the author (in this case two coeditors), the city of publication, the publisher, the date of publication, the length of the introduction, the number of pages, the size of the book (24 cm.) and the presence of a bibliography and an index.

There is no foolproof method for determining the quality of a book from a catalog card. The best way to judge a book is always to read it. But a catalog listing can reveal some useful clues if you know how to find them. Consider, for example, the date of publication. There is no reason to assume that new books are always better than old books, but unless you are researching a historical or literary topic you should be careful not to rely heavily upon material that may be out of date. Consider also the length of the book. A book with 300 pages is likely to provide more information than a book half that size. A book with a bibliography may help you to find more material. Finally, you might also consider the reputation of the publisher. Any conclusions that you draw at this point should be tentative. But some books are better than others, and it is your responsibility as a researcher to evaluate the material that you use. If you are fortunate enough to find several books on your subject, select the books that seem the most substantial.

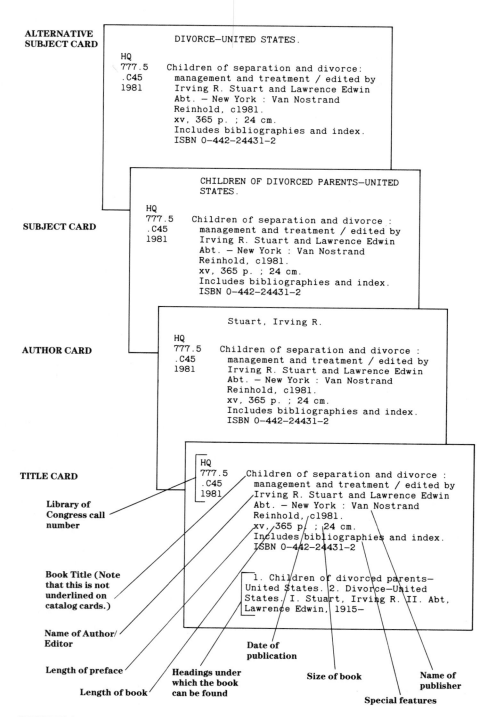

FIGURE 1

ALTERNATIVES TO THE CARD CATALOG

Because of the great amount of material being published, many libraries are now using systems that allow for material to be recorded in less space than a card catalog requires. When looking for books, you may need to use some type of microform—which means printed material which has been reduced in size through microphotography. Libraries that use microform provide researchers with special readers that magnify the material in question—whether it is available on microfilm or microfiche, which means a flat sheet of microfilm.

Increasing numbers of libraries are also now using computers to either supplement or replace their card catalogs. In addition to recording material in their own collections, these libraries usually subscribe to one or more database services which link individual libraries with computerized lists of material available throughout the United States and Canada. The most commonly used bibliographic networks are BRS (Bibliographical Retrieval Services), DIALOG (operated by Lockheed Information Systems), ERIC (Educational Research Information Center), RLIN (Research Libraries Information Network), and OCLC (Online Computer Library Center). Some libraries provide students with direct access to computers, especially if the library's own holdings are online; other libraries restrict the use of the computer to librarians.

Searching for material with the assistance of a computer requires a research strategy which is similar to the one you must use in order to locate material through a card catalog. You must be able to supply the computer with an important piece of information—either a specific book title, an author's name, or a subject heading. And as with a card catalog, you must use the correct subject heading in order to get results.

USING PERIODICAL INDEXES

A good researcher wants to be aware of the latest developments in his or her field. A scholarly book may be several years in the making; publication may be delayed, and another year or two pass before the book is purchased and cataloged by your library. You may also need to obtain detailed information on a particular subtopic that is discussed only briefly in the books that are available to you. Therefore, you will often need to turn to periodicals after searching for books. "Periodicals" means magazines, newspapers, and scholarly journals: material that is published "periodically." And there are numerous indexes to help you find literature of this sort.

The best known of these is the *Readers' Guide to Periodical Literature,* which has been published since 1900. It covers 150 magazines and journals, indexing material by subject and by author. The limitation of the *Readers' Guide* is that it covers only popular, mass-circulation periodicals. The articles you find on most subjects will often be relatively short and general.

Begin your search for periodical literature with the *Readers' Guide* if you wish. But most college libraries have a variety of specialized indexes that will lead you to more substantial material. Almost every field has its own index.

Detailed lists of such indexes and other reference books can be found in *Guide to Reference Books* by Eugene P. Sheehy and *American Reference Books Annual,* edited by Janet H. Littlefield. Among the specialized indexes most frequently used are:

The *Applied Science and Technology Index*	The *Humanities Index*
The *Art Index*	*Index to Legal Periodicals*
The *Biological and Agricultural Index*	*Index Medicus* (for medicine)
The *Business Periodicals Index*	The *Music Index*
The *Education Index*	The *Philosopher's Index*
	The *Science Citation Index*
	The *Social Sciences Index*

Anyone doing research in literature should also be familiar with the *MLA International Bibliography* (which appears annually and includes both books and articles written about English, American, and foreign language literature), and also with the *Essay and General Literature Index,* which indexes essays and articles which have appeared in books rather than in journals.

Although there is occasionally some overlapping from one index to another, you need to realize that each of these indexes covers different periodicals. The references that you find in one will usually be entirely different from the references you find in another. This is worth remembering for two reasons: (1) You should not get easily discouraged when searching for periodical literature. If you cannot locate any material in the last few years of one index, then you should try another index that sounds as if it might include references to your subject. (2) Many subjects of general interest will be found in more than one index, and if you consult more than one index, you are increasing the likelihood of being exposed to different points of view.

You may choose to do a research paper on one of the subjects discussed in Part Two of this book. But in order for you to see how different indexes lead to different types of material, let us take an example from outside of the book—pretending that you have decided to do a paper on divorce. This is a very broad subject, as you realize when you look it up in the *Readers' Guide.* See Figure 2 (p. 583) for an example. The list of articles under "Divorce" lacks a clear focus. It ranges as broadly as the subject itself. But the "See also" directs you to four related subjects. "Children of divorced parents" sounds promising. Perhaps you could do your paper on ways to minimize the effects of divorce upon children. This is still a big subject, but it is much more manageable than "Divorce," and as your reading progresses you may find ways of narrowing the topic further. Figure 3 (p. 584) shows what you will find when looking up "Children of divorced parents." It looks as if there is plenty of material on this subtopic, but looking closer you realize that three of the articles are only one page long, and your thesis may not be taken seriously if you base your argument upon material drawn from *Readers' Digest, Made-*

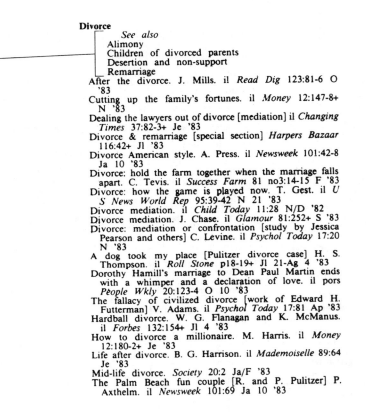

The *Guide* directs you to additional subject headings

Divorce

See also
Alimony
Children of divorced parents
Desertion and non-support
Remarriage

After the divorce. J. Mills. il *Read Dig* 123:81-6 O '83

Cutting up the family's fortunes. il *Money* 12:147-8+ N '83

Dealing the lawyers out of divorce [mediation] il *Changing Times* 37:82-3+ Je '83

Divorce & remarriage [special section] *Harpers Bazaar* 116:42+ Jl '83

Divorce American style. A. Press. il *Newsweek* 101:42-8 Ja 10 '83

Divorce: hold the farm together when the marriage falls apart. C. Tevis. il *Success Farm* 81 no3:14-15 F '83

Divorce: how the game is played now. T. Gest. il *U S News World Rep* 95:39-42 N 21 '83

Divorce mediation. il *Child Today* 11:28 N/D '82

Divorce mediation. J. Chase. il *Glamour* 81:252+ S '83

Divorce: mediation or confrontation [study by Jessica Pearson and others] C. Levine. il *Psychol Today* 17:20 N '83

A dog took my place [Pulitzer divorce case] H. S. Thompson. il *Roll Stone* p18-19+ Jl 21-Ag 4 '83

Dorothy Hamill's marriage to Dean Paul Martin ends with a whimper and a declaration of love. il pors *People Wkly* 20:123-4 O 10 '83

The fallacy of civilized divorce [work of Edward H. Futterman] V. Adams. il *Psychol Today* 17:81 Ap '83

Hardball divorce. W. G. Flanagan and K. McManus. il *Forbes* 132:154+ Jl 4 '83

How to divorce a millionaire. M. Harris. il *Money* 12:180-2+ Je '83

Life after divorce. B. G. Harrison. il *Mademoiselle* 89:64 Je '83

Mid-life divorce. *Society* 20:2 Ja/F '83

The Palm Beach fun couple [R. and P. Pulitzer] P. Axthelm. il *Newsweek* 101:69 Ja 10 '83

FIGURE 2
Sample page from *Readers' Guide*

moiselle, and *Seventeen.* You decide to continue your search elsewhere, grateful that the *Readers' Guide* has at least helped you to narrow your topic.

Since the *Social Sciences Index* includes material on sociology, education, and psychology (and other related fields) you decide that it would probably include references to articles on the children of divorced parents. See Figure 4 (p. 585). Reading over the list of citations from the *Social Sciences Index,* you can see that it directs you to material that looks substantial. Of the first three articles, two are thirteen pages long, and another is fourteen. All three of these articles include bibliographies, as do several others. And by using periodicals like *Child Development* and the *American Journal of Psychology,* you should be able to write with more authority than had you stayed with articles drawn exclusively from the *Readers' Guide.* These articles are going to be more difficult to read than articles in popular magazines.

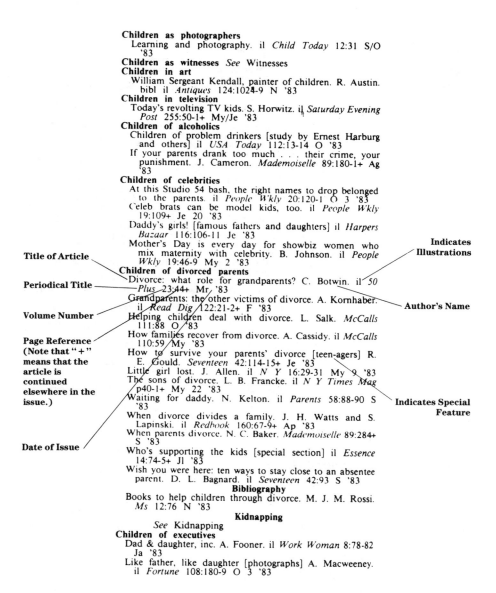

Children as photographers
　Learning and photography. il *Child Today* 12:31 S/O '83
Children as witnesses *See* Witnesses
Children in art
　William Sergeant Kendall, painter of children. R. Austin. bibl il *Antiques* 124:1024-9 N '83
Children in television
　Today's revolting TV kids. S. Horwitz. il *Saturday Evening Post* 255:50-1+ My/Je '83
Children of alcoholics
　Children of problem drinkers [study by Ernest Harburg and others] il *USA Today* 112:13-14 O '83
　If your parents drank too much . . . their crime, your punishment. J. Cameron. *Mademoiselle* 89:180-1+ Ag '83
Children of celebrities
　At this Studio 54 bash, the right names to drop belonged to the parents. il *People Wkly* 20:120-1 O 3 '83
　Celeb brats can be model kids, too. il *People Wkly* 19:109+ Je 20 '83
　Daddy's girls! [famous fathers and daughters] il *Harpers Bazaar* 116:106-11 Je '83
　Mother's Day is every day for showbiz women who mix maternity with celebrity. B. Johnson. il *People Wkly* 19:46-9 My 2 '83
Children of divorced parents
　Divorce: what role for grandparents? C. Botwin. il *50 Plus* 23:44+ Mr '83
　Grandparents: the other victims of divorce. A. Kornhaber. il *Read Dig* 122:21-2+ F '83
　Helping children deal with divorce. L. Salk. *McCalls* 111:88 O '83
　How families recover from divorce. A. Cassidy. il *McCalls* 110:59 My '83
　How to survive your parents' divorce [teen-agers] R. E. Gould. *Seventeen* 42:114-15+ Je '83
　Little girl lost. J. Allen. il *N Y* 16:29-31 My 9 '83
　The sons of divorce. L. B. Francke. il *N Y Times Mag* p40-1+ My 22 '83
　Waiting for daddy. N. Kelton. il *Parents* 58:88-90 S '83
　When divorce divides a family. J. H. Watts and S. Lapinski. il *Redbook* 160:67-9+ Ap '83
　When parents divorce. N. C. Baker. *Mademoiselle* 89:284+ S '83
　Who's supporting the kids [special section] il *Essence* 14:74-5+ Jl '83
　Wish you were here: ten ways to stay close to an absentee parent. D. L. Bagnard. il *Seventeen* 42:93 S '83
　　　　Bibliography
　Books to help children through divorce. M. J. M. Rossi. *Ms* 12:76 N '83
　　　　Kidnapping
　　　See Kidnapping
Children of executives
　Dad & daughter, inc. A. Fooner. il *Work Woman* 8:78-82 Ja '83
　Like father, like daughter [photographs] A. Macweeney. il *Fortune* 108:180-9 O 3 '83

Annotations (left margin):
Title of Article
Periodical Title
Volume Number
Page Reference (Note that "+" means that the article is continued elsewhere in the issue.)
Date of Issue

Annotations (right margin):
Indicates Illustrations
Author's Name
Indicates Special Feature

FIGURE 3
Sample page from *Readers' Guide*

But you can overcome this difficulty through proper preparation: Do not try to read articles in scholarly journals until you have completed preliminary reading in encyclopedias, books, and magazines.

Continuing your search, you should be able to find additional material in the *Education Index* (since teachers are involved with children) and the

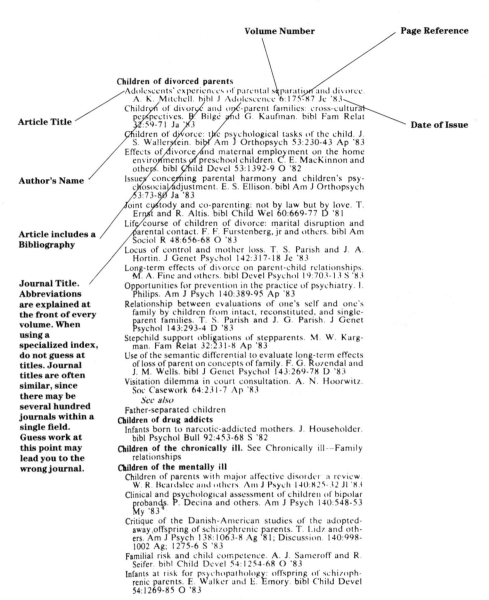

Volume Number

Page Reference

Article Title

Date of Issue

Author's Name

Article includes a
Bibliography

Journal Title.
Abbreviations
are explained at
the front of every
volume. When
using a
specialized index,
do not guess at
titles. Journal
titles are often
similar, since
there may be
several hundred
journals within a
single field.
Guess work at
this point may
lead you to the
wrong journal.

Children of divorced parents
　Adolescents' experiences of parental separation and divorce.
　　A. K. Mitchell. bibl J Adolescence 6:175-87 Je '83
　Children of divorce and one-parent families: cross-cultural
　　perspectives. B. Bilge and G. Kaufman. bibl Fam Relat
　　32:59-71 Ja '83
　Children of divorce: the psychological tasks of the child. J.
　　S. Wallerstein. bibl Am J Orthopsych 53:230-43 Ap '83
　Effects of divorce and maternal employment on the home
　　environments of preschool children. C. E. MacKinnon and
　　others. bibl Child Devel 53:1392-9 O '82
　Issues concerning parental harmony and children's psy-
　　chosocial adjustment. E. S. Ellison. bibl Am J Orthopsych
　　53:73-80 Ja '83
　Joint custody and co-parenting: not by law but by love. T.
　　Ernst and R. Altis. bibl Child Wel 60:669-77 D '81
　Life course of children of divorce: marital disruption and
　　parental contact. F. F. Furstenberg, jr and others. bibl Am
　　Sociol R 48:656-68 O '83
　Locus of control and mother loss. T. S. Parish and J. A.
　　Hortin. J Genet Psychol 142:317-18 Je '83
　Long-term effects of divorce on parent-child relationships.
　　M. A. Fine and others. bibl Devel Psychol 19:703-13 S '83
　Opportunities for prevention in the practice of psychiatry. I.
　　Philips. Am J Psych 140:389-95 Ap '83
　Relationship between evaluations of one's self and one's
　　family by children from intact, reconstituted, and single-
　　parent families. T. S. Parish and J. G. Parish. J Genet
　　Psychol 143:293-4 D '83
　Stepchild support obligations of stepparents. M. W. Karg-
　　man. Fam Relat 32:231-8 Ap '83
　Use of the semantic differential to evaluate long-term effects
　　of loss of parent on concepts of family. F. G. Rozendal and
　　J. M. Wells. bibl J Genet Psychol 143:269-78 D '83
　Visitation dilemma in court consultation. A. N. Hoorwitz.
　　Soc Casework 64:231-7 Ap '83
　　　See also
　Father-separated children
Children of drug addicts
　Infants born to narcotic-addicted mothers. J. Householder.
　　bibl Psychol Bull 92:453-68 S '82
Children of the chronically ill. See Chronically ill—Family
　relationships
Children of the mentally ill
　Children of parents with major affective disorder: a review.
　　W. R. Beardslee and others. Am J Psych 140:825-32 Jl '83
　Clinical and psychological assessment of children of bipolar
　　probands. P. Decina and others. Am J Psych 140:548-53
　　My '83
　Critique of the Danish-American studies of the adopted-
　　away offspring of schizophrenic parents. T. Lidz and oth-
　　ers. Am J Psych 138:1063-8 Ag '81; Discussion. 140:998-
　　1002 Ag; 1275-6 S '83
　Familial risk and child competence. A. J. Sameroff and R.
　　Seifer. bibl Child Devel 54:1254-68 O '83
　Infants at risk for psychopathology: offspring of schizoph-
　　renic parents. E. Walker and E. Emory. bibl Child Devel
　　54:1269-85 O '83

FIGURE 4
Sample page from *Social Sciences Index*

Index to Legal Periodicals (since lawyers are involved with divorce). The
articles would be different, but the form of the citations would be similar,
just as the citations in the *Social Sciences Index* are similar to those in the
Readers' Guide.

DIVORCE, Separations and Annulments — Cont

number of marriages rose 2%, to 2.5 million (S), Mr 16,16:6

Jamie Talan article on difficulty of arranging wedding ceremonies in cases where parents of bride or groom are divorced; drawing (M), Ap 3,XXI,10:3

Detroit, Mich, resident Vickie Alex files suit in Wayne County Circuit Court charging that her husband Joseph did not tell her he had herpes before they were married in Sept 1982; is seeking $100,000 in damages; husband filed for divorce on Feb 8 in separate suit and denies charges in new suit (S), Ap 11,II,8:3

Republic Insurance Group of Dallas to offer program intended to guarantee flow of child-support or alimony payments in event of default; program is available only through lawyers representing parties in divorce and arrangement can be made only during original negotiation or renegotiation of divorce; details of how program operates (M), Ap 12,IV,23:2

Article on Rhode Island schoolteacher Paul W Lataille, who has been jailed for failing to pay $15,000 in savings, legal fees and alimony that his wife was awarded in divorce judgment; Family Court Judge William Goldberg has vowed to keep Lataille in jail for contempt of court until he pays; Lataille's lawyer Mitchell S Riffkin comments (M), Ap 17,I,23:1

Linda Bird Francke article on studies showing that boys tend to be more handicapped by divorce of their parents than girls; drawing (L), My 22,VI,p40

NYS Assembly, 124-14, approves Assemblywoman May W Newburger's bill directing divorce courts to distribute property equally; Sen approval doubted (S), My 29,I,39:2

Michigan Appeals Court upholds Jan 1982 judgment governing divorce of Ann M Woodworth and Michael G Woodworth in which Ingham County Circuit Court Judge James Kallman ruled husband's law degree was marital property and therefore wife was entitled to share of his future earnings; Kallman had ordered Michael to pay Ann $2,000 annually for 10 years as her share of degree (S), Je 8,I,14:5

Joseph Cardinal Bernardin of Chicago becomes highest-ranking Roman Catholic prelate to celebrate mass for divorced and separated church members (S), Je 27,I,10:6

Bill that is designed to help Orthodox Jews who want to remarry within faith passes both houses of NYS Legislature; under bill, NYS cannot grant civil divorce until party suing for divorce swears he has removed any barriers to remarriage (S), Je 27,II,4:3

Letter by Rabbi Bernard M Zlotowitz and Albert Vorspan urges Gov Cuomo to veto bill passed by New York State Legislature; holds it would involve state in religion, Jl 18,I,14:5

Joan Gelman (Hers column) comment on social 'stresses' of children from intact homes who do not enjoy 'benefits' of competitive bidding by divorced parents wooing their young; drawing (S), Ag 4,III,2:1

NYS Gov Cuomo signs into law bill under which Jewish husbands who refuse to grant their wives divorces under Jewish religious law will be barred from obtaining civil divorces (M), Ag 10,II,7:1

Judge Linda Thomas of Family Court divorces 108 people at once, Dallas, Texas; all are clients of lawyer Averil Sweitzer (S), Ag 21,I,22:6

Georgia Dullea column Relationships discusses lawyer-client relationships in divorce cases; drawing (M), Ag 22,II,10:1

Article on program begun by child and adolescent out-patient division of Westchester division of New York Hospital-Cornell Medical Center to help families in first years of marital separation or those who are considering divorce; photo (M), S 4,XXII,18:3

Article on benefits to children of divorced parents of not breaking ties with relatives of noncustodial parent (M), S 5,I,29:1

Note that the New York Times Index gives you a one sentence summary of each article, rather than article titles. "drawing" tells you the article is illustrated. (L) means that this is a long article. The date of issue is May 22 (of 1983, the year of the volume consulted). "VI" means that the article is in section number six—on page 40 in this case.

Short article on your subject

Medium length article on your subject.

FIGURE 5

Sample page from the *New York Times Index*

USING A NEWSPAPER INDEX

There are indexes available for the *Wall Street Journal* and the *Christian Science Monitor,* and, since 1972, the *Newspaper Index* has provided information on articles in the *Chicago Tribune,* the *Los Angeles Times,* the *New Orleans Times-Picayune,* and the *Washington Post.* But if your library has an index for any one newspaper, it is most likely to be the *New York Times Index,* which has been published since 1913. Figure 5 (p. 586) is an example of what you would find if you consulted this index for your paper on the children of divorced parents. This is only part of the list of articles on divorce in one year of the *New York Times.* Several of the articles look as if they would be worth reading, but you may decide that you already have enough material on children and divorce without searching further. Bear in mind that the *New York Times* is especially useful when researching historical events or very contemporary topics that have only recently made news.

USING ABSTRACTING SERVICES

There is one other type of print resource usually available in a college library and that is an *abstract,* which means a summary of an article or book (see p. 264 for an example). Among the most important abstracting services are:

> *Abstracts in Anthropology*
> *Biological Abstracts*
> *Chemical Abstracts*
> *Historical Abstracts*
> *Physics Abstracts*
> *Psychological Abstracts*
> *Sociological Abstracts*
> *Women Studies Abstracts*

These abstracts are organized in different ways, and when you decide that you need to use an abstract, you can find instructions on how to proceed in the front of any volume. If you run into difficulties, remember that you can always ask a librarian for help. But here is an example of what you would find if you looked up "Divorce" in *Psychological Abstracts*—which is divided into two parts, the subject index being separate from the actual summaries. Figure 6 (p. 588) shows what you will find when consulting the subject index for "Divorce." The most important entry in the subject index is the number which appears at the end of each citation. This is not a page number. It is the number of the article being summarized. Article summaries can be found in numerical order, either at the front of the volume containing the subject index or in a separate volume (which will be shelved beside it) depending upon how your library decides to bind them. Figure 7 (p. 589) shows a partial

One-sentence
description of
article, not a
title.

Divorce

adjustment & feelings about parental separation, 12–18 yr olds from
separated or divorced 1-parent families, 10256

The entry
number under
which you can
find the article
abstract.

attitudes toward effects of Big Brother/Big Sister program on
children of divorce, participating parents & children & Big Brother
& Big Sister volunteers, 11023

attitudes toward marriage & divorce & children of divorce, 13 & 14 yr
olds from intact vs divorced homes, 5448

background factors vs compatibility vs unrealized expectations,
prediction of marriage failure, divorced & separated couples,
USSR, 3321

cognitive/social stimulation in home environment & sex typing in
child's room, 3–6 yr olds from intact/mother working vs nonwork-
ing vs divorced/mother working families, 3048

divorce, father-child relationship & psychiatric symptoms, fathers,
literature review, 930

divorce in inter- vs intraethnic marriages, Chinese & Japanese,
Hawaii, 9-yr longitudinal study, 10340

divorce rate, marital satisfaction, spouses, reanalysis of 1963 data &
implications for methodology in studies of social variables &
marital satisfaction, 6958

divorce, stress reaction & social support, 12575

divorce, stress reactions, 23–58 yr olds, 3304

family correlates, social adjustment following parental divorce, 2–18
yr olds, 10250

group counseling, persons in process of divorce, 4182

intact vs broken home & age & sex, personal adjustment, 10th
graders, 864

marital conflict & divorce & child behavior problems, literature
review, 1258

marriage & divorce rates, counties experiencing vs not experiencing
major natural disasters, 7784

FIGURE 6

Sample page from subject index of *Psychological Abstracts*

page of summaries, including one of the articles found in the subject index:
10250. Note that it is only at this point that you learn the author of the
article, the title of the article, and the journal, volume, date, and pages where
it can be found.

Abstracts can be cumbersome to use, especially at first. But they offer an
obvious advantage. Sometimes it is hard to tell from a title alone if an article
will be useful, and a summary can help you to decide whether or not you
want to read the entire article. A good rule to follow with abstracts is that if
you can't understand the summary, you probably won't understand the article. And there is one other point to remember when using abstracting services. Many of them are international in scope. Just because the article summary
is written in English does not mean that this is true of the article itself. But
if an article is written in a foreign language, that will be indicated—as in
numbers 10251 and 10252.

Author's Institutional Affiliation

10249. **Pepler, Debra J. & Rubin, Kenneth H.** (U Toronto Erindale Coll, Ctr for Research in Human Development, Mississauga, Canada) **Current issues in the study of children's play.** *Human Development,* 1982(Nov–Dec), Vol 25(6), 443–447. —Presents a review of the book, *Children's Play: Current Theory and Research,* edited by the present authors (1982). The theoretical bases for the role of play in development are reviewed, and the definitional and methodological problems that plague contemporary play research are examined. The developmental nature of play and the relations between different forms of play (e.g., fantasy activity) and indices of developmental competence (e.g., problem-solving) are considered. The effects of the ecological setting on children's play are examined. (17 ref)

Date of Issue

Volume & Issue Number

Page Ref.

Corresponding entry number (from subject index)

10250. **Pett, Marjorie G.** (U Utah Coll of Nursing, Salt Lake City) **Correlates of children's social adjustment following divorce.** *Journal of Divorce,* 1982(Sum), Vol 5(4), 25–39. —Examined family correlates of children's social adjustment following divorce. Data concerning 411 2–18 yr olds were collected from interviews with 206 randomly selected custodial parents. A social adjustment scale completed by the custodial parent served as the criterion measure of children's adjustment. The most significant factor related to children's satisfactory social adjustment (as measured by the Personal Adjustment and Role Skills Scale) was a positive relationship with the custodial parent. Other significant correlates included the custodial parent's own ability to maintain emotional and social adjustment, the parent's age and number of previous marriages, the children's current reaction to the divorce, and parental satisfaction with dating and friends. (25 ref) —*Journal abstract.*

Article title

Journal title

10251. **Polič, Marko; Dekleva, Bojan; Marjanovič, Ljubica & Umek, Peter.** **Pomenske in vedenjske značilnosti različnih okolij. / Meaningful and behavioural characteristics of different environments.** (Sloe) *Anthropos,* 1981, Vol 4–6, 207–217. —29 13–14 yr olds and 24 university students rated 4 environments differing on the dimensions of man-made vs natural, open vs closed, and few vs many inhabitants. On the average, the older group would pursue 46.25% of the activities suggested, and the younger group only 8.75%. This difference is attributed to differences in social roles arising from the age differences between the groups. The number of activities was least restricted in the natural environment and most restricted by the population of a given environment. While the populated environment was considered more meaningful, intimate, and stimulating, both groups rated the natural environment as most pleasant. (English abstract) (14 ref)

Indicates a bibliography with 25 sources.

Language of article

10252. **Research Group in the Study on Ideal, Motive and Interest of Adolescents.** **/ The study in ideal, motive and interest of adolescents in school in ten provinces and cities.** (Chin) *Acta Psychologica Sinica,* 1982, Vol 14(2), 199–210. —Research results show that most Chinese adolescents possess strong ideals and that these ideals provide the basis of their outlook on life. It is argued that education must arouse the students' motives, foster their interests, and deal with the relation between these factors and ideals. —*English abstract.*

Reminder that only this summary is in English

FIGURE 7
Sample page of summaries from *Psychological Abstracts*

COMPILING A PRELIMINARY BIBLIOGRAPHY

As you begin locating sources of possible value for your paper, you should be careful to record certain essential information about the books and articles you have discovered. You will need this information in order to compose a preliminary bibliography. For books, you need to record the full title, the full name of the author or authors, the city of publication, the publisher, and the date of publication. If you are using a particular part of a book, be sure to record the pages in question. And if you are using an article or a story included in an anthology edited by someone other than the author of the material you are using, make the distinction between the author and the title of the selection and the editor and title of the book as a whole. When you have located articles in periodicals, record the author(s) of the article, the title of the article, the title of the journal in which it was published, the volume number, the issue number (if there is one), the date of the issue, and the pages between which the article can be found.

The easiest way to compile a preliminary bibliography is to use a set of 3 × 5 note cards, recording separate sources on separate cards. This involves a little more trouble than jotting references down on whatever paper you have at hand, but it will be to your ultimate advantage. As your research progresses, you can easily eliminate any sources that you were unable to obtain—or that you have rejected as inappropriate for one reason or another. And by using this method, you will later find it easier to arrange your sources in the order in which they should appear in the formal typewritten bibliography which will be included at the end of your finished paper. But whatever method you use, be sure to keep accurate notes. No one enjoys discovering a failure to record an important reference—especially if this discovery comes after the paper is written and shortly before it must be handed in.

GOING OUTSIDE THE LIBRARY

A good college library should give you all the resources you need for most research papers, especially in introductory courses. But you may occasionally find it necessary to look beyond the library where you normally work. If you live in or near a city, there may be several other libraries that you can use. If this is not the case, remember that most libraries also provide an interlibrary loan service which allows you to request a book or a journal article that your own library does not possess. When a library offers interlibrary loan, you will be asked to provide bibliographical information about the material you are requesting. Librarians will then do the work of locating and securing a copy of the book or article for you. You should ask for material only if you are reasonably certain that it would be an important asset for you, and that an equivalent resource is not already available in your own library. You should also realize that interlibrary loan usually takes approximately two weeks, and sometimes longer. It is of no use to the student who defers his or her research to the week before the paper is due.

On some topics, you may want to interview people with expertise in that subject area. Interviews are usually inappropriate for literary and scientific papers, but they can be helpful for work in the social sciences. If writing a paper on the effects of divorce upon children, you might decide to interview both parents and children. But unless your instructor has encouraged you to do some interviews, you should check to make sure that interviews are acceptable for your assignment. Remember also that interviews need to be planned ahead, and you should have a list of questions before you go. But don't feel compelled to adhere rigidly to the questions you prepared in advance. A good interviewer listens carefully and knows how to ask a follow-up question that is inspired by a provocative response to an earlier question. Do not get so caught up in an interview, however, that you forget to take careful notes. (If you want to use a tape recorder, courtesy demands that you ask permission to do so when you arrange for the interview.) Since you will need to include the interview in your bibliography, record the date of the interview and the full name of the person you have interviewed.

TAKING NOTES

If you have never done a research paper before, you would be wise to take notes on 3×5 note cards. Note-taking is essential to research. Unfortunately, few researchers can tell in advance exactly what material they will want to include in their final paper. Especially during the early stages of your research, you may record information that will later seem unnecessary when you have become more expert on your subject and have a clear thesis. So you will probably have to discard some of your notes when you are ready to write your paper.

The advantage of the note card system is that it allows for flexibility when you are ready to move from research to composition. The odds are against discovering material in the exact order in which you will want to use it. By spreading your note cards out on a desk or table, you can study how they best fit together. You can arrange and rearrange note cards until you have them in a meaningful sequence. This system only works, however, when you have the self-restraint to limit yourself to recording one fact, one idea, or one quotation to a card. This means that many of your cards will have a lot of empty space that you may be tempted to fill. Don't. As soon as you decide to put two ideas on the same card, you have made an editorial decision that you may later regret. The cost of a set of note cards is minimal compared to the amount of time you must invest in doing a good research paper.

Sorting your note cards is also one of the easiest ways to determine if you have enough material to write a good paper. If your notes fall into a half-dozen different categories, your research might lack focus. In this case you should do some more research, concentrating on the category that interests you the most. If, on the other hand, your notes fall into a clear pattern, you may be ready to start writing. Of course, the point at which you move from research into writing will depend not only on your notes but also on the length of the paper you have in mind: Long papers usually involve more research than short papers. But if you classify your notes every few days during the process of doing your research, you will be in a position to judge when you have taken as many notes as you will need.

AVOIDING SELECTIVE RESEARCH

Although your research should have a clear focus, and you may have a tentative thesis in mind, you should formulate your final thesis only after your research is complete. Your research strategy should be designed to answer a question that you have posed to yourself, such as "How does divorce affect children?" This is very different from starting your research with your thesis predetermined. A student who is morally opposed to divorce may be tempted to take notes only from sources that discuss the harmful effects of divorce—rejecting as irrelevant any source that suggests that divorce can sometimes benefit children. Research, in this case, is not leading to greater knowledge or understanding. On the contrary, it is being used to reinforce personal beliefs that may border on prejudice.

We have seen that "anticipating the opposition" is important even in short essays of opinion. It is no less important in the research paper. Almost any topic worth investigating will yield up facts and ideas that could support different conclusions. The readings assembled in this book have demonstrated that it is possible to defend or attack mandatory drug testing, gun control, capital punishment, censorship, and animal experimentation—among other issues. As you may have already observed, some of the most opinionated people are also the most ignorant. Well-educated men and women are usually aware of how most problems are complex, and this is because they have been exposed to different points of view during their education. Good students remember this when they are doing research. They allow their reading to influence their thought, and not their thoughts to determine their reading. Your own research may ultimately support a belief that you already hold, but it could just as easily lead you to realize that you were misinformed. When taking notes, you should remember the question that you have posed for yourself so that you do not waste time recording information that is not relevant to the question. But you should not be tempted to overlook material that directly concerns your question just because you don't agree with what this material says. If you have a good reason to reject the conclusion of someone else's work, your paper will be stronger if you recognize that this disagreement exists and then demonstrate why you favor one position over another.

ORGANIZING YOUR PAPER

If you have used the note card system, you may be able to dispense with an outline and compose your first draft by working directly from your notes—assuming that you have sorted them carefully and arranged them into an easily understandable sequence. But many writers find it useful to outline the ideas they plan to cover. Students who lack experience in writing long papers are especially likely to benefit from taking the trouble to prepare an outline before attempting to write.

If you decide to outline your paper, you should use the standard format for a formal outline:

I. Major idea
   A. Supporting idea
      1. Minor idea
         a. Supporting detail
         b. Supporting detail
      2. Minor idea
   B. Supporting idea
II. Major idea

And so forth. Subdivisions only make sense when there are at least two categories—otherwise there would be no need to subdivide. So Roman numeral I usually implies the existence of Roman numeral II, and supporting idea "A" implies the existence of supporting idea "B." A good outline is usually parallel, with each part in balance with the others.

An outline may consist of complete sentences or simply of topics, but follow consistently whichever system you choose. (For an example of a topic outline, see page 574.) The extent to which you benefit from an outline is usually determined by the amount of effort you devote to preparing it. The more developed your outline, the more likely you are to have thought your essay through and considered how it can be best organized. Your outline may show you that you have much to say about one part of your paper and little about another. This could result in a lopsided paper if the parts should be of equal importance. In this case, your outline may lead you to do some additional research in order to obtain more information for the part of the paper that looks as if it is going to be weak. Or you may decide to rethink your essay and draft another outline, narrowing your paper to the discussion of the part that had most interested you. Either of these decisions would make it easier for you to write a well-organized paper by reducing the risk of introducing ideas you could not pursue.

You should remember that an outline is not an end in itself; it is only a device to help you write a good paper. You can rewrite an outline much more easily than you can rewrite a paper, so do not think of an outline as some sort of fixed contract which you must honor at all cost. Be prepared to rework any outline that does not help you to write better.

EDITING YOUR PAPER

Unless instructed otherwise, you should be guided by the following rules when preparing your final draft:

1. Research papers should be typed. Use nonerasable 8½-by-11 inch white, 20-pound paper. Type on one side of each page only. Doublespace all lines, leaving a margin of one inch on all sides.

2. In the upper left corner of page 1, or on a separate title page, include the following information: your name, your instructor's name, the course and section number, and the date the essay is submitted.

3. Beginning on page 2, number each page in the upper right corner, ½ inch from the top. Type your last name immediately before the number.

4. Make sure that any quotations in your essay fit in smoothly with the essay as a whole. Eliminate any quotation that seems "stuck in," or—if it is too important to cut—introduce it with a transition that will link it to whatever has come before it, and follow it with analysis or commentary that will make the significance of the quotation clear.

5. Long quotations (anything more than four lines) should be set off from the rest of the text. Begin a new line, indenting ten spaces to form the left margin for the quotation. The indentation means that you are quoting, so additional quotation marks are unnecessary in this case (except for quotations within the quotation).

6. In order to avoid the charge of "padding," you should try to edit long quotations whenever possible. Use the ellipsis (. . .) to indicate that you have omitted a word or phrase within a sentence. Leave a space before and after each period. Begin with a fourth period with no space before it when the ellipsis comes at the end of a sentence (. . . .).

7. Make sure that edited quotations are still grammatical and clear. If the addition of an extra word or two would help make the quotation more easily understandable, you can make an editorial interpolation enclosing the inserted material within square brackets [   ]. If your typewriter does not have brackets, you can draw them in by hand.

8. Make sure that you consistently follow a documentation style acceptable to your instructor, and give clear and adequate credit to all your sources.

9. Proofread your paper carefully. The research paper should be the product of many hours of work, and it should not look as if written in haste. Typographical errors or careless mistakes in spelling or grammar can cause your audience to lose confidence in you. If your instructor allows ink corrections, make them as neatly as you can. Retype any page that has numerous or lengthy corrections.

10. Use a paper clip to bind your work together. This allows your instructor to easily separate the pages of your paper if he or she wishes to do so.

IN CONCLUSION

The readings assembled in Part 2 have demonstrated the importance of research in the world behind the classroom. Extensive research is readily apparent in the articles by Bird, Burger, Gallistel, Mayo, Neuman, Singer, and

Shurr. But research also supports the arguments of Bruck, FitzGerald, Kates, O'Keefe, and Spitzer—among others. None of these works could have been written if their authors had not taken the trouble to become well informed on their chosen subjects.

Having studied these essays, you should be familiar with the way experienced writers use content notes to clarify various points in their arguments. Individual essays have also illustrated the major documentation styles: Gallistel and Mayo use the APA author/year system, as does Travis Knopf in his essay. Neuman provides an example of the author/date system and bibliography recommended by *The Chicago Manual of Style*. The essay by Tim Paetsch provides an example of a numbered system of references. James McClain, Pamela Schmidt, Connie Thompson, Janet Jurgella, and Kim Bassuener all use the MLA author/work style. For an example of the MLA author/work style in a longer paper, consider the following research paper by Richard Kaufman.

Richard Kaufman
Professor Molinaro
English 102, sec. 14
May 7, 1985

The Case for Robert Cohn:
The Unsung Hero of The Sun Also Rises

I.   Introduction
    A. What most critics think of Robert Cohn
       1. Quotation from Allen Tate
       2. Quotation from Leon Seltzer
       3. Quotation from Robert Cochran
       4. Quotation from Earl Rovit
    B. The historical background of the book
       1. The friends with whom Hemingway traveled to Spain
       in 1925
          a. Lady Duff Twysden and her companion Pat Guthrie
          b. Bill Smith, a boyhood friend of Hemingway's
       2. Harold Loeb, the model for Robert Cohn
          a. Loeb's biographical background
          b. Hemingway's feelings towards Loeb
II. How other characters in the book view Cohn
    A. Bill's point of view
       1. The importance of Cohn's religion
       2. Evidence that Bill is anti—Semitic
    B. Jake's point of view
       1. Positive information about Cohn provided by Jake
       2. Evaluation of negative details provided by Jake
III. My own view of Cohn
    A. Cohn as an idealist
       1. Evidence that he wants his life to be worthwhile
       2. Evidence that he is capable of falling seriously in
       love
    B. Cynicism the cause of other characters' resentment of
    Cohn
       1. Jake's and Bill's ridicule of romantic love
       2. Mike's relationship with Brett

      C. Critics who ridicule Cohn for being in love
         1. Quotation from Sheridan Baker
         2. Quotation from Mark Spilka
      D. Evidence from the book that shows Cohn's critics to be wrong
         1. Jake's speech to Brett about behaving badly
         2. Comparison of Cohn with Pedro Romero and other characters

IV. Conclusion
      A. Cohn's role in the book
         1. The significance of his status as an outsider
         2. Cohn's effect upon other characters
      B. Final Statement

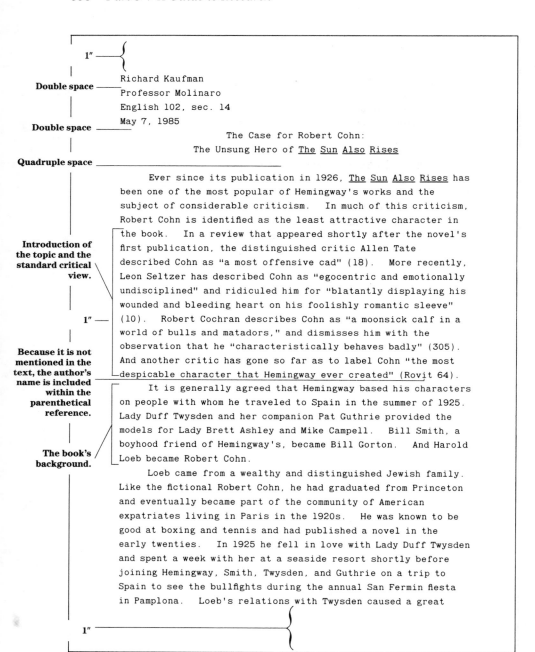

1"

Double space ——— Richard Kaufman
Professor Molinaro
English 102, sec. 14
Double space ——— May 7, 1985
                                    The Case for Robert Cohn:
                         The Unsung Hero of The Sun Also Rises
Quadruple space ———

                    Ever since its publication in 1926, The Sun Also Rises has
             been one of the most popular of Hemingway's works and the
             subject of considerable criticism.   In much of this criticism,
             Robert Cohn is identified as the least attractive character in
Introduction of   the book.   In a review that appeared shortly after the novel's
the topic and the first publication, the distinguished critic Allen Tate
standard critical described Cohn as "a most offensive cad" (18).   More recently,
view.   Leon Seltzer has described Cohn as "egocentric and emotionally
             undisciplined" and ridiculed him for "blatantly displaying his
             wounded and bleeding heart on his foolishly romantic sleeve"
1" ——   (10).   Robert Cochran describes Cohn as "a moonsick calf in a
             world of bulls and matadors," and dismisses him with the
Because it is not observation that he "characteristically behaves badly" (305).
mentioned in the   And another critic has gone so far as to label Cohn "the most
text, the author's despicable character that Hemingway ever created" (Rovit 64).
name is included
within the   It is generally agreed that Hemingway based his characters
parenthetical on people with whom he traveled to Spain in the summer of 1925.
reference.   Lady Duff Twysden and her companion Pat Guthrie provided the
             models for Lady Brett Ashley and Mike Campell.   Bill Smith, a
             boyhood friend of Hemingway's, became Bill Gorton.   And Harold
The book's   Loeb became Robert Cohn.
background.
                    Loeb came from a wealthy and distinguished Jewish family.
             Like the fictional Robert Cohn, he had graduated from Princeton
             and eventually became part of the community of American
             expatriates living in Paris in the 1920s.   He was known to be
             good at boxing and tennis and had published a novel in the
             early twenties.   In 1925 he fell in love with Lady Duff Twysden
             and spent a week with her at a seaside resort shortly before
             joining Hemingway, Smith, Twysden, and Guthrie on a trip to
             Spain to see the bullfights during the annual San Fermin fiesta
             in Pamplona.   Loeb's relations with Twysden caused a great

1" ——

Kaufman 2

deal of ill feeling.   After several days of building tension,
Hemingway and Loeb quarreled.   (They left a restaurant
intending to have a fist fight, but unlike Jake and Cohn they did
not actually come to blows.)

But if Hemingway had reason to resent Loeb, he also took
trouble to remain on good terms with him.   On the morning after
the quarrel, Hemingway sent Loeb a note of apology, the heart
of which reads as follows:

> I was terribly tight and nasty to you last night and
> I dont [sic] want you to go away with that nasty
> insulting lousiness as the last thing of the fiestas.
> I wish I could wipe out all the mean-ness [sic] and I
> suppose I cant [sic] but this is to let you know that
> I'm thoroly [sic] ashamed of the way I acted and the
> stinking, unjust uncalled for things I said.
>
> (Letters 166)

Hemingway may have remembered that the publication of his first
book, In Our Time, had recently been arranged for through
Loeb's intervention with his own publisher.   And there is
reason to believe that Hemingway may have been jealous of Loeb.
Sheridan Baker has described Loeb as "the Princeton man . . .
who could outplay Hemingway at tennis and outbox his twitching
eye, who had beaten him to publication and then too fortunately
helped him—had run off with the most desirable woman in Paris"
(41).   So if the original model for Robert Cohn was a man who
was worthy of some respect, it may be that his fictional
counterpart is something more than a fool.

At least part of Hemingway's resentment of Loeb can be
traced to anti-Semitism.   Discussing The Sun Also Rises while
he was still working on it, Hemingway is reported to have told
a friend, "I'm putting everyone in it and that kike Loeb is the
villain" (qtd. in C. Baker 154).   Cohn's religion is
emphasized throughout the novel.   It is, for example, one of
the first things the reader is told about him: "No one had ever
made him feel he was a Jew, and hence any different from
anybody else, until he went to Princeton" (4).   The

Student adds [sic] to a quotation in order to indicate that the errors are part of the quotation and have not been made in transcription.

Student introduces his own thesis.

An indirect source for a quotation. Author's first initial is included to distinguish him from another writer with the same last name.

Student begins to cite evidence from the book in support of his thesis.

½″

implication of this line is that a "Jew" <u>is</u> "different from
anybody else." Many readers come to like Bill Gorton, but it is
Bill who complains about Cohn's "Jewish superiority," (162)
refers to Cohn as "That kike!" (164) and sarcastically asks
Jake, "Haven't you got some more Jewish friends you could bring
along?" (101) Bearing these remarks in mind, an unbiased reader
should try to appraise Cohn more objectively. The victim of
prejudice, Cohn may be more admirable than the other characters
in the novel were able to recognize.

There are many positive references to Cohn within the
novel that are frequently overlooked. After describing Cohn's
boxing career at Princeton, Jake remarks, "I mistrust all frank
and simple people, especially when their stories hold together"
(4). The implication is that Cohn is "frank" and "simple" and
honest about his background. These are undeniably attractive
qualities. Jake also comments that Cohn was "a nice boy, a
friendly boy, and very shy" (4) when he went off to college--a
description that is at odds with attempts to portray Cohn as
egoistic and self-centered. Several chapters later, Jake
returns to the subject of Robert Cohn, offering a detailed
description which is worth quoting at length:

> Somehow I feel I have not shown Robert Cohn clearly.
> The reason is that until he fell in love with Brett,
> I never heard him make one remark that would in any
> way detach him from other people. He was nice to
> watch on the tennis-court, he had a good body, and he
> kept it in shape; he handled his cards well at
> bridge, and he had a funny sort of undergraduate
> quality about him. If he were in a crowd nothing he
> said stood out. He wore what used to be called polo
> shirts at school, and may be called that still, but
> he was not professionally youthful. I do not
> believe he thought about clothes very much.
> Externally he had been formed at Princeton.
> Internally he had been moulded by the two women who
> had trained him. He had a nice, boyish sort of

This is an unusually long quotation to be included in a research paper, but it is acceptable because it describes the character who is the subject of the paper. Quotation marks are not used because the passage is begun on a new line and indented ten spaces.

Kaufman 4

> cheerfulness that had never been trained out of him,
> and I probably have not brought that out.   He loved
> to win at tennis. . . .   On the other hand, he was
> not angry at being beaten.   When he fell in love
> with Brett his tennis game went all to pieces.
> People beat him who had never had a chance with him.
> He was very nice about it. (45)

The worst that is said about Cohn in this passage is that he did
not make clever remarks that would have made him stand out in a
crowd--and that he had been "trained" by the two women with
whom he had lived.   Neither of these observations is
especially damaging, although they do convey a sense that Cohn
was weak in some ways.   These two details aside, the rest of
the passage is positive.   The reader learns that Cohn had a
good body and kept it in shape and that he seemed young even
though he was not "professionally youthful"--which means he
did not work at seeming young.   Some critics have condemned
Cohn because he did not like to fish and was upset when he saw
horses gored at a bullfight (Ross 522; Cochran 305).   But to
value fishing and bullfighting over tennis, boxing, and bridge is
to judge Cohn by an arbitrary standard.   The point to grasp is
that Cohn is good at some games; they just don't happen to be
the games that Jake and Bill most like.   It's not as if Cohn
was entirely inept; there's nothing ridiculous about being good
at tennis and bridge.   Nor is there anything wrong about
dressing casually.   That Cohn did not fuss about his clothing
shows a commendable lack of pretension.   Most importantly, the
passage as a whole suggests that Cohn was "nice."   Surely a
character with a "nice, boyish sort of cheerfulness" is a
welcome relief within a novel full of characters who are
anything but nice.   And critics who emphasize Cohn's failings
should at least give him credit for being a good loser on the
tennis court.

But Cohn's greatest virtue has nothing to do with clothing
or sports.   He is an admirable character because he is an
idealist who expects more from life than sitting around getting

Student provides analysis of the quotation.

A summary of other views, cited within the same parenthetical reference.

Kaufman 5

drunk.   Consider the following conversation between Cohn and
Jake:

> "Listen, Jake. . . . .Don't you ever get the
> feeling that all your life is going by and you're not
> taking advantage of it?   Do you realize you've lived
> nearly half the time you have to live already?"
> "Yes, every once in a while."
> "Do you know that in about thirty-five years
> more we'll be dead?"
> "What the hell, Robert," I said.   "What the
> hell."
> "I'm serious."
> "It's one thing I don't worry about," I said.
> "You ought to." (11)

It may not be sophisticated to be so earnest about life, but
people can be too sophisticated for their own good.   Cohn
should be admired for thinking about his future and wanting to
make something of his life.

The worst charge that can be brought against Cohn is that
he shows bad judgment by falling in love with Brett Ashley—who
is superficial, promiscuous, and manipulative.   But the other
characters in the novel do not blame Cohn for loving Brett;
they blame him for <u>revealing</u> that he loves her—as if adults
should know better than to be open about how they feel.
Waiting at the Pamplona station for Brett's train, Jake
observes:

> I have never seen a man in civil life as nervous as
> Robert Cohn—nor as eager.   I was enjoying it.   It
> was lousy to enjoy it, but I felt lousy.   Cohn had a
> wonderful quality of bringing out the worst in
> anybody. (98)

Jake has a good reason for feeling "lousy."   He is impotent as
the result of a war wound and incapable of feeling the
excitement with which Cohn anticipates Brett's arrival.
Contemptuous of Cohn's open display of feeling, Jake seems to
believe that love is somehow ridiculous.   Thinking over the

**Quotation marks
are used despite
indentation
because dialogue
is involved.**

Kaufman 6

entire situation, Jake concludes:

> That damn Cohn.   He should have hit somebody the
> first time he was insulted, and then gone away.   He
> was so sure that Brett loved him.   He was going to
> stay, and true love would conquer all. (199)

The reference to "true love" is distinctly sarcastic, as if no
one could truly be in love.   Bill seems to share Jake's belief
that Cohn's devotion to Brett is foolish, as if fidelity were a
breach of good taste.   After Cohn fights with Pedro Romero and
unsuccessfully tries to take Brett away with him, Bill dryly
comments: "Wanted to make an honest woman of her, I imagine.
Damned touching scene" (201).   And Mike Campbell seems as
resentfully impotent as Jake Barnes.   He spends most of the
novel getting drunk and trying to overlook Brett's affairs with
other men.   He objects to her affairs with Cohn and Romero not
because she was being unfaithful to him, but because she was
being unfaithful to their social class: No one is ever allowed
to lose sight of the fact that Cohn is a Jew and Romero a
bullfighter.   After a scene in which he embarrasses everyone by
savagely ridiculing Cohn, Mike defends his behavior on grounds
that are worth noting, complaining that Cohn had joined a party
"where he damned well wasn't wanted" and then "hung around
Brett and just <u>looked</u> at her" (143).   The implication seems to
be that Mike wouldn't have minded Cohn doing more than just
"looking" and that he would have respected Cohn more if he had
been more aggressive.

Most critics have agreed with Mike's appraisal of Cohn's
behavior, as if love has no place in modern fiction.   According
to Sheridan Baker, Cohn is an "unrealist still living by
Victorian mottoes, springing to arms over imaginary insults to
a nonexistent lady. . ." (44).   Mark Spilka is a little more
sympathetic to Cohn.   But in an often cited essay, Spilka
argues that Cohn's predicament reveals the death of romantic
love:

> Cohn's romanticism explains his key position in the
> parable.   He is the last chivalric hero, the last

Student cites criticism with which he disagrees.

defender of an outworn faith, and his function is to
illustrate its present folly--to show us through the
absurdity of his behavior, that romantic love is
dead, that one of the great guiding codes of the past
no longer operates. (129)

But a conversation between Jake and Brett suggests that Cohn is
not "the last chivalric hero":

> "Everybody behaves badly," I said, "Give them
> the proper chance."
>
> "You wouldn't behave badly," Brett looked at
> me.
>
> "I'd be as big an ass as Cohn," I said. (181)

"Behaving badly," according to Brett and her friends, means
being serious and unwilling to treat life like a joke. Cohn
"behaves badly" by being seriously in love with Brett and
unwilling to pretend otherwise. Jake is smart enough to
realize that Cohn is only being human. Given the right
circumstances, "everybody" could act like Cohn--even the
world-weary Jake. And it is worth remembering that of all the
characters in the book, Jake comes closest to being Hemingway's
own counterpart. So Jake's recognition that he himself could
be like Cohn is significant.

In defense of Robert Cohn, it should also be noted that he
shares a number of qualities with Pedro Romero, a character who
is generally admired. They are both "fighters": Cohn is a
boxer, and Romero a bullfighter. They drink only moderately.
They have little sense of humor. And they both love Brett.
Romero is even more old-fashioned than Cohn; it is Romero,
after all, who expects Brett to grow her hair longer in order
to be more "womanly" (242). Comparing the two men, one critic
concludes that Cohn is "sadly incapable of the self-sufficient
manhood of Romero" (S. Baker 44). But this is not clearly
established by what actually happens in the book. There may
be something ridiculous in the fist fight between Cohn and Romero
over Brett, but surely Cohn deserves at least some credit for
being strong enough to knock the younger man down. When Cohn

First initial is used to distinguish the author from another writer with the same last name.

Kaufman 8

bends down to shake hands with his opponent, Romero hits him in
the face. Is this a "manly" act? And is Romero really all
that "self-sufficient"? He can't even get dressed by himself,
but has to rely upon a group of attendants who follow him
almost everywhere. And as far as self-sufficiency goes, it is
Romero, not Cohn, who actually wants to <u>marry</u> Brett.

Much has been made of the fact that Cohn breaks down and
cries after his fight with Romero, but his misery seems genuine.
Jake reports that Cohn was "crying without making any noise"
(194)--a fact that rescues Cohn from seeming merely pathetic.
It is to their discredit that the other characters in the novel
see Cohn's pain as still another reason to turn against him.
As Robert W. Lewis has argued in <u>Hemingway</u> <u>on</u> <u>Love</u>, "they hate
him because he suffers" (24). This is in part because his
unhappiness is spoiling their party, but it may also be because
Cohn's capacity for suffering underscores their own want of
feeling.

Robert Cohn provides a standard against which all the
other characters can be measured. It is for this reason that
he occupies such a central position in the book: The first two
words of the novel are "Robert Cohn," and Hemingway devotes the
entire first chapter to describing him. The other characters
eventually unite against him. Cohn is an "outsider" who can't
fit into their circumscribed little world of parties and deceit.
He makes them feel bad by revealing their own shortcomings.
They cannot forgive him for being different. "Do you think
you belong here among us?" Mike demands, "People who are out
to have a good time?" (177)

Student begins to move towards his conclusion, revealing why Cohn is an important character.

If life was meant to be nothing more than having "a good
time," then Mike could be excused for telling Cohn, "Go away.
Go away, for God's sake. Take that sad Jewish face away" (177).
But it may be "for God's sake" that Cohn remains where he is,
surrounded by people who know not what they do. He makes them
question their values--or lack of values--and tells them
truths they need to hear. After Jake has brought Brett and
Romero together, Cohn calls him a "damned pimp" (190). Jake

cannot forgive this because he knows that it is true.   And it
may very well be Cohn's "sad Jewish face" that eventually leads
Brett to decide, "I'm not going to be one of those bitches that
ruins children" (243).   Her decision to leave the nineteen
year old Romero represents something of a moral victory, as her
subsequent conversation with Jake reveals:

> "You know it makes one feel rather good
> deciding not to be a bitch."
>
> "Yes."
>
> "It's sort of what we have instead of God."
>
> "Some people have God," I said.   "Quite a
> lot." (245)

It is impossible to judge whether or not Robert Cohn is
one of the many people who still "have God" to guide them and
are not just dependent on whatever code of social behavior
happens to be momentarily fashionable.   But this much at least
is clear: It's good to be an outsider when the insiders are
corrupt.   Robert Cohn is the most attractive character in <u>The</u>
<u>Sun</u> <u>Also</u> <u>Rises</u> precisely because he doesn't fit in to a world
that is not worth fitting in with.

Kaufman 10

WORKS CITED

Baker, Carlos.   <u>Ernest Hemingway: A Life Story</u>. New York:
      Scribner's, 1969.

Baker, Sheridan.   "Jake Barnes and Spring Torrents." <u>Studies
      in The Sun Also Rises</u>.   Ed. William White.   Columbus:
      Merrill, 1969.   37—52.

Castillo—Puche, José.   <u>Hemingway in Spain</u>.   Trans. Helen R.
      Lane.   Garden City: Doubleday, 1974.

Cochran, Robert W.   "Circularity in <u>The Sun Also Rises</u>."
      <u>Modern Fiction Studies</u> 14 (1968): 297—305.

Hemingway, Ernest.   <u>Ernest Hemingway: Selected Letters 1917—
      1961</u>.   Ed. Carlos Baker.   New York: Scribner's, 1981.

———.   <u>The Sun Also Rises</u>.   New York: Scribner's, 1926.

Lewis, Robert W.   <u>Hemingway on Love</u>. 1965.   New York: Haskell,
      1973.

Nelson, Gerald B., and Glory Jones.   <u>Hemingway: Life and
      Works</u>.   New York: Facts On File, 1984.

Ross, Morton L.   "Bill Gorton, The Preacher in <u>The Sun Also
      Rises</u>." <u>Modern Fiction Studies</u> 18 (1972—73): 517—527.

Rovit, Earl.   "<u>The Sun Also Rises</u>: An Essay in Applied
      Principles." <u>Studies in The Sun Also Rises</u>.   Ed. William
      White.   Columbus: Merrill, 1969.   58—72.

Seltzer, Leon F.   "The Opportunity of Impotence: Count
      Mippipopolous in <u>The Sun Also Rises</u>." <u>Renascence</u> 21
      (1978): 3—14.

Spilka, Mark.   "The Death of Love in <u>The Sun Also Rises</u>."
      <u>Hemingway: A Collection of Critical Essays</u>.   Ed. Robert
      P. Weeks.   Englewood Cliffs: Prentice, 1962.   127—138.

Sprague, Claire.   "<u>The Sun Also Rises:</u> Its 'Clear Financial
      Basis'." <u>American Quarterly</u> 21 (1969): 259—266.

Tate, Allen.   "Hard—Boiled." <u>Studies in The Sun Also Rises</u>.
      Ed. William White.   Columbus: Merrill, 1969. 17—19.

———————Five spaces

Student cites two
works by same
author. Three
hyphens followed
by a period are
used instead of
repeating the
author's name.

Glossary of Useful Terms

ad hominem argument: An argument that makes a personal attack upon an opponent instead of addressing itself to the issue that is under dispute.

allusion: An informal reference that an audience is expected to understand without explanation.

analogy: A comparison that works on more than one level, usually between something familiar and something abstract.

anticipating the opposition: The process through which a writer or speaker imagines the most likely counterarguments that could be raised against his or her position.

audience: Whoever will read what you write. Your audience may consist of a single individual (such as your Congressman), a particular group of people (such as English majors), or a larger and more general group of people (such as "the American people"). Good writers have a clear sense of audience, which means that they never lose sight of whomever they are writing for.

authority: A reliable source that helps support an argument. It is important to cite authorities who will be recognized as legitimate by your opponents. This means turning to people with good credentials in whatever area is under consideration. If you are arguing about the economy, cite a prominent economist as an authority—not the teller at your local bank.

begging the question: An argument that assumes as already agreed upon whatever it should be devoted to proving.

bibliography: A list of works on a particular subject. One type of bibliography is the list of works cited that appears at the end of a research paper, scholarly article, or book. Another type of bibliography is a work in itself—a compilation of all known sources on a subject. An annotated bibliography is a bibliography that includes a brief description of each of the sources cited.

bogus claim: An unreliable or false premise; a questionable statement that is unsupported by reliable evidence or legitimate authority.

claim: Any assertion that can or should be supported with evidence. In the model for argument devised by Stephen Toulmin, the "claim" is the conclusion that the arguer must try to prove.

cliché: A worn-out expression; any group of words that are frequently and automatically used together. In "the real world" of "today's society," writers should avoid clichés because they are a type of instant language that makes writing seem "as dead as a doornail."

concession: Any point in an opposing argument that you are willing to recognize as valid. In argumentation, concessions help to diffuse the opposition by demonstrating that you are fair-minded.

connotation: The associations inspired by a word, in contrast to *denotation* (see below).

data: The evidence that an arguer uses to support a claim. It may take the form of personal experience, expert opinion, statistics, or any other information that is verifiable.

deduction: The type of reasoning through which a general observation leads to a specific conclusion.

denotation: The literal dictionary definition of a word.

diction: Word choice. Having good diction means more than having a good vocabulary; it means using language appropriately by using the right word in the right place.

documentation: The references that writers supply to reveal the source of the information they have reported.

equivocation: The deliberate use of vague, ambiguous language to mislead others. In writing, equivocation often takes the form of using abstract words to obscure meaning.

evidence: The experience, examples, or facts that support an argument. Good writers are careful to offer evidence for whatever they are claiming (see *claim*).

focus: The particular aspect of a subject upon which a writer decides to concentrate. Many things can be said about most subjects. Having a clear focus means narrowing a subject down so that it can be discussed without loss of direction. If you digress from your subject and begin to ramble, you have probably lost your focus.

generalization: Forming a conclusion that seems generally acceptable after citing several pieces of evidence. Argumentative writing demands a certain amount of generalization. It becomes a problem only when it is easily disputable. You have overgeneralized if someone can think of exceptions to what you have claimed. Be wary of words such as "all" and "every" since they increase the likelihood of overgeneralization.

hyperbole: A deliberate exaggeration for dramatic effect.

hypothesis: A theory that guides your research; a conditional thesis that is subject to change as evidence accumulates.

induction: The type of reasoning through which specific observations lead to a generally acceptable conclusion.

irony: A manner of speech or writing in which one's meaning is the opposite of what one has said.

jargon: A specialized vocabulary that is usually abstract and limited to a particular field, hence, difficult to understand for those outside the field.

loaded term: A word or phrase that is considered an unfair type of persuasion because it is either slanted or gratuitous within its context.

metaphor: A comparison in which two unlike things are declared to be the same; for example, "The Lord is my shepherd."

meter: The rhythm of poetry, in which stressed syllables occur in a pattern with regular intervals. In the analysis of poetry, meter is measured by a unit called a "foot," which usually consists of two or three syllables of which at least one is stressed.

non sequitur: Latin for "it does not follow"; a logical fallacy in which a writer bases a claim upon an unrelated point.

paradox: A statement or situation that appears to be contradictory but is nevertheless true; for example, "conspicuous by his absence."

paraphrase: Restating someone's words to demonstrate that you have understood them correctly or to make them more easily understandable.

personification: Giving human qualities to nonhuman objects; for example, "The sofa smiled at me, inviting me to sit down."

persuasion: A rhetorical strategy designed to make an audience undertake a specific action. Although there are many different types of persuasion, most involve an appeal to feeling that would not be part of a strictly logical argument.

plagiarism: Taking someone's words or ideas without giving adequate acknowledgment.

point of view: The attitude with which a writer approaches a subject. Good writers maintain a consistent point of view within each individual work.

post hoc, ergo propter hoc: Latin for "after this, therefore because of this"; a logical fallacy in which precedence is confused with causation.

premise: The underlying value or belief that one assumes as a given truth at the beginning of an argument.

rhetorical question: A question that is asked for dramatic effect, without expectation of a response.

rime scheme (or "rhyme"):   A fixed pattern of rimes that occurs throughout a poem.

simile: A direct comparison between two unlike things that includes such words as "like," "as," or "than"; for example, "My love is like a red, red rose."

stereotype: An unthinking generalization, especially of a group of people in which all the members of the group are assumed to share the same traits; for example, the "dumb jock" is a stereotype of high school and college athletes.

style: The combination of diction and sentence structure that characterizes the manner in which a writer writes. Good writers have a distinctive style, which is to say their work can be readily identified as their own.

summary: A brief and unbiased recapitulation of previously stated ideas.

syllogism: A three-stage form of deductive reasoning through which a general truth yields a specific conclusion.

thesis: The central idea of an argument; the point that an argument seeks to prove. In a unified essay, every paragraph helps to advance the thesis.

tone: The way a writer sounds when discussing a particular subject. Whereas point of view establishes a writer's attitude toward his or her subject, tone refers to the voice that is adopted in conveying this point of view to an audience. For example, one can write with an angry, sarcastic, humorous, or dispassionate tone when discussing a subject about which one has a negative point of view.

topic sentence: The sentence that defines the function of a paragraph; the single most important sentence in each paragraph.

transition: A link or bridge between topics that enables a writer to move smoothly from one subtopic to another so that every paragraph is clearly related to the paragraphs that surround it.

warrant: A term used by Stephen Toulmin for an implicit or explicit general statement that underlies an argument and establishes a relationship between the data and the claim.

Copyrights and Acknowledgments

Author-Title Index

A 8
B 9
C 0
D 1
E 2
F 3
G 4
H 5
I 6
J 7